Modern Pace
Handicapping

Modern Pace
Handicapping

TOM BROHAMER

WILLIAM MORROW AND COMPANY, INC.

New York

Library of Congress Cataloging-in-Publication Data

Brohamer, Tom.
    Modern pace handicapping / Tom Brohamer.
        p. cm.
    ISBN 0-688-08782-5
    1. Horse race betting. 2. Horses—Paces, gaits, etc. I. Title.
II. Title: Pace handicapping.
SF331.B77 1991
798.401—dc20   90-41050
                                                          CIP

Printed in the United States of America

        4 5 6 7 8 9 10

BOOK DESIGN BY BERNARD SCHLEIFER

To my loving wife, Shirley. None of this would have been possible without her support.

To my parents, John and Marion Brohamer. Thanks for everything.

Preface

Tom Brohamer's dream was to master the art and science of Thoroughbred Handicapping.

He wanted independence. He relished the thought of not having to rely on a job in commerce or industry to provide him with a steady income. He did not want his financial future dictated by the condition of the economy. In short, he aspired to become a professional handicapper.

Tom began honing his handicapping skills by reading and studying the books and procedures of every legitimate voice on the subject. From the beginning he learned that the socially perceived gambler and the successful handicapper were distinctly different entities. He approached handicapping like a medical student. He dissected and analyzed thousands of races. He tried every approach on the market. He tested and probed each racing variable like a micro-organism until he could thoroughly evaluate any given horse race. He became a superb diagnostician.

Brohamer joined me in 1983, studied the Sartin Methodology, and through the ensuing years contributed greatly to its effectiveness. Tom has the unique distinction of being a winner first and handicapping author second. Since 1983 I have watched him use his parimutuel profits to overcome all debts and allow him to retire at age forty-seven from a corporate executive to full time handicapping winner.

His chapter on the Sartin Methodology is fully authorized. It is a comprehensive work detailing the basic concepts of a handicapping procedure that has earned a place beside other recognized works.

The true purpose of any worthwhile handicapping book is to help guide horse racing aficionados in their quest to predict the future. The successful handicapper is as worthy as the surgeon, engineer, barrister, or physician. The Handicapper must never be confused with the random gambler.

Tom Brohamer will take you in depth on a handicapping odyssey that will demonstrate that horse racing is far more predictable than most authors would dare proclaim. In so doing he will share insights and procedures that will show you how, with diligence and hard work, you can make your dream a reality.

HOWARD G. SARTIN, PH.D.

Acknowledgments

As I SORTED and organized the essential material, I decided early on not to create this book in a vacuum. The newness and complexity of the material, and my own familiarity with the principles, were potential detriments to the clarity of the presentation. My efforts to avoid the problem placed a considerable burden on friends and colleagues. I imposed on several of them to read and digest the material, especially in the early draft stages.

Dick Schmidt has read the entire manuscript and has offered valuable criticism of clarity and style. Phil Hubbard, Jack Brohamer, Jr., and Mike Dally worked through the technical material and the arithmetic despite busy schedules. Hubbard was especially helpful with the accuracy of the numbers in the illustrations, a frustrating job in the first draft.

I would also like to thank Howard Sartin, whose creative genius is responsible for many of the concepts in the book.

And special thanks to James Quinn, the current "dean" of handicapping authors, who, more than anyone else, provided the encouragement I needed to undertake this project. I also appreciate his contributions to style and clarity, and for suggesting the title, *Modern Pace Handicapping*.

Contents

An Overview

THIS BOOK FILLS a fundamental gap in the contemporary literature of thoroughbred handicapping.

In the past two decades the study and practice of the great game of handicapping have been bulwarked by an unprecedented outpouring of texts that qualify as standards in the field.

Excellent treatments of the handicapping process as a whole, of speed, class, form analysis, trip, track biases, trainer intentions, parimutuel wagering, and even equine body language, have not only legitimized a previously dubious art as a respectable intellectual pursuit, but also have met with a surprisingly wide, hungry, and enthusiastic audience.

As scarcely nothing of lasting value had come before, the new books have represented a revolution. Handicapping today does not remotely resemble its notorious past. As never before, too, dedicated practitioners have a glorious chance to unravel a complicated game for not insignificant money. And thousands do.

Among the modern good books, glaringly missing has been a definitive treatment of pace.

Pace as a fundamental factor in handicapping has long been recognized as a final separation factor among a slate of contenders, but the ideas and methods proposed to accomplish the separating have been amazingly diverse, and largely ineffective.

Some have focused on the relationship between fractional time and final time, some on specific segments of a race, others on combinations of race segments, such as the first and third quarters of sprints, and others still on the rates of speed dem-

13

onstrated throughout the entire race. None has been shown to be associated with significantly greater percentages of winners.

In sum, the search for a meaningful pace methodology has ended at a variety of dead ends.

Now, at last, comes *Modern Pace Handicapping*, and with its publication a convincing resolution of even the thorniest problems of pace analysis. I predict without hesitation the book will stand for decades as the final authority on effective pace handicapping.

As presented here, pace is still concerned with the multitudinous relations among final times, fractional times, and running styles, but tradition ceases there. Fresh concepts, new ideas, original techniques, and a provocative array of innovative rating methods abound between these covers. The book literally opens a new frontier of figure handicapping.

The numbers in this book are, to be sure, unconventional. They are velocity ratings, a finer estimate of horses' true speed.

Final times and fractional times—the familiar fifths of seconds—express only points in time, not rates of speed, and can be considered relatively gross estimates of how fast racehorses actually run. Time is one-dimensional.

Velocity ratings, a function of distance divided by time, provide a two-dimensional measure, and are expressed as feet per second (fps). For example, Horse A ran to the second call of a six-furlong sprint in 58.65 fps. Velocity ratings capture a horse's actual rate of speed.

In an early chapter Brohamer guides the reader in a practical step-by-step routine of making the (velocity) calculations, using familiar points of call of races as points of departure. The reader's participation in the procedure, hands on, is almost indispensable to a command of later relationships. I urge that active participation. It will provide as well a first sense of how fast (in velocity rates) horses typically run at familiar pace intervals.

More broadly, these contents will be most immediately meaningful to handicappers prepared to deal actively with the numerical relationships they promote. Those relations are not overly complex, but they are new and unfamiliar, the numbers an abrupt change from common practice.

Brohamer's pace ratings might be considered a horseplayer's version of the new math. Trace the arithmetic yourself. Simulate the calculations on new data in the *Daily Racing Form*. Before proceeding, understand each relationship the numbers are intended to reflect. A habit of guided practice will serve understanding very well.

These contents also constitute a perfectly compatible marriage of substance and author. From the day he diverted his attention from speed figures to pace ratings, Tom Brohamer's mission was to advance a treatment of pace analysis that other practitioners might comprehend and implement. Understanding pace has brought it all together for Brohamer, his great leap forward.

For approximately fifteen seasons Brohamer had practiced his handicapping at the southern California tracks, experimenting widely with alternative ideas and methods, and winning consistently, notably with speed figures, until in 1982 he arrived at the most important conclusion of his career. The high-figure horses lost too often, not due to influences of class or form the figures did not satisfactorily represent, but due to the influences of pace.

Since then Brohamer has worked closely with the pace principles and computer programs promoted by Howard Sartin and his associates, delivering original contributions, and becoming in the bargain the quintessential Sartin practitioner and a big, consistent winner. Indeed, in these pages Brohamer credits Sartin with making the ultimate difference in his handicapping proficiency and success.

But the author's background is important, and if the rating methods they find here will be new to experienced handicappers, Brohamer's pace analyses, the crucial interpretations of the data, will be strikingly, and reassuringly, familiar.

Brohamer has succeeded impressively with these new power tools in no small measure because he was an outstanding handicapper to begin with. The pace methodology to be described here is not a system, not even a rigorously defined set of standard operating procedures. Method players overly dependent on procedure to obtain results will probably be disappointed.

To be successful, this book's disciples will be required to identify contenders, select representative pacelines, know their racetracks, and interpret a wide array of pace ratings intelligently. Brohamer's guidelines will help enormously on the final three counts, but nothing very meaningful will occur by glancing studiously for sixty seconds at a computer printout.

Modern Pace Handicapping will be a tremendous supplement to fundamental handicapping proficiency, but it will not substitute for it. Novices will be seriously stretched.

Brohamer's diversity of handicapping skills will shine through brightly at regular intervals in the book. Speed handicappers can contemplate my contention that his chapter on making daily track variants is the best treatment of that complicated topic on record. Figure handicappers will learn as well how to construct par-time charts for unfamiliar tracks from limited data.

I especially like Brohamer's tersely practical advice to recreational handicappers on arriving at the race books of Las Vegas—and, by extension, at OTB parlors, intertrack sites, or anywhere that unfamiliar racing, or local racing too long not visited, might be occurring. A few convenient practices enhance the possibility of catching a few additional winners.

Brohamer is especially expert at pace analysis, the kind of reasoning the numerical pace ratings are supposed to inform. Handicappers everywhere will be well-advised to pay attention in particular to the fine points.

Finally, *Modern Pace Handicapping* has been cleverly illustrated in the examples of races selected by the author. Most handicappers learn inductively, from a particular race to a general conclusion. The book supports that tendency admirably.

I also can report firsthand on the efficacy of these methods as a full-dress approach to handicapping.

In 1987, at Oak Tree at Santa Anita in the fall, I used the approach exclusively throughout thirty-two racing days. A novice user, my profits exceeded $3500. Aspects of pace methodology, techniques here called turn-time and early-energy distribution (percent of), have been staples of my handicapping regimen ever since.

In an arena of adult recreation where customer education has never been adequately extolled, the arrival of an important book on handicapping is always cause for celebration. This one is cause for jubilation.

—JAMES QUINN

Los Angeles

CHAPTER I

Introduction

The gate opens for a six-furlong sprint at Saratoga. The 1 and 2 horses break clear of the field, neither able to establish early superiority. As they hit the quarter in 21.3 seconds, it becomes apparent that if one doesn't crack the other soon, the off-pace runners will surely win.

The Modern Pace Handicapper had analyzed each pace segment and this "race within a race" was predictable.

As the field of horses enters the second fraction, it's clear to the entire crowd that the pace setters are too closely matched.

The handicapper's prerace analysis identified both as E or "Early Pace" runners only. To win, one must dominate the other. In the race, each is being asked for more than it can comfortably give and still go on to win. Bettors who believe pace analysis is merely determining the early leader are about to throw away tickets because of a superficial analysis. Neither horse figures to be around at the finish.

The 3 horse is beginning to cut into the advantage by launching a bid on the turn.

The "turn-time" horse is a "presser" that figured a couple lengths behind in the first of the "races within a race," but figured to win the battle of the second fraction. Visually, the move is impressive:

The 3 gains momentum while closing rapidly on the two leaders. The closers, not making a similar turn-time move, will be at a severe disadvantage in the third pace segment. The field hits the half in 44.4 seconds.

As the race enters the third pace segment, the final fraction, the pace presser has joined the two leaders. The horse has gained the momentum with only 1320 feet to the finish line.

In this scenario the pace handicapper's prerace analysis identified the turn-time move to be decisive. Too much "Early Pace," not enough "Sustained Pace." The horse with the best combination of both wins the race. The pace "presser" was the key to this match of contenders.

Let's look at the tools the Modern Pace Handicapper employed for the prerace analysis.

RACES WITHIN A RACE

Perhaps the single greatest factor defeating accurate speed figures is a potential weakness in the internal "splits" or fractions of a race. Too often, the high figure horse exits a race in which the rating was achieved by dominating one or two fractions to the extent that a weak fraction did not surface as a problem. If the domination was in the first two fractions, the horse is always a threat to repeat the high rating. When the first or second fraction surfaces as a weakness, the high speed-figure horse often loses to pressure exerted *throughout* the race. Many maiden winners face exactly that scenario.

Maiden wins are often accomplished by dominating the first fraction; posting a slow to moderate second fraction; and then, fresh from a "breather," the winner draws away late, recording a fast time in the process.

When asked to face winners, usually as a low odds underlay, the figure horse's second fraction weakness contributes to its defeat.

In *Modern Pace Handicapping* we'll learn to look at all three of the pace segments and analyze each as "a race within a race," and how each segment contributes to the overall match up.

Pace Segments

The fractional segments we'll consider are the first fraction (call), the second fraction, and the final fraction of a race. We will not use the stretch call. It is not unimportant to the outcome of races or to the process of contender selection, but the distance of the segment is too short to be of value in the analysis of feet-per-second velocities and pace ratings.

	1FR	2FR	3FR	AP	EP	SP	FX	%E
Horse 1	60.35	56.75	52.85	56.65	58.66	55.75	56.60	52.63%
Horse 2	60.11	56.90	52.94	56.65	58.66	55.80	56.52	52.63%
Horse 3	59.45	58.00	53.15	56.86	58.66	55.90	56.30	52.43%
Horse 4	57.40	57.35	54.85	56.53	57.39	56.12	56.12	51.06%
Horse 5	56.85	57.65	55.35	56.61	57.39	56.37	56.10	50.85%

AP = Average Pace; EP = Early Pace; SP = Sustained Pace; FX = Factor X; %E = Energy Distribution.

1Fr (first fraction): Also the first call. The first quarter-mile of sprint races and the first half-mile of routes (excluding marathon distances).

In our Saratoga example Horses 1 and 2 clearly lead the field with their 60+ feet-per-second (fps) first fractions. But both are closely matched, and unless they can withstand prolonged pace duels, the potential exists for an off-pace winner. Horse 3 is just behind the leaders, while 4 and 5 are well behind the early fraction and will have to gain much ground later.

2Fr (second fraction): The second fraction or "turn-time" of both sprints and routes is a quarter-mile. It is the difference between the first fraction and the second call. In our example:

44.4 (second call) minus 21.3 (1Fr) = 23.1 seconds (2Fr)

In the example race, the pace handicapper envisions a probable pace battle between 1 and 2, with the 3 horse cutting into their lead with a 58.00 fps turn-time fraction. The closers should be making some progress against the leaders, but are actually *losing* ground to 3 as that horse moves to challenge the lead.

Early Pace/Second Call: These are interchangeable terms and represent the time of the race after two of our mini-races have occurred. In a sprint the second call is a half-mile; in a route it's three quarters of a mile (six furlongs). The conceptual difference between the second *call* and the second *fraction* is essential to grasping the principles in this book.

The second call of the example race is *44.4*; the second fraction is *23.1* seconds. We'll discuss the fractions and calls in greater detail in the chapter "Feet-Per-Second Calculations."

3Fr: The third, or final fraction, of the race is the difference between final time and the second call. In our Saratoga race, if the final time had been 1:10.1, the final fraction:

3Fr = 1:10.1 minus 44.4, or *25.2* seconds

Horses 4 and 5 dominate the final fraction and may very well overhaul the two early leaders. They should not, however, threaten the 3 horse, who benefited from the pace duel and, by means of superior turn-time velocity, found itself in the "garden spot" as the field turned into the stretch. For us to bet closers, we'll demand a horse that can generate a move in the second fraction. This is another important point in pace analysis. A one-run closer, the horse possessing *only* a strong third fraction, is the *worst* kind of pace selection. Only when the early pace and presser scenario completely breaks down is this type of runner a viable selection. Even then they usually settle for the minor purse awards.

The three fractional points of call from the Eastern edition of the *Daily Racing Form:*

Don't Knock It — **Dk. b. or br. h. 5, by Best Native—Game Bid, by Cornish Prince**
$16,000 **Br.—Appleton Arthur I (Fla)**
Own.—S K S Stable **Tr.—Seewald Alan**

12Aug89- 7Mth	sly	6f	:22	:45⅕	1:10⅗	3↑Clm 25000	2	4	4^{2}	$5^{1\frac{1}{2}}$	2^{hd}	3^{2}	Krone J A		116	*1.70
22Jly89- 7Mth	fst	6f	:21⅗	:44⅖	1:10	3↑Clm 25000	1	4	$1^{1\frac{1}{2}}$	1^{2}	1^{1}	$3^{1\frac{3}{4}}$	Wilson R	b	116	*1.00
6Jly89- 7Mth	my	6f	:21⅖	:44	1:10	3↑Clm 50000	1	4	$1^{\frac{1}{2}}$	1^{hd}	1^{hd}	$4^{1\frac{3}{4}}$	Vigliotti M J	b	116	*1.60
24Jun89- 6Mth	fst	6f	:21⅖	:43⅘	1:09	3↑Alw 29000	5	1	$2^{\frac{1}{2}}$	2^{2}	2^{4}	$6^{8\frac{3}{4}}$	Vigliotti M J	b	115	6.10
7Sep88- 9Med	fst	6f	:22	:44⅖	1:09	3↑Alw 25000	2	1	$1^{1\frac{1}{2}}$	1^{1}	1^{hd}	$4^{5\frac{1}{2}}$	Wilson R	b	115	*1.50
27Aug88- 5Mth	fm	5f	[T]:22	:45⅖	:57⅘	3↑Helioscope	4	3	2^{hd}	$3^{\frac{1}{2}}$	$6^{5\frac{1}{2}}$	6^{8}	Wilson R	b	114	*1.50
27Aug88-Run in Divisions																
13Aug88- 3Mth	fst	6f	:21⅘	:43⅗	1:08⅗	3↑Eillo	1	3	$1^{\frac{1}{2}}$	1^{hd}	2^{1}	$2^{2\frac{1}{2}}$	Wilson R	b	117	1.70
19Jly88- 8Mth	fst	6f	:21⅗	:44⅕	1:08⅘	3↑Alw 25000	3	3	$1^{\frac{1}{2}}$	$1^{1\frac{1}{2}}$	$1^{2\frac{1}{2}}$	$2^{\frac{3}{4}}$	Wilson R	b	115	*1.50
4Jly88- 9Pha	fst	6f	:22	:44⅖	1:09⅘	3↑Quaker H	4	1	$1^{1\frac{1}{2}}$	$2^{\frac{1}{2}}$	2^{1}	$2^{\frac{1}{2}}$	Madrid A Jr	b	114	*1.00
7Jun88- 9Mth	fst	6f	:22⅕	:45⅕	1:09⅘	3↑Decathlon	3	4	$1^{\frac{1}{2}}$	1^{hd}	$1^{1\frac{1}{2}}$	2^{hd}	Krone J A	b	115	4.70

LATEST WORKOUTS Aug 7 Mth 4f fst :48⅗ H Jly 18 Mth 4f fst :47⅘ H Jun 1

Land at War — **Dk. b. or br. g. 4, by Wardlaw—Landera, by In Reality**
Br.—Carrion Jaime S (Fla)
Own.—Bottazzi P **Tr.—Costa Frank**

29Jly89- 2Mth	fst	1	:47⅖	1:11⅗	1:36⅖	3↑Elkwood	3	1	$1^{\frac{1}{2}}$	2^{1}	$4^{4\frac{1}{2}}$	4^{8}	Chavez J F	b	113	13.40
8Jly89- 3Mth	fst	$1\frac{1}{16}$	:45⅘	1:10⅖	1:42⅗	3↑Alw 29000	1	1	2^{hd}	1^{1}	$2^{\frac{1}{2}}$	$2^{1\frac{1}{2}}$	Chavez J F	b	115	22.80
24Jun89- 6Mth	fst	6f	:21⅖	:43⅘	1:09	3↑Alw 29000	3	5	5^{7}	5^{5}	5^{7}	$5^{7\frac{3}{4}}$	Santagata N	b	115	13.60
16Jun89- 7Mth	fst	6f	:21⅕	:44	1:10	3↑Alw 20000	2	4	$4^{4\frac{1}{2}}$	$3^{4\frac{1}{2}}$	2^{2}	$1^{\frac{1}{2}}$	Santagata N	b	116	11.60
7Jun89- 9Mth	sly	6f	:21⅗	:44⅗	1:10⅘	3↑Alw 20000	6	4	$5^{3\frac{1}{2}}$	$7^{6\frac{1}{4}}$	$8^{9\frac{1}{2}}$	$6^{8\frac{1}{4}}$	Santagata N	b	116	4.10
1Apr89-10Del	fst	6f	:22⅕	:45	1:10⅕	3↑Inaugural	6	1	1^{3}	2^{hd}	1^{hd}	4^{2}	Melendez J D		116	12.20
25Mar89-10GS	fst	6f	:22⅕	:45⅕	1:11⅖	3↑Equus H	1	1	$3^{\frac{1}{2}}$	$2^{\frac{1}{2}}$	$2^{1\frac{1}{2}}$	$4^{\frac{3}{4}}$	Alligood M A	b	109	24.50
4Mar89- 8GS	fst	6f	:22⅖	:45⅘	1:12	J Kilmer H	6	1	3^{2}	$4^{2\frac{3}{4}}$	5^{2}	$5^{4\frac{1}{4}}$	Bravo J	b	110	25.20
22Feb89- 9GS	sly	6f	:22⅖	:45⅗	1:11	Alw 14500	4	1	1^{hd}	2^{2}	2^{2}	2^{4}	Bravo J^{5}		113	*1.00[D]
22Feb89-Disqualified and placed fourth																
5Feb89- 8Pha	fst	6f	:22	:44⅖	1:09⅕	Alw 18000	6	2	$2^{\frac{1}{2}}$	2^{hd}	2^{hd}	2no	Bravo J^{5}		111	3.00

From the tabloid editions of the *Form:*

Don's Irish Melody *
STEVENS G L **117** **$80,000**
Own.—Coelho & Valenti **Lifetime 26 6 8 6 $343,625**

1Nov89-5SA	a6½f	(T):21^{1}	:43	1:12^{2}	fm	5/2	115	1^{hd}	2^{hd}	2^{hd}	$4^{1\frac{1}{2}}$	Stevens G L^{7}	100000	

1Nov89—Drifted in start												
18Oct89-8SA	6f	:21	:43^3	1:08 ft	11	114	2$^{3\frac{1}{2}}$	3$^{4\frac{1}{2}}$	3$^{5\frac{1}{2}}$	3$^{7\frac{1}{2}}$	Solis A^2	Anct Ttl H
18Oct89—Stumbled start												
26Sep89-12Fpx	6½f	:21^3	:45^1	1:16^{4}ft	8-5	116	2^1	1^1	1$^{1\frac{1}{2}}$	2no	PdrozMA 3	Gov Cup H
19Sep89-12Fpx	6f	:21^4	:44^2	1:09^{1}ft	*2	117	1^{hd}	2$^{\frac{1}{2}}$	2$^{\frac{1}{2}}$	4$^{7\frac{3}{4}}$	Pedroza MA 5	Aprisa H
3Aug89-8Dmr	6f	:21^3	:44^1	1:08^{4}ft	2¼	115	1$^{\frac{1}{2}}$	1^{hd}	2^{hd}	2^2	Castanon AL 6	Aw50000
4Jly89-7Hol	1	:44	1:08^1	1:33^{4}ft	23	114	2^{hd}	2$^{1\frac{1}{2}}$	2$^{3\frac{1}{2}}$	3$^{5\frac{1}{4}}$	Castanon A L 9	HcpO
29May89-8GG	6f	:21^1	:43^1	1:08^{1}ft	15	116	4^2	4^4	4^3	3^2	Castanon A L^5	Oak H
28Apr89-8GG	6f	:21^2	:43^2	1:08^{1}ft	5½	117	2$^{\frac{1}{2}}$	2$^{1\frac{1}{2}}$	3^2	2$^{1\frac{1}{2}}$	CstnonAL^7	[S]Mntclr H
5Apr89-8SA	6½f	:21^4	:44^1	1:14 ft	13	116	8$^{6\frac{1}{4}}$	8$^{8\frac{1}{2}}$	7^{10}	8^{10}	VlnzlPA^2	Ptro Grnd H
5Apr89—Grade III; Troubled trip												

Speedratic *

STEVENS G L **115**

Own.—Ustin S

							Lifetime	16	6	4	2	$451,820
21Oct89-8Aqu	1	:44^1	1:08	1:32^{4}ft	3¾	117	(1^1)	(2^{hd})	2^{hd}	(3^1)	PcLJr 6	N Y R A Ml H
1Oct89-11Fpx	a1⅛	:46	1:10^1	1:49^{1}ft	*7-5	122	2$^{\frac{1}{2}}$	1^1	1$^{1\frac{1}{2}}$	1^3	Pincay LJr 4	Pom Iv H
26Aug89-8Dmr	1⅛	:47^1	1:11^1	1:47 ft	2½	116	1$^{1\frac{1}{2}}$	1^2	1$^{1\frac{1}{2}}$	2$^{1\frac{3}{4}}$	StevnsGL 1	Cabrillo H
26Aug89—Grade III; Lugged out												
17Aug89-8Dmr	6½f	:22^1	:44^4	1:15^{1}ft	*7-5	117	2^{hd}	1^1	2^{hd}	2$^{1\frac{3}{4}}$	Stevens G L 4	Aw50000
17Aug89—Lugged out drive												
30Jly89-8Dmr	6f	:21^2	:43^4	1:08 ft	12	117	3^3	3^4	3^4	2^5	VlnzlPA 7	B Crosby H
30Jly89—Grade III; Wide												
5Feb89-8SA	1¼	:47^2	1:37^1	2:02^{1}m	3½	117	3^2	3^{nk}	3^3	4$^{11\frac{1}{2}}$	StvnsGL 3	C H Strub
5Feb89—Grade I												
15Jan89-8SA	1⅛	:46^4	1:10^1	1:47^{2}ft	9½	120	3$^{1\frac{1}{2}}$	1^{hd}	2^{hd}	2^{hd}	StvnsGL 10	Sn Frndo
15Jan89—Grade I; Veered out start												
26Dec88-8SA	7f	:22	:44	1:21^{3}ft	3	120	5^2	4^{nk}	4$^{2\frac{1}{2}}$	3^1	StvnsGL 11	Malibu
26Dec88—Grade II; Wide final 3/8												

In *Modern Pace Handicapping* we'll go beyond a simple analysis of fractional components and develop pace ratings that will effectively separate contenders from pretenders. The first of these ratings is actually another velocity number: Early Pace.

Early Pace (EP): Feet-per-second velocity to the second call of a race. In both sprints and routes "Early Pace" and "Second Call" are interchangeable terms and, as we'll see later, represent the most important point of call.

Sustained Pace (SP) is an average of the second call and third fraction velocities. In short, SP represents finishing ability related to second call position. When the Early Pace horse is also the top-ranked Sustained Pace runner, it's time to loosen the rubber band around the bankroll.

Average Pace (AP) is the average of all three fractions in sprints, and the average of EP and SP in routes. By itself, Average Pace is the most consistent winner-producer of any rating in the array.

Factor X (FX) is the average of the first and third fractions, and is a sprint rating only. The route races in this book will not use Factor X in any of the race arrays.

In our Saratoga example, Horse 3 is top rated in Average Pace, tied for the top rating in Early Pace, and rated a respectable third in Sustained Pace and Factor X.

Handicappers applying the principles in this book will know from their *Decision Models* and *Track Profiles* if Horse 3 possesses the right combination of ratings to win a six-furlong race at Saratoga. Horses that do not fit the "Model," or "Profile" are poor probabilities and are to be avoided at the betting windows.

In the analysis of our race, Horse 3 was designated as a pace "presser"; 1 and 2 as "early pace" only; and 4 and 5 as "sustained pace" runners. In the chapter on "ESP" we'll organize our entire analysis of pace around the running styles of the horses in the race.

Finally, any complete analysis of pace must also relate energy distribution patterns of contenders to the demands of the racetrack. The Modern Pace Handicapper's analysis of the race reveals that Horses 4 and 5 distribute their available energy too late to win a six-furlong race at Saratoga.

They may be betting possibilities at Belmont, but at Saratoga they will rally too late to be effective.

The designation %E, or Energy Distribution, is the relationship of energy expended at the second call to a horse's total available energy. A horse that's expending too much early energy seldom wins. A horse that expends its energy too late is the one-run type that depends on a complete breakdown of early and mid-race pace. We'll learn how to measure energy distribution and how to determine parameters for any racetrack.

SPEED VS PACE

Effective pace analysis is neither of the following:
   (1) Merely determining the early speed of the race.
   (2) Determining the "fastest" horse in the race, as indicated by final time.

1. When you've digested the material in this book, you will not apply a superficial "who will get the early lead" analysis to a race. Many otherwise sophisticated handicappers consider pace analysis to be an exercise intended to find the early leader in

the race. That's certainly an important part of the pace scenario, but a contender's ability to apply and withstand pressure in the various "races within a race" is far more reliable as a basis for winner selection.

In our example race it was the internal pressure exerted by Horse 3 that proved to be the key to winning. *Most* races are considerably more difficult than simply searching for the early leader.

2. *Of course* the "fastest" horse is an important factor to the outcome of any horse race. What we need to do, however, is redefine the term "fastest."

Speed figures, by themselves, are no longer a viable basis for long-term profits. The influence of top practitioners has served to underlay the odds of legitimate "figure" horses and force top players to combine speed handicapping with other approaches. Supplemented with trip and trainer analyses, speed figures are alive and may well be generating profits to top players. There is, however, no "fat" in the process. Whereas a competent pace handicapper may generate significant profits from one of the "mini-races" within a race, the figure horse is usually exposed to everyone at the track. This is a tough game to beat on a steady diet of low-priced underlays.

"Fastest," to pace handicappers, is the highest velocity in whichever pace segment, or segments, the match-up shows as most significant. Sometimes it's Early Pace; sometimes Sustained Pace. Just as often it may be internal pressure. Our definition does not emphasize how fast a horse runs its total race, but rather how fast it runs in the mini-races, and the manner in which it distributes its available energy.

Let's take another look at our hypothetical Saratoga race and the final times from which the pace numbers were generated:

Horse 1	1:10.0
Horse 2	1:10.0
Horse 3	1:09.4
Horse 4	1:10.0
Horse 5	1:09.4

Traditional speed figures indicate a tie between Horses 3 and 5, with the others one length behind. In our array of pace figures, that is *not* the case.

The rating that most closely approximates final time is Average Pace, and by virtue of the value of incremental velocity, 3 has a decisive edge in the rating. Horse 5 is actually tied with 1 and 2 with their final times of 1:10.0. Applying the additional tool of energy distribution further downgrades 5 as a possible selection, despite its high speed "figure." Both 1 and 2, each with lower "figures," would have been superior to 5 as betting selections. *Final time will not be the emphasis of this book.*

The use of a feet-per-second format will be discussed in a subsequent chapter. For now, though, please accept the idea that more precise figures result from their application. The effects of differing rates of velocity and the values of beaten lengths contribute to that precision.

Let's take a quick look at the effect of incremental velocity on the two best final-time horses in the example: Horses 3 and 5.

	1Fr	2Fr	3Fr
Horse 3	22.1	22.4	24.4
Horse 5	23.1	22.4	23.4

For sake of illustration, the numbers we've used in this example have been rounded to fifths of a second and are not an exact match to the array. If the two horses were pieces on a game board, handicappers would reason that the 5-length difference in the first fraction was nullified by Horse 5's superiority in the third. Not so.

As rates of velocity differ, so will the feet-per-second values. In the example, Horse 3's 5-length superiority in the first fraction will outweigh its final fraction deficiency. Let's look at the fps values for the first and third fractions only:

	1Fr	3Fr
Horse 3	59.45	53.22
Horse 5	56.89	55.46

By rounding to fifths, we've slightly dulled 3's advantage, but it is still significant. The difference in the first fraction is 2.56 fps in favor of 3, while the final fraction favors 5 by only 2.24 fps. Compounded into all three fractions, the ratings for

Average Pace are 56.85 and 56.74 respectively. The difference would have been greater had we not nullified Horse 3's turn-time edge by also rounding to fifths of a second.

The point should be clear: Horses that are active in the early part of a race will be advantaged by our approach to pace analysis. And that's how it should be.

GENERATING THE NUMBERS

Many readers may be put off by the apparent difficulty of the material. Don't be. At first glance the array of numbers and the technical terms may seem difficult to grasp and apply. I assure you, that's *not* the case.

Generating feet-per-second numbers will be the most technical of applications, but the math is relatively simple and, once mastered, will lead directly to all the numbers necessary to effective pace analysis. The terms "model," "profile," "energy distribution," "par charts," and "variants" are all extensions of feet-per-second calculations or traditional handicapping concepts modified for a more precise analysis of pace.

Consider feet-per-second calculation to be the speedometer attached to the neck of a horse; once you've learned to read that speedometer, *all* the numbers will fall neatly into place. Take the time to review the earlier array, and note how all the ratings and energy numbers were simply extensions of the three fractional components of a race.

Many of the tools we'll develop to analyze pace are nontechnical and will not require any math of the reader. The majority of the material, however, will not be an easy "read." To understand and effectively apply the principles of *Modern Pace Handicapping* will require a commitment of effort. Much of the material will be new and not quickly grasped. Stay with it. The reward will be a new clarity to your analysis of pace.

The use of a calculator is a necessity. I've included a feet-per-second chart at the end of the second chapter, but even with the chart, a calculator will be necessary to compound the ratings and generate energy percentages. The math is simple, and I advise the reader to continue with the material until mastering it.

For the reader versed in simple computer programming, the basic material is a natural for any of the handheld computers on today's market. The algorithms are straightforward and eas-ily adapted to those machines. For those unable to program for themselves, the Sartin group, PIRCO, has agreed to provide a basic program to generate the numbers in this book. I've in-cluded the necessary information at the conclusion of the chap-ter on the Sartin Methodology.

Now it's time to take out the calculator and learn the basis for most of the principles in the book: feet-per-second calcula-tions.

CHAPTER II

Feet-Per-Second Calculations

MUCH OF THIS BOOK is dependent upon converting the *Daily Racing Form*'s fifths of a second to feet-per-second numbers. Energy distribution, Sartin numbers, and energy variants all require the fps format. There is no more graphic or precise way to look at a race. However, it's a "good news, bad news" story. The good news is the accuracy and clarity of the format to the figures. The bad news is the math required to make the numbers. Without a computer, it can be tedious to the point of irritation. But the insights the figures provide into the pace picture are worth the effort. For the reader uncomfortable with the calculation of the numbers, I've included an fps chart at the end of the chapter. The chart covers the most frequently run fractional distances.

Consider the following races at six and seven furlongs.

| (A) 6F | 22.2 | 45.4 | 1:11.3 |
| (B) 7F | 22.3 | 45.4 | 1:24.0 |

In this format the pace handicapper has some work to do. He must extrapolate the fractions from the running lines. Much of pace analysis is dependent upon viewing the individual fractions and their interrelationships.

However, viewing the raw fractions is only marginally more helpful.

| (A) 6F | 22.2 | 23.2 | 25.4 |
| (B) 7F | 22.3 | 23.1 | 38.1 |

It is evident in both illustrations that A and B draw even in the second fraction. But what about the final fraction? Mix in another frequently run distance and the array becomes even more difficult to analyze.

(C) 6½F	22.2	23.1	32.3
		(45.3)	(1:18.1)
(A) 6F	22.2	23.2	25.4
(B) 7F	22.3	23.1	38.1

We have three different distances within a single distance structure and no common final fraction. Even with a parallel speed chart, which would interpret the final fractions, the player is left with a less than graphic portrayal. This is a basic reason for speed and pace figures. It is exceedingly difficult to grasp the subtleties of a race using a one-point-per-fifth-of-a-second format. Modern pace analysis requires greater precision. Handicappers wishing to include a cursory pace analysis in their approach can utilize one-fifth second = 1 length and not be too severely disadvantaged, but the pace player should not tolerate such imprecision.

Exclusive of possible bias considerations, which of the example races is the best performance? Reexamined in a feet-per-second format, the picture is clearer.

	1Fr	2Fr	3Fr
(A) 58.92	56.41	51.16
(B) 58.40	56.89	51.83
(C) 58.92	56.89	50.61

We'll talk later about determining fps values for beaten lengths, but the array highlights B as the top performer. It's close, but the final fraction is significantly superior to give B the edge. In the chapter on the Sartin Methodology, we'll compound the fractions into workable pace ratings. They'll also give the nod to B.

There is no more graphic way to analyze a race. When viewed in an fps format, a race can come to life. Internal moves, early pace advantages, and final fraction superiority are readily displayed to the pace analyst. I advise you to work through the chapter with a handheld calculator before programming the algorithms for a computer.

Likewise, you should learn the calculations before resorting to the use of the fps chart. It is not my intention to bury the reader by providing a course in basic racetrack mathematics. It *is* my intention, however, to offer an overall understanding and feel for the basics of a racetrack. Some of the example calculations will be rather lengthy. They are primarily for the reader who intends to adopt the principles as outlined. For the reader not as seriously intended, the numbers can be closely duplicated by the use of the fps chart at the end of the chapter. For the reader incapable of programming a computer, Dr. Sartin has agreed to provide a basic computer program at nominal cost.

FPS—THE BASIC LAYOUT

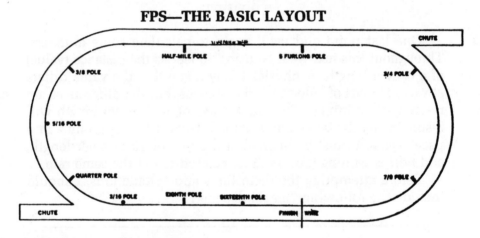

RACETRACK (LAYOUT)

Before jumping ahead to calculating fractional components of a race, we should spend some time with the basics of the track itself. Surprisingly few players are fully conversant with a racetrack layout. Most can point out the stretch call (eighth pole) and, possibly, the quarter pole; but very few can relate the charts and past performances to specific locations on the track. Successful application of pace handicapping principles demands a complete understanding of the racing surface and the track layout.

Let's get some of the basics out of the way. The points of call:

• Eighth poles. Beginning with the ⅞ pole, each is ⅛ mile

closer to the finish. Eighths, or furlongs, are the basic units of measurement of the racetrack. There are 660 feet in a furlong.

- Stretch Call. One-eighth mile from the finish line; at *all* distances.
- Quarter Pole. One-quarter mile from the finish line. There are 1320 feet in a quarter-mile.
- Half-Mile Pole. One-half mile to the finish line. There are 2640 feet in a half-mile.
- Three-quarter Pole. Three-quarter mile, or six furlongs to the finish line. There are 3960 feet in six furlongs.
- Sixteenth Poles. Subdivides the eighth poles. There are 330 feet in a sixteenth of a mile.
- The math symbols: $*$ = multiplication
  $/$ = division

One last point and we'll begin to calculate some numbers. Throughout this text we'll be using 10 feet as the distance (value) of a beaten length. A physicist may argue that the value differs at various rates of velocity and distances, but the differences are really quite minimal. The blanket use of 10 feet per length will result in highly satisfactory figures. Horses losing ground in a pace segment must be debited at the rate of 10 feet per length, and horses gaining ground must be credited at the same rate.

Before attempting the definitions and calculations, I should include the following "magic decoder."

BL = Beaten Lengths. (HD = .10   NK = .25   ½ = .50)

10 = Value of a length; 10 feet per

T1 = Time of the first fraction (also first *call*)

T2 = Time of second fraction

T3 = Time of final fraction

T4 = Time of second *call*

FEET-PER-SECOND CALCULATIONS—SPRINTS

First Fraction (1Fr) 1320 feet (also first *call*)

Throughout the examples, I'll be referring to the diagram of the basic layout. The first fraction starts in the backstretch chute and is run to the half-mile pole in six furlong races; to the 9/16 pole (not shown on the diagram) at 6½ furlongs; and to the 5/8 pole in seven-furlong races. At "bullring" layouts, and tracks with layouts longer than the standard one mile, the starting locations will vary with track lengths. The fraction, however, will still be completed at the same distance from the start of the race: one-quarter mile.

Fps figures reflect the *average* rate of velocity in each fraction. The computation:

$$1Fr = 1320 \text{ feet} - (BL * 10) / T1 \text{ (time of the fraction)}$$

Example: Horse A has led from the start of the race and has completed the first fraction in 22.1.
Calculation: 1320 / 22.2 = 58.92 fps
Example: Horse B is 7 lengths behind a 22.3 first fraction.
Calculation: 1320 − (7 * 10) or 1250 feet / 22.6 = 55.30 fps
(Note: the 22.3 must be converted to 22.6. Calculators work in *tenths*, not fifths.)

Second Fraction (2Fr) 1320 feet

In six-furlong sprints the middle fraction is run from the half-mile pole to the quarter pole; 6½ and seven furlongs differ proportionate to their respective starting points. At most tracks the second fraction in six-furlong races is run almost entirely around a turn. Hence the term "turn-time," arguably the most significant fraction in a sprint race. Since it must be extrapolated from the relationship of the first and second calls, it is also referred to as the "hidden fraction."

$$2Fr = 1320 \text{ feet} + \text{or} - (BL * 10) / T2$$

In the second fraction the calculation must account for the possibility of lengths *gained* as well as lost. The handicapper credits, or debits, 10 feet for every length gained, or lost, against the pace of the race. A runner 7 lengths (70 feet) behind the pace at the first call that gains to within 3 lengths at the second call, has gained 4 lengths (40 feet) on the pace of the race.

Example: The leader of the previous example (A) reaches the second call in 45.4, and B has gained 4 lengths between the first and second calls. The second fraction of the race is the difference between the second and first calls (T4 − T1) or 45.4 − 22.3 = 23.1.

Calculation: 1320 + (4 * 10) or 1360 / 23.2 = 58.62 fps

Example: Horse C loses 2 lengths in the second fraction of the same race.

Calculation: 1320 − (2 * 10) or 1300 / 23.2 = 56.03 fps
(Remember to convert fifths to tenths.)

Final Fraction (3Fr) 1320, 1650, or 1980 feet

The distance of the final fraction varies with the distance of the race. The number of feet in the segment is a simple calculation: feet in a furlong, multiplied by the furlongs in the fraction.

6F   660 * 2   = 1320 feet (¼ pole to finish)

6½F 660 * 2.5 = 1650 feet (⁵⁄₁₆ pole to finish)

7F   660 * 3   = 1980 feet (⅜ pole to finish)

I've not included 5 and 5½ furlong races because those races are best handicapped with final time.

3Fr = Number of feet in the fraction + or − (BL * 10) / T3

Example: Horse D maintains a lead from the second call to the finish of a six-furlong race. The "splits" of the race are 22.2 45.3   1:11.2.

Calculation: The final fraction of a six-furlong race is 2 furlongs times 660 feet per furlong = 1320 feet. The time of the fraction is the difference between the second call and the final time. In this example the third fraction is:

1:11.2 − 45.3 = 25.4. In tenths, the fraction is 25.8 and is determined by first converting the 1:11.2 to 71.4 and the 45.3 to 45.6. The calculator input/output is 71.4 − 45.6 = 25.8.

Horse D's final fraction is $1320 - (0 \text{ BL}) / 25.8 = 51.16$ fps.

Example: Horse E loses 3 lengths from the second call to the finish in the same race.

Calculation: $1320 - (3 * 10)$ or $1290 / 25.8 = 50.00$ fps.

Example: Horse F gains 5.25 lengths in the final fraction of a 6½-furlong race with splits of 22.2   45.2   1:17.3.

Calculation: The following preliminary calculations are necessary:

(1) $2.5 * 660 = 1650$ feet in the fraction

(2) $1:17.3 = 77.6$ final time in tenths

(3) $77.6 - 45.4 = 32.2$ final fraction in tenths (T4)

Horse F's final fraction:

$1650 + (5.25 * 10)$ or $1702.5 / 32.2 = 52.87$ fps

Summarizing the Sprint Calculations

First Fraction / First Call
$1\text{Fr} = 1320 - (10 * \text{BL}) / \text{T1}$
Second Fraction
$2\text{Fr} = 1320 + \text{or} - (10 * \text{BL}) / \text{T2}$
Third or Final Fraction
$3\text{Fr} = \text{feet in fraction} + \text{or} - (10 * \text{BL}) / \text{T3}$

Now let's add the most important calculation of all: the second call.

Second Call (2Call)

In sprints the second call occurs a half-mile, or four furlongs, into the race. It is also referred to as Early Pace (EP).

$$2\text{Call} = 2640 - (10 * \text{BL}) / \text{T4}$$

Some practical examples of the sprint calculations:

Maven's Pride		Ch. g. 4, by Maven—Sweet Lynn, by Brau Busher						
		Br.—Krumhorn Morris D (IN)	1989	3	2	0	0	$6,180
Own.—Shlofrock L & Dassouki M	**117**	Tr.—Dassouki Michael	1988	16	3	4	2	$17,007
		Lifetime 22 5 4 2 $23,946						

7Jly89-2AP	6f :23 :47 1:13¹ft	7 119	12½ 13 1⁴ 1¹	Diaz J L⁴	Ⓢ 5000 74-27 Maven'sPride,DiscoTco,Interction 11
15Jun89-1Haw	6f :22³ :46¹ 1:11⁴ft	2½ 119	3½ 21 43½ 7⁵½	Diaz J L⁸	Ⓢ 5000 73-24 ShadyFamily,JustZack,SonuvBoosh 8
15Jun89—Four wide.					
7Jun89-1Haw	6f :22¹ :46 1:11⁴ft	13 114	1½ 11½ 1ʰᵈ 11	MarquezCHJr²	Ⓢ 5000 82-18 Mven'sPrid,GoodHilrious,DiscoTco 7
6Dec88-5Bml	6f :22³ :47³ 1:14³ft	8½ 114	2² 21½ 32 2⁶	Razo A⁷	Ⓢ 5000 79-21 Zensheir,Maven'sPride,DavesHolme 8
6Dec88—Drifted out					
15Oct88-3Bml	6f :22² :46³ 1:13⁴ft	8½ 112	1¹ 1½ 35 6¹⁰	Diaz J L⁶	Ⓢ 5000 — — SeHbloIngls,DvsHolm,Mthw'sMrk 12

1. Maven's Pride 7Jly89
The filly ran wire-to-wire recording the following fractions:

1Fr   T1 = 23.0 1320 / 23.0 = 57.39 fps
2Fr   T2 = 24.0 1320 / 24.0 = 55.00 fps
3Fr   T3 = 26.1 1320 / 26.2 = 50.38 fps
2Call T4 = 47.0 2640 / 47.0 = 56.17 fps

The fps array we'll be working with throughout the text:

Contender	1Fr	2Fr	3Fr	2Call/EP
Maven's Pride	57.39	55.00	50.38	56.17

A few additional points before moving to another example:

- The third-fraction calculation should be a reminder that the use of a calculator requires the user to convert fifths of a second to tenths. Hence the *26.2* in the example.
- Second call and Early Pace are interchangeable terms.
- The second fraction is the difference between the second call and the first call. It is T2 = T4 − T1. Maven's Pride's second fraction was 47.0 − 23.0 = 24.0 seconds.

2. Maven's Pride 15Jun89
This trip she did not fare as well. The race fractions:

1Fr   T1 = 22.3 1320 − (.5 * 10) or 1315 / 22.6 = 58.18 fps
2Fr   T2 = 23.3 1320 − (.5 * 10) or 1315 / 23.6 = 55.72 fps
3Fr   T3 = 25.3 1320 − (8.5 * 10) or 1235 / 25.6 = 48.24 fps
2Call T4 = 46.1 2640 − (1   * 10) or 2630 / 46.2 = 56.92 fps

Contender	1Fr	2Fr	3Fr	2Call/EP
Maven's Pride	58.18	55.72	48.24	56.92

There are two additional points I should emphasize before proceeding.
1. The beaten lengths in each fraction were .5, .5, and 8.5.

The second call, however, is a "stand alone" and represents the cumulative beaten lengths of the first two fractions. Whereas they must be calculated with distance gained or lost during the fractions, the second call is calculated exactly as printed in the past performances. Maven's Pride was second, 1 length behind the leader at the call.

$$2\text{Call} = 2640 - (1 * 10) \text{ or } 2630 / 46.2 = 56.92 \text{ fps}$$

2. The trouble line "four wide" is significant and is usually an excuse to use another race as indicative of current ability. A pace setter running outside the other early pace on the turn is taking all the worst of it. The horse must be much the best to win. Do not, however, be tempted to modify the line by compensating for the trip with fps adjustments! Unless you're adept with a Ouija board, you will not be successful in your compensations. Simply use another paceline and mentally note the last performance as "better than looked." In actuality, the race was not a bad effort anyway. Remember, the second call (Early Pace) occurs two thirds of the way into a six-furlong race. One length behind at the 66.66% mark of the race, against a solid pace, is hardly a poor effort.

3. Drouilly' Boy 19Sep89
This one's a sustained pace runner (closer).

1Fr $T1 = 21.4$ $1320 - (8 \quad * 10)$ or $1240 / 21.8 = 56.88$ fps

2Fr $T2 = 22.3$ $1320 + (3.5 * 10)$ or $1355 / 22.6 = 59.95$ fps

3Fr   T3 = 24.4 1320 + (4.5 * 10) or 1365 / 24.8 = 55.04 fps

2Call T4 = 44.2 2640 − (4.5 * 10) or 2595 / 44.4 = 58.44 fps

Contender	1Fr	2Fr	3Fr	2Call/EP
Drouilly's Boy	56.88	59.95	55.04	58.44

An additional point regarding these calculations: In two of the fractions this horse *gained* on the pace of the race. In the lengths gained or lost scenario, keep in mind the timing of the fraction was based on the first horse to hit the point of call. Horses behind the leader may have run significantly more, or less, distance than did the leader. In the above race Drouilly's Boy was approximately 80 feet behind the leader at the first call. He must be debited for his failure to get the entire fraction completed by the time the race hit the 1320 feet mark. Conversely, in the second fraction, he *gained* 35 feet (the difference between first call BL 8.0 and second call BL of 4.5) and must be credited with running more feet in the second pace increment. Similarly, he has to be credited with an additional 45 feet gained in the final fraction.

Buy the Firm

Own.—Kinsman Stable

114

B. f. 3(May), by Affirmed—By the Hand, by Intentionally
Br.—Kinsman Stud Farm (Fla)
Tr.—Lenzini John J Jr

1989 5 2 0 1 $21,130
Turf 1 0 0 0 $200

Lifetime 5 2 0 1 $21,130

20Sep89-9Crc	6½f :22² :46 1:19³ft	3½ 113	65½ 53½ 1hd 14½	Valiente D⁴ ⑤Aw12600	87-16 BuytheFirm,MedievlPrincss,SuprNt 6
4Mar89-2GP	1½ :48 1:12² 1:46³ft	9½ 116	72½ 68½ 36 45½	Valiente D¹ ⑤Aw25000	62-18 EtofEtrnll,LovEmrgncy,GrlyWhrly 11
18Feb89-3GP	7f :22³ :45³ 1:26³ft	7½ 121	79½ 69½ 34 3hd	Chavez JF⁸ ⑤Aw21400	71-23 Up, Blushing Katy, Buy the Firm 8
2Feb89-8GP	al ①	1:36³fm 4½ 116	812 811 815 919	Santos J A⁹ ⑤Aw28000	68-15 Adira, Amad Key, Feliness 10
11Jan89-3GP	6f :22² :45⁴ 1:12³ft	13 121	45½ 35½ 21½ 1½	Chavez J F⁷ ⑥Mdn	76-21 Buy the Firm, To Win, Mama Bee 11

Oct 2 Aqu 5f sy 1:01 H (d)   Sep 16 Crc 4f ft :42 B   Sep 10 Crc 5f ft 1:02 B   Sep 4 Crc 6f ft 1:15³ B

4. Buy The Firm 20Sep89 6½ furlongs

1Fr   T1 = 22.2 1320 − (5.25 * 10) or 1267.5 / 22.4 = 56.58 fps

2Fr   T2 = 23.3 1320 + (1.5 * 10) or 1335   / 23.6 = 56.56 fps

3Fr   T3 = 33.3 1650 + (3.75 * 10) or 1687.5 / 33.6 = 50.22 fps

2Call T4 = 46.0 2640 − (3.75 * 10) or 2602.5 / 46.0 = 56.57 fps

Contender	1Fr	2Fr	3Fr	2Call/EP
Buy The Firm	56.58	56.56	50.22	56.57

In this example an additional point arises. The third fraction is not the neat 1320 associated with the earlier examples. This time we must work a little harder. At 6½ furlongs the last fraction is 2½ furlongs, or 1650 feet. At seven furlongs the final fraction is three furlongs or 1980 feet. The three possibilities: 1320, 1650, or 1980. Five- and 5½-furlong races are essentially all-out dashes and are best handicapped from final time. The final fractions are shorter than the internal fractions, and if employed in a pace rating scheme, tend to distort the ratings in favor of late runners.

5. Buy The Firm 18Feb89 seven furlongs

1Fr   T1 = 22.3 1320 − (9.25 * 10) or 1227.5 / 22.6 = 54.31 fps
2Fr   T2 = 23.0 1320 + (0   * 10) or 1320   / 23.0 = 57.39 fps
3Fr   T3 = 41.0 1980 + (9.15 * 10) or 2071.5 / 41.0 = 50.52 fps
2Call T4 = 45.3 2640 − (9.25 * 10) or 2547.5 / 45.6 = 55.86 fps

Contender	1Fr	2Fr	3Fr	2Call/EP
Buy The Firm	54.31	57.39	50.52	55.86

FEET-PER-SECOND CALCULATIONS—ROUTES

First Fraction (1Fr) 2640 feet (also the first *call*)

On the basic layout the first fraction starts in front of the grandstand and runs to the half-mile pole in one-mile races; the 9/16 pole at 1 1/16 miles; and to the 5/8 pole in 1 1/8 mile races.

$$1Fr = 2640 \text{ feet} - (BL * 10) / T1$$

Example: Horse A leads throughout the first call of a route race with a first call time of 47.3.
Calculation: 2640 − (0) / 47.6 = 55.46 fps
Example: Horse B was 4¼ lengths off a first call of 48.4.
Calculation: 2640 − 42.5 or 2597.5 / 48.8 = 53.22 fps
Example: Horse C was 13 lengths behind a first call of 47.2.
Calculation: 2640 − 130 or 2510 / 47.4 = 52.95 fps

Second Fraction (2Fr) 1320 feet

The middle fraction is 1320 feet and links the first and second calls. It is computed the same way in routes as in sprints.

$$2Fr = 1320 \text{ feet} + \text{or} - (BL * 10) / T2$$

Example: Horse B makes a run at the leaders of his race and gains 2¼ lengths against splits of 48.4   1:13.2. The second fraction is $73.4 - 48.8 = 24.6$ fps.

Calculation: $1320 + 22.5$ or $1342.5 / 24.6 = 54.57$ fps

Final Fraction (3Fr) Distance varies

The same as with the sprint races. For sake of easy reference, I'll restate the material.

The feet in the final fraction varies with the distance of the race. The number of feet in the segment is a simple calculation. Feet in a furlong, multiplied by the furlongs in the fraction.

Eight furlongs	= 1320 feet
Mile & 40 yards (8.18F)	= 1440 feet
Mile & 70 yards (8.42F)	= 1530 feet
8½ furlongs	= 1650 feet
Nine furlongs	= 1980 feet
Mile & 3⁄16 (9½F)	= 2310 feet

Calculate the final fraction using the same formula as in sprints:

$$3Fr = \text{Number of feet in the fraction} + \text{or} - (BL * 10) / T3 \text{ First}$$

Example: Horse D has a running line that looks like this:

8½F	47.3	1:12.1	1:45.1
BL	6	4	nk

Calculation:
(1) For the calculator, the final time of the race is 1:45 and 2⁄10 seconds. It is expressed as: 60 (seconds) + 45 (sec-

onds)+.2 (seconds)=105.2 seconds. The final fraction of the example is therefore: 105.2−72.2=33.0 seconds.
(2) Horse D ran: 1650+(3.75 * 10) or 1687.5 feet during the 33.0 seconds of the fraction.
(3) D's final fraction: 1687.5 / 33.0=51.13 fps

Example: Horse E has the following line:

9F	47.1	1:11.4	1:50.4
BL	2	2	5¾

Calculation:
(1) 1:10.8 (final time)−71.8 (second call)=39.0 seconds
(2) E ran 1980−(3.75 * 10) or 1942.5, losing 37.5 feet in the fraction.
(3) E's final fraction:
3Fr=1942.5 / 39.0=49.81 fps

Second Call (2Call & Early Pace)

In routes the second call occurs ¾ mile or six furlongs into the race. As in sprints it is a "stand alone" call and is computed separate from the fractions.

2Call=3960 feet−(BL * 10) / Time of the call (T4)

Example: Horse F is 7 lengths behind at the second call in the following race:

47.1   1:12.2   1:44.4

Calculation: 3960−(7 * 10) or 3890 / 72.4=53.73 fps

The Route Summary

First Fraction / First Call
    1Fr=2640−(10 * BL) / T1
Second Fraction
    2Fr=1320+ or−(10 * BL) / T2
Third or Final Fraction
    3Fr=D * 660+or−(10 * BL) / T3

Second Call or Early Pace
2Call = 3960 − (BL ∗ 10) / T4

To summarize the fractions and points of call for the most commonly run distances:

Dist	*1Fr*	*Pole*	*2Fr*	*Pole*	*3Fr*	*Pole*	*2Call*	*Pole*
6F	1320	½	1320	¼	1320	Fin	2640	¼
6½F	1320	9⁄16	1320	5⁄16	1650	Fin	2640	5⁄16
7F	1320	⅝	1320	⅜	1980	Fin	2640	⅜
8F	2640	½	1320	¼	1320	Fin	3960	¼
8½F	2640	9⁄16	1320	5⁄16	1650	Fin	3960	5⁄16
9F	2640	⅝	1320	⅜	1980	Fin	3960	⅜
9½F	2640	11⁄16	1320	7⁄16	2310	Fin	3960	7⁄16

Missing from the summary are the 5- and 5½-furlong dashes and the distances over 1 3⁄16 miles. We've discussed the reasoning behind the shorter races, but the marathon distances present the other end of the spectrum. In races over 1 3⁄16 miles, pace ratings become highly unreliable. That's not to say *pace* is not an important factor, but the ratings are suspect and unrepresentative. In the longer races, stamina, class, and pace *strategy* should be the focal points for the handicappers.

Route Examples

Aptostar — B. f. 4, by Fappiano—Stark Drama, by Graustark
Own.—Centennial Farms — 119 — Br.—Whitney T P (Fla) — Tr.—Jerkens H Allen
1989 5 1 2 1 $121,583
1988 7 4 1 1 $335,464
Lifetime 13 6 7 2 $487,047

25Jun89-8Bel 7f :22³ :45⁴ 1:22⁴ft *3-5 118 62¾ 3½ 1² 12¼ CrdrAJr⁷ ⒻVagrancyH 88-17 Aptostar, Toll Fee, Lambros 7
25Jun89—Grade III
8Jun89-8Bel 6f :21⁴ :44³ 1:09²gd 2¼ 122 33½ 3⁴ 2⁵ 2⁴ StsJA³ ⒻGenuine Rsk 88-14 SafelyKept,Aptostr,CgeyExuberncе 4
8Jun89—Grade II
13May89-8Bel 1⅛ :44⁴ 1:09 1:40⁴ft 5½e 115 4³ 41½ 6⁶ 611¾ KrnJA¹ ⒻShuvee H 86-16 Baker'sLdy,Ros'sCntin,GrcinFlight 7
13May89—Grade I
23Apr89-8Aqu 1⅛ :49¹ 1:13⁴ 1:51⁴ft 6½ 117 5⁶ 5⁴ 3³ 3⁶ KronJA² ⒻTop Flight 73-27 Banker'sLady,ColonilWters,Aptostr 5
23Apr89—Grade I
9Apr89-8Aqu 1 :45² 1:10 1:35²ft 2½ 118 3¹ 1hd 2½ 25¼ KrJA⁵ ⒻBed Roses H 84-17 Banker's Lady, Aptostar, Avie's Gal 5
9Apr89—Grade II
3Jly88-9Bel 1½ :48² 2:04⁴ 2:32⁴ft 2¾ 121 41½ 3¹ 2² 21¾ DvsRG² ⒻC C A Oaks 54-25 GoodbyeHalo,Aptostar,MakeChnge 6
3Jly88—Grade I
18Jun88-8Bel 1⅛ :45⁴ 1:10² 1:49⁴ft 8-5e 121 96¾ 65¼ 5³ 31¾ DsRG⁷ ⒻMther Goose 76-20 GoodbyeHalo,MakeChange,Aptostr 9
18Jun88—Grade I
21May88-8Bel 1 :45¹ 1:09² 1:34⁴ft *1e 121 42¾ 31½ 2½ 1³ DavisRG³ ⒻAcorn 91-11 Aptostar, Topicount, Avie's Gal 9
21May88—Grade I
●Aug 8 Sar 3f ft :36³ H ●Aug 4 Sar 6f ft 1:14 H Jly 18 Bel 4f ft :51⁴ B Jun 28 Bel tr.t 6f ft 1:15 B

1. Aptostar 9Apr89 One mile

1Fr T1 = 45.2 2640 $-(10*1$) or 2630 / 45.4 = 57.92 fps

2Fr T2 = 24.3 1320 $+(10*1$) or 1330 / 24.6 = 54.06 fps

3Fr T3 = 25.2 1320 $-(10*5.25)$ or 1267 / 25.4 = 49.89 fps

2Call T4 = 1:10.0 3960 / 70.0   = 56.57 fps

Contender	1Fr	2Fr	3Fr	2Call/EP
Aptostar	57.92	54.06	49.89	56.57

The second call of this race presents a new wrinkle to the subject. A calculator is incapable of accepting the 1:10.0 from the *Racing Form* past performances. The player must convert any number over one minute to the number of seconds and tenths of seconds: 1:10.0 is 70 seconds; 1:11.3 is 71.6 seconds; 1:35.3 would be 95.6 seconds; and so on.

2. Aptostar 13May89 1⅟₁₆ miles

1Fr T1 = 44.4 2640 $-(10*3$) or 2610 / 44.8 = 58.26 fps

2Fr T2 = 24.1 1320 $+(10*1.5)$ or 1335 / 24.2 = 55.16 fps

3Fr T3 = 31.4 $2.5*660 = 1650 - (10*10.25)$ or 1547.5 / 31.8 =
48.66 fps

·2Call T4 = 1:09.0 3960 $-(10*1.5)$ or 3945 / 69.0 = 57.17 fps

Contender	1Fr	2Fr	3Fr	2Call/EP
Aptostar	58.26	55.16	48.66	57.17

3. Aptostar 23Apr89 1⅛ miles

1Fr T1 = 49.1 2640 $-(10*6)$ or 2580 / 49.2 = 52.43 fps

2Fr T2 = 24.3 1320 $+(10*2)$ or 1340 / 24.6 = 54.47 fps

3Fr T3 = 37.2 $3*660 = 1980 - (10*2)$ or 1960 / 37.4 = 52.40 fps

2Call T4 = 1:13.4 3960 $-(10*4)$ or 3920 / 73.8 = 53.11 fps

Contender	1Fr	2Fr	3Fr	2Call/EP
Aptostar	52.43	54.47	52.40	53.11

I strongly recommend you work through the sprint and route examples until you can easily replicate the results of my calculations. Do not be concerned if the numbers are slightly different. Mine were created by the handheld computer I use in my daily calculations. The rounding-off procedures may create differences as high as .02 fps, and you should not be concerned. It is the essence of the calculations that must be mastered. Once you've gained an understanding of the concepts and composition of the numbers, by all means use a computer or even the charts in the back of the chapter. There are many inexpensive handheld computers on the market that will easily run these formulas.

The remainder of the text will assume the reader has mastered feet-per-second calculations. Many of the principles in this book will stand alone, and fps numbers will be unnecessary to many of the applications; however, much more of the text will be dependent upon understanding the calculations.

FPS VALUE OF A LENGTH

Handicappers who employ a feet-per-second methodology must eventually answer a basic question: What is the fps value of a beaten length? Just as surely, most will think through the process and land on the correct procedure to answer the question. It is my intention to shorten as much of the learning time as possible. Consider the following scenario:

A hypothetical racetrack has been favoring early pace in the extreme. The bias has been so strong that no horse has come from farther behind than 1¾ lengths at the second call. Racegoers will have witnessed a steady procession of wire-to-wire winners in both sprints and routes. The following field lines up at the starting gate for a 1¹⁄₁₆ mile route:

	1Fr	2Fr	3Fr	2Call/EP
Horse A	54.89	55.00	51.98	54.92
Horse B	56.43	54.06	49.69	55.61
Horse C	54.64	54.54	52.39	54.60
Horse D	56.41	53.79	49.90	55.51

This is a neat, compact little graphic. Everything is orderly and compartmentalized. *But* without additional understanding of the figures, the graphics are a bit self-serving. Much *can* be interpreted from the fps array without really addressing the key to the race: the bias. In the example, B and D are clearly in the lead at the first call, with A and C approximately 1.75 fps behind in average velocity. So what? How far behind the leader is 1.75 fps? I'll answer that in a moment. In the second fraction A gets into gear and closes the gap; somewhat. How much is "somewhat," and how far behind is the horse at the all-important second call? After all, the bias is so strong it is dictating the handicapping of the race itself.

The horses in the example race are actually very close if we were measuring for final time. We're not. When a strong bias exists, overall pace ratings and speed figures must take a back seat to a more basic pace analysis. Where do the horses in the race figure to be at the important points of call? In the example race they figure to be positioned as follows:

Horse B	0 BL
Horse D	1 BL
Horse A	7 BL
Horse C	10 BL

The final times are all comparable, but anyone willing to bet A or C had better stick to speed figures. At the six-furlong point in a race, one length is equivalent to about .15 fps. That's nice to know, but how is it determined and what is one length worth at other distances? I'll give you the most frequently encountered distances, but the calculations are quite simple.

(feet in the segment / time = fps rating)
3960 / 72.0 (1:12.0) = 55.00 fps
}diff. .16 fps
3960 / 72.2 (1:12.1) = 54.84 fps
}diff. .15 fps
3960 / 72.4 (1:12.2) = 54.69 fps
}diff. .15 fps
3960 / 72.6 (1:12.3) = 54.54 fps
}diff. .15 fps
3960 / 72.8 (1:12.4) = 54.39 fps

The average value per beaten length at 3960 feet is .15 fps.

Prove it to yourself and work through several distance/time relationships. The most common distances and their approximate values:

six furlongs	.15 fps
four furlongs	.25 fps
three furlongs	.28 fps
2½ furlongs	.33 fps
two furlongs	.53 fps

These are approximate and will vary at differing rates of speed. They are, however, good ball-park estimates, and can be used with confidence when estimating beaten lengths.

Before leaving this chapter, we should revisit the A-B-C-D scenario.

	1Fr	2Fr	3FR	2Call/EP
Horse A	54.89	55.00	51.98	54.92
Horse B	56.43	54.06	49.69	55.61
Horse C	54.64	54.54	52.39	54.60
Horse D	56.41	53.79	49.90	55.51

The bias at our hypothetical track dictates we play no horse that will not be within 1.75 lengths of the leader at the second call of the race (6F). Therefore, to be a possible play a runner must be within .26 fps (1.75 * .15) at the call. Any runner in the scenario with a second call rating less than 55.35 fps (B's 55.61 − .26 = 55.35) would be a poor betting proposition. In the chapter on creating a generic "model" for the racetrack, we'll relax that .26 a bit to reflect the minor "glitches" inherent in track speeds or variants.

One final look at the race: Let's superimpose another bias requirement. No winner has been farther behind than three lengths at the *first call*. The same procedure applies. No horse should be considered for play that is not within .75 fps (3 * .25) of Horse B's 56.43 fps. In the hypothetical scenario, any contender with a first call velocity of less than 55.68 should be summarily eliminated from consideration. Horses A and C should no longer be contenders for the win.

This chapter has required an extensive commitment by the reader. I said early on that the calculations can be quite tedious. Yet much of what comes later is dependent upon a working knowledge of the math involved. For the player who fully embraces a modern approach to pace analysis, the effort will have been time well invested.

Pace Chart—FPS

1½ fur (3/16 mile)	2 fur (¼ mile)	2½ fur (5/16 mile)	3 fur (⅜ mile)	4 fur (½ mile)	6 fur (¾ mile)
16—61.87	21—62.86	28—58.92	35—56.37	43—61.39	1:08—58.23
1—61.11	1—62.26	1—58.51	1—56.25	1—61.11	1—58.06
2—60.36	2—61.68	2—58.09	2—55.93	2—60.82	2—57.89
3—59.63	3—61.11	3—57.69	3—55.61	3—60.55	3—57.72
4—58.92	4—60.55	4—57.29	4—55.30	4—60.27	4—57.55
17—58.23	22—60.00	29—56.89	36—55.00	44—60.00	1:09—57.39
1—57.55	1—59.45	1—56.50	1—54.69	1—59.72	1—57.22
2—56.89	2—58.92	2—56.12	2—54.39	2—59.45	2—57.06
3—56.25	3—58.40	3—56.74	3—54.09	3—59.19	3—56.89
4—55.61	4—57.89	4—55.37	4—53.80	4—58.92	4—56.73
18—55.00	23—57.39	30—55.00	37—53.51	45—58.66	1:10—56.57
1—54.39	1—56.89	1—54.63	1—53.22	1—58.40	1—56.41
2—53.80	2—56.41	2—54.27	2—52.94	2—58.14	2—56.25
3—56.09	3—55.93	3—53.22	3—52.65	3—57.89	3—56.09
4—52.65	4—55.46	4—53.57	4—52.38	4—57.64	4—55.93
19—52.10	24—55.00	31—53.22	38—52.10	46—57.39	1:11—55.77
1—51.56	1—54.54	1—52.88	1—51.83	1—57.14	1—55.61
2—51.03	2—54.09	2—52.54	2—51.56	2—56.89	2—55.46
3—50.51	3—53.65	3—52.21	3—51.29	3—56.65	3—55.30
4—50.00	4—53.22	4—51.88	4—51.03	4—56.41	4—55.15
20—49.51	25—52.80	32—51.56	39—50.76	47—56.17	1:12—55.00
1—49.00	1—52.38	1—51.24	1—50.51	1—55.93	1—54.84
2—48.52	2—51.96	2—50.92	2—50.25	2—55.69	2—54.69
3—48.05	3—51.56	3—50.61	3—50.00	3—55.46	3—54.54
4—47.59	4—51.16	4—50.30	4—49.74	4—55.23	4—54.41
21—47.14	26—50.76	33—50.00	40—59.50	48—55.00	1:13—54.24
1—46.69	1—50.38	1—49.69	1—49.25	1—54.77	1—54.09
2—46.26	2—50.00	2—49.41	2—49.00	2—54.54	2—53.94
3—45.83	3—49.62	3—49.10	3—48.76	3—54.32	3—53.80
4—45.41	4—49.25	4—48.81	4—48.52	4—54.09	4—53.65
22—45.00	27—48.88	34—48.52		49—53.87	1:14—53.51
	1—48.52	1—48.24		1—53.65	1—53.36
	2—48.17	2—47.94		2—53.44	2—53.22
	3—47.82	3—47.68		3—53.22	3—53.08
	4—47.48	4—47.41		4—53.01	4—52.94
	28—47.14	35—47.14		50—52.80	1:15—52.80
		1—46.87		1—52.56	
		2—46.61		2—52.36	

CHAPTER III

Running Styles—ESP

IN THIS BOOK we spend a lot of time with velocity, energy, bias, and track models. They are the tools of the modern pace handicapper. Effective application of the principles depends on a thorough understanding of these tools. Profits are sized by the depth of that understanding and by the degree of belief in the concepts.

As with any method of play, there must be a firmness of resolve and a positive attitude. To "dabble" with any method is hazardous to the bankroll. Practitioners will often be wrong about personal adaptations. They will frequently be on the wrong path of a zigzag pattern. If you accept the concepts, and wish to adopt them, give yourself a chance to succeed. Apply them in the manner presented, at least until proficiency is achieved.

Having said that, I caution the inexperienced player. The computer, velocity numbers, and an existing bias may conspire against you. Races are won on the racetrack, by flesh and blood animals, not by computers or speed charts. Every race is a different scenario; very few are alike. While most handicapping principles apply in a general sense, they often do not apply in the specific.

Too many early pace horses in a race can be a setup for sustained pace. If the velocity numbers are closely matched, the early horses will usually engage in a pace duel. The track may be strongly biased early, and their velocity numbers superior, but the early pace horses do not have the advantage. Conversely, the lone pace setter is always a candidate to upset, no matter the velocity numbers or the bias. Experienced handicappers know that. Inexperienced handicappers are often blinded by methodologies, and steadfastly adhere to their "figures." That can be self-destructive.

As an instructor with PIRCO, the Sartin support group, I've observed too much dependence on computer output. The methodology is computer based, and it's natural to let the computer do all the work. It *will*, except in situations where it *won't*. That isn't doubletalk. There are races every day that match up in such a manner as to defy the general trends of winning performances.

Consider the following:

(1) The faint-hearted speedster who suddenly grabs the lead and never looks back, on a track strongly biased for closers.

(2) The late runner who wins on a day when every other race is won on the lead.

(3) The horse with clearly superior early pace velocity who doesn't challenge the early lead.

Needlessly, inexperienced handicappers will lose most races that do not conform to their expectation. The above races will usually result in losing bets. Many players lack the skill and confidence to visualize races before the running. Invariably they'll rely on the figures. In many situations, numbers are not enough. Fortunately, the alternative skills can be acquired almost mechanically.

ESP

The subject is not parapsychology. The letters ESP represent the dominant running styles of horses: Early, Sustained, and Presser. Every race should be handicapped from the same starting point: identification of running styles. Before contender selection, before paceline selection, before class evaluation, identify *how* the race figures to be run. PIRCO instructors were able to wean most clients from overdependence on computers by also focusing on running styles. We should do the same.

Identifying running styles seems like an easy task. It is. Yet most bettors have only the slightest idea of which horses will contend for the early lead; which will be content to push the pace; and which will be closing late. Fewer still have any idea as to the probable intensity of the pace. Aside from recognizing the obvious early and sustained runners, most handicappers are severely disadvantaged. The subtleties of many races go completely unnoticed. Pace handicappers should not let that happen. They should carefully designate running styles at the outset.

EARLY PACE

The trickiest piece of the pace scenario is the analysis of Early Pace. Most races are won on, or near, the lead. Therefore, much care should go into the labeling of early pace horses. A horse designated as "early" will figure in every scenario. If several are able to contend for the lead, a probable pace duel may ensue. Early pace runners with pace figures that indicate inability to gain the lead in a race should be considered noncontenders.

An early pace horse, an E, is a runner whose very best races are *on the lead*. The E horse is habitually on the lead, or within a length of the leader while attempting to lead. Wins are accomplished *only* in that manner. The E horse that can also lay just behind the pace should be labeled E/P, indicating pressing ability. We'll cover pressers shortly.

SUSTAINED

The horse labeled Sustained or S is the opposite of the E horse. This one comes on late in the race, often after the issue has been decided. It's habitually in the last third of the field at the early calls, and wins by catching the leaders in the last fraction. First-call beaten lengths can be deceiving. They'll often be within three or four lengths at the first call, but usually against slow fractions. *Position is the deciding factor as to running style; not velocity.*

PRESSER

Pressers, P, are often difficult to label. They lay 1 to 3 lengths off the leaders and then come on in the second and third fractions. They do not run from the back of the pack, and are usually positioned third or fourth in the early going. What makes them difficult to label is a close resemblance to the other styles.

There's usually a race or two in a presser's past performances that qualifies as E or S, but the predominant style will be to snug in close to the pace. Pressers are the most reliable horses at any racetrack. They're relatively immune to early pace velocity and are usually quick enough to maintain contact with the field. They'll usually run their race.

ESP—THE BALLERINA STAKES

8th Saratoga

7 FURLONGS. (1.20⅘) 11th Running THE BALLERINA (Grade I). Purse $100,000 Added. Fillies and mares, 3-year-olds and upward. By subscription of $200 each, which should accompany the nomination; $800 to pass the entry box; $800 to start, with $100,000 added. The added money and all fees to be divided 60% to the winner, 22% to second, 12% to third and 6% to fourth. Weights, 3-year-olds, 117 lbs. Older, 122 lbs. Winners of three races of $50,000 since May 1, 1989, an additional 2 lbs. Non-winners of two races of $35,000 since February 1 allowed 3 lbs. Of two such races in 1988–89, 6 lbs. Of a race of $25,000 in 1988–89, 9 lbs. Of two races of $20,000 in 1988–89, 12 lbs. Starters to be named at the closing time of entries. Trophies will be presented to the winning owner, trainer and jockey. Closed with 21 nominations.

Saratoga's Grade I Ballerina Stakes usually contains some of the best female sprinters on the East Coast. The 1989 edition was no exception. Add a couple of tough routers, and the August 11 race fits southern California handicapper Dick Mitchell's contentious race scenario. He would contend there will be several possible outcomes to the race, and to take a short price would be foolish. He'd be correct in advising you to shop for the overlays. Our handicapping of the race will be limited to the designation of running styles: ESP. I've included only the horses that seemed to have a reasonable chance of affecting the outcome of the race.

Early Pace (E)

Feel The Beat ✳

The Lukas filly has only one way to go: in front. She is strictly an E horse and has shown no willingness to ration her speed. Only twice did she fail to gain the lead at the first call, and both races were nonthreatening losses. She'll affect the running of any race in which she's entered. Her last race, since it was against lesser, is not a good indication of her ability to get seven furlongs. The win on 25Aug88 was accomplished on a sloppy track, midway through her three-year-old season. That race does not clearly prove her ability to go seven furlongs.

Bodacious Tatas

Own.—Kimmel John C   116

B. f. 4, by Distinctive Pro—Key to Paree, by L'Enjoleur
Br.—Kimmel John (Fla)
Tr.—Kimmel John C
Lifetime   33 .9 4 5 $275,880

This filly has been routing throughout her past performances. Her route speed is excellent, but hardly in a class with quality sprinters. Her confirmed style is an early pace type; mark her as an E.

As mentioned earlier, the pace handicapper must be aware that confirmed early pace horses incapable of gaining the lead should be relegated to noncontender status. That should be evident in the past performances of both these horses. Feel The Beat failed to lead only twice in her shown races. She finished a weak third and a distant eighth. Bodacious Tatas failed to lead three times in her races; all three were dismal efforts. She should not be able to gain the lead today.

Sustained (S)

Proper Evidence

Own.—Sampol H   116

Ch. f. 4, by 360W Sentence—Catch a Blessing, by Prince Blessed
Br.—West Edward J (Fla)
Tr.—Barton John L
Lifetime   28 7 4 5 $251,100

9Jly89-7WO 6f :213 :443 1:102ft 7 116 65¾ 56 44½ 1½ Duffy L3 ⒻHcp0 91-09 ProperEvidence,Zdrcrt,BientotGold 6
9Jun89-7WO 1 Ⓣ:4841:1411:39 fm 12 117 74½ 85¾ 810 89½ Duffy L8 ⒻAw35200 72-13 HanginOnaStar,Ptermagnt WeeDrm 8
27May89-9WO 7f :224 :444 1:232ft 17 116 65 64½ 44 1hd DffyL10 ⒻSeaway 91-17 ProperEvidence,FoxyAlexis,Anglia 10
27May89—Grade III
18May89-8WO 6½f :224 :46 1:17 ft 3½ 117 42½ 41 1½ 12½ Duffy L3 ⒻAw32800 88-14 ProperEvidenc,WDrm,CrystlSlippers 5
5May89-8WO 6f :221 :452 1:104sy 10 117 67½ 68½ 47½ 34½ Duffy L1 ⒻAw32800 84-20 Vness'sPride,SttlSngu,ProprEvidnc 7
16Feb89-7GP 6f :221 :452 1:104ft 9½ 119 66½ 710 612 411¾ GonzlzMA 1 ⒻAw24000 73-28 Waggley,Ataentsic,FairwayGoddess 8
Jly 24 WO 3f ft :39 B Jly 1 WO 5f ft 1:004 H Jun 25 WO 5f ft 1:011 H Jun 19 WO 4f ft :482 B

Proper Evidence is Canada's contribution to the race. The filly's best races are from well off the pace. Her race on 18May89 fits a presser's profile, but the preponderance of evidence points toward an S designation. The May 18 race had only five entrants, and she was running next to last at the second call. If in doubt as to best style, consider running position. She was fourth in a five-horse field. Proper Evidence is a classy filly with a lifetime bankroll of $251,180; and she's an effective sprinter.

Cagey Exuberance
Ch. m. 5, by Exuberant—Prudent Cagey, by Prudent Roman
Br.—Burbank L D (Fla) 1989 7 2 1 2 $133,285
Own.—Burbank Lindsay D 119 Tr.—Camac Robert W 1988 13 5 6 1 $316,080
Lifetime 37 18 9 4 $738,936
9Jly89-11Lrl 7f :232 :461 1:231ft 9-5 120 42½ 53½ 32 32¾ DsrKJ 1 ⒻMy Juliet H 88-20 Dessa, Shaviana, CageyExuberance 7
9Jly89—Bumped
8Jun89-8Bel 6f :214 :443 1:092gd 2½ 122 44½ 46½ 38 38 PrrtC 2 ⒻGenuine Rsk 84-14 SafelyKept,Aptostr,CgeyExuberncе 4
8Jun89—Grade II
20May89-9Pim 6f :23 :452 1:093ft *6-5 121 65 54½ 53¾ 24 DsrKJ 5 ⒻJacobFrnceh 94-10 Kerygma,CgeyExubernce,IntheCurl 6
15Apr89-8Pim 6f :231 :461 1:112sy *8-5 123 42 43 46 58½ DsrKJ 4 ⒻPrimonettaH 79-15 In the Curl, Kerygma, Cu'. Ice 6
26Feb89-8Aqu 6f ⊡:223 :46 1:104ft *4-5 122 3½ 22 1½ 1¾ MlrR 4 ⒻCorrection H 90-24 CgeyExubernc,Hdgbout,RcylRxson 6
12Feb89-10Lrl 7f :22 :444 1:212ft *2½ 122 86½ 84½ 64½ 411¼ StsJA 12 ⒻB Fritche H 92-11 Tappiano, Very Subtle,TopsInTaps 12
12Feb89—Grade III; Raced wide
1Jan89-8Aqu 6f ⊡:222 :453 1:102ft *4-5 121 64½ 62¾ 1hd 12 SntsJA 1 ⒻInterboro H 92-23 CgyExubrnc,Hdgbout,SunshnAlwys 8
1Jan89—Grade III
19Nov88-9Lrl 7f :233 :472 1:251sy *7-5 122 42½ 62½ 54 55½ CstdM 5 ⒻStrght DefH 79-19 Kerygma, Dessa, Nasty Affair 7
Aug 8 Pha 4f ft :49 B ●Aug 2 Pha 5f ft 1:012 B Jly 26 Pha 5f ft 1:034 B Jly 19 Pha 4f ft :493 B

Cagey Exuberance is another top-class runner. The mare has earned three-quarter-million dollars in her career, and she wins half her starts. She's always dangerous, although another runner in this race, Aptostar, beat her solidly on 8Jun89. Losing four in a row is an exceedingly negative sign with a horse of this quality. She may be in a serious decline. Her running style is also an S.

Presser (P)

Lambros
B. f. 4, by In Reality—Killaloe, by Dr Fager
Br.—Norsul John A Revocable Trust (Fla) 1989 4 2 0 1 $58,534
Own.—Norsul J A 116 Tr.—Dimitrijevic Spasoje 1988 9 3 1 1 $56,880
Lifetime 13 5 1 2 $115,414
21Jly89-6Bel 1 :461 1:112 1:381gd *6-5 119 32 1hd 1½ 12¾ Maple E5 ⒻAw47000 74-28 Lmbros,MissySlw,Tomorrow'sChild 6
21Jly89—Bore in; clear
25Jun89-8Bel 7f :223 :454 1:224ft 15 109 42 52½ 44 35½ MpleE4 ⒻVagrancy H 83-17 Aptostar, Toll Fee, Lambros 7
25Jun89—Grade III

14Apr89-8Aqu	1	:46³	1:11¹	1:37	ft	3½	121	2¹	2½	1½	12¾	Maple E7	ⒻAw33000	81-31	Lambros, Cherlindrea, Rose Park	7
13Jan89-9GP	6f	:22³	:45	1:11	ft	24	119	127¾	9⁴½	7⁶	87¼	GuerraWA9	ⒻAw22000	77-23	StanleysRun,SocialPro,PlteQueen	12
13Jan89—Broke poorly																
31Dec88-10Crc	7f	:22³	:45³	1:24	ft	48	110	84½	6⁴	55½	77¾	CrugutJ2	ⒻVirginia H	87-16	Tappiano, LeL'Argent,EasterMary	14
31Dec88—Off slowly																
28Nov88-7Aqu	7f	:23	:46²	1:24²	sy	4½	115	2¹	2hd	2hd	1hd	ImparatoJ1	ⒻAw38000	79-28	Lmbros,MtlyArrngd,Ms.StollyNight	5
28Nov88—Slow st,driving																
24Sep88-7Bel	6f	:22¹	:44⁴	1:09¹	ft	19	110	9⁹	9¹³	8¹⁴	7¹²	Cruguet J6	ⒻHcp0	81-15	CleverPower,LasMaits,FineTiming	10
3Sep88-6Bel	7f	:23	:47¹	1:25⁴	ft	2½	115	53¾	31½	1⁵	16½	Cruguet J8	ⒻAw27000	74-27	Lmbros,SwissExcellence,Consecrtd	8

Aug 9 Sar 3f ft :36⁴ H   Aug 4 Sar 4f ft :49⁴ H   Jly 18 Bel 4f ft :50⁴ B   Jly 9 Bel 4f ft :49³ B

Lambros is a pure presser. All four of her wins have been accomplished by being tightly positioned behind the pace. When too far off the pace, this filly fails to threaten and is usually beaten off decisively. Additionally, all of her wins have been against weaker. She's definitely a P, but figures to be well back of the pace. She should not be bet in any race where she'll be relegated to mid-pack. A closer she's not.

Lake Valley   Dk. b. or br. f. 4, by Mr Prospector—La Vue, by Reviewer
Own.—Mohammed Al Maktoum   113   Br.—King Ranch Inc (Ky)   1989 1 0 0 1 $4,920
Tr.—Schulhofer Flint S   1988 11 4 4 1 $177,885
Lifetime 15 5 6 2 $212,936

20Aug89-4Sar	7f	:21³	:44	1:22	ft	3½	115	4³	31½	43½	39¾	Santos J A6	ⒻAw41000	83-08	Topicount, FeelTheBeat,LakeValley	7
20Aug89—Stumbled start																
18Dec88-8Aqu	6f	⊡:22⁴	:45⁴	1:11¹	ft	9-5	112	31½	2³	2hd	12½	SantosJA4	ⒻHandicap	80-23	LakeVlley,CleverPower,Hedgebout	7
11Nov88-6Aqu	7f	:23¹	:47¹	1:25²	ft	*4-5	113	1hd	2hd	13½	1⁴	Santos J A2	ⒻAw41000	74-31	LkVlly,DwnsAdvoct,Kolactoo'sRby	7
30Oct88-8Aqu	7f	:23	:46³	1:24²	ft	*8-5e	111	51½	41½	67½	85¾	SrvisDA8	ⒻFrst Flt H	73-23	CgeyExuberace,MstyAffir,Intently	10
30Oct88—Grade III																
14Oct88-8Med	6f	:21³	:44²	1:09⁴	ft	*4-5	119	21½	4³	34½	32½	StsJA2	ⒻAbrahamClrk	90-05	Feel TheBeat,LostKitty,LakeValley	5
8Sep88-9Lrl	6½f	:22¹	:45¹	1:16²	ft	*2	120	6⁷	5⁶	22½	2no	SantosJA5	ⒻColumbia	90-13	CleverPower,LakeVlley,RedyJetGo	8
17Aug88-1Sar	7f	:21⁴	:44²	1:22⁴	ft	*2-5	112	2½	1½	1⁴	11½	Santos J A2	ⒻAw25000	88-14	Lake Valley, Toll Fee, Our Marie	6
4Aug88-8Sar	7f	:22²	:45¹	1:22³	ft	8½	114	4½	1¹	1hd	21½	SantosJA1	ⒻTest	88-11	Fara'sTeam,LkeVlley,ClssicCrown	10
4Aug88—Grade I																

Jly 29 Bel 4f ft :50⁴ B   Jly 24 Bel 5f ft 1:02¹ B   Jly 10 Bel 5f ft 1:01² H   Jly 10 Bel 4f ft :50 B

Combined Styles

As with all the other parts of the pace puzzle, there's a shaded area. Not all horses neatly fit our categories of running styles. Many horses are versatile enough to overlap the designations. They should be marked accordingly. This process is not a gratuitous exercise. Once labeled, each of the runners will be compared to the probable pace demands of the race. If the designations are accurate, the selection process will be more effective.

Lake Valley is an excellent example of a presser who can also win on the lead. If the pace is not to her liking, she can go to the lead. Against a fast pace, she's capable of relaxing just behind the leaders and waiting for a collapse. Let's label her as an E/P. There is no better bet than a horse that can employ that combination of styles. When in top form, they're always difficult to best. In the case of Lake Valley, she may be a race or two away from her best. The stretch run of her last race seemed to show the effects of 8½ months on the shelf.

Ready Jet Go B. f. 4, by Northjet—Rough Girl, by Lt Stevens
Br.—Jones Brereton C (Ky) 1989 9 2 4 1 $58,074
Own.—Rice Clyde D 116 Tr.—Rice Linda 1988 15 7 1 5 $272,797
Lifetime 24 9 5 6 $331,871
5Aug89-5Mth 6f :222 :444 1:091ft *1-2 117 2½ 1½ 13 15½ MadridAJr7 ⒻAw27000 94-13 Ready Jet Go, Hushi, Lena's Prayer 7
22Jly89-9Mth 6f :211 :44 1:091ft 2 122 22½ 21½ 22 21 MadridAJr9 ⒻAw27000 93-13 Feel The Beat, Ready Jet Go,Hushi 9
4Jly89-3Mth 6f :204 :431 1:083ft 3½ 116 35½ 36 39 25½ Madrid A Jr3 ⒻRegret 91-13 SafelyKept,RedyJetGo,FeelTheBet 4
25Jun89-8Bel 7f :223 :454 1:224ft 7½ 116 21 63 67½ 58½ MdrdAJr2 ⒻVagrncyH 78-17 Aptostar, Toll Fee, Lambres 7
25Jun89—Grade III
14Jun89-7Mth 6f :21 :44 1:093ft *1-2 122 44½ 21½ 2hd 2½ MadridAJr3 ⒻAw25000 91-12 DistinctiveSky,RdyJtGo,KlssyBrifcs 5
3Jun89-5Mth 6f :212 :44 1:084ft 2½ 115 2½ 1½ 14 13½ MadridAJr6 ⒻAw25000 96-10 Ready Jet Go, Norangle, Ira's Cat 6
15May89-9GS 5f :222 :46 :581ft *2-3 116 2½ 2hd 2½ 24½ Wilson R2 ⒻAw19500 85-18 Polly Wally, ReadyJetGo,FullCargo 6
6May89-9GS 6f :212 :44 1:083ft 2½ 116 57 48½ 917 918 MdrdAJr5 ⒻBdrsCupH 81-16 Safely Kept, Social Pro, Kerygma 9
6May89—Grade III
Aug 8 Pha 4f ft :513 Bg ●Aug 2 Mth 3f ft :341 H Jly 16 Mth 1 ft 1:41 B

Ready Jet Go also has that combination of early and presser styles. She should also be designated E/P. This one seems to lack the class to win a race of this magnitude. Against her own kind, she's a threat every time she steps onto the track.

Aptostar B. f. 4, by Fappiano—Stark Drama, by Graustark
Br.—Whitney T P (Fla) 1989 5 1 2 1 $121,583
Own.—Centennial Farms 119 Tr.—Jerkens H Allen 1988 7 4 1 1 $335,864
Lifetime 18 6 7 2 $487,847
25Jun89-8Bel 7f :223 :454 1:224ft *3-5 118 62½ 3½ 12 12½ CrdrAJr7 ⒻVagrancyH 88-17 Aptostar, Toll Fee, Lambres 7
25Jun89—Grade III
8Jun89-8Bel 6f :214 :443 1:092gd 2½ 122 33½ 34 25 24 StsJA3 ⒻGenuine Rsk 88-14 SafelyKept,Aptostr,CgeyExubernce 4
8Jun89—Grade II
13May89-8Bel 1 1/16 :444 1:09 1:404ft 5½e 115 43 41½ 66 611¾ KrnJA1 ⒻShuvee H 86-16 Baker'sLdy,Ros'sCntin,GrcinFlight 7
13May89—Grade I
23Apr89-8Aqu 1⅛ :491 1:134 1:511ft 6½ 117 56 54 33 36 KronJA2 ⒻTop Flight 73-27 Banker'sLady,ColonilWters,Aptostr 5
23Apr89—Grade I
9Apr89-8Aqu 1 :452 1:10 1:352ft 2½ 118 31 1hd 2½ 25½ KrJA5 ⒻBed Roses H 84-17 Banker's Lady, Aptostar, Avie's Gal 5
9Apr89—Grade II
3Jly88-9Bel 1½ :482 2:044 2:324ft 2½ 121 41½ 31 22 21¾ DvsRG2 ⒻC C A Oaks 54-25 GoodbyeHalo,Aptostar,MakeChnge 6
3Jly88—Grade I
18Jun88-8Bel 1⅛ :454 1:102 1:494ft 8-5e 121 96¾ 65½ 53 31¾ DsRG7 ⒻMther Goose 76-20 GoodbyeHalo,MakeChange,Aptostr 9
18Jun88—Grade I
21May88-8Bel 1 :451 1:092 1:344ft *1e 121 42½ 31½ 2½ 13 DavisRG3 ⒻAcorn 91-11 Aptostar, Topicount, Avie's Gal 9
21May88—Grade I
●Aug 8 Sar 3f ft :363 H ●Aug 4 Sar 6f ft 1:14 H Jly 10 Bel 4f ft :504 B Jun 28 Bel tr.t 6f ft 1:15 B

Aptostar is among the best of her generation. She's banked nearly half a million dollars and has competed in top class races. Her best style overlaps the sustained and presser designations. She's an S/P, and presents a common problem inherent to the process. At today's distance Aptostar should be considered an S horse. If the race was carded at a route distance, she'd be labeled P. It may seem like a minor point. It isn't. In the final analysis, the bet may be entirely dependent upon where the horse figures to be positioned during the running of the race. Aptostar should be *well* behind the early pace of the Ballerina Stakes.

ANALYZING EARLY PACE—THE BALLERINA STAKES

I made an earlier point that accurate identification of the early pace horses was the most important part of the process. Races are won or lost as the result of early pace match-ups. Races unbalanced with too many front runners are usually a setup for pressers and closers. Races with a lone front runner usually result in a wire-to-wire win. Front runners who have recently wired their fields regularly lose if confronted with too much pace pressure in their next start. Front runners, after losing pace duels, will often win at big prices when that pressure disappears.

A basic question must be asked by the handicapper: Who figures to lead today's race?

No matter the methodology, if this question goes unanswered, the player is inviting unnecessary losses. Of course it's not quite that simple. Not only must the likely leader be identified, *the intensity of the effort to lead* must also be evaluated.

Will the horse have an easy lead, or will it be all-out to gain command?

Can the horse withstand pressure and still go on to record a strong effort? In the case of multiple E's, does one horse qualify as the "speed of the speed"?

In other words, is one horse so quick early that it reduces the other E's to mid-pack runners?

All of these questions must be answered when analyzing early pace.

In the Ballerina Stakes there were two E type horses: Feel The Beat and Bodacious Tatas. Let's analyze the probable chances of each.

Feel The Beat: In this field she qualifies as the "speed of the speed." She is capable of throwing sub-45.0 half-miles at her opposition. That type is always dangerous and should be carefully considered for the win. In her case, however, the distance of the race is of major concern. She expends too much energy in the early stages of her races to win at seven furlongs against top company. We'll learn to quantify energy exertion in a subsequent chapter.

Her impact in this race is still considerable. A dominant early pace horse serves to eliminate the other E horses from consideration. The designation E should indicate the ability to win on the lead *only*. Once again, E horses unable to get the early lead usually finish well up the track, and should be considered noncontenders. If the horse has any ability to run second in a "parade" with the other pace setters, the designation should have been E/P.

Bodacious Tatas: A certain loser in the early pace scenario. She seems incapable of challenging seriously for the lead. All the evidence in her running lines indicates an unwillingness to rate. The shorter distance should not alter her basic tendencies. She's a noncontender, and should not affect the outcome.

PRESSERS—THE BALLERINA STAKES

When the dominant early pace horse fits the distance, class, and bias requirements of a specific racetrack, and is a fair price, it's time to head to the betting windows. There's no better bet in racing. That's hardly an earth-shattering observation. Unfortunately, pace handicapping is more complex than that. Most races have more pieces to the puzzle than simply determining who'll be in the early lead. In the Ballerina Stakes we've discounted the distance and class capabilities of the certain leader. Where to next?

The natural position of the P horse is just off the pace setters. If the leaders weaken, it's the presser that's in the "garden spot" and ready to take over.

However, they may also suffer the same basic weakness that eliminated Bodacious Tatas from consideration. Many pressers are dependent upon being very close to the leaders. When faced with a pace that makes that an unrealistic possibility, they're relegated to mid-pack positions. Unless there is evidence of some closing ability, an S/P designation, the presser is an unlikely winner.

Lambros: This is a nice horse, but she seems to lack the class to win at this level. More importantly, she fits the scenario of the presser without sufficient pressing speed. In two other races, she faced the kind of early pace she'll likely face in here. Both times she ran poorly.

Ready Jet Go: This one's in a very difficult spot. She's an E/P, but wants to be *just* off the early pace. Her best style is on the lead, and the presser designation is a little bit tenuous. The velocities of her final fractions indicate she's probably not very effective in the role of presser. There are class and distance clouds over her chances in this race. She is not a solid proposition in this pace scenario.

Lake Valley: She's a quality filly who *can* press a fast pace. This type is always difficult to beat; seldom do they beat themselves. She can handle seven furlongs, but her last race indicates she may want another conditioner before showing her best.

SUSTAINED—THE BALLERINA STAKES

At most racetracks seven furlongs is an ideal distance for the sustained pace horses. That's not to say earlier runners do not win at the distance, because they do. But general tendencies favor the sustained horses; especially the S/P variety. By virtue of the enormous influence of Feel The Beat, the Ballerina Stakes seems a certainty for an S horse. Among the pressers, only Lake Valley's style will survive a careful pace analysis; her current condition is suspect.

Aptostar: She's probably the best filly in the field. She wins races and seems at home at seven furlongs. So far she's the best fit to the pace scenario. If the price is adequate, she'd be a high probability investment. Aptostar should grab a major share of the purse.

Proper Evidence: This one's sharp and fits the pace demands of the race..She'll be running strongly in the late stages and should overhaul many of these down the stretch. There's a class question over her head, but her style and bankroll are positive indicators. A strong contender.

Cagey Exuberance: Another positive pace fit. The race should be won by one of the three S horses, and she has no class clouds. Her current condition *is* suspect. Once a high percentage winner begins to string together losses, the handicapper should look elsewhere.

EIGHTH RACE 7 FURLONGS. (1.20⅖) 11th Running THE BALLERINA (Grade I). Purse $100,000 Added.
Saratoga Fillies and mares, 3-year-olds and upward. By subscription of $200 each, which should
AUGUST 11, 1989 accompany the nomination; $800 to pass the entry box; $800 to start, with $100,000 added. The added money and all fees to be divided 60% to the winner, 22% to second, 12% to third and 6% to fourth. Weights, 3-year-olds, 117 lbs. Older, 122 lbs. Winners of three races of $50,000 since May 1, 1989, an additional 2 lbs. Non-winners of two races of $35,000 since February 1 allowed 3 lbs. Of two such races in 1988-89, 6 lbs. Of a race of $25,000 in 1988-89, 9 lbs. Of two races of $20,000 in 1988-89, 12 lbs. Starters to be named at the closing time of entries. Trophies will be presented to the winning owner, trainer and jockey. Closed with 21 nominations. Value of race $121,800; value to winner $73,090; second $26,796; third $14,516; fourth $7,308. Mutuel pool $385,135. Exacta Pool $447,887. Triple Pool $359,923.

Last Raced	Horse	Eqt.	A.	Wt	PP	St	¼	½	Str	Fin	Jockey	Odds $1
30Jly89 9WO5	Proper Evidence		4	116	3	11	11	8½	2½	1$2\frac{3}{4}$	Antley C W	42.60
25Jun89 8Bel1	Aptostar		4	119	11	8	8½	5½	4$1\frac{1}{2}$	2no	Cordero A Jr	a-.60
2Aug89 4Sar3	Lake Valley		4	114	7	2	4^{1}	4$1\frac{1}{2}$	3½	3nk	Santos J A	5.90
2Aug89 4Sar2	Feel The Beat		4	116	1	4	1$1\frac{1}{2}$	1$1\frac{1}{2}$	1^{2}	4½	Perret C	10.10
21Jly89 6Bel1	Lambros		4	116	8	10	10$2\frac{1}{2}$	9^{1}	6½	5$2\frac{1}{2}$	Maple E	22.00
5Aug89 5Mth1	Ready Jet Go		4	116	9	3	3$1\frac{1}{2}$	2½	5hd	6no	Madrid A Jr	13.80
2Aug89 4Sar1	Topicount	b	4	119	2	9	9½	11	8^{1}	7$2\frac{1}{2}$	Romero R P	a-.60
4Jly89 10Mth1	Bodacious Tatas		4	116	10	1	2hd	3½	9$1\frac{1}{2}$	8^{1}	Wilson R	9.20
9Jly89 11Lrl3	Cagey Exuberance	b	5	119	4	5	7$1\frac{1}{2}$	6½	7^{2}	9nk	Migliore R	11.50
22Jly89 5Bel6	Toll Fee	b	4	110	5	7	5hd	7hd	10^{5}	10$9\frac{1}{2}$	Samyn J L	43.80
2Aug89 4Sar7	Hardeeni	b	5	113	6	6	6½	10hd	11	11	McCauley W H	50.80

a–Coupled: Aptostar and Topicount.

OFF AT 5:24 Start good, Won driving. Time, :22⅘, :45⅘, 1:10⅘, 1:23⅕ Track fast.

$2 Mutuel Prices:				
	3–(C)–PROPER EVIDENCE	87.20	12.80	5.00
	1–(A)–APTOSTAR (a–entry)		2.40	2.10
	7–(G)–LAKE VALLEY			3.20

$2 EXACTA 3–1 PAID $195.00. $2 TRIPLE 3–1–7 PAID $940.00.

Ch. f, by Stiff Sentence—Catch a Blessing, by Prince Blessed. Trainer Dalton John L. Bred by Wiest Edward J (Fla).

PROPER EVIDENCE, away slowly, raced very wide into the stretch while rallying, came over slightly while moving to FEEL THE BEAT just inside the final furlong and drew clear. APTOSTAR rallied while racing well out in the track approaching te stretch, was steadied slightly between horses nearing the final furlong and continued on gamely to gain the place. LAKE VALLEY, close up early while saving ground, came out between horses to make a run entering the stretch but wasn't good enough. FEEL THE BEAT saved ground while making the pace, settled into the stretch with a clear advantage and weakened late. LAMBROS, steadied along early, moved just inside PROPER EVIDENCE while advancing approaching the stretch but failed to seriously menace with a mild late response. READY JET GO away in good order despite stumbling slightly at the start, remained a factor to the stretch while racing between horses and tired. TOPICOUNT failed to be a serious factor. BODACIOUS TATAS raced forwardly until near the stretch and gave way. CAGEY EXUBERANCE tired while saving ground. TOLL FEE was finished early. HARDEENI was finished early.

Owners— 1, Gampel H; 2, Centennial Farms; 3, Mohammed AL Maktoum; 4, Allen J; 5, Nerud J A; 6, Rice Clyde D; 7, Centennial Farms; 8, Kimmel John C; 9, Burbank Lindsay D; 10, Fox Ridge Farm; 11, Phelan Mary.

Trainers— 1, Dalton John L; 2, Jerkens H Allen; 3, Schulhofer Flint S; 4, Lukas D Wayne; 5, Dimitrijevic Spasoje; 6, Rice-Appleby Linda; 7, Jerkens H Allen; 8, Kimmel John C; 9, Camac Robert W; 10, Kelly Patrick J; 11, Preger Michael C.

Corrected weight: Hardeeni 113 pounds. **Overweight:** Lake Valley 1 pound.

ESP—Format

The analysis of the Ballerina did not consider overall velocity or internal fractions. In everyday use, ESP considerations must be in light of ability, as well as style. My point was to demonstrate the concept and its value to pace analysis. More than just a rough identification of running styles, ESP provides an organizational format for the analysis of pace. The pace handicapper is best served by following a regular format.

(1) First analyze the early part of a race. Evaluate the chances of the horses involved in that part of the scenario, and disqualify runners who do not measure up.

(2) Evaluate the pressers in the race. Most often, a weak early pace picture strongly favors this type and they must be given strong consideration.

(3) Consider the closers in the race. In most races these are the least probable winners. In races like the Ballerina, they may be all-important.

The format seems simplistic. Unfortunately, most players have little organization to their approach and often move too quickly to the betting decision. This format will give each type its proper due. It will also ensure an adequate understanding of the pace picture for the race about to be bet.

ESP—A COMPLETE PICTURE

Let's work through the entire process. The following race was run at Santa Anita on March 15, 1989.

9th Santa Anita

1 1-16 MILES
SANTA ANITA

1 1/16 MILES. (1.40⅘) CLAIMING. Purse $14,000. 4-year-olds and upward. Weight, 121 lbs. Non-winners of two races at one mile or over since December 25 allowed 3 lbs.; of such a race since then, 5 lbs. Claiming price $12,500; if for $10,500 allowed 2 lbs. (Claiming and starter races for $10,000 or less not considered.)

Jazz Island — Ch. g. 4, by Island Whirl—Jazz Era, by Olden Times
OLGUIN G L — 1115 — Br.—Koley & Lee (Cal) — Tr.—Schiewe David — $12,500
Own.—Villalba G
1989 4 0 2 0 $5,200
1988 7 2 0 2 $6,600
Lifetime 11 2 2 2 $11,800

26Feb89-1SA 1 1/16 :462 1:112 1:441ft 8½ 1125 11½ 11½ 1hd 2hd Olguin G L7 10000 80-14 Bcrtino, Jazz Island, Siraluovat 12
19Feb89-3SA 1 1/16 :462 1:113 1:464m 39 1115 21 1hd 11½ 2hd Olguin G L3 10000 67-25 Bortino, Jazz Island, Very Double 11
5Jan89-9SA 6½f :213 :443 1:162ft 26 115 3nk 31½ 57 1014 Douglas R R1 10000 74-16 ProudPoliticin,Tritquos,Tiffn'sToy 12
6Jan89-9SA 6f :213 :443 1:094ft 76 115 95 95½ 89½ 78½ Gryder A T7 14000 81-15 NkdJybird,HdlnNws,GoForBrodwy 10
29Dec88-4Hol 6f :221 :453 1:103sy 23 115 75 64½ 76½ 711¾ Baze R A2 16000 77-23 BooBoo'sBckr,AlsknJm,Ppoy'sCasl 8
19Nov88-7AC 6f :224 :452 1:094ft 2¾ 111 1½ 11 11½ 12½ Enriquez H F7 Aw5000 90-19 Jazz Island, Rare Tyson, Look Far 7
6Nov88-5AC 6f :224 :444 1:10 ft 9¾ 111 4nk 4nk 2hd 36 Martinez J C1 Aw5000 83-14 Bert Co., Raja Naif, Jazz Island 5
30Oct88-2AC 6f :224 :444 1:10 ft 2¾ 115 12 11 13 15 Enriquez H F1 M8000 89-16 JazzIsland,CountCopy,SierraSultan 6
23Oct88-6AC 6f :23 :453 1:114ft 4¾ 115 3nk 3½ 52½ 58 Bastida F M1 M12500 72-19 VonGnd,PtFitzptrick,Bb'sLuckyBoy 7
28Aug88-6Sac 6f :223 :451 1:101ft 3 115 41½ 2½ 23 44 Gonzalez R M 2 M12500 84-10 PtrPipr,MotorCityLd,AstroAction 12
Mar 10 SA 4f R :48 H

Dhaleem — B. h. 6, by Lyphard—Patia, by Don
DOMINGUEZ R E — 116 — Br.—de Chambure-Ouaki Est-Ades (Ky) — Tr.—O'Hara John — $12,500
Own.—Six-S Racing Stable
1989 5 0 0 0 $775
1987 17 0 3 2 $26,900
Turf 19 1 3 2 $30,444
Lifetime 25 1 3 2 $31,544

4Mar89-5SA 1⅛ Ⓣ:46 1:3512:014fm 44 118 811 914 917 710½ DominguzRE7 Aw35000 59-22 FlatteringNews,SpiritBay,Mikhtoun 9
4Feb89-9GG 1 1/16 :47 1:112 1:433m 19 117 713 710 79½ 512½ Campbell B C5 25000 68-20 NobleNBold,UncleAde,AnotherCod 7
21Jan89-7BM 1 1/16 Ⓣ:4741:1221:45 gd 19 116 99¾ 87¼ 79½ 56¼ Campbell B C1 25000 71-25 PardeLeder,ChiefOffFire,UncleAde 10
15Jan89-2BM 1 Ⓣ:4631:1141:391gd 11 116 913 811 712 77¼ Steiner J J6 Aw17000 69-20 Finlized,DublinO'Bron,SilverStrike 10
1Jan89-5SA 1 1/16 :453 1:102 1:423ft 71 120 1110 1015 1011 1015¼ Olivares F 8 Aw34000 72-10 Malo Malo, Sky High, Mispu 11
14Dec87-9Hol 1⅛ :47 1:113 1:49 ft 14 115 45½ 55¼ 59¼ 710½ FerndezAL 4 Aw36000 81-10 Fiction, The Great Prize, Sinforoso 7
28Nov87-7SA 1⅛ Ⓣ:4811:3832:041fm 3 117 86½ 83¾ 86¾ 77¾ Toro F 4 Aw38000 58-34 Convincing, Proud Cat, Unicopia 8
12Nov87—Steadied 3/16
14Oct87-5SA 1⅛ Ⓣ:4921:3742:041fm 12 118 87 98¾ 85 31 DelhoussyeE 8 Aw38000 65-34 Rough Passage, Feraud, Dhaleem 9
14Oct87—Wide in stretch
19Sep87-10Fpx 1 1/16 :46 1:133 1:451ft 17 118 106¼ 96¼ 98 109¼ FernndezAL 1 Aw27000 75-18 Bugarian, Proving Spark, Shrewdy 10
6Sep87-7Dmr 1 1/16 Ⓣ:4711:12 1:424fm 14 118 87 86¾ 67 78½ Kaenel J L 2 Aw24000 77-16 Rufus Dawes, Ima Bullet,ChiefPal 10
6Sep87—Rank 1/8
Feb 22 Hol 5f R 1:011 H   Jan 31 GG 4f R :482 H

Ancient Blue — B. g. 8, by Blue Times—Ancient Jewel, by Hail to Reason
TORO F — 118 — Br.—Jones A U (Ky) — Tr.—Blincoe Tom — $12,500
Own.—Blincoe & Just 4 Fun Stb
1989 3 1 0 1 $10,100
1988 11 1 2 0 $14,975
Turf 4 0 0 1 $3,100
Lifetime 54 6 9 7 $60,591

4Feb89-9SA 1⅛ :462 1:103 1:50 ft 7¾ 115 1110 99½ 78½ 76½ Toro F4 16000 72-16 OurBrndX.,SirTyson,Mischifinmnd 12
26Feb89—Broke slowly
3Jan89-2SA 1⅛ :463 1:113 1:504ft 9¾ 116 89¾ 66½ 45½ 34 Toro F5 16000 71-16 Mischifinmind,FlyingH.,AncintBlu 11
1Jan89-9SA 1 1/16 :47 1:112 1:434ft 31 116 77 44½ 41½ 11 Toro F12 12500 82-14 AncntBl,LovDn'sGtwy,MddlCanch 12
11Jan89—Wide on turns
4Dec88-1Hol 7f :22 :453 1:243m 12 116 911 89 79 711¼ Baze R A9 12500 70-23 King Clyde, Slam Dance, Nordicus 9

24Dec88—Wide into stretch
7Dec88-5Hol 1 1/16 :471 1:12 1:44 ft 25 115 913 89 76¾ 74¾ Ortega L E5 16000 75-17 Chili Hill, Kamp Out, Taplado 9
7Dec88—Off slowly
1Aug88-2Dmr 1 1/16 :463 1:11 1:424ft *4½ 118 108½ 98½ 911 46 Stevens G L10 c12500 80-17 LuckyBer,D.D.ThKid,ExoticArbitor 12
31Aug88—Wide final 3/8
3Aug88-8LA 1 1/16 :444 1:101 1:41 ft 5¾ 116 89¾ 46½ 31 15½ Stevens G L7 12500 103-07 Ancient Blue, Restage, Extranix 10
Jly88-9Hol 1 1/16 (T):46 1:10 1:401fm 102 116 1116 1110 1112 1016 Solis A6 Aw35000 77-04 Delegant,Whitstable,J.B.R.'sDream 11
25Jly88—Bumped start
3Jly88-9Hol 1 1/16 :46 1:112 1:441ft 26 115 1110 74½ 33½ 23½ Lambert J11 c10000 75-16 Gunburst,AncintBlu,Bkr'sCrossing 12
13Jly88—Wide
Jly88-3Hol 1⅛ :47 1:121 1:504ft 3 115 69½ 67 68½ 66½ Baze R A8 10000 76-17 ProvingSprk.RceBook,AnotherCod 8
Feb 15 SA 6f ft 1:164 H

Tricky Lad

Dk. b. or br. g. 4, by Clever Trick—Carefree Lass, by Exalted Rullah
GARCIA H J 1115 Br.—Klein Mr-Mrs E V (Cal) 1989 3 0 1 0 $3,775
Tr.—Stucki Wayne B $12,500 1988 15 0 2 3 $17,450
Own.—Stucki D B-W B-W B Lifetime 25 2 3 6 $59,825
24Feb89-9SA 1⅛ :462 1:103 1:50 ft 7½ 1115 87 1111 89¾ 88½ Valenzuela F H 1 16000 78-16 OurBrndX.,SirTyson,Mischifinmnd 12
25Jan89-2SA 1 1/16 :463 1.112 1:442ft 10 1105 41½ 31½ 2hd 2hd Valenzuela F H 2 12500 79-17 Bold Reach, Tricky Lad, Siraluovat 9
4Jan89-1SA 7f :223 :45 1:223m 10 1105 83 97½ 46½ 45 Valenzuela F H 1 12500 82-15 CatFisher,Precedence,Mn'sIntent 12
28Nov88-1SA 6f :213 :45 1:11 ft 12 116 118¾ 89½ 914 1019½ Solis A 8 28000 64-19 SrosBid,DrouillyFuisse,TuckyJohn 11
28Nov88—Wide final 3/8
22Oct88-7SA 6f :211 :442 1:102ft 23 1115 108¾ 910 67½ 66½ ValenzuelaFH 11 25000 79-12 MixedPlesure,ElusiveAgnt Mdcuff 12
22Oct88—Wide.
7Oct88-5SA 1 :451 1:094 1:372ft 20 1105 916 816 914 98¾ Valenzuela F H 1 40000 72-19 Lot'sCuriosity,MaloMlo,SpekHigh 10
18Sep88-1Dmr 6½f :213 :443 1:163ft 16 1095 99½ 87½ 63¾ 2½ Valenzuela F H 4 20000 88-12 Ship'sLog,TrickyLad,GoForBrodwy 9
29Aug88-3Dmr 6½f :22 :45 1:17 ft 11 116 53 22½ 22½ 64½ Solis A 2 25000 82-10 TmprT.,Bbb'sBllt,Somkndwondrfl 10
29Aug88—Wide 3/8 turn
19Aug88-3Dmr 6f :214 :45 1:094ft 3½ 115 118½ 64 44½ 25½ Solis A 8 (S) 20000 83-15 Aaron'sDewn,TrickyLd,FrncPrince 12
19Aug88—Very wide final 3/8
1Aug88-5Dmr 6f :214 :444 1:094ft 45 116 1212 99 84½ 35½ Solis A 9 20000 83-12 StuckWithYou,FrskMNot,TrckyLd 12
1Aug88—Bumped start; very wide in stretch
Mar 8 SA 6f ft 1:131 H Feb 19 SA 5f ft 1:011 H Jan 20 SA 6f ft 1:131 H

It's Never Dull

Dk. b. or br. g. 9, by What Luck—Sharp Pencil, by Olden Times
VALENZUELA F H 1115 Br.—Forrester Geri (Md) 1989 5 0 1 0 $5,250
Tr.—Shulman Sanford $12,500 1988 27 4 7 6 $55,438
Own.—Charles & ClearValleyStables Lifetime 90 14 16 13 $173,443 Turf 20 4 7 1 $52,070
22Feb89-2SA 1 1/16 :462 1:113 1:452ft 5 116 42 32½ 41½ 43½ Baze R A 6 c10000 78-18 SpruceSkipper,MimiBound,Shirke 12
3Feb89-9SA 7f :22 :444 1:214ft 9½e116 32½ 43 34½ 47 Baze R A 5 12500 84-17 Hillstrk,Emperor'sTurn,PowerFlet 10
3Feb89—Broke slowly
19Jan89-9SA 1⅛ :472 1:12 1:511ft 5½ 1115 1½ 2½ 1hd 2¾ Corral J R 8 c10000 72-23 Siraluovt,It'sNeverDull,Ack'sReply 10
6Jan89-9SA 1¼ :464 1:374 2:033gd 3½ 116 1½ 23½ 48½ 415½ Pedroza M A 1 10000 55-20 Bold Decree, Equilibre, Siraluovat 8
6Jan89—Hopped in air; lugged out stretch
2Jan89-9SA 1 1/16 :454 1:103 1:433ft 8½ 116 32½ 42½ 54 97 Pedroza M A 9 16000 76-13 K.'sCharger,ToB.ARuler,SlamDnce 12
26Dec88-9SA 1 1/16 :461 1:103 1:424ft 12 114 32 42½ 64½ 68½ Pedroza M A 7 22500 78-13 Shafy, Rakaposhi, Remar 8
9Dec88-3Hol 1 :453 1:104 1:361ft 3 116 1hd 3½ 41½ 510 Pedroza M A 6 20000 72-16 AngleArc,BooBoo'sBuckroo,Trnzer 8
27Nov88-5Hol 1⅛ :47 1:114 1:511gd 8 114 1hd 1½ 22 36 Pedroza M A 5 20000 75-24 Full Charm, Bugarian,It'sNeverDull 7
6Nov88-9SA 1 1/16 :46 1:104 1:432ft 9½ 116 1hd 1hd 2hd 1nk Pedroza M A 6 16000 84-17 It's Never Dull, Last Mote!,ChiliHill 9
27Oct88-9SA 1 1/16 :46 1:11 1:424ft 8½ 116 1hd 1½ 23 34½ Pedroza M A 12 12500 82-14 HloHtch,ToB.ARuler,It'sNeverDull 12
Mar 10 SA 4f ft :48 H Jan 29 SA 3f ft :374 H

Bortino

B. g. 5, by Balzac—Caprice, by Turn-to
BAZE R A 116 Br.—Plemmons J H (Ky) 1989 4 2 0 0 $15,950
Tr.—Miyadi Steve $12,500 1988 12 1 1 1 $10,870
Own.—B & C Ranch-Miccolo-Travato Lifetime 17 3 1 1 $26,820
26Feb89-1SA 1 1/16 :462 1:112 1:441ft 8 1135 21½ 21½ 2hd 1hd Garcia H J9 10000 80-14 Bortino, Jazz Island, Siraluovat 12
10Feb89-3SA 1 1/16 :462 1:113 1:464m 11 1105 44½ 43½ 21½ 1hd Garcia H J9 10000 67-25 Bortino, Jazz Island, Very Double 11
10Feb89—Fractious in gate
18Jan89-1SA 7f :222 :451 1:233ft 17 1115 52½ 42½ 43½ 43½ Olguin G L6 10000 78-17 RrTyson,RunCougrRun,SundncSqr 11
18Jan89—Wide into stretch
1Jan89-1SA 6½f :22 :451 1:171ft 18 115 42 42½ 54¾ 42½ Gryder A T2 10000 82-18 Tritequos,Petronck,BusinssSchool 10
11Dec88-1Hol 6½f :22 :453 1:172ft 55 1115 75 62½ 53½ 32¾ Olguin G L10 10000 85-17 Alaskan Jim, CoastalLove,Bortino 12
26Nov88-1Hol 6f :221 :453 1:111m 47 1115 86½ 56½ 79 57¾ Olguin G L1 10000 78-25 Romx,SundncSqur,KingOfCliforni 12
26Nov88—Broke against bit
18Nov88-2Hol 6½f :223 :46 1:17 ft 110 115 31 128½ 1215 1218¾ Sorenson D 1 10500 71-19 Angle Arc, Run CougarRun,BeaHo 12
18Nov88—Checked 1/4
12Aug88-11LA 6½f :213 :444 1:164ft 10 1115 76½ 64½ 43½ 42¾ Valenzuela F H 9 10000 90-10 ‡Our March, Big Craig, MajorShare 9
5Aug88-9LA 6f :214 :451 1:102ft 18 119 74½ 75¾ 76½ 66¾ Proctor L B 4 16000 84-13 Coursing Eagle, Oak Wine MelO'C. 8
1Aug88-4LA 6f :22 :461 1:123ft 4 120 74 63¾ 31 1½ Proctor L B 3 M18000 80-19 Bortino,Winemucca,CruiserManet 10
Mar 9 SA 4f ft :472 H Feb 20 SA 4f ft :481 H Feb 5 SA tr.t 6f gd 1:184 H Jan 27 SA 4f ft :483 H

Last Command ✳

PINCAY L JR	**116**	Ch. g. 6, by Bold Commander—Miss Hitting Away, by Hitting Away
Own.—Rubinsfeld N W		Br.—Kerr & Kerr & Kerr (Ky)
		Tr.—Shulman Sanford

1989 4 1 1 0 $10,150
1988 14 0 3 2 $32,525
$12,500
Lifetime 67 11 10 14 $311,539   Turf 6 1 0 1 $9,535

```
2Mar89-1SA    7f :22  :441 1:23 sy   *2 117   541 311 31 12     Pincay L Jr 5   c10000 85-18 LstCommnd,UnclFoss,BuenaAmnst 10
   2Mar89—Lugged in stretch
9Feb89-9SA    11/8:464 1:12 1:453m   41 117   32 11 121 541    Pincay L Jr 5    12500 68-23 Middle Concho, Equilibre,Tablado 11
28Jan89-3SA   11/8:47 1:112 1:50 ft   61 117   2hd 2hd 321 781  Pincay L Jr 2    20000 78-13 ToB.ARuler,Hagley'sLion,KampOut 8
14Jan89-5SA   11/8:454 1:103 1:44 ft   11 117   33 21 22 23     Pincay L Jr 4    16000 80-11 CrystlCttr,LstCommand,ExtcArbtr 11
   14Jan89—Lugged in stretch
31Dec88-1SA   61/2:212 :441 1:161ft   20 117   45 861 991 1191  Pincay L Jr 9    16000 79-10 Pppy'sConsul,MuiMlody,K:ngClyd 12
31Aug88-2Dmr  11/8:463 1:11 1:424ft    7 116   431 45 551 67    Ortega L E 4     12500 79-17 LuckyBer,D.D.ThKid,ExoticArbitor 12
28Aug88-9Dmr  11/8:461 1:11 1:431ft    81 116   54 311 741 78   Ortega L E 10    20000 76-15 ProperRidr,Convincing,It'sNvrDull 8
10Aug88-3Dmr  11/8:452 1:103 1:44 ft    41 116   771 43 43 321  Ortega L E 2     16000 77-17 ProvingSprk,KniDncr,LstCommand 10
   10Aug88—Steadied start
18July88-5Hol  1 :444 1:093 1:354ft    *21 117  321 311 2hd 311  Pincay L Jr 9    20000 83-10 Gossarone,ILoveRcing,LstCommand 8
   18July88—Lugged in; bumped late
30June88-7Hol 61/2:213 :443 1:102ft    13 1095  991 861 65 541   Corral J R 4     20000 85-15 HechizrDOro,ImprssivRsult,BidUs 11
   ●Feb 7 SA 3f gd :354 H
```

Hovering Presence ✳

NOGUEZ A M	**116**	Gr. g. 6, by Dust Commander—Puss in Cahoots, by The Axe II
Own.—Forster & Rodriguez		Br.—Franzheim Susan Beth (Ky)
		Tr.—Rodriguez Hugo

1989 3 0 0 0
1988 22 0 1 2 $10,380
$12,500   1988 $1,060
Lifetime 60 6 7 8 $84,389   Turf 2 0 0 1

```
1Mar89-9SA    7f :223 :454 1:234hy   59 116   1061 941 761 891  Noguez A M7     10000 72-14 Remar, Manhattan King, Darion 12
17Feb89-1SA   61/2f:213 :45 1:174ft   20 116   11141115101310931 Dominguez RE3   10000 71-21 SwetwtrSprings,RrTyson,Trilquos 12
   17Feb89—Wide into stretch
3Feb89-1SA    6f :214 :441 1:104ft   60 116   1213121210831 851 Dominguez RE6   10000 78-17 RllANtrl,SwtwtrSprngs,BsnssSchl 12
   3Feb89—7 wide into drive
25Sep88-9Fpx  6f :221 :453 1:102ft   32 1115  851 981 810 8101  Olguin G L4     12500 84-06 StrOrphn,JustTheFcts,RdwoodBoy 10
16Sep88-10Fpx 61/2f:221 :454 1:17 ft  20 1095  811 811 66 461   Corral J R5     10000 82-14 Silver Hero, MajorShare,RisingPine 8
15Sep88-9Dmr  7f :22  :451 1:231ft   16 116   909 811 1061 100  Ortega L E8     10000 78-14 RollANaturl,HloHtch,Mr.Edelweiss 12
11Aug88-9Dmr  61/2f:22 :451 1:173ft   19 116   1211106 1 751 66  Ortega L E3     10000 78-21 NkdJybird,LuckyAdvnc,WldPursut 12
38July88-9LA  6f :222 :453 1:103ft   23 116   86 441 45 561     Bazan J8        12500 83-09 CortWzrd,QckRondtrp,ChocoltBlks 10
15July88-7Sol  1 :474 1:11 1:361ft   20 115   712 551 46 39 1   † Bazan J6      14000 85-10 TrojnTrick,SnsRivl,‡HoveringPrsnc 8
   15July88—Disqualified and placed fifth; Drifted in 1/16
4July88-1Hol  7f :22  :451 1:231ft   20 1105  78 751 671 541    Olguin G L12    10000 83-08 StrOfAmeric,HijoElToro,DncenKid 12
   Feb 13 Fpx 4f gd :49 H   ●Jan 17 Fpx 6f ft 1:143 H
```

Kennedy Exchange

CORRAL J R	**114**	Ch. g. 6, by Kennedy Road—Exchanged Princess, by Prince John
Own.—Johnston Betty-E W-Judy		Br.—Old English Rancho (Cal)
		Tr.—Warren Donald

1989 1 0 1 0 $2,800
1988 13 1 2 2 $18,400
$10,500   Turf 1 0 0 0
Lifetime 25 1 4 4 $27,728

```
23Feb89-1SA   1 :453 1:104 1:394ft   11 1095  32 311 33 221    Corral J R 7   S 10500 71-20 RreTyson,KnndyExchng,Polysmous 8
10Oct88-12Fpx 11/16:491 1:384 2:17 ft 71 111   11 771 812 815   Gryder A T 1   H16000 75-09 Exotic Arbitor, Aleteen,SpiceTrade 9
24Sep88-12Fpx 11/16:47 1:391 2:181ft *21 117  32 31 1hd 31     Gryder A T 2   H12500 83-10 Aleteen,PrdeLeder,KenndyExchng 11
15Sep88-13Fpx px a11/8:491 1:134 1:513ft 71 113  21 21 23 241  Black C A 2    A12500 80-15 LuckyBer,KennedyExchng 2,Achirnt 8
18July88-10AC 6f :221 :442 1:092ft    91 115   521 631 1191 1191 Long D C 2     8000 82-14 Gaelic Money, Bakhit,BoldRooster 11
25Jun88-9AC   11/8:461 1:103 1:414ft  11 115   15 1hd 68 615    Long D C 1    Aw6000 81-16 Lafitte, Rafik, Forio 6
14May88-9AC   11/8:463 1:102 1:423ft  5 114   21 — — —         Enriquez H F 3 Aw6000 — — Lafitte, Faigh Abhaile, Rafik 7
   14May88—Sulked
24Apr88-9AC   11/16:471 1:103 1:483ft 11 112   11 1hd 951 10121  MrtnzJC7   ⒭Rnd Tbl H 83-14 Motivos, Faigh Abhaile,Starshield 10
27Mar88-9AC   11/8:47 1:101 1:42 ft   91 112   11 11 741 7101    MrtJC1     ⒭Phar Lap H 85-16 Motivos, Starshield, Cesar 8
28Mar88-9AC   6f :221 :45 1:093ft     21 115   3nk 3nk 411 451   Lopez A D5     Aw6000 86-16 Lafitte, Bold Rooster, Fill Up 8
   Mar 11 SA 5f ft 1:011 H   Mar 5 SA 4f ft :472 H   Feb 21 SA 3f ft :352 H   Feb 16 SA 7f ft 1:25 H
```

Bueno Amnistia

SOLIS A	**114**	Dk. b. or br. g. 5, by Kick—Zinghara, by Best Example
Own.—Belamy III & Bueno		Br.—Murty Farm (Ky)
		Tr.—Valenzuela A C

1989 4 0 0 1 $2,450
1988 5 0 0 0
$10,500   Turf 3 0 0 0
Lifetime 13 1 0 1 $11,250

```
2Mar89-1SA    7f :22  :441 1:23 sy   30 116   911 1061 531 32   Solis A 9      10000 83-18 LstCommnd,UnclFoss,BuenoAmnst 10
25Feb89-1SA   11/8:462 1:112 1:441ft 67 116   1011 891 561 5111  Solis A 3      10000 69-14 Bortino, Jazz Island, Siralovat 12
11Feb89-1SA   1 :473 1:132 1:404m   31 115   891 751 661 573   Solis A 1      10000 56-31 ManhattnKing,LuckyBer,StrRibot 10
3Feb89-1SA    6f :214 :441 1:104ft  60 116   11111111 981 1061  Solis A 2      10000 78-17 RllANtrl,SwtwtrSprngs,BsnssSchl 12
   3Feb89—Bumped start
14Dec88-9Hol  11/8:464 1:114 1:513ft 70 115   631 1118 11241 1132 Patterson A 7  12500 47-16 RationalApproch,Silor'sTle,Iberico 11
27Nov88-2Hol  11/8:472 1:123 1:451gd 37 115   851 1214 11241 1029 Patterson A 4  12500 45-24 Extrnix,Wher'sMchis,BrgirStndrd 12
   27Nov88—Wide final 3/8
9Nov88-9Hol   11/4①:47 1:1141:432fm 267 117  4321 1210 12201 2251 Patterson A 3 Aw25000 52-23 HollywdHl,NstyNskr,VgrsCmmndr 12
13Feb88-3SA   11/4①:4911:3912:04 fm 55 117  4131 641 891 813   Oldham D W 4 Aw34000 54-24 DefiniteSigns,SpruceSkipper,Deput 8
30Jan88-7SA   11/4①:46 1:3812:044fm 52 116  1115 99 610 611    Higuera A R2 Aw34000 52-30 ProudCat,HotStge,StelliteExpress 12
26Dec87-2SA   11/8:464 1:111 1:441ft 66 115  1015 1191 89 8101  Stevens S A11    40000 69-16 GretNegotitor,FstDelivry,Rkposhi 11
   Mar 13 SA 4f ft :492 H   Mar 9 SA 4f ft :49 H   Feb 18 Fpx 5f ft 1:85 H   Jan 29 SA 5f ft 1:00 H
```

```
Bucket Head                      B. g. 4, by Zamboni—Lady's Guard, by Advance Guard
                                 Br.—Wilson J R (Cal)                    1989  3 1 0 1      $4,000
  PEDROZA M A              116   Tr.—Greenman Dean          $12,500      1988  1 M 0 0
Own.—Greenman & Wilson          Lifetime   4 1 0 1   $4,000
 3Mar89-9SA   1⅛:47^1 1:11^3 1:51^1gd  79 114  8^6 7^4¾ 4^3 3^1¼  Douglas R R^1  10500 72-19 Lucky Bear, Chili Hill,BucketHead 10
     3Mar89—Bumped hard 1/16, 1st time around
17Feb89-3SA   6½f:22^1 :45^1 1:17^2ft  30 117  3^1 4^3 4^5 5^6¾  Solis A 10       10000 76-21 BiscayneBoy,CervantesSt.,WrDebt 10
22Jan89-1AC   6f :22^4 :45^4 1:11^1ft   6 120  4^2 4^1½ 1^1 1^3  Barsallo E 1   M10000 83-24 BucketHead,PatFitzptrick,Crpshot 6
14Dec88-4Hol  6f :21^3 :45^1 1:10^4ft  58 118  12^16 12^12 11^12 11^13¼ Pedroza M A 2 M32000 75-16 RaiderMrcus,GoldenVision,LddyV. 12
     14Dec88—Broke slowly
   Feb 24 SA 5f ft 1:01^3 H    Feb 13 SA tr.t 5f ft 1:03 H    ●Feb 4 AC 6f m 1:13^4 H    Jan 30 AC 5f ft 1:03^3 H

Precedence                       Gr. g. 5, by Keep Your Promise—Mrs Sanchez, by Sensitive
                                 Br.—Plimley B (BC-C)                    1989  3 0 1 0      $3,650
  CORRAL J R               114   Tr.—Ratchford Don          $10,500      1988 14 1 0 1      $9,930
Own.—Earner-Hubbard-MarlaEtal   Lifetime  36 6 7 2   $43,035
 8Feb89-9SA   1 1/16:46^4 1:12 1:45^3m  41 1115 10^9¼ 7^7½ 4^3½ 4^2  Corral J R 1  12500 71-23 Middle Concho, Equilibre,Tablado 11
     8Feb89—Steadied sharply 3 1/2 to avoid injured horse
28Jan89-9SA   7f :22^2 :45^1 1:22^2ft  12 116  5^3½ 9^9¾ 11^15 11^19¼ Castanon A L 6  10000 69-13 Hillstark,RollANaturl,MnhttnKing 11
 4Jan89-1SA   7f :22^3 :45 1:22^3m     35 115  7^2¾ 5^4 2^3 2^2½  Castanon A L 7  10500 84-15 CatFisher,Precedence,Mn'sIntent 12
21Dec88-9Hol  1 1/16:48^1 1:14 1:46^4sl 21 115 2^1 3^6½ 7^14 7^18  Rivera J V 1    10000 48-30 Extranix, Menelik, Bold Decree 11
19Oct88-9SA   1⅛:46^1 1:11^1 1:50^1ft  74 118  6^3¾ 5^2¾ 5^4½ 5^6½  Pedroza M A 6  10000 72-16 Halo Hatch, Iberico, Correoso 11
 6Oct88-9SA   1 1/16:46^3 1:11^3 1:44^2ft 24 118 7^8½ 6^6 9^8½ 7^14¼ Baze R A 4    10000 64-18 Halo Hatch, Correoso, Trump Up 11
28Sep88-10Fpx 1 1/16:45 1:10^2 1:42^4ft ¾ 119  4^5 4^6 4^9 4^16¾  Pedroza M A 8   10000 80-07 OurBrndX.,PocketTim,Don'tFightIt 8
 8Sep88-9Dmr  1 1/16:46 1:10^4 1:43^1ft 7 118  3^2 5^2½ 6^4½ 5^6½  Sibille R 6     10000 78-15 WtTllMondy,RsonToStudy Gunbrst 9
25Aug88-9Dmr  1⅛:46^1 1:10^4 1:49^4ft  6¾ 118  6^5 7^4¾ 5^5½ 3^5½  Baze R A 10    10000 75-18 Achirnte,GreyGuntlet,Precedence 12
17Aug88-9Dmr  1 1/16:46^4 1:11^2 1:43^2ft 5¾ 116 7^4½ 5^2½ 6^5¾ 6^10¾ Baze R A 3   12500 72-16 Amatar,Bigbadndmen,AnotherCode 8
     17Aug88—Rough start
   Feb 27 SA 6f ft 1:14^1 H    Jan 31 SA 6f ft 1:15^4 H
```

At the time this race was run, most of the Santa Anita routes were being won by early and presser types. Not many winners were more than four lengths behind at the first call. Fewer still were more than two lengths behind at the second. Armed with that information, the pace handicapper should have been focusing on running positions in the forward half of the field. Only a sustained horse with an *extreme* class edge, or in a field of suicidal E types, should have been given more than passing consideration.

Let's take them one at a time.

```
Jazz Island                      Ch. g. 4, by Island Whirl—Jazz Era, by Olden Times
                                 Br.—Koley & Lee (Cal)                   1989  4 0 2 0      $5,200
  OLGUIN G L              111^5  Tr.—Schiewe David          $12,500      1988  7 2 0 2      $6,600
Own.—Villalta G                 Lifetime  11 2 2 2   $11,800
25Feb89-1SA   1 1/16:46^2 1:11^2 1:44^1ft 8¾ 112^5 1^1½ 1^1½ 1^hd 2^hd Olguin G L^7 10000 80-14 Bcrtino, Jazz Island, Siraluovat 12
10Feb89-3SA   1 1/16:46^2 1:11^3 1:46^4m 30 111^5 2^1 1^hd 1^1½ 2^hd  Olguin G L^3 10000 67-25 Bortino, Jazz Island, Very Double 11
25Jan89-9SA   6½f:21^3 :44^3 1:16^2ft  26 115  3^nk 3^1½ 5^7 10^14  Douglas R R^1  10000 74-16 ProudPoliticin,Tritquos,Tiffn'sToy 12
16Jan89-9SA   6f :21^3 :44^3 1:09^4ft  76 115  9^5 9^5½ 8^8½ 7^8½  Gryder A T^7    14000 81-15 NkdJybird,HdlnNws,GoForBrodwy 10
24Dec88-4Hol  6f :22^1 :45^3 1:10^3sy  23 115  7^5 6^4½ 7^6½ 7^11¾  Baze R A^2     16000 77-23 BooBoo'sBckr,AlsknJm,Ppoy'sCnsl 8
19Nov88-7AC   6f :22^4 :45^2 1:09^4ft  2¾ 111  1½ 1^1 1^1½ 1^2½  Enriquez H F^7 Aw5000 90-19 Jazz Island, Rare Tyson, Look Far 7
 6Nov88-5AC   6f :22^4 :44^4 1:10 ft   9¾ 111  4^nk 4^nk 2^hd 3^6  Martinez J C^1 Aw5000 83-14 Bert Co., Raja Naif, Jazz Island 5
30Oct88-2AC   6f :22^4 :44^4 1:10 ft   2¾ 115  1^2 1^1 1^3 1^5  Enriquez H F^1   M8000 89-16 JazzIsland,CountCopy,SierraSultan 6
23Oct88-6AC   6f :23 :45^3 1:11^4ft    4¾ 115  3^nk 3½ 5^2½ 5^8  Bastida F M^1   M12500 72-19 VonGnd,PtFitzptrick,Bb'sLuckyBoy 7
28Aug88-6Sac  6f :22^3 :45^1 1:10^1ft   3 115  4^1½ 2½ 2^3 4^4  Gonzalez R M 9 M12500 84-10 PtrPipr,MotorCityLd,AstroAction 12
   Mar 10 SA 4f ft :48 H
```

His best races have been with the lead at the second call. Only in one of those races was he as far back as 1 length at the first call; and that was over a muddy surface. He's an E runner.

Dhaleem
DOMINGUEZ R E   **116**
Own.—Six-S Racing Stable

This one should have been harnessed for field work. In fact, most of his races appear as though he'd already been pulling a plow. He's an S type, but should also carry an NF or "no form" label. The NF ensures that he won't be reconsidered if the race later favors sustained runners.

Ancient Blue
TORO F   **118**
Own.—Blincoe & Just 4 Fun Stb

If this one gives you any trouble, go back and read the previous pages. He's an S in all his races.

Tricky Lad
GARCIA H J   **1115**
Own.—Stauchl B B—W B—W B

26Nov88-1SA 6f :213 :45 1:11 ft 12 116 119¾ 89½ 914 1019½ Solis A 8 20000 64-19 SrosBid,DrouillyFuisse,TuckyJohn 11
26Nov88—Wide final 3/8
22Oct88-7SA 6f :211 :442 1:102ft 23 1115 109¾ 910 67¾ 66¼ ValenzuelaFH 11 25000 79-12 MixedPlesure,ElusiveAgnt Mdcuff 12
22Oct88—Wide.
7Oct88-5SA 1 :451 1:094 1:372ft 28 1105 916 816 914 98¾ Valenzuela F H 1 40000 72-19 Lot'sCuriosity,MaloMio,SpekHigh 10
10Sep88-10mr 6½f:213 :443 1:163ft 16 1095 98¼ 87¾ 63¾ 2¾ Valenzuela F H 4 20000 88-12 Ship'sLog,TrickyLad,GoForBrodwy 9
29Aug88-3Dmr 6½f:22 :45 1:17 ft 11 116 53 22¾ 22¾ 64¼ Solis A 2 25000 82-18 TmprT.,Bbb'sBlt,Somkndwondrfl 10
29Aug88—Wide 3/8 turn
19Aug88-3Dmr 6f :214 :45 1:094ft 3¾ 115 119¾ 64 44¾ 25¼ Solis A 8 [S] 20000 83-15 Aaron'sDewn,TrickyLd,FrncPrince 12
19Aug88—Very wide final 3/8
1Aug88-5Dmr 6f :214 :444 1:094ft 45 116 1212 99 84¾ 35¼ Solis A 4 20000 83-12 StuckWithYou,FrskMNot,TrckyLd 12
1Aug88—Bumped start; very wide in stretch
Mar 8 SA 6f ft 1:131 H Feb 19 SA 5f ft 1:011 H Jan 28 SA 6f ft 1:131 H

This horse represents one of the major reasons for the procedure. When I presented this race at a seminar, there was extensive discussion as to his proper designation. The 25Jan89 race clearly fits a presser's profile. The fractions were legitimate, and he was no doubt pressing that pace. If we label him a P, we'll have to consider him in that light during the final analysis. That could prove costly.

Examine Tricky Lad's basic running style in nine of the ten races presented in the *Racing Form*. Is this guy really a presser, or was the January 25 race an aberrant performance? Probability indicates that 90 percent of the time he'll drop hopelessly out of contention. In his 24Feb89 race he *did* revert to type. Stick with the probabilities. Tricky Lad's an S, although the NF designation would not be inappropriate.

It's Never Dull Dk. b. or br. g. 8, by What Luck—Sharp Pencil, by Olden Times
Br.—Forrester Geri (Md) 1989 5 0 1 0 $5,250
VALENZUELA F H 1115 Tr.—Shulman Sanford $12,500 1988 27 4 7 6 $55,430
Own.—Charles & ClearValleyStables Lifetime 90 14 16 13 $173,443 Turf 20 4 7 1 $52,870
22Feb89-2SA 1$\frac{1}{16}$:462 1:113 1:452ft 5 116 42 32½ 41½ 43½ Baze R A 6 c10000 78-18 SpruceSkipper,MimiBound,Shirke 12
3Feb89-9SA 7f :22 :444 1:214ft 9½e116 32½ 43 34½ 47 Baze R A 3 12500 84-17 Hillstrk,Emperor'sTurn,PowerFlet 10
3Feb89—Broke slowly
19Jan89-9SA 1⅛:472 1:12 1:511ft 5½ 1115 1½ 2½ 1hd 2¾ Corral J R 8 c10000 72-23 Siraluovt,It'sNeverDull,Ack'sReply 10
6Jan89-9SA 1¼:464 1:374 2:033gd 3½ 116 1½ 23½ 48½ 415¼ Pedroza M A 1 10000 55-20 Bold Decree, Equilibre, Siraluovat 8
6Jan89—Hopped in air; lugged out stretch
2Jan89-9SA 1$\frac{1}{16}$:454 1:103 1:433ft 8½ 116 32½ 42½ 54 97 Pedroza M A 8 16000 76-13 K.'sCharger,ToB.ARuler,SlamDnce 12
26Dec88-9SA 1$\frac{1}{16}$:461 1:103 1:424ft 12 114 32 42½ 64½ 68¾ Pedroza M A 7 22500 78-13 Shafy, Rakaposhi, Remar 8
9Dec88-3Hol 1 :453 1:104 1:361ft 3 116 1hd 3½ 41½ 510 Pedroza M A 6 20000 72-16 AngleArc,BooBoo'sBuckroo,Trnzor 8
27Nov88-5Hol 1⅛:47 1:114 1:511gd 8 114 1hd 1½ 22 36 Pedroza M A 5 20000 75-24 Full Charm, Bugarian,It'sNeverDull 7
6Nov88-9SA 1$\frac{1}{16}$:46 1:104 1:432ft 9½ 116 1hd 1hd 2hd 1nk Pedroza M A 6 16000 84-17 It's Never Dull, Last Motel,ChiliHill 9
27Oct88-9SA 1$\frac{1}{16}$:46 1:11 1:424ft 8½ 116 1hd 1½ 23 34½ Pedroza M A 12 12500 82-14 HloHtch,ToB.ARuler,It'sNeverDull 12
Mar 10 SA 4f ft :48 H Jan 29 SA 3f ft :374 H

His last race can easily be construed as a pressing performance. But he was no real threat to win. His best style is an E, and he should be evaluated in the early pace scenario.

Bortino B. g. 5, by Balzno—Caprice, by Turn-to
BAZE R A 116 Br.—Piemmons J M (Ky) 1989 4 2 0 0 $15,950
Own.—B & C Rnch–Nicolo–Travato Tr.—Miyadi Steve $12,500 1988 12 1 1 1 $10,870
Lifetime 17 3 1 1 $26,820
26Feb89-1SA 1 1/16 :462 1:112 1:441ft 8 1135 2 1½ 2 1½ 2hd 1hd Garcia H J9 10000 80-14 Bortino, Jazz Island, Siralvovat 12
16Feb89-3SA 1 1/16 :462 1:113 1:464m 11 1105 4 4½ 4 3½ 2 1½ 1hd Garcia H J9 10000 67-25 Bortino, Jazz Island, Very Double 11
16Feb89—Fractious in gate
18Jan89-1SA 7f :222 :451 1:233ft 17 1115 3 2½ 4 2½ 4 3½ 4 3½ Olguin G L6 10000 78-17 RrTyson,RunCougrRun,SundncSqr 11
18Jan89—Wide into stretch
1Jan89-1SA 6½f :22 :451 1:171ft 10 115 42 4 2½ 5 4½ 4 2½ Gryder A T2 10000 82-10 Tritequos,Petronck,BusinssSchool 10
11Dec88-1Hol 6½f :22 :453 1:172ft 55 1115 75 6 2½ 5 3½ 3 2½ Olguin G L10 10000 85-17 Alaskan Jim, CoastalLove,Bortino 12
26Nov88-1Hol 6f :221 :453 1:111m 47 1115 8 6½ 5 6½ 79 5 7½ Olguin G L1 10000 78-25 Romx,SundncSqur,KingOfCliforni 12
26Nov88—Broke against bit
10Nov88-2Hol 6½f :223 :46 1:17 ft 110 115 31 12 8½ 12 15 12 18½ Sorenson D 1 10500 71-19 Angle Arc, Run CougarRun,BeaHo 12
10Nov88—Checked 1/4
12Aug88-11LA 6½f :213 :444 1:164ft 10 1115 7 6½ 6 4½ 4 3½ 4 2½ Valenzuela F H 2 10000 90-10 ‡Our March, Big Craig, MajorShare 9
5Aug88-9LA 6f :214 :451 1:102ft 18 119 7 4½ 7 5½ 7 6½ 6 6½ Proctor L B 4 16000 84-13 Coursing Eagle, Oak Wine MelO'C. 8
1Aug88-4LA 6f :22 :461 1:123ft 4 120 74 6 3½ 31 1½ Proctor L B 3 M10000 80-19 Bortino,Winemucca,CruiserManet 10
Mar 9 SA 4f ft :472 H Feb 20 SA 4f ft :481 H Feb 5 SA tr.t 6f gd 1:164 H Jan 27 SA 4f ft :483 H

As a sprinter, Bortino should be considered a sustained pace runner. As a router, 100 percent of the evidence dictates a P designation.

Last Command * Ch. g. 8, by Bold Commander—Miss Hitting Away, by Hitting Away
PINCAY L JR 116 Br.—Kerr & Kerr & Kerr (Ky) 1989 4 1 1 0 $10,150
Own.—Rubinfeld N W Tr.—Shulman Sanford $12,500 1988 14 0 3 2 $32,525
Lifetime 67 11 10 14 $311,530 Turf 6 1 0 1 $9,535
2Mar89-1SA 7f :22 :444 1:23 sy *2 117 5 4½ 3 1½ 31 12 Pincay L Jr 2 c10000 85-18 LstCommnd,UnclFoss,BuenoAmost 10
2Mar89—Lugged in stretch
8Feb89-9SA 1 1/16 :464 1:12 1:453m 4½ 117 32 11 1 2½ 5 4½ Pincay L Jr 5 12500 68-23 Middle Concho, Equilibre,Tablado 11
20Jan89-3SA 1 1/8 :47 1:112 1:50 ft 6½ 117 2hd 2hd 3 2½ 7 8½ Pincay L Jr 2 20000 70-13 ToB.ARuler,Hagley'sLion,KampOut 8
14Jan89-5SA 1 1/16 :454 1:103 1:44 ft 11 117 30 21 22 2½ Pincay L Jr 4 16000 80-11 CrystlCttr,LstCommnd,ExtcArbtr 11
14Jan89—Lugged in stretch
31Dec88-1SA 6½f :212 :441 1:161ft 20 117 45 8 6½ 9 9½ 11 9½ Pincay L Jr 9 16000 79-10 Pppy'sConsul,MuiMlody,KingClyd 12
31Aug88-2Dmr 1 1/16 :463 1:11 1:424ft 7 116 4 3½ 46 5 8½ 67 Ortega L E 4 12500 79-17 LuckyBer,D.D.ThKid,ExoticArbitor 12
20Aug88-9Dmr 1 1/16 :461 1:11 1:431ft 8½ 116 54 3 1½ 7 4½ 70 Ortega L E 10 20000 76-15 ProperRidr,Convincing,It'sNvrDull 12
10Aug88-3Dmr 1 1/16 :452 1:103 1:44 ft 4½ 116 7 7½ 43 43 3 2½ Ortega L E 2 16000 77-17 ProvingSprt,KniDncr,LstCommnd 10
10Aug88—Steadied start
10Jly88-5Hol 1 :444 1:093 1:354ft *2½ 117 3 2½ 3 1½ 2hd 3 1½ Pincay L Jr 8 20000 83-10 Gossarone,ILoveRcing,LstCommnd 8
10Jly88—Lugged in; bumped late
30Jun88-7Hol 6f :213 :443 1:102ft 13 1095 9 9½ 8 6½ 65 5 4½ Corral J R 4 20000 85-15 HechizrDOro,ImprssivRsult,BidUs 11
●Feb 7 SA 3f gd :354 H

He's an old class horse who once would have annihilated this bunch. These days he's on hard times. He should be designated E/P, but his two most recent routes suggest more early than presser.

Hovering Presence * Gr. g. 6, by Bust Commander—Puss in Cahoots, by The Axe II
NOGUEZ A M 116 Br.—Franzheim Susan Beth (Ky) 1989 3 0 0 0
Own.—Forster & Rodriguez Tr.—Rodriguez Hugo $12,500 1988 22 0 1 2 $10,300
Lifetime 60 6 7 8 $94,300 Turf 2 0 0 1 $1,050
1Mar89-9SA 7f :223 :454 1:234ft 59 116 10 6½ 9 4½ 7 6½ 8 9½ Noguez A M7 10000 72-14 Remar, Manhattan King, Darion 12
17Feb89-1SA 6½f :213 :45 1:174ft 28 116 11 14 11 15 10 13 9 9½ Dominguez RE3 10000 71-21 SwetwtrSprings,RrTyson,Tritquos 12
17Feb89—Wide into stretch

3Feb89-1SA	6f	:214 :444 1:104ft	68	116	1213 1212 108¾ 85¾	Dominguez RE6	10000	78-17	RllANtrl,SwtwtrSprngs,BsassSchl	12
3Feb89—7 wide into drive										
25Sep88-9Fpx	6f	:221 :453 1:102ft	32	1115	85¾ 98½ 810 810¾	Olguin G L4	12500	84-06	StrOrphn,JustTheFcts,RdwoodBoy	10
16Sep88-10Fpx	6½f	:221 :454 1:17 ft	20	1095	811 811 66 48¾	Corral J R5	16500	82-14	Silver Hero, MajorShare,RisingPine	8
1Sep88-9Dmr	7f	:22 :451 1:231ft	16	116	106¾ 89½ 108½ 108	Ortega L E8	10000	78-14	RollANaturl,HloHtch,Mr.Edelweiss	12
11Aug88-9Dmr	6½f	:22 :451 1:173ft	19	116	1211 106½ 75¾ 66	Ortega L E3	10000	78-21	NkdJybird,LuckyAdvnc,WildPursut	12
30Jly88-9LA	6f	:222 :453 1:103ft	23	116	86 44½ 45 56¾	Bazan J8	12500	83-09	CortWzrd,QckRondtrp,ChocoltBlls	10
16Jly88-7Sol	1	:474 1:11 1:361ft	20	115	712 55½ 46 38	† Bazan J6	14000	85-10	TrojnTrick,SnsRivl,‡HoveringPrsnc	8
†16Jly88—Disqualified and placed fifth; Drifted in 1/16										
4Jly88-1Hol	7f	:22 :451 1:231ft	20	1105	78 75½ 67½ 54¾	Olguin G L12	10000	83-08	StrOfAmerc,HijoElToro,DacenKid	12
Feb 13 Fpx 4f gd :483 H	●Jan 17 Fpx 6f ft 1:143 H									

An owner's worst nightmare. The gelding has no early pace ability, no real closing ability, and is probably bad-natured as well. What he seems to need is a small piece of lead inserted just behind the left ear, by a loaded revolver. He's an NF for no form.

Kennedy Exchange
CORRAL J R **114**
Own.—Johnston Betty-E W-Judy

Ch. g. 6, by Kennedy Road—Exchanged Princess, by Prince John
Br.—Old English Rancho (Cal) 1989 1 0 1 0 $2,800
Tr.—Warren Donald $10,500 1988 13 1 2 2 $18,400
Lifetime 25 1 4 4 $27,728 Turf 1 0 0 0

23Feb89-3SA	1	:453 1:104 1:384ft	11	1095	32 31½ 33 22½	Corral J R 7	[S] 10500	71-20	RreTyson,KnndyExchng,Polysmous	8
1Oct88-12Fpx	1⅝	:491 1:384 2:17 ft	7¾	111	1½ 77½ 812 815	Gryder A T 1	H16000	75-09	Exotic Arbitor, Aleteen,SpiceTrade	9
24Sep88-12Fpx	1⅝	:47 1:391 2:181ft	*2½	117	32 3½ 1hd 31	Gryder A T 2	H12500	83-10	Aleteen,PrdeLeder,KenndyExchng	11
15Sep88-13Fpx	a1⅛	:481 1:134 1:513ft	7½	113	21 21 23 24½	Black C A 7	A12500	80-15	LuckyBer,KennedyExchng,Achirnt	8
10Jly88-10AC	6f	:221 :442 1:092ft	9½	115	52¾ 63½ 118½ 118½	Long D C 7	8000	82-14	Gaelic Money, Bakhit,BoldRooster	11
26Jun88-9AC	1 1/16	:461 1:103 1:414ft	11	115	15 1hd 68 615	Long D C 1	Aw6000	81-16	Lafitte, Rafik, Forio	6
14May88-9AC	1 1/16	:463 1:102 1:423ft	5	114	21 — — —	Enriquez H F3	Aw6000	— —	Lafitte, Faigh Abhaile, Rafik	7
14May88—Sulked										
24Apr88-9AC	1⅛	:471 1:103 1:483ft	11	112	1½ 1hd 95¾ 1012½	MrtnzJC7	ⓢRod Tbl H	83-14	Motivos, Faigh Abhaile,Starshield	10
27Mar88-9AC	1 1/16	:47 1:101 1:42 ft	9½	112	11 1½ 74¾ 710¾	MrtzJC1	ⓢPhar Lap H	85-16	Motivos, Starshield, Cesar	8
20Mar88-9AC	6f	:221 :45 1:093ft	2¾	115	3nk 3nk 41½ 46½	Lopez A D5	Aw6000	86-16	Lafitte, Bold Rooster, Fill Up	8
Mar 11 SA 5f ft 1:011 H	Mar 5 SA 4f ft :472 H	Feb 21 SA 3f ft :352 H	Feb 16 SA 7f ft 1:25 H							

Exclude his Agua Caliente (AC) races from your evaluation. That's someplace horses go when they can sink no further. This horse's races against four-legged competition suggest an E/P style.

Bueno Amnistia
SOLIS A **114**
Own.—Belany III & Bueno

Dk. b. or br. g. 5, by Kick—Zinghara, by Best Example
Br.—Murty Farm (Ky) 1989 4 0 0 1 $2,450
Tr.—Valenzuela A C $10,500 1988 5 0 0 0
Lifetime 13 1 0 1 $11,250 Turf 3 0 0 0

28Mar89-1SA	7f	:22 :444 1:23 sy	38	116	911 106¾ 53½ 32	Solis A 2	10000	83-18	LstCommnd,UnclFoss,BunoAmnst	10
26Feb89-1SA	1 1/16	:462 1:112 1:441ft	67	116	1011 89¾ 56½ 511½	Solis A 2	10000	69-14	Bortino, Jazz Island, Siralrovat	12
11Feb89-1SA	1	:473 1:132 1:404m	31	115	89½ 75½ 66½ 57¾	Solis A 1	10000	56-31	ManhattnKing,LuckyBer,StrRibot	10
3Feb89-1SA	6f	:214 :444 1:104ft	60	116	1111 1111 98¾ 106¼	Solis A 2	10000	78-17	RllANtrl,SwtwtrSprngs,BsassSchl	12
3Feb89—Bumped start										
14Dec88-9Hol	1⅛	:464 1:114 1:513ft	70	115	63½ 1118 1124 1132	Patterson A 7	12500	47-16	RationalApproch,Silor'sTle,Iberico	11
27Nov88-2Hol	1 1/16	:472 1:123 1:451gd	37	115	85¾ 1214 1124 1029	Patterson A 4	12500	45-24	Extrnix,Wher'sMchis,BrgirStndrd	12
27Nov88—Wide final 3/8										
9Nov88-9Hol	1 1/16	①:47 1:114 1:432fm	267	117	53¾ 1210 1220 1225½	Patterson A 3	Aw25000	52-23	HollywdHl,MstyMskr,VgrsCmmndr	12
13Feb88-3SA	1¼	①:491 1:391 2:04 fm	55	117	41¾ 64½ 89½ 813	Oldham D W 4	Aw34000	54-24	DefiniteSigns,SpruceSkipper,Deput	8
30Jan88-7SA	1¼	①:46 1:381 2:044fm	52	116	1115 99 610 611	Higuera A R2	Aw34000	52-30	ProudCat,HotStge,StelliteExpress	12
26Dec87-2SA	1 1/16	:464 1:111 1:441ft	66	115	1015 119½ 89 810½	Stevens S A11	40000	69-16	GretNegotitor,FstDelivry,Rkposhi	11
Mar 13 SA 4f ft :482 H	Mar 9 SA 4f ft :48 H	Feb 10 Fpx 5f ft 1:05 H	Jan 29 SA 5f ft 1:00 H							

An S horse with no form. His last race was an improvement, but it was run on a sloppy track and is probably not representative. There isn't much in Bueno Amnistia's past performances to encourage even the most optimistic bettor.

Bucket Head B. g. 4, by Zamboni—Lady's Guard, by Advance Guard
PEDROZA M A 116 Br.—Wilson J R (Cal) 1989 3 1 0 1 $4,000
Tr.—Greenman Dean $12,500 1988 1 M 0 0
Own.—Greenman & Wilson Lifetime 4 1 0 1 $4,000

3Mar89-9SA	1⅛:471 1:113 1:511gd	79	114	86	74¾	43	31¼	Douglas R R1	10500	72-19	Lucky Bear, Chili Hill,BucketHead	10
3Mar89—Bumped hard 1/16, 1st time around												
17Feb89-3SA	6½f :221 :451 1:172ft	30	117	31	43	45	56¾	Solis A 10	10000	76-21	BiscayneBoy,CervantesSt.,WrDebt	10
22Jan89-1AC	6f :224 :454 1:111ft	6	120	42	41½	11	13	Barsallo E 1	M10000	83-24	BucketHead,PatFitzptrick,Crpshot	6
14Dec88-4Hol	6f :213 :451 1:104ft	58	118	1216	1212	1112	1113¾	Pedroza M A 2	M32000	75-16	RaiderMrcus,GoldenVision,LddyV.	12
14Dec88—Broke slowly												

Feb 24 SA 5f ft 1:013 H Feb 13 SA tr.t 5f ft 1:03 H ●Feb 4 AC 6f m 1:134 H Jan 30 AC 5f ft 1:003 H

This kind of horse always presents a problem. He's lightly raced and is sending confusing signals. He's clearly not much horse, but he must be dealt with effectively. Ignore the maiden win at Agua Caliente; 1:11.1 is a slow time over that surface. His last race is the best line in his past performances. After some trouble early, he came running strongly in the stretch. He flattened out badly when near the pace in his previous race, and may be best as a late runner. I labeled him an S. A valid argument might be made for S/P, although his trainer will probably ask for a duplication of his last race.

Precedence Gr. g. 5, by Keep Your Promise—Mrs Sanchez, by Sensitive
CORRAL J R 114 Br.—Plimley B (BC-C) 1989 3 0 1 0 $3,650
Tr.—Ratchford Don $10,500 1988 14 1 0 1 $8,930
Own.—Earner-Hubbard-MauriaEtal Lifetime 36 6 7 2 $43,035

8Feb89-9SA	1 1/16:464 1:12 1:453m	41	1115	109½	77½	43½	42	Corral J R 1	12500	71-23	Middle Concho, Equilibre,Tablado	11
8Feb89—Steadied sharply 3 1/2 to avoid injured horse												
28Jan89-9SA	7f :222 :451 1:222ft	12	116	53½	98¾	1115	1119¾	Castanon A L 6	10000	69-13	Hillstark,RollANaturl,MnhttnKing	11
4Jan89-1SA	7f :223 :45 1:223m	35	115	72¾	54	23	22½	Castanon A L 7	10500	84-15	CatFisher,Precedence,Mn'sIntent	12
21Dec88-9Hol	1 1/16:481 1:14 1:464sl	21	115	21	36½	714	718	Rivera J V 1	10000	48-30	Extranix, Menelik, Bold Decree	11
19Oct88-9SA	1⅛:461 1:111 1:501ft	74	118	63¾	52¾	54½	56½	Pedroza M A 6	10000	72-16	Halo Hatch, Iberico, Correoso	11
6Oct88-9SA	1 1/16:463 1:113 1:442ft	24	118	78½	66	98½	714½	Baze R A 4	10000	64-18	Halo Hatch, Correoso, Trump Up	11
28Sep88-10Fpx	1 1/16:45 1:102 1:424ft	3½	119	45	46	49	416¾	Pedroza M A 8	10000	80-07	OurBrndX.,PocketTim,Don'tFightIt	8
8Sep88-9Dmr	1 1/16:46 1:104 1:431ft	7	118	32	52½	64½	56½	Sibille R 6	10000	78-15	WtTilMondy,RsonToStudy Gunbrst	9
25Aug88-9Dmr	1⅛:461 1:104 1:494ft	6¾	118	65	74¾	55½	35½	Baze R A 10	10000	75-18	Achirnte,GreyGuntlet,Precedence	12
17Aug88-9Dmr	1 1/16:464 1:112 1:432ft	5½	116	74½	52½	65¾	610¾	Baze R A 3	12500	72-16	Amatar,Bigbadndmen,AnotherCode	8
17Aug88—Rough start												

Feb 27 SA 6f ft 1:141 H Jan 31 SA 6f ft 1:154 H

An S horse.

The Pace Picture

Early Pace

(1) Jazz Island
(2) It's Never Dull

(3) Last Command (E/P)

(4) Kennedy Exchange (E/P)

Pressers

(1) Bortino

(2) Last Command (E/P)

(3) Kennedy Exchange (E/P)

Sustained Pace

(1) Ancient Blue

(2) Tricky Lad

(3) Bucket Head

(4) Precedence

No Form

Dhaleem, Hovering Presence, and Bueno Amnistia.

This is not a gratuitous exercise. By segmenting the race into its component parts, the pace analyst organizes his approach around the manner in which races are run. In the Ninth at Santa Anita we can use this approach to attack the race most efficiently. The bias favors E and P types. By having spent a few minutes identifying styles, we're at the heart of the race. Let's continue.

Early Pace

The basic question: Who will lead in today's match up? There are four possibilities; Jazz Island, It's Never Dull, Last Command, and Kennedy Exchange. Of the four, only Jazz Island and It's Never Dull show any dedication to the role of pace setter. The majority of Last Command's races indicates greater comfort in the role of presser. He should now be labeled P in this match up.

Kennedy Exchange represents a problem worth discussing. The early velocity of this horse's last race illustrates a potential danger; overdependence upon pure numbers.

Kennedy Exchange's fractional times in the 23Feb89 race are the best recent early pace numbers in the field. But can they be relied upon? The answer is no. The computer, or calculator, output will show him leading comfortably at the first two calls.

Does Kennedy Exchange customarily grab the lead in his races? Excepting the Caliente races, only at the 1⅜ mile marathon distance did he lead against decent company. And that race was a disaster! In the February 23 race it appears he was "pulled" along behind a fast pace. He assumed his usual position and then went along for the ride. The dismal final time of the race, and his final quarter in 28.1, suggests he won't be asked for that kind of speed again. Don't hesitate to argue with the computer output. The ESP designations will keep the race in focus.

The legitimate early pace contention: Jazz Island and It's Never Dull. Let's look at them separately.

Jazz Island: In his two route efforts he's been on the lead with solid fractional splits. He also possesses excellent sprint speed (26Jan89) and can probably outrun most routers "sent" for the lead. He should reach the first call in about 46.2 and still be within himself. If the other early pace candidate can't match the fraction, Jazz Island qualifies as a lone E.

It's Never Dull: In recent races he's been unable to gain the early lead. The 47.2, 1:12.0 splits of the 19Jan89 race will stick him in the role of presser; a spot from which he has demonstrated he cannot win. The basic question: Does he have enough current early pace to outrun Jazz Island? His last race answers the question. Against $10,000 claimers he found himself behind *three* other horses in a 46.2 half-mile. Following the effort, he hit the second call in about 1:12.0 and came home in a poor 34.0 seconds. He should not threaten Jazz Island.

The early pace summary: Jazz Island is a lone E. He should lead with fractions that are well within his capabilities. Off a 1:11.2 second call, he's a tough one to catch. He wins the early pace match-up. Now for the pressers.

Pressers

Any presser worth considering in this scenario must be able to press the probable 46.2   1:11.2 pace of Jazz Island. With that in mind, let's analyze Kennedy Exchange, Bortino, and Last Command.

Kennedy Exchange: He's 1 for 25 lifetime, and has probably never won a race as a presser. At first glance his last race looks like a good effort. But when compared to the pace setter, the final time and closing fraction of the race are both weak. This is a bad horse. I can't envision a pace scenario that would favor Kennedy Exchange. He may be properly placed at the second call, but he lacks the finishing ability to defeat the weakest fields.

Bortino: A major threat to Jazz Island. He's managed to press the pace and beat Jazz Island in two successive races. It would be no surprise to see a repeat of that outcome.

Last Command: This is the favorite in the race, and he has the back class to win at the level. His best races are as a presser, and that's his role in this race.

The question: Does he fit today's scenario? In his last race he was dropped to the bottom of the Santa Anita class ladder, his second consecutive drop. Although he won the race (on a sloppy track), the pattern is not positive. As recently as January 14 he ran strongly through two very fast fractions. He narrowly missed winning the race. His next two races are the keys to his role today.

In both he pressed fractions significantly weaker than the 14Jan89 race and weakened badly. The first of those efforts started his slide down the class ladder. He may be forwardly placed in today's race, but his recent ability and current condition do not measure up.

Sustained Pace

Ancient Blue, Bucket Head, Tricky Lad, and Precedence. With the existing bias, only the prospect of a suicidal pace duel could possibly form an argument for selecting any of these. That's not likely to happen. There is a dominant pace setter (Jazz Island) who doesn't appear to face any significant pace pressure. Should any unforeseen pressure develop, the race should belong to a presser. Bortino fits that part of the scenario.

The S horses in this race should not win a major share of the purse. In this race the role of the closers is to overhaul the casualties of the early pace and pressers match-up. Only Jazz Island and Bortino survive the match-up. The others are vulnerable to the late runners.

The Final Decision

When you see the chart of the race, you'll probably agree this was an easy decision. *Bet both horses.* Jazz Island was 9–1 and Bortino 6–1. If that's not your cup of tea, the decision for one horse should go to Jazz Island. The pace of the race indicates an easy lead, and lone E types are among the most solid betting propositions in racing. When the bias favors early pace horses and pressers, the Jazz Islands will win more than a fair share of these races.

NINTH RACE
Santa Anita
MARCH 15, 1989

1 1/16 MILES. (1.40 4/5) CLAIMING. Purse $14,000. 4-year-olds and upward. Weight, 121 lbs. Non-winners of two races at one mile or over since December 25 allowed 3 lbs.; of such a race since then, 5 lbs. Claiming price $12,500; if for $10,500 allowed 2 lbs. (Claiming and starter races for $10,000 or less not considered.)

Value of race $14,000; value to winner $7,700; second $2,800; third $2,100; fourth $1,050; fifth $350. Mutuel pool $286,288. Exacta pool $495,541.

Last Raced	Horse	Eqt.	A.	Wt	PP	St	1/4	1/2	3/4	Str	Fin	Jockey	Cl'g Pr	Odds $1
26Feb89 ^{1}SA^{2}	Jazz Island		4	113	1	3	1^{1}	$1^{1/2}$	$1^{1/2}$	$1^{1/2}$	1^{1}	Olguin G L^{5}	12500	9.70
26Feb89 ^{1}SA^{1}	Bortino		5	116	6	2	2^{hd}	3^{2}	2^{2}	2^{3}	$2^{2\frac{1}{2}}$	Baze R A	12500	6.80
8Feb89 ^{9}SA^{4}	Precedence	b	5	114	12	6	8^{3}	$7^{1\frac{1}{2}}$	5^{2}	3^{2}	3^{5}	Stevens G L	10500	14.10
22Feb89 ^{2}SA^{4}	It's Never Dull	b	9	111	5	1	$3^{1\frac{1}{2}}$	$2^{1/2}$	$3^{1\frac{1}{2}}$	4^{4}	$4^{1\frac{1}{2}}$	Valenzuela F H^{5}	12500	9.50
3Mar89 ^{9}SA^{3}	Bucket Head	b	4	116	11	10	7^{hd}	8^{2}	7^{1}	$6^{1/2}$	5^{1}	Pedroza M A	12500	6.10
2Mar89 ^{1}SA^{3}	Bueno Amnistia	b	5	114	10	12	11^{hd}	11^{hd}	11^{5}	7^{1}	6^{hd}	Solis A	10500	28.00
24Feb89 ^{9}SA^{7}	Ancient Blue		8	118	3	8	$9^{1/2}$	9^{2}	9^{1}	$9^{1\frac{1}{2}}$	7^{hd}	Toro F	12500	4.90
23Feb89 ^{3}SA^{2}	Kennedy Exchange		6	114	9	5	4^{hd}	5^{2}	4^{hd}	$5^{1/2}$	$8^{1\frac{1}{2}}$	Corral J R	10500	13.00
2Mar89 ^{1}SA^{1}	Last Command	b	8	117	7	4	$5^{1\frac{1}{2}}$	4^{hd}	6^{hd}	$8^{1/2}$	9no	Pincay L Jr	12500	3.30
24Feb89 ^{9}SA^{8}	Tricky Lad	b	4	111	4	9	6^{3}	6^{hd}	$8^{1\frac{1}{2}}$	$10^{1/2}$	10^{1}	Garcia H J^{5}	12500	7.10
1Mar89 ^{9}SA^{8}	Hovering Presence		6	116	8	11	10^{3}	10^{4}	$10^{1/2}$	11^{3}	$11^{2\frac{1}{2}}$	Noguez A M	12500	99.40
1Mar89 ^{5}SA^{7}	Dhaleem	b	6	116	2	7	12	12	12	12	12	Dominguez R E	12500	44.40

OFF AT 5:14. Start good. Won driving. Time, :22 4/5, :46, 1:10 4/5, 1:36 4/5, 1:43 1/5 Track fast.

$2 Mutuel Prices:			
1–JAZZ ISLAND	21.40	11.20	7.40
6–BORTINO		7.00	5.80
12–PRECEDENCE			9.20

$5 EXACTA 1–6 PAID $179.00.

Additional Analysis

Most races fit the Jazz Island scenario. The race contained the usual mix of E, S, and P types. The handicapper should evaluate the probable pace match-up of every race using a similar format. Not doing so risks missing potential aberrant pace match-ups that can result in generous prices.

ESP as a formalized concept materialized for just that reason. In a Sartin Seminar in 1986 I presented a race wherein *all* the top computer-rated horses were eliminated by matching the running styles. To this day it's my favorite race. Of nine possible contenders, seven were E horses with matching velocity numbers. The race contained *one* presser and *one* closer, both in reasonably good form. They ran 1–2. The winner payed a hefty 20–1. Unless one of the E's can handle intense pressure and still run its race, that type of pace scenario belongs to the late runners; regardless of bias or velocity ratings.

THE LONE E

As a guest handicapper at a "day of the races" seminar, I was confronted with a popular misconception as to the basic focus of pace handicapping. The moderator, a good class/form handicapper, volunteered to guess my selection in one of the early races. He reasoned I was a "pace player" and must have selected the horse that would gain the lead in the first fraction. He was right about the early lead, but the horse didn't have the mid-race velocity to maintain the early advantage.

Certainly the chances of the early leader must be carefully resolved in the pace analysis. But the focus goes far beyond a superficial analysis. Bias, mid-race pressure, class, and general condition are all yardsticks by which the early pace horse must be measured. *However*, when the ESP labels identify a "best" horse on the lead scenario, don't forsake the opportunity.

Jack Brohamer, Jr., has been around athletics all of his twenty-one years; his father played nine years of major league baseball. Young Jack has personally seen many of the minor ailments that plague the human athlete, and he's carried that understanding over to the equine athlete. Jack also has a facility with numbers. Pace handicapping has become his first love, and college classes permitting, he spends most of his waking hours with the *Daily Racing Form*.

We celebrated his twenty-first birthday in the race books of Las Vegas. His strength, at this stage of his development, is the identification of horses with strong early pace advantages. He uses the ESP labels in every race he handicaps. In a series of five bets, at three different racetracks, he pinpointed four winners.

The best of these plays was in the seventh race at Arlington on August 6, 1989. Spend a few minutes with the race and identify the basic running styles. Then we'll analyze the race.

Early Pace: Maven's Pride . . . and nobody else!

7th Arlington

6 FURLONGS. (1.08) ALLOWANCE. Purse $20,900 (includes 10% from Illinois Thoroughbred Breeder's Fund). 3-year-olds and upward, Illinois registered, conceived and/or foaled, which have never won a race other than maiden, claiming or starter. Weight, 3-year-olds, 117 lbs.; older, 122 lbs. Non-winners of a race other than claiming since May 1 allowed 3 lbs.; of a race since March 15, 5 lbs.

Maven's Pride
Own.—Shlofrock L & Dassouki M 117
Ch. g. 4, by Maven—Sweet Lynn, by Brau Busher
Br.—Krumhorn Morris D (Ill) 1989 3 2 0 0 $6,180
Tr.—Dassouki Michael 1988 16 3 4 2 $17,007
Lifetime 22 5 4 2 $23,946
7Jly89-2AP 6f .23 :47 1:131ft 7 119 12½ 13 14 1½ Diaz J L4 S 5000 74-27 Maven'sPride,DiscoTco,Interction 11
15Jun89-1Haw 6f :223 :461 1:114ft 2¾ 119 3½ 21 43½ 79¼ Diaz J L8 S 5000 73-24 ShadyFamily,JustZack,SonuvBoosh 8
15Jun89—Four wide.
7Jun89-1Haw 6f :221 :46 1:114ft 13 114 1½ 11½ 1hd 11 MarquezCHJr2 S 5000 82-18 Mven'sPrid,GoodHilrious,DiscoTco 7
6Dec88-5Bml 6f :223 :473 1:143ft 8¼ 114 22 21½ 32 26 Razo A7 S 5000 79-21 Zensheir,Maven'sPride,DavesHolme 8
6Dec88—Drifted out
15Oct88-3Bml 6f :222 :463 1:134ft 8¾ 112 11 1½ 35 610 Diaz J L6 S 5000 — — SeHbloIngls,DvsHolm,Mthw'sMrk 12
5Oct88-5Haw 6f :222 :461 1:114ft 13 112 11½ 2½ 66½ 810¾ Meier R11 SAw18700 71-22 SilverOrs,HevyPockts,WhoopItUp 11
23Sep88-3Haw 6f :214 :451 1:104gd 15 112 12½ 12 1½ 84¾ Diaz J L2 8000 82-16 QuitclimDd,NoDllinc,MilwukWrror 10
17Aug88-3Haw 6f :22 :453 1:12 ft 2¾ 112 11½ 1½ 1hd 22½ Diaz J L6 S 5000 79-24 PocktPrsonlity,Mvn'sPrid,DiscoTco 8
22Jly88-5Haw 6f :223 :46 1:114ft 3½ 114 13½ 13½ 13 13½ Diaz J L1 S 7500 82-17 Mvn'sPrd,Dmtr'sSword,Krs'SprPt 10
13Jly88-2Haw 6½f :224 :461 1:184ft 13 111 13 11½ 1hd 1no † MarquezCHJr2 S 5000 79-16 ‡Mven'sPrid,Fthr'sPort,Enducmnt 11
†13Jly88—Disqualified and placed second
Jly 31 AP 4f ft :481 H Jly 18 AP 5f ft 1:04 B

Liberty County
Own.—Conkling Russell W 114
Ch. g. 3(Feb), by It's Freezing—Elegance, by Decies II
Br.—Conkling Russell W (Ill) 1989 4 0 2 0 $7,420
Tr.—Hazelton Richard P 1988 5 1 2 1 $9,655
Lifetime 9 1 4 1 $17,075
12Jly89-6AP 7f :223 :46 1:25 ft *6-5 112 33 23½ 716 716½ VelsquezJ 9 SAw18700 60-25 ZenTnTr,PlunderPrince,HeHndsom 9
2Jly89-3AP 6f :23 :472 1:13 ft 3½ 112 33 34 24 26½ Torres F C 5 SAw18700 68-31 SpyMesure,LibertyCounty,CshsHir 12
17Jun89-5Haw 6f :213 :442 1:11 ft 25 112 54 46½ 34½ 21¾ Torres F C 3 SAw18400 84-16 Sezincote,LibrtyCounty,HHndsom 11
10Jun89-6Haw 6½f :23 :461 1:173ft 9½ 112 72½ 32½ 512 712½ Torres F C 8 SAw18400 71-21 BoldlyCler,SlptheClown,Znthrwsu 12
9Dec88-2Bml 6f :23 :483 1:16 ft *1 122 22 2½ 13 13 Torres F C 7 SMdn 78-22 LibertyCounty,SilvrLion,NicndRdy 12
25Nov88-4Bml 6f :224 :48 1:153ft 3½ 122 74 53½ 24 22½ Torres F C 11 SMdn 77-21 Dsty'sLdr,LbrtyConty,StrongnBrv 12
11Nov88-4Bml 6f :223 :464 1:134ft 3¾ 122 54 34½ 25 27¼ Torres F C 9 SMdn — — Doc's Pill,LibertyCounty,FlySignal 12
28Oct88-4Bml 6f :23 :491 1:172ft 26 122 95½ 63¾ 3½ 36¼ Torres F C9 SMdn — — WldThndr,Robrto'sImg,LbrtyCnty 12
15Oct88-4Bml 6f :222 :471 1:161ft 4½ 122 54 48 48½ 410¾ Torres F C 1 SMdn — — JimmyHulsey,Robrto'sImg,SuchBld 8
Jly 30 AP 4f sy :524 B Jun 29 AP 4f ft :50 B Jun 9 Haw 3f ft :391 B

And Like That
Own.—Randolph Charles 1175
Ch. c. 4, by Spy Signal—Kashmire Sapphire, by Break Up the Game
Br.—Colven Farm & No LimitFarm (Ill) 1989 7 1 0 0 $6,662
Tr.—Salazar Marco P 1987 0 M 0 0
Lifetime 7 1 0 0 $6,662
27Jly89-6AP 6f :221 :45 1:104ft 106 1175 85¼ 814 1122 1122 Davis K M2 SAw20900 64-17 ChepSunglsses,‡WorldBurnr,TllTz 12
23Jun89-8Bml 6f :222 :462 1:124ft 30 122 3½ 43 1111 1211½ Jawny A3 SAw11385 78-12 Nn'sNcBoy,PlundrPrnc,MyLstPok 12
13Jun89-6Bml 2f :212gd 38 122 10 105½ 106¾ Jawny A1 Aw8800 — — FunnySideUp,ChsinLov,SilvrSingh 11
6Jun89-6Bml 6f :23 :473 1:134ft 10 1175 3nk 21 12 11½ Gomez A12 SMdn 84-14 AndLikeTht,Bromine,CountryRoyl 12
27May89-6Bml 6f ⊡:234 :482 1:16 ft 5 1175 12 12½ 43½ 58½ Robletto L C3 SMdn 71-20 GunCnyon,Georg'sPst,Nn'sNicBoy 10
30Apr89-2Bml 6f :233 :483 1:153ft *2½ 122 1hd 2hd 11½ 46¾ MrquzCHJr6 SM10000 68-22 Duke'sFool,NoVictim,DemonVntur 10
2Apr89-5Bml 6f :224 :47 1:141sy 5½ 122 85¾ 88½ 718 718¼ Torres J E8 SMdn 64-21 Hootnaney, HoldingPenalty,St.Killy 8
●Jly 24 Haw 3f ft :364 B Jly 4 Haw 6f ft 1:154 B

Quick Hot Stuff
Own.—Stein M et al 117
B. g. 3(May), by Hot Oil—Quick Tell, by Tell
Br.—Pitzer Lee & Peggy (Ill) 1989 4 1 0 1 $13,930
Tr.—Cristel Mark 1988 0 M 0 0
Lifetime 4 1 0 1 $13,930
18Jly89-9FP 6f :214 :444 1:103ft 11 114 55 59 67½ 56¼ HllndMA 2 SIll Sta Trl 84-16 Island Sage, Dee Quik, Roman Side7
18Jly89—Bumped early
3Jun89-9Haw 6f :223 :462 1:13 sy 8½ 113 42½ 34 48 45½ Diaz J L 7 SAw18400 71-23 Kel Irish, Sir Con, Home toRejoice 9
22May89-3Spt 6f :234 :472 1:132ft 2¾ 122 12½ 12½ 11 12 Diaz J L 4 SMdn 83-17 QckHotStff,PocktT.V.,Gnl'sZnston 9
30Apr89-3Spt 6f :233 :471 1:14 ft 3½ 122 34½ 35 32½ 32 Sellers S J6 SMdn 78-21 NoblBufflo,PocktT.V.,QckHotStff 10
Jly 11 FP 4f ft :494 B

Chief Chuck
Own.—Meadows Caryl 117
Ch. g. 3(Apr), by Tartar Chief—Chuckie Sue, by Chuckie Away
Br.—Garner L D (Ill) 1989 1 1 0 0 $11,220
Tr.—Meadows George F 1988 0 M 0 0
Lifetime 1 1 0 0 $11,220
22Jly89-7AP 6f :231 :472 1:123ft 9½ 115 79½ 46½ 1hd 1hd Razo E Jr6 SMdn 77-22 ChiefChuck,SpreBer,StonHrborJim 8
22Jly89—Lunged start.
Jly 11 AP 5f ft 1:022 B Jly 5 AP 4f ft :49 B Jun 26 AP 5f ft 1:024 Bg Jun 9 Haw 4f ft :50 B

Option Tony
Own.—Goldish Marc-Savoy Stable 112
Dk. b. or br. g. 3(Mar), by Royal Roberto—Dowager, by Honest Pleasure
Br.—Duchossois R L (Ill) 1989 3 0 2 0 $11,243
Tr.—Voelkner Robert G 1988 4 1 0 2 $8,655
Lifetime 7 1 2 2 $19,898
22May89-8Spt 1 :482 1:132 1:393ft *8-5 113 89½ 78¼ 47½ 22½ Clark K D4 SAw27025 79-17 Lwdy'sCommnd,OptonTony,TxtMhl 8
10Apr89-9Spt 1 :501 1:152 1:414ft *6-5 113 56 45 22½ 24½ Clark K D6 SAw22575 66-28 FlySgnl,OptonTony,Lwdy'sCommnd 9
30Mar89-7Spt 6½f :242 :483 1:203ft 15 113 108 97½ 69 43¾ Clark K D10 SAw22050 70-25 NoMorePipe,PushShot,HeHndsom 10
30Mar89—Wide stretch.

23Nov88-1Bml 6f :222 :471 1:142ft 11 122 108¼ 710 66½ 48¼ Clark K D7 [S]Aw9460 78-20 Lookouthrcom,JmmyHlsy,Znthrws 10
22Oct88-3Bml 6½f:23 :48 1:23 ft *6-5 122 98¾ 77¼ 21 1no Clark K D1 [S]Mdn — — OptionTony,Hightway,He'saTooter 12
5Oct88-4Haw 6f :222 :472 1:14 ft 3½ 119 86¼ 77¼ 44½ 34 Clark K D1 [S]Mdn 67-22 Ldy'sCmmnd,AggrssvPr,OptnTny 12
28Sep88-3Haw 6f :224 :472 1:131ft 6½ 119 109¾ 98¾ 38 36 Clark K D1 [S]Mdn 69-24 Ankls,Lwdy'sCommnd,OptionTony 12

Justa Hoping

Own.—Ashelman Jack 117
Dk. b. or br. g. 3(Mar), by Accipiter's Hope—Might Just, by Crozier
Br.—Crooks Dennis R (Ill) 1989 7 1 0 0 $12,595
Tr.—Darjean Paul Turf 1 0 0 0
Lifetime 7 1 0 0 $12,595

27Jly89-6AP 6f :221 :45 1:104ft 42 115 42 611 614 712½ Meier R6 [S]Aw20900 74-17 ChepSunglsses,‡WorldBurnr,TllTz 12
27Jly89—Checked turn
12Jly89-6AP 7f :223 :46 1:25 ft 18 115 22½ 34 616 817 Meier R4 [S]Aw18700 60-25 ZenTnTr,PlunderPrince,HeHndsom 9
2Jly89-5AP 1 Ⓣ:4821:1331:39 fm 29 112 74¾ 43 73¾ 97¼ Meier R6 [S]Aw20900 73-18 BonitDvil,Hrhm'sImpril,Mjor'sSstr 10
2Jly89—Four wide
17Jun89-10Haw 6f :22 :452 1:114ft 20 113 87¾ 711 67 66½ Meier R2 [S]Aw18400 75-16 Saybrook, ‡Pocket T. V., Millville 10
17Jun89—Placed fifth through disqualification
10Jun89-6Haw 6½f:23 :461 1:173ft 23 113 21 55 813 512½ Meier R3 [S]Aw18400 72-21 BoldlyCler,SlptheClown,Znthrwsu 12
25May89-2Spt 6f :234 :481 1:143gd 6 113 22 2hd 11½ 1½ Meier R3 [S]Mdn 77-22 JustHopng,SpyMsur,RturnofGylord 7
25May89—Bore out
15May89-5Spt 6½f:232 :473 1:20 ft 13 113 32½ 42½ 37 48½ Meier R6 Mdn 69-21 BoldlyCler,AggressivePowr,OplKlus 9
Jly 31 AP 6f ft 1:18 B Jun 30 AP 4f ft :51 B Jun 23 Haw 4f ft :512 B Jun 8 Haw 4f ft :50 B

Secret Plan

Own.—Vanier-Lauer-Roncari 117
Ch. c. 4, by Top Command—Lucina, by Buckfinder
Br.—Lauer, Victor & Vanier (Ill) 1989 2 0 0 0
Tr.—Vanier Harvey L 1988 11 1 2 2 $19,039
Lifetime 18 1 2 3 $20,977

27Jly89-6AP 6f :221 :45 1:104ft 8½ 119 64 1116 1016 812½ Day P10 [S]Aw20900 74-17 ChepSunglsses,‡WorldBur[illegible]TllTz 12
27Jly89—Checked turn
2Jly89-3AP 6f :23 :472 1:13 ft 9¾ 117 88¼ 712 616 614½ VelsquezJ7 [S]Aw18700 60-31 SpyMesure,LibertyCounty,CshsHir 12
24Aug88-7Haw 6½f:224 :46 1:191ft 20 115 73¾ 66 79¾ 79¼ Clark K D10 [S]Aw20900 68-27 PocktPrsonlty,WtchthSlt,Intrcton 10
28Jly88-6Haw 6½f:223 :46 1:191ft 3 114 4¾ 2hd 1hd 11¼ Clark K D2 [S]Mdn 77-12 SecretPln,MoccsinMike,TkethSuc 10
8Jly88-6Haw 170:473 1:134 1:444ft 2¼ 114 22 22 37 47¼ MrquezCHJr12 [S]Mdn 70-23 Dry Country, To Errer,IlliniPrince 12
2Jun88-9CD 1⅛:48 1:14 1:474sy 3¼ 112 98¾ 75¾ 52¾ 34 Fires E5 Mdn 65-22 Blues Fool, Egret, Secret Plan 12
13May88-9CD 1⅛:473 1:124 1:46 ft 4 111 77¼ 56 46 2no Fires E1 Mdn 78-15 RollingSmoke,ScrtPln,DryCountry 12
22Apr88-9Kee 1⅛:48 1:131 1:474ft *3-2e118 59 59½ 55½ 46 Fires E10 Mdn 61-22 Granduce, Evening Dress, Egret 12
14Apr88-4Kee 1⅛:481 1:14 1:472ft 5¾ 118 48 33½ 22 21½ Fires E3 Mdn 68-20 FunnyFeeling,SecretPln,Wilmette 10
9Mar88-6Crc 1⅛:484 1:143 1:492ft 27 120 1011 613 413 39 Fires E11 Mdn 63-19 Kid Ory, Get the Net, Secret Plan 12
Aug 4 AP 5f sy 1:032 B Aug 3 AP 4f ft :482 H Jly 25 AP 4f ft :492 B Jly 19 AP 5f m 1:032 B

Slap the Clown

Own.—Fair Systems Inc 112
Dk. b. or br. g. 3(Feb), by Mara Lark—Miss Curtain Call, by Stage Director
Br.—Hartwig J & Ryan T V (Ill) 1989 8 0 2 0 $10,480
Tr.—Mitchell Paraskevas 1988 2 1 1 0 $9,284
Lifetime 10 1 3 0 $19,764

12Jly89-3AP 7f :23 :464 1:263ft 7 114 53½ 41½ 35 514¾ Razo E Jr7 [S]Aw18700 54-25 PostOffice,WorldBurner,MichelBell 7
17Jun89-10Haw 6f :22 :452 1:114ft 3 113 77½ 57 43½ 54½ Razo E Jr6 [S]Aw18400 77-16 Saybrook, ‡Pocket T. V., Millville 10
17Jun89—Placed fourth through disqualification; Crowded early
10Jun89-6Haw 6½f:23 :461 1:173ft 20 113 11 11½ 24 24½ Razo E Jr6 [S]Aw18400 79-21 BoldlyCler,SlptheClown,Znthrwsu 12
17May89-7Spt 6½f:23 :47 1:191ft 19 113 63½ 43½ 65¾ 77¾ Razo E Jr10 [S]Aw26450 73-21 ChngingthGurd,MovingDncr,TllTz 10
28Apr89-9Spt 1 :492 1:151 1:421sy 7½ 114 23 34½ 48 716½ Ward W A1 [S]Aw24675 53-30 CblloDlSol,PushShot,MrqurtAvnu 10
10Apr89-9Spt 1 :501 1:152 1:414ft 4 114 11 22½ 33 48 Ward W A2 [S]Aw22575 63-28 FlySgnl,OptonTony,Lwdy'sCommnd 9
17Mar89-9Spt 6f :234 :481 1:142sy 3½ 114 812 713 714 711¾ Guidry M1 [S]Aw19845 66-24 Zenascus, Dr. Mora, Kel Irish 9
27Feb89-5Spt 6f :25 :484 1:142ft 2¾ 114 31 3nk 4nk 21½ Guidry M8 [S]Aw18900 76-20 OutofthRd,SlpthClown,SmiChocolt 8
29Dec88-7Bml 6f :221 :461 1:123ft 9-5e122 57½ 55½ 43 2hd Guidry M7 [S]Aw12760 95-02 RainPasser,SlaptheClown,Zenascus 7
16Dec88-5Bml 6½f:224 :462 1:191ft 22 122 31 41½ 12 11 Guidry M8 [S]Mdn 96-05 SlptheClown,FlySignl,LittleMonis 12
Jun 7 Haw 4f ft :493 B

Sun Money

Own.—Bar R J Stable 112
B. c. 3(May), by Solar City—Galla Bux, by Well Spent
Br.—Bar R-J Stables (Ill) 1989 5 1 0 0 $5,149
Tr.—Tomillo Thomas F 1988 5 M 1 1 $3,748
Lifetime 10 1 1 1 $8,897 Turf 1 0 0 0

29Jly89-3AP 1⅛Ⓣ:4921:1421:46 fm 29 111 54½ 54¾ 66 711 Diaz J L4 [S]Aw22000 66-22 ALittleMuck,Dr.Mora,MoccsinMike 9
29Jly89—Wide early
10Jun89-6Haw 6½f:23 :461 1:173ft 36 112 41½ 1010 1023 1022½ RydwskSR5 [S]Aw18400 62-21 BoldlyCler,SlptheClown,Znthrwsu 12
10Jun89—Bled
22May89-8Spt 1 :482 1:132 1:393ft 38 112 2½ 22½ 27 58½ RydwskSR7 [S]Aw27025 73-17 Lwdy'sCommnd,OptonTony,TxtMhl 8
30Apr89-2Spt 6½f:231 :473 1:214ft 4 113 44½ 32 1hd 12 RydowskSR5 [S]M10000 68-21 Sun Money, RitzyTroy,BurngaeBoy 9
19Apr89-2Spt 6f :234 :491 1:16 m 8½ 113 23 1½ 2hd 44½ RydowskSR6 [S]M10000 66-29 Mlt'sSprPt,Mr'sMgc,OnthNghtShft 9
11Nov88-4Bml 6f :223 :464 1:134ft *3 122 65 47 814 717¾ Rydowski SR11 [S]Mdn — — Doc's Pill,LibertyCounty,FlySignal 12
28Oct88-4Bml 6f :23 :491 1:172ft *2 122 119¾ 99¼ 89¼ 714½ Rydowski S R6 [S]Mdn — — WldThndr,Robrto'sImg,LbrtyCnty 12
14Oct88-4Bml 6f :223 :473 1:15 ft 6½ 122 34½ 32½ 22½ 22 Rydowski SR10 [S]Mdn — — Ron Mik, SunMoney,Daniri'sRuler 12
28Sep88-5Haw 6f :23 :472 1:141ft 7 119 78½ 710 69½ 55½ Rydowski S R1 [S]Mdn 64-24 MichelBelle,AggrssvPowr,RonMik 10
8Sep88-2Haw 6f :222 :463 1:131ft 14 119 57½ 45 49½ 310½ Rydowski S R3 [S]Mdn 65-21 BabyGrnd,WillingAction,SunMoney 9
Jly 15 AP 6f ft 1:164 H Jly 1 AP 5f ft 1:033 B

Merry Performer

Own.—Bestwina Rudolph & Pauline **117**

B. c. 3(Apr), by Command Performer—Merry Carrie, by Ingrained
Br.—Bestwina Mr & Mrs Rudolph (Ill) **1989 7 1 0 0 $9,799**
Tr.—King George A **1988 0 M 0 0**
Lifetime 7 1 0 0 $9,799

23Jly89-7AP	1	$:46^4$	$1{:}12^2$	1:38 ft	83	114	$4^{1\frac{1}{2}}$	5^7	10^{25}	$10^{27\frac{1}{2}}$	Gabriel R E 4	[S]Aw22000	43-25	Wht'sAtStke,Zentherwsu,GmFllow	10
12Jly89-3AP	7f	:23	$:46^4$	$1{:}26^3$ ft	50	115	3^1	$5^{1\frac{3}{4}}$	5^6	$4^{10\frac{1}{4}}$	SrrwsAGJr 1	[S]Aw18700	59-25	PostOffice,WorldBurner,MichelBell	7
12Jly89—Steadied															
24Jun89-8Haw	170	$:46^3$	$1{:}12^2$	$1{:}43^1$ ft	59	114	5^{11}	8^{15}	11^{18}	$11^{21\frac{3}{4}}$	Gabriel R E 8	[S]Aw17600	58-19	BonitDvil,U.JokrsFntsy,PlyfullJoy	12
12Jun89-9Haw	6f	:22	:47	$1{:}15^1$ sy	54	115	7^7	$7^{8\frac{3}{4}}$	$3^{2\frac{1}{2}}$	$1^{2\frac{1}{2}}$	Sayler B 6	[S]Mdn	65-28	MrryPrfrmr,KhnjrHlt,AnnsGldnBy	11
22May89-1Spt	6f	$:23^3$	$:47^4$	1:13 ft	73	122	6^{10}	$6^{9\frac{1}{2}}$	7^{13}	$7^{13\frac{1}{4}}$	Baird E T 1	[S]Mdn	72-17	AggrssvPowr,Who'sCkn,Rhmbhdrn	8
30Mar89-3Spt	6f	$:24^1$	$:49^1$	$1{:}14^4$ ft	27	122	4^3	$5^{4\frac{1}{4}}$	10^{17}	$10^{15\frac{1}{2}}$	Baird E T 9	[S]Mdn	60-25	Caballo Del Sol, Maram,LaGantlet	10
16Mar89-3Spt	6f	$:24^1$	$:48^2$	1:15 ft	17	113	$5^{7\frac{1}{2}}$	5^{11}	5^{11}	5^{17}	Evans R D 2	[S]Mdn	58-31	Uno Sol, Tartar Sting, Penadonte	7

Several of the others have demonstrated a race or two as an early pace runner, but none have been recent. Additionally, those races were clearly aberrant performances.

Pressers: Slap The Clown, Justa Hoping, and Liberty County. The others have shown no recent ability to press the pace. Even these three are questionable.

Sustained: Why bother? For sake of the drill, the rest of the field should be labeled S or S/NF.

Jack had one question: Was the class barrier from $5000 claiming to state-bred allowances too steep for the horse to handle? The answer is no. Maven's Pride possessed an enormous pace advantage in a very weak field. With the exception of California, Kentucky, and possibly Florida, races restricted to state-bred horses are uniformly inferior. Horses running in state-bred nonwinners allowance races are among the slowest horses on the grounds. Low level claiming horses often move into those races and win decisively. In the case of Maven's Pride, she brought along a huge pace advantage. Is the lone E dangerous? She won by 5½ lengths at 6–1!

SEVENTH RACE
Arlington
AUGUST 6, 1989

6 FURLONGS. (1.08) ALLOWANCE. Purse $20,900 (includes 10% from Illinois Thoroughbred Breeder's Fund). 3–year–olds and upward, Illinois registered, conceived and/or foaled, which have never won a race other than maiden, claiming or starter. Weight, 3–year–olds, 117 lbs.; older, 122 lbs. Non–winners of a race other than claiming since May 1 allowed 3 lbs.; of a race since March 15, 5 lbs.

Value of race $20,900; value to winner $12,540; second $4,180; third $2,299; fourth $1,254; fifth $627. Mutuel pool $166,282. Quin pool, $42,853; Per Pool, $27,094; Tri Pool, $136,532.

Last Raced	Horse	Eqt.	A.	Wt	PP	St	¼	½	Str	Fin	Jockey	Odds $1
7Jly89 ^{2}AP^1	Maven's Pride		4	117	1	4	1^2	$1^{2\frac{1}{2}}$	1^5	$1^{5\frac{1}{2}}$	Diaz J L	6.20
12Jly89 ^{3}AP^5	Slap the Clown	b	3	112	9	1	3^1	2^{hd}	2^4	2^2	Velasquez J	8.30
22Jly89 ^{7}AP^1	Chief Chuck		3	117	5	8	9^3	$8^{2\frac{1}{2}}$	$6^{3\frac{1}{2}}$	$3^{1\frac{1}{2}}$	Razo E Jr	2.80
27Jly89 ^{6}AP^8	Secret Plan	b	4	117	8	9	8^{hd}	$7^{1\frac{1}{2}}$	4^{hd}	4^{hd}	Bruin J E	7.90
29Jly89 ^{3}AP^7	Sun Money	b	3	112	10	2	5^{hd}	4^{hd}	5^{hd}	$5^{\frac{3}{4}}$	Gryder A T	43.10
27Jly89 ^{6}AP^7	Justa Hoping	b	3	117	7	5	2^{hd}	3^3	3^{hd}	$6^{\frac{1}{2}}$	Meier R	26.00
22May89 ^{8}Spt^2	Option Tony		3	112	6	10	11	10^5	$7^{1\frac{1}{2}}$	7^4	Clark K D	6.30
12Jly89 ^{6}AP^7	Liberty County	b	3	114	2	11	$10^{1\frac{1}{2}}$	9^{hd}	9^5	8^{hd}	Torres F C	3.50
18Jly89 ^{9}FP^5	Quick Hot Stuff	b	3	117	4	7	4^{hd}	6^{hd}	8^1	9^7	Sellers S J	5.70
23Jly89 ^{7}AP^{10}	Merry Performer	b	3	117	11	3	6^4	5^1	10^8	$10^{10\frac{1}{2}}$	Johnson P A	85.00
27Jly89 ^{6}AP^{11}	And Like That		4	117	3	6	7^{hd}	11	11	11	Gomez A^5	85.90

OFF AT 4:15. Start good. Won ridden out. Time, :23, :47, 1:12⅘ Track fast.

$2 Mutuel Prices:

1–MAVEN'S PRIDE	14.40	8.00	5.20
9–SLAP THE CLOWN		8.20	4.20
5–CHIEF CHUCK			3.40

$2 QUIN (1–9) PD $56.60; $2 PER (1–9) PD $140.60; $2 TRI (1–9–5) PD $489.80.

CHAPTER IV

Turn-Time

WHICH PART OF A horse's performance represents its true form and condition? Several leading authorities have promoted the final fraction as the most reliable because by then a runner is relatively exhausted and is calling upon reserve power and condition.

But most studies prove the final fraction is the *least* reliable predictor of subsequent winning performances. Too much of the race has already been decided, leaving noncontenders and closers to record the strong final fractions. Horses that have determined the outcome of the race have spent their available energy earlier and are either winners or also-rans.

Conversely, the first fraction represents the other side of the energy spectrum. Certainly, the earliest part of the race can represent a runner's sharpness, but even relatively unfit animals can sustain speed through the first quarter of a sprint or the first half-mile of a route.

Picture yourself a runner. You are probably not in ideal condition, and so unable to sustain yourself over longer amounts of real estate. Yet you can move relatively well for short distances before doing your impression of a pretzel.

The latter part of the run represents what occurred before. Your downfall probably came in the middle of the run, when your body was asked to extend itself and respond to the pressure from the other runners. Likewise, I offer another argument as to which fractional time component reflects improving and peaking form—the middle fraction.

The second fraction of a race, designated here as "turn-time," offers virgin territory from which to extract winners. Several years ago Howard Sartin and his researchers began using mid-race velocity as a highly predictive source of winners. Within this fraction the race becomes most intense and pretenders are exposed. During the second fraction, run on the turn at most distances, classier horses "look their lessers in the eye" and then proceed to contest the outcome of the race.

Runners that exceed par for the middle fraction tend to figure strongly in most races, and many develop high win percentages. Visualize a sprint at the three-eighths pole as the field begins the turn. As the runners negotiate the turn, some will be moving at the pace or drawing away from the field. That's the turn-time move we'll explore throughout this chapter.

Every bettor has experienced the helpless feeling of watching a selection inhaled on the turn by a superior turn-time horse. Consider the following example:

```
Olympic Prospect              Ch. g. 5, by Northern Jove—Brilliant Future, by Forli
                              Br.—Christiana Stables (Ky)          1989  1  1  0  0    $32,800
  SOLIS A               123   Tr.—Sadler John W                    1988  9  6  1  0   $311,890
Own.—Alsdorf-Opas-Sinatra     Lifetime  20 10  2  2  $444,270      Turf  1  1  0  0    $86,450
22Jly89-10LaD 6f :21^3 :44    1:09^4ft  *3-5 112   12½ 16  16  111½ Solis A 8    Bd Br Cp   93-19 OlympcProspct,TwcArnd,IllstrsHgh 8
3Dec88-9Hol   6f :21^3 :44^2 1:09^3ft  *6-5 124   1hd 1½  12½ 4nk  PincyLJr 1  Ntl Spt Chp 94-12 GllntSilor,Reconnoitering VrySubtl7
    3Dec88—Grade III
5Nov88-4CD    6f :21   :44^1 1:10^2sy   6½ 126    1hd 1½  2hd 74¼  PncLJr 11 Br Cp Sprnt   87-20 Gulch, Play The King, Afleet     13
    5Nov88—Grade I
19Oct88-8SA   6f :21   :43^3 1:09 ft   *2-3 123   1hd 12½ 14  11¾  PincyLJr 5  Ancnt Ttl H 93-16 OlympicProspct,Sbrof,Rconnoitrng6
24Aug88-8Dmr  6f :21^1 :43^2 1:08^4ft    2 121    1½  13½ 13  11¼  Solis A 3   B Crsby H   94-11 Olympic Prospect, Faro, S:brof   6
    24Aug88—Grade III
2Jly88-8Hol   6f (T):22^1 :44^1 1:08 fm*4-5 120   11½ 11½ 13  1hd  PincyLJr 3  Bd Br Cp H 97-07 OlympcPrspct,SylvnEprss LrdRcks 6
11Jun88-8Hol  6f :21^3 :43^4 1:08^4ft  *9-5 116   12½ 13  13½ 11¾  Solis A 4        L A H  98-13 OlympcPrspct,HppInSpc,S'vnEprss 7
    11Jun88—Grade III; Broke out, bumped
1Jun88-7Hol   6f :21^4 :44^1 1:09 ft   *3-5 118   12  15  15  16½  Pincay L Jr 6 Aw42000  97-15 OlympcPrspct,GldnGntlt,Dggr'sRst 7
14May88-7Hol  6f :21^3 :44^2 1:09^4ft  *3-5 117   13½ 13  12  21¾  Pincay L Jr 3 Aw52000  91-15 MyGllntGm,OlympcProspct,Tomcm 8
9Apr88-7SA    6f :21^1 :43   1:08 ft   *6-5e117   12  16  17  17½  Pincay L Jr 7 Aw38000  98-13 OlympicProspct,DncForL,LnsMnus 9
 ●Jly 20 Hol 3f ft :34^4 H     Jly 13 Hol 6f ft 1:12^4 H     ●Jly 6 Hol 6f ft 1:14^2 H     Jun 29 Hol 5f ft :59^4 H
```

Olympic Prospect is a classic example of a runner capable of dominating the middle of a race. After running strongly through the first fraction of a race, Olympic Prospect regularly records a turn-time velocity of 22.0 to 22.2. That middle move ensures the demise of other pace setters. After drawing off on the turn, Olympic Prospect is practically guaranteed to be a factor at the end of nearly all his races. That's reflected by his win percentage.

Even as a three-year-old in maiden claiming events, this guy was able to throw incredible fractions at the opposition. Once he learned what the game was about, not only did he begin to win the majority of his races, but he also spelled sudden death for other early pace types. Let's spend some time with his past performances.

By now I hope it's clear the race, in its entirety, is a matter of early acceleration and then continuing deceleration. "Acceleration" in the second fraction is actually a comparison of the rates of deceleration within a field of runners or against an established par. What appears to be a quickening of velocity is actually a slower rate of deceleration with all horses except those without a trace of early speed.

Occasionally a plodder *does* quicken its pace in the second fraction, but seldom does that lend value to turn-time as a predictor. A horse that expends little or no energy in the first fraction *should* have something to offer in the ensuing parts of the race. The turn-time velocity of one-run closers should be minimized by the handicapper.

Now consider Olympic Prospect's race at Louisiana Downs on 22Jly89.

"Turn-time" is the difference between the first and second calls of the race, and since it is not readily displayed in the past performances, is often referred to as the "hidden fraction." The splits were most impressive, with the quarter in 21.3 and the half in 44.0. But the way the fractions were recorded was even more impressive. The acceleration on the turn was 22.2 following a 21.3 first quarter, and that's flying.

Few front-running horses can keep up with that kind of pace. High quality pressers or sustained types may wait out the leader's exhaustion, but most fields would be hard put to stay within striking position. In feet-per-second velocity numbers the race appears as follows: 61.11   58.92   51.16.

The 58.92 second fraction is faster than a majority of horses are capable of achieving in their first fractions. Very few can sustain that velocity through the half-mile.

Early pace types capable of matching the 21.3 or 61.11 fps first quarter are usually gutted in the second quarter. If I owned a quality early pace horse I would go to great extremes to avoid Olympic Prospect; the result of a duel might have long-range effects on my runner. Now consider his performance in the 1988 renewal of the Bing Crosby at Del Mar's seaside course. He ran through fractions of 21.1 and 43.2 en route to a final clocking of 1:08.4. Turn-time velocity in this race was a sizzling 22.1 following the 21.1 first quarter. The horse increased his lead three lengths in the quarter, opening a 3½-length lead that could not be overcome. The feet-per-second array is 62.26   59.45   51.96— a 59.45 second segment *after* a 62.26 first quarter. And that leads us to a discussion of the racetrack itself.

To maintain a proper perspective when considering different turn-time values, it must be in light of the surface over which the horse has performed. A 22.2 turn-time fraction over a race-track that regularly allows times of 22.1 hardly qualifies as an exceptional performance. Therefore, a basic understanding of class pars is necessary. Again, consider the 1988 Bing Crosby.

At Del Mar top quality horses sprint six furlongs in 21.3 44.2 1:08.4. The turn-time par is the difference between the 21.3 and the 44.2, or 22.4 seconds. The par quantified: 61.11   57.89   54.09.

Now let's compare the par to Olympic Prospect's performance:

| 61.11 | 57.89 | 54.09 | par |
| 62.26 | 59.45 | 51.96 | 1988 Crosby |

Insist on about a 2-length variation from par before becoming too excited about a horse's performance in the turn of a race. The above example is far beyond such a guideline and surely qualifies as an exceptional performance. In actual practice, however, the meaningful measurement is horse against horse and how one field matches up against another. We'll examine that a bit later. Let's first consider another race that subsequently became a key race during the 1989 Santa Anita meeting.

The 1989 MALIBU STAKES

The beginning of the winter Santa Anita meeting features a series of races for quality four-year-olds that culminates in the Charles H. Strub Stakes run at about the one-third point in the meeting. The Strub is run at 1¼ miles on the main track, and has for years been an exceedingly important race in sorting out the previous year's three-year-olds.

Ancient Title, Affirmed, and Spectacular Bid are just three champions who have participated in the series.

EIGHTH RACE

Santa Anita

DECEMBER 26, 1988

7 FURLONGS. (1.20) 37th Running of THE MALIBU STAKES (Grade II).(Allowance) $100,000 added. 3-year-olds. By subscription of $100 each to accompany the nomination, $250 to pass the entry box and $750 additional to start, with $100,000 added, of which $20,000 to second, $15,000 to third, $7,500 to fourth and $2,500 to fifth. Weight, 126 lbs. Non-winners of two races of $100,000 in 1988 allowed 3 lbs.; of a race of $100,000 or two of $60,000 in 1988, 6 lbs.; of a race of $35,000 since October 4, $50,000 in 1988, or a race of $100,000 in 1987, 9 lbs.; of a race of $30,000 in 1987-88, 12 lbs. Starters to be named through the entry box by the closing time of entries. A trophy will be presented to the owner of the winner. Closed Wednesday, December 14, 1988 with 23 nominations.
Value of race $115,550; value to winner $70,550; second $20,000; third $15,000; fourth $7,500; fifth $2,500. Mutuel pool $1,258,097.

Last Raced	Horse		Eqt.A.Wt	PP	St	¼	½	Str	Fin	Jockey	Odds $1
13Nov88 5Hol1	Oraibi		3 117	3	6	4¹	1hd	11½	1½	Pincay L Jr	6 00
14Dec88 8Hol1	Perceive Arrogance	b	3 120	7	7	6hd	5½	5¹	2nk	Cordero A Jr	11 40
26Nov88 8Hol1	Speedratic	b	3 120	11	1	5¼	4²	4hd	3no	Stevens G L	2 90
26Nov88 8Hol5	Mi Preferido		3 123	2	8	8³	6²	3½	4¼	McCarron C J	2 30
2Dec88 8Hol7	Prospectors Gamble	b	3 120	6	4	1hd	2hd	2½	5nk	Baze R A	12 30
18Nov88 9Med2	Unzipped		3 117	9	9	9¹	8hd	8²	62¾	Delahoussaye E	7 30
14Dec88 8Hol2	Bosphorus		3 114	1	10	10½	11hd	9½	7hd	Black C A	*9 40
25Nov88 8Aqu1	Star Attitude		3 114	5	13	12½	12hd	10²	8¼½	Sibille R	f–10 40
17Dec88 4BM1	No Commitment		3 120	4	5	3¼	3hd	6¹½	9no	Campbell B C	56 00
26Nov88 8Hol3	Smart Guy		3 114	8	11	11²	9¼	7hd	102¼	Toro F	f–10 40
26Nov88 8Hol2	Blade Of The Ball		3 114	12	12	13	13	113½	11⁶	Solis A	70 90
4Dec88 7Hol2	Frontline Fable	b	3 114	13	2	7¹	10¼	12hd	12¹	Valenzuela F H	f–10 40
2Apr88 11Crc11	Havanaffair	b	3 116	10	3	2¼	7¹¼	13	13	Valenzuela P A	57 20

f—Mutuel field.

OFF AT 4:07. Start good. Won driving. Time, :22, :44, 1:08⅖, 1:21⅖ Track fast.

$2 Mutuel Prices:

4-ORAIBI	14.00	7.00	5.00
7-PERCEIVE ARROGANCE		9.60	5.80
10-SPEEDRATIC			4.00

Ch. c, by Forli—Dancing Liz, by Northern Dancer. Trainer Mandella Richard. Bred by Todd R E & Aury (Ky).

ORAIBI forced the issue early while saving ground, vied for the lead around the far turn while continuing to save ground, edged clear in the upper stretch, responded willingly through the final furlong and had enough left late to prevail. PERCEIVE ARROGANCE, never far back, came into the stretch five wide, gained in the drive but could not get up. SPEEDRATIC, always prominent after an alert start, vied for the lead around the far turn while four wide, entered the stretch four wide, then kept to his task in the drive to gain the show. MI PREFERIDO, outrun early, moved up to get within close range of the lead before going a half, was boxed in around the far turn, kept to his task through the drive while along the inner rail and just missed the show. PROSPECTORS GAMBLE vied for the early lead to the stretch, then weakened slightly. UNZIPPED, outrun early and wide down the backstretch, came into the stretch six wide and was full of run late. STAR ATTITUDE, wide down the backstretch after breaking slowly, was four wide into the stretch. NO COMMITMENT vied for the lead to the stretch and gave way. BLADE OF THE BALL, wide down the backstretch, was six wide into the stretch. FRONTLINE FABLE, wide down the backstretch, was four wide into the stretch. HAVANAFFAIR vied for the early lead, was shuffled back while in traffic nearing the far turn, faltered and was five wide into the stretch. DROUILLY'S BOY (1) WAS WITHDRAWN. ALL WAGERS ON HIM IN THE REGULAR POOLS WERE ORDERED REFUNDED AND ALL OF HIS PICK NINE AND LATE TRIPLE SELECTIONS WERE SWITCHED TO THE FAVORITE, MI PREFERIDO (3).

Owners— 1, Todd R E & Aury; 2, Laken G B; 3, Kerlan-L4Stable-UstinEtal; 4, Barrera & Saiden; 5, Siegel M-Jan-Samantha; 6, Perkins B W; 7, Naify Valerie; 8, Teinowitz P; 9, Northgate Ranch & Hagan; 10, Banche Mr-Mrs N C; 11, Abtahi(Lse)-Brown-MaddyEtal; 12, Coutu-Konis-Sigband et al; 13, Mevorach & Monroe.

Trainers— 1, Mandella Richard; 2, Barrera Albert S; 3, Mitchell Mike; 4, Barrera Lazaro S; 5, Mayberry Brian A; 6, Perkins Ben Jr; 7, Headley Bruce; 8, Schulhofer Flint S; 9, Mason Lloyd C; 10, Jory Ian; 11, Stute Melv n F; 12, Murphy Marcus J; 13, Stute Melvin F.

Overweight: Oraibi 3 pounds; Havanaffair 2.

Scratched—Drouilly's Boy (2Dec88 8Hol6).

The first of these races is the seven-furlong Malibu Stakes, which is followed by the 1⅛-mile San Fernando Stakes. The 1989 version of the Malibu did not produce anything resembling a champion; it did, however, turn into the most productive "key race" of the meeting. Pace players tuned in to the importance of the internal fraction made this a "race to watch" as soon as the charts became available for inspection.

The overall figure of the race was not overly impressive, nor were the first and second calls—at least at first inspection. The

22.0 first quarter was actually quite leisurely, and the second call was only slightly faster than par. However, the route *to* the second call *was* exceptional.

First, the par for this type of race at Santa Anita: 21.4   44.2 1:22.0

Now let's examine the running of the race. After that leisurely 22.0, the internal pressure of the race became intense with runner after runner taking a shot at the pace. *Seven* horses were within 2½ lengths of each other as they entered the turn. What *is* truly impressive was the velocity of the fraction: 22.0! Only razor-sharp, talented sprinters can apply and withstand that kind of pressure.

And to what value is all of this? *Five* of these horses came back to win their next starts, beginning with Prospectors Gamble at 6–1.

One horse's performance is deserving of further mention inasmuch as it seems to best illustrate my point. Speedratic was sent off at 9–1 in the San Fernando Stakes, only to lose a narrow photo to another horse from this race—Mi Preferido.

In the Malibu, Speedratic was four wide versus that 22.0 second quarter, dropped back two lengths and then came on again late.

Spend a few moments absorbing that running line. Against a turn-time superior to par by *three lengths*, this guy had the worst of it and then displayed enough stamina/condition to again gain on the pace. Time and again the astute player will be generously rewarded by having paid due attention to this particular aspect of the race.

AS A MEASUREMENT OF CURRENT FORM: TRUST FUND

Without question the most consistent part of a horse's performance is its turn-time ability. While the other fractions are subject to early urging and end-race exhaustion, the second fraction remains a tightly perimetered boundary within which a runner records highly reliable numbers. Within the framework of same or similar racetracks, seldom does the turn-time number vary more than a couple of lengths.

Trust Fund's past performances are worth inspecting.

Trust Fund Dk. b. or br. m. 5, by Better Believe Me—Fund, by Speak John
DAVIS R G 116 Br.—Osborne Farm (Wash) 1989 12 3 2 0 $31,275
Own.—BCLRcingStb–Ross–TtrultEt Tr.—Ellis Ronald W $25,000 1988 13 1 1 0 $12,442
Lifetime 28 5 3 0 $46,117

15Jly89-5Hol	6½f	:214	:443	1:164ft	*3-2	116	21	11½	13½	11½	Davis R G 7	Ⓕ c20000	91-11	TrustFund,PlyingTps,SovrignAppl	10
4Jly89-2Hol	6f	:22	:451	1:103ft	7	116	3½	1½	11½	11	Davis R G 10	Ⓕ c16000	88-12	Trust Fund, Lacrosse, OurOleLady	10
23Jun89-5Hol	7f	:22	:444	1:23 ft	5	116	1hd	11	12	1½	Davis R G 3	Ⓕ c12500	89-15	TrustFund,ShwSy,SovereignAppel	11
20May89-2Hol	6f	:214	:443	1:093ft	13	116	42½	66¼	1012	1014¾	Solis A 11	Ⓕ c16000	78-07	Priscll'sCrown,SldJt,Lt'sDrnkDnnr	11
3May89-1Hol	6f	:221	:453	1:11 ft	14	116	1hd	1hd	2hd	4nk	Solis A 7	Ⓕ 16000	86-15	NelliMlb,FrdomInMyEys,S'd'sLdy	11
22Apr89-1SA	6f	:22	:451	1:104ft	2¾	1115	31	2½	2hd	21	NakataniCS 3	Ⓕ c12500	83-17	FrdomInMyEys,TrustFund,Swtnss	10
13Apr89-5SA	6f	:214	:444	1:101ft	17	1115	4¾	3½	32½	53¾	Nakatani C S 6	Ⓕ 16000	83-15	Lcrosse,JustAsFleet,GreySeptmbr	12
13Apr89—Wide 3/8 turn															
1Apr89-2SA	6f	:214	:453	1:12 ft	16	1115	98	98½	109¾	88½	Nakatani C S 5	Ⓕ 20000	69-16	Valhll,TouchOfTudor,GoldenGrden	11
4Mar89-1SA	6f	:213	:451	1:102ft	*2¼	116	31½	3nk	2hd	44¾	Pedroza M A 7	Ⓕ 20000	81-12	DefndYourMn,GrySptmbr,MlynLdy	7
4Mar89—Stumbled start															
26Jan89-5SA	6f	:213	:45	1:10 ft	7½	117	52¼	42½	34	55½	Pincay L Jr 11	Ⓕ 20000	82-16	Holdrm,Crusn'TwoS,PlyngThrogh	12

Jly 1 Hol 3f ft :361 H Jun 19 SA 5f ft 1:01 H Jun 14 SA 4f ft :481 H Jun 9 SA 3f ft :354 H

At the midpoint of the season this mare had become as reliable on the racetrack as she was at the claiming box. Claimed in five of her last six races, she produced wins off four of the claims. She won again on the day of these past performances. Early in the year this was just another claimer who won infrequently, often failing at short prices.

Her move into top form was signaled by improved performances in the middle fraction of her races. Prior to her race on 13Apr89, Trust Fund was racing in soft form, sometimes collecting a minor check without threatening to win a race. Her usual turn-time figure was 23.2 to 23.3.

On April 13 she improved dramatically while racing wide through a 23.0 second fraction before tiring a bit late. Her next race was a narrow loss while recording a sub 23.1 turn-time, and she was claimed in the process. After reverting to her earlier 23.2-type clockings in the races on 3May89 and 20May89, she began to show the improvement signaled a few races earlier.

Her winning seven-furlong race on 23Jun89 was run through a 22.4 which, by virtue of a longer run into the turn, is about the equivalent of a 23.0 quarter in a six-furlong race. Her win on 4Jly89 was against a 23.1 turn-time within which she gained half a length and two positions.

On July 15 she threw her best yet: a 22.3 turn-time clocking.

This mare is razor sharp, and until her turn-time performance declines, she deserves to be played. Yes, her next win was even more impressive.

SECOND RACE
Del Mar
JULY 26, 1989

6 FURLONGS. (1.07⅘) CLAIMING. Purse $20,000. Fillies and mares. 3-year-olds and upward. Weights, 3-year-olds, 115 lbs.; older, 121 lbs. Non-winners of two races since June 1 allowed 3 lbs.; a race since then, 5 lbs. Claiming price $25,000; if for $22,500 allowed 2 lbs. (Races when entered for $20,000 or less not considered.)

Value of race $20,000; value to winner $11,000; second $4,000; third $3,000; fourth $1,500; fifth $500. Mutuel pool $457,614.

Last Raced	Horse	Eqt.	A.	Wt	PP	St	¼	½	Str	Fin	Jockey	Cl'g Pr	Odds $1
15Jly89 5Hol1	Trust Fund	b	5	116	8	2	2hd	23	22½	12½	Davis R G	25000	1.30
4Nov88 7SA9	Moni Marlena		4	109	6	1	12	11	1hd	2¾	Castanon J L5	22500	14.30
19Jly89 5Hol5	Sense Of Romance		4	116	2	7	71½	72	51½	3¾	Black C A	25000	5.10
6Jly89 5Hol2	Afloat	b	5	117	5	5	5½	51½	41½	44	Pincay L Jr	25000	4.10
4Jly89 3Hol6	Queens Guard	b	5	116	1	4	41	4hd	3hd	52¾	Sibille R	25000	24.50
6Jly89 5Hol4	Distant Hour	b	4	111	3	8	8	8	72	63	Garcia H J5	25000	23.00
8Dec88 7Hol2	Table Clique		4	116	4	3	31	3hd	61½	73½	McCarron C J	25000	4.30
6Jly89 5Hol6	Valhalla	b	4	111	7	6	65	61	8	8	Nakatani C S5	25000	13.90

OFF AT 2:37. Start good. Won driving. Time, :21⅘, :45, :57⅘, 1:10 Track fast.

$2 Mutuel Prices:			
8–TRUST FUND	4.60	4.00	3.00
6–MONI MARLENA		10.00	6.20
2–SENSE OF ROMANCE			3.40

Dk. b. or br. m, by Better Believe Me—Fund, by Speak John. Trainer Ellis Ronald W. Bred by Osborne Farm (Wash).

TRUST FUND, prominent early, engaged for the lead turning into the stretch and drew away in the final sixteenth. MONI MARLENA set the early pace and could not stay with TRUST FUND in the last sixteenth. SENSE OF ROMANCE, devoid of early speed, was going strongly late. AFLOAT, outrun early, lacked the needed response in the final quarter. QUEENS GUARD, in contention early while saving ground, weakened in the drive. TABLE CLIQUE, close up early, gave way.

Owners— 1, BCLRcngSt-Ross-TetreaultEtal; 2, Tricar Stables; 3, Grbrg-Norris-ThndrHllsRcgEtal; 4, Mitrovich M P. 5, Six-S Racing Stable; 6, Baker R N or Dolly; 7, Vadnais Mr-Mrs E J; 8, LaTorre-Maycock-Oda Et Al.

Trainers— 1, Ellis Ronald W; 2, Silva Jose; 3, Mulhall Richard W; 4, Peterson Douglas R; 5, O'Hara John; 6, Jackson Bruce L; 7, Hess R B Jr; 8, Palma Hector O.

Overweight: Afloat 1 pound.

Scratched—Predicted Winner (19Jly89 5Hol7).

AS A SIGNPOST OF APPROACHING FORM: TRITEAMTRI

The 1989 Santa Anita Handicap will never be remembered as a classic renewal. Few top-class older dirt runners were on the grounds, and when the race was contested, most of the betting went to the Strub Stakes winner Nasr el Arab, a proven turf performer. When the race ended, we were looking at a pair of 40–1 shots and a classified allowance rating. Subsequent performances bore out the weakness of the rating. The second finisher, at $29.80 to place, was an interesting story. Triteamtri was a top-class three-year-old in Europe but had only an allowance win at Santa Anita prior to his runner-up effort in the "Big Cap."

The race preceding that allowance win is worth examining.

EIGHTH RACE
Santa Anita
JANUARY 15, 1989

1 ⅛ MILES. (1.45⅘) 37th Running of THE SAN FERNANDO STAKES (Grade I). $200,000 added. 4-year-olds. By subscription of $200 each to accompany the nomination, $2,000 additional to start, with $200,000 added, of which $40,000 to second, $30,000 to third, $15,000 to fourth and $5,000 to fifth. Weight, 126 lbs. Non-winners of two races of $100,000 at one mile or over or three such races of $50,000 in 1988–89 allowed 3 lbs.; of such a race of $30,000 or

two such races of $50,000 in 1988, 6 lbs.; of a race of $50,000 since December 25, or two of $30,000 or one of $50,000 in 1988 or a race of $100,000 in 1987, 9 lbs.; of a race of $30,000 in 1988 or one of $30,000 at one mile or over in 1987, 12 lbs. Starters to be named through the entry box by the closing time of entries. A trophy will be presented to the owner of the winner. Closed Wednesday, January 4, 1989 with 21 nominations.

Value of race $228,200; value to winner $138,200; second $40,000; third $30,000; fourth $15,000; fifth $5,000. Mutuel pool $1,016,458.

Last Raced	Horse	Eqt.	A.	Wt	PP	St	¼	½	¾	Str	Fin	Jockey	Odds $1
26Dec88 $^{8}SA^{4}$	Mi Preferido		4	123	1	1	$1^{1\frac{1}{2}}$	$1^{\frac{1}{2}}$	$2^{2\frac{1}{2}}$	1^{hd}	1^{hd}	McCarron C J	4.10
26Dec88 $^{8}SA^{3}$	Speedratic	b	4	120	10	9	4^{1}	3^{hd}	1^{hd}	2^{4}	$2^{4\frac{1}{2}}$	Stevens G L	9.40
26Dec88 $^{8}SA^{2}$	Perceive Arrogance	b	4	120	5	3	$3^{\frac{1}{2}}$	$4^{\frac{1}{2}}$	6^{hd}	5^{hd}	3no	Santos J A	4.00
30Dec88 $^{8}SA^{2}$	Claim		4	117	11	6	$7^{\frac{1}{2}}$	$6^{\frac{1}{2}}$	3^{hd}	3^{1}	4^{1}	Gryder A T	6.70
26Dec88 $^{8}SA^{11}$	Blade Of The Ball		4	114	12	10	8^{1}	8^{1}	$8^{1\frac{1}{2}}$	$6^{\frac{1}{2}}$	5^{2}	Pedroza M A	45.30
10Dec88 $^{8}Aqu^{2}$	Dynaformer	b	4	126	2	7	$9^{\frac{1}{2}}$	10^{4}	$11^{1\frac{1}{2}}$	$9^{1\frac{1}{2}}$	6^{nk}	Cordero A Jr	7.30
7Dec88 $^{8}Hol^{4}$	Undercut		4	114	9	5	5^{hd}	5^{1}	7^{1}	8^{hd}	7no	Black C A	39.80
13Nov88 $^{8}Hol^{9}$	Triteamtri		4	120	4	12	10^{4}	$7^{\frac{1}{2}}$	$4^{\frac{1}{2}}$	$7^{1\frac{1}{2}}$	$8^{1\frac{1}{2}}$	Meza R Q	24.60
26Dec88 $^{8}SA^{8}$	Star Attitude		4	115	7	11	12	$11^{1\frac{1}{2}}$	10^{hd}	$10^{1\frac{1}{2}}$	$9^{\frac{1}{2}}$	Sibille R	5.90
2Jan89 $^{7}SA^{6}$	Drouilly's Boy	b	4	114	6	8	$11^{\frac{1}{2}}$	12	12	12	$10^{2\frac{3}{4}}$	Olivares F	130.80
26Dec88 $^{8}SA^{1}$	Oraibi		4	120	8	2	$2^{\frac{1}{2}}$	2^{1}	$5^{1\frac{1}{2}}$	$4^{1\frac{1}{2}}$	$11^{1\frac{3}{4}}$	Pincay L Jr	4.30
31Dec88 $^{8}SA^{4}$	Raykour		4	114	3	4	6^{hd}	$9^{\frac{1}{2}}$	9^{hd}	11^{hd}	12	Hawley S	50.00

OFF AT 4:23. Start good for all but TRITEAMTRI. Won driving. Time, :23, :46$\frac{4}{5}$, 1:10$\frac{1}{5}$, 1:34$\frac{3}{5}$, 1:47$\frac{4}{5}$ Track fast.

$2 Mutuel Prices:			
1–MI PREFERIDO	10.20	6.60	4.80
10–SPEEDRATIC		9.20	7.00
5–PERCEIVE ARROGANCE			3.40

Dk. b. or br. c, by Island Whirl—Exacting Lady, by Disciplinarian. Trainer Barrera Lazaro S. Bred by Saiden A (Fla).

MI PREFERIDO set the early pace without being hustled after breaking alertly, battled for the lead while inside SPEEDRATIC throughout the final four furlongs and prevailed by a narrow margin in a game effort. SPEEDRATIC, off a bit awkwardly, moved up to get within close range of the lead before going a quarter, advanced while wide early in the run down the backstretch to engage for the lead soon after going a half, battled for the lead throughout the final four fourlongs, while outside MI PREFERIDO, lost a close decision while giving his all and was cleary second best. PERCEIVE ARROGANCE, close up early, steadily dropped back after a half, saved ground around the far turn, came back on in the final drive when finding renewed energy and got up for the show. CLAIM, never far back, was close up around the far turn but weakened a bit in the drive. BLADE OF THE BALL, outrun early, rallied on the far turn while wide, came into the stretch five wide and was going well late. DYNAFORMER, outrun early, was steadied and shuffled back while in traffic soon after entering the clubhouse turn, improved his position after six furlongs, entered the stretch four wide and could not gain the necessary ground in the drive. UNDERCUT was four wide into the stretch. TRITEAMTRI stumbled at the start, made a move on the backstretch while wide to look dangerous nearing the far turn but gave way in the last quarter. STAR ATTITUDE, far back early and wide down the backstretch, was never dangerous and came into the stretch five wide. DROUILLY'S BOY, wide down the backstretch, was six wide into the stretch. ORAIBI forced the early pace, stayed in contention on the far turn and in the upper stretch, then faltered in the final furlong.

Owners— 1, Barrera & Saiden; 2, Kerlan-L4Stable-UstinEtal; 3, Laken G B; 4, Claiborne Farm; 5, Abtahi(L-se)-Brown-MaddyEtal; 6, Allen Joseph; 7, Juddmonte Farm; 8, Warner M; 9, Teinowitz P; 10, Bartsch-Franklin-Fowler et al; 11, Todd R E & Aury; 12, Milhous P & R.

Trainers— 1, Barrera Lazaro S; 2, Mitchell Mike; 3, Barrera Albert S; 4, Proctor Willard L; 5, Stute Melvin F; 6, Lukas D Wayne; 7, Gregson Edwin; 8, Frankel Robert; 9, Schulhofer Flint S; 10, Spawr William; 11, Mandella Richard; 12, Vienna Darrell.

Overweight: Star Attitude 1 pound.

The San Fernando Stakes proved to be a nightmare for Triteamtri. He broke poorly and then tried to move wide into a hotly contested pace. He did manage to gain one length and three positions before tiring late, and to his credit, still finished in front of four runners.

In his next race I made him the best bet of the day based on his turn-time performance under those troubled conditions. How strong was the figure earned in the San Fernando?

First we need the turn-time par for that class level: 24.1 following a half-mile in about 46.2. In the race, Triteamtri rallied wide and gained ground into a 23.2 third quarter. As the pace of the race intensified, this guy was still trying to overcome his bad start.

Clearly, this was an exceptional performance. How exceptional? Take a look at the chart of his next race . . .

SEVENTH RACE
Santa Anita
FEBRUARY 11, 1989

1 MILE. (1.33½) THE POMPEII COURT HANDICAP. $60,000 added. 4-year-olds and upward. Nominations closed Wednesday, February 8 at $50 each. Weights were published the same day. High weights preferred.

Value of race $60,900; value to winner $33,900; second $12,000; third $9,000; fourth $4,500; fifth $1,500. Mutuel pool $404,378. Exacta pool $505,766.

Last Raced	Horse	Eqt.A.Wt PP St	¼	½	¾	Str	Fin	Jockey	Odds $1
15Jan89 8SA8	Triteamtri	4 118 4 1	1½	1¹	1⁴	1⁶	1¹⁰	Stevens G L	3.70
1Feb89 7SA2	Gorky	5 117 1 2	4⁷	4²	4²	2⁵	2⁴½	Pincay L Jr	3.10
29Jan89 8SA4	He's A Saros	6 118 5 3	2³	2²	2½	3½	3½	Valenzuela P A	5.00
25Jan88 7Arg1	Pranke	5 120 3 5	5	5	5	4½	4⁶	Delahoussaye E	1.40
1Feb89 7SA3	He's A Cajun	b 4 116 2 4	3½	32½	3½	5	5	Meza R Q	5.80

OFF AT 3:42. Start good. Won ridden out. Time, :23½, :47½, 1:12½, 1:25¾, 1:38½ Track muddy.

$2 Mutuel Prices:

6-TRITEAMTRI	9.40	4.60	3.20
1-GORKY		3.60	2.40
7-HE'S A SAROS			2.80

$5 EXACTA 6-1 PAID $92.00.

B. c. by Tri Jet—Special Team, by Specialmente. Trainer Frankel Robert. Bred by Warner M L (Fla).

TRITEAMTRI made the early pace while inside HE'S A SAROS and drew off in the final three furlongs. GORKY, outrun early but not far back, was no match for the winner in the last quarter but had enough of a response in the drive to prove clearly best of the rest. HE'S A SAROS forced the early pace while outside TRITEAMTRI and lacked the needed response in the final quarter. PRANKE trailed early after breaking awkwardly and lacked the necessary rally. HE'S A CAJUN, close up in the early stages after hopping slightly in the air at the break, faltered. HE'S A SAROS wore mud calks. MARK CHIP (3) AND SABONA (5) WERE WITHDRAWN. ALL WAGERS ON THEM IN THE REGULAR AND EXACTA POOLS WERE ORDERED REFUNDED AND ALL OF THEIR PICK SIX, PICK NINE AND DAILY TRIPLE SELECTIONS WERE SWITCHED TO THE FAVORITE, PRANKE (4).

Owners— 1. Warner M; 2. Broccoli Mr-Mrs A; 3. Green Thumb Farm Stable; 4. Sanchez H M; 5. C & K Stable
Trainers— 1. Frankel Robert; 2. Winick Randy; 3. Manzi Joseph; 4. Gregson Edwin; 5. Roberts Craig
Overweight: Gorky 1 pound.
Scratched—Mark Chip (29Jan89 8SA2); Sabona (18Jan89 7SA1).

Not a bad price for a solid selection in a short field.

PRACTICAL APPLICATIONS—DARINGLY

Turn-time as a viable factor in the pace scenario is not limited to the major tracks or by class structure. It is, in fact, probably more valuable as an indicator of positive form and improvement on the cheaper circuits. The ability to handle the turn in an efficient manner is a characteristic of a fit horse.

Conversely, those in lesser condition tend to lose ground and record times slower than when in peak form. Avoid horses whose current form demonstrates inability to maintain position during the middle part of their races.

It doesn't matter whether the problem is soreness or lack of ability; this kind seldom re-rallies into a winning position. Those that do manage to remount a rally, unless the weak turn performance was caused by trouble, are not often winners and tend to burn money in subsequent starts.

The next example should prove informative in the use of turn-time as an indicator of approaching form.

Most of my play is concentrated on the southern California circuit, which should explain the predominance of examples from that area. However, I do play frequently in Las Vegas, which provides an excellent opportunity to apply my skills in less familiar surroundings.

On this particular trip I was with James Quinn, a good friend and frequent playing partner, who has adapted the turn-time concept to his own game. Quinn is an excellent all-around handicapper, and we trust one another's judgment.

Jim had already isolated the probable winner of the second race at Garden State, an $18,000 claiming event for three-year-old fillies, and suggested I look at the first race. Our intent was to bet the daily double. After an initial revulsion to the race and a verbal declaration to the effect that no one could win, I did become interested in one of the entrants.

The heavy favorite in the race was Secret Chimes, who had finished second in two consecutive races. In maiden claiming races this kind often continues to run close without delivering the win promised by the close finishes. That win may never come.

The right approach is to look for something else or pass altogether. In this race a definite possibility existed: Daringly may have more talent than the 3–5 favorite. The key to that talent is the turn-time performance within her brief five-race career:

Daringly's career began with a pair of maiden claiming sprints at Philadelphia Park. She showed the ability to beat half the field in her second try, but her overall rating and turn-time ability gave no indication of an approaching win.

On 21Feb89 she gained 5 lengths against a 24.1 internal fraction: giving her a 23.1 turn-time and, according to the chart maker, she was very wide in the process! A definite improvement, but by no means a bet in her next race.

As noted earlier, a horse that does nothing in the early stages of a race *should* show something in the later fractions. It is encouraging that Daringly's run was in the second fraction and not the final fraction. The late-running sprinter can often be a heartbreaker, and represents a poor overall investment.

The key race in Daringly's past performances came with the inexplicable move to a higher-class racetrack, Pimlico.

Her trainer must have been impressed with this filly's improvement to have shipped her to another circuit. Although she defeated only two horses and was beaten 11 lengths, she ran the race of her young life. She was actually in the top half of her field at the second call, and had recorded a 23.1 turn-time. Major improvement in both categories.

In light of her improved form, she deserved a long look in this, her next race, the first half of the daily double. Of all the other horses in the race, only Secret Chimes could handle the turn in 23.4 to 24.0; and she was the type of odds-on favorite that should always be played against. None of the others could run at all.

Daringly represents a type of bet that has become a "knee jerk" reaction for me. By no means do I suggest you isolate turn-time as the single factor in the selecting of winners. Much more is involved than simply isolating the horse with the best velocity in the middle fraction. But in some of these weaker races where overall figures are sub par and most of the entrants cannot run, turn-time can become the dominating factor in the race.

Quinn and I cashed our daily double.

FIRST RACE
Garden State
MAY 16, 1989

6 FURLONGS. (1.08⅘) MAIDEN CLAIMING. Purse $7,000, Fillies 3-year-olds, weights, 122 lbs. Claiming price $16,000! for each $2,000 to $14,000 2 lbs. (86TH NIGHT. WEATHER SHOWERY. TEMPERATURE 60 DEGREES).

Value of race $7,000; value to winner $4,200; second $1,400; third $770; fourth $420; fifth $210. Mutuel pool $33,291. Exacta Pool $47,550.

Last Raced	Horse	Eqt.	A.	Wt	PP	St	¼	½	Str	Fin	Jockey	Cl'g Pr	Odds $1
17Apr89 ^{5}Pim^{7}	Daringly	b	3	122	3	4	1^{hd}	1^{2}	1^{5}	1^{8}	Alligood M A	16000	5.20
19Apr89 ^{6}GS^{6}	Princess of Power		3	122	4	7	5^{3}	4^{1}	$4^{2\frac{1}{2}}$	2^{hd}	Cabrera S	16000	48.30
2May89 ^{7}GS^{4}	Stormy Sea		3	122	6	1	2^{1}	2^{2}	2^{2}	3^{nk}	King E L Jr	16000	3.70
2May89 ^{7}GS^{2}	Secret Chimes	b	3	117	7	2	3^{2}	3^{2}	3^{hd}	4^{4}	Bravo J^{5}	16000	.70
22Apr89 ^{5}Del^{5}	Wish Sara Wish		3	122	2	5	$6^{\frac{1}{2}}$	6^{3}	6^{4}	$5^{\frac{1}{2}}$	Capanas S	16000	9.60
2May89 ^{7}GS^{6}	Our Fine Misty	b	3	120	1	3	$4^{1\frac{1}{2}}$	5^{4}	5^{2}	6^{5}	Allen K Kt	14000	59.10
25Apr89 ^{3}GS^{3}	Gattor's Princess		3	120	8	6	7^{1}	8	7^{1}	$7^{3\frac{1}{2}}$	Colton R E	14000	23.30
24Mar89 ^{3}GS	Anna's High	b	3	122	5	8	8	7^{hd}	8	8	Lukas M	16000	8.50

OFF AT 7:35. Start good, Won driving. Time, :22⅗, :46⅗, 1:13 Track sloppy.

Official Program Numbers↘

$2 Mutuel Prices:			
3-DARINGLY	12.40	7.80	4.00
4-PRINCESS OF POWER		28.00	13.80
6-STORMY SEA			4.40

$2 EXACTA 3-4 PAID $350.00

TURN-TIME AS A KEY PREDICTOR—OVERBROOK

The following example at Santa Anita, on January 28, 1989, is a fairly common play at racetracks across the country. Our interest lies with Overbrook's performance on 5Jan89.

Overbrook Dk. b. or br. c. 4, by Water Bank—Countless Times, by Timeless Moment
VALENZUELA F H 1115 Br.—Robertson C J (Ky) 1989 1 0 0 0
Own.—Saren Stable Tr.—Jones Gary 1988 7 2 0 1 $43,975
Lifetime 11 3 1 1 $127,425 Turf 1 0 0 0 $500
5Jan89-7SA 6½f :212 :434 1:161m *3 114 4nk 1hd 51¾ 77½ Pedroza MA 6 Aw48000 81-17 Zelphi, CrystalRun,WhatADiplomat 7
5Jan89—Wide 3/8 turn; lost whip 1/8
20Nov88-8BM 6f :22 :44 1:091ft 8¾ 111 65 65¼ 89¼ 87 Hansen R D 7 Sar H 86-17 RobrtoGrnd,SnnyBlossom,HghHok 8
23Oct88-9SA 6f :213 :44 1:092ft 5¾ 116 1½ 11½ 11½ 32 ValenzuelPA 4 Aw33000 89-16 Speedratic,LagunaNtive,Overbrook 7
9Oct88-5SA a6½f Ⓣ:214 :4431:151fm 7½ 115 75¾ 55¼ 56¼ 57 ♦ Baze R A 5 Aw40000 76-14 Dr.Brent,WhtADiplomt,LgunNtive 10
♦ 9Oct88—Dead heat
1Sep88-8Dmr 6½f :22 :443 1:152ft 5¼ 115 2hd 62½ 64¼ 77¾ Baze R A 4 Aw38000 87-14 Peaked, Pewter, Golden Gauntlet 7
1Sep88—Wide 3/8 turn
21Aug88-7Dmr 6½f :214 :443 1:153ft 2¾ 114 51¼ 43 56 58¼ McCarronCJ 7 Aw45000 85-12 FstAccount,MiPrfrido,BrodwyPoint 7
21Aug88—Lugged in late
24Jly88-7Hol 6f :214 :444 1:091ft *2¾ 115 52¾ 4¾ 4¾ 1no McCarronCJ 5 Aw36000 96-12 Overbrook, Lans Manus, BurnAnnie 7
24Jly88—Brushed late
8Jan88-5SA 6f :212 :441 1:094ft *4-5 120 2hd 1½ 13 14 Hawley S 2 Aw32000 89-19 Overbrook, Gran Musico,TemperT. 10
20Dec87-8Hol 1 :45 1:091 1:343ft 11 121 32 31½ 47 49½ Hawley S 1 Hol Fut 80-08 Tejano, Purdue King, Regal Classic 8
20Dec87—Grade I; Off slowly
22Nov87-4Hol 6f :213 :443 1:094ft 3½e 117 32 2hd 1½ 14½ Hawley S 3 Mdn 93-14 Overbrook, Switch Codes, Peace 11
Jan 22 Hol 5f ft 1:011 H Jan 17 Hol 5f ft 1:03 H ●Jan 12 Hol 4f ft :472 H Dec 29 Hol 5f ft 1:012 H

The other possibilities in the race:

Laguna Native Ro. h. 5, by Ruthie's Native—Laguna Pearl, by Deep Diver
DELAHOUSSAYE E 117 Br.—Chandler W C (Ky) 1989 1 0 0 1 $6,000
Own.—Chandler & Zimmerman Tr.—Ellis Ronald W 1988 8 1 2 1 $40,900
Lifetime 17 3 4 3 $108,225 Turf 4 1 1 1 $27,200
14Jan89-3SA 6f :212 :44 1:082ft 3¾ 116 2½ 21½ 23 33½ DelhoussyeE1 Aw40000 92-11 RonBon,WesterlyWind,LagunNtive 6
2Dec88-8Hol 6f :214 :443 1:091ft 9¾ 116 32 63 54½ 54 DelhoussyeE5 Aw35000 92-15 On The Line, Claim, Caballo DeOro 9
2Dec88—Bumped start
23Oct88-9SA 6f :213 :44 1:092ft 14 119 32 33 32½ 21 Gryder A T6 Aw33000 90-16 Speedratic,LagunaNtive,Overbrook 7
23Oct88—Broke out, bumped
9Oct88-5SA a6½f Ⓣ:214 :4431:151fm 4½ 120 2hd 1hd 2hd 32 Gryder A T3 Aw40000 81-14 Dr.Brent,WhtADiplomt,LgunNtive 10
18Sep88-10Fpx 6½f :212 :451 1:17 ft 3 120 42½ 22 2½ 1nk Gryder A T5 Aw32000 91-16 LagunaNative,ElegntBrgin SrosBid 9
7Aug88-3Dmr 1 :444 1:10 1:354ft 11 118 22 2hd 44 59¼ Meza R Q2 Aw33000 80-13 Speedratic, Redoble II, NoCanLose 6
26Jly88-10LA 1$\frac{1}{16}$:453 1:111 1:441ft *8-5 117 2½ 2hd 41¾ 613 Black C A6 Ⓡ O C Cen 74-21 Khlil,Preeminently,Keepminstitchs 9
3Jly88-9Hol 1$\frac{1}{16}$ Ⓣ:4621:1011:41 fm *1 116 32½ 52½ 45 67¼ DelhoussyeE2 Aw40000 82-11 WildBehvior,Roundlet,BestSolution 8
4Jun88-5Hol 1$\frac{1}{16}$ Ⓣ:48 1:1141:421fm 6 115 11 1½ 11 2nk DelhoussyeE4 Aw40000 83-16 Hot Stage, LagunaNative,Nilambar 7
13May87-8Hol 1$\frac{1}{16}$ Ⓣ:4711:1121:412fm *1 114 15 13½ 11½ 1hd DelhoussyeE2 Aw24000 87-13 LgunNtive,ContctGm,Mountincmlli 8
Jan 9 SA 5f ft :592 H Dec 27 SA 5f ft 1:003 H ●Dec 20 SA 4f ft :464 H Dec 11 SA 4f ft :464 H

Westerly Wind B. h. 5, by Inverness Drive—Pet Label, by Petrone
SIBILLE R 117 Br.—Jelks J R Sr (Ky) 1989 2 0 1 0 $9,000
Own.—Jelks J R Sr Tr.—Wheeler Robert L 1988 13 2 1 0 $44,700
Lifetime 24 3 4 2 $81,875 Turf 4 1 0 0 $19,250
14Jan89-3SA 6f :212 :44 1:082ft 49 116 31½ 31½ 33 23½ Sibille R 2 Aw40000 92-11 RonBon,WesterlyWind,LagunNtive 6
5Jan89-7SA 6½f :212 :434 1:161m 17 117 2hd 4¾ 63¼ 57 Sibille R 3 Aw40000 82-17 Zelphi, CrystalRun,WhatADiplomat 7
5Jan89—Lost whip 5/16
4Nov88-8SA a6½f Ⓣ:22 :4511:162fm 6½ 119 31 3nk 53½ 87 Toro F 5 Aw33000 70-14 RsonblRj,MobiusStrip,WhtADplomt 8
4Nov88—Checked 3/16
16Oct88-5SA a6½f Ⓣ:214 :4411:15 fm 14 116 2½ 2hd 2½ 1no Toro F 12 Aw35000 84-12 WestrlyWind,SuprbKing,Rformdo 12
2Sep88-5Dmr 6½f :213 :442 1:154ft 57 117 64¾ 66¼ 78 69½ Solis A 5 Aw34000 83-15 Lin, Cresting Water, Hard ToMiss 10
2Sep88—Bumped start; wide into stretch
19Aug88-7Dmr 6f :213 :441 1:092ft 37 1125 63½ 66½ 56 67 ValenzuelFH 1 Aw33000 84-15 Peaked, IrishRobbery,BraveCapade 8
19Aug88—Lugged out badly, steadied 1/2
7Aug88-7Dmr 6½f :212 :434 1:162ft 9 117 74 77¾ 99¼ 87¾ Sibille R 8 Aw31000 82-13 Valdad, Irish Robbery, Peaked 9

7Aug88—Wide final 3/8
27Jly88-5Dmr 1 1/16 Ⓣ:48^{2}1:12^{1}1:43^{3}fm 37 117 1½ 2^{hd} 4^{4}½ 8^{7}½ Sibille R 9 Aw33000 74-13 Mulhollande,SwordDance,JazzPlyer 9
27Jly88—Hopped in air
1Jly88-7Hol 6½f :21^{4} :44^{2} 1:15^{4}ft 22 119 3^{1} 3½ 2^{1}½ 5^{7}½ Sibille R 1 Aw36000 91-17 Athlone, Lans Manus, Dry Ridge 10
9Jun88-8Hol 6f :21^{2} :44^{1} 1:10 ft 11 122 5^{7} 5^{9} 4^{9} 7^{9}¼ Baze R A 4 Aw36000 83-18 BasicRate,Threegees,CesarEdurdo 12
Jan 4 SA 3f ft :37^{2} H Dec 23 SA 5f ft 1:00^{4} H Dec 13 SA 5f ft 1:00 H Dec 1 SA 4f ft :49 H

Perfecting
STEVENS G L **116**
Own.—Harbor View Farm
Dk. b. or br. c. 4, by Affirmed—Cornish Colleen, by Cornish Prince
Br.—Harbor View Farm (Ky) **1989 1 0 0 0 $3,000**
Tr.—Barrera Lazaro S **1988 11 3 5 1 $187,869**
Lifetime 13 3 5 1 $190,869 **Turf 9 2 4 1 $167,319**

14Jan89-3SA 6f :21^{2} :44 1:08^{2}ft 3½ 115 5^{4} 5^{3}¼ 4^{4} 4^{4}¼ Stevens G L^{4} Aw40000 92-11 RonBon,WesterlyWind,LagunNtive 6
21Aug88-8Dmr 1⅛Ⓣ:47 1:11 1:49 fm 3¼ 118 2½ 1½ 1^{2} 2^{hd} StnsGL^{2} Dmr Dby H 88-16 SilverCircus,Prfcting,Robr'o'sDncr 8
21Aug88—Grade II
7Aug88-8Dmr 1 1/16 Ⓣ:47 1:11 1:41^{3}fm 5 116 4^{2} 3½ 1^{hd} 1^{1}¾ StevnsGL^{8} La Jolla H 92-12 Prfcting,Robrto'sDncr,ProvSplndid 8
7Aug88—Grade III
27Jly88-8Dmr 1 Ⓣ:46^{4}1:11 1:36 fm 7 118 1^{1}½ 1^{1} 1^{1}½ 2^{1} StvnsGL^{6} ⓇOceanside 90-13 SilverCircus,Perfecting,CrownPlsur 9
8Jly88-8Hol 6f Ⓣ:22^{1} :44^{3}1:08^{2}fm *1 120 2^{hd} 2^{hd} 2^{1}½ 3^{4}¾ Stevens G L^{2} Aw35000 90-06 CrownPleasure,Madcuff,Perfecting 8
8Jly88—Bumped start
10Jun88-8Hol 1⅛Ⓣ:47^{1}1:10^{3}1:46^{4}fm 9¼ 115 1^{1} 1½ 3^{1}½ 7^{6}¾ GrydrAT^{3} Cinema H 87-09 Pece,BldeOfTheBll,Roberto'sDncer 8
10Jun88—Grade II
29May88-8Hol 1 1/16 Ⓣ:46 1:09^{2}1:40^{1}fm 5½ 115 1^{1} 1^{1}½ 1^{2} 2^{1}¾ StvnsGL^{2} W Rgrs H 91-09 WordPirte,Perfecting,Robrto'sDncr 9
29May88—Grade II
18May88-9Hol 1 1/16 Ⓣ:45^{4}1:09^{4}1:41 fm*4-5 114 1^{hd} 1^{2} 1^{4} 1^{3} Stevens G L^{2} Aw35000 89-11 Perfecting,FildOfViw,JustAsLucky 10
29Apr88-5Hol 1 Ⓣ:46^{1}1:09^{3}1:34^{2}fm*9-5 117 1½ 2^{hd} 2^{hd} 2½ Stevens G L^{3} Aw34000 91-08 Peace, Perfecting, Field Of View 8
6Apr88-5SA a6½f Ⓣ:21^{2} :43^{4}1:14^{2}fm 3 114 2^{hd} 1^{hd} 2^{hd} 4^{3}¼ Stevens G L^{4} Baldwin 84-13 ExclsvNryv,ProspctrsGmbl,Mhmtsk 9
6Apr88—Jumped crossing dirt track, again at 1 1/16; Run in divisions
Jan 2 SA 5f ft :58^{4} H Dec 27 SA 5f ft :59^{1} H ●Dec 20 Hol 4f m :47^{4} H Dec 14 Hol 3f ft :36 H

As it should be with any race we handicap, the early pace horses must be identified. Overbrook, Westerly Wind, and Laguna Native all surface as possible pace setters, but only Overbrook seems dedicated and talented enough to lead in this field.

Our dilemma: Is he sharp enough to take these all the way through the 6½ furlongs?

Consider his January 5 race, just 23 days earlier. From an outside post, and a muddy racetrack, he vied for the early lead to the second call before tiring a bit late. How strong a race was this?

The Santa Anita par for this level is *21.3 44.2 1:16.0* on a track with a *Daily Racing Form* variant of about 17.

Turn-time par is 22.4.

On January 5 Overbrook, the 3–1 favorite, took all the worst of it against a 21.2 first quarter followed by a 22.2 turn-time. Overbrook's fps array:

Overbrook	*61.56*	*59.04*	48.61
Par	61.11	57.89	52.21

After such a favorable comparison to par, I'll generally begin my walk to the betting windows. In this race, however, I began to reach deeper into my pockets than usual.

Overbrook added Lasix in this race, strongly suggesting he

had bled on January 5. Any concerns about his weak final fraction were considerably lessened with that information.

Now to compare the main contenders and their pacelines:

Laguna Native	(14 Jan)	61.44	57.96	53.27
Overbrook	(5 Jan)	61.56	59.04	48.61
Perfecting	(14 Jan)	59.81	58.62	53.81
Westerly Wind	(14 Jan)	60.98	58.40	53.40

The final analysis of this race should consider the *Daily Racing Form* variant for the two races shared by the contenders. It suggests the common race of the three other contenders was run on a significantly faster racetrack than the Overbrook race (DRF 16 vs 11).

In support of that conclusion, Westerly Wind was involved in both races and performed better in the six-furlong race. I submit that in light of running lines, track condition, and the addition of the bleeder medication, Overbrook is a standout selection.

He figures to match Laguna Native for the first quarter, and then, based on his superior turn-time numbers, should put away that rival. He should also draw off from the rest of the field.

There are few better bets in racing than a solid front-running type capable of dominating his main rivals in the second fraction.

Can we get a price here? Not from each other, but thanks to a less sophisticated public, Overbrook paid a generous 9–2. Several races later he won a two turn mile in 1:34.2 and paid $30.80 for the effort.

FIFTH RACE
Santa Anita
6 ½ FURLONGS. (1.14) ALLOWANCE. Purse $41,000. 4-year-olds and upward which are non-winners of $3,000 three times other than maiden, claiming or starter. Weights, 4-year-olds, 120 lbs.; older, 121 lbs. Non-winners of two such races since December 1 allowed 2 lbs.; of such a race since then, 4 lbs.
JANUARY 28, 1989

Value of race $41,000; value to winner $22,550; second $8,200; third $6,150; fourth $3,075; fifth $1,825. Mutuel pool $445,500. Exacta pool $531,777.

Last Raced	Horse	EqLA.Wt PP St	¼	½	Str	Fin	Jockey	Odds $1
5Jan89 7SA7	Overbrook	b 4 111 3 3	2¹	11½	1⁴	14½	Valenzuela F H⁵	4.00
14Jan89 3SA3	Laguna Native	5 117 2 6	1hd	2¹	2¹½	2no	Delahoussaye E·	2.70
14Jan89 3SA2	Westerly Wind	b 5 117 7 1	4hd	3¹	3¹½	3¹½	Sibille R	7.90
23Sep88 4Eng¹	Martial Law	4 116 6 4	8	8	5¹½	4hd	Pedroza M A	7.70
20Nov88 9Hol⁶	Jonleat	5 117 4 7	6³	6hd	4¹	54½	Meza R Q	27.10
18Jan89 5SA3	Country Side	4 111 1 5	7½	7hd	62½	65½	Olguin G L⁵	45.60
14Jan89 3SA4	Perfecting	4 116 5 8	3¹½	5¹½	7¹	72½	Stevens G L	1.40
19Nov88 8BM7	Grand Chelem	5 117 8 2	5½	4½	8	8	Baze R A	17.50

OFF AT 2:47. Start good. Won driving. Time, :21¾, :43¾, 1:08¾, 1:15¾ Track fast.

$2 Mutuel Prices:
3-OVERBROOK	11.60	5.80	4.40
2-LAGUNA NATIVE		3.80	3.00
7-WESTERLY WIND			4.00

$5 EXACTA 3-2 PAID $111.00.

A PRACTICAL APPLICATION—
DANAWEE PROSPECTOR

With the advent of year-round racing, more and more of our racetracks are presenting handicappers with two almost insurmountable problems: short fields and cheap races. Sheer greed, by both management and legislators, has weakened the fabric of racing to the extent that many of our prestigious races have become virtual walkovers. They have also become havens for allowance horses that once had no chance in these races.

As bettors we must either exercise great restraint or open our play into areas many of us would never have previously touched.

Fortunately, a solid understanding of pace characteristics within class levels can open the door to regular profits.

In these weaker races final time is *not* the route to profits. Most runners with strong final numbers are severely overbet and, by virtue of lower-class infirmities, are probably already on the downside of the form cycle.

Trip handicappers have an edge in these races because their data is relatively hidden from the average players.

Pace handicappers are also blessed with a strong advantage.

The nature of these races favors the horse that can establish position and then apply pressure on the turn. Many of these fields are loaded with sore and untalented horses incapable of contending beyond the first fraction.

Closers in these fields are generally one-run types that fire every few races. They are overly dependent upon what has occurred earlier in the race, and represent poor investment possibilities.

The first race at Hollywood Park on 22Jly89 is an almost daily occurrence.

These are the only possibilities either early or late. The pacelines selected are, in all cases, the last race. Each contender's basic ability is fairly represented, and it was unnecessary to go beyond the last race.

1st Hollywood

6 FURLONGS. (1.08) MAIDEN CLAIMING. Purse $16,000. 3-year-olds and upward. Weights, 3-year-olds, 116 lbs.; older, 122 lbs. Claiming price $32,000; if for $28,000 allowed 2 lbs.

Slew's Bandit

CORTEZ A **116**
Own.—Big Train Farm
Gr. g. 3(Apr), by Slick Slew—Rising Peak, by Elevation
Br.—Coleman B (La) 1989 4 M 1 0 $5,775
Tr.—Van Berg Jack C $32,000 1988 0 M 0 0
Lifetime 4 0 1 0 $5,775

28Apr89-2Hol	6½f	:22^1	:45^2	1:17 ft	*3	113	3^{nk}	3^2	8^9	$11^{17\frac{1}{4}}$	Davis R G^2	M35000	73-15
13Apr89-6SA	1$\frac{1}{16}$	:46^4	1:11^3	1:42^{2}ft	4¼	116	1^{hd}	2^{hd}	$6^{6\frac{3}{4}}$	$7^{16\frac{3}{4}}$	ValenzuelaPA^4	M45000	72-15
5Apr89-6SA	6f	:21^3	:44^3	1:10^{4}ft	2½	118	$3^{\frac{1}{2}}$	$3^{2\frac{1}{2}}$	$4^{3\frac{1}{2}}$	$4^{1\frac{1}{2}}$	McCarron C J^2	M50000	82-14
5Apr89—Stumbled start													
8Mar89-6SA	6f	:22	:45^2	1:11 ft	15	116	1^1	2^{hd}	2^{hd}	2^2	McCarron C J^4	M45000	81-15

Jly 11 Hol 5f ft 1:02^3 H **Jun 24 Hol 5f ft 1:02^4 H** **Jun 2 Hol 4f ft :47^3 H**

Danawee Prospector

MCCARRON C J **116**
Own.—Marellee Racing Stable
B. c. 3(Jan), by Naevus—Crawley Beauty, by Go Marching
Br.—Marellee Racing Stable (Cal) 1989 2 M 0 0
Tr.—Hofmans David $32,000 1988 1 M 1 0 $5,400
Lifetime 3 0 1 0 $6,400

7Jly89-4Hol	6½f	:21^3	:44^3	1:15^{3}ft	12	116	2½	1^{hd}	5^6	$5^{16\frac{1}{4}}$	Davis R G 4	[S]M50000	81-13
24Jun89-4Hol	6f	:22	:45^3	1:10^{3}ft	*9-5	117	3^1	4^2	$4^{6\frac{1}{2}}$	$5^{8\frac{1}{4}}$	Pincay L Jr^1	M50000	80-11
31Dec88-4SA	6f	:21	:43^4	1:09^{2}ft	42	117	$3^{1\frac{1}{2}}$	2^4	3^5	$3^{8\frac{1}{2}}$	Pedroza M A^6	[S]Mdn	82-10
31Dec88—Awarded second purse money													

Jly 17 Hol 5f ft 1:01^4 H **Jly 4 Hol 4f ft :49 Hg** **Jun 21 Hol 5f ft 1:02^2 H** **Jun 16 Hol 5f ft 1:01^4 H**

Mild Reproach

DELAHOUSSAYE E **122**
Own.—Hartstone & Levine
Ch. g. 4, by Aggravatin'—Im Perposing, by Dumpty Humpty
Br.—Hartstone G D (Cal) 1989 3 M 1 0 $3,200
Tr.—Hartstone George D $32,000 1988 2 M 0 0 $1,875
Lifetime 5 0 1 0 $5,075

8Jly89-2Hol	6f	:22^1	:45^3	1:10^{3}ft	10	120	2½	$4^{1\frac{1}{2}}$	2^3	2^2	DelhoussyeE^{11}	M28000	86-12
8Jun89-1Hol	6f	:22^1	:45^4	1:11^{1}ft	6½	120	4^2	4^2	$5^{3\frac{1}{2}}$	6^3	Sibille R^5	M28000	82-14
25May89-2Hol	7f	:22	:45^1	1:23^{4}ft	3	122	2^{hd}	$4^{2\frac{1}{2}}$	4^2	$7^{5\frac{1}{2}}$	DelahoussyeE^6	M32000	79-12
18Aug88-6Dmr	6f	:21^3	:44^4	1:10^{3}ft	10	111^5	$5^{2\frac{1}{2}}$	$7^{3\frac{3}{4}}$	$9^{6\frac{3}{4}}$	$9^{8\frac{3}{4}}$	Corral J R^{11}	M50000	76-18
18Aug88—Lugged out badly 3/8 turn													
30Jly88-4Dmr	6f	:21^3	:44^3	1:08^{3}ft	28	110^5	3^1	3^3	3^5	$4^{10\frac{1}{4}}$	Corral J R^2	[S]Mdn	85-08

Jly 16 Hol 4f ft :49^1 H **Jly 2 Hol 4f ft :47^1 H** **Jun 25 Hol 5f ft 1:01^2 H** **Jun 21 Hol 4f ft :47^4 H**

Captain Casey

CASTANON J L **109^5**
Own.—Valpredo J
B. g. 3(May), by Captain Nick—Up First, by Dimaggio
Br.—Valpredo & Sellers Mmes (Cal) 1989 5 M 0 0 $1,250
Tr.—Tinsley J E Jr $28,000 1988 0 M 0 0
Lifetime 5 0 0 0 $1,250

8Jly89-2Hol	6f	:22^1	:45^3	1:10^{3}ft	71	116	3½	3^1	4^7	$10^{15\frac{1}{2}}$	Castanon AL^{12}	M32000	72-12
21Jun89-2Hol	6½f	:21^4	:44^4	1:16^{2}ft	12	116	4^4	$4^{6\frac{1}{2}}$	5^{11}	5^{15}	ValenzuelFH^{11}	M32000	78-17
29May89-2Hol	7f	:22	:45^1	1:23^{4}ft	7¾	115	1½	3^1	8^{15}	$8^{18\frac{1}{4}}$	Black C A^6	M32000	67-13
17Feb89-2SA	6f	:22	:45^2	1:11^{3}ft	10	112^5	1^{hd}	2^{hd}	2^{hd}	$5^{5\frac{1}{2}}$	VlenzuelFH^4	[S]M32000	74-21
17Feb89—Bumped start													
27Jan89-2SA	6f	:22	:45^4	1:12^{2}ft	15	113^5	1^{hd}	1^{hd}	$2^{2\frac{1}{2}}$	$5^{5\frac{3}{4}}$	Olguin G L^5	M32000	70-21

Jly 15 Hol 5f ft 1:00^4 H **Jun 29 Hol 7f ft 1:31^2 H** **Jun 15 Hol 5f ft 1:02^3 H** **Jun 8 Hol 7f ft 1:30 H**

Misaki

PINCAY L JR **116**
Own.—Winner C & Anne
Ch. c. 3(Mar), by Miswaki—Laughing Allegra, by His Majesty
Br.—Hosta V-Sally & Vazzana J (Ky) 1989 5 M 1 2 $8,625
Tr.—Aguilera Humberto $32,000 1988 2 M 0 0
Lifetime 7 0 1 2 $8,625

8Jly89-2Hol	6f	:22^1	:45^3	1:10^{3}ft	*2¾	117	$4^{3\frac{3}{4}}$	2^1	3^3	3^4	Pincay L Jr 4	M32000	84-12
8Jun89-1Hol	6f	:22^1	:45^4	1:11^{1}ft	4¼	117	2^1	2½	$2^{1\frac{1}{2}}$	$3^{1\frac{1}{2}}$	Pincay L Jr 10	M32000	83-14
11Feb89-4SA	7f	:22^4	:46^4	1:27^{3}m	10	118	1½	$1^{1\frac{1}{2}}$	2½	2^7	Solis A 8	M32000	55-31
16Jan89-2SA	7f	:22^2	:45^3	1:25^{2}ft	13	118	1½	2½	3^5	$5^{6\frac{3}{4}}$	Solis A 5	M32000	67-15
2Jan89-4SA	6f	:21^3	:44^4	1:10^{1}ft	64	118	2^{hd}	3½	$5^{6\frac{1}{2}}$	$11^{15\frac{1}{4}}$	Castanon A L 3	M32000	72-13
9Dec88-2Hol	6f	:22	:46	1:11^{2}ft	87	118	1^1	3½	2^4	$7^{10\frac{1}{2}}$	Solis A^4	M40000	74-16
15Jun88-4Hol	5½f	:22	:46	1:05 ft	50	117	$10^{9\frac{1}{4}}$	11^{12}	11^{17}	11^{25}	Solis A^7	M50000	64-16
15Jun88—Broke out, bumped													

Jly 2 Hol 6f ft 1:12 H **Jun 25 Hol 6f ft 1:14^3 H** **Jun 16 Hol 5f ft 1:01^1 H** **Jun 3 Hol 6f ft 1:12^2 H**

Slew's Bandit	59.34	56.14	xx.xx
Danawee Prospector	60.87	57.60	xx.xx
Mild Reproach	59.23	55.98	52.60
Captain Casey	59.23	56.19	xx.xx
Misaki	59.12	56.30	51.60

None of these cheapies can be designated as closers, although the velocity characteristics of Mild Reproach are those of a presser. In his races, however, he has shown a tendency to battle for the lead, which would be self-destructive here.

Danawee Prospector's first fraction of 21.3 changes the running characteristics of all the other contenders to mid-pack.

Once that occurs in a race, the bettor is faced with two alternatives, one clearly superior to the other. Look for closers capable of running down the lone pace setter, or analyze the race in terms of turn-time ability.

The high speed-figure horse in this race is Mild Reproach. He is probably the only contender with the energy to continue on when the bulk of the field stops chasing Danawee Prospector. Unfortunately, this type of horse will often remain a short-priced maiden for a long time, frustrating even the most patient bettors.

Turn-time analysis is the key to most of these races. Many experienced players still perceive pace to be a quest to determine which horse will gain the early lead. That's of great importance, but the real key is the middle of the race.

What happens after the lead is established? Will the pace setter lose the momentum on the turn to a presser or to another early pace type, or will he retain his margin and draw away?

If the latter is the case, the final fraction of the horse is seldom a major consideration unless you're dealing with an habitual quitter.

With that in mind, what should happen in this match-up? Danawee Prospector's 21.3 should establish a solid early lead, and then his sub 23.0 turn-time should put away the entire field.

None of the other front-running types have any chance to regain lost ground from the first fraction and are no threat in the race. The best recent turn-time of the others is 23.2.

The pace battle is "no contest." Only the possibility of Danawee Prospector stopping on his own should cause any concern. That is seldom the case, and if the price is right, he's a strong play.

Surprisingly, these kinds are often held at overlaid prices and produce significant profits every season.

FIRST RACE

Hollywood

JULY 22, 1989

6 FURLONGS. (1.08) MAIDEN CLAIMING. Purse $16,000. 3-year-olds and upward. Weights, 3-year-olds, 116 lbs.; older, 122 lbs. Claiming price $32,000; if for $28,000 allowed 2 lbs. 66th DAY. WEATHER CLEAR. TEMPERATURE 83 DEGREES.

Value of race $16,000; value to winner $8,800; second $3,200; third $2,400; fourth $1,200; fifth $400. Mutuel pool $304,872.

Last Raced	Horse	Eqt. A. Wt	PP	St	¼	½	Str	Fin	Jockey	Cl'g Pr	Odds $1
7Jly89 4Hol5	Danawee Prospector	b 3 116	2	1	1$\frac{1}{2}$	13$\frac{1}{2}$	15	16	McCarron C J	32000	*3.70
8Jly89 2Hol2	Mild Reproach	4 122	3	4	4hd	4$\frac{1}{2}$	3hd	2$\frac{1}{2}$	Delahoussaye E	32000	3.70
3Sep88 5B M	Eratone	b 4 122	9	9	71	5$\frac{1}{2}$	53$\frac{1}{2}$	31$\frac{1}{2}$	Davis R G	32000	3.90
8Jly89 2Hol6	Lucky Busty	b 3 116	5	6	51	6$\frac{1}{2}$	4$\frac{1}{2}$	44	Stevens G L	32000	7.00
8Jly89 2Hol3	Misaki	b 3 116	8	2	32	2hd	2$\frac{1}{2}$	52	Pincay L Jr	32000	4.20
23Jun89 2Hol11	Saratoga Looie	b 3 116	7	12	11$\frac{11}{2}$	102	6$\frac{11}{2}$	6$\frac{11}{2}$	Sorenson D	32000	122.70
	Kid Mustang	4 122	6	8	6hd	7$\frac{11}{2}$	7$\frac{1}{2}$	7nk	Baze R A	32000	6.90
7Jly89 1Hol9	Removed	4 120	10	10	92	8hd	8$\frac{1}{2}$	8$\frac{11}{2}$	Sibille R	28000	84.80
3May89 2Hol7	Opening Ceremony	b 3 116	11	3	2hd	31	91	9nk	Desilva A J	32000	74.70
28Apr89 2Hol11	Slew's Bandit	3 116	1	5	81	9$\frac{1}{2}$	101	10$\frac{11}{2}$	Cortez A	32000	30.70
8Jly89 2Hol18	Captain Casey	3 109	4	7	102	11hd	112	112$\frac{1}{2}$	Castanon J L5	28000	47.10
	Cool Captain	3 109	12	11	12	12	12	12	Jaureguı L H5	28000	27.00

*—Actual Betting Favorite.

OFF AT 1:33. Start good. Won handily. Time, :22⅖, :45⅖, :58, 1:11 Track fast.

Official Program Numbers

$2 Mutuel Prices:

2-DANAWEE PROSPECTOR	9.40	5.40	4.40
3-MILD REPROACH		5.00	3.60
9-ERATONE			4.40

B. c, by Naevus—Crawley Beauty, by Go Marching. Trainer Hofmans David. Bred by Marellee Racing Stable (Cal). DANAWEE PROSPECTOR, a pace factor from the start, drew away after three furlongs and was under oily a mild hand ride through the final sixteenth. MILD REPROACH, in contention early after being bumped in the initial strides, was no match for DANAWEE PROSPECTOR in the drive but gained the place. ERATONE, outrun early and wide down the backstretch, came into the stretch five wide and did not have the needed response in the drive. LUCKY BUSTY, in contention early after being jostled in the opening strides, entered the stretch four wide and also did not have the needed response in the drive. MISAKI, hustled to vie for the early lead, gave way. KID MUSTANG was four wide into the stretch. REMOVED, wide down the backstretch, was six wide into the stretch. OPENING CEREMONY vied for the early lead and faltered. CAPTAIN CASEY, bumped and jostled in the initial strides, was five wide into the stretch. COOL CAPTAIN was wide early.

Owners— 1, Marellee Racing Stable; 2, Hartstone & Levine; 3, Baccala & Ross; 4, Bernstein & Giulianc; 5, Winner C & Anne; 6, Diamond M Ranch; 7, Manning-Platt-Swendener; 8, Jimenez J R; 9, Clark J A; 10, Big Train Farm; 11, Valpredo J; 12, Cavanagh Mr-Mrs T M.

Trainers— 1, Hofmans David; 2, Hartstone George D; 3, Sadler John W; 4, Bernstein David; 5, Agu Iera Humberto; 6, Brooks L J; 7, Manning Dennis R; 8, Jimenez James; 9, Heap Blake; 10, Van Berg Jack C, 11, Tirsley J E Jr; 12, Peterson Douglas R.

Scratched—Class Scholar (18Jly89 6Hol7); Le Roc (18Jly89 6Hol3)

A PRACTICAL APPLICATION—TEACH A TRON

The selection of the following race may well be interpreted as too simplistic by the experienced racegoer. I assure you it is not.

At this point in the text I hope I've imparted an understanding of the value of turn-time in the analysis of pace. If so, selecting the winner of this race will be a real "no brainer."

As to being too easy for the experienced player: If that were the case, the 5–1 price on the winner must have been the result of a computer malfunction.

The first race at Del Mar on August 14, 1989:

1st Del Mar

6 ½ FURLONGS. (1.13⅘) CLAIMING. Purse $15,000. 3-year-olds. Bred in California. Weight, 120 lbs. Non-winners of two races since June 1, allowed 2 lbs.; of a race since then, 4 lbs. Claiming price $16,000; if for $14,000, allowed 2 lbs. (Races when entered for $12,500 or less not considered.)

Stadium Stud — Ch. g. 3(May), by Dimaggio—Delightful Debbie, by Windy Sands
Br.—Old English Rancho (Cal) 1989 3 1 0 1 $10,488
BLACK C A 118 Tr.—Headley Bruce $16,000 1988 0 M 0 0
Own.—Siegel M-Jan-Samantha Lifetime 3 1 0 1 $10,488
31Jly89-5Dmr 6f :21^2 :44^2 1:10^{3}ft 26 118 4^4 5^7 6^6 6^{6}½ Black C A 7 25000 79-16 Rketmnsch,GoDogsGo,NturllyWys 12
7Jly89-2Hol 6f :22^1 :45^3 1:11^{3}ft *2¼ 116 2^{hd} 1^{hd} 1^{1}½ 1^{nk} Black C A 5 M32000 83-13 StdumStud,VgulyIrsh,ShrpEydBoy 10
7Jly89—Bumped hard start
18May89-2Hol 6f :22 :45^3 1:09^{4}ft 9 115 4^{1}½ 3^1 2^6 3^{9}¼ ♦ Patterson A 5 Ⓢ M32000 83-07 FiercComptitor,Obnd,StdiumStud 12
♦18May89—Dead heat
Jly 22 Dmr 5f ft 1:01^2 H Jly 2 SA 3f ft :37 H Jun 21 SA 5f ft 1:02 H ●Jun 16 SA 5f ft :59^2 H

Lucky Busty — Ch. g. 3(Feb), by What Luck—Donna Domestic, by Don B
Br.—Giuliano S R (Cal) 1989 10 1 2 1 $14,450
GARCIA H J 109^5 Tr.—Bernstein David $14,000 1988 1 M 0 0
Own.—Bernstein & Giuliano Lifetime 11 1 2 1 $14,450
7Aug89-5LA 6f :22^1 :45^3 1:11^{1}ft 2 115 3^1 2½ 1^{hd} 1^{hd} Black C A 9 M12500 87-13 Lucky Busty,TahitianHarry,J.A.Pest
31Jly89-5LA 6f :22^1 :45^4 1:12^{4}ft *8-5 115 2^{hd} 3^{1}½ 2^2 2no Black C A 2 M20000 79-18 NorthrnAngl,LuckyBusty,MgcOfTm
22Jly89-1Hol 6f :22^2 :45^3 1:11 ft 7 116 5^{2}½ 6^{5}½ 4^{5}½ 4^{8}½ Stevens G L 5 M32000 77-16 DnweProspctor,MildRproch,Erton 1
22Jly89—Wide final 3/8
8Jly89-2Hol 6f :22^1 :45^3 1:10^{3}ft 12 116 6^{2}¾ 7^5 5^{7}¼ 6^{11}½ McCarron C J 1 M32000 76-12 NaturalCandy,MildReproach,Miski 1
8Jly89—Bothered by loose horse 3/8
8Jun89-1Hol 6f :22^1 :45^4 1:11^{1}ft 10 115 3^{1}½ 3^{1}½ 3^{2}½ 4^{1}¾ McCarronCJ 12 M32000 83-14 Joytiltwo, Regally Gold, Misaki
31May89-1Hol 1$\frac{1}{16}$:46^4 1:11^3 1:44^{2}ft 5 115 2^1 2^2 6^{11} 6^{17} Stevens GL 1 Ⓢ M32000 61-15 NeverInLc,FlingFbulous,SonOfOn
12May89-6Hol 7f :21^4 :44^3 1:23 ft *8-5 117 5^{4}½ 5^{4}¾ 6^8 8^{15}¼ Pincay L Jr 2 M40000 74-14 ForEric,Imhedinforthebrn,ChrlieO. 1
28Apr89-6Hol 6f :22^2 :45^4 1:11 ft 5¼ 113 3^{1}½ 3^2 2^1 3^{3}¾ Olivares F 5 Ⓢ M45000 82-15 Egl'sPrdis,JunglJklin,LuckyBusty 1
14Apr89-4SA 7f :22 :44^3 1:22^{4}ft 7¼ 118 3^{1}½ 2^{1}½ 2½ 2^{4}½ Olivares F 4 M40000 81-12 DomntdDbt,LckyBsty,RghtOvrFct 1
29Mar89-4SA 6f :21^4 :45 1:11^{1}ft 6¼ 118 7^{1}¾ 7^{4}¼ 7^6 6^{3}½ Olivares F 4 Ⓢ M32000 78-17 Far Trip,PaintedTiger,StateCoach 1
29Mar89—Broke slowly
Jly 29 SA 3f ft :36^3 B Jly 2 SA 5f ft 1:00^2 H Jun 24 SA 3f ft :36^4 H

Allo's Natural — Ch. g. 3(Mar), by Surgeon Sam—Naturalmente, by New Policy
Br.—Sultan A (Cal) 1989 5 1 2 1 $17,80
PINCAY L JR 118 Tr.—Lewis Craig A $16,000 1988 0 M 0 0
Own.—Sultan A Lifetime 5 1 2 1 $17,800
31Jly89-5Dmr 6f :21^2 :44^2 1:10^{3}ft 9 118 5^{5}½ 9^{12} 10^{11} 10^{10}¼ Pincay L Jr 1 25000 75-16 Rketmnsch,GoDogsGo,NturllyWys
31Jly89—Broke out, bumped
13Jly89-1Hol 6f :22^1 :45^2 1:11 ft 4¼ 119 4^4 6^{4}½ 4^3 2^{3}½ Pincay L Jr 7 Ⓢ 25000 82-14 JaklinLomaLad,Allo'sNaturl,Chlden
14Jun89-1Hol 6f :22 :45^3 1:11^{1}ft 2½ 118 1½ 1^{1}½ 1^{1}½ 1¾ Pincay L Jr 6 Ⓢ M32000 85-15 Allo'sNturl,OhDtFox,Cptin'sHolidy
14Jun89—Bumped at start
11May89-2Hol 1 :45^2 1:11 1:36^{2}ft *2¾ 117 1^1 1½ 1^{hd} 3^{2}½ Pincay L Jr 7 Ⓢ M32000 78-16 CatfishPurdy,GoStark,Allo'sNaturl
26Apr89-2Hol 6f :22 :45^1 1:10^{2}ft 19 114 1^1 1^{hd} 1^{1}½ 2^2 Black C A 4 M28000 87-10 PeaceCall,Allo'sNatural,Villa'sBeu
26Apr89—Lugged out backstretch
Jly 19 Hol 3f ft :36 H Jun 29 Hol 5f ft 1:01^4 H

Chief Kennedy — B. g. 3(Feb), by Kennedy Road—Chief Fred, by Tom Tulle
Br.—Ward & Williams (Cal) 1989 6 1 1 0 $15,9
DELAHOUSSAYE E 116 Tr.—Williams George L $16,000 1988 4 M 0 0 $7
Own.—Strand & Williams Lifetime 10 1 1 0 $16,700
10Jly89-7Hol 7f :21^4 :44^3 1:23^{2}ft 15 116 7^{7}¾ 6^7 3^5 2^{3}½ Stevens G L 7 16000 83-12 GreekMyth,ChiefKennedy,Gloryizd
10Jly89—Wide
16Jun89-9Hol 1$\frac{1}{16}$:46^1 1:11^3 1:45 ft 6½ 116 7^{12} 6^{10} 6^{10} 4^{11} DelahoussayeE 6 16000 64-13 Such A Wager, MonteCarlo,SlyGu
16Mar89-9SA 1 :46^1 1:10^4 1:37^{2}ft 25 113^5 7^{6}½ 6^9 6^8 5^9 Valenzuela F H 6 32000 72-16 PrccsKnght,MrclMystry,MlcsPrtr
16Mar89—Broke slowly
24Feb89-4SA 1$\frac{1}{16}$:46^3 1:11^2 1:46^{1}ft 5¼ 117 6^{4}¾ 6^{5}½ 4^{1}¾ 1no DelahoussyeE 6 M32000 70-16 ChiefKennedy,SlemSe,ResilintNti
26Jan89-2SA 1$\frac{1}{16}$:47^2 1:12^4 1:45^{4}ft 23 112^5 8^{4}¾ 6^{2}¼ 4^3 5^{4}½ Olguin G L 10 M32000 68-16 SumDndy,Mr.Termintor,FettleKttl
5Jan89-2SA 6½f :21^4 :45 1:17^{2}ft 39 112^5 8^{8}¾ 6^6 5^8 4^7 Olguin G L 6 Ⓢ M32000 76-13 BtOutOfHll,FlingThBlus,RockSuk
5Jan89—Broke very slowly

24Dec88-2Hol 6½f :22 :454 1:18 m 46 118 121111112 99¾ 814¾ Olguin G L2 M32000 70-23 NonEdwrdo,BtOutOfHll,RockSukr
8Dec88-4Hol 6f :221 :451 1:094ft 114 118 85½ 64½ 67¼ 510 CastnonAL8 [S]M32000 83-12 MyLckyLynn,ScrtAccmplc,RckSkr
8Dec88—Bumped hard start
25Aug88-2Dmr 6f :223 :454 1:11 ft 11 117 85 57 57¾ 714¼ Solis A1 [S]M32000 69-18 Colorful Hitter, Try Raja, Latour
25Aug88—Bumped 5/16
8Aug88-2Dmr 6f :222 :462 1:104ft 8 117 97¾ 86¼ 68 513¼ DelhoussyE5 [S]M32000 71-15 Forceten Road, Jazz, Try Raja
8Aug88—Wide 3/8 turn
Aug 7 Dmr 5f ft 1:023 H Aug 2 Dmr 4f ft :481 H Jly 13 Hol 4f ft :50 H Jly 8 Hol 3f ft :363 H

Bargain Bob
Dk. b. or br. g. 3(Feb), by Bargain Day—Rebarbara, by Pass the Glass
NAKATANI C S 1095
Br.—Klinger R H (Cal) 1989 11 2 2 1 $22,500
Tr.—Mason Lloyd C $14,000 1988 4 M 1 0 $1,200
Own.—Klinger & Two Rivers Farm
Lifetime 15 2 3 1 $23,700
2Aug89-2Dmr 1 1/16 :461 1:111 1:441ft 9¼ 116 86¾ 108½ 88 77¾ McCarron C J8 16000 71-15 PrinceOfAck,SuchAWgr,Amwinnr 10
27Jun89-10Pln 170 :47 1:12 1:434ft 4¼ 115 42½ 41½ 22½ 2½ Warren R J Jr3 16000 74-22 Steeplechase,BargainBob,LeliaLove 7
27Jun89—Bumped start
9Jun89-3GG 1 :453 1:102 1:373ft 5¼ 117 32 21 21½ 2nk Gryder A T7 [S] 10000 77-20 RomntcGroom,BrgnBb,DncOnWtr 10
20May89-2GG 6f :214 :444 1:101ft 4¼ 117 43 46½ 612 711¼ Chapman T M8 16000 77-13 TexsHtchetmn,Heyrobbin,KingZoot 8
11May89-9GG 1 :46 1:103 1:37 ft 3¾ 117 69 67¾ 69¾ 510¾ Hansen R D2 25000 69-19 RockSuker,LeliaLove,IslndMinstrel 7
29Apr89-3GG 6f :22 :452 1:101gd 14 117 63½ 65½ 64¼ 64¾ Gryder A T2 Aw20000 83-18 Roni Bo, Pukkaraki, Vote 6
24Mar89-7GG 1 1/16 :471 1:12 1:444gd 5¼ 117 33 31 22 32½ Loseth C6 Aw19000 72-27 Arc Of Tawa,StrungUp,BargainBob 9
11Mar89-8GG 1 :454 1:12 1:39 m 15 113 85¾ 88½ 75¾ 55½ CpbllBC4 [R]Lfyt Iv H 64-25 MysticlWizrd,Terrorizd,PrinCptn 12
20Feb89-8GG 6f :214 :443 1:092ft 9¼ 115 55 53 54½ 46½ CmpbllBC5 Gldn Bear 85-21 DowntownDvy,RsAStnz,WrkTllDwn 5
5Feb89-7GG 6f :223 :462 1:103gd 11 115 2½ 1hd 11½ 16 Campbell B C4 18000 86-24 BargainBob,LaCostRoyle,GoldCdet 9
Aug 6 Dmr 4f ft :482 H Jly 13 GG 5f ft 1:012 H Jun 19 GG 3f ft :352 H

Teach A Tron
Dk. b. or br. g. 3(Apr), by Boitron (Fra)—School Marm, by Tree of Knowledge
CASTANON J L 1115
Br.—Mamakos J (Cal) 1989 6 1 0 0 $9,525
Tr.—Mamakos Jason $14,000 1988 0 M 0 0
Own.—Mamakos J L
Lifetime 6 1 0 0 $9,525
Entered 12Aug89- 2 DMR
10Jly89-7Hol 7f :214 :443 1:232ft 3¼ 119 13 12½ 21½ 67½ Pedroza M A 3 16000 79-12 GreekMyth,ChiefKennedy,Gloryizd 9
24Jun89-3Hol 6f :22 :444 1:093ft 29 116 52½ 911 915 918½ Pedroza M A 7 40000 75-11 Agitated Mike, Go Dogs Go,Skisit 10
24Jun89—Lugged out
2Jun89-2Hol 6½f :214 :444 1:162ft *8-5 115 12 11½ 15 14 PedrozaMA 6 [S]M32000 93-10 TeachATron,NobleValiant,GoBigAl 12
4May89-6Hol 1 :452 1:101 1:364ft 12 113 12½ 11½ 2½ 65 Pedroza M A 10 M35000 74-15 CrnkyKd,Smrst'sTrn,Mr.DndyDncr 11
15Mar89-4SA 6f :22 :451 1:103ft 11 1135 1½ 2hd 22 46½ Garcia H J2 [S]M32000 78-14 CommnderDowns,Chlden,GoBigAl 12
15Mar89—Lugged out badly backstretch, 3/8 turn
2Feb89-2SA 6f :213 :444 1:104ft 14 1135 99½ 1011 1116 1120¼ VlenzuelFH9 [S]M40000 64-18 Puttn'ForEgl,IslndLgcy,FblosStff 12
2Feb89—Steadied sharply start; wide into stretch
Aug 5 Dmr 3f ft :351 H Jly 6 Hol 4f ft :494 H Jun 28 Hol 4f ft :473 H Jun 14 Hol 4f ft :501 H

Papa Stan
B. g. 3(Apr), by Stanstead—Theresa's Star, by Olympiad King
SOLIS A 116
Br.—Holt L (Cal) 1989 8 1 1 1 $19,050
Tr.—Holt Lester $16,000 1988 1 M 0 0
Own.—Holt L
Lifetime 9 1 1 1 $19,050
3Aug89-1Dmr 6f :22 :451 1:111ft 19 116 96½ 76¼ 56 32 Solis A 7 16000 80-14 Ex Beau, Allo's Wish, Papa Stan 11
3Aug89—Bumped start
7Jun89-6Hol 6f :22 :45 1:10 ft 14 116 87½ 77½ 67¼ 49¾ Solis A 2 20000 81-15 AgitldMik,Brillintzd,PocktfulOfAcs 8
24May89-4Hol 1 1/16 :483 1:124 1:44 ft 24 119 41½ 41¼ 66 610¾ Guerra W A 7 25000 69-15 HourFinder,GreekMyth,SuchAWger 7
5May89-5Hol 1 :451 1:101 1:36 ft 28 119 52½ 53 54½ 56½ Valenzuela F H 9 32000 76-16 ‡SySyBoom,RcerRex,MliciousPrtnr 9
21Apr89-4SA 1 1/16 :461 1:113 1:453ft 3¼ 118 12½ 1½ 12½ 12½ Solis A 2 M32000 73-17 PapaStan,BoundingBear,PeaceCll 11
29Mar89-4SA 6f :214 :45 1:111ft 5¼ 118 61¼ 52 53 43¼ Baze R A 11 [S]M32000 79-17 Far Trip,PaintedTiger,StateCoach 12
29Mar89—Wide 3/8 turn
17Feb89-2SA 6f :22 :452 1:113ft 3¼ 117 31 42 66 79¼ Meza R Q 8 [S]M32000 71-21 BettorRoger,FarTrip,AnotherSros 10
27Jan89-2SA 6f :22 :454 1:122ft 9 118 51¼ 41¾ 44 23 Meza R Q11 M32000 73-21 Totally Fun, Papa Stan, Tonzatilt 12
27Jan89—Bumped start
31Dec88-2SA 6f :211 :441 1:10 ft 40 117 78 78 89 78¼ Meza R Q5 [S]Mdn 79-10 Giglio, Stylish Stud, Morry's Lad 9
31Dec88—Broke against bit, hit gate start
Jly 22 Dmr 6f ft 1:151 H Jly 15 SA 5f ft 1:023 H Jly 10 SA 5f ft 1:034 H Jly 5 SA 4f ft :482 H

Golden Messenger
Ch. c. 3(Jan), by Golden Eagle II—Little Avalanche, by Against the Snow
PEDROZA M A 116
Br.—Heover D R (Cal) 1989 4 1 0 1 $3,285
Tr.—Garcia Victor $16,000 1988 1 M 0 1 $360
Own.—Heover D R
Lifetime 5 1 0 2 $3,645
3Aug89-1Dmr 6f :22 :451 1:111ft 7 116 52½ 33½ 33½ 42 DelahoussayeE 6 16000 80-14 Ex Beau, Allo's Wish, Papa Stan 11
3Aug89—Bumped twice
28May89-4Hol 6½f :214 :442 1:162ft 28 119 76½ 87½ 88¼ 914¾ McCarron C J1 25000 78-11 Go Dogs Go, BelieveItToMe,ReRun 9

2May89-6AC 6f :23¹ :45² 1:10⁴ft 6½ 119 52½ 54 43½ 1no Mercado F³ AlwM 85-15 GldnMssngr,MnfstDstny,L'sDfndnt 9
6May89-9AC 6f :22¹ :44¹ 1:09²ft 6½ 119 64¾ 74½ 63¾ 32 Flores D R⁶ AlwM 90-12 StedySilver,Lucifer,GoldenMssngr 11
16Oct88-1AC 6f :22³ :45² 1:11²ft 2½ 1107 6⁶ 6⁶ 52¼ 32 Castanon J G¹ AlwM 80-17 CkForQn,Acrossword,GoldnMssngr 6
Aug 11 Dmr 4f ft :50 H   Aug 2 Dmr 4f ft :48⁴ Hg   Jly 28 Dmr 7f ft 1:26² H   Jly 22 Dmr 6f ft 1:15² H

I have omitted two runners from minor tracks with virtually no probability of winning the race, leaving eight runners for consideration. We'll look at them individually.

Stadium Stud: This guy is dropping two levels from an even effort against $25,000 horses. His previous was a maiden claiming win after gamely battling on the pace the entire trip. His usual turn-time figure is 23.3 after a 22.1 first quarter. His best race was on the lead, and with those early numbers, this field will have to be empty for him to have any chance to win. We'll designate him an early pace type.

Lucky Busty: His two races at Los Alamitos were against much weaker horses. He wants to force the pace but lacks speed to do that effectively. He'll be mid-pack in most fields, and his usual 22.3+ 23.3 first two quarters should have no impact here.

Allo's Natural: The *Daily Racing Form* selectors have made him their consensus selection. He drops a couple of levels, but with younger horses this is not as significant as it appears. The age bracket tends to be overvalued, and most of these are just looking for a spot to earn a check. His best style seems to be as an early pace type, and he can run the first quarter in 22.0 on his best days. His turn-time, following the 22.0, is about 23.2. His latest races are not encouraging.

Chief Kennedy: The consensus second choice. He has no early pace ability, and figures to win only if all the early pace runners self-destruct. His turn-time in sprints does not figure to impact the pace by any significant amount.

In an earlier section I made the point that the closers worth backing are those that can begin to overhaul the pace in the second fraction of a sprint. The one-run types will often break your heart and seldom fatten your bankroll.

Chief Kennedy is a closer or sustained pace runner.

Bargain Bob: Except for the Golden Bear Stakes, run earlier in his career, he has no early pace ability and is capable of only a 23.2+ turn-time. He would be a surprise in here.

Teach A Tron: An easily identified early pace horse. He is definitely capable of a 21.4 to 22.0 first fraction, and should easily lead in here. Beyond his early momentum, he should sustain his pace through a middle fraction of about 23.0. He'll lead this field into the stretch.

Papa Stan: Another sustained pace horse. In recent races Papa Stan has shown no early pace but has managed the turn in about 23 seconds. Against all but Teach A Tron, this one should be making some impact in the middle of the race.

Golden Messenger: A mid-pack runner who figures to be well off the pace today. His last race fractions of 22.2, 23.2 make him an outside possibility only. His previous turn-time fraction of 22.4 should be minimized. He was going nowhere and had expended little effort early. It's important to evaluate horses off races in which they showed their basic ability.

The Early Pace Match-up of the Race

	1Fr	2Fr		
Stadium Stud	59.45	55.93	(22.1	23.3)
Lucky Busty	58.40	55.93	(22.3	23.3)
Allo's Natural	60.00	56.41	(22.0	23.2)
Chief Kennedy	55.93	57.39	(23.3	23.0)
Bargain Bob		no factor		
Teach A Tron	60.55	57.39	(21.4	23.0)
Papa Stan	56.89	57.39	(23.1	23.0)
Golden Messenger	58.92	56.41	(22.2	23.2)

The paper race figures to follow this scenario: Teach A Tron almost certainly will lead through the first fraction, with Allo's Natural, Lucky Busty, and Golden Messenger vying for the second spot. The rest of the field should be well back and praying for pace casualties. When they enter the turn, those casualties should occur.

By virtue of a dominant second fraction versus the other close-up types, Teach A Tron figures to open up without extending himself beyond his demonstrated ability. The other early pace and presser types will either fall back several lengths or attempt to extend beyond their previously shown abilities.

In either case the up-close runners should not figure in the possible outcome of the race. Only the sustained pressers and closers have any chance for a major share of this purse. Once early pace runners have been outrun on the turn, they seldom finish well enough to hit the board. Teach A Tron should enter the stretch with a 3- or 4-length lead and still be well within himself. His backers will be looking for the sustained pace runners and hoping they run out of room.

Of the Chief Kennedy–Papa Stan match-up, Papa Stan is the more solid play because of his superior early position and matching turn-time ability.

On paper this one looks easy, and in actual application, it is just that. *But* is it easy for players not tuned into the value of turn-time in the pace match-up? Take a look at the DRF consensus and the results chart of the race and the answer is self-evident.

	TRACKMAN	HANDICAP	ANALYST	HERMIS	SWEEP	CONSENSUS	
1	ALLO'S NATURAL PAPA STAN CHIEF KENNEDY	CHIEF KENNEDY JEN U WINE JOE PAPA STAN	CHIEF KENNEDY PAPA STAN JEN U WINE JOE	ALLO'S NATURAL CHIEF KENNEDY TEACH A TRON	ALLO'S NATURAL TEACH A TRON CHIEF KENNEDY	ALLO'S NATURAL CHIEF KENNEDY PAPA STAN	15 14 5

DEL MAR RESULTS

Monday's Races

Copyright 1989 by NEWS AMERICA PUBLICATIONS INC.

2154 – FIRST RACE. 6½ furlongs. 3 year olds Bred in California. Claiming prices 16,000-14,000. Purse $15,000.

Horse and Jockey	Wgt.	PP	ST.	¼	½	¾	Str.	Fin.	To$1
Teach A Tron (Castanon)	111	6	1	1-1½	1-3½	–	1-5	1-2½	5.80
Papa Stan (Solis)	116	7	9	8-hd	5-1	–	2-2½	2-3½	3.60
Bargain Bob (Nakatani)	109	5	7	7-3½	7-2	–	5-hd	3-2½	14.90
Chief Kennedy (Delahoussaye)	116	4	10	10	8-hd	–	7-1½	4-1¾	8.10
Stadium Stud (Black)	118	1	6	3-½	6-½	–	6-1	5-¾	10.80
Allo's Natural (Pincay)	118	3	4	2-hd	3-½	–	3-1	6-hd	4.00
Lucky Busty (Garcia)	109	2	8	9-6	9-½	–	9-5	7-1½	33.10
Golden Messenger (Pedroza)	116	8	5	6-1½	4-1	–	4-hd	8-5½	6.20
Jen U Wine Joe (Olivares)	116	10	3	5-hd	2-hd	–	8-½	9-7½	4.20
Long Way To Come (Cortez)	116	9	2	4-½	10	–	10	10	77.10

Scratched – none.
Claimed – Stadium Stud-Kuebler & Sears-16,000-tr Washington Willaim
Claimed – Jen U Wine-Greene HF & Janet-$16,000-Tr Hess Rb Jr

Teach A Tron	13.60	6.80	4.20
Papa Stan		4.80	3.80
Bargain Bob			9.20

TIME – 0:21.4, 0:45.0, 1:10.2, 1:17.0. Clear & Fast. Winner – DBB G 86 Boltron School Marm. Trained by Mamakos Jason. Mutuel pool – $225,307. Ex pool – $216,093.

$2 Exacta (6-7) Paid $64.60

TURN-TIME AS A NEGATIVE INFLUENCE

So far we've examined only the positive influence of turn-time on the outcome of a race. The early pace horse able to dominate the first fraction, and then run through the second fraction without sacrificing any of its early advantage, is always a tough customer. Unless that runner is intrinsically faint-hearted, there is no better wager in racing.

But what happens when the dominant turn-time horse is a confirmed quitter? The answer to that question sets the observant pace analyst apart from the crowd. Consider the following match-up:

	Contender		Racing Characteristics
Horse A	22.1	23.1	Early pace
Horse B	22.1	23.3	Early pace
Horse C	22.2	23.2	Early pace
Horse D	23.0	23.1	Presser

In this scenario Horse A figures to contend with B and C through the first quarter and then draw off convincingly on the turn. With an honest runner that's usually the race in a nutshell.

There are, however, many horses at every racetrack that simply cannot sustain an advantage, no matter how significant. Their influence on the race is still considerable and must be examined carefully, or the bettor is liable to back a noncontender.

Once a runner has demonstrated that his best efforts are as an early pace type, his fortune is then determined by the velocity and determination of the other need-to-lead types. It would be asking a lot to expect this runner to lay off the pace and then come on to win late. Especially if the best early horse has drawn away on the turn.

In the example, when Horse A pulls away on the turn, the other early pace horses are relegated to mid-pack performers. Horses B and C then become poor bets and should always be avoided. Even the unsophisticated handicapper will recognize Horse A's tendency to stop in his races, but will still often back one of the other early pace runners.

That's a serious mistake unless the runner has shown some of the characteristics of a pace presser. If the analyst has designated running styles properly, that should not be the case.

As a result of Horse A's negative influence on the other pace setters, Horse D is a high probability play. This is an excellent bet and should be aggressively pursued. Witness the second race at Del Mar on August 13, 1989:

2nd Del Mar

6 FURLONGS. (1.07¾) CLAIMING. Purse $24,000. 3-year-olds. Weight, 121 lbs. Non-winners of two races since June 15 allowed 3 lbs.; of a race since then, 5 lbs. Claiming price $32,000; for each $2,000 to $28,000 allowed 1 lb. (Races when entered for $25,000 or less not considered).

Go Dogs Go — **STEVENS G L** — 116
Own.—Dye G V Jr
Ch. g. 3(Apr), by Beau's Eagle—Lotta Line, by Roman Line
Br.—Iron Horse Stables (Cal) 1989 8 2 3 1 $36,150
Tr.—Grissom O Dwain $32,000 1988 0 M 0 0
Lifetime 8 2 3 1 $36,150

31Jly89-5Dmr 6f :21^2 :44^2 1:10^{3}ft *2-3 116 65¾ 35½ 2½ 21½ Stevens G L 4 c25000 84-16 Rketmnsch,GoDogsGo,NturllyWys 12
31Jly89—Steadied at 5 1/2
15Jly89-3Hol 6f :21^3 :44^3 1:10^{2}ft 5¾ 116 77 54 34 2¾ Stevens G L 2 40000 88-11 ShelterUs,GoDogsGo WorkTillDawn 8
15Jly89—Wide into stretch
24Jun89-3Hol 6f :22 :44^4 1:09^{3}ft 4¾ 116 73¾ 32½ 23 23½ Stevens G L 5 40000 89-11 Agitated Mike, Go Dogs Go, Sksit 10
11Jun89-5Hol 6f :22^2 :45^1 1:10^{1}ft *8-5 119 41½ 43 33½ 32¼ Pincay L Jr 1 c32000 88-10 BlckDuzy,BelieveItToM GoDogsGo 8
28May89-4Hol 6½f :21^4 :44^2 1:16^{2}ft *2¼ 119 2½ 2½ 1½ 12½ Pincay L Jr 5 c25000 93-11 Go Dogs Go, BelieveItToMe ReRun 9
20May89-4Hol 1 :44^3 1:09^1 1:35 ft 8¼ 117 46 45½ 53¾ 44¼ Pincay L Jr 4 40000 84-07 RghtOvrFct,CrtThDwn,GldImprssr 9
20May89—Lugged in stretch
7May89-5Hol 6f :21^4 :45 1:10 ft 41 113 62¾ 63¾ 64½ 79¼ Solis A 2 [S]Aw27000 83-10 Pt'sPocktful,ElGorrion,BgOfMgc 13
7May89—Checked mid-turn
24Apr89-4SA 7f :22^3 :46^3 1:26^{2}ft *9-5 118 31½ 1hd 13 13 Pincay L Jr 1 [S]M32000 68-22 Go Dogs Go, Latour, La zam 12

Burnt Adobe — **SIBILLE R** — 116
Own.—Triple AAA Ranch
Ch. g. 3(May), by First Draft Choice—Classy Stamp, by Outing Class
Br.—Triple AAA Ranch (Ariz) 1989 7 2 0 0 $30,503
Tr.—Owens R Kory $32,000 1988 3 2 0 0 $5,330
Lifetime 10 4 0 0 $35,833

5Aug89-3Dmr 6f :22 :45^1 1:10^{2}ft 6 116 32 43 54 63¼ Solis A 6 40000 83-15 Rindo Try, Way Wild,AgitatedMike 7
15Apr89-11TuP 6½f :21^2 :43^4 1:16^{1}ft 9-5 120 21½ 2hd 1hd 42½ McGurn C 4 Aw10000 87-15 PleaseMeSaros,GoBoberib,Cfeton 8
25Mar89-10TuP 1$\frac{1}{16}$:47 1:11^1 1:44^{3}ft *2e 122 2hd 2hd 65 812¾ McGurn C 10 Tu P Dby 62-18 Stalaxis, Well Aware, Stage King 12
11Mar89-9TuP 1 :45^1 1:11 1:38^{1}ft *2-5 122 2½ 2hd 2½ 45 McGurn C 8 Dby Trl 73-18 StgKing,LuckyStblBoy,BoogiMyW 9
25Feb89-10TuP 1 :46^1 1:11^1 1:37^{1}ft 3¾ 118 11½ 11 12 1nk McGurnC 6 Dr Fager H 83-18 BurntAdobe,PlesMSros,HonstMik 12
11Feb89-10TuP 6f :21^2 :44 1:08^{4}ft 16 114 11½ 11½ 12½ 14 McGrnC 5 Crfty Drn H 90-18 BurntAdob,HstyDoubl,BoldEgoRsr 11
14Jan89-10TuP 1 :46^2 1:11^2 1:38 ft 4¾ 117 1hd 52 75¾ 88¾ MlgriniTM 1 Affrmd H 70-22 WyykinRx,FoolishBt,DkothThundr 12
26Dec88-10TuP 6½f :21^3 :43^4 1:15^{3}ft 2½e 119 3nk 95½ 914 912¾ MalgariniTM 6 Tup Fut 80-17 Hasty Double, MyTreat,RoyalPlan 11
14Dec88-6TuP 6f :22^2 :45^2 1:10^{2}ft 4¾ 119 1½ 2½ 2hd 11 Malgarini TM 4 Fut Trl 82-20 Burnt Adobe, Elrino, Extors on 10
19Nov88-4TuP 6f :22^3 :46 1:11^{1}ft 3¼ 118 3½ 1hd 1½ 13 Malgarini T M 12 Mdn 78-20 BrntAdob,PlsMSros,FoodFrThght 12
Jly 30 Dmr 5f ft :59^3 H — Jly 22 SA 5f ft 1:01 Hg — ●Jly 18 Pre 4f ft :49^1 H — ●Jly 7 Pre 3f ft :36^3 H

Mr. Don — **VALENZUELA P A** — 116
Own.—Klinger & Two Rivers Farm
Dk. b. or br. g. 3(Mar), by Don B—Amazing Urmanski, by Banners Image
Br.—Klinger R H (Cal) 1989 9 2 3 1 $33,400
Tr.—Mason Lloyd C $32,000 1988 7 2 1 1 $14,825
Lifetime 16 4 4 2 $48,225

11Jun89-9GG 6f :22 :44^1 1:08^{3}ft 5½ 120 42 43½ 57 615 Gryder A T 5 Aw22000 81-14 SummrSl,Movinglkwnnr,AmdoTucc 6
27May89-7GG 6f :21^4 :44^3 1:09^{2}ft 6 117 1hd 1hd 1hd 11½ McCarronCJ 1 Aw20000 92-15 Mr. Don, Rip Curl, Just Deeds 10
13May89-1GG 6f :21^4 :45 1:10^{3}ft 14 117 1½ 1½ 12 2½ Gryder A T 1 Aw20000 85-19 First Loyalty, Mr. Don, Vote 6
13May89—Bobbled start
29Apr89-1GG 6f :22 :44^3 1:10^{1}ft 5¾ 117 21 2hd 1hd 31 Gryder A T 5 32000 87-18 Eagle Leash, WorkTillDawn,Mr.Don 6
20Apr89-7GG 6f :22 :44^4 1:10^{2}ft 4¾ 117 1hd 2hd 1hd 1¾ Gryder A T 1 25000 87-13 Mr. Don, Eagle Leash, Dress Array 9
22Mar89-6GG 6f :21^3 :44^4 1:10^{3}ft 7½ 117 21 21 21 21½ Gryder A T 6 25000 84-17 GreekEqualizer,Mr Don,EagleLeash 7
8Mar89-6GG 6f :22 :45^2 1:10^{3}sy 5¼ 117 3½ 3nk 2½ 56 Gryder A T 6 32000 80-21 Roni Bo, Such A Wager, Heyrobbin 6
4Feb89-4GG 6f :22^2 :46^2 1:11^{4}m 5 117 1hd 2hd 2½ 22½ Gryder A T 4 32000 77-20 Heyrobbin, Mr. Don,NisquallyWally 6
25Jan89-7GG 6f :21^3 :44^1 1:08^{3}ft 17 117 — — — — Gryder A T 3 Aw18000 — — AvengingForce,RockyNils,Trrorizd 11
25Jan89—Lost rider
15Dec88-7BM 6f :22^3 :45^4 1:11 ft 5¼ 110^5 3½ 21 1½ 1hd Hubbard N J 4 16000 84-21 Mr.Don,OhHowJust,HwiinExpress 11
Aug 11 Dmr 3f ft :36 H — Aug 6 Dmr 6f ft 1:13^4 H — Jly 30 Dmr 5f ft 1:01 H — Jly 24 Dmr 4f ft :51^3 H

Naturally Weyes
NAKATANI C S 1105
Own.—Osher B
Dk. b. or br. c. 3(Apr), by L'Natural—Weyes Guise, by Grenfall
Br.—Osher B (Cal) 1989 8 1 1 1 $15,500
Tr.—Mulhall Richard W $30,000 1988 2 M 0 0
Lifetime 10 1 1 1 $15,500

31Jly89-5Dmr 6f :212 :442 1:103ft 24 118 13 15 11½ 34¾ Solis A 10 25000 80-16 Rketmnsch,GoDogsGo,NturllyWys 12
31Jly89—Veered out early drive
15Jly89-3Hol 6f :213 :443 1:102ft 32 116 11 2½ 65½ 811 Solis A 4 40000 78-11 ShelterUs,GoDogsGo,WorkTillDawn 8
10Jun89-8GG 6f :212 :44 1:093ft 6½ 117 32 43 57 67½ ValenzuelFH 7 Aw20000 83-11 Desert Rival, Vote, Just Deeds 8
2Jun89-5GG 6f :214 :441 1:093ft 3¾ 118 12 14 18 17 ChapmanTM 10 M32000 91-14 NturllyWeyes,Morwell,MoreGoldn 10
26Apr89-4Hol 6f :214 :444 1:09 ft 5 115 42 55½ 69 611¾ Davis R G 2 M32000 84-10 ShltrUs,CourgousPirt,GoldnVision 12
12Apr89-2SA 6f :213 :444 1:102ft *2½ 118 1hd 2hd 2½ 22½ Davis R G 5 Ⓢ M32000 83-14 MisterMx,NturllyWys,CtfishPurdy 12
12Apr89—Veered in start
1Mar89-2SA 6f :211 :442 1:094ft *2¾ 118 13 11 21 48¾ VlenzuelPA 9 Ⓢ M32000 80-14 AnnulDte,NeverInLce,Steffi'sEgle 12
1Mar89—Wide into stretch
8Feb89-6SA 6f :211 :442 1:113m 3½ 1115 11 11 2½ 55½ ValenzuelaFH 1 M45000 74-23 ChzNck,HollywoodScott,SndyDons 7
31Dec88-4SA 6f :21 :434 1:092ft 4¾ 117 21½ 34 47½ 714 Stevens G L 8 Ⓢ Mdn 77-10 VlintPet,TruEnough,DnwProspctor 9
11Dec88-6Hol 6f :214 :45 1:111ft 3½ 1135 32½ 31 54½ 77¾ Valenzuela FH 9 Ⓢ Mdn 78-17 BlueEydDnny,FistDISol,Morry'sLd 10
11Dec88—Lugged out
Jly 25 Dmr 4f ft :482 H Jly 7 SA 6f ft 1:133 H Jun 30 SA 6f ft 1:142 H Jun 25 SA 5f ft 1:043 H

Black Duzy
BLACK C A 116
Own.—Flying Lizard Stable
Dk. b. or br. g. 3(Apr), by Stutz Blackhawk—First Queen, by Iron Ruler
Br.—October House Farm (Fla) 1989 10 2 0 1 $32,425
Tr.—Zucker Howard L $32,000 1988 7 1 0 1 $7,440
Lifetime 17 3 0 2 $39,865 Turf 1 0 0 0

5Aug89-3Dmr 6f :22 :451 1:102ft 10 116 54 53½ 42½ 73½ Black C A 1 40000 82-15 Rindo Try, Way Wild,AgitatedMike 7
22Jun89-8Hol 1 Ⓣ:4911:1311:363fm 19 115 42 31½ 67 69 Guerra W A 4 Aw31000 72-18 Friendly Ed, Art Work,OrneryGuest 7
11Jun89-5Hol 6f :222 :451 1:101ft 17 116 62¾ 21½ 21½ 11 Guerra W A 8 32000 90-10 BlckDuzy,BelieveItToM,GoDogsGo 8
18May89-5Hol 6½f :22 :45 1:16 ft 12 114 42 3nk 32½ 37 Guerra W A 7 30000 88-07 RestlessGlxy,Rud'sGrtLgs,BlckDuzy 7
29Apr89-1GG 6f :22 :443 1:101ft 4¾ 119 65 54 53 53½ SchvneveldtCP 4 32000 84-18 Eagle Leash, WorkTillDawn,Mr.Don 6
17Mar89-1SA 6½f :214 :444 1:164ft 12 115 72¼ 43 34 47¼ Black C A 8 40000 79-20 ‡AdvntrsomLov,ClvrSpch,BttrRgr 10
26Feb89-3SA 6f :22 :452 1:11 ft 32 116 62¼ 31 3nk 11½ Black C A 7 32000 83-14 BlckDuzy,CleverSpch,MgicJohnson 8
16Feb89-1SA 6f :214 :451 1:111ft 41 115 73¼ 53½ 64¾ 43¾ Meza R Q 4 25000 78-21 MiracleMystery,WaltzingSss,Trgo 12
19Jan89-5SA 1 :462 1:12 1:39 ft 12 116 75¾ 64 54 56 DelahoussayeE 2 32000 67-23 Dime Time,Bargainaul,Caro sRuler 10
19Jan89—Wide into stretch
6Jan89-5SA 1 :46 1:113 1:381m 64 114 86¾ 74¼ 55½ 56½ Black C A 8 40000 70-20 AgnKing,Prt'sAdvntur,John'sRvng 10
6Jan89—Bumped early drive
Jly 31 Dmr 4f ft :482 H Jly 18 SA 3f ft :374 H

Regally Gold
DAVIS R G 118
Own.—Liber M
B. g. 3(Mar), by Regal and Royal—Gold Eyes (Fra), by Ortis III
Br.—Peskoff S (Fla) 1989 3 1 1 0 $12,575
Tr.—Garvey Robert W $32,000 1988 0 M 0 0
Lifetime 3 1 1 0 $12,575

22Jly89-2Hol 6f :221 :454 1:12 ft 5¾ 116 78 66 52¾ 12 Davis R G 1 M32000 81-16 RegllyGold,ConcordChoir,Btsy'sBt 10
22Jly89—Broke slowly
6Jly89-6Hol 1 :454 1:104 1:353ft 14 1105 86½ 65 66¾ 510¼ Garcia H J 3 M50000 75-17 ImmrtlScrpt,FlyngCndymn,SpkJsh 12
8Jun89-1Hol 6f :221 :454 1:111ft 166 1105 64½ 64½ 43 21½ Garcia H J 3 M32000 83-14 Joytiltwo, Regally Gold, Misaki 12
8Jun89—Raced greenly
Aug 11 Dmr 4f ft :494 H Aug 4 Dmr 5f ft :59 H Jly 20 SA 4f ft :481 H Jly 13 SA 3f ft :353 H

Brilliantized
PINCAY L JR 116
Own.—Meadowbrook Farms Inc
Ch. g. 3(Apr), by If This Be So—Brilliant Move, by Effervescing
Br.—Meadowbrook Farms Inc (Fla) 1989 11 2 2 0 $29,125
Tr.—La Croix David $32,000 1988 4 1 1 0 $13,075
Lifetime 15 3 3 0 $42,200

30Jly89-3Dmr 6½f :213 :443 1:164ft 8¼ 117 63¼ 52½ 53½ 2½ Pincay L Jr 4 32000 83-10 Mr Baldski, Brilliantized,ShelterUs 7
30Jly89—Wide into stretch
12Jly89-7Hol 1 :444 1:094 1:351ft 16 1115 21 21½ 45½ 411½ Nakatani C S 4 40000 75-16 FeelingFabulous,Jazz,ClassicKnight 8
22Jun89-3Hol 7f :221 :444 1:234ft *9-5 117 1hd 11 13 11½ Pincay L Jr 6 25000 85-12 Brilliantized,IslandLegcy,SrosFntsy 7
7Jun89-6Hol 6f :22 :45 1:10 ft 18 1115 52½ 32½ 24 25 Nakatani C S 8 20000 86-15 AgittdMik,Brilintzd,PocktfulOfAcs 8
7Jun89—Wide final 3/8
11May89-9GG 1 :46 1:103 1:37 ft 20 117 3½ 32 55¾ 610¾ Warren R J Jr 3 25000 69-19 RockSuker,LeliaLove,IslndMinstrel 7
27Apr89-3GG 6f :214 :452 1:111ft *8-5 117 1½ 11 11 11½ Warren R J Jr 5 16000 83-19 Brilliantized,PiaMan,InTissr sPride 7
2Apr89-5GG 6f :214 :443 1:102ft 14 117 1½ 2hd 3½ 54¾ Lambert J 1 20000 82-16 King Zoot,Heyrobbin,Raketmensch 8
23Mar89-1SA 6½f :213 :45 1:183ft 47 114 104½ 99¼ 89½ 811 Olivares F 10 18000 66-19 WltzngSss,MgcJhnsn,LghtnngPrt 11
16Feb89-1SA 6f :214 :451 1:111ft 23 115 51¾ 64½ 1010 1011¼ Sibille R 11 25000 71-21 MiracleMystery,WaltzingSss,Trgo 12
16Feb89—Wide into stretch
1Feb89-5SA 6f :22 :451 1:101ft 30 116 64 78½ 812 813¾ Meza R Q 6 50000 73-15 Gntlmn'sStyl,MgcJhnsn,SpcyYllti 10
1Feb89—Bumped start; checked 5 1/2
Aug 10 Dmr 4f ft :482 H Jly 27 Dmr 3f ft :372 H Jly 4 Hol 4f ft :482 H

```
Naskra's Waltz                    Dk. b. or br. g. 3(Feb), by Naskra—Waltz of Joy, by Delta Judge
                                  Br.—Mamakos & McAnally (Cal)              1989 7 1 0 0      $12,225
  MEZA R Q                   116  Tr.—Wright Robert          $32,000       1988 2 M 0 0
Own.—Rescigno Josephine          Lifetime   9 1 0 0   $12,225              Turf 3 0 0 0      $2,325
 7Jly89-9Hol  1 1/16 Ⓣ:482 1:122 1:43 fm  37 115  31½ 3½ 75¼ 79¾  Meza R Q3   Aw31000 69-19 Double Found, Isnad, King Armour 8
22Jun89-8Hol  1 Ⓣ:491 1:131 1:363fm  62 115  2½ 21 34 44¾  Meza R Q7   Aw31000 76-18 Friendly Ed, Art Work,OrneryGuest 7
27Apr89-7Hol  1 Ⓣ:464 1:11 1:36 fm  56 115  53 54 914 1016  Meza R Q6   Aw28000 68-16 Skisit,Presidentil,Plymeonmortim 12
30Mar89-3SA   1 :453 1:104 1:371ft  16 119  67½ 69 815 821¼  Sibille R 3   25000 61-16 GrekMyth,SumDndy,MurtMunson 10
10Mar89-7SA   7f :221 :443 1:223ft  36 118  810 79¾ 815 820¾  Black C A 5 ⓈAw32000 66-17 Mr. Bolg, Shady Pine, Saros Town 8
26Jan89-2SA   1 1/16 :472 1:124 1:454ft  *2¾ 117  3½ 1hd 21½ 78  ValenzuelPA 5 Mc32000 64-16 SumDndy,Mr.Termintor,FettleKttl 12
11Jan89-2SA   1 :462 1:114 1:381ft  23 117  31½ 2½ 2½ 23  Meza R Q 4   M32000 74-14 ItsRoyalty,Naskra'sWltz,Dr.Hughes 9
     11Jan89—Awarded first purse money
10Dec88-4Hol  6f :22 :451 1:11 ft  26 118  86 88¾ 812 812¾  Meza R Q7   M32000 74-17 LghtnngPrt,MrclMystry,SctOfFrtn 12
     10Dec88—Bumped start
12Sep88-6Dmr  6f :223 :46 1:104ft  12 118  52 66 813 816¾  Baze R A3   M62500 67-19 Gum, Charlie O., Pope's Warning 9
  Aug 5 Dmr 5f ft 1:004 H     Jly 30 Dmr 7f ft 1:281 H     Jly 24 Dmr 5f ft 1:012 H     Jly 18 SA 4f ft :474 H

Jungle Jaklin                     B. g. 3(Feb), by Jaklin Klugman—Petite Savage, by Jungle Savage
                                  Br.—Klugman&ElRanchoDeJaklin (Cal)        1989 8 1 3 0      $21,775
  SOLIS A                    118  Tr.—Fanning Jerry          $32,000       1988 0 M 0 0
Own.—El Rancho de Jaklin         Lifetime   8 1 3 0   $21,775
28Jly89-2Dmr  6f :221 :452 1:101ft  *7-5 116  1hd 11½ 11½ (11½)  Solis A1   ⓈM32000 87-16 JunglJkln,JustBoogn'By,Frnk'sGy 10
20Jly89-6Hol  6f :22 :452 1:11 ft  *2 116  32 31½ 32 21½  Solis A11   ⓈM40000 84-23 GreekTurf,JunglJklin,Prtndr'sGold 12
 7Jly89-1Hol  6f :222 :454 1:111ft  4¼ 116  72¾ 61¾ 42 2nk  Solis A5   M32000 85-13 Johnl'sLrk,JunglJklin,ThIrishTout 12
     7Jly89—Broke slowly
 8Jun89-1Hol  6f :221 :454 1:111ft  *6-5 116  53½ 53 63½ 52¾  DelhoussyeE11 M32000 82-14 Joytiltwo, Regally Gold, Misaki 12
     8Jun89—Wide 3/8
10May89-6Hol  1 :453 1:102 1:351ft  5½ 116  87½ 79 68½ 617½  DelhoussyE1 ⓈM50000 69-12 CorgosPrt,RoylActon,ConcordChor 8
28Apr89-6Hol  6f :222 :454 1:11 ft  4 116  52¼ 53 43 22  DelhoussyE3 ⓈM50000 84-15 Egl'sPrdis,JunglJklin,LuckyBusty 10
16Apr89-2SA   7f :221 :451 1:233ft  12 118  42½ 66 66 55½  Sibille R1   Mdn 76-16 DamskStr,ProudIrish,LiveTheDrem 9
     16Apr89—Broke slowly
15Mar89-2SA   6f :214 :451 1:11 ft  8½ 118  31½ 2½ 2½ 44  McCrronCJ2 ⓈM32000 79-14 IslndLgcy,JustBoogin'By,I'mFstst 12
  Jly 16 Hol 4f ft :471 H     Jun 30 Hol 5f ft 1:001 H     Jun 23 Hol 6f ft 1:131 H

Saros Night Wind                  Dk. b. or br. c. 3(Mar), by Saros—Time for Petting, by New Prospect
                                  Br.—Stephenson Jacqueline A (Cal)         1988 3 1 1 0      $5,510
  BAZE R A                   116  Tr.—Raub Bennie            $32,000
Own.—Raub Marella M              Lifetime   3 1 1 0   $5,510
26Dec88-10TuP 6½f :213 :434 1:153ft  7¾ 119  61 74 1114 1113½  Lozoya D A 8  Tup Fut 79-17 Hasty Double, MyTreat,RoyalPlan 11
14Dec88-7TuP  6f :221 :45 1:102ft  5 119  1½ 11 11 11  Lozoya D A2   Fut Trl 82-20 SrosNightWind,MyTrt,SlkyDmond 10
 7Oct88-2Haw  6f :213 :45 1:11 ft  5¾ 119  1½ 1½ 23 26½  Torres F C 5   Mdn 79-21 ShockTrtmnt,SrosNghtWnd,Brbth 12
  Aug 10 GD tr.t 5f ft 1:02 H     Jly 26 GD tr.t 6f ft 1:133 H     Jly 18 GD tr.t 5f ft 1:004 H     ●Jly 10 GD tr.t 4f ft :481 Hg
```

The negative influence in this race is Naturally Weyes. He's a confirmed early pace horse who regularly throws a first quarter of 21.3 seconds. Off that fraction he sustains a turn-time of 23.0 en route to a 44.3 second call. Any front-running type drawn against him had better be extremely quick or have the ability to also run as a presser.

The other early pace horses in this race: Burnt Adobe, Mr. Don, Brilliantized, Saros Night Wind.

Of this group only Brilliantized has demonstrated the versatility to lay off the pace and finish. Based upon the negative pace influence of Naturally Weyes, the others should be relegated to noncontenders. (Mr. Don's races at Golden Gate Fields are somewhat misleading. That medium-class track regularly allows sub 23.0 turn-time velocities.)

That leaves the following possibilities and their estimated fractions from recent efforts:

Go Dogs Go	22.3	22.4
Black Duzy	23.0	23.0
Regally Gold	23.1	23.2
Brilliantized	22.2	22.4
Jungle Jaklin	22.2	23.1

The bettor's task is to determine which of these contenders will have the momentum when the pace setter begins to fold.

By now the answer should be automatic. The two horses with the best combination of early pace and turn-time ability are Brilliantized and Go Dogs Go. Of the two, Brilliantized has the more versatile style, while Go Dogs Go was recently dropped two levels off a race he very nearly won. That's always a negative sign.

The $7.80 on Brilliantized won't make you rich, but this kind of analysis will contribute greatly to stronger overall play.

SECOND RACE
Del Mar
AUGUST 13, 1989

6 FURLONGS. (1:07⅘) CLAIMING. Purse $24,000. 3-year-olds, Weight, 121 lbs. Non-winners of two races since June 15 allowed 3 lbs.; of a race since then, 5 lbs. Claiming price $32,000; for each $2,000 to $28,000 allowed 1 lb. (Races when entered for $25,000 or less not considered).

Value of race $24,000; value to winner $13,200; second $4,800; third $3,600; fourth $1,800; fifth $600. Mutuel pool $560,854.

Last Raced	Horse	Eqt.	A.	Wt	PP	St	¼	½	Str	Fin	Jockey	Cl'g Pr	Odds $1
30Jly89 3Dmr2	Brilliantized	b	3	117	7	1	3^{3}	$3^{1\frac{1}{2}}$	3^{2}	$1^{1\frac{1}{2}}$	Pincay L Jr	32000	2.90
5Aug89 3Dmr7	Black Duzy	b	3	116	5	4	5^{hd}	5^{3}	5^{1}	2no	Black C A	32000	6.50
31Jly89 5Dmr2	Go Dogs Go	b	3	116	1	10	$6^{1\frac{1}{2}}$	$4^{\frac{1}{2}}$	4^{1}	$3^{1\frac{1}{2}}$	Stevens G L	32000	3.30
28Jly89 2Dmr1	Jungle Jaklin		3	118	9	5	$8^{\frac{1}{2}}$	6^{1}	$6^{1\frac{1}{2}}$	4^{hd}	Solis A	32000	8.10
26Dec88 10TuP11	Saros Night Wind	b	3	116	10	7	1^{hd}	$2^{1\frac{1}{2}}$	2^{hd}	$5^{1\frac{1}{2}}$	Baze R A	32000	20.90
31Jly89 5Dmr3	Naturally Weyes	b	3	110	4	2	$2^{\frac{1}{2}}$	1^{hd}	1^{hd}	6^{1}	Nakatani C S5	30000	11.10
22Jly89 2Hol1	Regally Gold		3	118	6	9	$7^{\frac{1}{2}}$	7^{hd}	7^{2}	$7^{1\frac{1}{2}}$	Davis R G	32000	24.10
5Aug89 3Dmr6	Burnt Adobe	b	3	116	2	3	4^{1}	$8^{1\frac{1}{2}}$	8^{3}	$8^{1\frac{1}{2}}$	Sibille R	32000	10.70
7Jly89 9Hol7	Naskra's Waltz		3	116	8	8	10	10	$9^{1\frac{1}{2}}$	9^{3}	Meza R Q	32000	14.30
11Jun89 9GG6	Mr. Don		3	116	3	6	$9^{1\frac{1}{2}}$	$9^{\frac{1}{2}}$	10	10	Valenzuela P A	32000	4.60

OFF AT 2:40. Start good. Won driving. Time, :21⅘, :44⅘, :57⅗, 1:10⅘ Track fast.

$2 Mutuel Prices:			
7-BRILLIANTIZED	7.80	4.40	2.80
5-BLACK DUZY		6.80	4.40
1-GO DOGS GO			3.00

Ch. g. (Apr), by If This Be So—Brilliant Move, by Effervescing. Trainer La Croix David. Bred by Meadowbrook Farms Inc (Fla).

BRILLIANTIZED, always prominent, took command leaving the furlong marker and drew clear. BLACK DUZY, outrun early, came into the stretch five wide and rallied for the place. GO DOGS GO, outrun early after he broke slowly, came into the stretch four wide, rallied and just missed the place. JUNGLE JAKLIN, devoid of early speed and wide down the backstretch, was going well late. SAROS NIGHT WIND dueled for the lead to the furlong marker and weakened a bit. BURNT ADOBE, in contention early, dropped out of contention before going a half. NASKRA'S WALTZ, wide down the backstretch, was four wide into the stretch. MR. DON showed little.

Owners— 1, Meadowbrook Farms Inc; 2, Flying Lizard Stable; 3, Dye G V Jr; 4, El Rancho de Jaklin; 5, Raub Marella M; 6, Osher B; 7, Liber M; 8, Triple AAA Ranch; 9, Rescigno Josephine; 10, Klinger & Two Rivers Farm.

Trainers— 1, La Croix David; 2, Zucker Howard L; 3, Grissom O Dwain; 4, Fanning Jerry; 5, Raub Bennie; 6, Mulhall Richard W; 7, Garvey Robert W; 8, Owens R Kory; 9, Wright Robert; 10, Mason Lloyd C.

Overweight: Brilliantized 1 pound.

Black Duzy was claimed by Redman L & Ida; trainer, Murphy Marcus J.

TURN-TIME AND CLASS DEMANDS

In 1987 I did a seminar with James Quinn, copresenting several approaches to the same basic conclusions. The most important point of agreement concerned the repeated failures of top speed-figure horses to successfully negotiate the next level on the class ladder.

The failure of the "figure" horse, in condition and without serious reservations as to connections or distance, is a speed handicapper's worst nightmare.

My own development as a handicapper featured a long love affair with speed figures. The loss of these "cinches," often at ridiculous prices, led me to the analysis of pace as the basis for my handicapping. The example used to make our point was the class jump from claiming races into the nonwinners allowance series. Most readers are familiar with Quinn's classic text *The Handicapper's Condition Book,* and will probably remember the next example. Only two horses are necessary to make the point: Jim Burke and Will Win.

Jim Burke: An older claimer with more than 33 lifetime starts and still eligible for a nonwinners of one allowance race (NW1). He had recently defeated a band of $40,000 claimers with the following line:

21.4   44.4   1:09.2 . . . turn-time 23.0

Will Win: A lightly raced runner with only two tries at this level. Both were good efforts. His last race was at 6½ furlongs:

21.4   44.2   1:15.4 . . . turn-time 22.3

In the race, Jim Burke was 3–1 and Will Win was held at 5½–1. The race was run with the following fractions and final time: *21.2   44.0   1:09.0.*

Based on what we've learned about turn-time as an indicator, how would you predict the running of the race?

No doubt you'll be right. They both hit the quarter at the same time, but when they entered the turn, Will Win threw a 22.3 turn-time fraction and the race was over. As the result of attempting more than his basic capabilities, Jim Burke failed the class test and finished a badly beaten last.

The point is, there's nearly always a "Will Win" waiting at the next class level. Each level demands increasingly more from its participants, and final-time ability is not a satisfactory approach to successful play.

Each higher class level, claiming or nonclaiming, is littered with the carcasses of impressive lower-class winners unable to cope with the pace demands of the higher level. Learn the pace pars for each class at your racetrack, especially the relationship between maidens and nonwinners-of-one allowances.

SOME FINAL THOUGHTS

Turn-time as a predictor should not be employed as an independent factor in the handicapping process. Too often, bettors become dependent upon single factors, thereby diluting their overall importance. This is one of those factors.

I made an earlier point that turn-time is most dependable in the cheaper races. There is usually a lack of quality pressers and closers in those races.

One look at Olympic Prospect's performance in the 1988 Breeders' Cup should prove that point. He did attempt to draw away on the turn, but the other horses patiently ran to their own abilities and went by him late. That's often the case in high quality races.

A few remaining points:

1. Route turn-times are less reliable than their shorter counterparts. A full half-mile has already been negotiated, and the general fast/slow characteristics of the race have already been determined. The middle fraction may not be of importance. Then again, it may. A better than par second fraction must be carefully evaluated against first-fraction performance. A strong move off a fast half-mile is just as significant as it was in sprints. Just use extra care in analysis.

2. At certain distances "turn-time" is actually a misnomer. The fraction is run mostly on a straightaway and not around the turn. Only the rate of velocity is different: the value to winner selection remains unchanged.

3. Recent maiden winners are most vulnerable when the maiden win has the soft underbelly of a weak turn-time. Short-priced failures of otherwise impressive maiden winners can

usually be traced to this factor. Make it a practice to analyze the maiden win in the context of the internal demands of today's class level. The analysis will save a lot of grief.

4. The value of the factor varies with the demands of the racetrack. If the track promotes sustained pace in the extreme, the lead established early may be of no consequence. Application may be in the determination of which closer will begin to rally on the turn. That's local knowledge and relatively easy to obtain.

Finally, what's significant about the following race?

| SIXTH RACE | 7 FURLONGS. (1.20) MAIDEN. Purse $28,000. 3-year-olds. Weight, 118 lbs. (Non-starters for |
| **Santa Anita** | a claiming price of $32,000 or less in their last three starts preferred.) |

APRIL 1, 1989

Value of race $28,000; value to winner $15,400; second $5,600; third $4,200; fourth $2,100; fifth $700. Mutuel pool $527,387.

Last Raced	Horse	Eqt.A.Wt PP St	¼	½	Str	Fin	Jockey	Odds $1
19Mar89 6SA8	Northern Drama	b 3 118 1 6	1½	1²	1²	1²	Meza R Q	19.00
12Mar89 6SA6	Histrion	3 118 8 1	5¹	4hd	4½	2¹	Davis R G	17.20
12Mar89 6SA4	Bride Groom	3 118 3 8	9²½	9²½	5hd	3¹½	Patterson A	6.60
4Dec88 4Hol10	The Reader	b 3 113 10 2	7¹½	6¹	6¹	4hd	Valenzuela F H5	a-22.80
4Mar89 2SA8	Alyone	3 118 2 7	4½	3¹½	2hd	5½	Stevens G L	1.80
18Feb89 4SA6	What's At Stake	3 118 7 9	8¹	8hd	7²	6¹½	Baze R A	a-22.80
8Mar89 6SA5	Icy Resolution	3 118 5 10	10	10	9⁸	7¹½	Pedroza M A	32.40
	Proud Irish	b 3 118 6 4	3¹½	2¹	3²½	8⁴	Valenzuela P A	6.20
18Mar89 6SA6	Tokatee	b 3 118 9 3	6¹½	5³	8¹½	9¹²	Pincay L Jr	2.90
	Ocala Buck	b 3 118 4 5	2hd	7¹½	10	10	Black C A	6.90

a-Coupled: The Reader and What's At Stake.

OFF AT 3:49. Start good. Won driving. Time, :22, :44½, 1:09¾, 1:23 Track fast.

$2 Mutuel Prices:	2-NORTHERN DRAMA	40.60	14.00	6.60
	9-HISTRION		12.20	6.20
	4-BRIDE GROOM			5.00

I've used enough examples from Santa Anita to give the reader a general feel for significant performances over that surface. The 22.1 turn-time of the Northern Drama win borders on spectacular. *Five* winning races emerged from this single event, two by Northern Drama.

CHAPTER V

Sartin Methodology

IN THE mid-1980s the Sartin Methodology began to receive attention from journalists and authors of national prominence. While the reviews of the method were uniformly positive, Sartin's support group, PIRCO, was usually described as "cult-like," a religious sect, replete with high priests and inviolable doctrine. The word "cult" is defined as "a religious system with its adherents showing a faddish devotion." Briefly, let's explore the "cult" label.

PIRCO stands for Parimutuel Information and Research Company, and was created for one purpose: to lessen the workload of its founder, Howard Sartin, a clinical psychologist from Beaumont, California. When Sartin introduced the Sartin Methodology, he offered free follow-up service throughout the learning period. The fledgling handicapper or "client" enters an informal contract. It includes a conscientious effort to learn in exchange for follow-up consultation.

The "Methodology" was a critical success at introduction; clients by the hundreds entered into the teacher-student covenant. The demands on Sartin's time prompted him to solicit users capable of teaching his material to others.

In my case, I was so impressed with the concepts and potential of the method that I readily became part of the support group. I reasoned the best way to learn the intricacies of this powerful method was to teach it. Most of the other PIRCO charter members participated for the same reason.

Much of the "cult" rap probably stems from the friendship and respect the PIRCO people feel toward Dr. Sartin and each

108

other and the unconventional computer-based aspects of the material. Their charter was to provide assistance during the difficult learning process. As long as the client extended a "good faith" effort, there were no constraints on the substance or length of the commitment.

So, what is this "methodology"? Is it an easy "system"? Will it automatically pick winners? Will it magically transport the player from the world of losers to the rarefied air of winners? Let's talk about that.

To label the Sartin Methodology a "system" is to mislabel the intent and content of the material. A system imposes a rigid application of rules, leaving little room for individual interpretation. Every user lands on the same selections every time—at least in theory.

A "method" is intended to provide a basic framework while still allowing individual styles and abilities to assert themselves. Ideally, it provides a methodical approach to selection without dictating final selections or individual styles. The better the player, the more effective the methodology.

On that score, the Sartin material does very well indeed. It is not a system. Nor is it rigid in application. There are few rules in the Sartin Methodology. In this text we'll examine the basic tenets of the Sartin material and spend some time with application and interpretation. The pace ratings we'll use are the basis for the Sartin Methodology and are exactly as I use them in everyday play. It will be the first time this material has been presented to the general public with the sanction of Doc Sartin.

EVOLUTION

Howard Sartin, as noted, is a clinical psychologist. In 1975 he was given a choice of therapy groups: alcoholics or gamblers. Ever the maverick, Sartin reasoned that one had been done to the extreme, so he chose to treat the gamblers.

The group he counseled consisted of truck drivers who had been convicted of gambling-related felonies and serious misdemeanors. All entered therapy as a condition of probation. This was not your everyday therapy group. Many were capable of breaking the good doctor as if he were dry kindling. Sartin's tack? He reasoned the basic problem, in most cases, was losing, not gambling. If a chronic loser can be turned into a winner, there is no problem. Sartin's thesis: "The cure for losing is winning!" Now, there's a novel idea.

"Therapy" consisted of developing a winning approach to thoroughbred racing. The group organized around specific task assignments. Their intention was to isolate factors that consistently exerted positive influences on the outcome of horse races. They assembled a data base of 13,000 races, which eventually grew to more than 18,000. They examined 143 variables considered by experts as exerting the most influence on the outcome of races. Variables ranged from post positions and points of call to jockeys and post-time odds. Nearly all exerted *some* influence on a race. Only a few met the basic criterion set by the group: to be viable, any factor or variable must consistently rank the winner in the top four in the race. "Consistently" was defined as 67 percent. The following factors survived the test:

(1) Second Call velocity
(2) Average Pace (a compounding of factors)
(3) Sustained Pace (also a compounding of factors)

It is interesting to note that only second call velocity (Early Pace) was able to stand alone in the analysis. The others, as you'll soon learn, depend heavily on the second call. Final time was discarded because of easy accessibility by the general public and the accompanying lack of betting value.

A "near miss" to the final three is another compounded variable that the Methodology refers to as "Factor X." That factor's value to winner selection is limited by distance and does not have universal application. We'll use Factor X, but within the limits of its effectiveness.

Now what to do with these findings?

The group applied the factors to conventional handicapping procedures, only to find those procedures did not withstand close scrutiny.

Commonly accepted rules regarding recency requirements were abandoned in favor of more relaxed guidelines. Guidelines were developed for selecting "pacelines," the races most likely to represent a horse's current form/ability. A procedure was established to interpret the array of feet-per-second numbers and pace ratings resulting from the process. In short, a new methodology was developed for selecting the winners of thoroughbred races.

Throughout the developmental process, the group was making forays to the Mexican race books. Paper tests may steer a right course, but the acid test requires real money. They took regular beatings, to be sure. They did, however, show genuine progress toward the goal of consistent winning. Sartin did not forget the original charge. The psychological side of gambling did not go unaddressed. Sartin reasoned that frequent trips to the cashier's window significantly bolster a player's attitude and confidence. After all, doesn't a winner visit that window?

The two-horse win bet became a basic tenet of the method. Sartin insists the two-horse scheme was a defense mechanism on his part. What reasonable man wants to be on the other side of the border with truck drivers who have just lost money using his strategies? He also insists if a five- or six-horse strategy had been profitable, he would have further ensured his well-being!

The goal was to select 63 percent winners employing a two-horse betting strategy. That target still remains part of his methodology. The commitment to the new client is for technical and psychological support to that level of proficiency.

Eventually, the therapy group developed a workable method that was showing consistent profits. Did the individual players go on to be consistent racetrack winners? Who knows. Once they began to show a profit, most lost interest in the subject and resumed their real vocation: driving trucks. Sartin had earned his fees.

Where to now? The doctor was in possession of a method which, in the right hands, was capable of providing regular profits at the racetrack. Why not market the material on a limited basis? With the intent of working with a maximum client base of a thousand, probably much less, he placed a threadbare ad in the *Daily Racing Form*. The method was an instant success, and the follow-up provision forced him to seek additional support or abandon the informal contracts. His solution was the PIRCO support group.

PIRCO

PIRCO. Parimutuel Information and Research Company. This is the part of the Sartin experience that I cannot reproduce in this book. This has been the key to transforming many players without an extensive knowledge/experience base into certifiable winners. It is part psychological and part technological. I'm a member of that support group. An introduction to some of the other members seems appropriate.

Jim "The Hat" Bradshaw: Sartin's right-hand man. "The Hat" is the perfect flip side to Sartin. What Howard conceptualizes, Bradshaw implements. The two have collaborated on most of the computer programs offered to PIRCO clients. A native of Oklahoma, Bradshaw was a high school track coach for more than thirty years. In that role, he developed a keen understanding of energy exertion/depletion patterns in the human athlete. The knowledge is transferable to the racetrack. He's particularly adept at matching horse against horse. To quote Bradshaw: "Hell, son, it ain't nothin' but a horse race. One horse goes out and gets the lead and the others try to catch up. That's all it is."

Bob Purdy: PIRCO's ex-Marine. One of the original members of the group, and originator of "Synergism"—a unique computer program that creates its own variant from the pacelines of race contenders. Bob's a successful southern California businessman and an excellent computer programmer. With some exceptions, most of the PIRCO software has been written by Bradshaw or Purdy. Bob's a courageous bettor and believes strongly in the Sartin material. A quick insight into the type of person Sartin solicited for his support group: after waiting several minutes for a New York mutuel clerk to gather additional $100 bills to pay off his winning tickets, Bob promptly handed the windfall to a client he had just met. It seems the man was facing an operation for cataract removal and did not have health insurance. Bob thought it the right thing to do.

Michael Pizzolla: Graduate of NYU Law School. Practiced Wall Street attorney. Professional magician who has performed before four of the last five U.S. Presidents. Accomplished actor. Successful handicapper. Pizzolla demonstrates his skills in the midst of New York's sharpest handicappers. This is not the stereotypical "horseplayer" of Damon Runyon's world. Pizzolla's articulate and smooth, strengths he utilizes very effectively in addressing PIRCO clientele.

Bert Mayne: Another PIRCO charter member who is unique in the group. A hulk of a man with a deep, resonant voice, Bert spent ten years as a road musician singing in "saloons" prior to taking his college degree. He lives in Carlisle and plays the Finger Lakes racetrack in upstate New York. So what's unique about *this* guy? His preference for "bottom of the barrel" racing and his "shady" past suggest he may be the group's only stereotypical "horseplayer." Not so. Bert Mayne is a Presbyterian minister serving *two* churches!

Dick Schmidt: Nope, he doesn't fit the term "punter" any more than the others. A former insurance company executive and writer, he's the newest addition to Sartin's charter group. Bright, literate, with a nice comic touch, Schmidt edits Sartin's bimonthly *Follow-Up* journal and is a frequent contributor to the instruction manuals. His entire handicapping experience has been accumulated in the last five or six years. No bad habits. No outdated racetrack "truths." Dick brings a perspective that is commonly shared by most new clients. He can relate to the learning experience.

Other prominent members of PIRCO include Virginia Butler in the Pacific Northwest, Tom Hambleton in Los Angeles, Marion Jones in San Diego, Bill Conklin in Louisiana, Bob Cochran in Chicago, and Elton Smith in Kansas City.

Much of what has become the terminology of modern pace handicappers has its origins in the Sartin Methodology. Early Pace, Sustained Pace, Average Pace, Energy expenditure, Brohamer Models, Track profiles, are concepts developed and tested by the Sartin-PIRCO collaboration. I owe many of the insights in this book to my association with this loose framework of handicappers. I value that experience. It's a matter of credit due.

SARTIN "FIGURES"

	1Fr	2Fr	3Fr	AP	EP	SP	FX	%E
Horse A	59.45	56.41	51.56	55.78	57.89	54.72	55.51	52.89%
Horse B								
Horse C								

This is the array we'll be using, in one form or another, throughout the rest of this book. It represents the basic Sartin Methodology. In this chapter we'll discuss Early Pace (EP) and then develop the most important of the compounded ratings: Sustained Pace (SP), Average Pace (AP), and Factor X (FX). I'll also discuss contender and paceline selection.

In subsequent chapters I'll explain energy distribution (%E), a concept original with this methodology; variants; adjustment techniques for track to track comparisons; and several modeling techniques designed to separate contenders.

It is important to understand the distinction between pure velocity in feet-per-second and compounded ratings. The building blocks for the pace handicapper are the velocity figures from the individual fractions. They're the only "uncontaminated" figures in the array. No race should be bet without analyzing fps relationships among contenders. Strengths and weaknesses of each runner, in each pace segment, should be identified. Once compounded, they no longer represent pure velocity and become pace "ratings."

To be sure, compounded ratings are exceedingly important to the pace handicapper and should be employed enthusiastically. They should not, however, be employed at the expense of actual performance data from the running lines.

The Sartin Methodology, as with any feet-per-second method, is best implemented with a data processor. A handheld computer or programmable calculator is sufficient. The use of fps charts can be of value, but must still be used with a calculator to obtain the necessary pace ratings.

In either case, I again caution the reader to avoid blind adherence to the output of machines. Unfortunately, horses are unaware of their ratings and perform according to style and competitiveness rather than to a handicapper's sense of order. Too bad; the game would be much easier if horses had the same thought processes as handicappers. At least some handicappers.

Early Pace (EP)

Early pace and second call are interchangeable terms. EP is the only "rating" we'll be discussing that is also a velocity number and can be expressed in fps. Earlier, I advanced the argument that the second call is, unquestionably, the most important point of call on the racetrack. The handicapper should focus on the importance of where the call occurs in a race. Examine the following:

	Total Feet in Race	2Call Dist.	% of Total
6F	3960	2640	66.6%
6½F	4290	2640	62.0%
7F	4620	2640	57.0%
8F	5280	3960	75.0%
8½F	5610	3960	71.0%
9F	5940	3960	66.0%

At the very least, 57 percent of the entire race has been completed upon reaching the second call. At some distances, considerably more.

Many players lose sight of exactly how important that is. Most races have been decided at the second call. The *winner* hasn't necessarily been identified, but horses still *capable* of winning are clearly in focus. The cumulative effect of the first and second fractions is influencing the leaders. Too slow to the second call, and the leaders are home free. Too fast, and the leaders will be showing signs of fatigue. Closers will be moving in for the kill. Most racetrack biases center around second-call position.

Certainly, many races are won or lost in the first fraction, especially in routes. Many pace plays will center around perceived first-fraction advantages. On a closer's racetrack, other bets will result from final-fraction advantages. But the majority of races are determined by second-call position. The second call is the "hinge" for most ratings in any methodology using modern pace concepts.

The formula to compute Early Pace (second call): EP = feet in the segment minus beaten lengths (BL) divided by the time of the segment (T4).

Sprints:
$$EP\ (2Call) = 2640 - (10 * BL) / T4$$
Routes:
$$EP\ (2Call) = 3960 - (10 * BL) / T4$$

Sustained Pace (SP)

Sustained pace is the average of early pace and the final fraction (3Fr). It is designed to relate second-call position and finishing ability. It is probably evident by now that second-call velocity exerts a strong influence on the SP rating. As a result, the best early horse is often the best sustained horse as well.

EP = 2Call

3Fr = feet in fraction, plus or minus BL, divided by time of fraction
          (T3)

SP = EP + 3Fr / 2

Average Pace (AP)

In terms of winner selection, AP is the most important rating. Sartin's therapy group found Average Pace to consistently exert the greatest influence on the outcome of thoroughbred races. Sartin clients know the factor as Factor W, a somewhat less descriptive term. Under either designation, it can be employed singularly as a key rating factor. When an accurate variant is applied, it is the dominant "figure" for the race.

Routes are calculated by averaging Early Pace and Sustained Pace.

$$AP = EP + SP / 2$$

Sprints are calculated a bit differently. As a concession to the dramatic importance of final time in sprint races, the optimal calculation for average pace is the sum of the three fractions divided by three.

$$AP = 1Fr + 2Fr + 3Fr / 3$$

Our concession to the importance of final time does not dilute the value of compounded pace. Horses that perform well in the internal pace segments still have a ratings advantage over horses achieving fast final times through a single, powerful fraction. Consider another Horse A and Horse B scenario:

A   6F   22.0   45.0   1:10.0   Beaten lengths   0   0   0
          60.00 + 57.39 + 52.80 / 3 = $\boxed{56.73}$

B   6F   22.0   45.0   1:10.0   Beaten lengths   6   6   0
          57.27 + 57.39 + 55.20 / 3 = $\boxed{56.62}$

A has a noticeable edge in average pace over B, who performed strongly in the final fraction only. On-pace horses *should* have the edge in any pace methodology.

Factor X (FX)

is the average of the sum of the first and third fractions.

$$FX = 1FR + 3FR / 2$$

This is the "near miss" I alluded to earlier in the chapter. Factor X has a distance qualifier to its effectiveness. It is a powerful predictor of winning performance in sprint races. As distances increase beyond a mile, X no longer meets the original study group's criteria for predicting winners. Additionally, the importance of the rating tends to vary from track to track. Generally, it is most effective at lesser class tracks where first-quarter position and final-fraction ability may be most important. We'll use the factor within the confines of its effectiveness.

Let's look at a few examples to familiarize ourselves with the format.

T. V. Screen
Ch. g. 3(Feb), by Silent Screen—T V Miss, by T V Lark
Br.—Li J F (Cal)
BAZE R A 115 Tr.—Hronec Philip
1989 3 2 0 0 $27,500
1988 1 M 0 0
Own.—Li & Ridgewood Racing Stb Lifetime 4 2 0 0 $27,500
11Aug89-8Dmr 7f :21⁴ :44¹ 1:21³ft 4½ 115 4² 55¼ 76¼ 79 Baze R A 1 ⑤RI Gd DI 85-15 Mr. Bolg, Timeless Answer, Brulio 7
11Aug89—Checked at 3/8
31Jly89-7Dmr 6½f :21⁴ :44² 1:15³ft 2¼ 115 1hd 2½ 1hd 1½ Baze R A 5 ⑤Aw30000 90-16 T. V. Screen, Comical, Shady Pine 9
7Jly89-4Hol 6½f :21³ :44³ 1:15³ft 2½ 116 3³ 3nk 1⁴ 1⁷ Baze R A 8 ⑤M50000 97-13 T. V. Screen, Interpol, FiestaDelSol 8
31Dec88-2SA 6f :21¹ :44¹ 1:10 ft 10 117 4³ 6⁵ 7⁹ 8¹¹½ Baze R A 2 ⑤Mdn 77-10 Giglio, Stylish Stud, Morry's Lad 9
31Dec88—Steadied start; rank backstretch
●Sep 1 Dmr 5f ft :58¹ H Aug 26 Dmr 5f ft 1:02⁴ H Aug 20 Dmr 3f ft :36 H Aug 9 Dmr 3f ft :38⁴ H

1. T.V. Screen 11Aug89

1Fr $\quad 1320 - 20 / 21.8 = 59.63$ fps

2Fr $\quad 1320 - 35 / 22.4 = 57.37$ fps

3Fr $\quad 1980 - 35 / 37.4 = 52.00$ fps

2Call $\quad 2640 - 55 / 44.2 = 58.48$ fps

The fractional array:

	1Fr	2Fr	3Fr	AP	EP	SP	FX
T.V. Screen	59.63	57.37	52.00		58.48		

And, the compounded ratings:

Average Pace: $59.63 + 57.37 + 52.00 / 3 = 56.33$
Early Pace: 58.48 (2Call)
Sustained Pace: $58.48 + 52.00 / 2 = 55.24$
Factor X: $59.63 + 52.00 / 2 = 55.81$

The completed array:

	1Fr	2Fr	3Fr	AP	EP	SP	FX
T.V. Screen	59.63	57.37	52.00	56.33	58.48	55.24	55.81

2. T.V. Screen 31Jly89

1Fr $1320 / 21.8 = 60.55$ fps
2Fr $1320 - 5 / 22.6 = 58.18$ fps
3Fr $1650 + 5 / 31.2 = 53.04$ fps
2Call $2640 - 5 / 44.4 = 59.34$ fps

The fractional array:

	1Fr	2Fr	3Fr	AP	EP	SP	FX
T.V. Screen	60.55	58.18	53.04		59.34		

The compounded ratings:

Average Pace: $60.55 + 58.18 + 53.04 / 3 = 57.25$
Early Pace: 59.34 (2Call)
Sustained Pace: $59.34 + 53.04 / 2 = 56.19$
Factor X: $60.55 + 53.04 / 2 = 56.79$

The completed array:

	1Fr	2Fr	3Fr	AP	EP	SP	FX
T.V. Screen	60.55	58.18	53.04	57.25	59.34	56.19	56.79

Before moving on, let's look at a route race.

Good Deliverance ✳

VALENZUELA P A		**117**	
Own.—Laiacono F & Carol			

Ch. g. 4, by Defense Verdict—Auto Lady, by Pretense
Br.—DominickLongoRevocblTrust (Ky)
Tr.—Ippolito Steve
Lifetime 27 5 6 5 $113,575

1989	12	1 4 2	$54,350
1988	15	4 2 3	$59,225
Turf	7	0 2 2	$20,800

27Aug89-7Dmr 1 :454 1:101 1:344ft   4½ 117   31½ 2½ 2hd 2½   ValenzuelPA4 Aw38000 91-11 Alandvon,GoodDeliverance,MloMlo 7
  27Aug89—Bumped start
16Aug89-7Dmr 6½f:22   :444 1:16 ft   10 117   63¾ 74¾ 42 31   ValenzuelPA4 Aw35000 87-14 Sbulose,Gentlmn'sStyl,GocdDlivrnc 8
2Aug89-7Dmr 1 :461 1:102 1:351ft   7½ 116   43 43½ 68 510   Stevens G L5 62500 80-15 CaptainValid,RoylCmeronin,Decore 6
  2Aug89—Wide
3Jly89-7Hol 6f :22   :45 1:093ft   *9-5 118   77½ 68½ 66 65½   Pincay L Jr3 Aw31800 88-10 WnchstrDrv,TmFrAccrcy,BgOfMgc 7
10Jun89-7Hol 1 :451 1:10 1:35 ft   4½ 117   52 3½ 1½ 1hd   Pincay L Jr7   50000 88-13 GoodDeliverncy,Dcor,RoylCmronin 11
  10Jun89—Wide final 3/8
29May89-7Hol 1¼:462 1:103 1:421ft   6½ 115   1hd 2hd 52½ 68½   Davis R G1 Aw30000 80-13 MagnumPlus,MloMlo,Rogue'sRelm 6
17May89-7Hol 1 :451 1:094 1:35 ft   7½ 115   53½ 52 22 22   Davis R G6 Aw30000 86-11 Henbne,GoodDelivernce,ScrtMtIng 8
24Apr89-7SA 6½f:212 :442 1:162ft   23 116   68½ 67¾ 43½ 31   Toro F4   Aw37000 87-22 SmWho,BlckJckRod,GoodDelivernc 6
  24Apr89—Wide into stretch
1Apr89-5SA a6½f①:211 :4311:143fm   11 1115   75½ 76 87 98½   VlenzuelFH12 Aw37000 77-20 MjorCurrent,IcyAmber,Superbest 12
12Mar89-3SA a6½f①:22 :4411:144fm   23 1115   53½ 55½ 25 23½   ValenzuelFH1 Aw36000 81-13 BraveCpde,GoodDelivernce,Drmtis 10
  Sep 5 Dmr 5f ft 1:022 H   ● Aug 29 Dmr 3f ft :34 H   Aug 24 Dmr 5f ft :59 H   Aug 11 Dmr 5f ft 1:01 H

3. Good Deliverance 27Aug89

1Fr $2640 - 15 / 45.8 = 57.31$ fps

2Fr $1320 + 10 / 24.4 = 54.50$ fps

3Fr $1320 / 24.6 = 53.65$ fps

2Call $3960 - 5 / 70.2 = 56.33$ fps

The fractional array:

	1Fr	2Fr	3Fr	AP	EP	SP	FX
Good Deliverance	57.31	54.50	53.65		56.33		

The compounded ratings:

Early Pace :   56.33 (2Call)

Sustained Pace: $56.33 + 53.65 / 2 = 54.99$

Average Pace: $56.33 + 54.99 / 2 = 55.66$

(Remember, Average Pace is calculated differently in routes.)

Factor X: a sprint rating only.

The completed array:

	1Fr	2Fr	3Fr	AP	EP	SP	FX
Good Deliverance	57.31	54.50	53.65	55.66	56.33	54.99	

As an instructor with PIRCO I've seen countless good handicappers abandon their skills in favor of the computer. That's a *serious* mistake. The Sartin Methodology is powerful because it utilizes your skills, but it doesn't replace them. No method can compensate for poor handicapping fundamentals.

Learn to qualify contenders. Learn to pick pacelines. Practice makes perfect. In the hands of a competent handicapper, the Sartin figures can be impressive. In the hands of an excellent handicapper, they can be deadly.

CONTENDERS

PIRCO instructors have developed mechanical procedures for picking contenders. They were designed, primarily, for clients unable to come to grips with the complexities of a difficult game, and for inexperienced players lacking an adequate knowledge base.

Most readers of handicapping books have already exorcised the demons plaguing beginners. Whatever winnowing procedures that worked previously will work with this approach. Handicappers who include too many contenders in their analyses will soon get the message. Too many contenders needlessly confuse the scenario, but may not have tragic consequences. Players unable to get a race down to the few horses capable of winning should read the works of Quirin, Beyer, Quinn, Davidowitz, Ainslie, and Selvidge.

PACELINE SELECTION

The subject of paceline selection *must* be addressed. Ill-conceived choices of pacelines have hastened the end of many a bankroll. Aside from adjustments and variants, selecting pacelines is the biggest problem for the player new to the methodology.

"Paceline" is a key concept in the pace handicapper's terminology. Simply, it is the race(s) upon which a contender's ability is to be based. Speed handicappers have been choosing running lines for years. Any handicapper who has analyzed running ability, in the context of any rating procedure, has done the same.

So what's difficult about choosing pacelines? Nothing. Aside from considerations as to probable pace, the procedures are the same. Yet players new to the methodology consistently struggle with handicapping fundamentals.

Within the framework of a few guidelines, picking pacelines is a highly intuitive skill best developed through constant repetition. Good handicappers have refined the skill to an instinctive level, and for them, picking representative lines is automatic. It is "pattern recognition," best cultivated by picking hundreds of pacelines. Like the route to Carnegie Hall, it's "practice, practice, practice."

I offer the following guidelines to experienced and inexperienced players alike.

1. Pacelines *must* reflect current form and condition. The last race, while not necessarily the best choice of paceline, must be part of the analysis. Handicappers who regularly ignore the importance of the last running line fight an uphill battle. Horses go in and out of form too quickly to cavalierly ignore the last performance. If the effort is excusably bad, by all means look for another race indicative of current form. If inexcusable, the last race should be selected as today's probability of performance.

Don't be too forgiving of bad races. Even horses encountering serious trouble, or racing at unsuitable class levels, should show *something*. Early pace ability, mid-race or late moves, are indicators of continuing form. Beware the in-form runner that suddenly misbehaves at the gate or breaks poorly and fails to show any signs of form. When you're in doubt as to whether to excuse a bad performance, write your reasons on a sheet of paper. The most often encountered reason is "because." "Because" is not a satisfactory reason for risking a hard-earned bankroll.

2. Within the framework of current form and condition, the paceline should reflect *today's probable pace*. Estimate the pace of the race and then select a paceline that shows a good effort against the estimated pace. Many horses perform well only in certain pace situations and should be rated accordingly. If unable to perform well against your estimated pace, make the horse a noncontender.

3. When possible, do not base a horse's ability on a single race. Choose a paceline that represents the horse's usual running style and pace characteristics. *If in doubt as to the suit-*

ability of a running line, draw a line through the race and find another that will give the same indications. Handicappers are too eager to base betting decisions on a single running line. If unable to find another paceline that supports the line in question, choose a race that represents the "preponderance of evidence."

Let's handicap several races using fps numbers, the basic Sartin ratings, and the ESP designations we developed previously. In subsequent chapters we'll develop additional tools for separating contenders.

The following race was carded on October 5, the second day of the 1989 Oak Tree at Santa Anita season. It was run at 8½ furlongs.

9th Santa Anita

Ancient Blue B. g. 8, by Blue Times—Ancient Jewel, by Hail to Reason
Br.—Jones A U (Ky) 1989 9 1 0 1 $11,820
TORO F 116 Tr.—Blincoe Tom $10,000 1988 11 1 2 0 $14,975
Own.—Blincoe Maraye D Lifetime 60 6 9 7 $62,311 Turf 4 0 0 1 $3,100
27Sep89-10Fpx 1 1/16:46² 1:12² 1:45 ft 3¾ 116 10⁸¼ 8⁵¼ 6⁵½ 5⁷ Flores D R1 10000 79-16 Beret Scout, Renzo, Forty Grand 10
27Sep89—5-Wide into lane
18Sep89-10Fpx 1 1/16:46 1:11³ 1:44²ft 17 116 9¹¹ 7⁷½ 7⁵¾ 5³ Flores D R9 10000 86-12 Alignment, Forty Grand,KampOut 10
18Sep89—Wide throughout
23Aug89-9Dmr 1 1/16:46 1:11 1:42⁴ft 23 115 10⁷½10⁷¾10⁸¾ 8¹⁰¼ Toro F10 10000 76-14 SlvteTel,ResonToStudy,FortyGrnd 12
23Aug89—Wide final 3/8
9Aug89-9LA 1 1/16:46⁴ 1:12³ 1:44²ft 4¾ 116 9⁵ 8⁵¾ 6⁶¼ 6⁶¼ Ortega L E2 10000 77-19 Grey Writer, Honor Flag, Pas Plus 10
2Aug89-9LA 6½f :21⁴ :45² 1:16 ft 7½ 116 10¹²10¹¹ 9⁹¾ 7¹⁰¼ Ortega L E4 10000 85-12 Walt, Bold Crusader, Gallic Writer 10
2Aug89—Pinched at start
15Mar89-9SA 1 1/16:46 1:10⁴ 1:43¹ft 5 118 9⁹¾ 9⁹¾ 9¹² 7¹¹ Toro F3 12500 74-14 Jazz Island, Bortino, Precedence 12
15Mar89—Wide into stretch
24Feb89-9SA 1⅛:46² 1:10³ 1:50 ft 7½ 115 11¹⁰ 9⁹¾ 7⁸¼ 7⁶¼ Toro F4 16000 72-16 OurBrndX.,SirTyson,Mischifinmnd 12
24Feb89—Broke slowly
29Jan89-2SA 1⅛:46³ 1:11³ 1:50⁴ft 9½ 116 8⁹¾ 6⁶¾ 4⁵¼ 3⁴ Toro F5 16000 71-16 Mischifinmind,FlyingH.,AncintBlu 11
11Jan89-9SA 1 1/16:47 1:11² 1:43⁴ft 31 116 7⁷ 4⁴¾ 4¹½ 1¹ Toro F12 12500 82-14 AncntBl,LovDn'sGtwy,MddlConch 12
11Jan89—Wide on turns
24Dec88-1Hol 7f :22 :45³ 1:24³m 12 116 9¹¹ 8⁹ 7⁹ 7¹¹¼ Baze R A9 12500 70-23 King Clyde, Slam Dance, Nordicus 9
24Dec88—Wide into stretch

I'll Be The Judge B. g. 4, by Naskra—Pervasive, by Raise a Native
Br.—Feather Ridge #5 (Ky) 1989 9 1 2 0 $22,805
PEDROZA M A 116 Tr.—Borick Robert $10,000 1988 0 M 0 0
Own.—Four Four Forty Farms Lifetime 9 1 2 0 $22,805
17Sep89-9Fpx 1 1/16:46¹ 1:11¹ 1:43²ft 6¾ 116 2hd 1¹ 4²½ 6¹⁰¼ Flores D R 2 16000 84-10 Bugarian, Emigrant Gap,Ki-Nobre 10
30Aug89-9Dmr 1 1/16:45¹ 1:10¹ 1:42³ft 3½ 116 3⁵½ 2² 1½ 2² Stevens G L 11 c12500 85-13 Dolly'sVldz,I'llBThJudg,OnBrodwy 12
10Aug89-9Dmr 1 1/16:46² 1:11¹ 1:43⁴ft 4½ 116 1¹ 2hd 2hd 2nk Black C A 2 16000 81-20 QuickRoundtrip,I'llBeThJudg,Drion 9
30Jly89-9Dmr 6f :22 :44⁴ 1:10 ft 10 116 7³¼ 5²¼ 6⁴½ 5⁴¼ Black C A 11 16000 84-10 Robrt'sLd,DonB.Blu,AmzingCourg 12
30Jly89—Wide final 3/8
15Jly89-7Hol 6f :22¹ :45¹ 1:09¹ft 32 122 7⁵ 7⁵¼ 7⁹ 7¹⁰ Davis R G1 Aw30000 85-11 Saros Town,NevadaEon,Mehmetski 8
9Mar89-5SA 6f :21² :44 1:08³ft 8½ 120 10⁶ 10⁷¾10¹¹10¹⁷½ ValenzuelPA7 Aw32000 77-15 BlckJckRod,FirstToArriv,Mgnifico 10
9Mar89—Hopped at start
24Feb89-3SA 6½f :21² :44¹ 1:15¹ft 11 119 4² 4³ 4⁴¾ 6¹⁰¼ ValenzuelPA1 Aw32000 84-16 FrostFree,SecretSlction,SnowPrch 8
24Feb89—Bumped hard at intervals down chute, backstretch
12Jan89-2SA 6f :21⁴ :44⁴ 1:09²ft *8-5 118 2hd 2hd 1¹½ 1½ Stevens G L5 Mdn 91-12 I'llBThJudg,WstrnRgnt,Zid'sBstMn 9
1Jan89-4SA 6½f :21⁴ :44⁴ 1:16 ft 7½ 119 10⁹¾ 9⁸¼ 6⁹ 4⁷¾ Stevens G L5 Mdn 82-10 FrstToArrv,Khld'sRdr,Lorn'sSrprs 12
1Jan89—Hopped in air
Sep 29 SA 5f ft 1:01³ H Sep 23 SA tr.t 4f ft :49² H Sep 11 Dmr 4f ft :49³ H Aug 23 Dmr 5f ft 1:01 H

On Broadway Ch. g. 4, by Broadway Forli—Stylish Model, by Drone
Br.—Alexander T (Ky) 1989 15 1 0 2 $11,465
ORTEGA L E 118 Tr.—Ippolito Steve $10,000 1988 7 1 0 0 $12,600
Own.—Ippolito S Lifetime 22 2 0 2 $24,065 Turf 1 0 0 0
17Sep89-9Fpx 1 1/16:46¹ 1:11¹ 1:43²ft 11 116 1hd 2¹ 7⁹½ 7¹⁹¼ Castanon A L 9 16000 75-10 Bugarian, Emigrant Gap,Ki-Nobre 10
17Sep89—Bumped hard start
10Sep89-1Dmr 1 :45¹ 1:10 1:36¹ft 3½ 116 1² 1²½ 1³ 1³½ Ortega L E 1 10000 85-10 OnBroadway,Renzo,Bigbadandmean 8
30Aug89-9Dmr 1 1/16:45¹ 1:10¹ 1:42³ft 20 116 1² 1² 3¹ 3⁵½ Ortega L E 7 12500 81-13 Dolly'sVldz,I'llBThJudg,OnBrodwy 12
10Jly89-2Hol 6f :22 :44⁴ 1:10¹ft 24 117 8⁶¼ 6⁴ 4³½ 5⁵ Sibille R 2 10000 85-12 SpndTwoBcks,GoldnStks,PrncO'Fr 9
22Jun89-5Hol 7f :22 :44⁴ 1:22⁴ft 38 116 4² 4¾ 5⁵ 10¹¹¾ Fernandez A L 5 10000 78-12 FighAbhil,BlzingZulu,MnhttnKing 11
22Jun89—Fanned wide late
3Jun89-1Hol 6f :22² :45² 1:10¹ft 3 117 4¹½ 4²½ 5⁶ 5⁶¾ Guerra W A 6 10000 83-11 Nazaret,JoseSentMe,Maid'sMistake 8
27May89-1Hol 6f :21⁴ :45 1:10 ft 50 117 4³½ 3¹ 2²½ 3⁴ Fernandez AL 10 10000 87-10 Cracksman, Pain, On Broadway 12
27May89—Wide final 3/8
13May89-2Hol 6f :22¹ :44³ 1:10¹ft 19 116 2¹ 3¹ 3³½ 6⁶¾ Fernandez A L 7 10000 83-11 RcknghrsDrm,LJllSpdstr,MtthT.Prr 8
4May89-1Hol 7f :22¹ :45 1:23¹ft 4¾ 117 4¹½ 3nk 5⁷½11¹⁵¼ Cedeno A 5 10000 72-15 Polysemous, Wild Pursuit, Darion 11
4May89—Bumped at 4 1/2
21Apr89-5SA 7f :22² :45 1:23²ft 34 116 4¹ 1hd 4²½ 7⁷¼ Fernandez A L 1 16000 76-17 Rare Tyson, FlyingH.,TrusT.Danus 12
Sep 29 SA 4f ft :47 H ●Aug 22 Dmr 5f ft :58² H Aug 16 Dmr 4f ft :51 H

Quick Roundtrip — B. g. 7, by Flight to Glory—Fleet Ali, by Fleet Mel
CEDENO A — 118 — Br.—Garcia W G & Anne (Cal) — 1989 16 1 3 1 $19,740
Own.—Di Fiore Dr F — Tr.—DiFiore Leslie $10,000 — 1988 15 2 1 1 $17,780
Lifetime 65 11 8 6 $112,785

14Sep89-10Fpx	1 1/16	:453	1:111	1:452ft	2½	119	1hd	21½	56	612¼	Cedeno A1	12500	72-16	Emperdori,SilverSurfer,Icecapation	9
26Aug89-9Dmr	1 1/16	:46	1:11	1:43 ft	9½	116	2hd	2hd	3nk	44¾	Cedeno A2	16000	80-09	SpiritBay,MonLegionnire,TresSuve	9
10Aug89-9Dmr	1 1/16	:462	1:111	1:434ft	18	116	21	1hd	1hd	1nk	Cedeno A1	10000	81-20	QuickRoundtrip,I'llBeThJudg,Drion	9
29Jly89-12LA	1 1/16	:452	1:111	1:424ft	4	116	2nk	52¾	612	615	Cedeno A7	10000	76-11	Exotic Arbitor, All Cat, Don's Tryst	7
15Jly89-1Hol	1 1/16	:473	1:12	1:443ft	21	115	2½	2hd	2hd	2½	Cedeno A9	10000	76-11	Rossco,QuickRoundtrip,Percntstr	12
6Jly89-1Hol	6f	:22	:452	1:104ft	21	117	52¾	63¾	76½	76½	Cedeno A3 Ⓢ	10000	80-17	OrchrdSng,BrgnStndrd,LJllSpdstr	12
22Jun89-5Hol	7f	:22	:444	1:224ft	40	116	2½	1hd	21½	45	Cedeno A6	10000	85-12	FighAbhil,BlzingZulu,MnhttnKing	11
11Jun89-1Hol	6½f	:214	:442	1:171ft	46	117	53½	65½	65½	78½	Cedeno A5	10000	80-10	Premiere,Contravene,BiscayneBoy	12
2Jun89-9Hol	6½f	:22	:444	1:164ft	6¾	117	41½	51¾	86¼	89	Cedeno A9 Ⓢ	10000	82-10	Loverue, Contravene,Smilin'Smiley	9
2Jun89—Wide 3/8 turn															
12May89-1Hol	6f	:224	:452	1:101ft	3	116	4¾	2hd	32½	35	Fernandez A L9	10000	85-14	SwtchCods,Mdcuff,QuckRoundtrp	12

Sir Sparkler — Ch. c. 4, by Leashi Gold—Grace and Savour, by His Majesty
FLORES D R — 116 — Br.—Hobby Horse Farms (Ky) — 1989 11 1 1 4 $4,932
Own.—Big Train Farm — Tr.—Barrera Lazaro S $10,000 — 1988 2 M 0 0 $180
Lifetime 13 1 1 4 $5,112

22Sep89-11Fpx	1 1/16	:454	1:111	1:452ft	10	116	55	55	53½	54¼	Flores D R 3	12500	80-15	FghAbhl,SouthrnSprc,JornyThrTm	7
14Sep89-13Fpx	a1⅛	:471	1:123	1:52 ft	9	113	35	45½	47	68	Flores D R 4	A12500	75-16	MonLgionnir,PssAnothrTb,GryWrtr	9
18Jun89-2AC	1	:46	1:103	1:37 ft	7¾	120	46¼	1hd	11½	14	Mercado F 3	M10000	85-13	SirSparkler,HiggieBaby,PureCutlss	7
18Jun89—Stumbled start															
11Jun89-1AC	6f	:22	:44	1:101ft	37	120	73¾	66¼	65¾	33¼	Mercado F 8	M10000	84-12	GoldenStakes,Billdancer,SirSprkler	8
4Jun89-1AC	6f	:22	:44	1:09 ft	25	120	45½	46½	36½	38½	Martinez J C 3	M8000	85-13	FlashyNGood,Beau'sWay,SirSprkler	6
14May89-3AC	6f	:222	:443	1:101ft	7½	120	41¾	46	46	34¾	Jeronimo A V 1	M6250	83-15	Truely Bold,Beau'sWay,SirSparkler	6
15Apr89-2AC	6f	:222	:441	1:094ft	15	119	42½	46	49	53¼	Escalona G S 5	M9000	86-13	Josefa,PatFitzptrick,WebelosScout	8
19Mar89-2AC	7f	:233	:453	1:234ft	8½	120	43½	43½	54	68	Mercado F 7	M10000	91-12	Scholstcllyhgh,ZoomZoom,SrousSr	8
11Mar89-2AC	6f	:223	:451	1:101ft	5	118	3nk	2½	42	55¾	Mercado F 3	AlwM	82-14	Bufw,GoldenStkes,Scholsticllyhigh	8
19Feb89-2AC	6f	:223	:442	1:101ft	5½	120	21½	22	2½	23	Mercado F 5	M10000	85-14	AlbertoCrlos,SirSprkler,ScreenGirl	9

Sep 30 SA 5f ft 1:014 H — Sep 21 SA 3f ft :353 H — Sep 7 Bmr 5f ft :593 H — Aug 30 Bmr 4f ft :474 H

Middle Concho * — B. g. 4, by Dandy Bingo—Runculus, by Cutlass
DELAHOUSSAYE E — 118 — Br.—Stinson M C (Tex) — 1989 5 2 0 1 $17,525
Own.—Farr-Lawrence-Stinson — Tr.—Lawrence Renn $10,000 — 1988 11 1 0 1 $17,437
Lifetime 19 4 0 3 $46,512 — Turf 1 0 0 0

4Sep89-10BM	1 1/16 Ⓣ	:472	1:122	1:443fm	21	117	77	87	913	915	PattersonA12	Aw17000	65-20	Uncultivtd,ILovRcng,AwrdForAlln	12
14Aug89-9Dmr	1	:454	1:111	1:371ft	4	116	34	1½	1½	1hd	DelahoussayeE1	10000	89-19	MiddleConcho,MnhttnKing,BlzFlm	8
3Mar89-6GG	1⅛	:474	1:113	1:493ft	6¾	116	42	55½	45½	45	Doocy T T3	H12500	72-23	GllntHwk,BoldDecree,WonderPlum	6
8Feb89-9SA	1 1/16	:464	1:12	1:453m	13	1105	87½	67½	22½	1nk	Garcia H J8	12500	73-23	Middle Concho, Equilibre,Tablado	11
8Feb89—Altered path 1/16															
11Jan89-9SA	1 1/16	:47	1:112	1:434ft	43	1105	44	54¾	3½	31	Garcia H J8	-12500	81-14	AncntBl,LovDn'sGtwy,MddlConch	12
21Dec88-9Hol	1 1/16	:481	1:14	1:464sl	8	112	55	48	48	48¼	DominguezRE11	10000	58-30	Extranix, Menelik, Bold Decree	11
21Dec88—Wide 7/8															
9Dec88-9Hol	1 1/16	:462	1:114	1:444ft	72	115	43½	41½	52¾	64	Patterson A3	16000	72-16	Hgly'sLion,ComfortblLd,Bsngstok	11
5Nov88-12BM	1	:454	1:103	1:362ft	4¾	117	811	1014	918	716¼	Hansen R D10	20000	70-18	Jlt'sDncr,SlfContnd,MowshkDncr	10
22Oct88-6BM	1	:461	1:11	1:371ft	11	117	77¾	54½	57	44½	Douglas R R8	25000	77-16	WuzWinder,DnvilleGold,MistrPppG.	8
9Oct88-2SA	6f	:21	:44	1:10 ft	71	115	67½	48½	58½	87½	Black C A1	20000	80-16	GoForBrodwy,RecklessOne,LeTch	12

Sep 25 SA 5f ft 1:023 H — Sep 15 SA 5f ft 1:034 H — Aug 6 SA 5f ft 1:024 H

The opening-day card left doubts as to preferred running styles in route races. Two routes sent mixed signals to the handicapper: one winner with a pressing style, the other from far off the early pace. Neither race contained an early pace runner with the class and ability to win. Fortunately, there were two routes run earlier on the October 5 card. Both won by S horses from well off the early pace. Both winners were 4 lengths behind the pace at the second call and easily gained the necessary ground to win. Even with such limited data, handicappers should be giving the edge to sustained pace runners.

Reason To Study *
B. g. 6, by Coulee Man—Mag's Deck, by Mo Bay
SOLIS A 116
Br.—Smith & Quisenberry (Cal) 1989 8 1 2 3 $19,025
Tr.—Truman Eddie $10,000 1988 9 2 1 0 $17,370
Own.—Academic Farms Inc Lifetime 35 6 6 4 $71,820

23Aug89-9Dmr 1 1/16 :46 1:11 1:42⁴ft *3¼ 115 64½ 52¼ 52¼ 22¼ Stevens G L 5 10000 83-14 SlvteTel,ResonToStudy,FortyGrnd 12
23Aug89—Broke in, bumped
10Aug89-1Dmr 1 1/16 :45³ 1:11 1:44 ft *3¼ 116 58½ 46½ 35½ 35¾ Davis R G 4 10000 74-20 MtthewT.Prker,Nec,ResonToStudy 8
22Apr89-10SA 1 1/16 :46³ 1:11³ 1:44³ft 6¼ 116 76¼ 86½ 89¼ 510 Valenzuela P A 9 12500 68-17 Mt. Erin, Tricky Lad, Beret Scout 9
22Apr89—Bumped 7 1/2, wide 7/8 turn, into stretch
6Apr89-9SA 1 1/16 :46 1:11¹ 1:44²ft 6¼ 116 69½ 75½ 42 1½ Stevens G L 1 10000 79-14 ReasonToStudy,Rosasco,ShmsEgo 12
17Mar89-9SA 1¼ :46² 1:37¹ 2:03²ft 4½ 116 48 37½ 35 33¼ Stevens G L 5 10000 69-20 Fmillion,OurBrndX.,ResonToStudy 11
10Feb89-3SA 1 1/16 :46² 1:11³ 1:46⁴m *2¼ 116 69 79½ 66¼ 45¼ Valenzuela P A 2 10000 62-25 Bortino, Jazz Island, Very Double 11
27Jan89-3SA 1 1/16 :47¹ 1:12¹ 1:45⁴ft *2¼ 117 66 55½ 62¾ 21¾ Baze R A 6 [S] 10000 70-21 DePillo'sPride,ResonToStudy,Murt 8
13Jan89-1SA 1 :46⁴ 1:11³ 1:37³ft 4¼ 116 53½ 55½ 45 37¼ Baze R A 2 [S] 10000 73-15 J.C.Architct,OnwrdMl,RsonToStudy 9
13Jan89—Stumbled start
4Nov88-9SA 1⅛ :47¹ 1:11³ 1:51¹ft 4¾ 116 74½ 75¾ 53 42½ Baze R A 2 10000 70-18 Extranix, Bold Decree, Tablado 11
13Oct88-3SA 1 :46 1:11² 1:38⁴ft *2 118 55½ 75½ 54½ 42¼ Stevens G L 5 [S] 10000 72-19 Remar, Siraluovat, Comets Flare 9
13Oct88—Fanned wide 1/4
Oct 1 SA 6f ft 1:14 H Sep 25 SA 6f ft 1:14³ H Sep 16 SA 5f ft 1:01 H Sep 9 Dmr 4f ft :48³ H

ESP: S

Paceline: 23Aug89. The last race is always the best indicator of current condition. Although troubled ("broke in"), the race is a good effort and represents his usual running style. Don't be overly concerned with the 42 days between races. Del Mar and Oak Tree are separated by the Los Angeles County Fair meeting (Fairplex Park) and many trainers avoid the "bullring."

Alignment
B. g. 4, by Lyphard's Wish—Maria Line, by Roman Line
DAVIS R G 118
Br.—Payson V K (Ky) 1989 4 1 0 0 $7,700
Tr.—Fulton Jacque $10,000 1988 7 2 0 1 $19,183
Own.—Four D Stable Lifetime 11 3 0 1 $26,883 Turf 7 2 0 1 $19,183

18Sep89-10Fpx 1 1/16 :46 1:11³ 1:44²ft 7 116 12 13 13½ 11¾ Olivares F 10 10000 89-12 Alignment, Forty Grand,KampOut 10
2Aug89-1Dmr 6f :21⁴ :44⁴ 1:10¹ft 12 111⁵ 85½ 1212 1218 1222¾ Nakatani C S 7 10000 64-15 ChiefPl,RiseAPound,MtthwT.Prkr 12
18Jun89-5Hol 6f :21⁴ :45 1:10¹ft 32 116 3hd 43½ 912 1216 DelahoussayeE 2 20000 74-12 BickerBear,LansMnus,InspiredToo 12
1Jun89-7Hol 6f :21⁴ :44¹ 1:09¹ft 58 117 31½ 46 716 720 Davis R G 2 62500 75-13 Shigmb,Wtch'nWin,EightyBlowZro 7
21Nov88♦3Toulouse(Fra) a1 : gd — 128 ① 69 Boeuf D Px Mrqs d Tric Jilgueno,Kolkwitzi,SturdyEvening 10
21Nov88—No time taken
26Oct88♦6Marseille(Fra) a1¼ : gd — 128 ① 8 BinchiG Px Colonl Maldn Magawika, Tiki Boy, Brown Chick 12
26Oct88—No time taken
3Oct88♦4Toulouse(Fra) a1 : gd 3 119 ① 1¾ Bianchi G Px Cntlause Alignment, Los Verdes, Kadanchou 8
3Oct88—No time taken
11Sep88♦4Cavaillon(Fra) a1 : gd 5¾ 129 ① 11½ DupoyS Px MrceLfra H Alignment, Tiki Boy, Satin Flash 13
11Sep88—No time taken
29Jly88♦6Evry(Fra) a7f 1:25¹gd 17 119 ① 77 SamaniH PxLeSancy Indicted, Astronef, Silver Head 9
4Jly88♦7Evry(Fra) a1⅛ 1:58¹sf 12 123 ① 12 PlpprM Px d Champigny BlueNile,Barbarik,MyCherieAmour 13
Sep 10 Dmr 3f ft :35¹ H Aug 12 Dmr 4f ft :46⁴ Hg

ESP: E

Paceline: 18Sep89. A case of apples and oranges. Fairplex Park is considerably slower than Del Mar and requires an adjustment to pacelines taken from that surface. The approximate 1989 adjustments were:

First call: 1 length
Second call: 3 lengths
Final time: 5 lengths

The adjusted paceline for Alignment should be: 45.4 1:11.0 1:43.2.

Ancient Blue B. g. 8, by Blue Times—Ancient Jewel, by Hail to Reason
TORO F 116 Br.—Jones A U (Ky) 1989 9 1 0 1 $11,820
Own.—Blincoe Marnye D Tr.—Blincoe Tom $10,000 1988 11 1 2 0 $14,975
Lifetime 68 6 9 7 $62,311 Turf 4 0 0 1 $3,100
27Sep89-10Fpx 1 1/16 :46² 1:12² 1:45 ft 3¾ 116 10⁹¼ 8⁵¼ 6⁵½ 5⁷ Flores D R¹ 10000 79-16 Beret Scout, Renzo, Forty Grand 10
27Sep89—5-Wide into lane
18Sep89-10Fpx 1 1/16 :46 1:11³ 1:44²ft 17 116 9¹¹ 7⁷½ 7⁵¾ 5³ Flores D R⁹ 10000 86-12 Alignment, Forty Grand,KampOut 10
18Sep89—Wide throughout
23Aug89-9Dmr 1 1/16 :46 1:11 1:42⁴ft 23 115 107½107¾108¾ 8¹⁰¼ Toro F¹⁰ 10000 76-14 SlvteTel,ResonToStudy,FortyGrnd 12
23Aug89—Wide final 3/8
9Aug89-9LA 1 1/16 :46⁴ 1:12³ 1:44²ft 4¾ 116 9⁵ 8⁵¾ 6⁶¼ 6⁸¼ Ortega L E² 10000 77-19 Grey Writer, Honor Flag, Pas Plus 10
2Aug89-9LA 6½f :21⁴ :45² 1:16 ft 7½ 116 10¹²10¹¹ 9⁹¾ 7¹⁰¼ Ortega L E⁴ 10000 85-12 Walt, Bold Crusader, Gallic Writer 10
2Aug89—Pinched at start
15Mar89-9SA 1 1/16 :46 1:10⁴ 1:43¹ft 5 118 9⁸¾ 9⁹¾ 9¹² 7¹¹ Toro F³ 12500 74-14 Jazz Island, Bortino, Precedence 12
15Mar89—Wide into stretch
24Feb89-9SA 1 1/8 :46² 1:10³ 1:50 ft 7½ 115 11¹⁰ 9⁹¼ 7⁸¼ 7⁶½ Toro F⁴ 16000 72-16 OurBrndX,SirTyson,Mischifinmnd 12
24Feb89—Broke slowly
29Jan89-2SA 1 1/8 :46³ 1:11³ 1:50⁴ft 9½ 116 8⁹¾ 6⁶½ 4⁵½ 3⁴ Toro F⁵ 16000 71-16 Mischifinmind,FlyingH.,AncintBlu 11
11Jan89-9SA 1 1/16 :47 1:11² 1:43⁴ft 31 116 7⁷ 4⁴½ 4¹½ 1¹ Toro F¹² 12500 82-14 AncntBl,LovDn'sGtwy,MddlConch 12
11Jan89—Wide on turns
24Dec88-1Hol 7f :22 :45³ 1:24³m 12 116 9¹¹ 8⁹ 7⁹ 7¹¹¼ Baze R A⁹ 12500 70-23 King Clyde, Slam Dance, Nordicus 9
24Dec88—Wide into stretch

ESP: S/NF. Except for a single win in January, Ancient Blue hasn't been a threat in 1989.

Paceline: none required

I'll Be The Judge B. g. 4, by Naskra—Pervasive, by Raise a Native
PEDROZA M A 116 Br.—Feather Ridge #5 (Ky) 1989 9 1 2 0 $22,885
Own.—Four Four Forty Farms Tr.—Borick Robert $10,000 1988 0 M 0 0
Lifetime 9 1 2 0 $22,885
17Sep89-9Fpx 1 1/16 :46¹ 1:11¹ 1:43²ft 6½ 116 2hd 1¹ 4²½ 6¹⁰¼ Flores D R 2 16000 84-10 Bugarian, Emigrant Gap,Ki-Nobre 10
30Aug89-9Dmr 1 1/16 :45¹ 1:10¹ 1:42³ft 3½ 116 3⁵½ 2² 1½ 2² Stevens G L 11 c12500 85-13 Dolly'sVldz,I'llBThJudg,OnBrodwy 12
10Aug89-9Dmr 1 1/16 :46² 1:11¹ 1:43⁴ft 4½ 116 1¹ 2hd 2hd 2nk Black C A 2 16000 81-20 QuickRoundtrip,I'llBeThJudg,Drion 9
30Jly89-9Dmr 6f :22 :44⁴ 1:10 ft 10 116 7³½ 5²½ 6⁴½ 5⁴½ Black C A 11 16000 84-10 Robrt'sLd,DonB.Blu,AmzingCourg 12
30Jly89—Wide final 3/8
15Jly89-7Hol 6f :22¹ :45¹ 1:09¹ft 32 122 7⁵ 7⁵½ 7⁹ 7¹⁰ Davis R G¹ Aw30000 85-11 Saros Town,NevadaEon,Mehmetski 8
9Mar89-5SA 6f :21² :44 1:08³ft 8½ 120 10⁶ 107½10¹¹10¹⁷½ ValenzuelPA⁷ Aw32000 77-15 BlckJckRod,FirstToArriv,Mgnifico 10
9Mar89—Hopped at start
24Feb89-3SA 6½f :21² :44¹ 1:15¹ft 11 119 4² 4³ 4⁴½ 6¹⁰½ ValenzuelPA¹ Aw32000 84-16 FrostFree,SecretSlction,SnowPrch 8
24Feb89—Bumped hard at intervals down chute, backstretch
12Jan89-2SA 6f :21⁴ :44⁴ 1:09²ft *8-5 118 2hd 2hd 1¹½ 1½ Stevens G L⁵ Mdn 91-12 I'llBThJudg,WstrnRgnt,Zid'sBstMn 9
1Jan89-4SA 6½f :21⁴ :44⁴ 1:16 ft 7½ 119 10⁹¼ 9⁹¼ 6⁹ 4⁷¾ Stevens G L⁵ Mdn 82-10 FrstToArrv,Khld'sRdr,Lorn'sSrprs 12
1Jan89—Hopped in air
Sep 29 SA 5f ft 1:01³ H Sep 23 SA tr.t 4f ft :49² H Sep 11 Dmr 4f ft :48³ H Aug 23 Dmr 5f ft 1:01 H

ESP: A difficult call. This gelding has two races that indicate an E designation and one race indicating an alternate P label. The pressing performance appears to have been a result of another horse running away early and relegating other early pace horses to the role of pressers. The fractional times, and I'll Be The Judge's late collapse, support an E as his preferred style. His last race, a pace battle with On Broadway, further supports that conclusion.

Paceline: 30Aug89. With the presence of On Broadway in this race, the pace will likely duplicate the August 30 race. That leaves this early horse in the role of presser; not his preferred style.

On Broadway — Ch. g. 4, by Broadway Forli—Stylish Model, by Drone

ORTEGA L E — 118 — Br.—Alexander T (Ky) — Tr.—Ippolito Steve — $10,000

Own.—Ippolito S — Lifetime 22 2 0 2 $24,065 — 1989 15 1 0 2 $11,465 — 1988 7 1 0 0 $12,600 — Turf 1 0 0 0

17Sep89-9Fpx 1 1/16 $:46^1$ $1:11^1$ $1:43^2$ft 11 116 1^{hd} 2^1 $7^{9\frac{1}{2}}$ $7^{19\frac{1}{4}}$ Castanon A L 9 16000 75-10 Bugarian, Emigrant Gap,Ki-Nobre 10

17Sep89—Bumped hard start

10Sep89-1Dmr 1 $:45^1$ 1:10 $1:36^1$ft 3½ 116 1^2 $1^{2\frac{1}{2}}$ 1^3 $1^{3\frac{1}{2}}$ Ortega L E 1 10000 85-10 OnBroadway,Renzo,Bigbadandmean 8

30Aug89-9Dmr 1 1/16 $:45^1$ $1:10^1$ $1:42^3$ft 20 116 1^2 1^2 3^1 $3^{5\frac{1}{2}}$ Ortega L E 7 12500 81-13 Dolly'sVldz,I'llBThJudg,OnBrodwy 12

10Jly89-2Hol 6f :22 $:44^4$ $1:10^1$ft 24 117 $8^{6\frac{1}{4}}$ 6^4 $4^{3\frac{1}{2}}$ 5^5 Sibille R 2 10000 85-12 SpndTwoBcks,GoldnStks,PrncO'Fr 9

22Jun89-5Hol 7f :22 $:44^4$ $1:22^4$ft 38 116 4^2 $4^{\frac{3}{4}}$ 5^5 $10^{11\frac{3}{4}}$ Fernandez A L 5 10000 78-12 FighAbhil,BlzingZulu,MnhttnKing 11

22Jun89—Fanned wide late

3Jun89-1Hol 6f $:22^2$ $:45^2$ $1:10^1$ft 3 117 $4^{1\frac{1}{4}}$ $4^{2\frac{1}{2}}$ 5^6 $5^{6\frac{3}{4}}$ Guerra W A 6 10000 83-11 Nazaret,JoseSentMe,Maid'sMistake 8

27May89-1Hol 6f $:21^4$:45 1:10 ft 58 117 $4^{3\frac{1}{2}}$ 3^1 $2^{2\frac{1}{2}}$ 3^4 Fernandez AL 10 10000 87-10 Cracksman, Pain, On Broadway 12

27May89—Wide final 3/8

13May89-2Hol 6f $:22^1$ $:44^3$ $1:10^1$ft 19 116 2^1 3^1 $3^{3\frac{1}{2}}$ $6^{6\frac{3}{4}}$ Fernandez A L 7 10000 83-11 RckneghrsDrm,LJllSpdstr,MtthT.Prr 8

4May89-1Hol 7f $:22^1$:45 $1:23^1$ft 4¾ 117 $4^{1\frac{1}{2}}$ 3^{nk} $5^{7\frac{1}{2}}$ $11^{15\frac{1}{2}}$ Cedeno A 5 10000 72-15 Polysemous, Wild Pursuit, Darion 11

4May89—Bumped at 4 1/2

21Apr89-5SA 7f $:22^2$:45 $1:23^2$ft 34 116 4^1 1^{hd} $4^{2\frac{1}{2}}$ $7^{7\frac{1}{4}}$ Fernandez A L 1 16000 76-17 Rare Tyson, FlyingH.,TrusT.Danus 12

Sep 29 SA 4f ft :47 H ●Aug 22 Dmr 5f ft $:59^2$ H Aug 16 Dmr 4f ft :51 H

ESP: E

Paceline: 30Aug89. His win on 10Sep89 was accomplished at a shorter distance and without mid-race pressure. No horse mounted a challenge from the quarter pole to the eighth pole, and On Broadway was home-free. I'll Be The Judge assures pressure in this mid-race scenario.

Quick Roundtrip — B. g. 7, by Flight to Glory—Fleet Ali, by Fleet Mel

CEDENO A — 118 — Br.—Garcia W G & Anne (Cal) — Tr.—DiFiore Leslie — $10,000

Own.—Di Fiore Dr F — Lifetime 65 11 8 6 $112,785 — 1989 16 1 3 1 $19,740 — 1988 15 2 1 1 $17,780

14Sep89-10Fpx 1 1/16 $:45^3$ $1:11^1$ $1:45^2$ft 2½ 119 1^{hd} $2^{1\frac{1}{2}}$ 5^6 $6^{12\frac{1}{4}}$ Cedeno A^1 12500 72-16 Emperdori,SilverSurfer,Icecapation 9

26Aug89-9Dmr 1 1/16 :46 1:11 1:43 ft 9½ 116 2^{hd} 2^{hd} 3^{nk} $4^{4\frac{3}{4}}$ Cedeno A^2 16000 80-09 SpiritBay,MonLegionnire,TresSuve 9

10Aug89-9Dmr 1 1/16 $:46^2$ $1:11^1$ $1:43^4$ft 18 116 2^1 1^{hd} 1^{hd} 1^{nk} Cedeno A^1 10000 81-20 QuickRoundtrip,I'llBeThJudg,Drion 9

29Jly89-12LA 1 1/16 $:45^2$ $1:11^1$ $1:42^4$ft 4 116 2^{nk} $5^{2\frac{3}{4}}$ 6^{12} 6^{15} Cedeno A^7 10000 76-11 Exotic Arbitor, All Cat, Don's Tryst 7

15Jly89-1Hol 1 1/16 $:47^3$ 1:12 $1:44^3$ft 21 115 2½ 2^{hd} 2^{hd} 2½ Cedeno A^9 10000 76-11 Rossco,QuickRoundtrip,Percntstr 12

6Jly89-1Hol 6f :22 $:45^2$ $1:10^4$ft 21 117 $5^{2\frac{3}{4}}$ $6^{3\frac{3}{4}}$ $7^{6\frac{1}{4}}$ $7^{6\frac{1}{2}}$ Cedeno A^3 Ⓢ 10000 88-17 OrchrdSng,BrgnStndrd,LJllSpdstr 12

22Jun89-5Hol 7f :22 $:44^4$ $1:22^4$ft 40 116 2½ 1^{hd} $2^{1\frac{1}{2}}$ 4^5 Cedeno A^6 10000 85-12 FighAbhil,BlzingZulu,MnhttnKing 11

11Jun89-1Hol 6½f $:21^4$ $:44^2$ $1:17^1$ft 46 117 $5^{3\frac{1}{2}}$ $6^{5\frac{1}{2}}$ $6^{5\frac{1}{2}}$ $7^{8\frac{1}{2}}$ Cedeno A^5 16000 80-10 Premiere,Contravene,BiscayneBoy 12

2Jun89-9Hol 6½f :22 $:44^4$ $1:16^4$ft 6¾ 117 $4^{1\frac{1}{2}}$ $5^{1\frac{3}{4}}$ $8^{6\frac{1}{4}}$ 8^9 Cedeno A^9 Ⓢ 10000 82-10 Loverue, Contravene,Smilin'Smiley 9

2Jun89—Wide 3/8 turn

12May89-1Hol 6f $:22^4$ $:45^2$ $1:10^1$ft 3 116 4¾ 2^{hd} $3^{2\frac{1}{2}}$ 3^5 Fernandez A L^9 10000 85-14 SwtchCods,Mdcuff,QuckRoundtrp 12

ESP: E. His win on 10Aug89 was accomplished while competing for the lead and does not support a pressing style.

Paceline: 10Aug89. The race supports his normal second-call velocity of approximately 1:11.1, and it was at this level. His 26Aug89 race against $16,000 claimers was a good effort. It was two levels above today's race and indicates continuing good form. The race at the Fairplex "bullring" can be excused because of the track and the 45.3 first call; too fast for that surface.

Sir Sparkler — Ch. c. 4, by Lembi Gold—Grace and Savour, by His Majesty
FLORES D R — 116 — Br.—Hobby Horse Farms (Ky) — 1989 11 1 1 4 $4,932
Tr.—Barrera Lazaro S — $10,000 — 1988 2 M 0 0 $180
Own.—Big Train Farm — Lifetime 13 1 1 4 $5,112

22Sep89-11Fpx	$1\frac{1}{16}$	$:45^4$	$1:11^1$	$1:45^2$ft	10	116	5^5	5^5	$5^{3\frac{1}{2}}$	$5^{4\frac{1}{4}}$	Flores D R3	12500	80-15	FghAbhl,SouthrnSprc,JornyThrTm	7
14Sep89-13Fpx	a$1\frac{1}{8}$	$:47^1$	$1:12^3$	1:52 ft	9	113	3^5	$4^{5\frac{1}{2}}$	4^7	6^8	Flores D R4	A12500	75-16	MonLgionnir,PssAnothrTb,GryWrtr	9
18Jun89-2AC	1	:46	$1:10^3$	1:37 ft	$7\frac{3}{4}$	120	$4^{6\frac{1}{4}}$	1^{hd}	$1^{1\frac{1}{2}}$	1^4	Mercado F3	M10000	85-13	SirSparkler,HiggieBaby,PureCutlss	7
18Jun89—Stumbled start															
11Jun89-1AC	6f	:22	:44	$1:10^1$ft	37	120	$7^{3\frac{1}{4}}$	$6^{6\frac{1}{2}}$	$6^{5\frac{3}{4}}$	$3^{3\frac{1}{2}}$	Mercado F8	M10000	84-12	GoldenStakes,Billdancer,SirSprkler	8
4Jun89-1AC	6f	:22	:44	1:09 ft	25	120	$4^{5\frac{1}{2}}$	$4^{6\frac{1}{2}}$	$3^{6\frac{1}{2}}$	$3^{8\frac{1}{2}}$	Martinez J C3	M8000	85-13	FlashyNGood,Beau'sWay,SirSprkler	6
14May89-3AC	6f	$:22^2$	$:44^3$	$1:10^1$ft	$7\frac{1}{2}$	120	$4^{1\frac{3}{4}}$	4^6	4^6	$3^{4\frac{1}{2}}$	Jeronimo A V1	M6250	83-15	Truely Bold,Beau'sWay,SirSparkler	6
15Apr89-2AC	6f	$:22^2$	$:44^1$	$1:09^4$ft	15	119	$4^{2\frac{1}{2}}$	4^6	4^9	$5^{3\frac{1}{2}}$	Escalona G S5	M9000	86-13	Josefa,PatFitzptrick,WebelosScout	8
19Mar89-2AC	7f	$:23^3$	$:45^3$	$1:23^4$ft	$8\frac{1}{2}$	120	$4^{3\frac{1}{2}}$	$4^{3\frac{1}{2}}$	5^4	6^8	Mercado F7	M10000	91-12	Scholstcllyhgh,ZoomZoom,SrousSr	8
11Mar89-2AC	6f	$:22^3$	$:45^1$	$1:10^1$ft	5	118	3^{nk}	$2^{\frac{1}{2}}$	4^2	$5^{5\frac{3}{4}}$	Mercado F3	AlwM	82-14	Bufw,GoldenStkes,Scholsticllyhigh	8
19Feb89-2AC	6f	$:22^3$	$:44^2$	$1:10^1$ft	$5\frac{1}{2}$	120	$2^{1\frac{1}{2}}$	2^2	$2^{\frac{1}{2}}$	2^3	Mercado F5	M10000	85-14	AlbertoCrlos,SirSprkler,ScreenGirl	9

Sep 30 SA 5f ft $1:01^4$ H   Sep 21 SA 3f ft $:35^3$ H   Sep 7 Dmr 5f ft $:59^3$ H   Aug 30 Dmr 4f ft $:47^4$ H

A noncontender. His maiden win at Caliente does not qualify him as a contender at Santa Anita. The two races at Fairplex were dull efforts, and he should not be competitive here.

Middle Concho * — B. g. 4, by Dandy Bingo—Ruscutus, by Cutlass
DELAHOUSSAYE E — 118 — Br.—Stinson M C (Tex) — 1989 5 2 0 1 $17,525
Tr.—Lawrence Renn — $10,000 — 1988 11 1 0 1 $17,437
Own.—Farr-Lawrence-Stinson — Lifetime 19 4 0 3 $46,512 — Turf 1 0 0 0

4Sep89-10BM	$1\frac{1}{16}$ Ⓣ	$:47^2$	$1:12^2$	$1:44^3$fm	21	117	7^7	8^7	9^{13}	9^{15}	PattersonA12	Aw17000	65-20	Uncultivtd,ILovRcng,AwrdForAlln	12
14Aug89-9Dmr	1	$:45^4$	$1:11^1$	$1:37^1$ft	4	116	3^4	$1^{\frac{1}{2}}$	$1^{\frac{1}{2}}$	1^{hd}	DelahoussayeE1	10000	80-19	MiddleConcho,MnhttnKing,BlzFlm	8
3Mar89-6GG	$1\frac{1}{8}$	$:47^4$	$1:11^3$	$1:49^3$ft	$6\frac{3}{4}$	116	4^2	$5^{5\frac{1}{2}}$	$4^{5\frac{1}{2}}$	4^5	Doocy T T3	H12500	72-23	GllntHwk,BoldDecree,WonderPlum	6
8Feb89-9SA	$1\frac{1}{16}$	$:46^4$	1:12	$1:45^3$m	13	110^5	$8^{7\frac{1}{2}}$	$6^{7\frac{1}{2}}$	$2^{2\frac{1}{2}}$	1^{nk}	Garcia H J8	12500	73-23	Middle Concho, Equilibre,Tablado	11
8Feb89—Altered path 1/16															
11Jan89-9SA	$1\frac{1}{16}$	:47	$1:11^2$	$1:43^4$ft	43	110^5	4^4	$5^{4\frac{3}{4}}$	$3^{\frac{1}{2}}$	3^1	Garcia H J8	-12500	81-14	AncntBl,LovDn'sGtwy,MddlConch	12
21Dec88-9Hol	$1\frac{1}{16}$	$:48^1$	1:14	$1:46^4$sl	8	112	5^5	4^8	4^8	$4^{8\frac{1}{4}}$	DominguezRE11	10000	58-30	Extranix, Menelik, Bold Decree	11
21Dec88—Wide 7/8															
9Dec88-9Hol	$1\frac{1}{16}$	$:46^2$	$1:11^4$	$1:44^4$ft	72	115	$4^{3\frac{1}{4}}$	$4^{1\frac{1}{2}}$	$5^{2\frac{3}{4}}$	6^4	Patterson A3	16000	72-16	Hgly'sLion,ComfortblLd,Bsngstok	11
5Nov88-12BM	1	$:45^4$	$1:10^3$	$1:36^2$ft	$4\frac{3}{4}$	117	8^{11}	10^{14}	9^{18}	$7^{16\frac{1}{2}}$	Hansen R D10	20000	70-18	Jlt'sDncr,SlfContnd,MowshkDncr	10
22Oct88-6BM	1	$:46^1$	1:11	$1:37^1$ft	11	117	$7^{7\frac{3}{4}}$	$5^{4\frac{1}{2}}$	5^7	$4^{4\frac{1}{2}}$	Douglas R R8	25000	77-16	WuzWinder,DnvilleGold,MistrPppG.	8
9Oct88-2SA	6f	:21	:44	1:10 ft	71	115	$6^{7\frac{1}{4}}$	$4^{8\frac{1}{2}}$	$5^{8\frac{1}{2}}$	$8^{7\frac{1}{2}}$	Black C A1	20000	80-16	GoForBrodwy,RecklessOne,LeTch	12

Sep 25 SA 5f ft $1:02^3$ H   Sep 15 SA 5f ft $1:03^4$ H   Aug 6 SA 5f ft $1:02^4$ H

ESP: S. The race on 14Aug89 borders on a presser's performance, but it was following a layoff of five months. "Fresh" horses often show more early pace ability than normal. Middle Concho's other races support the S designation.

Paceline: A difficult decision. The use of Middle Concho's 14Aug89 race conflicts with his sustained running style. He pressed the pace and then recorded a final fraction of 26 seconds; not his usual closing ability. A better paceline selection is the 11Jan89 race. That's further back than I normally like to go, but the horse is in form and a strong contender in this race. He deserves a fair evaluation. Santa Anita is slower than Del Mar and requires the following paceline adjustments:

First call: 2 lengths

Second call: 1 length

Final time: 3 lengths

(We'll talk later about a method for determining track-to-track comparisons.) The adjusted paceline for Middle Concho's 11Jan89 race should be: 46.3   1:11.1   1:43.1

Feet-Per-Second Array

First, a quick review.

Reason To Study   46.0   1:11.0   1:42.4
          BL   4.5   2.25   2.5

1Fr	2640 − 45 or 2595 / 46.0 = 56.41 fps
2Fr	1320 + 22.5 or 1342.5 / 25.0 = 53.70 fps
3Fr	1650 − 2.5 or 1647.5 / 31.8 = 51.81 fps
EP	3960 − 22.5 or 3937.5 / 71.0 = 55.45 fps
SP	55.45 + 51.81 / 2 = 53.63
AP	55.45 + 53.63 / 2 = 54.54

	1Fr	2Fr	3Fr	AP	EP	SP	FX
Reason To Study	56.41	53.70	51.81	54.54	55.45	53.63	n/a
Alignment	57.64	52.38	50.92	54.56	55.77	53.35	"
I'll Be The Judge	57.19	54.20	50.92	54.82	56.12	53.52	"
On Broadway	58.40	52.80	49.22	54.61	56.41	52.81	"
Quick Roundtrip	56.68	53.62	50.61	54.36	55.61	53.11	"
Middle Concho	55.79	53.37	52.71	54.39	54.95	53.83	"

Ranking the Contenders

Let's set some order to the ratings by ranking the contenders in each category. We'll rank average pace, early pace, and sustained pace considering .04 to be a tie.

Average Pace:

(1) I'll Be The Judge	54.82
(2) On Broadway	54.61
(3) Alignment	54.56
(3) Reason To Study	54.54
(5) Middle Concho	54.39
(5) Quick Roundtrip	54.36

Early Pace:

(1) On Broadway	56.41
(2) I'll Be The Judge	56.12
(3) Alignment	55.77
(4) Quick Roundtrip	55.61
(5) Reason To Study	55.45
(6) Middle Concho	54.95

Sustained Pace:

(1) Middle Concho	53.83
(2) Reason To Study	53.63
(3) I'll Be The Judge	53.52
(4) Alignment	53.35
(5) Quick Roundtrip	53.11
(6) On Broadway	52.81

Summary:	AP	EP	SP
I'll Be The Judge	1	2	3
On Broadway	2	1	6
Alignment	3	3	4
Reason To Study	3	5	2
Middle Concho	5	6	1
Quick Roundtrip	5	4	5

At this stage of the analysis many players focus on the ratings and lose sight of the probable race scenario. Clearly, the best balance of early and late belongs to I'll Be The Judge. On an unbiased track, and with proven ability to successfully press the pace, he would be an excellent betting proposition. But in the ESP evaluation we concluded he is not capable of winning with a pressing style.

The handicapper should focus attention on the horses ranked strongly in the Sustained Pace category. Reason To Study with a 3–5–2 ranking, and Middle Concho's 5–6–1, are in tune with the demands of this surface. Don't run to the window just yet. Even on a sustained racetrack a runaway early pace horse will still be dangerous and must be considered. Before making the bet, evaluate the race; there are often major surprises.

Early Pace Scenario

On Broadway: 2–1–6 ranked. The first fraction of the array indicates a solid lead for On Broadway. His style is to gun for the lead and let the rest of the race take care of itself. That may be a successful tactic on a track biased toward early pace, or in a race devoid of late runners, but this track is favoring sustained pace.

Alignment: 3–3–4. He may present a problem early. The first fraction of his race at Fairplex was very fast for that surface, and he may have more early pace ability than the array suggests. His second fraction, however, is a weak 52.38 and indicates a relaxed quarter-mile in that race. In today's match-up he'll not have the luxury of a "breather" on the turn. That will have a serious effect on his final fraction of 50.92. Once energy is expended in the early stages, there is no recovery.

I'll Be The Judge: 1–2–3. He also has a very fast first fraction. His 57.19 figures to place him 4 to 5 lengths back at the first call, but he possesses the dominant second fraction (turn-time) in the race. He should move strongly into the turn and join the leaders before they reach the quarter pole. If I'll Be The Judge were a presser, he'd be the ideal horse for this situation. We've already established that he's best as an E type and probably cannot win as a P.

Quick Roundtrip: 5–4–5. Another horse whose best races have been on the pace. He should reach a contending position by the second call, but his races suggest he cannot win from off the early pace. If he's "used" to get position early, he'll suffer late.

The race shapes up as a battle for the early lead all the way to the second call. All of the early horses have fast early fractions and each seems dedicated to the early lead. None has shown ability to win after battling on a fast pace. Only Quick Roundtrip has won after a pace duel, but on slower fractions. In light of the indicated bias, this race should be won from off the pace.

Sustained Pace

There were no pressers in the ESP evaluation, leaving only S types to evaluate. There are two in-form sustained pace runners: Middle Concho and Reason To Study.

Reason To Study: 3–5–2. By virtue of a "three" ranking in Average Pace, he rates strongly in here. The composition of the Average Pace ranking is indicative of overall running ability. It utilizes the second call more fully than any of the other compounded ratings. Consider the algorithm $AP = EP + SP / 2$. EP is pure second-call velocity, and SP uses the second call as 50 percent of the rating. In both ratings second-call velocity is paramount.

An Average Pace ranking of 3 is always a threat to win. Since we've eliminated the four E horses from consideration, the 5 ranking in Early Pace is of no concern. The 2 ranking in Sustained Pace, coupled with the AP ranking, makes Reason To Study the most attractive horse in the scenario.

Middle Concho: 5–6–1. The 1 ranking in Sustained Pace on a closer's racetrack is a strong plus for this horse. He has a weakness in Average Pace, but only compared with Reason To Study. The other four horses have been eliminated in the early pace match-up. Middle Concho is the second most probable winner in this race and must be included in the betting decision.

The Race

Price permitting, bettors employing a two-horse betting strategy should have included both of the sustained pace horses. The one-horse bettor should have bet Reason To Study and taken an exacta box with Middle Concho. In the race, Middle Concho made a winning move on the turn, only to encounter serious traffic trouble inside the quarter pole. He flattened out late and had to settle for the show. Quick Roundtrip showed surprising gameness by forcing the leaders and then running strongly to the wire. Reason To Study came along late to win the race.

NINTH RACE
Santa Anita
OCTOBER 5, 1989

$1\frac{1}{16}$ MILES. ($1.40\frac{4}{5}$) CLAIMING. Purse $12,000. 3-year-olds and upward. Weights, 3-year-olds, 117 lbs.; older, 121 lbs. Non-winners of two races at one mile or over since July 25 allowed 3 lbs.; of such a race since then, 5 lbs. Claiming price $10,000. (Races when entered for $8,500 or less not considered.)

Value of race $12,000; value to winner $6,600; second $2,400; third $1,800; fourth $900; fifth $300. Mutuel pool $176,606. Exacta pool $272,882.

Last Raced	Horse	Eqt.	A.	Wt	PP	St	¼	½	¾	Str	Fin	Jockey	Cl'g Pr	Odds $1
23Aug89 ^{9}Dmr^{2}	Reason To Study	b	6	116	1	5	6^{3}	$6^{3\frac{1}{2}}$	6^{hd}	$4^{1\frac{1}{2}}$	$1^{\frac{1}{2}}$	Solis A	10000	2.90
14Sep89 ^{10}Fpx^{6}	Quick Roundtrip		7	118	6	4	4^{1}	4^{1}	2^{1}	$1^{\frac{1}{2}}$	$2^{1\frac{1}{4}}$	Cedeno A	10000	14.90
4Sep89 ^{10}BM^{9}	Middle Concho		4	118	8	8	7^{4}	7^{5}	7^{4}	$3^{1\frac{1}{2}}$	3^{3}	Delahoussaye E	10000	3.90
17Sep89 ^{9}Fpx^{6}	I'll Be The Judge	b	4	116	4	3	3^{6}	3^{6}	1^{1}	$2^{\frac{1}{2}}$	4^{5}	Pedroza M A	10000	3.30
27Sep89 ^{10}Fpx^{5}	Ancient Blue		8	116	3	6	8	8	8	$6^{1\frac{1}{2}}$	5^{hd}	Dominguez R E	10000	7.90
22Sep89 ^{11}Fpx^{5}	Sir Sparkler	b	4	116	7	7	$5^{1\frac{1}{2}}$	$5^{\frac{1}{2}}$	4^{1}	5^{4}	6^{14}	Flores D R	10000	20.10
17Sep89 ^{9}Fpx^{7}	On Broadway	b	4	118	5	2	$2^{1\frac{1}{2}}$	$2^{1\frac{1}{2}}$	$5^{\frac{1}{2}}$	7^{6}	7^{10}	Ortega L E	10000	7.50
18Sep89 ^{10}Fpx^{1}	Alignment		4	118	2	1	1^{1}	1^{hd}	3^{hd}	8	8	Davis R G	10000	5.20

OFF AT 5:22. Start good. Won driving. Time, $:22\frac{3}{5}$, $:46\frac{1}{5}$, $1:11\frac{3}{5}$, $1:37\frac{4}{5}$, 1:44 Track fast.

$2 Mutuel Prices:

1–REASON TO STUDY	7.80	4.40	2.80
6–QUICK ROUNDTRIP		11.80	4.20
8–MIDDLE CONCHO			2.80

$5 EXACTA 1–6 PAID $287.50.

B. g, by Coulee Man—Mag's Deck, by Mo Bay. Trainer Truman Eddie. Bred by Smith & Quisenberry (Cal).

REASON TO STUDY, devoid of early speed, came into the stretch five wide while on the move, sustained his rally in the drive and was up in time. QUICK ROUNDTRIP, outrun early, made a move to take the lead coming into the stretch but could not outfinish REASON TO STUDY. MIDDLE CONCHO, far back early after he broke slowly, closed strongly to menace a quarter of a mile out, was steadied and altered course leaving the quarter pole to secure a clear path when full of run, threatened from along the inside rail through the last furlong but had to settle for the show. I'LL BE THE JUDGE, close up early, took over nearing the five sixteenths marker but then weakened in the drive. ANCIENT BLUE was six wide into the stretch. SIR SPARKLER, outrun early after he broke slowly and veered

The next race was at six furlongs on August 25, 1989.

7th Del Mar

6 FURLONGS. ($1.07\frac{4}{5}$) CLAIMING. Purse $27,000. 3-year-olds. Weight, 121 lbs. Non-winners of two races since July 1, allowed 3 lbs.; of a race since then, 5 lbs. Claiming price $40,000; if for $35,000, allowed 2 lbs. (Races when entered for $32,000 or less not considered.)

Brilliantized
PINCAY L JR **116**
Own.—Meadowbrook Farms Inc

Ch. g. 3(Apr), by If This Be So—Brilliant Move, by Effervescing
Br.—Meadowbrook Farms Inc (Fla) 1989 12 3 2 0 $42,325
Tr.—La Croix David $40,000 1988 4 1 1 0 $13,075
Lifetime 16 4 3 0 $55,400

13Aug89-2Dmr	6f	$:21^{4}$	$:44^{4}$	$1:10^{2}$ft	*3	117	$3^{\frac{1}{2}}$	$3^{1\frac{1}{2}}$	3^{nk}	$1^{1\frac{1}{2}}$	Pincay L Jr 7	32000	86-14	Brilliantized,BlackDuzy,GoDogsGo	10
30Jly89-3Dmr	$6\frac{1}{2}$f	$:21^{3}$	$:44^{3}$	$1:16^{4}$ft	$8\frac{1}{4}$	117	$6^{3\frac{1}{2}}$	$5^{2\frac{1}{2}}$	$5^{3\frac{1}{2}}$	$2^{\frac{1}{2}}$	Pincay L Jr 4	32000	83-10	Mr. Baldski, Brilliantized,ShelterUs	7
30Jly89—Wide into stretch															
12Jly89-7Hol	1	$:44^{4}$	$1:09^{4}$	$1:35^{1}$ft	16	111^{5}	2^{1}	$2^{1\frac{1}{2}}$	$4^{5\frac{1}{2}}$	$4^{11\frac{1}{2}}$	Nakatani C S 4	40000	75-16	FeelingFabulous,Jazz,ClassicKnight	8
22Jun89-3Hol	7f	$:22^{1}$	$:44^{4}$	$1:23^{4}$ft	*9-5	117	1^{hd}	1^{1}	1^{3}	$1^{1\frac{1}{2}}$	Pincay L Jr 6	25000	85-12	Brilliantized,IslandLegcy,SrosFntsy	7
7Jun89-6Hol	6f	:22	:45	1:10 ft	18	111^{5}	$5^{2\frac{1}{2}}$	$3^{2\frac{1}{2}}$	2^{4}	2^{5}	Nakatani C S 8	20000	86-15	AgittdMik,Brillintzd,PocktfulOfAcs	8
7Jun89—Wide final 3/8															
11May89-9GG	1	:46	$1:10^{3}$	1:37 ft	20	117	$3^{\frac{1}{2}}$	3^{2}	$5^{5\frac{3}{4}}$	$6^{10\frac{3}{4}}$	Warren R J Jr 3	25000	69-19	RockSuker,LeliaLove,IslndMinstrel	7
27Apr89-3GG	6f	$:21^{4}$	$:45^{2}$	$1:11^{1}$ft	*8-5	117	$1^{\frac{1}{2}}$	1^{1}	1^{1}	$1^{1\frac{1}{2}}$	Warren R J Jr 6	16000	83-19	Brilliantized,PiaMan,InTisr'sPride	7
2Apr89-5GG	6f	$:21^{4}$	$:44^{3}$	$1:10^{2}$ft	14	117	$1^{\frac{1}{2}}$	2^{hd}	$3^{\frac{1}{2}}$	$5^{4\frac{3}{4}}$	Lambert J 1	20000	82-16	King Zool,Heyrobbin,Raketmensch	8
23Mar89-1SA	$6\frac{1}{2}$f	$:21^{3}$	:45	$1:18^{3}$ft	47	114	$10^{4\frac{1}{2}}$	$9^{9\frac{1}{2}}$	$8^{9\frac{1}{2}}$	8^{11}	Olivares F 10	18000	66-19	WltzngSss,MgcJhnsn,LghtnngPrt	11
16Feb89-1SA	6f	$:21^{4}$	$:45^{1}$	$1:11^{1}$ft	23	115	$5^{1\frac{3}{4}}$	$6^{4\frac{1}{2}}$	10^{10}	$10^{11\frac{1}{4}}$	Sibille R 11	25000	71-21	MiracleMystery,WaltzingSss,Trgo	12
16Feb89—Wide into stretch															

Aug 18 Dmr 4f ft $:48^{2}$ H **Jly 27 Dmr 3f ft $:37^{2}$ H** **Jly 4 Hol 4f ft $:48^{2}$ H**

Maison Maestro
TORO F **116**
Own.—Daley & Wynne

B. c. 3(Mar), by Mamaison—Raja's Song, by Raja Baba
Br.—Daley R-Jean-M (Ky) 1989 6 0 1 1 $11,675
Tr.—Mandella Richard $40,000 1988 2 1 1 0 $16,500
Lifetime 8 1 2 1 $28,175 Turf 2 0 0 0 $700

4Jun89-7Hol	1	Ⓣ$:45^{1}$	$1:09^{4}$	$1:35^{1}$fm	$6\frac{1}{4}$	115	5^{8}	$5^{2\frac{1}{4}}$	7^{6}	6^{6}	Toro F 1	90000	82-10	FrindlyEd,ArtWork,DoublProsprty	12
4Jun89—Bumped 1/8															
18May89-8Hol	$1\frac{1}{16}$	Ⓣ:47	$1:11^{1}$	$1:42^{3}$fm	31	117	$6^{2\frac{3}{4}}$	4^{2}	$5^{2\frac{1}{4}}$	5^{3}	Baze R A 4	Aw28000	78-19	Presidential, Mr. O. P., Tokatee	10
18May89—Checked 1/8															
15Apr89-7GG	6f	$:21^{1}$	$:43^{3}$	$1:09^{2}$ft	*$2\frac{1}{4}$	117	$6^{6\frac{1}{2}}$	6^{7}	$5^{6\frac{1}{4}}$	$3^{2\frac{1}{2}}$	Toro F 5	Aw20000	89-15	SummrSl,PorcupinRidg,MsonMstro	9
15Apr89—Bumped start															
24Mar89-7SA	6f	$:22^{1}$	:46	$1:10^{2}$ft	$5\frac{1}{2}$	116	6^{3}	$2^{\frac{1}{2}}$	$2^{\frac{1}{2}}$	2^{1}	McCarron C J 3	62500	85-20	Dmskim,MisonMestro,CleverSpech	7
5Mar89-7SA	1	$:45^{1}$	$1:09^{3}$	$1:35^{3}$ft	10	116	6^{6}	7^{5}	$7^{6\frac{3}{4}}$	$7^{7\frac{1}{2}}$	DelhoussyeE 1	Aw35000	82-07	RunwyDunwy,NotoriousPlesur,Copt	8
5Mar89—Wide into stretch															

7Jan89-7SA 6f :212 :444 1:101ft 6 120 101110 9 78 58½ DelhoussyE10 Aw31000 78-14 SttngAppl,RomnAv,NotorousPlsur 10
18Dec88-4Hol 6½f :224 :47 1:191sy *6-5 118 2½ 21 1hd 1nk Delahoussaye E1 Mdn 79-23 MaisonMestro,Lyscent,KingArmour 8
26Nov88-2Hol 6f :222 :462 1:122m 8¼ 118 89½ 64¾ 42 21¼ DelahoussayeE11 Mdn 79-25 Clumr,MisonMestro,CleverSpeech 12
Aug 19 Dmr 5f ft :583 H Aug 7 Dmr 5f ft 1:024 H Jly 9 Hol 5f ft 1:00 H Jly 3 Hol 4f ft :473 H

Number One Tuto
B. c. 3(May), by J O Tobin—Chachita, by Princely Native
CASTANON J L 1115
Br.—Barrera L S (Ky) 1989 6 1 2 0 $23,050
Tr.—Barrera Lazaro S $40,000 1988 0 M 0 0
Own.—Barrera L S
Lifetime 6 1 2 0 $23,050
16Aug89-5Dmr 6f :213 :443 1:092ft 3¾ 115 2hd 42 78½ 814½ Stevens G L 2 50000 76-14 Comicl,MightBeRight,Pt'sPocktful 8
13May89-6Hol 7f :221 :444 1:21 ft 7½ 116 52 64 67¾ 616¼ Cortez A 3 Aw27000 83-11 Lode, Saros Town, Splurger 7
13May89—Broke slowly
6May89-3Hol 6f :22 :45 1:094ft 3½ 116 3½ 1hd 11½ 2nk McCarron C J 3 62500 92-09 Gntlmn'sStyl,NmbrOnTto,FrstLylty 9
19Apr89-6SA 6f :213 :444 1:103ft *1 118 2½ 2hd 2hd 11½ Stevens G L 11 M50000 85-14 NumberOnTuto,ClssyPlyr,I'mFstst 11
8Apr89-4SA 6f :214 :444 1:094ft *2¼ 118 52½ 53½ 46 48¼ Stevens G L2 Mdn 81-12 OvrThPol,PrmiumAwrd,VlrtinWin 10
8Apr89—Bumped start
22Mar89-6SA 6f :213 :444 1:104ft *2¾ 118 52½ 43½ 23 22½ Stevens G L5 M50000 81-17 Skisit, Number One Tuto,WayWild 12
22Mar89—Broke slowly
Aug 12 Dmr 5f ft :584 H ●Aug 1 Dmr 5f ft :581 H Jly 26 Dmr 4f ft :50 H ●Jun 29 Hol 5f ft :592 H

Fiesta Del Sol
B. g. 3(Mar), by Habitony—Princess Torsion, by Torsion
DELAHOUSSAYE E 116
Br.—Mabee Mr-Mrs J C (Cal) 1989 4 1 0 1 $13,750
Tr.—Jery Ian $40,000 1988 5 M 2 1 $16,075
Own.—Golden Eagle Farm
Lifetime 9 1 2 2 $29,825
10Aug89-3Dmr 1 :462 1:11 1:353ft 3½e 116 31½ 42½ 35 611¾ DelhoussyeE 5 Aw35000 76-20 Splurger, True Potential, Histrion 9
10Aug89—Rank to place 3/4
27Jly89-2Dmr 6f :221 :452 1:094ft *9-5 117 51¾ 3½ 11½ 15 DelahoussyeE 6 M32000 89-16 FiestaDelSol,B.Sharp,IntoTheMot 11
27Jly89—Wide 3/8 turn
7Jly89-4Hol 6½f :213 :443 1:153ft *2½ 116 43 52¼ 34½ 38¼ DelhoussyE 5 Ⓢ M50000 89-13 T. V. Screen, Interpol, FiestaDelSol 8
7Jly89—Checked stretch
18Jun89-6Hol 6½f :22 :444 1:162ft 5½ 116 1hd 11 32½ 45¾ Delahoussaye E 1 Mdn 87-12 Nevada Eon, Just Go For 't, Ole' 6
31Dec88-2SA 6f :211 :441 1:10 ft 3½ 117 53½ 42½ 44½ 44½ Sibille R 4 Ⓢ Mdn 83-10 Giglio, Stylish Stud, Morry's Lad 9
31Dec88—Wide into stretch
11Dec88-6Hol 6f :214 :45 1:111ft 4¼ 118 53½ 52¼ 21½ 21¼ DelahoussyeE3 Ⓢ Mdn 85-17 BlueEydDnny,FistDlSol,Mcrry'sLd 10
2Dec88-6Hol 6f :214 :443 1:104ft *1 118 55 54½ 55½ 43¼ DelhoussyeE10 Ⓢ Mdn 85-15 DistntPowr,BluEydDnny,BggrBoy 10
20Nov88-3Hol 7f :214 :45 1:23 ft 3¾ 118 2hd 1hd 21½ 23¼ Sibille R8 Ⓢ Mdn 85-12 DontsToDollrs,FstDlSol,RollngDnt 10
5Nov88-8SA 6f :213 :443 1:092ft 5½ 117 53½ 33 36½ 311 Ortega L E11 Ⓢ Mdn 80-13 Mr.Bolg,DonutsToDollrs,FistDlSol 12
5Nov88—Bumped start
●Aug 20 Dmr 4f ft :461 H Jly 20 Hol 6f ft 1:144 H Jun 29 Hol 4f ft :472 H

Eager Play
B. c. 3(Apr), by Eager Eagle—Via Play, by Via Venuto
GARRIDO O L 114
Br.—Burrow C W (Cal) 1989 2 1 0 0 $2,284
Tr.—Gale Bryce $35,000 1988 0 M 0 0
Own.—Burrow C W
Lifetime 2 1 0 0 $2,284
6Apr89-11TuP 6½f :22 :443 1:172ft 11 120 76¼ 73¼ 55 52½ Lowry G Q3 Aw4600 81-20 StalwartExpress,ChuckFul',FrmBoy 7
26Mar89-4TuP 6f :231 :50 1:21 hy 23 114 96¼ 77¾ 32 1nk Lowry G Q3 Mdn 29-66 EgerPly,WhlrCnyon,OnMorBrothr 10
Aug 19 Fpx 6f ft 1:173 H Aug 11 LA 5f ft 1:04 H Aug 5 LA 5f ft 1:034 H

Rindo Try
Gr. c. 3(Mar), by Drone—Patty's Fault, by Bronze Babu
VALENZUELA P A 118
Br.—Clay A G (Ky) 1989 10 2 0 0 $31,250
Tr.—Palma Hector O $40,000 1988 1 M 0 0 $400
Own.—Tsurumaki T
Lifetime 11 2 0 0 $31,650 Turf 1 0 0 0
16Aug89-5Dmr 6f :213 :443 1:092ft 13 116 77¼ 64½ 67 57¼ Valenzuela P A 3 50000 84-14 Comicl,MightBeRight,Pt'sPocktful 8
16Aug89—Wide into stretch
5Aug89-3Dmr 6f :22 :451 1:102ft 27 116 43½ 32 32½ 1½ Valenzuela P A 7 40000 86-15 Rindo Try, Way Wild,AgitatedMike 7
24Jly89-7Hol 6f :221 :451 1:09 ft 27 116 44 43½ 55 79¼ Dominguez RE 6 50000 87-11 JklinLomLd,AgittdMk,WorkTllDwn 7
15Jun89-5Hol 1 :444 1:093 1:353ft 31 116 73¼ 75¼ 710 713 Valenzuela F H 5 62500 72-19 DominatedDebut,Lyscent,WellAwre 9
15Jun89—Wide final 3/8
28May89-3Hol 1 :45 1:093 1:343ft 53 115 52½ 53 54 56½ ValenzuelFH 3 Aw28000 83-11 Damask Star, Splurger,Waterscape 6
13May89-6Hol 7f :221 :444 1:21 ft 42 116 42 52½ 57¼ 514½ Pedroza MA 2 Aw27000 84-11 Lode, Saros Town, Splurger 7
27Apr89-7Hol 1 Ⓣ:464 1:11 1:36 fm 16 116 21½ 21 43½ 74¾ ValenzuelPA 5 Aw28000 79-16 Skisit,Presidentil,Plymeonmortim 12
16Apr89-7SA 1 1/16 :462 1:11 1:43 ft 21 1115 52¼ 42 55¼ 45¾ ValenzuelFH 3 Aw36000 80-16 NotorousPlsur,ImprlLd,PrncColony 6
5Apr89-6SA 6f :213 :443 1:104ft 40 118 63½ 64¼ 31½ 1hd ValenzuelaFH 1 M50000 84-14 Rindo Try, Flying Raja, Alias Alias 12
18Mar89-6SA 7f :221 :45 1:231ft 96 117 117¾ 118½ 1010 1013¼ Pedroza M A 12 Mdn 71-15 Lode, Prince Colony, Trebizond 12
Jly 21 Hol 4f ft :493 H Jly 13 Hol 5f ft 1:02 H Jly 6 Hol 4f ft :483 H Jun 29 Hol 4f ft :484 H

Black Duzy
Dk. b. or br. g. 3(Apr), by Stutz Blackhawk—First Queen, by Iron Ruler
BLACK C A 116
Br.—October House Farm (Fla) 1989 11 2 1 1 $37,225
Tr.—Murphy Marcus J $40,000 1988 7 1 0 1 $7,440
Own.—Redman L & Ida
Lifetime 18 3 1 2 $44,665 Turf 1 0 0 0
13Aug89-2Dmr 6f :214 :444 1:102ft 6½ 116 54½ 53½ 53¼ 21½ Black C A 5 c32000 84-14 Brilliantized,BlackDuzy,GoDogsGo 10
13Aug89—Wide into stretch

5Aug89-3Dmr 6f :22 :451 1:102ft 10 116 54 531 421 731 Black C A 1 40000 82-15 Rinde Try, Way Wild,Agit:tadMike 7
22Jun89-8Hol 1 ①:4911:1311:363fm 19 115 42 311 67 69 Guerra W A 4 Aw31000 72-18 Friendly Ed, Art Work,OrneryGuest 7
11Jun89-5Hol 6f :222 :451 1:101ft 17 116 623 213 211 11 Guerra W A 9 32000 90-10 BlckDuzy,BelieveItToM,GcDogsGo 8
18May89-5Hol 61f :22 :45 1:16 ft 12 114 42 3nk 321 37 Guerra W A 7 30000 88-07 RestlessGlxy,Rud'sGrtLgs,9lckDuzy 7
29Apr89-1GG 6f :22 :451 1:101ft 43 119 65 54 53 531 SchvneveldtCP 4 32000 84-18 Eagle Leash, WorkTillDawn,Mr.Don6
17Mar89-1SA 61f :214 :444 1:164ft 12 115 721 43 34 471 Black C A 9 40000 79-20 ‡AdvntrsomLov,ClvrSpch,BttrRgr 9
26Feb89-3SA 6f :22 :452 1:11 ft 32 116 621 31 3nk 11 Black C A 7 32000 83-14 BlckDuzy,CleverSpch,MgicJohnson 8
16Feb89-1SA 6f :214 :451 1:111ft 41 115 731 531 643 431 Meza R Q 4 25000 79-21 MiracleMystery,WaltzingSss,Trgo 12
19Jan89-5SA 1 :462 1:12 1:39 ft 12 116 753 64 54 56 DelahoussayeE 3 32000 67-23 Dime Time,Bargainaul,Caro'sRuler 10
  19Jan89—Wide into stretch
  Aug 23 Dmr 4f ft :48 H   Jly 31 Dmr 4f ft :482 H   Jly 18 SA 3f ft :374 H

Olympic Brat
B. g. 3(Mar), by Hollywood Brat—Olympic Skies, by Royal Ski
Br.—E L Allee Ranch (Cal)   1989 2 1 0 0 $9,350
PEDROZA M A   116   Tr.—Garcia Victor $40,000   1988 1 M 0 1 $360
Own.—Allee & Garcia   Lifetime 3 1 0 1 $9,710
12Aug89-1Dmr 6f :221 :452 1:10 ft 2 116 11 11 121 11 Pedroza M A 2 M32000 80-13 Olympic Brat, My Niriko, Svelte 12
29Jly89-4Dmr 6f :212 :442 1:092ft 71 116 113 213 57 7141 Pedroza M A 4 ⑤Mdn 76-10 MrcoAndMe,Interline,Don'tUpstgM 8
11Jun89-1AC 41f :231 :46 :521ft 21117 6 511 421 323 Lopez A D 4 Mdn 90-07 ApprovedToFly,Jn'sRj,OlympicBrt 10
  Aug 22 Dmr 4f ft :502 H   Aug 9 Dmr 5f ft :592 H   Jly 27 Dmr 3f ft :364 H   Jly 23 Dmr 6f ft 1:193 H

Go Steady Lad
B. g. 3(Mar), by Run of Luck—Up to Juliet, by First Balcony
Br.—Whitney W & Rowan L R (Cal)   1989 5 4 0 0 $16,920
JAUREGUI L H   1115   Tr.—Moreno Henry $40,000   1988 0 M 0 0
Own.—Alfred E C   Lifetime 5 4 0 0 $16,920
10Aug89-6LA 61f :214 :454 1:171ft 5 1105 631 411 1hd 111 Jauregui L H 9 20000 89-13 GoStdyLd,MgicJohnson,WltzingSss 8
8Jly89-12Rui 71f :232 :471 1:332ft *21 118 21 32 813 812 WhitedDW 2 Jky Clb H 77-17 StrightRlity,LoosLipsCsh,StwingSd 9
10Jun89-11Rui 6f :222 :454 1:113ft *6-5 117 411 42 34 12 CunninghmV 1 Aw4400 89-19 GoStdyLd,BrdlysKhli,KyTcChrism 10
27May89-8Rui 5f :222 :462 :594ft *21 121 841 65 441 111 Yoakum J 3 Aw3800 88-16 GoSteadyLd,StinsEgo,PrincBobbiD 10
22Apr89-6TuP 6f :214 :45 .1:181ft 3 120 56 41 13 17 McGurn C 9 Mdn 83-19 GoSteadyLad,Mnilius,PrivteEscort 10
  22Apr89—Fractious at gate
  Jly 31 LA 4f ft :534 H   Jly 24 LA 3f ft :364 H   Jly 2 Rui 5f ft 1:051 B   Jun 25 Rui 7f ft 1:313 H

Got The Bug
Ch. c. 3(Feb), by Naevus—Niponese Bug, by Wajima
Br.—Kanowsky V (Cal)   1989 2 1 0 0 $6,600
STEVENS G L   116   Tr.—Stepp William T $40,000   1988 0 M 0 0
Own.—Crash H   Lifetime 2 1 0 0 $6,600
7Aug89-5Dmr 6f :211 :441 1:091ft 20 114 811 811 812 8161 Pedroza MA 6 Aw32000 75-15 M Single M,Doncareer,LoadedJuan 10
28Jly89-9LA 6f :214 :452 1:104ft 6 1105 421 2nk 121 143 Nakatani C S 2 M32000 89-15 GotTheBug,ElGrnSid,ChuckNAgin 10
  Jly 26 SA 3f ft :357 Hg   Jly 22 SA 4f ft :473 Hg   Jly 14 SA 5f ft 1:023 H   Jly 6 SA 5f ft 1:012 H

First Loyalty
B. c. 3(Mar), by Top Command—Ellis Island, by First Landing
Br.—Financial C (Ky)   1989 9 1 1 1 $25,300
PATTON D B   116   Tr.—Wilmot William B $40,000   1988 2 1 0 0 $16,500
Own.—Freed R   Lifetime 11 2 1 1 $41,800
1Aug89-10LA 61f :221 :461 1:163ft 21 115 99 851 753 783 Black C A 7 ⑤Mcfdn 83-13 ‡Charlatan,SnowPerch,BearInMind 9
  1Aug89—Placed sixth through disqualification
24Jly89-7Hol 6f :221 :451 1:09 ft 41 116 751 651 781 69 Black C A 5 50000 87-11 JklinLomLd,AgittdMk,WorkTllDwn 7
13May89-1GG 6f :214 :45 1:103ft 21 117 43 32 22 11 Patton D B 3 Aw20000 86-19 First Loyalty, Mr. Don, Vote 6
6Mar89-3Hol 6f :22 :45 1:094ft 21 116 861 741 54 331 Guerra W A 8 62500 86-08 Gntlmn'sStyl,NmbrOnTto,FrstLylty 9
21Apr89-3SA 6f :214 :442 1:093ft *2 117 44 441 421 23 Pincay L Jr 3 c50000 89-17 ClvrSpch,FirstLoyltty,MgicJohnson 7
  21Apr89—Broke in a tangle; finished wide
24Mar89-7SA 6f :221 :46 1:102ft 6 118 211 42 45 4101 Meza R Q 2 62500 75-20 Dmskim,MisonMestro,CleverSpech 7
  24Mar89—Broke through gate
2Mar89-7SA 61f :213 :443 1:152sy 29 119 31 55 5121 Meza R Q 3 Aw32000 81-18 SundySilenc,HroicTyp,MightBRight 7
5Feb89-3SA 1 :463 1:123 1:401sy 13 118 31 34 614 8251 Meza R Q 5 Aw35000 41-21 Bbyitscoldoutside,Copt,BrirticChif 7
  5Feb89—Veered out start; lugged out badly 7/8
  Jly 28 SA 5f ft 1:004 H   ●Jly 14 SA 5f ft :594 H   ●Jly 8 SA 5f ft :591 H   Jly 2 SA 4f ft :47 H

Jet Echo
Ch. g. 3(Mar), by If This Be So—Jetting Polly, by Tri Jet
Br.—Hooper F W (Fla)   1989 5 1 0 1 $15,050
BAZE R A   118   Tr.—Russell John W $40,000   1988 2 M 0 0 $625
Own.—Bronson & Russell   Lifetime 7 1 0 1 $15,675
10Aug89-3Dmr 1 :462 1:11 1:353ft 19 116 42 32 551 5111 Baze R A 8 Aw35000 76-20 Splurger, True Potential, Histrion 9
24Jly89-7Hol 6f :221 :451 1:09 ft 91 116 651 761 651 561 DelahoussayeE 2 50000 89-11 JklinLomLd,AgittdMk,WorkTllDwn 7
10Jly89-6Hol 6f :214 :45 1:10 ft *1 116 31 2hd 12 12 Stevens G L 4 M40000 91-12 Jet Echo, Prospector'sHope,LeRoc 8
25Jun89-4Hol 1 :451 1:102 1:354ft 27 116 2hd 31 551 5111 DelahoussayeE 3 Mdn 72-19 EdgyDiplomat,KingArmour,Brcoy 10
8Jun89-6Hol 6f :223 :462 1:104ft 15 115 64 651 451 33 Solis A 1 M32000 94-14 Chaldean, SerranoDancer,JetEcho 12
21Aug88-6Dmr 1 :461 1:114 1:38 ft 91 116 643 531 661 671 McCarron C J 5 Mdn 70-12 Hwkster,FriendlyEd,EdgyDiplomt 10
27Jly88-6Dmr 51f :212 :443 1:024ft 83 118 89 761 631 5181 Baze R A 4 Mdn 87-11 Sabulose, Texian, Friendly Ed 11
  Aug 19 Dmr 5f ft :594 H   Aug 7 Dmr 5f ft 1:013 H   Aug 1 Dmr 5f ft 1:031 H   Jly 20 Hol 5f ft 1:021 H

Most Del Mar sprints were being won by E or P horses able to stay within 2½ lengths at the second call. Once we obtain our readouts, we'll insist that any betting possibility be within .75 fps (3 lengths) at the second call (EP).

Brilliantized — Ch. g. 3(Apr), by If This Be So—Brilliant Move, by Effervescing
PINCAY L JR — 116 — Br.—Meadowbrook Farms Inc (Fla) — 1989 12 3 2 0 $42,325
Own.—Meadowbrook Farms Inc — Tr.—La Croix David — $40,000 — 1988 4 1 1 0 $13,075
Lifetime 16 4 3 0 $55,400

13Aug89-2Dmr	6f	:214	:444	1:102ft	*3	117	3½	31½	3nk	11½	Pincay L Jr 7	32000	86-14	Brilliantized,BlackDuzy,GoDogsGo	10
30Jly89-3Dmr	6½f	:213	:443	1:164ft	8¼	117	63½	52½	53½	2½	Pincay L Jr 4	32000	83-10	Mr. Baldski, Brilliantized,ShelterUs	7
30Jly89—Wide into stretch															
12Jly89-7Hol	1	:444	1:094	1:351ft	16	1115	21	21½	45½	411½	Nakatani C S 4	40000	75-16	FeelingFabulous,Jazz,ClassicKnight	8
22Jun89-3Hol	7f	:221	:444	1:234ft	*9-5	117	1hd	11	13	11½	Pincay L Jr 6	25000	85-12	Brilliantized,IslandLegcy,SrosFntsy	7
7Jun89-6Hol	6f	:22	:45	1:10 ft	18	1115	52½	32½	24	25	Nakatani C S 8	20000	86-15	AgittdMik,Brillintzd,PocktfulOfAcs	8
7Jun89—Wide final 3/8															
11May89-9GG	1	:46	1:103	1:37 ft	20	117	3½	32	55¾	610¾	Warren R J Jr 3	25000	69-19	RockSuker,LeliaLove,IslndMinstrel	7
27Apr89-3GG	6f	:214	:452	1:111ft	*8-5	117	1½	11	11	11½	Warren R J Jr 6	16000	83-19	Brilliantized,PiaMan,InTisr'sPride	7
2Apr89-5GG	6f	:214	:443	1:102ft	14	117	1½	2hd	3½	54¾	Lambert J 1	20000	82-16	King Zoot,Heyrobbin,Raketmensch	8
23Mar89-1SA	6½f	:213	:45	1:183ft	47	114	104½	99¼	89½	811	Olivares F10	18000	66-19	WltzngSss,MgcJhnsn,LghtnngPrt	11
16Feb89-1SA	6f	:214	:451	1:111ft	23	115	51¾	64½	1010	1011¼	Sibille R 11	25000	71-21	MiracleMystery,WaltzingSss,Trgo	12
16Feb89—Wide into stretch															

Aug 10 Dmr 4f ft :482 H — Jly 27 Dmr 3f ft :372 H — Jly 4 Hol 4f ft :482 H

ESP: E/P. He has the ability to take the lead or rate just off the pace. That's the most dangerous type of all.

Paceline: 13Aug89. The race reflects his best running style and is the most current in his past performances.

Maison Maestro — B. c. 3(Mar), by Mamaison—Raja's Song, by Raja Baba
TORO F — 116 — Br.—Daley R-Jean-M (Ky) — 1989 6 0 1 1 $11,675
Own.—Daley & Wynne — Tr.—Mandella Richard — $40,000 — 1988 2 1 1 0 $16,500
Lifetime 8 1 2 1 $28,175 — Turf 2 0 0 0 $700

4Jun89-7Hol	1	ⓣ:451	1:094	1:351fm	6¼	115	58	52¼	76	66	Toro F 1	90000	82-10	FrindlyEd,ArtWork,DoublProsprty	12
4Jun89—Bumped 1/8															
18May89-8Hol	1 1/16	ⓣ:47	1:111	1:423fm	31	117	62¾	42	52¼	53	Baze R A 4	Aw28000	78-19	Presidential, Mr. O. P., Tokatee	10
18May89—Checked 1/8															
15Apr89-7GG	6f	:211	:433	1:092ft	*2¼	117	66½	67	56¼	32½	Toro F 6	Aw20000	89-15	SummrSl,PorcupinRidg,MsonMstro	9
15Apr89—Bumped start															
24Mar89-7SA	6f	:221	:46	1:102ft	5½	116	63	2½	2½	21	McCarron C J 3	62500	85-20	Dmskim,MisonMestro,CleverSpech	7
5Mar89-7SA	1	:451	1:093	1:353ft	10	116	66	75	76¾	77½	DelhoussyeE1	Aw35000	82-07	RunwyDunwy,NotoriousPlesur,Copt	8
5Mar89—Wide into stretch															
7Jan89-7SA	6f	:212	:444	1:101ft	6	120	1011	109	78	58½	DelhoussyE10	Aw31000	78-14	SttngAppl,RomnAv,NotorousPlsur	10
18Dec88-4Hol	6½f	:224	:47	1:191sy	*6-5	118	2½	21	1hd	1nk	Delahoussaye E1	Mdn	79-23	MaisonMestro,Lyscent,KingArmour	8
26Nov88-2Hol	6f	:222	:462	1:122m	8¼	118	89½	64¾	42	21¼	DelahoussayeE11	Mdn	79-25	Clumr,MisonMestro,CleverSpeech	12

Aug 19 Dmr 5f ft :583 H — Aug 7 Dmr 5f ft 1:024 H — Jly 9 Hol 5f ft 1:00 H — Jly 3 Hol 4f ft :473 H

ESP: S in all his recent races

Paceline: None. The 2½-month layoff, followed by a $50,000 drop in class, are signs that not all is well with this one. As if those weren't enough negatives, his running style is contrary to the existing bias toward forwardly placed runners.

```
Number One Tuto                B. c. 3(May), by J O Tobin—Chachita, by Princely Native
                               Br.—Barrera L S (Ky)                     1989  6 1 2 0   $23,050
  CASTANON J L          1115   Tr.—Barrera Lazare S          $40,000    1988  0 M 0 0
Own.—Barrera L S               Lifetime   6 1 2 0   $23,050
16Aug89-5Dmr 6f  :213 :443 1:092ft  3¾ 115  2hd 42  78½ 814½ Stevens G L 2    50000 76-14 Comicl,MightBeRight,Pt'sPocktful 8
13May89-6Hol 7f  :221 :444 1:21 ft  7½ 116  52  64  67¾ 616¼ Cortez A 3     Aw27000 83-11 Lode, Saros Town, Splurger 7
    13May89—Broke slowly
6May89-3Hol  6f  :22  :45  1:094ft  3½ 116  3½  1hd 11½ 2nk  McCarron C J 3   62500 92-09 Gntlmn'sStyl,NmbrOnTto,FrstLylty 9
19Apr89-6SA  6f  :213 :444 1:103ft  *1 118  2½  2hd 2hd 11½  Stevens G L 11  M50000 85-14 NumberOnTuto,ClssyPlyr,I'mFstst 11
8Apr89-4SA   6f  :214 :444 1:094ft *2¼ 118  52½ 53½ 46  48¾  Stevens G L2       Mdn 81-12 OvrThPol,PrmiumAwrd,VlrtinWin 10
    8Apr89—Bumped start
22Mar89-6SA  6f  :213 :444 1:104ft *2¾ 118  52½ 43½ 23  22½  Stevens G L5    M50000 81-17 Skisit, Number One Tuto,WayWild 12
    22Mar89—Broke slowly
  Aug 12 Dmr 5f ft :584 H   ●Aug 1 Dmr 5f ft :581 H   Jly 26 Dmr 4f ft :50 H   ●Jun 29 Hol 5f ft :592 H
```

ESP: E/P. When in form, he showed some versatility of style with good races from on, and slightly off, the pace.

Paceline: None. His last race should have been an improvement with the class drop to a field of three-year-old claimers. With older horses, the apparent drop from NW1 to $50,000 is actually a step up in class. Even in August, three-year-olds' claiming prices are still inflated in an attempt to offer protection to relatively unclassified runners. The pace of Number One Tuto's last race is similar to what Brilliantized can record, so this spot should not be much softer. Losing two lengths on the turn versus a 23.0 quarter is also a negative. Number One Tuto is a noncontender.

```
Fiesta Del Sol                 B. g. 3(Mar), by Habitony—Princess Torsion, by Torsion
                               Br.—Mabee Mr-Mrs J C (Cal)               1989  4 1 0 1   $13,750
  DELAHOUSSAYE E         116   Tr.—Jory Ian                  $40,000    1988  5 M 2 1   $16,075
Own.—Golden Eagle Farm         Lifetime   9 1 2 2   $29,825
10Aug89-3Dmr 1   :462 1:11 1:353ft 3½e116  31½ 42½ 35  611¾ DelhoussyeE 5 Aw35000 76-20 Splurger, True Potential, Histrion 9
    10Aug89—Rank to place 3/4
27Jly89-2Dmr 6f  :221 :452 1:094ft *9-5 117 51¾ 3½  11½ 15   DelahoussyeE 6 M32000 89-16 FiestaDelSol,B.Sharp,IntoTheMot 11
    27Jly89—Wide 3/8 turn
7Jly89-4Hol  6½f :213 :443 1:153ft *2¾ 116 43  52¼ 34½ 38¼  DelhoussyE 5 [S]M50000 89-13 T. V. Screen, Interpol, FiestaDelSol 8
    7Jly89—Checked stretch
18Jun89-6Hol 6½f :22  :444 1:162ft 5½ 116  1hd 11  32½ 45¾  Delahoussaye E 1 Mdn 87-12 Nevada Eon, Just Go For 't, Ole' 6
31Dec88-2SA  6f  :211 :441 1:10 ft 3½ 117  53½ 42½ 44½ 44½  Sibille R 4      [S]Mdn 83-10 Giglio, Stylish Stud, Morry's Lad 9
    31Dec88—Wide into stretch
11Dec88-6Hol 6f  :214 :45  1:111ft 4¼ 118  53½ 52¼ 21½ 21¼  DelahoussyeE3   [S]Mdn 85-17 BlueEydDnny,FistDlSol,Mcrry'sLd 10
2Dec88-6Hol  6f  :214 :443 1:104ft *1 118   55  54½ 55½ 43¼  DelhoussyeE10   [S]Mdn 85-15 DistntPowr,BluEydDnny,BggrBoy 10
20Nov88-3Hol 7f  :214 :45  1:23 ft 3¾ 118  2hd 1hd 21½ 23½  Sibille R8       [S]Mdn 85-12 DontsToDollrs,FstDlSol,RollngDnt 10
5Nov88-8SA   6f  :213 :443 1:092ft 5½ 117  53½ 33  36½ 311  Ortega L E11    [S]Mdn 80-13 Mr.Bolg,DonutsToDollrs,FistDlSol 12
    5Nov88—Bumped start
  ●Aug 20 Dmr 4f ft :461 H   Jly 28 Hol 6f ft 1:144 H   Jun 29 Hol 4f ft :472 H
```

ESP: P. He's attempted wire-to-wire tactics twice with poor results. His best style is from slightly off the pace, and that's sure to be today's strategy.

Paceline: 27Jly89. The race is current and reflects his best style.

Eager Play — B. c. 3(Apr), by Eager Eagle—Via Play, by Via Venuto
GARRIDO O L — 114 — Br.—Burrow C W (Cal) — 1989 2 1 0 0 $2,284
Own.—Burrow C W — Tr.—Gale Bryce — $35,000 — 1988 0 M 0 0
Lifetime 2 1 0 0 $2,284
6Apr89-11TuP 6½f :22 :443 1:172ft 11 120 76¼ 73¼ 55 52½ Lowry G Q3 Aw4600 81-20 StalwartExpress,ChuckFul',FrmBoy 7
26Mar89-4TuP 6f :231 :50 1:21 hy 23 114 96¼ 77¾ 32 1nk Lowry G Q3 Mdn 29-66 EgerPly,WhlrCnyon,OnMorBrothr 10
Aug 19 Fpx 6f ft 1:173 H Aug 11 LA 5f ft 1:04 H Aug 5 LA 5f ft 1:034 H

A noncontender. Turf Paradise is approximately 1.5 solar systems away from Santa Anita.

Rindo Try — Gr. c. 3(Mar), by Drone—Patty's Fault, by Bronze Babu
VALENZUELA P A — 118 — Br.—Clay A G (Ky) — 1989 10 2 0 0 $31,250
Own.—Tsurumaki T — Tr.—Palma Hector O — $40,000 — 1988 1 M 0 0 $400
Lifetime 11 2 0 0 $31,650 — Turf 1 0 0 0
16Aug89-5Dmr 6f :213 :443 1:092ft 13 116 77¼ 64½ 67 57¼ Valenzuela P A 3 50000 84-14 Comicl,MightBeRight,Pt'sPocktful 8
16Aug89—Wide into stretch
5Aug89-3Dmr 6f :22 :451 1:102ft 27 116 43½ 32 32½ 1½ Valenzuela P A 7 40000 86-15 Rindo Try, Way Wild,AgitatedMike 7
24Jly89-7Hol 6f :221 :451 1:09 ft 27 116 44 43½ 55 79¼ Dominguez R E 6 50000 87-11 JklinLomLd,AgittdMk,WorkTllDwn 7
15Jun89-5Hol 1 :444 1:093 1:353ft 31 116 73¼ 75¼ 710 713 Valenzuela F H 5 62500 72-19 DominatedDebut,Lyscent,WellAwre 9
15Jun89—Wide final 3/8
28May89-3Hol 1 :45 1:093 1:343ft 53 115 52½ 53 54 56¼ ValenzuelFH 3 Aw28000 83-11 Damask Star, Splurger,Waterscape 6
13May89-6Hol 7f :221 :444 1:21 ft 42 116 42 52½ 57¼ 514½ Pedroza M A 2 Aw27000 84-11 Lode, Saros Town, Splurger 7
27Apr89-7Hol 1 ⓣ:464 1:11 1:36 fm 16 116 21½ 21 43½ 74¾ ValenzuelPA 5 Aw28000 79-16 Skisit,Presidentil,Plymeonmortim 12
16Apr89-7SA 1 1/16 :462 1:11 1:43 ft 21 1115 52¼ 42 55¼ 45¾ ValenzuelFH 3 Aw36000 80-16 NotorousPlsur,ImprlLd,PrncColony 6
5Apr89-6SA 6f :213 :443 1:104ft 40 118 63½ 64¼ 31½ 1hd ValenzuelaFH 1 M50000 84-14 Rindo Try, Flying Raja, Alias Alias 12
18Mar89-6SA 7f :221 :45 1:231ft 96 117 117¾ 118½ 1010 1013¼ Pedroza M A 12 Mdn 71-15 Lode, Prince Colony, Treb'zond 12
Jly 21 Hol 4f ft :493 H Jly 13 Hol 5f ft 1:02 H Jly 6 Hol 4f ft :483 H Jun 29 Hol 4f ft :484 H

ESP: S, although an argument might also be made for an alternate P designation. Because of his usual first-fraction placement, we'll anticipate a sustained pace effort. He's been in the rear half of the field in most of his races.

Paceline: The 5Aug89 race was at this level and was free of the trouble encountered in his last race. The difference between $40,000 and $50,000 three-year-olds is not all that significant, making his last effort some cause for concern.

Black Duzy — Dk. b. or br. g. 3(Apr), by Stutz Blackhawk—First Queen, by Iron Ruler
BLACK C A — 116 — Br.—October House Farm (Fla) — 1989 11 2 1 1 $37,225
Own.—Redman L & Ida — Tr.—Murphy Marcus J — $40,000 — 1988 7 1 0 1 $7,440
Lifetime 18 3 1 2 $44,665 — Turf 1 0 0 0
13Aug89-2Dmr 6f :214 :444 1:102ft 6½ 116 54½ 53½ 53¼ 21½ Black C A 5 c32000 84-14 Brilliantized,BlackDuzy,GoDogsGo 10
13Aug89—Wide into stretch
5Aug89-3Dmr 6f :22 :451 1:102ft 10 116 54 53½ 42½ 73½ Black C A 1 40000 82-15 Rindo Try, Way Wild,AgitatedMike 7
22Jun89-8Hol 1 ⓣ:491 1:131 1:363fm 19 115 42 31½ 67 69 Guerra W A 4 Aw31000 72-18 Friendly Ed, Art Work,OrneryGuest 7
11Jun89-5Hol 6f :222 :451 1:101ft 17 116 62¾ 21½ 21½ 11 Guerra W A 8 32000 90-10 BlckDuzy,BelieveItToM,GoDogsGo 8
18May89-5Hol 6½f :22 :45 1:16 ft 12 114 42 3nk 32½ 37 Guerra W A 7 30000 88-07 RestlessGlxy,Rud'sGrtLgs,BlckDuzy 7
29Apr89-1GG 6f :22 :443 1:101ft 4¾ 119 65 54 53 53½ SchvneveldtCP 4 32000 84-18 Eagle Leash, WorkTillDawn,Mr.Don 6
17Mar89-1SA 6½f :214 :444 1:164ft 12 115 72¼ 43 34 47¼ Black C A 8 40000 79-20 ‡AdvntrsomLov,ClvrSpch,BttrRgr 10
26Feb89-3SA 6f :22 :452 1:11 ft 32 116 62¼ 31 3nk 11¾ Black C A 7 32000 83-14 BlckDuzy,CleverSpch,MgicJohnson 8
16Feb89-1SA 6f :214 :451 1:111ft 41 115 73¼ 53½ 64¾ 43¾ Meza R Q 4 25000 76-21 MiracleMystery,WaltzingSss,Trgo 12
19Jan89-5SA 1 :462 1:12 1:39 ft 12 116 75¾ 64 54 56 DelahoussayeE 2 32000 67-23 Dime Time,Bargainaul,Caro'sRuler 10
19Jan89—Wide into stretch
Aug 23 Dmr 4f ft :48 H Jly 31 Dmr 4f ft :482 H Jly 18 SA 3f ft :374 H

ESP: S. Nearly a clone of the previous runner. This one's more consistent and will probably run well off the claim.

Paceline: 13Aug89. A good closing effort to Brilliantized.

Olympic Brat B. g. 3(Mar), by Hollywood Brat—Olympic Skies, by Royal Ski
PEDROZA M A 116 Br.—E L Allee Ranch (Cal) 1989 2 1 0 0 $9,350
Own.—Allee & Garcia Tr.—Garcia Victor $40,000 1988 1 M 0 1 $360
Lifetime 3 1 0 1 $9,710
12Aug89-1Dmr 6f :221 :452 1:10 ft 2 116 1½ 1½ 12½ 1½ Pedroza M A 7 M32000 88-13 Olympic Brat, My Niriko, Svelte 12
29Jly89-4Dmr 6f :212 :442 1:092ft 7½ 116 11½ 21½ 57 714¾ Pedroza M A 4 [S]Mdn 76-10 MrcoAndMe,Interline,Don'tUpstgM 8
11Jun88-1AC 4½f :231 :46 :521ft 2½e117 6 51¼ 42¼ 32¾ Lopez A D4 Mdn 90-07 ApprovedToFly,Jn'sRj,OlympicBrt 10
Aug 22 Dmr 4f ft :502 H Aug 9 Dmr 5f ft :592 H Jly 27 Dmr 3f ft :364 H Jly 23 Dmr 6f ft 1:193 H

ESP: E

Paceline: 12Aug89. A recent maiden claiming winner, but the figures are strong and three-year-olds often do well out of these races.

Go Steady Lad B. g. 3(Mar), by Run of Luck—Up to Juliet, by First Balcony
JAUREGUI L H 1115 Br.—Whitney W & Rowan L R (Cal) 1989 5 4 0 0 $16,920
Own.—Allred E C Tr.—Moreno Henry $40,000 1988 0 M 0 0
Lifetime 5 4 0 0 $16,920
10Aug89-6LA 6½f :214 :454 1:171ft 5 1105 63½ 41¼ 1hd 11¼ Jauregui L H 8 20000 89-13 GoStdyLd,MgicJohnson,WltzingSss 8
8Jly89-12Rui 7½f :232 :471 1:332ft *2¾ 118 2½ 32 813 812 WhitedDW 7Jky Clb H 77-17 StrightRlity,LoosLipsCsh,StwingSd 9
10Jun89-11Rui 6f :222 :454 1:113ft *6-5 117 41½ 42 34 1¾ CunninghmV 1 Aw4400 89-19 GoStdyLd,BrdlysKhli,KyTcChrism 10
27May89-8Rui 5f :222 :462 :594ft *2½ 121 84½ 65 44½ 11¼ Yoakum J 3 Aw3800 88-16 GoStedyLd,StinsEgo,PrincBobbiD 10
22Apr89-6TuP 6f :214 :45 1:101ft 3 120 56 41 13 17 McGurn C9 Mdn 83-19 GoSteadyLad,Mnilius,PrivteEscort 10
22Apr89—Fractious at gate
Jly 31 LA 4f ft :534 H Jly 24 LA 3f ft :364 H Jly 2 Rui 5f ft 1:051 B Jun 25 Rui 7f ft 1:313 H

ESP: S.

Paceline: A noncontender. His Los Alamitos and Ruidoso Downs races are not credentials for success at a major southern California racetrack.

Got The Bug Ch. c. 3(Feb), by Naevus—Niponese Bug, by Wajima
STEVENS G L 116 Br.—Kanowsky V (Cal) 1989 2 1 0 0 $6,600
Own.—Crash H Tr.—Stepp William T $40,000 1988 0 M 0 0
Lifetime 2 1 0 0 $6,600
7Aug89-5Dmr 6f :211 :441 1:091ft 20 114 811 811 812 816½ Pedroza MA6 Aw32000 75-15 M Single M,Doncareer,LoadedJuan 8
28Jly89-9LA 6f :214 :452 1:104ft 6 1105 42½ 2nk 12½ 14¾ Nakatani C S2 M32000 89-15 GotTheBug,ElGrnSid,ChuckNAgin 10
Jly 26 SA 3f ft :352 Hg Jly 22 SA 4f ft :473 Hg Jly 14 SA 5f ft 1:023 H Jly 6 SA 5f ft 1:012 H

Another noncontender. His one try at Del Mar showed a distinct lack of talent.

First Loyalty B. c. 3(Mar), by Top Command—Ellis Island, by First Landing
PATTON D B 116 Br.—Financial C (Ky) 1989 9 1 1 1 $25,300
Own.—Freed R Tr.—Wilmot William B $40,000 1988 2 1 0 0 $16,500
Lifetime 11 2 1 1 $41,800
1Aug89-10LA 6½f :221 :461 1:163ft 2¾ 115 99 85½ 75¾ 70¾ Black C A7 [R]Mcfdn 83-13 ‡Charlatan,SnowPerch,BearInMind 9
1Aug89—Placed sixth through disqualification
24Jly89-7Hol 6f :221 :451 1:09 ft 4¼ 116 75½ 65¼ 76¼ 69 Black C A5 50000 87-11 JklinLomLd,AgittdMk,WorkTllDwn 7
13May89-1GG 6f :214 :45 1:103ft 2¼ 117 43 32 22 1½ Patton D B3 Aw20000 86-19 First Loyalty, Mr. Don, Vote 6

6Mar89-3Hol　6f :22　:45 1:094ft　2½ 116　86½ 74½ 54　33¾　Guerra W A⁸　62500 80-09 Gntlmn'sStyl,NmbrOnTto,FrstLylty 9
21Apr89-3SA　6f :214 :442 1:093ft　*2 117　44　44½ 42½ 2¾　Pincay L Jr³　c50000 89-17 ClvrSpch,FirstLoylty,MgicJohnson 7
　21Apr89—Broke in a tangle; finished wide
24Mar89-7SA　6f :221 :46 1:102ft　6 118　21½ 42　45　410½　Meza R Q²　62500 75-20 Dmskim,MisonMestro,CleverSpech 7
　24Mar89—Broke through gate
2Mar89-7SA　6½f:213 :443 1:152sy　29 119　2ʰᵈ 3¹　55　512½　Meza R Q³　Aw32000 81-18 SundySilenc,HroicTyp,MightBRight 7
5Feb89-5SA　1 :463 1:123 1:40¹sy　13 118　3½　3⁴ 6¹⁴ 825¾　Meza R Q⁵　Aw35000 41-20 Bbyitscoldoutside,Copt,BrirticChif 9
　5Feb89—Veered out start; lugged out badly 7/8
Jly 20 SA 5f ft 1:00⁴ H　　●Jly 14 SA 5f ft :59⁴ H　　●Jly 8 SA 5f ft :59¹ H　　Jly 2 SA 4f ft :47 H

ESP: S. His earlier races indicated an early pace style, but maturity and declining form have contributed to a sustained running style.

Paceline: None. His last two races are dull efforts against horses similar to those he's facing today.

Jet Echo　　Ch. g. 3(Mar), by If This Be So—Jetting Polly, by Tri Jet
BAZE R A　　　Br.—Hooper F W (Fla)　　　　　1989 5 1 0 1　　$15,050
Own.—Bronson & Russell　118　Tr.—Russell John W　$40,000　1988 2 M 0 0　　$625
　　　　　Lifetime　7 1 0 1　$15,675
10Aug89-3Dmr　1 :462 1:11 1:353ft　19 116　42　32 55½ 511¾　Baze R A⁸　Aw35000 76-20 Splurger, True Potential, Histrion 9
24Jly89-7Hol　6f :221 :451 1:09 ft　9½ 116　65½ 76½ 65½ 56½　DelahoussayeE² 50000 89-11 JklinLomLd,AgittdMk,WorkTllDwn 7
10Jly89-6Hol　6f :214 :45 1:10 ft　*1 116　3½ 2ʰᵈ 12 13　Stevens G L⁸　M40000 91-12 Jet Echo, Prospector'sHoçe,LeRoc 8
25Jun89-4Hol　1 :451 1:102 1:354ft　27 116　2ʰᵈ 3½ 55¾ 511¼　Delahoussaye E³ Mdn 72-19 EdgyDiplomat,KingArmour,Brcoy 10
8Jun89-6Hol　6f :223 :454 1:104ft　15 115　64 65½ 45½ 33　Solis A¹　M32000 84-14 Chaldean, SerranoDancer,JetEcho 12
21Aug88-6Dmr　1 :461 1:114 1:38 ft　9½ 116　64¾ 53½ 66¾ 67½　McCarron C J⁵　Mdn 70-12 Hwkster,FriendlyEd,EdgyDiplomt 10
27Jly88-6Dmr　5½f:212 :443 1:024ft　83 117　8⁹ 78½ 69½ 510½　Baze R A⁴　Mdn 87-11 Sabulose, Texian, Friendly Ed 11
Aug 19 Dmr 5f ft :59⁴ H　Aug 7 Dmr 5f ft 1:01³ H　Aug 1 Dmr 5f ft 1:03¹ H　Jly 20 Hol 5f ft 1:02¹ H

ESP: S. His maiden win was accomplished in excellent time and with a pressing style. His other races do not support anything other than a weak S designation. The two races following the maiden win are each weaker than the previous, not a promising sign.

Paceline: None.

Contenders

(1) Brilliantized E/P
(2) Fiesta Del Sol P
(3) Rindo Try S
(4) Black Duzy S
(5) Olympic Brat E

Feet-Per-Second Array

Once again, a quick review:

Brilliantized	21.4	44.4	1:10.2
BL	0.5	1.5	0

1Fr	1320 − 5 or 1315 / 21.8 = 60.32 fps
2Fr	1320 − 10 or 1310 / 23.0 = 56.95 fps
3Fr	1320 + 15 or 1335 / 25.6 = 52.14 fps
EP	2640 − 15 or 2625 / 44.8 = 58.59 fps
SP	58.59 + 52.14 / 2 = 55.37
AP	60.32 + 56.95 + 52.14 / 3 = 56.47
FX	60.32 + 52.14 / 2 = 56.23

	1Fr	2Fr	3Fr	AP	EP	SP	FX
Brilliantized	60.32	56.95	52.14	56.47	58.59	55.37	56.23
Fiesta Del Sol	58.69	57.41	54.30	56.79	58.03	56.17	56.49
Rindo Try	58.40	57.54	53.17	56.36	57.96	55.56	55.79
Black Duzy	58.48	57.82	52.34	56.21	58.14	55.24	55.41
Olympic Brat	59.45	56.89	53.65	56.65	58.14	55.90	56.55

Ranking the Contenders

Let's sort the race by the four compounded ratings: Average Pace, Early Pace, Sustained Pace, and Factor X.

	AP	EP	SP	FX
Fiesta Del Sol	1	4	1	2
Olympic Brat	2	2	2	1
Brilliantized	3	1	4	3
Rindo Try	4	5	3	4
Black Duzy	5	2	5	5

As with the previous example, I caution the handicapper not to focus only on the ranking categories. Remember, these races are being won by horses close to the pace and possessing

E and P running styles. First let's focus on probable second-call (EP) position.

Early Pace:

Brilliantized	58.59
Olympic Brat	58.14
Black Duzy	58.14
Fiesta Del Sol	58.03
Rindo Try	57.96

We began this race by stipulating that we'd accept no horse as a bet unless they figured to be within .75 fps (3 lengths) at the second call. At this point we'll eliminate only Rindo Try as a betting possibility. Rindo Try is close to the cutoff but is labeled an S and will probably position himself toward the rear of the field.

I've cautioned several times not to become overdependent on the computer output. Black Duzy is an excellent example of the danger of blindly accepting the readouts. His 2 ranking in Early Pace is misleading and should not be accepted at face value. We gave him an S designation, and if correct, he should be positioned mid-pack at the second call. If your decision is to bet the top early pace horses, consider his running style before using him as an "early" horse.

Only three horses remain in this scenario: Brilliantized, Olympic Brat, and Fiesta Del Sol. Each possesses the proper running style and enough early pace ability to be well positioned at the second call. The leader, based on the velocity ratings, should be Brilliantized. With his versatility of running style, however, don't be surprised to see him placed behind Olympic Brat should that one be gunned for the lead.

The Bet

Exclusive of daily variant considerations, Fiesta Del Sol and Olympic Brat possess most of the top rankings from the rating categories. Both will be close enough to the early pace to effectively "police" Brilliantized and avoid possible runaway tactics. Exacta players will probably use all three of the main contenders.

The Race

Most Del Mar sprints were won exactly in the manner of this race. The first three horses to hit the second call were also the first three finishers. The only surprise was the 16–1 on Olympic Brat. The betting public must have reasoned that the maiden claiming race he was exiting was inferior to the company he was facing today. That's generally true. But occasionally the speed and pace figures from those races are competitive with claiming winners, and handicappers must be prepared to make allowances. Those unwilling to back recent maiden claimers missed both the top finishers in favor of a bet on Brilliantized. At least he was a strong contender.

SEVENTH RACE
Del Mar
AUGUST 25, 1989

6 FURLONGS. (1.07⅗) CLAIMING. Purse $27,000. 3-year-olds. Weight, 121 lbs. Non-winners of two races since July 1, allowed 3 lbs.; of a race since then, 5 lbs. Claiming price $40,000; if for $35,000, allowed 2 lbs. (Races when entered for $32,000 or less not considered.)

Value of race $27,000; value to winner $14,850; second $5,400; third $4,050; fourth $2,025; fifth $675. Mutuel pool $320,616. Exacta Pool $396,413.

Last Raced	Horse	Eqt.	A. Wt	PP	St	¼	½	Str	Fin	Jockey	Cl'g Pr	Odds $1
10Aug89 ^{3}Dmr^{6}	Fiesta Del Sol	b	3 116	4	8	$4^{\frac{1}{2}}$	$3^{1\frac{1}{2}}$	3^{2}	$1^{\frac{1}{2}}$	Delahoussaye E	40000	3.30
12Aug89 ^{1}Dmr^{1}	Olympic Brat	b	3 116	8	3	$2^{1\frac{1}{2}}$	$2^{1\frac{1}{2}}$	$2^{\frac{1}{2}}$	$2^{\frac{3}{4}}$	Pedroza M A	40000	16.60
13Aug89 ^{2}Dmr^{1}	Brilliantized	b	3 117	1	4	$1^{\frac{1}{2}}$	1^{1}	$1^{1\frac{1}{2}}$	$3^{3\frac{1}{2}}$	Pincay L Jr	40000	3.40
13Aug89 ^{2}Dmr^{2}	Black Duzy	b	3 116	7	5	5^{1}	5^{hd}	$5^{1\frac{1}{2}}$	4^{nk}	Black C A	40000	10.50
4Jun89 ^{7}Hol^{6}	Maison Maestro	b	3 116	2	11	$8^{\frac{1}{2}}$	4^{hd}	4^{1}	5^{2}	Toro F	40000	7.00
16Aug89 ^{5}Dmr^{5}	Rindo Try	b	3 118	6	9	$10^{1\frac{1}{2}}$	9^{3}	$6^{1\frac{1}{2}}$	$6^{1\frac{3}{4}}$	Valenzuela P A	40000	11.10
10Aug89 ^{3}Dmr^{5}	Jet Echo		3 118	12	2	9^{1}	7^{hd}	$8^{\frac{1}{2}}$	7^{hd}	Baze R A	40000	7.50
16Aug89 ^{5}Dmr^{8}	Number One Tuto	b	3 111	3	10	$7^{\frac{1}{2}}$	8^{hd}	$9^{1\frac{1}{2}}$	$8^{1\frac{1}{2}}$	Castanon J L^{5}	40000	6.50
10Aug89 ^{6}LA^{1}	Go Steady Lad	b	3 111	9	6	3^{hd}	6^{1}	7^{hd}	$9^{2\frac{1}{2}}$	Jauregui L H^{5}	40000	15.50
1Aug89 ^{10}LA^{6}	First Loyalty		3 116	11	1	$11^{2\frac{1}{2}}$	$10^{1\frac{1}{2}}$	10^{4}	10^{6}	Patton D B	40000	31.70
7Aug89 ^{5}Dmr^{8}	Got The Bug		3 116	10	7	6^{hd}	11^{4}	11^{6}	11^{8}	Stevens G L	40000	35.70
6Apr89 ^{11}TuP^{5}	Eager Play		3 114	5	12	12	12	12	12	Garrido O L	35000	114.50

OFF AT 5:21. Start good. Won driving. Time, :22, :44⅘, :56⅘, 1:09⅘ Track fast.

$2 Mutuel Prices:			
4-FIESTA DEL SOL	8.60	5.60	3.60
8-OLYMPIC BRAT		13.20	7.20
1-BRILLIANTIZED			3.20

$5 EXACTA 4-8 PAID $272.00.

B. g, (Mar), by Habitony—Princess Torsion, by Torsion. Trainer Jery Ian. Bred by Mabee Mr–Mrs J C (Cal).

FIESTA DEL SOL, never far back, came on to engage for the lead leaving the sixteenth marker and had the needed late response to prevail. OLYMPIC BRAT forced the early pace, also came on to engage for the lead leaving the sixteenth marker and gained the place. BRILLIANTIZED, a pace factor from the outset, could not outfinish the top two. BLACK DUZY was four wide into the stretch. MAISON MAESTRO, well back early after being bumped and pinched back in the first few strides, advanced to reach contention on the far turn, saved ground on the far turn, then did not have the necessary further response in the drive. RINDO TRY was bumped in the initial strides. JET ECHO, wide down the backstretch, was five wide into the stretch. NUMBER ONE TUTO was bumped and shuffled back in the first few strides. GO STEADY LAD, close up early, gave way and was five wide into the stretch. FIRST LOYALTY, wide down the backstretch, was six wide into the stretch. GOT THE BUG, in contention early, was done after three furlongs. EAGER PLAY broke a bit awkwardly and was bumped in the opening strides.

"FROM A SPRINT TO A ROUTE AND BACK AGAIN"

Probably the most difficult of all handicapping problems is determining which sprinters will route successfully and which will not. Aside from breeding and basic running style, handicappers have little data upon which to base a decision. In the chapter

"Energy Distribution" we'll base our evaluation of probable route performance on how a horse distributes its available energy in sprint races. From that data it's possible to be remarkably accurate in assessing distance capabilities of first-time routers and horses stretching out after a series of sprint races. Energy distribution patterns do not, however, gauge *how fast* a horse will route.

Traditional handicapping methods usually employ parallel time charts to answer the central question of how fast a sprinter can be expected to route. In the absence of a suitable route paceline upon which to base a decision, handicappers attempt to match the rate of velocity in a sprint race to a comparable rate of velocity in a route. For example, the following material is excerpted from a later chapter on par-time charts (fractional times are in tenths of seconds, final times in fifths:

100   22.2   45.2   1:10.3   46.8   1:11.6   1:44.2   100

The class level 100 is for $10,000 claiming horses and represents the par for winning performances at Hollywood Park. In theory, a horse running a six-furlong race in 1:10.3 should also run a route in 1:44.2. "In theory" is a key phrase here. What's missing from this, or any other par-time chart, is the horse's willingness and capability of extending beyond a sprint distance.

Use of the chart to project a sprinter's probable route performance implies that handicappers are realistic in their assessment of capability and are prepared to be wrong a fair percentage of the time. With that in mind, let's develop the sprint-to-route adjustments for our feet-per-second ratings.

SPRINT TO ROUTE

The procedure is actually quite simple and is based on the pars for any class level at your racetrack. We'll use the $10,000 claiming par at Hollywood Park to develop the adjustments. In subsequent chapters we'll discuss the procedure for developing pars for any racetrack(s). Fractions are in tenths, final times in fifths:

100   22.2   45.2   1:10.3   46.8   1:11.6   1:44.2   100

The first step is to determine the numerical ratings for Early Pace, Sustained Pace, and Average Pace for the two par times. We'll use the array from earlier in the chapter:

	1Fr	2Fr	3Fr	AP	EP	SP	FX
Sprint Par	59.45	57.39	51.96	56.26	58.40	55.18	n/a
Route Par	56.41	53.22	50.30	54.05	55.30	52.80	n/a

To accurately assess the probable route performance of the sprinter, we should adjust the three "ratings" by each of the numerical differences. That will require the use of *three* separate sprint-route adjustments.

Consider the three pace ratings we use to select winners:

	AP	EP	SP
Sprint Par	56.26	58.40	55.18
Route Par	54.05	55.30	52.80
Diff.	2.21	3.10	2.38

The numerical differences between the sprint and route ratings are considerable. For the sake of simplicity, most fps methods *do* employ a single adjustment, but to average the three is to create needless error in each. With a little extra effort we can do better. At Hollywood Park, for sprinters matched against routers, this author applies the following adjustments to the *sprinter's* ratings:

Average Pace	−2.20
Early Pace	−3.10
Sustained Pace	−2.40

Example: A sprinter is entered in a route with the following paceline:

6F	22.2	45.3	1:11.1
BL	3	2	1

	1Fr	2Fr	3Fr	AP	EP	SP	FX
Sprint	57.59	57.32	51.95	55.62	57.45	54.70	n/a
Sprint-route adjustments:				−2.20	−3.10	−2.40	
Adjusted ratings:				53.42	54.35	52.30	

With the adjustments, at least we're in the ball park when it's time to match the sprinters and the routers. If you've properly evaluated the sprinter's suitability to a route, the ratings should serve well in application. Fortunately, not all routes mix sprinters and routers, and the numbers of runners requiring sprint-to-route adjustments are minimal.

Fractional Adjustments

Any adjustments to the sprinter's fractions will be unsatisfactory. The first fraction of a sprint is 1320 feet and is run at top speed by competitors. The route is run immediately into a turn, with riders employing rating tactics to save as much horse as possible. Why attempt to equate such dissimilar circumstances?

The second fraction, while the same distance in both races (1320 feet), occurs after the router has already traveled a half-mile; the sprinter only a quarter-mile.

Final fractions also occur after entirely dissimilar trips. Any attempt to equate them is simply a case of apples and oranges; the margin of error is too large for us to base decisions on internal match-ups.

In short, don't adjust the sprinter's fractions. Just use the adjusted pace ratings and energy distribution patterns of contenders to evaluate the chances of sprinters in routes.

ROUTE TO SPRINT

The opposite problem. Fortunately, the solution is much simpler and more reliable. It is acceptable to reverse sprint-to-route adjustments when routers are competing at seven furlongs. Providing the router shows enough speed to be competitive at the shorter distance, reversing the adjustments will produce its fair share of winners. Simply *add* your three adjustments to each of the pace ratings.

At sprint distances shorter than seven furlongs, reversing the sprint-to-route adjustments is an unsatisfactory application. The dissimilarity of the distance structures (sprints vs routes) is just too great. Horses without front-running speed in routes have little chance in most sprint races, no matter what their route rating. The Sartin Methodology handles the problem quite satisfactorily.

Before accepting the router as a contender in a sprint, handicappers must satisfy themselves that the horse has enough speed to compete at the shorter distance. Mid-pack routers are usually deep closers in sprints, a losing play at most racetracks. Front-running routers, to be forwardly placed in sprints, must show high route speed or be relegated to the role of mid-pack closer. Once satisfied with the sprint potential of the router, the handicapper can apply the following procedure.

(1) The *final time* of the new paceline will be the second call of the route *minus 2 lengths*, thus compensating for the nearness of the turn and rating tactics of the route.

(2) The *second call* of the new line will be the first fraction of the route, *also minus 2 lengths.*

(3) The *first fraction* of the contrived sprint line is one half the new second call, *minus 1 length* (round downward).

(4) *Beaten lengths* for each of the calls are halved for the new line. This is not as severe as it may first sound. If the router shows many beaten lengths in the internal fractions of the route, handicappers should question their use of the horse as a contender in a sprint race.

It's actually a very simple procedure and has produced consistent profits for this author from season to season.

Take a route that shows the following paceline:

8½F	46.1	1:10.4	1:44.1
BL	2	2	5

(1) *Final time:* 1:10.4 (route second call) minus 2 lengths = 1:10.2

(2) *Second call:* 46.1 (route first fraction) minus 2 lengths = 45.4

(3) *First fraction:* 45.4 (45.8) divided by 2 = 22.9

minus one length (two tenths) = 22.7
rounded downward = 22.6 = *22.3*

(4) *Final beaten lengths:* BL at each of the route calls, halved for the new line, are *one* at each call.

Finally, use the beaten lengths at the second call of the new paceline as beaten lengths at the first fraction of the new line.

The router's paceline for today's sprint race:

6F	22.3	45.4	1:10.2
BL	1	1	1

A PRACTICAL EXAMPLE—10DEC89

The following race was for three-year-old claimers at six furlongs.

3rd Hollywood

START
6 FURLONGS
HOLLYWOOD PARK
FINISH

6 FURLONGS. (1.08) CLAIMING. Purse $19,000. 3-year-olds. Weight, 122 lbs. Non-winners of two races since October 22 allowed 3 lbs.; a race since then, 6 lbs. Claiming price $40,000; for each $2,500 to $35,000 allowed 2 lbs. (Races when entered for $32,000 or less not considered.)

Ask The Man — Ch. g. 3(May), by Glamor Kid—Bubblin Belle, by Wild Lark
STEVENS G L 116 — Br.—Proctor J & W L (Tex) — 1989 8 2 1 0 $35,885
Tr.—Canani Julio C $40,000 — Turf 1 0 0 0 $1,025
Own.—Doe-Segal-Vallone et al — Lifetime 8 2 1 0 $35,885

15Nov89-5Hol 1$\frac{1}{16}$:45^3 1:10^1 1:42^{3}ft 3$\frac{1}{2}$ 116 3^{nk} 2^{hd} 31$\frac{1}{2}$ 6^{11} Stevens G L^6 50000 76-19 RacingRascal,WellAware,M'gnetized 8
15Nov89—Broke in a tangle
3Nov89-9SA 1$\frac{1}{16}$:47 1:11^3 1:42^{4}ft *8-5 116 31$\frac{1}{2}$ 3$\frac{1}{2}$ 31$\frac{1}{2}$ 44$\frac{3}{4}$ Sibille R^7 40000 85-14 RdrAlert,GhettoBuster,Nn'sHppiStr 7
3Nov89—Wide 7/8 turn
25Oct89-7SA 1 :45^2 1:10^1 1:36^{3}ft *3-2 116 7^{10} 57$\frac{1}{2}$ 56$\frac{1}{2}$ 66$\frac{3}{4}$ Stevens G L^8 50000 79-21 ScoutOfFortune,JustDeeds,WllAwr 9
25Oct89—Off very slowly
30Sep89-10Fpx 6$\frac{1}{2}$f :21^3 :45 1.17 ft 3$\frac{1}{4}$ 111 31$\frac{1}{2}$ 31$\frac{1}{2}$ 2^{hd} 24$\frac{1}{2}$ Castanon JL^1 Aw33000 86-13 Charlatan,AskTheMn,CleverReturn 7
8Sep89-3Dmr 1 ⓣ:47^{4}1:12^{1}1:37 fm 4$\frac{3}{4}$ 116 2^{hd} 1^{hd} 1$\frac{1}{2}$ 55$\frac{1}{4}$ Sibille R^1 80000 81-14 Strogien, Beau's Alliance, Lyscent 6
8Sep89—Rank 7/8 turn
30Aug89-5Dmr 1 :44^4 1:09^3 1:36 ft 3$\frac{1}{4}$ 116 2^{hd} 1^2 1^3 1^2 Sibille R^1 c40000 86-13 AskThMn,BtOutOfHll,Bonri'sMrk 10
7Aug89-5Dmr 6f :21^1 :44^1 1:09^{1}ft 3$\frac{1}{4}$ 115 4^5 52$\frac{3}{4}$ 42$\frac{1}{2}$ 4^5 Sibille R^7 Aw32000 87-15 M Single M,Doncareer,LoadedJuan 8
4Jly89-4Hol 6f :22^1 :45^2 1:10^{2}ft 5 116 2$\frac{1}{2}$ 2^{hd} 12$\frac{1}{2}$ 16$\frac{1}{2}$ Sibille R^{10} M32000 89-12 AskThMn,ChopmOnThBd,B.J.Bcks 12

Speed Index: Last Race: -1.0 3-Race Avg.: +0.6 3-Race Avg.: +0.6 Overall Avg.: -1.2
Dec 5 Hol 5f ft 1:00^2 H Nov 29 Hol 5f ft 1:03 H Nov 23 Hol 3f ft :36^4 H ●Oct 20 SA 4f ft :46^4 H

Route paceline: 45.3 1:10.1 1:42.3
New final time: 1:10.1 minus 2 lengths = *1:09.4*
New 2Call time: 45.3 minus 2 lengths = 45.1
New 1Fr: 45.1 / 2 = 22.6 minus 1 length = 22.4 = *22.2*

The Feet-Per-Second Array

	1Fr	2Fr	3Fr	AP	EP	SP	FX	%E
Ask The Man	58.81	57.96	53.65	56.80	58.38	56.02	56.23	n/a
Maharesred	59.41	57.39	53.44	56.73	58.38	55.91	56.42	n/a
Por D.J.	59.09	57.60	53.20	56.62	58.33	55.76	56.14	n/a
Stadium Stud	58.46	56.95	54.08	56.49	57.69	55.88	56.27	n/a
Brilliantized	58.91	57.86	51.94	56.23	58.38	55.16	55.42	n/a

The Rankings

	AP	EP	SP	FX
Ask The Man	1	1	1	2
Maharesred	2	1	2	1
Por D.J.	3	4	4	4
Stadium Stud	4	5	2	2
Brilliantized	5	1	5	5

Ask The Man rates clearly best in the most important ratings: Average Pace, Early Pace, and Sustained Pace. The fractional array shows him close up the entire trip, with enough closing ability to outfinish the field. The only question is whether the internal fractions of a route transfer well to sprint races. You answer the question.

Note: Readers interested in obtaining the basic computer programs necessary to generate the fps numbers and compounded pace ratings may contact Dr. Howard Sartin at the following address:

PIRCO
1390 E. 6th St. #6
Beaumont, CA 92223

CHAPTER VI

Negative Class Drops

"Psst, hey buddy, com'ere." The raspy voice startles the handicapper and diverts his attention from the *Daily Racing Form.* A wiry little man with a plaid coat, plaid slacks, and a paisley shirt, is standing too close. The odor of stale beer, his cocktail-lounge pallor and leathery skin, dead giveaways as to his usual whereabouts. What could Harry the Hustler possibly want? "Got a deal for ya in the ninth race. There's this horse that's worth $32,000 we're giving away for only $10,000, and I want you to be the first to know."

What's the natural response to that scenario? A call to security? At the very least, you'd head in another direction. Certainly, we wouldn't consider buying into such a ridiculous situation. True? Maybe; maybe not. What if Harry changed his appearance and, through a more subtle approach, offered the same scenario? What if Harry appeared as a past performance in the *Racing Form?* Same basic situation, but now the handicapper may be willing to buy into what this little guy is selling. Ridiculous? Take a look at the past performances of Bicker Bear shown on the following page.

This is a figure handicapper's worst nightmare. Bicker Bear has the top rankings in nearly every rating category a handicapper could consider important to the outcome of a thoroughbred horse race. Yet he represents the "deal" previously offered. What if this disgusting little guy verbally presented the following argument:

"Bicker Bear was claimed for $20,000, a race he won, and then ran a powerful second in a NW1 allowance race at Del Mar. Equated to claiming values, an NW1 on the southern Cal-

10th Fairplex

6 FURLONGS. (1.08⅘) CLAIMING. Purse $13,000. 3-year-olds and upward. Weights, 3-year-olds, 117 lbs.; older, 122 lbs. Non-winners of two races since July 25, allowed 3 lbs.; of a race since then, 6 lbs. Claiming price $10,000. (Maiden, claiming and starter races for $8,500 or less not considered.)

Bicker Bear — B. g. 4, by Color Bearer—Bickeree, by Bicker
BLACK C A — 119 — Br.—Nielsen K G (Cal) — 1989 14 3 1 1 $41,550
Own.—Handicapping Kid Stable — Tr.—Hess R B Jr — $10,000 — 1988 2 1 0 0 $8,250
Lifetime 16 4 1 1 $49,800

27Aug89-3Dmr 6½f :22 :443 1:154ft 12 118 711 710 53¾ 2nk DlhoussyE 1 [S] Aw32000 89-15 JklinLomLd,BickerBer,IntoTheMot 8
27Aug89—Broke slowly
20Aug89-7Dmr 1 1/16 :454 1:10 1:414ft 6¾ 118 55½ 55½ 78½ 710½ Stevens GL 10 Aw35000 80-12 Eighty Eight Keys,Bracoy,Amatar 10
5Aug89-9Dmr 1 1/16 :461 1:11 1:433ft *3 116 73¾ 42½ 2hd 14½ Stevens G L 1 c20000 82-15 Bicker Bear, Nomad Boi,TresSuave 8
5Aug89—Wide into stretch
19Jly89-7Hol 7f :22 :443 1:224ft 4 117 76½ 64¾ 64¾ 43½ Stevens G L 2 25000 86-18 UndrAndOvr,Arn'sDn,Amnthrbrthr 9
19Jly89—Bumped hard break
30Jun89-8Hol 6½f :212 :441 1:162ft 12 119 611 610 57 47 StevensGL 4 [S] Aw30000 86-16 WickedIdea,ImperialLad,S-osTown 6
18Jun89-5Hol 6f :214 :45 1:101ft 4½ 115 107¾ 74¾ 32 11½ Stevens G L 5 20000 90-12 BickerBear,LansMnus,InspiredToo 12
18Jun89—Bumped at start
4Jun89-5Hol 1 :453 1:103 1:362ft 3½ 115 72½ 74¾ 53½ 44 Guerra W A 9 20000 77-14 MountLaguna,Polysemous,Kmikze 12
4Jun89—Wide final 3/8
17May89-5Hol 7f :221 :443 1:231ft 8½ 117 86¾ 75¾ 53½ 41 Guerra W A 1 [S] 16000 87-11 Polysemous, Uncle Foss,RareTyson 8
17May89—Steadied 1/16
6May89-1Hol 6½f :22 :444 1:16 ft 10 117 75¾ 74 35½ 34¾ Guerra W A 1 16000 90-09 WellInTheAir,ExplodedJr.,BickrBr 11
6May89—Altered course1/8
15Apr89-5SA 6f :211 :44 1:092ft 4½ 118 108 1011 913 811¾ Valenzuela P A 9 25000 79-15 WllB.Gold,KnKnght,HollywoodHys 10
15Apr89—Bumped start; wide into stretch
Sep 21 SA 5f ft 1:004 H — Sep 11 Dmr 5f ft 1:00 H — Jly 30 Dmr 5f ft :592 H
R. e. 5. by Formidable—Freia, by Rheingold

ifornia circuit is worth about $32,000." Such a deal! Thanks to Harry's generosity we can get $32,000 worth of racehorse for a measly $10,000! How long has this been going on? Let's push our way to the front of the line before the bargain disappears!

Bicker Bear was held at 6–5 odds until two minutes to post and then late money flowed in against the horse, driving him up to 2–1. At post time he was still the public favorite. He broke down before the half-mile and was vanned from the racetrack.

This is not an uncommon occurrence. Every day, at every track, the *Racing Form* past performances play the part of Harry the Hustler. They often mislead the betting public into mistakes that, if considered with a modicum of common sense, should never occur. Let's stay with Bicker Bear for a moment longer.

If the trainer of this horse had approached individual bettors in the same manner and style that Harry approached our hypothetical handicapper, would Bicker Bear have still been a solid race favorite? If the answer to that is yes, you don't have a lot of faith in your fellow man. Bicker Bear would have been shunned in the betting for the suspicious commodity that he was. Yet because the impartial *Racing Form* p.p.'s presented a black and white picture of the best horse, people jumped like lemmings into the sea.

Bicker Bear is one of the more obvious situations. There are many more subtle variations of the same basic theme: horses that look too good to be true.

While it is true the majority of races are won by horses dropping in class, there is a distinct difference between a positive drop and one that is clearly intended to rid a stable of a troublesome commodity. It is this second category that poses a major threat to our success as investors, by offering the promise of a quick and safe return on the bet. In actuality, there is no greater threat to our bankrolls; unless you include pickpockets and the IRS in that category. By way of recognition, I'm talking of the claiming horse that is winning or threatening—position at the stretch call is an excellent yardstick for gauging "threat"— to win at a higher level than today's class, and is now offered for sale at a reduced price. Invariably, this runner will look superior to today's field and will be highly ranked versus the other contenders in the race.

Harry the Hustler worked overtime on September 26 at Fairplex. In an earlier six-furlong race with a claiming price of $16,000, the public made the following horse a very heavy betting favorite:

Dial Dusty

Dial Dusty is a little more subtle. Although she clearly belongs at much higher claiming levels, the betting public will reason that she's "dropping for the money." In truth, she is.

Horses dropping in class win more than their fair share of races. During the period of August 1988 through March 1989,

57 percent of the claiming races in southern and northern California were won by horses dropping one or two levels in class. Therefore, class droppers should be given strong consideration. That's a given. But the overwhelming majority of those races were won by horses clearly *needing* a drop in class. In other words, horses successfully competing at the higher levels should not be dropped.

In the case of Dial Dusty, she's clearly worth the $25–32,000 she's been competing for. At $16,000 she should cause a long line at the claim box if she's undamaged goods. When horses are threatening to win at higher levels, it just doesn't make sense to "drop for the money." They already *have* the money!

Let's examine the record of Dial Dusty.

15Jun89 & 14Jly89

Her races on the Hollywood turf course indicated two things: (1) she did not like turf racing and (2) she was overmatched. The logical move was to return her to the dirt course and drop her back in with her "friends."

26Jly89 & 10Aug89

Both races showed sharp improvement and a class "fit" at the $32,000 level. The class drop was a positive one and should not have been cause for concern on the part of the handicapper. What else can be done when a horse lacks the ability to successfully compete at a higher level?

19Aug89 & 6Sep89

Now it's time to become concerned. She wins this sprint as the 2–1 favorite, but a three-year-old filly dropping off a win, or near win, is an especially negative sign. At three, most of her racing career is still in front of her, and it just doesn't make sense to begin discounting her value. Additionally, she's a win type, which should make the bargain price that much more attractive. Note that in her win and subsequent near miss on

6Sep89, no one claimed her; her problems must be well-documented.

26Sep89

On September 26 trainer Spawr could not have sent a clearer message: this horse is seriously damaged goods. Bettors might just as well have received personal telegrams announcing her condition. Yet they lined up in droves to force the filly to odds-on, leaving all the other contenders at overlaid prices. She finished up the track and proceeded to do the same thing in her next race, also at a short price. In the September 26 race bettors could have bet *all* the other contenders and shown a significant profit. This happens every day at every track in the country.

The next horse should be even more obvious.

26Apr89

A sensational maiden win. The second-place finisher stepped up to a maiden $50,000 and won convincingly, validating Shelter Us's performance. On 10May89, he moved up in class and won a $40,000 claiming race in the excellent time of 1:16.0 for 6½ furlongs. This is a developing youngster.

26May89

The positive thing to do; jump him in class or risk losing the horse at the claiming box. He responded with a big race, losing a photo in the closing strides. Now, interject yourself into the role of trainer and visualize the conditions of his next start. At the very least, another try at the $62,500 level. If he's still on the improve, why not try NW1 allowance horses? There are several options, the least of which would be a drop in class. Gary Jones is one of the finest trainers on the southern California circuit and is noted for placing his horses where they belong. So, what does he do with Shelter Us?

The horse's reappearance, after 50 days, was in another $40,000 claiming race; a drop of $22,500! With the For Sale sign clearly around his neck, Shelter Us staggered home at $3.20. The second and third finishers encountered much trouble on the backstretch before nearly wearing him down in the final fraction.

30Jly89

Another negative drop in class. This time even the most inexperienced bettor should have been alerted that something was seriously wrong. I caution the reader to begin to avoid these short-priced decliners at the first opportunity. Once the class slide begins, there's no way of knowing to what depths the horse will eventually sink. The right play is a horse, especially a three-year-old, on the way up the class ladder. The negative droppers are seriously overbet. If the trainer is apparently giving up on the horse, it doesn't make sense for the bettor to do otherwise.

Shelter Us lost at even money.

25Aug89

Today's race. He's in for $16,000, the bottom level for a southern California three-year-old. The public wises up, right? They finally get the idea, and avoid the horse in favor of other betting opportunities, right? Nope, they hammer the horse down to a short-priced favorite and watch him lose again.

Let's sum up the betting action on Shelter Us: three bets at short prices. The public cashed once for $3.20. Think I was exaggerating when I described the influence of Harry the Hustler? Not for a minute.

The handicapper willing to deal aggressively with suspect class droppers is well ahead of the game. At first, it's not an easy thing to do. Most often the dropper has all the important numbers from class to pace to speed. The betting public, in their haste to capitalize on a "good thing," exerts enormous pressure as well. As the price falls, most players have difficulty maintaining their resolve. After all, if that many people feel otherwise, who am I to go against the grain? Crowd opinion, as reliable as it may be in the long run, is incredibly naive when dealing with suspect favorites.

And that's precisely what you're after: the betting public's commitment to a false favorite. Do not take the tack that dropdowns make the race unplayable. The opposite is true. Consider the amount of betting probability that disappears when an odds-on doesn't figure to win. Horses that should be 3–1 are 5–1; legitimate 5–1 shots are 10–1; 10–1 shots are 20–1; and so on. Run, don't walk, to the betting windows and take advantage of the bargain: betting against the suspicious drop-down. They occasionally win, as did Shelter Us, but the prices are ridiculously low and will never compensate for the short-priced losers.

Take a look at the past performances of the filly Summer Ambo, the even-money favorite on June 4, 1989.

Julio Canani's charge is a perfect example of the dilemma we face as handicappers. We can all see the following: a top trainer, a top rider, a perfect distance, and a drop to a level this filly should handle without drawing a deep breath. The purse is hers for the taking, right? *Wrong.* This filly is taking an extremely negative class drop and, despite holding most of the 1's in our ranking categories, should be avoided like the plague. Put yourself in Canani's shoes for a moment and reason your way through the situation. Let's go through this together.

Granted, they only paid $25,000 for this filly, but she has clearly established greater worth through her narrow losses in the $50–60,000 range. With the ability to earn major shares at much higher purse levels, why should she drop to today's level? Do you suppose someone has information that the general public doesn't? The answer to that question seems to be obvious: of course they do.

This is no longer the filly showing in the past performances, and will probably be claimed on the drop, drowning many players in the process. You should note, in most instances, trainers claiming this type of dropper are not the leading claiming trainers on your circuit. The good ones are especially sensitive to improving versus declining horses; their livelihoods are at stake.

FOURTH RACE
Hollywood
JUNE 4, 1989

1 $\frac{1}{16}$ MILES. (1.40) CLAIMING. Purse $17,000. Fillies and mares. 4-year-olds and upward. Weight, 122 lbs. Non-winners of two races at a mile or over since April 16, allowed 3 lbs, such a race since then, 6 lbs. Claiming price $25,000; if for $22,500, allowed 2 lbs. (Races when entered for $20,000 or less not considered.)

Value of race $17,000; value to winner $9,350; second $3,400; third $2,550; fourth $1,275; fifth $425. Mutuel pool $378,139. Exacta Pool $472,296.

Last Raced	Horse	Eqt	A.	Wt	PP	St	¼	½	¾	Str	Fin	Jockey	Cl'g Pr	Odds $1
24May89 1Hol1	Broad Street		7	117	4	1	$4^{1\frac{1}{2}}$	$4^{1\frac{1}{2}}$	$4^{\frac{1}{2}}$	$1^{1\frac{1}{2}}$	$1^{2\frac{1}{2}}$	Pincay L Jr	25000	3.80
24May89 9Hol1	Exodus From Rome	b	5	119	7	6	7^{6}	7^{7}	$5^{2\frac{1}{2}}$	$5^{3\frac{1}{2}}$	$2^{\frac{3}{4}}$	Baze R A	25000	7.30
12May89 3Hol4	Arcady Miss	b	4	116	8	7	3^{1}	$3^{\frac{1}{2}}$	$3^{2\frac{1}{2}}$	$2^{\frac{1}{2}}$	$3^{1\frac{1}{2}}$	Valenzuela P A	25000	7.80
18May89 6Hol1	Snow Spirit		4	114	3	8	8	8	8	$7^{\frac{1}{2}}$	4^{nk}	Garcia H J5	25000	49.40
18May89 7Hol3	Summer Ambo	b	4	116	5	2	$1^{1\frac{1}{2}}$	$1^{2\frac{1}{2}}$	1^{hd}	$3^{1\frac{1}{2}}$	5^{3}	Stevens G L	25000	1.00
10May89 5Hol2	Playing Taps	b	5	116	2	5	$6^{\frac{1}{2}}$	6^{hd}	6^{hd}	$6^{\frac{1}{2}}$	$6^{\frac{1}{2}}$	Black C A	25000	24.10
13May89 5Hol5	Retrograde		4	116	6	3	$2^{1\frac{1}{2}}$	$2^{1\frac{1}{2}}$	$2^{\frac{1}{2}}$	4^{2}	$7^{6\frac{1}{2}}$	McCarron C J	25000	9.70
24May89 1Hol2	Lady Charmin	b	4	116	1	4	$5^{2\frac{1}{2}}$	$5^{\frac{1}{2}}$	$7^{3\frac{1}{2}}$	8	8	Delahoussaye E	25000	9.10

OFF AT 3:13. Start good. Won ridden out. Time, $:22\frac{4}{5}$, $:46\frac{1}{5}$, $1:11\frac{3}{5}$, $1:37\frac{4}{5}$, $1:44\frac{4}{5}$ Track fast.

$2 Mutuel Prices:			
4-BROAD STREET	9.60	5.00	3.40
7-EXODUS FROM ROME		7.40	5.20
8-ARCADY MISS			5.00

$2 EXACTA 4–7 PAID $61.40.

Dk. b. or br. m, by Austin Mittler—Clemency, by George Lewis. Trainer Lage Armando. Bred by Magerman A P (Cal).

BROAD STREET, outrun early, got through along the inner rail to take command in the upper stretch, had a clear lead at the furlong marker and maintained a clear advantage through the final furlong. EXODUS FROM ROME, devoid of early speed and wide down the backstretch, came into the stretch five wide and rallied to gain the place. ARCADY MISS, never far back after being a bit slow to begin, engaged for the lead a quarter of a mile out while three wide but weakened a bit in the drive after entering the stretch four wide. SNOW SPIRIT, far back while trailing early, came into the stretch four wide, gained in the drive but found her best stride too late. SUMMER AMBO, the early pacesetter, weakened in the drive. RETROGRADE prompted the early pace, vied for the lead around the far turn, then gave way in the drive. LADY CHARMIN had no apparent mishap.

Owners— 1. Byrne III & Carr; 2. B C L Rcng St-Rss-TtrlEtal; 3. Friendly E; 4. Erickson R & Avis; 5. Doe-Segal-Vallone et al; 6. Jahnke C R; 7. Hollendorfer & Madden; 8. Alesia & Cappelli.
Trainers— 1. Lage Armando; 2. Ellis Ronald W; 3. Fulton Jacque; 4. Moreno Henry; 5. Canani Julio C; 6. Guidos John; 7. Sadler John W; 8. Eurton Pete.
Overweight: Broad Street 1 pound.
Broad Street was claimed by Gravina R; trainer, Carava Jack.

Let's look at a couple more examples; they appear several times on just about every racing card.

6th Hollywood

6 FURLONGS. (1.08) CLAIMING. Purse $15,000. 3-year-olds. Weight, 122 lbs. Non-winners or two races since April 23, allowed 3 lbs.; a race since then, 6 lbs. Claiming price $20,000; if for $18,000, allowed 2 lbs. (Races when entered for $16,000 or less not considered.)

Rudee's Great Legs			Gr. c. 3, by Swing Till Dawn—Jeanne Behave, by Ambehaving						
CORTEZ A		116	Br.—Backer J W (Ky)			1989 4 1 1 1			$16,050
Own.—Koch Ruth			Tr.—State Melvin F	$20,000		1988 1 M 0 0			
			Lifetime 5 1 1 1 $16,050						
18May89-5Hol	6½f :22 :45 1:16 ft	9½ 119	3½ 2nd 12 21	Valenzuela P A 5	32000	94-07	RestlessGlxy,Rud'sGrtLgs,BlckDuzy7
5May89-5Hol	1 :45¹ 1:10¹ 1:36 ft	16 116	3nk 64 91⁰ 915½	Guerra W A 2	32000	67-16	‡SySyBoom,RcerRex,MliciousPrtnr 9
6Apr89-2SA	6f :21¹ :44¹ 1:104ft	3½ 118	22½ 21 1hd 13½	ValenzuelPA 11	M32000	84-14	Rud'sGrtLgs,BcklUndr,CorgosPrt 12
6Apr89—Lugged in late							
9Feb89-2SA	6f :22 :45² 1:114sy	4½ 118	2nd 32 32½ 35½	Black C A 5	M32000	73-24	RockSukr,PunctlLord,Rd'sGrtLgs 12
1Jly88-4Hol	6f :22 :45³ 1:121ft	10 117	1211129½111³11114½	Black C A9	M50000	66-17	ThrTmsOldr,JstBogn'By,ClstClwn 12
1Jly88—Veered out sharply start; wide 3/8							
Jun 6 Hol 3f ft :38² H		May 31 Hol 5f ft 1:01¹ H		May 25 Hol 4f ft :49⁴ H		May 16 Hol 3f ft :38 H	

Rudee's Great Legs appears to be an improving three-year-old, whom I made a "Horse to Watch" off his narrow loss at $32,000 on 18May89, just 20 days before today's start. This guy is bet down to cofavorite at 5–2 and has the figure to justify a probable bet; at least it seems that way. But why don't we stop and ask a simple question: What would *we* do with a young horse with a clearly established worth of $32,000? With all the sharp trainers waiting to gobble up any reasonable value, I think we should run Rudee at $40,000 or stand the risk of winding up with an empty stall. That would be the sound tactic, *unless* we know that "Harry" is at work again and the past performances aren't telling the whole story. If that's the situation, the trainer is probably using this opportunity to unload damaged goods by offering a "too good to be true" bargain. You can see from the results that this guy not only lost, but wound up with a new owner as well. Of the three claims in the race, only Rudee was claimed by a low-percentage trainer.

SIXTH RACE
Hollywood
JUNE 7, 1989

6 FURLONGS. (1.08) CLAIMING. Purse $15,000. 3-year-olds. Weight, 122 lbs. Non-winners of two races since April 23, allowed 3 lbs.; a race since then, 6 lbs. Claiming price $20,000; if for $18,000, allowed 2 lbs. (Races when entered for $16,000 or less not considered.)

Value of race $15,000; value to winner $8,250; second $3,000; third $2,250; fourth $1,125; fifth $375. Mutuel pool $303,708.

Last Raced	Horse	Eqt.	A.Wt	PP	St	¼	½	Str	Fin	Jockey	Cl'g Pr	Odds $1
17May89 11TuP1	Agitated Mike	b	3 119	5	3	11	11½	14	15	McCarron C J	20000	2.30
11May89 9GG6	Brilliantized	b	3 111	8	1	52	3½	2½	22¾	Nakatani C S5	20000	17.70
13May89 1Hol5	Pocketful Of Aces	b	3 117	6	4	4hd	41½	3hd	32	Pincay L Jr	20000	8.50
24May89 4Hol6	Papa Stan	b	3 116	2	8	8	71½	61½	4hd	Solis A	20000	13.60
13May89 1Hol7	Lightning Port	b	3 116	7	2	2½	21	42½	51½	Stevens G L	20000	3.00
18May89 5Hol2	Rudee's Great Legs	b	3 116	1	7	61½	6½	71½	62	Cortez A	20000	2.50
28May89 4Hol6	Totally Fun		3 116	4	5	31	52½	5hd	71½	Valenzuela F H	20000	8.30
26Apr89 3Hol5	Muscle Bound		3 116	3	6	71½	8	8	8	Meza R Q	20000	44.40

OFF AT 4:01 Start good. Won ridden out Time, :22, :45, :57⅕, 1:10 Track fast.

$2 Mutuel Prices:			
5-AGITATED MIKE	6.60	5.40	4.00
8-BRILLIANTIZED		14.80	7.20
6-POCKETFUL OF ACES			5.60

Dk. b. or br. g, by Mike Fogarty—Double Agitate, by Agitate. Trainer Proctor Harry A. Bred by Pascoe III & Willie Williamson (Cal).

AGITATED MIKE outsprinted rivals for the early lead and drew out in the stretch. BRILLIANTIZED, in contention early and wide down the backstretch, came into the stretch four wide, was no match for AGITATED MIKE in the stretch but proved second best. POCKETFUL OF ACES, in contention early, lacked the needed response in the drive. PAPA STAN trailed early, steadily improved his position after a quarter but failed to menace. LIGHTNING PORT forced the early pace and gave way. RUDEE'S GREAT LEGS, outrun early, was never dangerous and entered the stretch four wide. TOTALLY FUN, prominent early, faltered.

Owners— 1, Wide Horizon Thoroughbreds; 2, Meadowbrook Farms Inc; 3, Bradley & Englekirk; 4, Holt L; 5, Shulman & Wild Oak Ranch; 6, Koch Ruth; 7, Greene H F or Janet; 8, Four Four Forty Farms.

Trainers— 1, Proctor Harry A; 2, La Croix David; 3, Marikian Charles M; 4, Holt Lester; 5, Shulman Sanford; 6, Stute Melvin F; 7, Hess R B Jr; 8, Borick Robert.

Overweight: Pocketful Of Aces 1 pound.

Agitated Mike was claimed by Charles & Cir Valley Stable; trainer, Shulman Sanford; Rudee's Great Legs was claimed by Collins J M; trainer, Klayman Eyal; Totally Fun was claimed by Landsburg A; trainer, Corin Vladimir.

Priscilla's Crown
DAVIS R G **122**
Own.—Oakmont Stable Ltd

B. m. 7, by Salem—Hidden Royalty, by Tentam
Br.—Franks J (La)
Tr.—Threewitt Noble **$10,000**
Lifetime 42 9 11 9 $179,300

1989	6	2	1	1
1988	11	1	4	3
Turf	4	0	1	1

20May89-2Hol	6f	:214	:443	1:093ft	6¾	116	21	1hd	13	12	Davis R G3	Ⓕ	16000	93-07	Priscll'sCrown,SldJt,Lt's'
4May89-5Hol	6f	:22	:451	1:102ft	2	118	32	21½	22½	24	Davis R G4	Ⓕ	c12500	85-15	Mrs.V.,Priscilla'sCrown,J
4May89—Wide in stretch															
27Apr89-1Hol	6½f	:221	:452	1:161ft	5½	116	1hd	11½	15	16½	Davis R G11	Ⓕ	10000	94-10	Priscll'sCrown,KnghtsBt
14Apr89-1SA	6f	:213	:443	1:10 ft	5¾	116	86½	67½	57	69	Davis R G8	Ⓕ	10000	79-12	Lager, Miss Liz, Clement
8Mar89-1SA	6f	:214	:453	1:111ft	*2¾	116	31	1hd	2hd	33½	Solis A10	Ⓕ	10000	78-15	NlliMlb,OurCoqutt,Prisci
9Feb89-3SA	6f	:22	:453	1:114sy	3¾	116	64½	22½	33	45¾	Solis A10	Ⓕ	10000	73-24	ClementsCrk,QuitLuck,G
9Feb89—Broke slowly															
27Jly88-2Dmr	6½f	:222	:452	1:164ft	*9-5	1105	73¼	94¼	55	35	Corral J R1	Ⓕ	16000	83-11	TBImprssv,DblDcrtd,Prs
4Jun88-9Hol	1 1/16	:464	1:114	1:442ft	3½	116	1½	1½	1½	25	Gryder A T3	Ⓕ	32000	73-16	Sir'sNwHop,Priscill'sCro
28May88-1Hol	7f	:212	:442	1:231ft	4¾	116	11½	11½	1hd	22½	Gryder A T8	Ⓕ	32000	86-13	Vianora, Priscilla's Crow
28May88—Bumped at 1/8															
19May88-9Hol	1 1/16	:461	1:112	1:451ft	7	115	1½	1hd	12½	32	Gryder A T10	Ⓕ	25000	72-19	Sr'sNwHop,RjctdLov,Prs

May 16 Hol 4f ft :484 H

One last example and, unfortunately, it also involves one of my Horses to Watch. After a smashing win at $16,000, Priscilla's Crown was unceremoniously dropped to the bottom class level, a move which says physical problems have once again gotten the best of this one-time classy mare. Please do not support this kind of bankroll killer. Take the opportunity to bet against a suspicious and overbet favorite; the worst that can happen is you lose to a short-priced underlay. That's hardly a major catastrophe.

Last Raced	Horse	Eqt.A.Wt PP St	¼	½	Str	Fin	Jockey	Cl'g Pr	Odds $1
2Jun89 3Hol³	Dynamite Kiss	b 5116 8 1	5²	4½	2²	15½	Sorenson D	10000	4.10
18May89 1Hol¹	Hanevir	b 6119 3 5	3hd	3½	4½	2²	Pedroza M A	10000	5.80
1Jun89 2Hol³	Curious Princess	b 6116 5 4	6hd	7³½	6⁴	3¹½	Cedeno A	10000	7.10
2Jun89 3Hol⁴	Sabinal Rose	b 4116 7 6	7³½	6½	5²½	4¹½	Fernandez A L	10000	14.90
20May89 1Hol⁴	Miss San Diego	6111 6 2	1hd	1hd	3¹	5⁴	Meza M D⁵	10000	21.90
20May89 2Hol¹	Priscilla's Crown	7122 4 3	2¹½	2²	1¹½	6¹½	Davis R G	10000	.90
11May89 5Hol⁵	Catch The Show	b 9116 2 7	8	8	8	7²½	Baze R A	10000	11.30
1Jun89 2Hol⁷	Official Note	4116 1 8	4¹	5hd	7¹	8	Sibille R	10000	33.10

OFF AT 5:35. Start good. Won driving. Time, :22½, :45½, 1:11, 1:17½ Track fast.

NINTH RACE
Hollywood
JUNE 9, 1989

6 ½ FURLONGS. (1.15) CLAIMING. Purse $11,000. Fillies and mares. 4-years-old and upward. Weight, 122 lbs. Non-winners of two races since April 23 allowed 3 lbs.; a race since then, 6 lbs. Claiming price $10,000.

Value of race $11,000; value to winner $6,050; second $2,200; third $1,650; fourth $825; fifth $275. Mutuel pool $207,606. Exacta pool $334,561.

$2 Mutuel Prices:	8-DYNAMITE KISS	10.20	5.00	3.20
	3-HANEVIR		5.40	3.20
	5-CURIOUS PRINCESS			3.80

$2 EXACTA 8-3 PAID $47.60.

Dk. b. or br. m, by Pass the Glass—Soft Kiss, by Tilt Top. Trainer Jackson Bruce L. Bred by Landon's Tb Horses (Cal).
DYNAMITE KISS, outrun early and wide down the backstretch, took command approaching the sixteenth marker and drew out while under a drive. HANEVIR, close up early, was no match for DYNAMITE KISS in the stretch but proved second best. CURIOUS PRINCESS, outrun early, came into the stretch four wide, improved her position in the drive but was never a threat. SABINAL ROSE, also outrun early, failed to menace. MISS SAN DIEGO vied for the early lead while outside PRISCILLA'S CROWN and gave way. PRISCILLA'S CROWN vied for the early lead while inside MISS SAN DIEGO, put away that rival to open a clear advantage in the upper stretch, was overtaken by DYNAMITE KISS approaching the sixteenth marker, was eased in deep stretch when suddenly in distress and broke down to be pulled up shortly after crossing the finish. CATCH THE SHOW was four wide into the stretch. OFFICIAL NOTE broke slowly, moved up to get into contention early, then was finished after a half.

A few words regarding strategy. There are a great many players who subscribe to the premise that these drop-downs render a race unplayable. A good friend was with me at Fairplex the day of the Bicker Bear race. He declared, somewhat sadly, that he'd like to bet the race but Bicker Bear's presence made it unplayable. The two horses he liked ran 1–2 and produced an exacta worth $145 for a $5 bet. He had taken the same stance in the Dial Dusty race earlier on the card. He also pegged the winner of that race.

I encourage you to accept the opposite approach and aggressively attack races that contain such runners. Once you've eliminated that much betting probability, virtually *everything* in the race becomes playable. Apply a multiple-horse betting strategy and catch the other contenders at overlaid prices. I consider this a "win-win" situation and I nearly *always* get involved in the betting of these races. You should, too.

Before we leave this subject, let's revisit the last of Shelter Us's races. With the drop to $16,000, Harry was sticking his hand in the betting public's collective pockets. The For Sale sign was clearly out, and handicappers should have taken a solid stand against the false favorite. In this instance more bettors *did* line up against the favorite than in any of his other drop-down races. However, he was still a short price. I bet three horses, including the eventual winner. Let's work through the race:

2nd Del Mar

6 FURLONGS. (1.07⅗) CLAIMING. Purse $15,000. 3-year-olds. Weight, 121 lbs. Non-winners of two races sicne June 15, allowed 3 lbs.; of such a race since then, 5 lbs. Claiming price $16,000; for each $1,000 to $13,000, allowed 1 lb. (Races when entered for $12,500 or less not considered.)

Paris Boldger

Gr. c. 3(Jan), by Bolger—Paris Escapade, by Al Hattab
VALENZUELA F H 116 **Br.—Oak Crest Farm (Wash)** 1989 6 1 2 0 $7,615
Tr.—Rothblum Steve $16,000 1988 1 M 0 0 $450
Own.—Mangano Mary A Lifetime 7 1 2 0 $8,065

4Aug89-6LA 6f :22 :451 1:11 ft *2-3 115 1hd 11 13 14¼ ValenzuelaFH 1 M12500 88-11 PrisBoldger,AllOnSky,ChifHuchuc 10
29Jly89-4LA 6f :22 :452 1:113ft 2½ 115 2hd 2hd 2½ 2¾ ValenzuelaFH 7 M12500 84-11 IrishBmbino,PrisBoldgr,ThitinHrry 8
15Jly89-3Sol 1 :484 1:131 1:401ft 3½ 115 11 13 12½ 22 SchvnevldtCP 4 M16000 71-16 Raj'sGrnBb,PrisBoldger,NoFilFox 10
2Jun89-2GG 6f :214 :45 1:111ft *2¼ 118 62¾ 74¼ 913 1117 Gryder A T 4 M20000 66-14 RegalTropics,GrayWhale,MistrlJet 11
26Apr89-2Hol 6f :22 :451 1:102ft 2¾ 115 21 42 54½ 67¼ Pedroza M A 3 M32000 82-10 PeaceCall,Allo'sNatural,Vi'la'sBeu 12
26Apr89—Bobbled break; lugged in stretch
9Mar89-4SA 6f :213 :451 1:104ft 4¼ 118 52½ 63 46 49 Pedroza M A8 M32000 75-15 Gold Impression, LastDay,Galleon 12
14Dec88-6Hol 6f :221 :453 1:112ft 4¾ 115 3½ 3nk 52¼ 57½ Douglas R R7 M55000 77-16 ClevrSpch,AnnulDt,ChllngingPoint 9
14Dec88—Bumped start
Aug 18 SA tr.t 3f ft :364 H Jly 8 GG 5f ft 1:00 H Jly 1 GG 3f ft :373 H

Good Matkas

B. g. 3(Apr), by Northern Ringer—Best Intent, by Intentionally
PINCAY L JR 116 **Br.—Drakos C (Ky)** 1989 4 1 0 1 $3,840
Tr.—Kooba Paul $16,000 1988 0 M 0 0
Own.—Lebowitz L Lifetime 4 1 0 1 $3,840

3Aug89-1Dmr 6f :22 :451 1:111ft 9¾ 117 2½ 1hd 2½ 62¼ Pincay L Jr 9 16000 80-14 Ex Beau, Allo's Wish, Papa Stan 11
3Aug89—Jostled start
3Jun89-3Hol 1 :452 1:103 1:364ft 5¾ 1115 52½ 53¼ 77½ 718½ Jauregui L H2 c20000 60-11 SchAWgr,IslndLgcy,WtTllTomorrw 7
13May89-1Hol 6f :22 :452 1:111ft 67 1115 66½ 75¾ 63½ 31¾ Jauregui L H4 20000 83-11 CndySlew,BelieveItToM,GoodMtks 9
13May89—Bumped hard start
9Apr89-3AC 6f :224 :452 1:104ft 9 119 1hd 1hd 1hd 1½ Uribe M R1 M12500 85-18 GoodMtks,ScndTmLcky,L'sDfndnt 9
Aug 19 Dmr 5f ft 1:012 H Aug 13 Dmr 3f ft :362 H Jly 29 Dmr 4f ft :493 H

Eagle's Paradise

Ch. g. 3(Jan), by Beau's Eagle—Poncherosa, by Raise a Native
NAKATANI C S 1115 **Br.—Relatively Stable (Cal)** 1989 6 1 1 0 $15,450
Tr.—Rose Larry $16,000 1988 0 M 0 0
Own.—Relatively Stable & Magnin Lifetime 6 1 1 0 $15,450

12Aug89-2Dmr 6f :213 :442 1:10 ft 27 116 52¼ 44 57 58¼ Davis R G 5 20000 80-13 Ex Beau, Gum Swapper, Chaldean 12
31Jly89-5Dmr 6f :212 :442 1:103ft 8¼ 116 23 47 87 86¾ DelahoussayeE 8 25000 78-16 Rketmnsch,GoDogsGo,NturllyWys 12
31May89-4Hol 6f :22 :45 1:103ft 4¼ 119 1½ 2½ 2hd 44 Pincay L Jr 2 [S] 40000 84-15 TiniklingDncr,MstrMx,MgcJohnson 7
31May89—Broke stride 1/8
7May89-5Hol 6f :214 :45 1:10 ft 27 115 2hd 74¼ 910 1017¼ Sibille R6 [S]Aw27000 74-10 Pt'sPocktful,ElGorrion,BgOfMgic 10
7May89—Steadied stretch
28Apr89-6Hol 6f :222 :454 1:11 ft *8-5 117 11½ 1½ 11 12 Pincay L Jr4 [S]M50000 86-15 Egl'sPrdis,JunglJklin,LuckyBusty 10
28Apr89—Lugged out badly
20Apr89-4SA 6f :212 :443 1:102ft 3¾ 118 2hd 1hd 2hd 22 Pincay L Jr5 M32000 84-16 RoadBlaster,Egle'sPrdise,Morwell 12
Aug 22 Dmr 4f ft :49 H ●Aug 8 Dmr 3f ft :351 H Jly 30 Dmr 3f ft :372 H Jly 25 Dmr 4f ft :49 H

Shelter Us

B. g. 3(Apr), by Shelter Half—School Play, by Hale
SIBILLE R 118 **Br.—Blue Seas Music Inc (Md)** 1989 6 3 1 1 $40,000
Tr.—Jones Gary $16,000 1988 0 M 0 0
Own.—Bacharach B Lifetime 6 3 1 1 $40,000

30Jly89-3Dmr 6½f :213 :443 1:164ft *1 118 2hd 1½ 1½ 32 McCarron C J 1 32000 82-10 Mr. Baldski, Brilliantized,ShelterUs 7
15Jly89-3Hol 6f :213 :443 1:102ft *2-3 116 21 1½ 13½ 1¾ McCarron C J 8 40000 89-11 ShelterUs,GoDogsGo,WorkTillDawn 8
26May89-5Hol 6½f :214 :44 1:161ft *2-3 116 1½ 1hd 11½ 2hd McCarron C J 3 62500 94-09 ForEric,ShelterUs,SagaciousPrince 6
26May89—Bobbled at start
10May89-7Hol 6½f :22 :45 1:16 ft *3-2 116 1hd 11 12 12¾ McCarron C J 6 40000 95-12 ShelterUs,BurntTwice,ColorfulHittr 7
26Apr89-4Hol 6f :214 :444 1:09 ft 7 115 31½ 1hd 12 11½ McCarron C J 3 M32000 96-10 ShltrUs,CourgousPirt,GoldnVision 12
26Apr89—Lugged in stretch
22Mar89-6SA 6f :213 :444 1:104ft 5 118 1½ 2hd 45½ 1112½ McCarron C J 9 M50000 71-17 Skisit, Number One Tuto,WayWild 12
Aug 18 Dmr 4f ft :48 H Aug 9 Dmr 4f ft :473 H Jly 9 Hol 5f ft 1:003 H Jly 4 Hol 6f ft 1:133 H

Island Legacy — Ch. g. 3(Apr), by Bold Tropic—Zaytoon, by Semi-pro
BAZE R A 116
Br.—Cardiff Stud Farm (Cal) 1989 10 1 3 1 $22,900
Tr.—Shulman Sanford $16,000 1988 0 M 0 0
Own.—Lindo DP-Amy O-Anela M Lifetime 10 1 3 1 $22,900

11Aug89-2Dmr 1 :462 1:11 1:371ft 4 117 41 32½ 56½ 610 Pincay L Jr 2 20000 70-19 CremToTheTop,SuchAWger,Joropo 9
30Jun89-3Hol 1 :454 1:11 1:372ft 2½ 117 31 11½ 1½ 31¾ Pincay L Jr 2 20000 74-16 SuchAWgr,MliciousPrtnr,IslndLgcy 8
22Jun89-3Hol 7f :221 :444 1:234ft 2 116 41½ 42½ 23 21½ Stevens G L 5 25000 83-12 Brilliantized,IslandLegcy,SrosFntsy 7
3Jun89-3Hol 1 :452 1:103 1:364ft 4½ 117 3½ 1hd 2hd 2½ Pincay L Jr 4 20000 78-11 SchAWgr,IslndLgcy,WtTllTomorrw 7
3May89-5Hol 6f :22 :451 1:104ft 9½ 114 85½ 85¾ 65½ 56 Stevens G L 2 22500 81-15 ChiefRunninBlze,Telvizd,B'ivItToM 8
7Apr89-5SA 6f :22 :46 1:113ft 8 118 84¼ 73¾ 74¾ 55¼ Davis R G 2 25000 75-19 GrkMyth,SpcyYllowtl,PcktflOfAcs 10
7Apr89—Lacked room 3/8
29Mar89-9SA 1 :46 1:104 1:363ft 17 112 51¾ 72¾ 86 88¾ Davis R G 4 35000 76-17 HonstOnyx,MghtyFr,HollywodRprtr 9
29Mar89—Lacked room far turn
15Mar89-2SA 6f :214 :451 1:11 ft *3-2 118 64¾ 53 31 1¾ Pincay L Jr 11 [S]M32000 83-14 IslndLgcy,JustBoogin'By,I'mFstst 12
15Mar89—Brushed 3/16; lugged in stretch
17Feb89-4SA 7f :222 :454 1:24 ft 4½ 118 52½ 52 54½ 68¾ Pedroza M A 10 M40000 71-21 StylshStd,Inconspcos,RghtOvrFct 12
2Feb89-2SA 6f :213 :444 1:104ft *2¾ 118 65 44 33 22¾ Pincay L Jr 10 [S]M40000 81-18 Puttn'ForEgl,IslndLgcy,FblosStff 12
Aug 5 Dmr 5f ft 1:021 H Jly 28 Dmr 5f ft 1:002 H Jly 10 Hol 5f ft 1:003 H

Forceten Road — B. c. 3(Jan), by Forceten—Abridge, by Kennedy Road
CEDENO A 116
Br.—Walker A J Jr (Cal) 1989 5 0 0 0 $925
Tr.—Verhoest Therese $16,000 1988 1 1 0 0 $8,250
Own.—Verhoest E R Lifetime 6 1 0 0 $9,175

11Aug89-9Dmr 1 :461 1:11 1:363ft 8½ 114 21½ 31½ 35 54½ Cedeno A 7 18000 78-19 Bonn'sMrk,Nn'sHppStr,MrfstDstny 9
11Aug89—Bumped early
2Aug89-2Dmr 1 1/16 :461 1:111 1:441ft 29 116 33½ 32½ 44 52½ Cedeno A 5 16000 76-15 PrinceOfAck,SuchAWgr,Amwinnr 10
2Aug89—Wide into drive
13Jly89-1Hol 6f :221 :452 1:11 ft 16 116 78½ 712 714 720½ Castanon AL 4 [S] 25000 65-14 JaklinLomaLad,Allo'sNaturl,Chlden 7
11Jun89-5Hol 6f :222 :451 1:101ft 6 116 52½ 65 77½ 79¾ Dominguez RE 7 32000 80-10 BlckDuzy,BelieveItToM,GoDogsGo 8
26May89-7Hol 7f :214 :44 1:213ft 26 113 76½ 710 89½ 78¾ DmngzRE 3 [S]Aw27000 87-09 Bag Of Magic,SarosTown,OneDrink 8
8Aug88-2Dmr 6f :222 :462 1:104ft 26 117 31½ 3nk 11½ 16½ DmngzRE 9 [S]M32000 84-15 Forceten Road, Jazz, Try Raja 10
Jly 27 SLR tr.t 5f ft 1:014 H Jly 7 SLR tr.t 4f ft :491 H Jly 1 SLR tr.t 6f ft 1:134 H

Searching Native — Ch. g. 3(Mar), by Be a Native—Always Searching, by Search for Gold
DOMINGUEZ R E 116
Br.—Spinelli R & Josie B (Cal) 1989 8 0 0 0 $2,080
Tr.—Spinelli Gary $16,000 1988 3 1 0 1 $11,200
Own.—Spinelli R & Josie B Lifetime 11 1 0 1 $13,280

10Aug89-6LA 6½f :214 :454 1:171ft 6½ 115 53½ 54½ 79½ 714 Black C A 7 28000 75-13 GoStdyLd,MgicJohnson,W'tzingSss 8
2Jly89-5Hol 6f :22 :451 1:102ft 36 1115 129½ 129¾ 911 810½ Jauregui L H 6 20000 78-13 StlwrtExpress,CndySlw,Mr.Bldski 12
2Jly89—Bumped hard break
21Jun89-3Hol 1 1/16 :462 1:12 1:444ft 26 116 66½ 54¾ 59 518½ Sibille R 1 25000 58-17 CtfshPurdy,AmrcnForc,AnothrSros 7
7Jun89-3Hol 1 1/16 :47 1:121 1:444ft 37 116 53½ 54 55 59 Sibille R 3 32000 67-15 Gold Impression,Jazz,CatfishPurdy 7
5May89-5Hol 1 :451 1:101 1:36 ft 20 116 85¼ 86 77½ 69 Sibille R 4 32000 74-16 ‡SySyBoom,RcerRex,MliciousPrtnr 9
5May89—Bumped at start
21Apr89-3SA 6f :214 :442 1:093ft 34 116 66 67½ 66 66½ Sibille R 1 50000 83-17 ClvrSpch,FirstLoylty,MgicJohnson 7
24Mar89-7SA 6f :221 :46 1:102ft 34 116 78 65 66½ 510½ Olivares F 7 62500 75-20 Dmskim,MisonMestro,CleverSpech 7
24Mar89—Steadied late
10Mar89-7SA 7f :221 :443 1:223ft 61 118 79½ 811 69½ 610½ Olivares F 4 [S]Aw32000 76-17 Mr. Bolg, Shady Pine, Saros Town 8
10Oct88-4Fpx 6f :221 :461 1:114ft 5½ 118 95¾ 69½ 42½ 12 Olivares F 4 [S]M32000 88-09 SrchngNtv,ScrtAccomplc,Cro'sRlr 10
25Sep88-2Dmr 6f :221 :46 1:114ft 12 118 1210 97¾ 76¾ 74¾ Gryder A T 7 M32000 74-15 BllyCrRod,BllStrod,ScrtAccomplc 12
●Aug 5 SA 4f ft :474 H Jly 29 SA 5f ft 1:014 H ●Jly 23 SA 4f ft :462 Hg Jly 17 SA 4f ft :474 H

Tuff Boss — Ch. g. 3(Apr), by Dust Commander—Kribot, by Exclusive Ribot
MCCARRON C J 116
Br.—McMurry Farm (Wash) 1989 4 1 0 1 $10,950
Tr.—Jones Gary $16,000 1988 2 M 0 1 $2,700
Own.—Prestonwood Farm Inc Lifetime 6 1 0 2 $13,650

12Aug89-2Dmr 6f :213 :442 1:10 ft 3 116 41½ 32½ 910 1114¼ McCarron C J 8 20000 74-13 Ex Beau, Gum Swapper, Chaldean 12
24Jun89-3Hol 6f :22 :444 1:093ft 18 116 41¾ 67½ 814 817½ McCarron C J 6 40000 75-11 Agitated Mike, Go Dogs Go,Skisit 10
29Apr89-2Hol 6f :221 :454 1:103ft *6-5 115 1½ 1½ 12 14½ McCarron C J 9 M32000 88-10 TffBoss,HnstJhnSlvr,StrctCnfdnc 11
23Mar89-4SA 6f :221 :454 1:11 ft *7-5 118 1½ 12 12 21 † McCarron C J 3 M32000 82-19 PostonUnclr,‡TuffBoss,SrnoDncr 12
†23Mar89—Disqualified and placed third; Drifted out late
15Aug88-6Dmr 6f :222 :46 1:112ft 5¾ 117 52¾ 31 54½ 813 McCarron C J 6 M50000 68-20 Irish, Corazon Bravo, My Viriko 9
15Aug88—Veered in, bumped start; wide 3/8 turn
3Aug88-6Dmr 6f :221 :453 1:104ft 8¾ 118 52½ 22½ 25 312½ McCarron C J 6 M50000 72-11 TersInMyEyes,SerrnoStr,TuffBoss 12
3Aug88—Broke in, bumped
●Aug 6 Dmr 5f ft :583 H Aug 1 Dmr 5f ft 1:001 B ●Jly 27 Dmr 4f ft :461 H Jly 22 Hol 5f ft :594 H

Say Say Boom B. g. 3(Feb), by Time to Explode—Bayasa, by Leon II
GUYMON T F 1115 Br.—Mamakos J (Ky) 1989 9 1 1 2 $24,475
Tr.—Bacorn Herbert $16,000 1988 1 M 0 0 $400
Own.—Bacorn Elizabeth Lifetime 10 1 1 2 $24,875
31Jly89-5Dmr 6f :212 :442 1:103ft 23 1115 86¾ 1114 1214 1213½ Nakatani C S 11 25000 71-16 Rketmnsch,GoDogsGo,NturllyWys 12
12Jly89-7Hol 1 :444 1:094 1:351ft 15 116 54 815 826 842½ Baze R A 7 40000 44-16 FeelingFabulous,Jazz,ClassicKnight 8
7Jun89-3Hol 1 1/16 :47 1:121 1:444ft 5½ 116 75½ 74¼ 75¼ 711½ Baze R A 1 c32000 64-15 Gold Impression,Jazz,CatfishPurdy 7
5May89-5Hol 1 :451 1:101 1:36 ft 6½ 116 2hd 11 11½ 1hd † McCarron C J 7 32000 83-16 ‡SySyBoom,RcerRex,MliciousPrtnr 9
† 5May89—Disqualified and placed second; Ducked in 1/16
24Apr89-2SA 1 :462 1:121 1:39 ft 10 118 2hd 2hd 21½ 45½ Solis A 2 40000 67-22 MightyFir,DomntdDbut,AnothrSros 8
12Apr89-9SA 1 1/16 :454 1:103 1:433ft 13 117 21½ 22¼ 25 35½ Solis A 2 32000 77-14 HollywoodRportr,FttlKttl,SySyBom 9
17Mar89-4SA 1 1/16 :454 1:111 1:461ft 7 118 43 41¼ 11 11 Baze R A 7 M40000 78-20 SaySayBoom,NeverInLce,Ldyized 12
17Feb89-4SA 7f :222 :454 1:24 ft 11 118 86¾ 85 65½ 56¾ Baze R A3 M40000 73-21 StylshStd,Inconspcos,RghtOvrFct 12
17Feb89—Wide into stretch
25Jan89-6SA 6f :214 :452 1:112ft 10 116 42½ 63¼ 53¼ 34 Baze R A1 M45000 77-17 ByNoMens,LtestRelese,SySyBoom 12
9Dec88-2Hol 6f :22 :46 1:112ft *9-5 118 53 51¼ 44¼ 56¾ Pincay L Jr 8 M40000 78-16 GumSwpper,RightOvrFct,NvrInLc 12
9Dec88—Rough start
●Jly 24 Hol 5f ft :59 H Jly 2 Hol 5f ft :593 H

Overidge B. g. 3(Mar), by L'Natural—Fleet Hi, by Don B
STEVENS G L 118 Br.—Hudon E A (Cal) 1989 3 1 0 0 $9,175
Tr.—Luby Donn $16,000 1988 0 M 0 0
Own.—Hudon E A Lifetime 3 1 0 0 $9,175
15Jly89-3Hol 6f :213 :443 1:102ft 33 1095 66½ 88½ 88½ 79 Castanon J L 6 35000 80-11 ShelterUs,GoDogsGo,WorkTillDawn 8
24Jun89-2Hol 6½f :214 :45 1:172ft *2½ 116 1½ 1hd 12 1¾ McCarron C J 4 M32000 88-11 Overidge,BlzBorlis,SummrTimFlys 12
2Jun89-2Hol 6½f :214 :444 1:162ft 4½ 115 55 43½ 46½ 58½ Meza R Q3 [S]M32000 84-10 TeachATron,NobleValiant,GoBigAl 12
Aug 18 Dmr 5f ft 1:004 H ●Aug 8 Fpx 3f ft :353 H ●Aug 1 Fpx 4f ft :483 H ●Jly 10 Fpx 4f ft :483 H

Bold Bolide B. g. 3(Mar), by Bel Bolide—Bett's Mandy, by Beau Gar
DAVIS R G 116 Br.—Sokol E I (Cal) 1989 12 2 2 3 $12,283
Tr.—Vienna Darrell $16,000 1988 1 M 0 0
Own.—Herrick W J Lifetime 13 2 2 3 $12,283 Turf 2 0 0 0 $210
11Aug89-6LA 6½f :213 :46 1:181ft 4 117 12 1hd 3½ 33 Black C A 10 12500 81-13 BelleCnyon,ChuckFull,BoldBolide 10
2Aug89-7LA 6½f :221 :464 1:173ft 9 114 13 11 13 22¼ Black C A 5 10000 85-12 SirM.AndM.,BoldBolide,NoMsSirVs 9
14Jly89-7Sol 6f :222 :443 1:103ft 3¼ 115 1½ 1½ 11½ 12 SchvaneveldtCP 6 8000 88-18 Bold Bolide, JericoJake,SunkenTub 9
30Jun89-10Pln 6f :221 :45 1:113ft 21 112 21½ 22 2hd 75¾ SchvnevldtCP 10 12500 78-18 Employer,Vistd'Aquil,ThIrishLook 10
30Jun89—Ducked in start
16Jun89-3Stk 6f :223 :454 1:101ft 5 116 11 11½ 16 19 SchvnevldtCP 3 M12500 96-06 BoldBolide,BigDukeAl,Cne'sGypsy 10
20May89-6TuP 1 1/16 Ⓣ:47 1:121 1:452fm 8¾ 114 22 52¼ 820 726¾ Munsell G R 9 Mdn 58-09 MonteCrlo,GoldN'Surf,BlivAPromis 9
7May89-7TuP a1 Ⓣ:49 1:142 1:42 fm 4½ 114 11 1½ 1hd 43 Guerrero A 8 Mdn 79-18 SensitiveTom,WindsOfTim,JyWolf 10
25Mar89-10TuP 1 1/16 :47 1:111 1:443ft 63 122 3½ 4¾ 98 1015¼ Munsell GR 9 Tu P Dby 60-18 Stalaxis, Well Aware, Stage King 12
11Mar89-9TuP 1 :451 1:11 1:381ft 11 122 1½ 42¼ 510 619 Guerrero A 9 Dby Trl 59-18 StgKing,LuckyStblBoy,BongiMyWy 9
11Feb89-6TuP 1 :462 1:111 1:373ft 3¼ 112 11 1½ 2½ 34 Dittfach H 5 Mdn 77-18 StanleyStomp,GoldBlst,BoldBolide 8
Jly 12 BM tr.t 3f ft :391 H Jun 25 BM 4f ft :494 H

Pocketful Of Aces B. g. 3(Apr), by Full Pocket—Nona's Review, by Reviewer
CASTANON J L 1115 Br.—Wood Mrs M L (Ky) 1989 15 0 0 2 $7,250
Tr.—Marikian Charles M $16,000 1988 4 1 0 0 $9,350
Own.—Bradley & Englekirk Lifetime 19 1 0 2 $16,600
19Aug89-2Dmr 6f :221 :452 1:103ft 22 1095 74 73¼ 74½ 76¼ Castanon J L 6 20000 79-14 Televized, Road Blaster, Agiwin 9
3Aug89-1Dmr 6f :22 :451 1:111ft 19 1115 62¼ 43¾ 66½ 86½ Nakatani C S 11 16000 75-14 Ex Beau, Allo's Wish, Papa Stan 11
3Aug89—Wide final 3/8
2Jly89-5Hol 6f :22 :451 1:102ft 33 116 117 96¼ 79 79¾ Valenzuela F H 5 20000 80-13 StlwrtExpress,CndySlw,M'Bldski 12
2Jly89—Bumped at break
22Jun89-3Hol 7f :221 :444 1:234ft 25 116 62¾ 54½ 69 610½ Baze R A 2 25000 74-12 Brilliantized,IslandLegcy,SrosFntsy 7
7Jun89-6Hol 6f :22 :45 1:10 ft 8¼ 117 42½ 43 34½ 37¾ Pincay L Jr 6 20000 83-15 AgittdMik,Brillintzd,PocktfulOfAcs 8
13May89-1Hol 6f :22 :452 1:111ft 12 1115 42 31 31 52 Nakatani C S 2 20000 83-11 CndySlew,BelieveItToM,GoodMtks 9
3May89-5Hol 6f :22 :451 1:104ft 28 116 73¾ 75¼ 77 711½ Pedroza M A 5 25000 75-15 ChiefRunninBlze,Telvizd,BlivItToM 8
20Apr89-1SA 6f :214 :451 1:094ft 9¼ 1125 77¼ 54¾ 44 46¼ Valenzuela F H 5 20000 83-16 GrkMyth,LightningPort,WltzingSss 7
7Apr89-5SA 6f :22 :46 1:113ft 57 1115 73¾ 52¼ 32¼ 33¼ Olguin G L 3 25000 77-19 GrkMyth,SpcyYllowtl,PcktflOfAcs 10
7Apr89—Troubled trip
26Mar89-3SA 6f :221 :453 1:103ft 27 1125 43 54¼ 68½ 614¾ Olguin G L 3 32000 78-16 BttorRogr,MrclMystry,GoldImprssn 6
Aug 10 Dmr 5f ft 1:012 H Aug 1 Dmr 3f ft :352 H Jly 23 Dmr 4f ft :483 H

Del Mar sprints were consistently being won by horses that were within 2½ lengths of the leader at the second call. Handicapping these races consisted mainly of identifying the horses that would be forwardly placed in the early running. Closers were of no concern unless all the runners in a race were early pace types with no ability to rate. Few races fit that criterion.

Paris Boldger: His Los Alamitos races show some speed, but in his races at the major tracks he showed little ability. A maiden $12,500 race in California is as bad as it gets.

Good Matkas: He shows some ability to be near the pace. In his last he hit the second call in around 45.1 seconds.

Eagle's Paradise: Another with some early speed and, with the exception of Shelter Us, he comes out of the fastest races. He broke his maiden for $50,000, a statement the rest of these can't make.

Shelter Us: The reason we're considering betting this bottom-level race.

Island Legacy: His recent six-furlong races show no early pace ability, and he's been running longer distances. His last four races should not help his early speed.

Forceten Road: A router with no early pace ability in sprints. He broke his maiden as a two-year-old by forcing a dreadfully slow pace. He hasn't been close to the lead in a sprint since.

Searching Native: An awful horse with no semblance of current form.

Tuff Boss: He showed a bit of speed in his last before a complete collapse. His maiden win was on the pace, but against very slow (45.4) fractions. At 6–1 he's a good one to bet against.

Say Say Boom: This one has no early speed and has been steadily declining since the claim on 7Jun89.

Overidge: A definite possibility. The drop is severe, but not all that suspicious. He clearly doesn't belong with $40,000 types and should be dropped.

Bold Bolide: He has speed but may lack class. He's yet to run at a major racetrack, but is from a good barn and gets the services of Robbie Davis. The step up in class is an encouraging sign.

Pocketful Of Aces: This is a horrible horse with no speed and apparently no heart. Other than those two minor problems, he's a terrific animal.

Summary

Only five horses were capable of being forwardly placed during the early running of the race. Shelter Us is eliminated for all the reasons mentioned earlier. That leaves the following horses and their post-time odds:

(1) Good Matkas 8–1
(2) Bold Bolide 23–1
(3) Eagle's Paradise 25–1
(4) Overidge 7–2

Realistically, in many of these races it may be asking a lot to expect the handicapper to isolate the single horse most likely to upset the false favorite. When that's possible, by all means go for it with both hands. In this race it wasn't necessary to isolate *the* horse that should win, just the *horses* that should win. The prices of the main contenders fitting the bias opened a lot of possibilities. I left Overidge off the ticket because of his price and the precipitous class drop. Fortunately, one of the others ran well enough to defeat Shelter Us as he continued to decline in form. Don't back away from these situations; they provide great opportunities to kick "Harry" in the butt.

SECOND RACE
Del Mar
AUGUST 25, 1989

6 FURLONGS. (1.07⅗) CLAIMING. Purse $15,000. 3-year-olds. Weight, 121 lbs. Non-winners of two races sicne June 15, allowed 3 lbs.; of such a race since then, 5 lbs. Claiming price $16,000; for each $1,000 to $13,000, allowed 1 lb. (Races when entered for $12,500 or less not considered.)

Value of race $15,000; value to winner $8,250; second $3,000; third $2,250; fourth $1,125; fifth $375. Mutuel pool $403,178.

Last Raced	Horse	Eqt	A	Wt	PP	St	¼	½	Str	Fin	Jockey	Cl'g Pr	Odds $1
12Aug89 ^{2}Dmr^{5}	Eagle's Paradise	b	3	116	3	2	1^{hd}	2^{2}	1^{hd}	1^{hd}	Solis A†	16000	25.50
30Jly89 ^{3}Dmr^{3}	Shelter Us	b	3	118	4	3	$2^{1\frac{1}{2}}$	1^{hd}	$2^{2\frac{1}{2}}$	$2^{1\frac{3}{4}}$	Sibille R	16000	1.60
15Jly89 ^{3}Hol^{7}	Overidge	b	3	118	8	5	4^{hd}	$3^{\frac{1}{2}}$	$3^{1\frac{1}{2}}$	3^{2}	Stevens G L	16000	3.60
11Aug89 ^{6}LA^{3}	Bold Bolide	b	3	116	11	1	3^{hd}	$4^{1\frac{1}{2}}$	$4^{2\frac{1}{2}}$	$4^{2\frac{1}{2}}$	Davis R G	16000	23.40
10Aug89 ^{6}LA^{7}	Searching Native	b	3	116	5	11	12	12	$6^{\frac{1}{2}}$	5^{1}	Ortega L E	16000	71.60
31Jly89 ^{5}Dmr^{12}	Say Say Boom	b	3	111	7	6	7^{1}	$7^{1\frac{1}{2}}$	$5^{1\frac{1}{2}}$	6^{2}	Guymon T F^{5}	16000	56.30
4Aug89 ^{6}LA^{1}	Paris Boldger	b	3	116	1	12	$11^{3\frac{1}{2}}$	$11^{1\frac{1}{2}}$	$7^{1\frac{1}{2}}$	$7^{1\frac{1}{2}}$	Valenzuela F H	16000	37.60
11Aug89 ^{2}Dmr^{6}	Island Legacy	b	3	116	9	10	$10^{2\frac{1}{2}}$	8^{hd}	$8^{1\frac{1}{2}}$	$8^{1\frac{1}{2}}$	Baze R A	16000	10.20
11Aug89 ^{9}Dmr^{5}	Forceten Road	b	3	116	10	9	$9^{\frac{1}{2}}$	$10^{\frac{1}{2}}$	$10^{1\frac{1}{2}}$	9no	Cedeno A	16000	9.50
19Aug89 ^{2}Dmr^{7}	Pocketful Of Aces	b	3	111	12	7	8^{hd}	9^{hd}	9^{hd}	10^{3}	Castanon J L^{5}	16000	44.10
12Aug89 ^{2}Dmr^{11}	Tuff Boss	b	3	116	6	4	$5^{2\frac{1}{2}}$	$5^{1\frac{1}{2}}$	11	11	McCarron C J	16000	6.30
3Aug89 ^{1}Dmr^{6}	Good Matkas	b	3	117	2	8	$6^{\frac{1}{2}}$	6^{hd}	—	—	Pincay L Jr	16000	7.90

Good Matkas, Broke down.

OFF AT 2:36. Start good. Won driving. Time, :21⅘, :44⅘, :57⅕, 1:10⅗ Track fast.

$2 Mutuel Prices:			
3–EAGLE'S PARADISE	53.00	16.20	9.20
4–SHELTER US		4.20	3.00
8–OVERIDGE			4.00

Ch. g. (Jan), by Beau's Eagle—Poncherosa, by Raise a Native. Trainer Rose Larry. Bred by Relatively Stable (Cal).

EAGLE'S PARADISE dueled for the lead from the start while inside SHELTER US, brushed at intervals with that rival in the final furlong and narrowly prevailed SHELTER US vied for the lead from the start while outside EAGLE'S PARADISE, brushed at intervals with that rival in the last furlong and lost a narrow decision OVERIDGE, jostled in the initial strides, and close up all the way, gained the show. BOLD BOLIDE, wide early while close up, lacked the needed response in the drive. SEARCHING NATIVE broke a bit awkwardly, lagged far back early and gained his best stride too late SAY SAY BOOM was four wide into the stretch ISLAND LEGACY, jostled in the opening strides, was checked while in traffic nearing the stretch and was five wide into the stretch FORCETEN ROAD, wide down the backstretch, was seven wide into the stretch. POCKETFUL OF ACES, wide down the backstretch, was six wide into the stretch. TUFF BOSS, close up early, faltered. GOOD MATKAS broke down after a half.

Owners— 1, Relatively Stable & Magnin; 2. Bacharach B; 3, Hudon E A; 4, Herrick W J; 5, Spinelli R & Josie B; 6, Bacorn Elizabeth; 7, Mangano Mary A; 8, Lindo DP-Amy O-Anela M; 9, Verhoest E R; 10, Bradley & Englekirk; 11, Prestonwood Farm Inc; 12, Lebowitz L

Trainers— 1, Rose Larry; 2, Jones Gary; 3, Luby Donn, 4, Vienna Darrell; 5, Spinelli Gary; 6, Bacorn Herbert; 7, Rothblum Steve; 8, Shulman Sanford; 9, Verhoest Therese; 10, Marikian Charles M; 11, Jones Gary; 12, Kooba Paul.

† **Apprentice allowance waived:** Eagle's Paradise 5 pounds **Overweight:** Good Matkas 1 pound

Scratched—Howdy Kid (12Aug89 ^{2}Dmr^{6}); Long Way To Come (14Aug89 ^{1}Dmr^{10}); Chief Runnin Blaze (19Aug89 ^{2}Dmr^{4}); Smooth Rider (10Aug89 ^{10}LA^{6}).

CHAPTER VII

The Decision Model

THERE ARE MORE WAYS than one to skin this handicapping cat. Class, speed, pace, trip, and angle handicappers, can all carve a niche at the racetrack. While philosophy and methodology may differ among skillful players, there is one universal thread: *winning players keep records.* I don't know a *single* long-term winner who does not. Style and content may differ, depending on methodology employed, but winning players are in touch with their personal skills and with the demands of the racetrack.

Pace and speed handicappers are acutely aware of par times, dominant running styles, and daily variants.

Class handicappers must know the intricacies of their class hierarchy or suffer missed betting opportunities and run the risk of losing amateurish bets.

Trip and angle handicappers depend on videotapes, back issues of the *Form*, and personal notes.

All keep betting records and can recite probability, average mutuel, and return on investment. It's the rare handicapper who can maintain long-term success without the data necessary to conduct "reality checks" on this most difficult pursuit. Only a minuscule percentage of "horseplayers" are consistent long-term winners. It's also true that a minuscule percentage of handicappers keep extensive records. The relationship between winning and record keeping is *not* casual. It is direct and must be maintained over time. The effort can be discouraging when you're playing at your worst, but the long-term rewards will be significant. Personal insights are not the least of the benefits to be gained.

My personal experience as a handicapper evolved through numerous methods and approaches. A personal style was developed by choosing tested ideas from established approaches and discarding those my records showed to be of little value. More important to my development were the insights gained regarding my personal play. I found I was able to maintain peak performance for relatively short periods of time before needing the recuperative attributes of other, less demanding pursuits. The bulk of my serious play is at Santa Anita's winter meeting, which begins the day after Christmas each year. By mid-February I'm ready for two weeks away from daily play. From the middle of May through the beginning of Oak Tree at Santa Anita, in October, I'm a casual player, making only one or two trips to the track each week. I also take the six weeks off between the end of Oak Tree in November and the main Santa Anita meeting.

No part of that schedule is by chance. Prior to pursuing the sport on a full-time basis, I assumed I would be a permanent fixture in all the grandstands of the southern California racetracks. My record keeping clearly shows the return on more extensive play is not worth that considerable effort.

I'm going to suggest you begin to objectively analyze your own performance. As to betting records, I recommend any of Dick Mitchell's or Huey Mahl's material. In this book we'll be addressing two records absolutely vital to successful pace analysis:

(1) A decision *model* constructed from the figures and ratings of races previously handicapped.
(2) A *track profile* detailing the characteristics of a specific racetrack.

The rest of this chapter will be concerned with creating, analyzing, and applying a decision model for a specific racetrack. In the next chapter we'll do the same for a track profile.

Experienced handicappers already know a painful "truth" about their game: It's not enough to merely have accurate figures. Without the interpretive skills necessary to effectively apply those figures, the handicapper is doomed to mediocrity. Certainly it's necessary to have accurate figures, but it's even more important to have the knowledge of which ratings work in which situations. I assure you, a bias exists at your racetrack, and it probably differs between sprints and routes.

Before proceeding, I should define the term "bias" as used

in this material. "Track bias" has become an increasingly popular term in recent years, as well it should be. To be successful,
handicappers must be capable of describing general pace, post-
position, trip, and running-style characteristics required to win
at their racetracks. For example, knowing the winner must be
in the top one third of the field at the second call is valuable
information for any player. To the pace handicapper, it is *vital*
information. Without that insight, it is virtually impossible to
unravel and apply the data from an array of ratings and feet-
per-second numbers.

But "bias" goes beyond general characteristics. Even at a
supposedly unbiased racetrack there will exist a bias within the
pace ratings. It may favor early pace; it may favor sustained pace;
or, if the track is truly unbiased, the ratings will favor average
pace. But, in nearly all cases, a "ratings bias" *will* exist. Consider the following two-horse array:

	AP	EP	SP
Horse A	1	1	4
Horse B	1	4	1

The two horses are tied for the top ranking in average pace,
but the early and sustained pace relationships are complete opposites. Horse A leans strongly in the direction of Early Pace,
while Horse B leans heavily toward Sustained Pace.

The question to the handicapper: which of the two profiles
fits today's track and distance requirements?

If the player is unable to confidently answer the question,
there is a definite problem. That very question is at the heart of
any pace handicapping methodology. The ability to separate the
four or five contenders under consideration is the key to consistent long-term winnings for the modern pace handicapper.

At the Fairgrounds, in New Orleans, Horse B will *usually*
possess a significant advantage over its rival in both sprints and
routes. On-pace horses have historically been at a disadvantage
over the Fairgrounds course, leaving most races to sustained pace
types.

Santa Anita sprints will *usually* favor Horse A in the scenario. On-pace horses are always tough to beat over that surface, especially in sprint races.

At both tracks, however, the ratings bias will frequently

change, thus reversing the preferred styles. It is the responsibility of a winning player to be aware of both long- and short-term characteristics, and to capitalize on both. The material in this chapter is offered with that in mind.

The "model" we'll be developing is a decision model based on day-to-day record keeping and will detail the results of races previously handicapped. It is intended to analyze the pace characteristics of a specific racetrack within the framework of our pace ratings. It will also serve as a "reality check" on the work of the individual handicapper.

Let's start by revisiting the Reason To Study race from the chapter on the Sartin Methodology.

	AP	EP	SP
I'll Be The Judge	1	2	3
On Broadway	2	1	6
Alignment	3	3	4
Reason To Study	3	5	2
Middle Concho	5	6	1
Quick Roundtrip	5	4	5

In the absence of specific data concerning the racetrack, a perfectly acceptable method of application is to total the rankings. For example: I'll Be The Judge totals 6, On Broadway 9, Alignment 10, and so on. Since the lower scores *should* reflect the best horses, the approach is not without merit.

Totaling the horizontal "line scores" will produce winners on a consistent basis, especially at a track without a specific pace bias. For several years it was the proper application of the Sartin Methodology. The value of the approach is that it forces organization into the decision-making process. At a racetrack new to the handicapper, it's the only approach available until enough races have been handicapped to develop a working model.

In the example race, however, there was a definite bias toward a single rating: Sustained Pace. To have bet the lowest totals in this race would have been to oppose the demonstrated pace requirements of the racetrack.

Interestingly, the same track, in the same time frame, was favoring average and early pace in sprint races. When a track presents a paradoxical sprint vs route bias, it can be enormously profitable for the bettor. The majority of players tend to bet the same characteristics in both sprints and routes, winning just enough bets to encourage their play. Handicapper's recognizing the paradox are in the enviable position of avoiding the zigzag pattern affecting their competitors.

At Santa Anita in 1984 a group of PIRCO members met for several days of concentrated play. On the first day, I presented a worksheet and a decision model developed from my own record keeping and handicapping. Sprint races were bet from Early Pace ratings and routes from Sustained Pace ratings.

Measured by the number of trips to the cashier's window, the results of the visit were spectacular. Beyond those three days, the data disclosed that 88 percent of all routes were won by the top three rankings in Sustained Pace. Betting decisions were simplified to the bone: consider only the top three sustained pace rankings. The concept of the "Brohamer Model" was added as basic material in the Sartin Methodology.

The only real change from the use of the horizontal line scores was to target specific ratings that are producing winners *now*, *today*. It is much easier to select winners from a specific ratings category (or two) than from the myriad possibilities within an array of ratings and raw numbers.

An additional benefit of using previously handicapped races to build your model is the ability to identify strengths and weaknesses of the individual handicapper. Players unable to skillfully pick pacelines or select contenders are in for a rude awakening. The model from their efforts will be erratic and too often will not include the eventual winner in the ratings array. That may be to the chagrin of the handicapper, but reality is not always pleasant. The potential for overall improvement is worth a few painful moments of regression.

The following worksheet is an adequate vehicle for recording the necessary data:

Date	Dist	AP	EP	SP	FX

Date	Dist	AP	EP	SP	FX

THE NECESSARY DATA

With concessions to date and distance as peripheral items necessary to effective interpretation, the data entered onto the worksheet are the *prerace ratings* of winning horses in races you've handicapped. I mentioned previously that in using prerace figures and rankings, there are dual benefits. Not only does the player acquire an understanding of current track bias, but he also gains insight into personal handicapping skills. The mechanics are very simple.

Again, consider the rankings from the Reason To Study race:

	AP	EP	SP
I'll Be The Judge	1	2	3
On Broadway	2	1	6
Alignment	3	3	4
Reason To Study	3	5	2
Middle Concho	5	6	1
Quick Roundtrip	5	4	5

The winner of the race was Reason To Study, and we'll concern ourselves with his rankings in each rating category. He ranked 3 in Average, 5 in Early and 2 in Sustained Pace. Record the data on the worksheet in each of the categories:

Date	Dist	AP	EP	SP	·FX
10–5	8½	3	5	2	

Again, our intent is to isolate track bias, and bias within your handicapping procedures. Knowing whether your prerace rankings generally place the winner in the top two or three in a given category is very valuable information. Therefore, the 1's, 2's, and 3's in any category represent the winner's rankings against the other contenders in that race. With few exceptions, those rankings should have been generated before the races were run.

Occasionally you'll find it necessary to rerate a race that seems to contradict your understanding of the bias. That's not only acceptable, but highly advisable. The idea is to develop pattern-recognition skills, and the practice involved in redoing races can be of great benefit. Take every step necessary to solve the bias puzzle; in it lies the key to the money room.

Record the date of the race with the intent of later isolating days that may have presented unusual bias requirements. The edge is significant to the handicapper who can confidently excuse, or upgrade, a performance earned contrary to the particular demands of the surface. Early pace types who managed to overcome, or at least challenge a sustained bias, may be excellent plays in subsequent starts. The reverse is also true. Sustained horses managing to impact a race strongly favoring early pace have also recorded efforts worth upgrading.

The distance of each race is important to the overall model. Six- and 6½-furlong races are often identical in bias requirements, while seven-furlong races may be significantly more sustained. It is important to segment races, even within a single distance structure.

The other categories reflect the ratings used in the handicapping of the race.

One race hardly constitutes a trend, so let's view additional races from later in the 1989 Oak Tree meeting.

A ROUTE MODEL

Date	Dist	AP	EP	SP	FX
10–18	8½	2	4	1	x
10–18	8½	1	1	1	
10–19	8½	1	1	5	
10–19	8½	2	2	2	

Date	Dist	AP	EP	SP	FX
10–20	8	1	3	1	
10–20	8½	3	3	3	
10–21	8½	1	2	2	
10–21	8	1	1	1	
10–21	9	1	1	2	
10–22	8½	4	4	1	
10–22	8½	3	4	2	
10–22	8½	1	2	1	

The worksheet represents my handicapping of one week's worth of nonmaiden routes for three-year-olds and older. Although limited to twelve races, the data is conclusive and is representative of the first three weeks of the meeting. The data cells reflect the relative rankings of the winners versus the other contenders in each race handicapped. It validates the decision-making criterion we used in the Reason To Study race: sustained pace.

The most effective use of the data is to quantify each of the rating categories. For example, the average ranking in average pace for the twelve-race sample is 21 (total of AP column) / 12 (races in column) = 1.75. For best results I try to include five contenders in each race used on the worksheet. An average ranking of 1.75 in a five-horse field is considerably more meaningful than in a field of three horses. (In races where it doesn't make sense to include more than three contenders, simply make the bet, cash your tickets, and don't use the race data to construct your model.)

With that in mind, the 1.75 ranking in average pace is exceedingly powerful. Let's view a larger profile of the typical winner:

AP	EP	SP	FX
1.75	2.33	1.83	X

This is one of the tighter models you'll encounter. Although leaning toward sustained pace, the data reflects a *relatively* unbiased racetrack. Factor X is a sprint rating and is of no concern to this particular model.

Let's finish the decision model by setting the following profile as the ideal in a route race:

AP   EP   SP

2   3   2

The profile indicates the ideal relationships between each of the rating categories. For the two-horse win bettor, the decision-making process is fairly simple: bet the top two ranked horses in either average pace or sustained pace. In either case, at least 9 of the 12 races were won by the top two.

Pay attention to the prices paid from each category and base the betting strategy accordingly. From the example model, I would base my play on Sustained Pace. Almost universally, horses selected on the basis of Sustained Pace are financially more rewarding than the easier-to-spot Early Pace or Average Pace types.

The one-horse bettor has a more complex decision. The number-one-ranked Average Pace horse produced the winner in 7 of the 12 races, but that may be unrealistic when related to the longer term. Certainly, the top Average Pace horse is a satisfactory selection criterion in this particular example, but it's not often that easy.

More likely, the bet should reflect the top two or three in Average Pace and a minimum ranking in one of the other categories. In this model I would lean heavily to the use of Average *and* Sustained Pace, requiring a high ranking in both categories. The 3 in Early Pace merely indicates the horse cannot be a deep closer and must be somewhere in the middle of a typical field.

The Reason To Study race was run before the bulk of this data was accumulated, but the race was a solid fit to the subsequent model. One more time, let's look at that race:

	AP	EP	SP
I'll Be The Judge	1	2	3
On Broadway	2	1	6
Alignment	3	3	4
Reason To Study	3	5	2
Middle Concho	5	6	1
Quick Roundtrip	5	4	5

The model relationship of Early to Sustained Pace, 3–2, reflects an imbalance toward Sustained. The ideal selection in this situation, for the one-horse bettor, should be highly ranked in Average Pace with a definite tendency toward a Sustained Pace running style.

On Broadway's profile of 1–6 is an automatic elimination.

Quick Roundtrip falls short in AP and his Early/Sustained relationship leans in the wrong direction.

Alignment's 3–4 is also slightly out of balance in the wrong direction, and in light of the tie in Average Pace, he should be compared directly to Reason To Study's 5–2 profile. In terms of the model, the latter's imbalance toward Sustained Pace is decisive.

Middle Concho falls by the wayside because of the deficiency in AP; a 5 is an unsuitable ranking for Average Pace in this model.

The difficult comparison is between Reason To Study and I'll Be The Judge. The latter, without consideration of the ESP match-up, ranks very highly in all categories. Despite the imbalance toward Early Pace, if using the horizontal line scores as the decision-making vehicle, the "Judge" is a stickout. But the ESP match-up and the requirement for Sustained Pace ability clearly favor Reason To Study as the proper bet. When in doubt, check the numbers upon which the rankings were based.

The numbers to the right of the following array are the numerical differences between the Early and Sustained ratings of each horse. They are often useful in gauging the balance between Early and Sustained Pace.

	EP	SP	EP–SP
I'll Be The Judge	56.12	53.52	2.60
Reason To Study	55.45	53.63	1.82

Since the composition of Sustained Pace is an equal mix of Early Pace and the final fraction, the impact of a high Early Pace rating is considerable. "Balance" is best measured by comparing the ratings of each horse being considered (deduct Sustained Pace from Early Pace). In this example, the relationship of the two factors is much tighter in the case of Reason To Study (1.82 compared to 2.60), thus indicating a greater emphasis on Sustained Pace.

A correlative conclusion is that the final fraction of Reason To Study must be significantly greater than his competitor. And it is: 51.81 to 50.92 fps. When compared to Reason To Study, I'll Be The Judge's profile clearly favors Early Pace and does not fit the current decision model.

WHICH RACES TO USE

A central question in our approach to bias analysis is: Which races should be used to build a reliable model?

To recommend the use of races with the most predictive value is to oversimplify the answer to the question. Those races may not easily be determined. It's necessary for individual handicappers to fully understand the basic class hierarchy at their racetracks. Each circuit reflects the personality of the individual racing secretaries. Restricted claiming races, state-bred limitations, and starter allowances are a few of the possible idiosyncratic offerings on an individual circuit. In southern California, races offered to the handicapper are straightforward to the extent of being dull and uninteresting. There *are* guidelines I recommend for every racing circuit:

1. Avoid the cheapest races carded at the track.

In southern California, currently, the cheapest are $10,000 claiming races, the weakest claiming division on the grounds. Many of the horses competing at that level would be entered for $5000 if that level were available. In actuality, many of those so-called $10,000 horses did drop to that level during the Fairplex and Los Alamitos meetings. Races at the lowest rung on the claiming ladder are usually won by form/condition default, often defying logical analysis.

For the same reasons, I exclude northern California races at the $6250 level.

2. Avoid the highest class at the track.

There is a flip side to the previous argument. The highest-class races consistently contradict an existing bias. In the chapter on energy distribution we'll talk about this to a greater extent; for now, please accept that the higher the class, the more likely a contender will run fast early *and* late. Class *will* tell, and the best horse usually overcomes whatever bias may exist.

3. Avoid the youngest horses on the grounds.

Early-season three-year-olds, and late-season two-year-olds, are not very predictable in terms of energy or model analysis. These youngsters are still learning to run, and many of the races—especially among fillies—become a matter of who can "put away" who. Races are usually decided by all the horses running as fast as they can, as far as they can. The final fraction can often be duplicated by the tractors positioning the starting gate.

This is not to say that races in these categories are unbettable. In many instances they *are* bettable and produce significant profits. Just exclude them from the model worksheet.

4. Avoid maiden claiming races.

These races are also among the weakest on the grounds. Many of the competitors have found permanent homes in the maiden ranks and are incapable of winning, no matter what the bias. When a dropper from the open maiden category wins one of these races, the manner in which they won is usually not important. The class edge was the deciding factor. Similarly, when one of the culls actually wins one of these races, the manner of the win usually has no predictive value to future bias concerns.

Now, which races *should* we use? The races with the most predictive value at any racetrack are the mid-range claiming to the conditioned allowance levels. Day in and day out, these races maintain a predictability that is consistent over time. In southern California those races include $16,000 claiming through nonwinners-of-three allowances. Races above those levels present other problems of class and form best dealt with in other ways. For overall predictability, stay within the recommended boundaries.

As a rule of thumb for other circuits, use claiming races two levels above the lowest level carded at the track. The top side of the scale remains relatively unchanged, although in some areas the local stakes races are merely NW2 races in disguise.

A FEW ADDITIONAL POINTS

1. Maintain separate sprint and route models for dirt and turf races. More often than not, the sprint and route biases will be opposites. For example, the long range profiles for Santa Anita dirt races are:

	AP	EP	SP
Sprints	2	2	4
Routes	3	4	2

Players not distinguishing between the two distance structures at Santa Anita are apt to be working in the wrong direction half the time. How do we achieve high win percentages and high returns on investment (ROI) in that situation? We don't.

2. Maintain a separate place model, especially if you're into exotics. Nothing is more frustrating than predicting the winner of an exacta race and then eating tickets because you missed the place horse.

It's not true that the second most probable winner is the most logical place horse. In actual practice, you'll find that "opposites attract" and the place horse often has a running style just the reverse of the winning profile.

Even in the face of a strong bias toward Early Pace, defeated front runners often give away the secondary awards to late runners catching tiring speed. Conversely, on a sustained track, the Early Pace horse, while not winning, frequently holds on for place.

3. With the intent of constructing a winning model, use only races that you have handicapped. I reemphasize an earlier point. One of the major benefits is the insight gained into your own handicapping skills. If you're weak at picking pacelines, selecting contenders, or adjusting between racetracks, those problems will surface, painfully.

A few words about betting from your model. Much effort has gone into the accumulating of data and subsequent analysis. If the data says bet the top two sustained pace horses, then bet them. Trust your conclusions; don't begin a "what if?" process that is certain to convolute established truths about your handicapping. It's human nature to overanalyze just about everything from motor skills to sex drive; but to do so here can be self-destructive. If you're fortunate enough to discover a dominant ratings bias, then trust your homework and bet with both hands. Go for it.

In the midst of what you've determined to be a strong sustained pace bias, don't be holding tickets on the early pace horse the "experts" may have pushed as a best bet. Have the courage of your convictions and optimize your "inside knowledge." If the winning profile is clear in your mind, then push it the maximum.

DURATION OF THE MODEL

What is the practical life of a decision model? For this question there is no absolute answer. I cannot say, beyond certain guidelines, that a model has any precise life expectancy. During the 1984 Santa Anita meeting I maintained a seven-week uninterrupted route model favoring sustained pace. In 1989 Santa Anita still supports that model as its general tendency. Yet during the 1989 meeting, there were four separate models upon which to base my play.

Weather, time of year, and track maintenance activity and directly influence the racing surface, and the bettor must be able to adjust to changes in tendency. That is both the pain and the pleasure of what we're about. Without those external factors, everyone would perceive the exact bias, and mutuels would plummet.

The answer to the question is: The model is good as long as it's good.

Say what?

Cashing a bet depends upon *today's* reality, not long-term dependability. The fact that we can count on a sustained pace bias at Santa Anita or Belmont Park over time means little today. Adhering to the general trends of a racetrack may produce profits over the long haul, but we can do better. Knowing what happened yesterday, and earlier today, is what produces maximum profits.

Coping with short-term trends is what our decision model is all about. I personally maintain a model until two or three races contradict what I know to be reality. At that point I begin to construct a separate model while still maintaining records for both the new and existing worksheets. If the trend continues, I use only the new material and file the old for future reference. I mentioned earlier the value of matching performance to bias. When the bias changes again, or reverts to type, repeat the process.

The Reason To Study race was based on four route races,

two the previous day and two earlier on the day of his race. It's not coincidental that the four-race model was still valid three weeks later.

THE ROUTE MODEL—APPLICATION

Let's put our newfound insights to work and handicap an Oak Tree route. The following race was run on October 22, 1989, and subsequently became the twelfth race on the worksheet presented earlier.

9th Santa Anita

1 1-16 MILES
SANTA ANITA

1 $\frac{1}{16}$ MILES. (1.40½) CLAIMING. Purse $16,000. 3-year-olds and upward. Weights, 3-year-olds, 117 lbs.; older, 121 lbs. Non-winners of two races at one mile or over since August 15 allowed 3 lbs.; of such a race since then, 5 lbs. Claiming price $16,000; if for $14,000 allowed 2 lbs. (Races when entered for $12,500 or less not considered.)

Polysemous

Ch. g. 5, by Prijinsky—Violet Charm, by Imbros

BAZE R A — 116

Br.—Mazzulli P P (Cal) — Tr.—Mollica Michael A — $16,000

Own.—Pessin S or Marilyn

1989 15 4 1 4 — $44,680
1988 13 0 3 1 — $15,315
Lifetime 42 6 7 6 $70,673

9Oct89-3SA	6½f :213 :442 1:152ft	13 115	6⁹ 68½ 71¹ 816½	Baze R A⁶	25000	76-13 Romaxe, Wicked Idea, HardToMiss 9
30Sep89-9Fpx	6½f :22 :453 1:171ft	3½ 115	53¾ 52½ 42½ 5²	Valenzuela F H ³	22500	88-13 Hard To Miss, Overidge, DonB.Blue8
23Sep89-8Fpx	6½f :452 1:17 ft	6½ 115	64½ 66½ 67 31½	Valenzuela F H ⁶	22500	90-10 Mr. Spade, Tiz Stealin, Polysemous9
23Sep89-Wide into stretch						
13Aug89-1Dmr	7f :222 :451 1:224ft	3 118	5⁴ 6⁴ 4² 11½	Davis R G⁹	16000	88-14 Polysemous, Exploded Jr., Pain 10
13Aug89-Wide final 3/8						
5Aug89-1Dmr	6½f :22 :452 1:163ft	19 114	9⁷ 95½ 63¾ 1nk	Davis R G ¹⁰	18000	85-15 Polysmous,Droully'sBoy,GrnMsco 11
5Aug89-Wide into stretch						
21Jly89-3Hol	6f :222 :452 1:11 ft	4 117	5⁴ 4⁴ 43½ 41¾	Valenzuela P A ¹	20000	84-14 GrnMusco,DscovrdGold,FrstToArrv6
9Jly89-4Hol	6½f :221 :45 1:161ft	2½ 117	2½ 2hd 3³ 35¼	Meza R Q ⁴	20000	88-12 Flying H.,Lark'sLegacy,Polysemous 5
30Jun89-5Hol	6½f :22 :45 1:163ft	3 119	64½ 52½ 32½ 3½	Stevens G L ⁹	c16000	91-16 NtiveConqust,FlyingH.,Polysmous 12
4Jun89-5Hol	1 :453 1:103 1:362ft	*3 115	82½ 3² 21½ 2²	Stevens G L ²	20000	79-14 MountLaguna,Polysemous,Kmikze 12
17May89-5Hol	7f :221 :443 1:231ft	5 117	74¾ 54½ 43 1½	Stevens G L ³ 🇸	16000	88-11 Polysemous, Uncle Foss,RareTyson 8

Sep 16 SA 6f ft 1:13³ H — Sep 9 Dmr 4f ft :49³ H

Matthew T. Parker

Dk. b. or br. g. 7, by Rock Talk—Dee's Might, by Might

FLORES D R — 116

Br.—Lege F M III (Md) — Tr.—Lage Armando — $16,000

Own.—Burke G W

1989 14 2 2 3 — $28,165
1988 1 0 0 0 — $312
Lifetime 37 4 11 5 $206,607
Turf 2 0 0 0 — $1,200

21Sep89-13Fpx	a1⅛ :474 1:122 1:511ft	3 114	2hd 1½ 2hd 31½	Flores D R⁵	A16000	86-14 DnB.Bl,WngOtThWrld,MtthwT.Prkr 7
21Sep89-Drifted out 1/4						
8Sep89-5Dmr	7f :222 :45 1:224ft	4½ 117	41½ 31½ 21½ 2hd	Pincay L Jr⁵	16000	88-12 NtvCnqst,MtthwT.Prkr,BldAndGrn 10
10Aug89-1Dmr	1⅟₁₆:453 1:11 1:44 ft	4½ 117	32½ 2¹ 1⁵ 11¾	Pincay L Jr³	10000	80-20 MtthewT.Prker,Nec,ResonToStudy 8
2Aug89-1Dmr	6f :214 :444 1:101ft	16 1135	7⁴ 52½ 43½ 31	Jauregui L H⁸	10000	86-15 ChiefPl,RiseAPound,MtthwT.Prkr 12
2Aug89-Wide into stretch						
4Jly89-1Hol	6½f :22 :451 1:163ft	6½ 1135	62½ 62¾ 7⁶ 76½	Jauregui L H⁶	10000	85-12 Sandy Mack, Chary Joy,WinedOut 12
18Jun89-1Hol	7f :221 :451 1:234ft	7½ 1125	3½ 1hd 2hd 1hd	Jauregui L H⁵	10000	85-12 MtthwT.Prkr,MnLgnnr,Smln'Smly 11
27May89-1Hol	6f :214 :45 1:10 ft	5¾ 117	64½ 6⁵ 76¾ 9⁷	Guerra W A²	10000	84-10 Cracksman, Pain, On Broadway 12
27May89-Steadied 4 1/2						
13May89-2Hol	6f :221 :443 1:101ft	4½ 116	3¹ 2¹ 2² 32½	Guerra W A ⁹	10000	88-11 RcknghrsDrm,LJllSpdstr;MtthT.Prr 8
4May89-1Hol	7f :221 :45 1:231ft	4½ 117	2½ 2hd 32½ 46½	Guerra W A ¹¹	10000	82-15 Polysemous, Wild Pursuit, Darion 11
27Apr89-5Hol	6f :221 :451 1:094ft	13 117	52¾ 42½ 75¾ 78½	Corral J R ⁶	18000	84-10 Vancealot, Barnhart, Bugarian 8

Oct 15 SA 7f ft 1:28³ H — Oct 9 SA 5f ft 1:00³ H — Oct 2 SA 5f ft 1:01² H — Sep 3 Dmr 5f ft :59⁴ H

G. G.'s Love

BLACK C A	**116**	B. g. 5, by Pappy—Gigi Roni, by Kings Favor
Own.—Dobson D (Lessee)		Br.—Horton & Gretchen (Wash) 1989 7 0 1 3 $6,830
		Tr.—Medeiros Beverly $16,000 1988 12 2 3 2 $7,627
		Lifetime 26 3 4 8 $16,515

80ct89-2SA 1 :463 1:104 1:36 ft 21 116 711 712 711 6151 Dominguez RE5 25000 71-17 Remar,FlyingH.,AManToRemember 8
80ct89—Wide into stretch
23Sep89-7L ga 6f :221 :452 1:094ft 51 113 771 65 54 4nk Boulanger G6 [S] 20000 87-15 TroopsPrmr,BgBdBombr,WndyPrr 8
17Sep89-4L ga 11/16 :471 1:113 1:434ft 41 113 52 211 211 2hd Boulanger G4 16000 80-18 Hydrostatic,G.G.'sLove,Lwschoolld 6
8Sep89-9L ga 1 :462 1:11 1:371ft 61 111 34 32 211 311 Perrine L L6 20000 81-24 OchocoPss,FlnkerNinetn,G.G.'sLov 7
26Aug89-8L ga 1 :454 1:101 1:36 ft 5 116 761 761 761 641 Baze G6 20000 84-20 Sndoonr,SpltCommsson,VwpntAhd 8
17Aug89-9L ga 61f :212 :443 1:161ft 7 116 661 44 56 331 Lamance C8 20000 84-20 PrintsChrming,Hydrosttc,G.G.'sLov 9
4Aug89-8L ga 6f :22 :45 1:094ft 19 116 67 67 441 32 Best F1 20000 85-23 CordovaRed,Sylvia'sBby,G.G.'sLove 6
240ct80-10Pla 170:462 1:104 1:394ft 31 121 631 641 66 57 RennkerL2 Au Rvor H 91-09 Cocolalla Kid, Top Change,SirLyon 6
90ct88-10Pla 1 :464 1:104 1:36 ft 36 115 631 431 43 33 SmmsMW7 Pla Mile H 94-15 Native Act, RegalVixen,G.G.'sLove 10
24Sep88-10Pla a61f :23 :471 1:15 ft 13 117 75 64 541 421 Ochoa A2 Trbltr H — — GeneralKirk,NtiveAct,WynChmpion 9
Oct 19 SA 5f ft 1:014 H   Oct 6 SA 4f ft :493 H   Sep 15 Lga 3f ft :382 B   Sep 2 Lga 3f m :301 B

Triquitraque

SOLIS A	**116**	B. g. 4, by Tantoul—La Pistola, by Riva Ridge
Own.—Flamingo Stable		Br.—Hirsch C L (Cal) 1989 12 0 0 1 $4,540
		Tr.—Silvera Gerald Jr $16,000 1988 11 1 4 3 $47,181
		Lifetime 34 1 4 4 $53,846 Turf 2 0 0 0 $1,406

10ct89-8F px 11/16 :462 1:112 1:44 ft 8 116 761 76 753 641 Castanon J L 7 20000 87-11 Bugarian, Shirkee, Flying H. 9
25Sep89-13F px 11/16 :462 1:113 1:433ft 7 116 973 863 541 321 Ortega L E 7 16000 90-12 RunCougrRun,Ki-Nobre,Triquitrqu 9
25Sep89—Rough start
30Jun89-5Hol 61f :22 :45 1:163ft 41 117 1215 1215 981 541 Pincay L Jr 11 c16000 87-16 NtiveConqust,FlyingH.,Polysmous 12
30Jun89—Wide into stretch
10Jun89-2Hol 61f :22 :45 1:163ft 91 117 971 961 851 523 Pincay L Jr 8 25000 89-13 UndrAndOr,WllInThAr,MnMdnssl 11
10Jun89—Wide final 3/8
26May89-7Hol 7f :214 :44 1:213ft 19 120 811 811 78 651 Solis A 8 [S]Aw27000 91-09 Bag Of Magic,SarosTown,OneDrink 8
26May89—Wide into stretch
14May89-2Hol 61f :221 :444 1:162ft 71 117 1113 1183 863 613 Pincay L Jr 11 20000 91-09 John'sRtrt,Brnhrt,JournyThruTim 11
14May89—Wide into stretch
30Apr89-5Hol 1 :453 1:102 1:353ft 41 117 710 761 741 551 Pincay L Jr 2 20000 80-13 Ono Gummo, Kamp Out, Kamikaze 7
12Apr89-5SA 61f :211 :434 1:151ft 25 116 1293 1215 873 8101 Solis A 2 32000 84-14 Desperte,KevinsDefense,Mgnifico 12
12Apr89—Broke slowly; fanned wide into stretch
11Mar89-2SA 7f :221 :451 1:233ft 12 116 531 411 633 871 Solis A 1 c20000 75-14 GoldnGntlt,TropclWhp,CorsngEgl 11
26Feb89-2SA 61f :213 :442 1:161ft 32 115 1011 873 711 673 Solis A 3 32000 81-14 Pop'sRuling,RdAndBlu,HrdToMiss 10
26Feb89—Wide 3/8 turn
Sep 18 Hol 6f ft 1:144 H   Sep 12 SA 6f ft 1:141 H   ●Sep 6 SA 3f ft :343 H

Spirit Bay

CASTANON J L	**1135**	B. h. 5, by Sir Ivor—Ocean Choir, by Foolish Pleasure
Own.—Branson-Mouslim-Sundquist		Br.—Kinghaven Farms Limited (Ont-C) 1989 17 2 2 2 $46,625
		Tr.—Shulman Sanford $16,000 1988 8 0 3 3 $19,763
		Lifetime 28 3 5 5 $69,380 Turf 9 0 2 1 $20,725

40ct89-9SA 11/16 :473 1:121 1:443ft 21 118 68 56 513 313 4 Pincay L Jr 1 16000 76-20 Our Brave, K.'s Charger, Spirit Bay 7
4 40ct89—Dead heat; Wide into stretch
26Aug89-9Dmr 11/16 :46 1:11 1:43 ft 3 116 763 623 411 1hd Stevens G L 1 c16000 85-09 SpiritBay,MonLegionnire,TresSuve 9
26Aug89—Bumped 1/8
19Aug89-9Dmr 11/16 :454 1:102 1:431ft 16 116 710 771 46 43 Stevens G L 5 20000 81-13 K.'sCharger,BelAirDancer,FlyingH. 10
16Jly89-1Hol 11/8 :47 1:121 1:514ft 51 117 671 311 11 111 Pincay L Jr 8 12500 78-16 SpiritBay,DePillo'sPride,SalvateTel 9
4Jly89-9Hol 11/8 ①:4741:1211:484fm 47 116 1112 117 1093 963 Baze R A 4 Aw31000 75-12 HowVryTochng,SpkHgh,ThM.V.P. 12
21Jun89-8GG 11/8 ①:4741:1221:502fm 45 117 47 47 541 543 Warren R J Jr 2 Aw23000 91-08 AlibiBrgin,SecondLegnd,TuckyJohn 5
10Jun89-9Hol 11/8 ①:4811:1221:482fm 39 115 883 863 853 761 Black C A 3 80000 80-15 Sperry, Point D'Artois, Banuz 8
25May89-8GG 11/8 ①:4811:12 1:503fm 51 119 613 413 35 22 Kaenel J L 2 Aw23000 — — Chief Of Fire, Spirit Bay, Blue Guy 6
6May89-3GG 13/8 ①:4931:4042:181fm 3 117 11 11 11 311 Kaenel J L 1 32000 73-26 PirdAndPintd,TrvldInSrch,SpiritBy 7
6May89—Drifted out 1/16
23Apr89-9SA 11/4 ①:4721:3722:023fm 71 117 69 731 741 451 Pincay L Jr 2 62500 69-26 Everso, Aiglefin, Proud Cat 8
23Apr89—Wide
Oct 14 SA 5f ft 1:004 H   Sep 21 SA 5f ft 1:033 H   Sep 12 Dmr 4f ft :504 H

Dolly's Valdez

SIBILLE R	**116**	Ch. g. 4, by Valdez—In True Form, by Imasmartee
Own.—Nyssen J M		Br.—Green Dolly (Ky) 1989 9 1 1 0 $14,655
		Tr.—Dorfman Leonard $16,000 1988 14 2 2 3 $38,050
		Lifetime 31 3 4 5 $62,405 Turf 2 0 0 0 $875

110ct89-9SA 11/16 :473 1:114 1:493ft 21 118 34 34 571 512 Pincay L Jr 1 c12500 63-12 PssAnothrTb,WondrPlm,Ack'sRply 9
17Sep89-9F px 11/16 :461 1:111 1:432ft 5 116 981 741 641 451 Sibille R 1 16000 83-10 Bugarian, Emigrant Gap,Ki-Nobre 10
17Sep89—Steadied 3/16
30Aug89-9Dmr 11/16 :451 1:101 1:423ft 41 117 811 57 21 12 Pincay L Jr 2 c12500 87-13 Dolly'sVldz,I'llBThJudg,OnBrodwy 12
30Aug89—Wide final 3/8
18Aug89-9Dmr 11/16 :452 1:101 1:501ft *21 117 813 812 711 563 Pincay L Jr 4 12500 72-14 Nec,WonderPlum,MmorisOfBronz 11
18Aug89—Bumped hard start

4Aug89-9Dmr 1 1/16 :464 1:111 1:424ft 8½ 116 86 75 46 26½ Pincay L Jr 7 12500 79-17 King'sHed,Dolly'sVldez,RoylReltiv 11
4Aug89—Wide into stretch
20Jly89-7Hol 1 :452 1:103 1:363ft 9½ 116 3½ 32 88¼ 810¾ Pedroza M A 1 16000 69-23 Ki-Nobre,EmigrntGp,DrouillyFuisse 9
9Jly89-5Hol 1 1/16 :464 1:112 1:43 ft 11 115 33½ 53 66½ 56½ Pedroza M A 5 25000 78-12 HollywoodHys,KntuckyStr,PrExpns 8
25Jun89-5Hol 1 1/16 :46 1:11 1:442ft 14 116 45 66½ 57 56½ Pedroza M A 1 20000 71-19 KentuckyStr,K.'sChrger,BiscynBoy 9
25Jun89—Clipped heels, bobbled 5/16
8Jan89-9SA 1⅛ :464 1:111 1:493ft 4½ 115 84½ 64¾ 54½ 42½ Solis A 1 c20000 78-13 ComfortblLd,HddnRoylty,FrskMNt 9
8Jan89—Wide into stretch
22Dec88-9Hol 1 1/16 :471 1:13 1:463gd 8 114 810 64½ 31 31½ Solis A 8 30000 66-27 Rssuring,SumKindGold,Dolly'sVldz 9
Oct 19 SA 5f ft 1:031 H Oct 7 SA 7f ft 1:281 H Oct 2 SA 5f ft 1:002 H Sep 27 SA 4f ft :494 H

Emperdori
VALENZUELA F H 116
Own.—Tons Of Fun Stable
Ch. h. 7, by Golden Act—Snow Empress, by Young Emperor
Br.—Floyd W & M B (Ky)
Tr.—Martin John F $16,000
Lifetime 56 10 11 8 $353,884
1989 3 2 1 0 $20,660
1988 10 2 1 0 $44,730
Turf 33 4 6 5 $170,659
29Sep89-10Fpx 1 1/16 :462 1:12 1:451ft *1 119 64½ 41 1hd 1no Black C A 4 c12500 85-15 Emperdori,JustAGigolo,GreyWritr 10
23Sep89-9Fpx 1⅜ :494 1:391 2:174ft *6-5 120 3nk 1hd 11½ 2¾ Nakatani C S 4 H12500 85-15 MonLegionnire,Emprdori,GryWritr 6
14Sep89-10Fpx 1 1/16 :453 1:111 1:452ft *3-2 116 56½ 33½ 21½ 12½ Black C A 5 12500 84-16 Emperdori,SilverSurfer,Icecapation 9
14Sep89—Lugged in late
10Dec88-5Hol 1 1/16 :464 1:111 1:434ft *3½ 116 99 76¾ 64¾ 65¾ DelahoussayeE 3 25000 75-15 ProperRider,NoMoneyDown,Shafy 11
19Nov88-9Hol 1 1/16 :461 1:102 1:42 ft 11 116 1212 119¾ 58½ 26½ DelahoussayeE 7 25000 83-11 Bizeboy, Emperdori, Rakaposhi 12
19Nov88—Wide final 3/8
30Oct88-9SA 1 1/16 :473 1:112 1:423ft 3 116 83½ 85½ 1013 1016¾ Valenzuela P A 6 32000 71-13 PassPassPssed,AceroRojo,Monroe 11
30Oct88—Steadied 1st turn
2Oct88-12Fpx 1⅜ :483 1:374 2:162ft 2½ 118 34 31 12 1½ Gryder A T 4 H25000 93-07 Emperdori, Bugarian, Amatar 8
23Sep88-13Fpx a1⅛ :474 1:113 1:50 ft *7-5 113 46½ 24 21½ 11½ Gryder A T 6 A25000 93-08 Emperdori, At The Ritz, Passer II 8
17Sep88-8Fpx 6½f :203 :451 1:162ft 7 116 1011 87 66½ 42½ Gryder A T 2 25000 92-15 Pialor, John's Retreat, Gerril 10
17Sep88—Broke slowly
7Sep88-7Dmr 1 1/16 :453 1:10 1:414ft 12 115 67 67 78½ 712½ Black C A 6 50000 78-17 Power Forward, Armin, Shafy 7
7Sep88—Wide into stretch; lugged in late
Oct 9 Fno 5f ft 1:044 H Sep 5 SA 7f ft 1:303 H Aug 29 SA tr.t 6f ft 1:183 H Aug 22 SA tr.t 5f ft 1:041 H

Emigrant Gap
NAKATANI C S 111[5]
Own.—Benowitz-Calhoun-Lackey
B. g. 4, by Impressive—Winter Tobin, by Tobin Bronze
Br.—Kerr-Kerr-Kerr (Cal)
Tr.—Sinne Gerald M $16,000
Lifetime 27 4 6 1 $59,330
1989 15 2 4 1 $30,405
1988 8 2 1 0 $25,500
28Sep89-11Fpx 6½f :214 :453 1:173ft 7½ 116 74½ 85¾ 811 918½ Pedroza M A1 16000 78-14 CoursingEgle,Pin,SecretSelection 10
28Sep89—Veered in 7/8
24Sep89-8Fpx 6f :22 :451 1:11 ft 3½ 116 31½ 22 2½ 1hd Pedroza M A9 c12500 92-10 Emigrant Gap, Pain, Will B. Gold 10
17Sep89-9Fpx 1 1/16 :461 1:111 1:432ft 8 116 3½ 31 2hd 21¾ Pedroza M A7 16000 92-10 Bugarian, Emigrant Gap,Ki-Nobre 10
8Sep89-5Dmr 7f :222 :45 1:224ft 7½ 116 31 42 43½ 42½ Davis R G10 16000 86-12 NtvCnqst,MtthwT.Prkr,BldAndGrn 10
20Aug89-2Dmr 6½f :214 :444 1:164ft 29 111[5] 65 75 97½ 87½ Jauregui L H8 25000 77-13 RdAndBl,Amnothrbrothr,Jhn'sRtrt 11
20Aug89—Bumped backstretch
5Aug89-1Dmr 6½f :221 :452 1:163ft 14 116 74½ 106¾ 107 918½ DelahoussyeE1 c20000 74-15 Polysmous,Droully'sBoy,GrnMsco 11
5Aug89—Took up 3/16
20Jly89-7Hol 1 :452 1:103 1:363ft *4-5 116 1hd 2½ 2½ 2no McCarron C J9 16000 80-23 Ki-Nobre,EmigrntGp,DrouillyFuisse 9
25Jun89-1Hol 1 :454 1:111 1:371ft 4½ 115 21 1hd 11 1nk McCarron C J8 12500 77-19 EmigrntGp,DonB.Blu,NturllyMitch 12
8Jun89-5Hol 7f :214 :443 1:224ft 5½ 116 44 45 44½ 22¾ DelahoussayeE2 12500 87-14 NtivConqust,EmigrntGp,Crcksmn 12
19May89-2Hol 7f :22 :443 1:221ft 4½ 116 64½ 62¾ 41¾ 2¾ DelhoussyeE2 Ⓢ 16000 92-08 NtrllyMtch,EmgrntGp,LodThWgn 11
●Oct 16 Fpx 6f ft 1:151 H Oct 8 Fpx 6f ft 1:144 H Sep 3 Bmr 5f ft 1:002 H

***Ki-Nobre**
ALMEIDA G 116
Own.—Arcangelli T
Ch. g. 6, by Elliot—Hors Concours, by Nordic
Br.—Haras Dom Octavio (Brz)
Tr.—Perdomo Pico $16,000
Lifetime 28 6 3 7 $38,146
1989 8 1 1 1 $13,710
1988 9 1 1 3 $1,974
Turf 6 2 0 2 $9,392
25Sep89-13Fpx 1 1/16 :462 1:113 1:433ft 6½ 116 74¾ 54½ 32½ 22½ Almeida G6 16000 91-12 RunCougrRun,Ki-Nobre,Triquitrqu 9
25Sep89—Rough trip
17Sep89-9Fpx 1 1/16 :461 1:111 1:432ft 24 116 88 84¾ 32 31¾ Almeida G3 16000 92-10 Bugarian, Emigrant Gap,Ki-Nobre 10
19Aug89-9Dmr 1 1/16 :454 1:102 1:431ft 24 116 811 99½ 67½ 56½ Toro F7 20000 77-13 K.'sCharger,BelAirDancer,FlyingH. 10
5Aug89-9Dmr 1 1/16 :461 1:11 1:433ft 9 111[5] 85¾ 87 77½ 68 Nakatani C S7 20000 74-15 Bicker Bear, Nomad Boi,TresSuave 8
5Aug89—Clipped heels5/16
20Jly89-7Hol 1 :452 1:103 1:363ft 49 116 98 74¾ 32 1no Toro F6 16000 80-23 Ki-Nobre,EmigrntGp,DrouillyFuisse 9
8Jly89-5Hol 1 :451 1:094 1:351ft 39 115 87½ 88 76½ 79½ Toro F9 20000 77-12 ILovRcng,Amnothrbrothr,BscynBy 9
22Jun89-7Hol 6½f :22 :45 1:162ft 80 117 56½ 65½ 611 615½ Castanon A L 2 32000 78-12 BrghtAndRght,RchTgr,UndrAndOvr 6
22Jun89—Checked start
10Jun89-7Hol 1 :451 1:10 1:35 ft 125 112 107½ 107¾ 98½ 914½ Cortez A11 45000 74-13 GoodDelivernc,Dcor,RoylCmronin 11
26Sep88♦5CidadeJardim(Brz a7f : ft — 126 3 Pr Jst Rllr Further, Information, NotAvailable 8
5Sep88♦3CidadeJardim(Brz a7f : fm — 126 ① 3 Pr Falafre Further, Information, NotAvailable 7
Oct 15 Hol 6f ft 1:163 H Sep 8 Bmr 3f ft :351 H Aug 30 Bmr 4f ft :471 H

The profile we'll be looking for once we generate our numbers will be:

AP	EP	SP
2	3	2

We won't be too restrictive in terms of average pace, but we'll insist the bet be one of the top two sustained pace horses. Only if the ESP match-up singles a lone front runner with a class edge will we reconsider our strategy.

Polysemous — Ch. g. 5, by Prijinsky—Violet Charm, by Imbros
BAZE R A — 116 — Br.—Mazzulli P P (Cal) — 1989 15 4 1 4 $44,680
Own.—Pessin S or Marilyn — Tr.—Mellica Michael A — $16,000 — 1988 13 0 3 1 $15,315
Lifetime 42 6 7 6 $70,673

9Oct89-3SA 6½f :213 :442 1:152ft 13 115 69 68½ 711 816½ Baze R A 6 25000 76-13 Romaxe, Wicked Idea, HardToMiss 9
30Sep89-9Fpx 6½f :22 :453 1:171ft 3½ 115 53¾ 52½ 42½ 52 Valenzuela F H 3 22500 88-13 Hard To Miss, Overidge, DonB.Blue 8
23Sep89-8Fpx 6½f :22 :452 1:17 ft 6½ 115 64¼ 66¼ 67 31¼ Valenzuela F H 6 22500 90-10 Mr. Spade, Tiz Stealin, Polysemous 9
23Sep89—Wide into stretch
13Aug89-1Dmr 7f :222 :451 1:224ft 3 118 54 64 42 11¼ Davis R G 2 16000 88-14 Polysemous, Exploded Jr., Pain 10
13Aug89—Wide final 3/8
5Aug89-1Dmr 6½f :221 :452 1:163ft 19 114 97 95¼ 63¾ 1nk Davis R G 10 18000 85-15 Polysmous, Droully'sBoy, GrnMsco 11
5Aug89—Wide into stretch
21Jly89-3Hol 6f :222 :452 1:11 ft 4 117 54 44 43½ 41¾ Valenzuela P A 1 20000 84-14 GrnMusco, DscovrdGold, FrstToArrv 6
9Jly89-4Hol 6½f :221 :45 1:161ft 2½ 117 2½ 2hd 33 35½ Meza R Q 4 20000 88-12 Flying H., Lark'sLegacy, Polysemous 5
30Jun89-5Hol 6½f :22 :45 1:163ft 3 119 64½ 52¼ 32½ 3½ Stevens G L 8 c16000 91-16 NtiveConqust, FlyingH., Polysmous 12
4Jun89-5Hol 1 :453 1:103 1:362ft *3 115 82½ 32 21½ 22 Stevens G L 2 20000 79-14 MountLaguna, Polysemous, Kmikze 12
17May89-5Hol 7f :221 :443 1:231ft 5 117 74¾ 54¼ 43 1½ Stevens G L 3 [S] 16000 88-11 Polysemous, Uncle Foss, RareTyson 8
Sep 16 SA 6f ft 1:133 H — Sep 9 Dmr 4f ft :493 H

ESP: He's been sprinting long enough to suggest he may have more speed than in his one-turn mile of 4Jun89. We'll designate him as mid-pack or P. The class drop (to $16,000 today) usually suggests an improved effort, but his last race is so bad, at a level at which he's been recently competitive, we'll label him a non-contender. When a horse with a dismal, inexcusable last race beats you, it's not a tragedy; just go on to the next bet and don't look back.

Paceline: none

Matthew T. Parker — Dk. b. or br. g. 7, by Rock Talk—Dee's Might, by Might
FLORES D R — 116 — Br.—Lege F M III (Md) — 1989 14 2 2 3 $28,165
Own.—Burke G W — Tr.—Lage Armando — $16,000 — 1988 1 0 0 0 $312
Lifetime 37 4 11 5 $286,607 — Turf 2 0 0 0 $1,200

21Sep89-13Fpx a1⅛ :474 1:122 1:511ft 3 114 2hd 1½ 2hd 31½ Flores D R5 A16000 86-14 DnB.Bl, WngOtThWrld, MtthwT.Prkr 7
21Sep89—Drifted out 1/4
8Sep89-5Dmr 7f :222 :45 1:224ft 4½ 117 41½ 31½ 21½ 2hd Pincay L Jr5 16000 88-12 NtvCnqst, MtthwT.Prkr, BldAndGrn 10
10Aug89-1Dmr 1 1/16 :453 1:11 1:44 ft 4½ 117 32½ 21 15 11¾ Pincay L Jr3 10000 80-20 MtthewT.Prker, Nec, ResonToStudy 8
2Aug89-1Dmr 6f :214 :444 1:101ft 16 1135 74 52½ 43½ 31 Jauregui L H8 10000 86-15 ChiefPl, RiseAPound, MtthwT.Prkr 12
2Aug89—Wide into stretch
4Jly89-1Hol 6½f :22 :451 1:163ft 6¾ 1135 62¾ 62¾ 76 76½ Jauregui L H6 10000 85-12 Sandy Mack, Chary Joy, WinedOut 12
18Jun89-1Hol 7f :221 :451 1:234ft 7½ 1125 3½ 1hd 2hd 1hd Jauregui L H5 10000 85-12 MtthwT.Prkr, MnLgnnr, Smln'Smly 11
27May89-1Hol 6f :214 :45 1:10 ft 5¾ 117 64¾ 65 76¾ 97 Guerra W A2 10000 84-10 Cracksman, Pain, On Broadway 12
27May89—Steadied 4 1/2
13May89-2Hol 6f :221 :443 1:101ft 4¾ 116 31 21 22 32¼ Guerra W A 8 10000 88-11 RcknghrsDrm, LJllSpdstr, MtthT.Prr 8
4May89-1Hol 7f :221 :45 1:231ft 4¾ 117 2½ 2hd 32½ 46½ Guerra W A 11 10000 82-15 Polysemous, Wild Pursuit, Darion 11
27Apr89-5Hol 6f :221 :451 1:094ft 13 117 52¾ 42½ 75¾ 78¼ Corral J R 8 18000 84-10 Vancealot, Barnhart, Bugarian 8
Oct 15 SA 7f ft 1:283 H — Oct 9 SA 5f ft 1:003 H — Oct 2 SA 5f ft 1:012 H — Sep 3 Dmr 5f ft :594 H

ESP: He's run well recently on, and slightly off, the pace. He's an E/P.

Paceline: Use the 21Sep89 race at Fairplex. The fractional and final times at Santa Anita are slightly faster than Fairplex, so we must adjust the paceline by deducting 2 lengths from each pace segment and the final time. The adjusted paceline: 47.2 1:12.0 1:50.4.

G. G.'s Love
BLACK C A
Own.—Dobson D (Lessee)

B. g. 5, by Pappy—Gigi Roni, by Kings Favor
Br.—Horton & Gretchen (Wash)
Tr.—Medeiros Beverly

116

$16,000

| | | | 1989 | 7 | 0 | 1 | 3 | $6,830 |
| | | | 1988 | 12 | 2 | 3 | 2 | $7,627 |

Lifetime 26 3 4 8 $16,515

| 8Oct89-2SA | 1 :463 1:104 1:36 ft | 21 116 | 711 712 711 6151 | Dominguez RE5 | 25000 71-17 Remar,FlyingH.,AManToRemember 8 |
8Oct89—Wide into stretch
23Sep89-7L ga	6f :221 :452 1:094ft	51 113	771 65 54 4nk	Boulanger G6 S 20000 87-15 TrooprsPrmr,BgBdBombr,WndyPrr 8
17Sep89-4L ga	11/16:471 1:113 1:434ft	41 113	52 211 211 2nd	Boulanger G4 16000 80-18 Hydrostatic,G.G.'sLove,LwschoolLd 6
8Sep89-9L ga	1 :462 1:11 1:371ft	61 111	34 32 211 311	Perrine L L6 20000 81-24 OchocoPss,FlnkerNinetn,G.G.'sLov 7
26Aug89-8L ga	1 :454 1:101 1:36 ft	5 116	761 761 761 641	Baze G6 20000 84-20 Sndoonr,SpltCommsson,VwpntAhd 8
17Aug89-9L ga	61/2f:212 :443 1:161ft	7 116	661 44 56 331	Lamance C8 20000 84-20 PrintsChrming,Hydrosttc,G.G.'sLov 9
4Aug89-8L ga	6f :22 :45 1:094ft	19 116	67 67 441 32	Best F1 20000 85-23 CordovaRed,Sylvia'sBby,G.G.'sLove 6
24Oct88-10Pla	170:462 1:104 1:394ft	31 121	631 641 66 57	RennkerL2 Au Rvor H 91-09 Cocolalla Kid, Top Change,SirLyon 6
9Oct88-10Pla	1 :464 1:104 1:36 ft	36 115	631 431 43 33	SmmsMW7 Pla Mile H 94-15 Native Act, RegalVixen,G.G.'sLove 10
24Sep88-10Pla	a61/2f:23 :471 1:15 ft	13 117	75 64 541 421	Ochoa A2 Trbltr H — — GeneralKirk,NtiveAct,WynChmpion 9

Oct 19 SA 5f ft 1:014 H   Oct 6 SA 4f ft :493 H   Sep 15 Lga 3f ft :382 B   Sep 2 Lga 3f m :381 B

ESP: His dominant style is S, but his last race, and his inability to win at the same approximate level at a lesser track, caused me to eliminate him as a contender.

Paceline: none

Triquitraque
SOLIS A
Own.—Flamingo Stable

B. g. 4, by Tantoul—La Pistola, by Riva Ridge
Br.—Hirsch C L (Cal)
Tr.—Silvera Gerald Jr

116

$16,000

			1989	12	0	0	1	$4,540
			1988	19	1	4	3	$47,181
			Turf	2	0	0	0	$1,406

Lifetime 34 1 4 4 $53,045

| 10Oct89-8Fpx | 11/16:462 1:112 1:44 ft | 8 116 | 761 76 751 641 | Castanon J L 2 20000 87-11 Bugarian, Shirkee, Flying H. 9 |
| 25Sep89-13Fpx | 11/16:462 1:113 1:433ft | 7 116 | 971 861 541 321 | Ortega L E 2 16000 90-12 RunCougrRun,Ki-Nobre,Triquitrqu 9 |
25Sep89—Rough start
| 30Jun89-5Hol | 61/2f:22 :45 1:163ft | 41 117 | 12151215 981 541 | Pincay L Jr 11 c16000 87-16 NtiveConqust,FlyingH.,Polysmous 12 |
30Jun89—Wide into stretch
| 10Jun89-2Hol | 61/2f:22 :45 1:163ft | 91 117 | 971 961 851 521 | Pincay L Jr 8 25000 89-13 UndrAndOr,WllInThAr,MnMdnssI 11 |
10Jun89—Wide final 3/8
| 26May89-7Hol | 7f :214 :44 1:213ft | 19 120 | 811 811 78 651 | Solis A 8 Aw27000 91-09 Bag Of Magic,SarosTown,OneDrink 8 |
26May89—Wide into stretch
| 14May89-2SA | 61/2f:221 :444 1:162ft | 71 117 | 11131181 861 611 | Pincay L Jr 11 20000 91-09 John'sRtrt,Brnhrt,JournyThruTim 11 |
14May89—Wide into stretch
| 30Apr89-5Hol | 1 :453 1:102 1:353ft | 41 117 | 710 761 741 551 | Pincay L Jr 2 20000 80-13 Ono Gummo, Kamp Out, Kamikaze 7 |
| 12Apr89-5SA | 61/2f:211 :434 1:151ft | 25 116 | 12931215 871 8101 | Solis A 2 32000 84-14 Desperte,KevinsDefense,Mgnifico 12 |
12Apr89—Broke slowly; fanned wide into stretch
| 11Mar89-2SA | 7f :221 :451 1:233ft | 12 116 | 531 411 631 871 | Solis A 1 c20000 75-14 GoldnGntlt,TropclWhp,CorsngEgl 11 |
| 26Feb89-2SA | 61/2f:213 :442 1:161ft | 32 115 | 1011 871 711 671 | Solis A 3 32000 81-14 Pop'sRuling,RdAndBlu,HrdToMiss 10 |
26Feb89—Wide 3/8 turn

Sep 18 Hol 6f ft 1:144 H   Sep 12 SA 6f ft 1:141 H   ●Sep 6 SA 3f ft :343 H

ESP: This is a truly bad horse. He lags early and then makes an ineffective late run. He's 1 for 34 lifetime, and why trainer Rivera decided to assume the liability on 30Jun89 is beyond comprehension. A noncontender.

Paceline: none

```
Spirit Bay                          B. h. 5, by Sir Ivor—Ocean Choir, by Foolish Pleasure
                                    Br.—Kinghaven Farms Limited (Ont-C)        1989 17 2 2 2     $46,625
  CASTANON J L              1135    Tr.—Shulman Sanford          $16,000       1988  8 0 3 3     $19,763
Own.—Branson-Moualim-Sundquist      Lifetime  28 3 5 5  $69,388                Turf  9 0 2 1     $20,725
4Oct89-9SA    1 1/16:473 1:121 1:443ft  2¾ 118  68  56  51¾ 31¾ ♦Pincay L Jr 1  16000 76-20 Our Brave, K.'s Charger, Spirit Bay 7
  ♦ 4Oct89—Dead heat; Wide into stretch
26Aug89-9Dmr  1 1/16:46 1:11 1:43 ft    3 116   76¾ 62¾ 41¼ 1hd  Stevens G L 1  c16000 85-09 SpiritBay,MonLegionnire,TresSuve 9
  26Aug89—Bumped 1/8
19Aug89-9Dmr  1 1/16:454 1:102 1:431ft  16 116  710 77½ 46  43   Stevens G L 5   20000 81-13 K.'sCharger,BelAirDancer,FlyingH. 10
16Jly89-1Hol  1⅛:47 1:121 1:514ft       5¼ 117  67½ 31½ 11  1¾   Pincay L Jr 6   12500 78-16 SpiritBay,DePillo'sPride,SalvateTel 9
4Jly89-9Hol   1⅛Ⓣ:4741:1211:484fm       47 116  11121117 109¼ 98¾ Baze R A 4   Aw31000 75-12 HowVryTochng,SpkHgh,ThM.V.P. 12
21Jun89-8GG   1⅛Ⓣ:4741:1211:502fm       4¼ 119  47  47  54¼ 54¾  Warren RJJr 2 Aw23000 91-08 AlibiBrgin,SecondLegnd,TuckyJohn 6
10Jun89-9Hol  1⅛Ⓣ:4811:1221:482fm       39 115  88¾ 86¾ 85¾ 76¼  Black C A 8     80000 80-15 Sperry, Point D'Artois, Banuz 8
25May89-8GG   1⅛Ⓣ:4811:12 1:503fm       5½ 119  613 413 35  22   Kaenel J L 2  Aw23000 — — Chief Of Fire, Spirit Bay, Blue Guy 6
6May89-3GG    1⅜Ⓣ:4931:4042:181fm       3 117   1½  1½  1½  31¼  Kaenel J L 1    32000 73-26 PirdAndPintd,TrvldInSrch,SpiritBy 7
  6May89—Drifted out 1/16
23Apr89-9SA   1¼Ⓣ:4721:3722:023fm       7½ 117  69  73¼ 74¼ 45¼  Pincay L Jr 2   62500 69-26 Everso, Aiglefin, Proud Cat 8
  23Apr89—Wide
 Oct 14 SA 5f ft 1:004 H        Sep 21 SA 5f ft 1:033 H        Sep 12 Dmr 4f ft :504 H
```

ESP: S

Paceline: 4Oct89. That line represents his current form/condition, and was over today's surface. Especially with claiming types, the more current the paceline, the more reliable the figures.

ESP: S

```
Dolly's Valdez                      Ch. g. 4, by Valdez—In True Form, by Imacmartee
                                    Br.—Green Dolly (Ky)                       1989  9 1 1 0     $14,695
  SIBILLE R                  116    Tr.—Dorfman Leonard          $16,000       1988 14 2 2 3     $38,050
Own.—Nyssen J M                     Lifetime  31 3 4 5  $52,605                Turf  2 0 0 0     $875
11Oct89-9SA   1⅛:473 1:114 1:493ft     2¾ 118  34  34  57½ 512  Pincay L Jr 2  c12500 69-12 PssAnothrTb,WondrPlm,Ack'sRply 9
17Sep89-9Fpx  1 1/16:461 1:111 1:432ft 5 116   98¼ 74¾ 64½ 45¼ Sibille R 1      16000 89-10 Bugarian, Emigrant Gap,Ki-Nobre 10
  17Sep89—Steadied 3/16
30Aug89-9Dmr  1 1/16:451 1:101 1:423ft 4½ 117  811 57  2½  12   Pincay L Jr 2  c12500 87-13 Dolly'sVldz,I'llBThJudg,OnBrodwy 12
  30Aug89—Wide final 3/8
18Aug89-9Dmr  1⅛:452 1:101 1:501ft    *2¾ 117  813 812 711 56¾  Pincay L Jr 4   12500 72-14 Nec,WonderPlum,MmorisOfBronz 11
  18Aug89—Bumped hard start
4Aug89-9Dmr   1 1/16:464 1:111 1:424ft 8¼ 116  86  75  46  26½  Pincay L Jr 7   12500 79-17 King'sHed,Dolly'sVldez,RoylReltiv 11
  4Aug89—Wide into stretch
20Jly89-7Hol  1 :452 1:103 1:363ft     9½ 116  3½  32  88½ 810¾ Pedroza M A 1   16000 69-23 Ki-Nobre,EmigrntGp,DrouillyFuisse 9
9Jly89-5Hol   1 1/16:464 1:112 1:43 ft 11 115  33½ 53  66½ 56½  Pedroza M A 5   25000 78-12 HollywoodHys,KntuckyStr,PrExpns 8
25Jun89-5Hol  1 1/16:46 1:11 1:442ft   14 116  45  66½ 57  56½  Pedroza M A 1   20000 71-19 KentuckyStr,K.'sChrger,BiscynBoy 9
  25Jun89—Clipped heels, bobbled 5/16
8Jan89-9SA    1⅛:464 1:111 1:493ft     4¼ 115  84¼ 64¾ 54½ 42½  Solis A 1      c20000 78-13 ComfortblLd,HddnRoylty,FrskMNt 9
  8Jan89—Wide into stretch
22Dec88-9Hol  1 1/16:471 1:13 1:463gd  8 114   810 64½ 31  31¼  Solis A 8       30000 66-27 Rssuring,SumKindGold,Dolly'sVldz 9
 Oct 19 SA 5f ft 1:031 H     Oct 7 SA 7f ft 1:281 H     Oct 2 SA 5f ft 1:002 H     Sep 27 SA 4f ft :494 H
```

Paceline: None. His declining form culminated in a 12-length defeat at 5–2 odds. It will take more than the claim for this one to regain the form of his 30Aug89 race. A 3 for 31 win record isn't encouragement to expect a bounce-back effort.

Emperdori — Ch. h. 7, by Golden Act—Snow Empress, by Young Emperor
VALENZUELA F H — 116 — Br.—Floyd W & M B (Ky) — 1989 3 2 1 0 $20,660
Own.—Tons Of Fun Stable — Tr.—Martin John F — $16,000 — 1988 10 2 1 0 $44,730
Lifetime 56 10 11 8 $353,884 — Turf 33 4 6 5 $170,659
29Sep89-10Fpx 1 1/16 :46^2 1:12 1:45^{1}ft *1 119 6$^{4\frac{1}{2}}$ 4^1 1^{hd} 1no Black C A4 c12500 85-15 Emperdori,JustAGigolo,GreyWritr 10
23Sep89-9Fpx 1 3/8 :49^4 1:39^1 2:17^{4}ft *6-5 120 3^{nk} 1^{hd} 1$^{1\frac{1}{2}}$ 2$^{\frac{3}{4}}$ Nakatani C S4 H12500 85-15 MonLegionnire,Emprdori,GryWritr 6
14Sep89-10Fpx 1 1/16 :45^3 1:11^1 1:45^{2}ft *3-2 116 5$^{6\frac{1}{4}}$ 3$^{3\frac{1}{2}}$ 2$^{1\frac{1}{2}}$ 1$^{2\frac{1}{2}}$ Black C A5 12500 84-16 Emperdori,SilverSurfer,Icecapation 9
14Sep89—Lugged in late
10Dec88-5Hol 1 1/16 :46^4 1:11^1 1:43^{4}ft *3/4 116 9^9 7$^{6\frac{3}{4}}$ 6$^{4\frac{3}{4}}$ 6$^{5\frac{3}{4}}$ DelahoussayeE3 25000 75-15 ProperRider,NoMoneyDown,Shafy 11
19Nov88-9Hol 1 1/16 :46^1 1:10^2 1:42 ft 11 116 12^{12}11$^{9\frac{3}{4}}$ 5$^{8\frac{1}{2}}$ 2$^{6\frac{1}{2}}$ DelahoussayeE7 25000 83-11 Bizeboy, Emperdori, Rakaposhi 12
19Nov88—Wide final 3/8
30Oct88-9SA 1 1/16 :47^3 1:11^2 1:42^{3}ft 3 116 8$^{3\frac{1}{4}}$ 8$^{5\frac{1}{4}}$10^{13}10$^{16\frac{3}{4}}$ Valenzuela P A6 32000 71-13 PassPassPssed,AceroRojo,Monroe 11
30Oct88—Steadied 1st turn
2Oct88-12Fpx 1 3/8 :48^3 1:37^4 2:16^{2}ft 2 1/4 118 3^4 3^1 1^2 1$^{\frac{1}{2}}$ Gryder A T4 H25000 93-07 Emperdori, Bugarian, Amatar 8
23Sep88-13Fpx a1 1/8 :47^4 1:11^3 1:50 ft *7-5 113 4$^{6\frac{1}{2}}$ 2^4 2$^{1\frac{1}{2}}$ 1$^{1\frac{1}{2}}$ Gryder A T6 A25000 93-08 Emperdori, At The Ritz, Passer II 8
17Sep88-8Fpx 6 1/2f :20^3 :45^1 1:16^{2}ft 7 116 10^{11} 8^7 6$^{6\frac{1}{2}}$ 4$^{2\frac{1}{4}}$ Gryder A T9 25000 92-15 Pialor, John's Retreat, Gerril 10
17Sep88—Broke slowly
7Sep88-7Dmr 1 1/16 :45^3 1:10 1:41^{4}ft 12 115 6^7 6^7 7$^{8\frac{1}{4}}$ 7$^{12\frac{1}{2}}$ Black C A6 50000 78-17 Power Forward, Armin, Shafy 7
7Sep88—Wide into stretch; lugged in late
Oct 9 Fno 5f ft 1:04^4 H — Sep 5 SA 7f ft 1:30^3 H — Aug 29 SA tr.t 6f ft 1:18^3 H — Aug 22 SA tr.t 5f ft 1:04^1 H

ESP: Only at the marathon distance of 1⅜ miles is he anything other than an S.

Paceline: 29Sep89. Adjust the line as we did with Matthew T. Parker: 2 lengths at all calls: 46.0 1:11.3 1:44.4.

Emigrant Gap — B. g. 4, by Impressive—Winter Tobin, by Tobin Bronze
NAKATANI C S — 111^5 — Br.—Kerr-Kerr-Kerr (Cal) — 1989 15 2 4 1 $30,405
Own.—Benewitz-Calhoun-Lackey — Tr.—Sinne Gerald M — $16,000 — 1988 8 2 1 0 $25,500
Lifetime 27 4 6 1 $59,330
28Sep89-11Fpx 6 1/2f :21^4 :45^3 1:17^{3}ft 7 1/2 116 7$^{4\frac{1}{2}}$ 8$^{5\frac{3}{4}}$ 8^{11} 9$^{18\frac{1}{4}}$ Pedroza M A1 16000 70-14 CoursingEgle,Pin,SecretSelection 10
28Sep89—Veered in 7/8
24Sep89-8Fpx 6f :22 :45^1 1:11 ft 3 1/2 116 3$^{1\frac{1}{2}}$ 2^2 2$^{\frac{1}{2}}$ 1^{hd} Pedroza M A9 c12500 92-10 Emigrant Gap, Pain, Will B. Gold 10
17Sep89-9Fpx 1 1/16 :46^1 1:11^1 1:43^{2}ft 8 116 3$^{\frac{1}{2}}$ 3^1 2^{hd} 2$^{1\frac{3}{4}}$ Pedroza M A7 16000 92-10 Bugarian, Emigrant Gap,Ki-Nobre 10
8Sep89-5Dmr 7f :22^2 :45 1:22^{4}ft 7 1/2 116 3^1 4^2 4$^{3\frac{1}{2}}$ 4$^{2\frac{1}{4}}$ Davis R G10 16000 86-12 NtvCnqst,MtthwT.Prkr,BldAndGrn 10
20Aug89-2Dmr 6 1/2f :21^4 :44^4 1:16^{4}ft 29 111^5 6^5 7^5 9$^{7\frac{1}{2}}$ 8$^{7\frac{1}{4}}$ Jauregui L H8 25000 77-13 RdAndBl,Amnothrbrothr,Jhn'sRtrt 11
20Aug89—Bumped backstretch
5Aug89-1Dmr 6 1/2f :22^1 :45^2 1:16^{3}ft 14 116 7$^{4\frac{1}{2}}$10$^{6\frac{3}{4}}$10^7 9$^{10\frac{1}{2}}$ DelahoussyeE1 c20000 74-15 Polysmous,Droully'sBoy,GrnMsco 11
5Aug89—Took up 3/16
20Jly89-7Hol 1 :45^2 1:10^3 1:36^{3}ft *4-5 116 1^{hd} 2$^{\frac{1}{2}}$ 2$^{\frac{1}{2}}$ 2no McCarron C J9 16000 80-23 Ki-Nobre,EmigrntGp,DrouillyFuisse 9
25Jun89-1Hol 1 :45^4 1:11^1 1:37^{1}ft 4 1/2 115 2^1 1^{hd} 1^1 1^{nk} McCarron C J8 12500 77-19 EmigrntGp,DonB.Blu,NturllyMitch 12
8Jun89-5Hol 7f :21^4 :44^3 1:22^{4}ft 5 3/4 116 4^4 4^5 4$^{4\frac{1}{2}}$ 2$^{2\frac{3}{4}}$ DelahoussayeE2 12500 87-14 NtivConqust,EmigrntGp,Crcksmn 12
19May89-2Hol 7f :22 :44^3 1:22^{1}ft 4 1/2 116 6$^{4\frac{1}{2}}$ 6$^{2\frac{3}{4}}$ 4$^{1\frac{3}{4}}$ 2$^{\frac{3}{4}}$ DelhoussyeE2 Ⓢ 16000 92-08 NtrllyMtch,EmgrntGp,LodThWgn 11
●Oct 16 Fpx 6f ft 1:15^1 H — Oct 8 Fpx 6f ft 1:14^4 H — Sep 3 Dmr 5f ft 1:00^2 H

ESP: E/P

Paceline: None. The excuse "veered in at the 7/8" is quite serious at a "bullring" track. The turns are tight, and failure to effectively negotiate them has caused more than a few defeats.

Then why have I eliminated Emigrant Gap as a contender?

This horse has twice shown a strong liking for the sharp turns at Fairplex, both times from the disadvantaged outside posts. Therefore, when he blows the first turn from an inside post and then fails to make a serious move of any kind, we're probably looking at a rapidly declining horse. Don't expect this kind to bounce back with a peak effort.

ESP: S

Paceline: 17Sep89. His last race was with a "rough trip," and since both of the last two were good efforts, it makes sense to use the untroubled race. My Fairplex adjustments are based on a *Daily Racing Form* variant of 13, and with the 10 attached to this paceline, we'll leave the race unadjusted. (In a subsequent chapter, we'll develop a method for adjusting the *Form* variant.)

Contenders

(1) Matthew T. Parker E/P
(2) Spirit Bay S
(3) Emperdori S
(4) Ki-Nobre S

Feet-Per-Second Array

	1Fr	2Fr	3Fr	AP	EP	SP	FX
Matthew T.	55.67	53.69	50.70	53.92	55.00	52.85	n/a
Spirit Bay	53.78	54.47	52.23	53.57	54.01	53.12	"
Emperdori	56.47	52.81	50.00	53.87	55.16	52.58	"
Ki-Nobre	55.41	54.10	52.17	54.25	54.95	53.56	"

The Rankings

	AP	EP	SP	FX
Ki-Nobre	1	3	1	X
Matthew T. Parker	2	2	3	X
Emperdori	3	1	4	X
Spirit Bay	4	4	2	X

	AP	EP	SP
Target Profile	2	3	2

Earlier in this chapter I briefly mentioned that one of the major benefits of keeping a model was the honing of pattern recognition skills. Ki-Nobre's 1–3–1 should be like a magnet in drawing the handicapper's attention. He is ideal in all categories, exceeding our standard in the two most important: Average and Sustained Pace. Only Ki-Nobre and Spirit Bay favor Sustained Pace, a requirement we drew earlier in analyzing the model, but Spirit Bay falls well short of his rival in average pace.

In the absence of a solid front-running type capable of overturning the bias by stealing a paceless race, Ki-Nobre is a prime bet.

The price on Ki-Nobre indicates the southern California crowd has some difficulty equating Fairplex races with Santa Anita or

Del Mar. In later chapters we'll gain a significant edge by developing track-to-track adjustments and learning to effectively apply the *Racing Form* variants.

NINTH RACE
Santa Anita
OCTOBER 22, 1989

1 1/16 MILES. (1.40⅕) CLAIMING. Purse $16,000. 3-year-olds and upward. Weights, 3-year-olds, 117 lbs.; older, 121 lbs. Non-winners of two races at one mile or over since August 15 allowed 3 lbs.; of such a race since then, 5 lbs. Claiming price $16,000; if for $14,000 allowed 2 lbs. (Races when entered for $12,500 or less not considered.)

Value of race $16,000; value to winner $8,800; second $3,200; third $2,400; fourth $1,200; fifth $400. Mutuel pool $318,245. Exacta pool $562,056.

Last Raced	Horse	Eqt.	A.	Wt	PP	St	¼	½	¾	Str	Fin	Jockey	Cl'g Pr	Odds $1
25Sep89 ^{13}Fpx^{2}	Ki-Nobre		6	116	9	9	7^{4}	$5^{1\frac{1}{2}}$	4^{1}	$1^{1\frac{1}{2}}$	$1^{3\frac{1}{2}}$	Almeida G	16000	9.90
8Oct89 ^{2}SA^{6}	G. G.'s Love		5	116	3	4	4^{5}	4^{4}	5^{4}	$4^{\frac{1}{2}}$	2^{2}	Black C A	16000	12.30
21Sep89 ^{13}Fpx^{3}	Matthew T. Parker		7	116	2	2	3^{2}	$3^{1\frac{1}{2}}$	3^{1}	2^{1}	$3^{\frac{3}{4}}$	Flores D R	16000	2.80
4Oct89 ^{9}SA^{3}	Spirit Bay	b	5	113	5	6	5^{hd}	$6^{\frac{1}{2}}$	6^{hd}	5^{2}	4^{1}	Castanon J L^{5}	16000	2.40
9Oct89 ^{3}SA^{8}	Polysemous	b	5	116	1	3	1^{hd}	1^{hd}	1^{hd}	3^{1}	$5^{1\frac{3}{4}}$	Baze R A	16000	6.40
11Oct89 ^{9}SA^{5}	Dolly's Valdez	b	4	116	6	5	$6^{1\frac{1}{2}}$	7^{6}	7^{7}	$6^{2\frac{1}{2}}$	6^{2}	Sibille R	16000	15.50
29Sep89 ^{10}Fpx^{1}	Emperdori	b	7	116	7	7	8^{6}	8^{5}	8^{4}	7^{3}	$7^{1\frac{1}{2}}$	Valenzuela F H	16000	10.30
1Oct89 ^{8}Fpx^{6}	Triquitraque		4	116	4	8	9	9	9	9	$8^{1\frac{1}{4}}$	Solis A	16000	10.80
28Sep89 ^{11}Fpx^{9}	Emigrant Gap		4	111	8	1	2^{1}	2^{1}	2^{hd}	$8^{2\frac{1}{2}}$	9	Nakatani C S^{5}	16000	9.10

OFF AT 5:15. Start good. Won ridden out. Time, :23⅕, :46⅘, 1:11⅗, 1:37⅘, 1:43⅘ Track good.

$2 Mutuel Prices:			
10-KI-NOBRE	21.80	10.80	6.60
3-G. G.'S LOVE		18.80	6.60
2-MATTHEW T. PARKER			4.20

$5 EXACTA 10-3 PAID $1,111.50.

Ch. g, by Elliot—Hors Councours, by Nordic. Trainer Perdomo Pico. Bred by Haras Dom Octavio (Brz).

KI-NOBRE, devoid of early speed after he broke slowly, circled rivals to reach the front a quarter of a mile out while our wide and drew away. G. G.'S LOVE, never far back, was shuffled back a bit on the far turn, came into the stretch four wide and had enough of a response in the drive to prove second best. MATTHEW T. PARKER forced the early pace, engaged for the lead from along the inside rail nearing the end of the backstretch but weakened in the drive. SPIRIT BAY, outrun early, lacked the needed rally. POLYSEMOUS vied for the lead through the early stages and gave way. DOLLY'S VALDEZ was six wide into the stretch. EMPERDORI broke through the gate prior to the start, then was never prominent after getting away on terms with the field. EMIGRANT GAP, a pace factor for a little more than six furlongs, faltered while lugging out and was five wide into the stretch. HYDROSTATIC (5) WAS SCRATCHED BY THE STEWARDS ON THE ADVICE OF THE VETERINARIAN. ALL WAGERS ON HIM IN THE REGULAR AND EXACTA POOLS WERE ORDERED REFUNDED AND ALL OF HIS PICK NINE SELECTIONS WERE SWITCHED TO THE FAVORITE, SPIRIT BAY (6).

Owners— 1, Arcangelli T; 2, Dobson D (Lessee) & Horton; 3, Burke G W; 4, Branson-Moualim-Sundquist; 5, Pessin S or Marilyn; 6, Nyssen J N; 7, Tons Of Fun Stable; 8, Flamingo Stable; 9, Benowitz-Calhoun-Lackey.

Trainers— 1, Perdomo Pico; 2, Medeiros Beverly; 3, Lage Armando; 4, Shulman Sanford; 5, Mollica Michael A; 6, Dorfman Leonard; 7, Martin John F; 8, Silvera Gerald Jr; 9, Sinne Gerald M.

Scratched—Hydrostatic (17Sep89 ^{4}Lga^{1}).

THE SPRINT MODEL

The development, interpretation, and application of a sprint model is identical to the route model. The following worksheet is for the same period of the 1989 Oak Tree at Santa Anita meeting. We'll take the time to develop the model with the specific reason of using it for the final chapter of the book: one week's worth of racing at Oak Tree.

Date	*Dist*	*AP*	*EP*	*SP*	*FX*
10–18	7	2	3	2	3
"	6½	1	1	3	2

"	6	2	2	3	2
"	6	1	1	1	1
10–19	6	1	1	3	1
10–20	6	1	2	1	1
"	6½	2	1	3	3
10–21	6½	1	1	4	1
10–22	6	1	1	1	1
"	6	2	1	4	1

The seven-furlong race on 10–18–89 should be dropped from the calculation of the model. The race leans toward Sustained Pace, while nearly all the other profiles favor an imbalance in the other direction. That's typical for that distance.

AP	EP	SP	FX
1.55	1.22	2.55	1.77

This is another very tight model which, like the route model, represents the long-term paradoxical characteristics of the Santa Anita surface. The sprints strongly favor Early Pace and Average Pace, the opposite pattern from routes. The material we're analyzing represents my handicapping over a ten-race sample and does not reflect all the races carded for the five days. I did not bet all of these races, nor did I win all the races I did play. The period, however, *was* successful and led to an excellent follow-up week using the data from the model.

The decision model we'll be using later:

AP	EP	SP	FX
2.0	2.0	3.0	2.0

Unlike the route model, the imbalance is toward Early Pace. Potential bets should be in the top two early, with a strong ranking in Average Pace. Based on the short 3 ranking in Sustained Pace, potential plays cannot be the weakest finishers of our contenders. In other words, it will not be wise to blindly play the number-one-ranked Early Pace horse.

Prior to the 1986 Santa Anita meeting Early Pace was so dominant that 2–5 (Early-Sustained) profiles were frequent winners, usually leaving the late runners with only minor awards. The introduction of a higher sand content to the surface changed the characteristics of the racetrack. Where early speed was once dominant in the extreme, today there must be a reasonable balance between Early and Sustained Pace. Fortunately for the perceptive player, Santa Anita's "speed crazy" reputation still persists. You and I will cash a lot of bets using the knowledge from our decision models.

SUMMARY

I purposely did not use a larger sample of races. My intent was to demonstrate the effectiveness of the procedure in identifying the immediate characteristics of the track we intend to play. I assure you, the models we developed are closely in tune with the long-term biases at Santa Anita. In a small sample of races we accurately identified profiles that will serve us over the longer term.

In no way is this material limited in application. The principles are applicable at all tracks, in all parts of the country. When I visit other racetracks, I handicap six to ten races from several days prior to the visit and construct a working model from the data. Granted, I may already know the results of those races and may not be accurately assessing my choice of contenders and pacelines, but the model is usable and always worth the effort.

CHAPTER VIII

The Track Profile

IN THE PREVIOUS CHAPTER I detailed the importance of analyzing races you've handicapped with the expressed intent of developing a decision model. The model served to detail the effectiveness of a handicapping methodology *and* the reality of the racetrack. Players maintaining a model stay in touch with their current skill levels and the demands of the racetrack.

Unfortunately, not all handicappers can handicap on a daily basis, and often find a changed reality from session to session. In this chapter we'll talk about a less time-consuming and only marginally less effective approach to bias analysis. We'll use the results charts to develop a track profile with which we can make many of the same analytical judgments we made in the previous chapter.

Our goal is to answer the following three questions:

(1) Where must a typical winner be positioned at the first call of the race?

(2) Where must a typical winner be positioned at the second call of the race?

(3) Is there a most effective running style at this racetrack?

Any handicapper unable to *confidently* answer all three questions is missing an opportunity to gain an advantage over the competition. Top handicappers, regardless of methodology, are able to rattle off the answers without hesitation. Pace handicappers unable to do so are playing the game with one hand tied behind their backs. More than with any other selection approach, pace analysis demands handicappers know *exactly* how races are being won.

The procedure we'll develop only requires a few minutes each day with the results charts, yet will accurately answer all three questions. *Any* handicapping methodology will be strengthened from the effort.

THE WORKSHEET

Dist	Ent	1Call	2Call	%E	ESP
				N/A	

Data Entries

Dist: The distance of the race. Separate profiles *must* be kept for sprints and routes, and for unique distances within a single distance structure. Seven-furlong races, for example, often require a different running style from the shorter sprints. Likewise, eight furlongs, especially a one-turn mile, can differ significantly from the longer routes.

Ent: The number of entries in the race. The significance of fourth position early in the race is far greater in a twelve-horse field than in a field of six runners. Many of our conclusions will be based on probable position in a race.

1Call: Position *and* beaten lengths of the winners at the first call. Both items of information are valuable to our analysis.

2Call: Position and beaten lengths of the winners at the second call.

%E: The winner's percentage of early energy expenditure. For now, we'll leave this blank. In the chapter on energy distribution we'll develop a procedure for establishing basic parameters for energy exertion. The track profile is an excellent vehicle for maintaining the data.

ESP: The running style of the winner; early pace, sustained pace, or presser.

Procedure

The material that follows was prepared by the author during a trip to Las Vegas in the summer of 1989. My intent was to play the new Arlington track in addition to my home track, Del Mar. Unlike Del Mar, however, I had no track variants or par times with which to aid my Chicago handicapping. The trip lasted only a few days, so creating variants more elaborate than the *Daily Racing Form* variant was out of the question. A track profile, aided by the *DRF* variant, can be a powerful tool in that situation.

The data used to develop the profile consisted of results from three days of racing: August 19, 20, and 21. I've included the 19Aug89 races, and part of the card on 20Aug89, so we can work together on the profile. We'll record the characteristics of winning performances in sprints, routes, and turf races. Once completed, we'll discuss the interpretation of the data and how best to apply the profile to the handicapping process.

FIRST RACE

Arlington

AUGUST 19, 1989

6 FURLONGS. (1.08) CLAIMING. Purse $8,500. 3-year-olds and upward. Weight, 3-year-olds, 117 lbs.; older, 122 lbs. Non-winners of two races since July 15 allowed 3 lbs.; of a race since then, 5 lbs. Claiming price $12,500; for each $1,000 to $10,500 allowed 2 lbs. (Races when entered to be claimed for $8,500 or less not considered.) 46TH DAY. WEATHER CLEAR. TEMPERATURE 77 DEGREES.

Value of race $8,500; value to winner $5,100; second $1,700; third $935; fourth $510; fifth $255. Mutuel pool $148,180. Quinella pool $43,379. Perfecta pool $35,828.

Last Raced	Horse	Eqt.A Wt PP St	¼	½	Str	Fin	Jockey	Cl'g Pr	Odds $1
9Aug89 5AP2	Adam Bomb	b 5 117 4 2	41	41½	31½	1¾	Bartram B E	12500	2.50
30Jly89 3AP4	Paris Venture	b 6 117 6 1	1hd	1hd	21½	2nk	Diaz J L	12500	1.20
9Aug89 5AP3	I'm Super Duper	b 6 119 2 6	6hd	52½	58	3nk	Torres F C	12500	10.70
31Jly89 9AP7	Dash The Music	b 5 117 7 3	31	21	1hd	44	Meier R	12500	10.30
21Jly89 6AP5	Max B.	6 117 5 5	21	31	4½	55	Silva C H	12500	5.70
6Aug89 2AP2	Great Jason	b 4 113 1 4	5½	7	7	6½	Bruin J E	10500	9.60
19Aug88 8Haw6	Stay Happy	b 4 113 3 7	7	6½	6hd	7	Sellers S J	10500	15.00

OFF AT 1:31. Start good. Won driving. Time, :22⅖, :46⅕, 1:11 Track fast.

The First race on August 19 was at six furlongs for three-year-olds and older with seven horses entered.

ARLINGTON

ARLINGTON HEIGHTS, ILL., SATURDAY, AUGUST 19, 1989—ARLINGTON
Meeting scheduled for ninety-five days (June 28 to October 15). No racing Tuesdays except July 4, No racing July 5.
(Main Course, 1-1/8 miles. Turf Course, 1 mile)

OWNERS, TRAINERS LISTED IN ORDER OF HORSES' ORIGINAL FINISH POSITION.

Off Times in Local P.M. Time Unless Otherwise Noted.

FIRST RACE
Arlington
AUGUST 19, 1989

6 FURLONGS. (1.08) CLAIMING. Purse $8,500. 3-year-olds and upward. Weight, 3-year-olds, 117 lbs.; older, 122 lbs. Non-winners of two races since July 15 allowed 3 lbs.; of a race since then, 5 lbs. Claiming price $12,500; for each $1,000 to $10,500 allowed 2 lbs. (Races when entered to be claimed for $8,500 or less not considered.) 46TH DAY. WEATHER CLEAR. TEMPERATURE 77 DEGREES.

Value of race $8,500; value to winner $5,100; second $1,700; third $935; fourth $510; fifth $255. Mutuel pool $148,180. Quinella pool $43,379. Perfecta pool $35,828.

Last Raced	Horse	Eqt.	A.	Wt	PP	St	¼	½	Str	Fin	Jockey	Cl'g Pr	Odds $1
9Aug89 5AP2	Adam Bomb	b	5	117	4	2	4 1	4 1½	3 1½	1 ¾	Bartram B E	12500	2.50
30Jly89 3AP4	Paris Venture	b	6	117	6	1	1 hd	1 hd	2 1½	2 nk	Diaz J L	12500	1.20
9Aug89 5AP3	I'm Super Duper	b	6	119	2	6	6 hd	5 2½	5 8	3 nk	Torres F C	12500	10.70
31Jly89 9AP7	Dash The Music	b	5	117	7	3	3 1	2 1	1 hd	4 4	Meier R	12500	10.30
21Jly89 6AP5	Max B.		6	117	5	5	2 1	3 1	4 ½	5 5	Silva C H	12500	5.70
6Aug89 2AP2	Great Jason	b	4	113	1	4	5 ½	7	7	6 ½	Bruin J E	10500	9.60
19Aug88 8Haw6	Stay Happy	b	4	113	3	7	7	6 ½	6 hd	7	Sellers S J	10500	15.00

OFF AT 1:31. Start good. Won driving. Time, :22⅘, :46⅕, 1:11 Track fast.

SECOND RACE
Arlington
AUGUST 19, 1989

6 FURLONGS. (1.08) MAIDEN. SPECIAL WEIGHT. Purse $18,700 (includes 10% from Illinois Thoroughbred Breeder's Fund). Fillies. 3 and 4-year-olds, Illinois registered, conceived and/or foaled. Weight, 3-year-olds, 117 lbs.; 4-year-olds, 122 lbs.

Value of race $18,700; value to winner $11,220; second $3,740; third $2,057; fourth $1,122; fifth $561. Mutuel pool $154,981. Quinella pool $61,563. Perfecta pool $69,364.

Last Raced	Horse	Eqt.	A.	Wt	PP	St	¼	½	Str	Fin	Jockey	Odds $1
3Aug89 9AP2	Playa Zen		3	117	8	9	5 3	4 3	1 3	1 3½	Allen K K	.30
3Aug89 9AP6	Thomson's Sugar		3	117	5	2	8 2½	6 1	4 2½	2 4	Gabriel R E	50.40
3Aug89 9AP7	Pretty Darlin		3	117	2	5	2 2½	2 1½	2 1½	3 nk	Bruin J E	24.50
29Jun89 3AP6	Kaycanyouhearme		3	117	10	8	7 2½	7 4	6 3	4 hd	Velasquez J	6.40
	Orea Kori		3	117	4	4	4 ½	5 ½	5 ½	5 2½	Focareto S	13.00
31Jly89 2AP2	L. M.'s Noble Miss		4	122	6	3	9 ½	8 2	8 4	6 ¾	Marquez C H Jr	9.70
3Aug89 6AP3	Whispering Spy		3	117	1	6	1 hd	1 hd	3 hd	7 5	Meier R	10.10
3Aug89 6AP8	On a Carousel	b	3	117	7	1	3 1	3 ½	7 ½	8 2	Sellers S J	74.00
9Jun89 2Haw12	Rossi Architect	b	3	112	3	7	6 ½	9 5	9 3	9 ½	Gomez A5	61.20
7Aug89 3AP8	Persian Coin		3	117	9	10	10	10	10	10	Suman S	80.00

OFF AT 1:57. Start good. Won handily. Time, :22⅘, :47, 1:13⅖ Track fast.

THIRD RACE
Arlington
AUGUST 19, 1989

6 FURLONGS. (1.08) ALLOWANCE. Purse $19,000. Fillies. 3-year-olds which have never won two races. Weight, 121 lbs. Non-winners of a race other than claiming since June 15 allowed 3 lbs.; of such a rae since March 1, 5 lbs.

Value of race $19,000; value to winner $11,400; second $3,800; third $2,090; fourth $1,140; fifth $570. Mutuel pool $199,284. Quinella pool $75,282. Perfecta pool $76,657.

Last Raced	Horse	Eqt.	A.	Wt	PP	St	¼	½	Str	Fin	Jockey	Odds $1
2Aug89 6AP5	Sovereign Coin		3	116	6	2	3 hd	2 ½	1 ½	1 1¾	Bartram B E	15.30
6Aug89 6AP5	Evaluating		3	116	3	1	1 1	1 hd	2 1	2 ½	Clark K D	5.70
2Aug89 6AP2	Weekend Spree		3	116	7	6	6 6	3 2	3 2	3 ½	Allen K K	1.60
26Jly89 1AP1	Cynpamdeb		3	121	2	5	4 hd	5 1	4 1½	4 2½	Bruin J E	2.90
9Aug89 6AP1	Don't Leave Home		3	116	4	4	5 ½	6 6	5 3½	5 6	Smith M E	11.80
2Aug89 6AP3	Purplette		3	116	5	3	2 1½	4 hd	6 4	6 5	Velasquez J	2.80
4Aug89 4AP	Erythronium	b	3	118	1	7	7	7	7	7	Johnson P A	32.20

OFF AT 2:22. Start good. Won driving. Time, :23, :46⅕, 1:10⅗ Track fast.

FOURTH RACE
Arlington
AUGUST 19, 1989

6 FURLONGS. (1.08) MAIDEN. SPECIAL WEIGHT. Purse $18,700 (includes 10% from Illinois Thoroughbred Breeder's Fund). Fillies. 3 and 4-year-olds, Illinois registered, conceived and/or foaled. Weight, 3-year-olds, 117 lbs.; 4-year-olds, 122 lbs.

Value of race $18,700; value to winner $11,220; second $3,740; third $2,057; fourth $1,122; fifth $561. Mutuel pool $200,827. Quinella pool, $74,863; Perfecta pool, $72,590.

Last Raced	Horse	Eqt.	A.	Wt	PP	St	¼	½	Str	Fin	Jockey	Odds $1
3Aug89 9AP4	Cos Shesa Winner	b	3	117	9	1	4 hd	2 hd	2 2½	1 2½	Diaz J L	6.90
	Temttate's Sister	b	3	117	8	7	6 2½	4 1½	4 1	2 ½	Lindsay R	11.40
3Aug89 9AP3	Rainbows Glitter		3	117	1	2	1 1	1 ½	1 hd	3 hd	Gryder A T	2.10
	Summer Debt		3	117	7	6	7 1½	6 8	5 3	4 1½	Meier R	19.10
23Jly89 2AP9	Final Type		3	117	3	3	5 ½	5 2	3 hd	5 2	Velasquez J	5.70
3Aug89 6AP2	Silver Purse		3	117	6	5	2 ½	3 1	6 12	6 10	Marquez C H Jr	1.50
	Showboat Iron		3	117	4	9	9	9	7 hd	7 nk	Schaefer G A	38.50

Last Raced	Horse	Eqt.A.Wt	PP	St	¼	½	Str	Fin	Jockey	Odds $1
23Jly89 2AP8	Grande Dame	b 3 117	2	8	8^{5}	$7^{1\frac{1}{2}}$	8^{6}	8^{8}	Razo E Jr	21.00
22Jly88 4Haw12	Sharlago	3 117	5	4	3^{hd}	8^{hd}	9	9	Gabriel R E	63.20

OFF AT 2:50. Start good. Won driving. Time, :22⅘, :46⅖, 1:12 Track fast.

FIFTH RACE
Arlington
AUGUST 19, 1989

6 FURLONGS. (1.08) MAIDEN. SPECIAL WEIGHT. Purse $17,000. Fillies. 2-year-olds. Weight, 119 lbs.

Value of race $17,000; value to winner $10,200; second $3,400; third $1,870; fourth $1,020; fifth $510. Mutuel pool $207,499. Quinella pool $79,073. Perfecta pool $33.80.

Last Raced	Horse	Eqt.A.Wt	PP	St	¼	½	Str	Fin	Jockey	Odds $1
29Jly89 4AP2	Can I Cope	2 119	3	5	1^{1}	1^{3}	1^{6}	$1^{7\frac{1}{2}}$	Fires E	.70
29Jly89 4AP6	Power On Ice	2 119	10	1	4^{hd}	5^{4}	$2^{1\frac{1}{2}}$	$2^{3\frac{1}{2}}$	Smith M E	13.30
29Jly89 4AP4	Sultry Miss	2 119	8	4	8^{1}	8^{hd}	4^{hd}	3^{2}	Allen K K	a-11.10
	Spinetingler	2 119	11	11	9^{2}	$9^{1\frac{1}{2}}$	$7^{1\frac{1}{2}}$	4^{2}	Hill B D	25.50
	Bal Harbour Miss	2 119	5	9	12	12	9^{3}	$5^{1\frac{1}{2}}$	Razo E Jr	a-11.10
	Sentimentally	2 119	7	6	$3^{1\frac{1}{2}}$	$3^{3\frac{1}{2}}$	3^{7}	$6^{1\frac{1}{4}}$	Clark K D	10.60
	Frunzi	2 119	2	10	$11^{2\frac{1}{2}}$	10^{2}	$8^{2\frac{1}{2}}$	7^{nk}	Velasquez J	7.20
19Jly89 5AP5	Outsmart	2 119	12	2	7^{2}	$7^{2\frac{1}{2}}$	6^{hd}	8^{3}	Marquez C H Jr	14.40
	Showtime Christel	2 119	6	8	5^{hd}	4^{hd}	5^{hd}	$9^{4\frac{1}{2}}$	Gryder A T	31.70
19Jly89 5AP3	Kara Koo	2 119	4	12	$10^{\frac{1}{2}}$	11^{3}	11^{1}	10^{4}	Bruin J E	10.90
7Aug89 5AP11	Miss Slew	b 2 119	9	3	6^{1}	6^{hd}	12	$11^{\frac{3}{4}}$	Schaefer G A	71.50
	China Joy	2 119	1	7	2^{1}	2^{hd}	$10^{1\frac{1}{2}}$	12	Johnson P A	26.00

a-Coupled: Sultry Miss and Bal Harbour Miss.

OFF AT 3:18. Start good. Won ridden out. Time, :21, :45⅘, 1:11⅘ Track fast.

SIXTH RACE
Arlington
AUGUST 19, 1989

1 $\frac{1}{16}$ MILES.(Turf). (1.41⅖) ALLOWANCE. Purse $24,000. Fillies and mares. 3-year-olds and upward which have never won three races other than maiden, claiming or starter. Weight, 3-year-olds, 115 lbs.; older, 122 lbs. Non-winners of a race other than maiden or claiming at a mile or over since May 15 allowed 3 lbs.

Value of race $24,000; value to winner $14,400; second $4,800; third $2,640; fourth $1,440; fifth $720. Mutuel pool $235,653. Perfecta pool $91,687. Quinella pool $94,360.

Last Raced	Horse	Eqt.A.Wt	PP	St	¼	½	¾	Str	Fin	Jockey	Odds $1
21Jun89 7CD7	Bangkok Lady	b 3 112	1	3	10^{hd}	10^{1}	$10^{1\frac{1}{2}}$	$3^{1\frac{1}{2}}$	$1^{3\frac{1}{4}}$	Fires E	5.70
23Jly89 9Cby7	Bainoville	4 122	8	12	$9^{1\frac{1}{2}}$	9^{1}	$8^{\frac{1}{2}}$	$4^{\frac{1}{2}}$	2^{hd}	Johnson P A	16.40
29Jly89 7AP2	Straight Up Long	4 119	5	2	2^{hd}	$2^{2\frac{1}{2}}$	$2^{1\frac{1}{2}}$	$1^{\frac{1}{2}}$	$3^{1\frac{1}{2}}$	Razo E Jr	4.50
30Jly89 8AP2	Luthier's Launch	3 115	6	8	$5^{\frac{1}{2}}$	$5^{\frac{1}{2}}$	$5^{\frac{1}{2}}$	$2^{\frac{1}{2}}$	$4^{4\frac{1}{2}}$	Bruin J E	1.40
31Jly89 4AP3	La Fey Morgan	5 119	4	4	4^{2}	4^{2}	$3^{\frac{1}{2}}$	$5^{2\frac{1}{2}}$	$5^{\frac{1}{2}}$	Allen K K	25.50
9Aug89 7AP6	Cyanna	3 112	7	11	12	12	11^{3}	8^{hd}	$6^{\frac{1}{2}}$	Meier R	74.60
29Jly89 7AP5	Obeah	b 4 122	3	10	8^{hd}	8^{hd}	$9^{1\frac{1}{2}}$	$9^{\frac{1}{2}}$	$7^{1\frac{1}{2}}$	Clark K D	8.70
5Aug89 9FP8	Blooming Jil	4 122	9	5	7^{1}	7^{hd}	$6^{\frac{1}{2}}$	6^{1}	$8^{1\frac{1}{2}}$	Gryder A T	7.90
29Jly89 7AP6	La Ice Queen	b 4 119	2	1	$6^{\frac{1}{2}}$	6^{hd}	7^{1}	$10^{1\frac{1}{2}}$	9^{nk}	Silva C H	71.70
3Aug89 5AP1	Slewsbasque	b 4 122	11	9	$11^{1\frac{1}{2}}$	$11^{1\frac{1}{2}}$	12	11^{4}	10^{3}	Sellers S J	21.10
30Jly89 5AP4	April Stride	b 4 122	10	6	$1^{2\frac{1}{2}}$	$1^{1\frac{1}{2}}$	$1^{\frac{1}{2}}$	7^{hd}	11^{4}	Torres F C	41.90
29Jly89 7AP8	Chapilca	3 112	12	7	$3^{1\frac{1}{2}}$	3^{hd}	4^{hd}	12	12	Velasquez J	15.10

OFF AT 3:48. Start good. Won ridden out. Time, :22⅘, :47⅗, 1:13⅗, 1:39⅕, 1:45⅘ Course firm.

SEVENTH RACE
Arlington
AUGUST 19, 1989

6 FURLONGS. (1.08) ALLOWANCE. Purse $20,900 (includes 10% from Illinois Thoroughbred Breeder's Fund). 3-year-olds and upward, Illinois registered, conceived and/or foaled, which have never won two races. Weight, 3-year-olds, 117 lbs.; older, 122 lbs. Non-winners of a race other than claiming since June 1 allowed 3 lbs.; of such a race since February 15, 5 lbs.

Value of race $20,900; value to winner $12,540; second $4,180; third $2,299; fourth $1,254; fifth $627. Mutuel pool $199,349. Qui pool $57,750. Perf pool $31,577. Tri pool $148,762.

Last Raced	Horse	Eqt.A.Wt	PP	St	¼	½	Str	Fin	Jockey	Odds $1
6Aug89 7AP2	Slap the Clown	3 112	10	1	6^{3}	$4^{2\frac{1}{2}}$	$2^{\frac{1}{2}}$	$1^{3\frac{1}{2}}$	Velasquez J	3.70
6Aug89 4AP5	Home to Rejoice	b 3 112	8	4	1^{1}	1^{1}	$1^{\frac{1}{2}}$	$2^{\frac{1}{2}}$	Johnson P A	53.60
2Aug89 5AP1	Stone Harbor Jim	3 117	2	3	$4^{\frac{1}{2}}$	3^{2}	3^{1}	$3^{\frac{1}{2}}$	Gryder A T	4.30
6Aug89 4AP2	Zentherewasu	b 3 112	3	5	$5^{1\frac{1}{2}}$	5^{4}	5^{4}	4^{hd}	Sellers S J	3.30
6Aug89 4AP4	Glenstare	3 117	7	8	2^{1}	2^{hd}	$4^{1\frac{1}{2}}$	5^{3}	Fires E	7.50
6Aug89 7AP3	Chief Chuck	3 117	4	11	$8^{1\frac{1}{2}}$	6^{3}	6^{hd}	6^{nk}	Razo E Jr	6.00
27Jly89 6AP2	Tall Taz	b 5 112	5	12	11^{3}	8^{hd}	8^{3}	$7^{\frac{1}{2}}$	Gomez A5	11.80
29Jly89 3AP6	Michael Belle	3 113	6	6	10^{2}	7^{2}	7^{1}	$8^{2\frac{1}{4}}$	Bruin J E	23.20
11Aug89 6AP9	Alexandra's Velvet	3 113	11	2	12	11^{4}	9^{hd}	9^{nk}	Diaz J L	70.60
6Aug89 4AP3	Solid Fuel	4 122	12	10	$7^{\frac{1}{2}}$	10^{2}	10^{1}	$10^{3\frac{1}{2}}$	Sorrows A G Jr	15.30
29Jly89 3AP5	Millville	4 112	9	9	9^{hd}	9^{3}	11^{5}	$11^{9\frac{1}{2}}$	Smith M E	9.90
6Aug89 7AP9	Quick Hot Stuff	b 3 117	1	7	3^{hd}	12	12	12	Clark K D	61.70

OFF AT 4:18. Start good. Won driving. Time, :22⅗, :45⅘, 1:11⅗ Track fast.

NINTH RACE
Arlington
AUGUST 19, 1989

1 $\frac{3}{16}$ MILES.(Turf). (1.53⅘) 28th Running ROUND TABLE STAKES ALLOWANCE (Grade III). $75,000 Added. 3–year–olds. By subscription of $75 each, which should accompany the nomination, $350 to pass the entry box, an additional $350 to start, with $75,000 added, of which 60% of all monies to the owner of the winner, 20% to second, 11% to third, 6% to fourth and 3% to fifth. Weight, 123 lbs. Non–winners of two races of $50,000 at a mile or over in 1989 allowed 3 lbs.; of two races of $30,000 at a mile or over in 1989, 5 lbs.; of two races of $15,000 at a mile or over in 1989, 8 lbs.; of two races of $12,000 at a mile or over, 11 lbs. This event will be limited to fourteen starters. Should more than fourteen pass the entry box, the starters will be determined at that time with preference given to winners of graded stakes, next preference, those that accumulated the highest earnings in 1989. As many as six horses may be placed on the also eligible list. Starters to be named through the entry box by the usual time of closing. A trophy to the owner of the winner. (Closed with 33 nominations.)

Value of race $85,875; value to winner $51,525; second $17,175; third $9,446; fourth $5,153; fifth $2,576. Mutuel pool $281,618. Quinella pool $95,512. Perfecta pool $74,340.

Last Raced	Horse	Eqt.A.Wt	PP	St	¼	½	¾	Str	Fin	Jockey	Odds $1
5Aug89 9AP7	Ebros	3 118	5	4	7^{hd}	9^{2}	9^{4}	4^{4}	1^{hd}	Velasquez J	1.60
5Aug89 9AP2	Dispersal	b 3 115	6	6	$2^{\frac{1}{2}}$	$2^{2\frac{1}{2}}$	$1^{\frac{1}{2}}$	$1^{1\frac{1}{2}}$	$2^{1\frac{1}{4}}$	Fires E	2.10
2Aug89 8AP1	Jake McKeown	3 113	3	1	$4^{1\frac{1}{2}}$	$5^{\frac{1}{2}}$	3^{1}	2^{hd}	3^{3}	Clark K D	50.60
31Jly89 7AP2	Ruszhinka	b 3 112	11	9	5^{1}	$4^{\frac{1}{2}}$	5^{hd}	3^{hd}	$4^{1\frac{1}{4}}$	Allen K K	7.60
15Jly89 7AP2	Prince Randi	3 113	7	8	$11^{2\frac{1}{2}}$	$10^{3\frac{1}{2}}$	$10^{2\frac{1}{2}}$	6^{1}	$5^{1\frac{1}{2}}$	Bruin J E	9.20
24Jly89 6AP1	Ankles	3 112	4	5	6^{hd}	$7^{2\frac{1}{2}}$	$6^{1\frac{1}{2}}$	$5^{\frac{1}{2}}$	6no	Gryder A T	30.60
22Jly89 11Aks6	Ridge Escape	b 3 115	12	12	8^{hd}	8^{hd}	8^{hd}	$7^{3\frac{1}{2}}$	7^{5}	Johnson P A	26.30
5Aug89 11LaD4	Gauntlett Boy	b 3 114	10	10	$9^{1\frac{1}{2}}$	6^{hd}	$7^{3\frac{1}{2}}$	$9^{1\frac{1}{2}}$	$8^{1\frac{1}{4}}$	Razo E Jr	27.20
28Jly89 8AP1	Tex's Zing	3 118	9	7	$1^{\frac{1}{2}}$	$1^{\frac{1}{2}}$	$2^{1\frac{1}{2}}$	8^{2}	9^{1}	Gabriel R E	7.70
31Jly89 7AP4	Priceless Peace	3 115	8	11	$10^{1\frac{1}{2}}$	12	12	10^{4}	10^{5}	Marquez C H Jr	83.40
12Aug89 6AP5	The Count	b 3 112	1	3	12	11^{hd}	$11^{\frac{1}{2}}$	12	$11^{\frac{1}{2}}$	Smith M E	111.20
21Jly89 5AP1	Northern Drama	b 3 118	2	2	3^{3}	$3^{1\frac{1}{2}}$	$4^{\frac{1}{2}}$	$11^{1\frac{1}{2}}$	12	Silva C H	26.00

OFF AT 5:21. Start good. Won driving. Time, :24⅘, :49⅕, 1:14⅕, 1:39⅘, 1:58⅖ Course firm.

TENTH RACE
Arlington
AUGUST 19, 1989

1 MILE.(Turf). (1.35) CLAIMING. Purse $13,000. 3–year–olds and upward. Weight, 3–year–olds, 115 lbs.; older, 122 lbs. Non–winners of a race at a mile or over since July 31 allowed 3 lbs.; of such a race since July 15, 5 lbs. Claiming price $25,000; for each $2,500 to $20,000 allowed 2 lbs. (Races when entered to be claimed for $18,000 or less not considered.)

Value of race $13,000; value to winner $7,800; second $2,600; third $1,430; fourth $780; fifth $390. Mutuel pool $167,268. Quinella pool $37,972. Perf pl $27,104. Trif pl $17,405.

Last Raced	Horse	Eqt.A.Wt	PP	St	¼	½	¾	Str	Fin	Jockey	Cl'g Pr	Odds $1
2Aug89 8AP5	Sir Roberto	4 117	10	8	$9^{\frac{1}{2}}$	$8^{\frac{1}{2}}$	8^{3}	6^{2}	$1^{\frac{1}{2}}$	Velasquez J	25000	3.20
2Aug89 9AP3	Jack the Hack	5 117	3	10	$8^{1\frac{1}{2}}$	7^{3}	$7^{1\frac{1}{2}}$	$3^{1\frac{1}{2}}$	$2^{\frac{3}{4}}$	Diaz J L	25000	6.20
26Feb89 11GP8	Plum Wine	7 117	7	5	6^{2}	$6^{1\frac{1}{2}}$	6^{hd}	$5^{\frac{1}{2}}$	3^{4}	Bartram B E	25000	2.10
2Aug89 9AP5	Thatsfaysrainbow	b 5 109	6	4	5^{3}	$5^{2\frac{1}{2}}$	$5^{\frac{1}{2}}$	8^{8}	$4^{\frac{1}{2}}$	Gomez A5	20000	8.70
5Mar89 9FG1	Affable Joe	b 5 117	11	6	3^{1}	$3^{\frac{1}{2}}$	3^{1}	4^{hd}	$5^{\frac{1}{2}}$	Razo E Jr	25000	33.70
2Aug89 9AP1	Explosively Great	b 4 122	4	2	$1^{\frac{1}{2}}$	$1^{1\frac{1}{2}}$	$2^{1\frac{1}{2}}$	2^{1}	6^{hd}	Sellers S J	25000	4.50
30Jly89 3AP2	Real Courtin	4 117	2	1	2^{2}	2^{2}	1^{hd}	$1^{\frac{1}{2}}$	$7^{1\frac{1}{4}}$	Clark K D	25000	18.50
24Jly89 9AP2	Top Monarch	b 3 112	5	3	4^{hd}	$4^{1\frac{1}{2}}$	4^{1}	7^{hd}	8^{5}	Fires E	25000	11.70
5Aug89 10AP6	Time for Trouble	b 4 113	1	11	11	11	11	11	9^{2}	Smith M E	20000	38.40
13Aug89 3AP5	Trucking Bucks	b 4 117	8	9	$7^{\frac{1}{2}}$	9^{2}	9^{1}	$9^{1\frac{1}{2}}$	$10^{1\frac{1}{4}}$	Johnson P A	25000	28.80
30Jly89 9AP8	Majestic Mikey	b 3 111	9	7	10^{5}	10^{6}	10^{8}	$10^{\frac{1}{2}}$	11	Gryder A T	25000	54.20

OFF AT 5:51. Start good. Won driving. Time, :23⅗, :47⅖, 1:12⅘, 1:38⅕ Course firm.

ARLINGTON

Copyright © 1989 By News America Publications Inc.

ARLINGTON HEIGHTS, ILL., SUNDAY, AUGUST 20, 1989—ARLINGTON
Meeting scheduled for ninety-five days (June 28 to October 15). No racing Tuesdays except July 4, No racing July 5.
(Main Course, 1-1/8 miles. Turf Course, 1 mile)
Vice President C. K. Dunn. American Totalisator. United Starting Gate. Film Patrol. American Teletimer, Complete finish of each race confirmed by Eye-in-the Sky Camera. Trackman, John Brown.
Length of stretch from last turn to finish, 1,029 feet.

FIRST RACE
Arlington
AUGUST 20, 1989

1 MILE. (1.32⅕) CLAIMING. Purse $8,500. 3–year–olds. Weight, 122 lbs. Non–winners of a race at a mile or over since July 31 allowed 3 lbs.; of such a race since July 15, 5 lbs. Claiming price $10,000; for each $500 to $9,000 allowed 2 lbs. (Races for $8,000 or less not considered.) 47TH DAY. WEATHER CLEAR. TEMPERATURE 81 DEGREES.

Value of race $8,500; value to winner $5,100; second $1,700; third $935; fourth $510; fifth $255. Mutuel pool $108,834. Quinella pool $29,243. Perfecta pool $25,309.

Last Raced	Horse	Eqt.	A.	Wt	PP	St	¼	½	¾	Str	Fin	Jockey	Cl'g Pr	Odds $1
4Aug89 ^{2}AP^{3}	Feels Like Far		3	117	2	6	4^{hd}	3^{2}	$3^{2\frac{1}{2}}$	2^{3}	1^{7}	Velasquez J	10000	.80
11Aug89 ^{3}AP^{6}	Trogan	b	3	109	6	3	2^{7}	2^{10}	$1^{\frac{1}{2}}$	$1^{\frac{1}{2}}$	2^{nk}	Gomez A^{5}	9000	9.30
11Aug89 ^{5}AP^{6}	Mickey's Place		3	117	7	2	$5^{1\frac{1}{2}}$	$5^{\frac{1}{2}}$	4^{8}	4^{8}	$3^{7\frac{1}{2}}$	Sellers S J	10000	18.20
11Aug89 ^{5}AP^{3}	Tri For Charlie		3	113	3	5	6^{10}	6^{10}	$5^{3\frac{1}{2}}$	5^{10}	$4^{\frac{3}{4}}$	Smith M E	9000	6.40
2Aug89 ^{3}AP^{3}	Peachmeister	b	3	117	4	1	$1^{\frac{1}{2}}$	$1^{\frac{1}{2}}$	2^{6}	3^{hd}	5^{7}	Fires E	10000	2.40
2Aug89 ^{3}AP^{5}	Bleu Chanson	b	3	113	1	7	7	7	7	$6^{1\frac{1}{2}}$	6^{6}	Ward W A	9000	33.10
9Aug89 ^{3}AP^{7}	Threshold's Image	b	3	117	5	4	3^{1}	4^{1}	6^{2}	7	7	Bartram B E	10000	19.90

OFF AT 1:30. Start good. Won ridden out. Time, :23, :45⅘, 1:10⅘, 1:37⅖ Track fast.

FOURTH RACE
Arlington
AUGUST 20, 1989

1 ⅛ MILES. (1.46⅕) MAIDEN. SPECIAL WEIGHT. Purse $18,000. 3 and 4-year-olds. Weight, 3-year-olds, 115 lbs. 4-year-olds, 122 lbs. (Originally scheduled to be run at 1 1/8 miles on the turf).

Value of race $18,000; value to winner $10,800; second $3,600; third $1,980; fourth $1,080; fifth $540. Mutuel pool $174,283. Perfecta pool $60,989. Quinella pool $74,738.

Last Raced	Horse	Eqt.	A.	Wt	PP	St	¼	½	¾	Str	Fin	Jockey	Odds $1
10Aug89 ^{5}AP^{2}	Toga Dancer	b	4	122	2	10	7^{2}	7^{3}	5^{hd}	1^{1}	$1^{1\frac{1}{4}}$	Clark K D	4.70
28Jly89 ^{5}AP^{3}	General Canoechee		3	115	8	2	$3^{\frac{1}{2}}$	$3^{\frac{1}{2}}$	2^{2}	2^{hd}	$2^{1\frac{1}{4}}$	Velasquez J	1.60
21Jly89 ^{6}Cby^{2}	Jersey Splash	b	3	115	7	9	6^{hd}	6^{hd}	4^{2}	$3^{\frac{1}{2}}$	$3^{\frac{1}{2}}$	Fires E	5.10
28Jun89 ^{4}AP^{7}	Wolfie		3	115	1	1	$1^{1\frac{1}{2}}$	$1^{2\frac{1}{2}}$	1^{1}	4^{4}	4^{4}	Gryder A T	19.30
30Jly89 ^{9}AP^{2}	Little Cognac	b	3	115	4	6	$5^{\frac{1}{2}}$	5^{hd}	6^{8}	6^{8}	$5^{1\frac{1}{2}}$	Smith M E	5.10
30Jly89 ^{9}AP^{3}	Screen the Call		3	115	6	3	2^{hd}	2^{hd}	3^{hd}	5^{hd}	$6^{4\frac{3}{4}}$	Bruin J E	5.40
7Aug89 ^{9}AP^{4}	Tanjee Miss	b	3	114	5	8	$9^{1\frac{1}{2}}$	$9^{2\frac{1}{2}}$	9^{hd}	$8^{\frac{1}{2}}$	$7^{1\frac{1}{4}}$	Solomone M	32.30
7Jly89 ^{7}AP^{4}	Proud Baron		4	122	9	4	10	10	10	9	$8^{3\frac{1}{2}}$	Ward W A	27.40
11Aug89 ^{4}AP^{8}	Steven's Capt.	b	3	115	3	7	8^{5}	8^{8}	7^{4}	7^{hd}	9	Sorrows A G Jr	24.10
2Aug89 ^{9}AP^{10}	Allie's Joy	b	4	122	10	5	4^{1}	4^{2}	8^{3}	—	—	Marquez C H Jr	61.10

Allie's Joy, Eased.

OFF AT 3:05. Start good. Won driving. Time, :24⅗, :48⅘, 1:13⅗, 1:40⅕, 1:53⅘ Track good.

SEVENTH RACE
Arlington
AUGUST 20, 1989

1 MILE. (1.32⅕) ALLOWANCE. Purse $20,000. Fillies and mares. 3-year-olds and upward, which have never won a race other than maiden, claiming or starter. Weight, 3-year-olds, 115 lbs.; older, 122 lbs. Non-winners of a race other than claiming at a mile or over since May 15 allowed 3 lbs. (Originally scheduled to be run at 1 1/16 miles on the turf). (Originally scheduled to be run at one and one-sixteenth mile on the turf).

Value of race $20,000; value to winner $12,000; second $4,000; third $2,200; fourth $1,200; fifth $600. Mutuel pool $152,834. Qui pool $37,623. Per pool $24,096. Tri pool $129,568.

Last Raced	Horse	Eqt.	A.	Wt	PP	St	¼	½	¾	Str	Fin	Jockey	Odds $1
10Aug89 ^{8}AP^{3}	Brattice Cloth		3	113	2	6	6^{hd}	4^{1}	$1^{\frac{1}{2}}$	$1^{\frac{1}{2}}$	1^{hd}	Bruin J E	1.00
27Jly89 ^{5}AP^{1}	Grandma G.		3	115	7	5	5^{2}	$6^{\frac{1}{2}}$	3^{hd}	2^{3}	$2^{3\frac{1}{2}}$	Smith M E	7.00
7Aug89 ^{9}AP^{1}	Dibs		3	115	5	8	7^{10}	7^{12}	6^{1}	$3^{3\frac{1}{2}}$	3^{7}	Allen K K	3.50
29Jly89 ^{4}Cby^{1}	Miss Kathy S.		4	122	4	2	$2^{\frac{1}{2}}$	$3^{\frac{1}{2}}$	5^{hd}	$4^{2\frac{1}{2}}$	$4^{6\frac{1}{2}}$	Fires E	6.00
4Aug89 ^{4}AP^{2}	Miss Harvey		3	113	8	1	$1^{2\frac{1}{2}}$	1^{hd}	2^{1}	5^{3}	5^{1}	Clark K D	8.70
7Aug89 ^{1}AP^{2}	Determined to Win	b	3	114	6	4	$4^{\frac{1}{2}}$	5^{hd}	7^{15}	6^{1}	6^{5}	Schaefer G A	17.00
28Jly89 ^{6}AP^{4}	Lil Streaker	b	4	114	3	3	3^{2}	$2^{1\frac{1}{2}}$	$4^{\frac{1}{2}}$	7^{12}	7^{15}	Gomez A^{5}	23.70
6Aug89 ^{10}RD^{1}	Marine Waltz		6	119	1	7	8	8	8	8	8	Ward W A	42.30

The winner should be recorded as:

1Call: fourth, 2 lengths behind the leader

2Call: fourth, 2 lengths behind the leader

ESP: Presser

Dist	*Ent*	*1Call*	*2Call*	*%E*	*ESP*
6	7	4/2L	4/2L	N/A	P

A reminder: Beaten lengths in results charts are read just the opposite from past performances. At the first call the winner of this race (Adam Bomb) was fourth, one length in front of the fifth horse, *not* one length behind the leader. To determine lengths behind the leader, the reader must add the beaten lengths of every horse in front of Adam Bomb at the call being evaluated. The first call in the example:

Paris Venture: first by a head
Dash The Music: second by 1 length
Max B.: third by 1 length

Adam Bomb was behind by the cumulative lengths of the horses in the first three running positions: head + 1 length + 1 length = 2.1 lengths. Round off at 2 lengths.

SECOND RACE
Arlington
AUGUST 19, 1989

6 FURLONGS. (1.08) MAIDEN. SPECIAL WEIGHT. Purse $18,700 (includes 10% from Illinois Thoroughbred Breeder's Fund). Fillies. 3 and 4-year-olds, Illinois registered, conceived and/or foaled. Weight, 3-year-olds, 117 lbs.; 4-year-olds, 122 lbs.

Value of race $18,700; value to winner $11,220; second $3,740; third $2,057; fourth $1,122; fifth $561. Mutuel pool $154,981. Quinella pool $61,563. Perfecta pool $69,364.

Last Raced	Horse	Eqt.	A.	Wt	PP	St	¼	½	Str	Fin	Jockey	Odds $1
3Aug89 ^{9}AP^{2}	Playa Zen		3	117	8	9	5^{3}	4^{3}	1^{3}	$1^{3\frac{1}{2}}$	Allen K K	.30
3Aug89 ^{9}AP^{6}	Thomson's Sugar		3	117	5	2	$8^{2\frac{1}{2}}$	6^{1}	$4^{2\frac{1}{2}}$	2^{4}	Gabriel R E	50.40
3Aug89 ^{9}AP^{7}	Pretty Darlin		3	117	2	5	$2^{2\frac{1}{2}}$	$2^{1\frac{1}{2}}$	$2^{1\frac{1}{2}}$	3^{nk}	Bruin J E	24.50
29Jun89 ^{3}AP^{6}	Kaycanyouhearme		3	117	10	8	$7^{2\frac{1}{2}}$	7^{4}	6^{3}	4^{hd}	Velasquez J	6.40
	Orea Kori		3	117	4	4	$4^{\frac{1}{2}}$	$5^{\frac{1}{2}}$	$5^{\frac{1}{2}}$	$5^{2\frac{1}{2}}$	Focareto S	13.00
31Jly89 ^{2}AP^{2}	L. M.'s Noble Miss		4	122	6	3	$9^{\frac{1}{2}}$	8^{2}	8^{4}	$6^{\frac{3}{4}}$	Marquez C H Jr	9.70
3Aug89 ^{6}AP^{3}	Whispering Spy		3	117	1	6	1^{hd}	1^{hd}	3^{hd}	7^{5}	Meier R	10.10
3Aug89 ^{6}AP^{8}	On a Carousel	b	3	117	7	1	3^{1}	$3^{\frac{1}{2}}$	$7^{\frac{1}{2}}$	8^{2}	Sellers S J	74.00
9Jun89 ^{2}Haw^{12}	Rossi Architect	b	3	112	3	7	$6^{\frac{1}{2}}$	9^{5}	9^{3}	$9^{\frac{1}{2}}$	Gomez A^{5}	61.20
7Aug89 ^{3}AP^{8}	Persian Coin		3	117	9	10	10	10	10	10	Suman S	80.00

OFF AT 1:57. Start good. Won handily. Time, :22⅘, :47, 1:13⅘ Track fast.

The Second race was at six furlongs for Illinois-bred maidens, with ten horses entered. Avoid using maiden claiming or two-year-olds in this procedure; straight maidens are marginal in their value to the profile. I used the race to expand the available data. The winner should be recorded as:

1Call: fifth, 4 lengths behind the leader
2Call: fourth, 2 lengths behind the leader
ESP: Presser/Sustained

I chose to label the winner as Presser/Sustained. The running line borders on both. Don't be too restrictive in designating running styles. Without past performances to corroborate the line, we're better served by being liberal in our designations.

Dist	*Ent*	*1Call*	*2Call*	*%E*	*ESP*
6	7	4/2L	4/2L	N/A	P
6	10	5/4L	4/2L	"	P/S

THIRD RACE
Arlington
AUGUST 19, 1989

6 FURLONGS. (1.08) ALLOWANCE. Purse $19,000. Fillies. 3-year-olds which have never won two races. Weight, 121 lbs. Non-winners of a race other than claiming since June 15 allowed 3 lbs.; of such a rae since March 1, 5 lbs.

Value of race $19,000; value to winner $11,400; second $3,800; third $2,090; fourth $1,140; fifth $570. Mutuel pool $199,284. Quinella pool $75,282. Perfecta pool $76,657.

Last Raced	Horse	Eqt.A.Wt	PP	St	¼	½	Str	Fin	Jockey	Odds $1
2Aug89 ^{6}AP^{5}	Sovereign Coin	3 116	6	2	3^{hd}	$2^{\frac{1}{2}}$	$1^{\frac{1}{2}}$	$1^{1\frac{3}{4}}$	Bartram B E	15.30
6Aug89 ^{6}AP^{5}	Evaluating	3 116	3	1	1^{1}	1^{hd}	2^{1}	$2^{\frac{1}{2}}$	Clark K D	5.70
2Aug89 ^{6}AP^{2}	Weekend Spree	3 116	7	6	6^{6}	3^{2}	3^{2}	$3^{\frac{1}{2}}$	Allen K K	1.60
26Jly89 ^{1}AP^{1}	Cynpamdeb	3 121	2	5	4^{hd}	5^{1}	$4^{1\frac{1}{2}}$	$4^{2\frac{1}{2}}$	Bruin J E	2.90
9Aug89 ^{6}AP^{1}	Don't Leave Home	3 116	4	4	$5^{\frac{1}{2}}$	6^{6}	$5^{3\frac{1}{2}}$	5^{6}	Smith M E	11.80
2Aug89 ^{6}AP^{3}	Purplette	3 116	5	3	$2^{1\frac{1}{2}}$	4^{hd}	6^{4}	6^{5}	Velasquez J	2.80
4Aug89 ^{4}AP	Erythronium	b 3 118	1	7	7	7	7	7	Johnson P A	32.20

OFF AT 2:22. Start good. Won driving. Time, :23, :46⅕, 1:10⅗ Track fast.

The Third race was also at six furlongs, for NW1 allowance horses, with seven horses entered. The winner:

1Call: third, 2½ lengths behind the leader
2Call: second, a head behind the leader
ESP: Presser

Dist	*Ent*	*1Call*	*2Call*	*%E*	*ESP*
6	7	4/2L	4/2L	N/A	P
6	10	5/4L	4/2L	"	P/S
6	7	3/2½	2/hd	"	P

The rest of the sprints for August 19, 20, and 21:

	Dist	Ent	1Call	2Call	%E	ESP
19Aug89	6	7	4/2L	4/2L	N/A	P
	6	10	5/4L	4/2L	"	P/S
	6	7	3/2½	2/hd	"	P
	6	9	4/1½	2/½	"	P
	6	12	6/4L	4/3L	"	P/S
20Aug89	6	9	4/1½	4/2	"	P
	6	8	4/4½	4/4½	"	P/S
	6	10	1/1	1/1½	"	E
	6	8	2/hd	1/2½	"	E
21Aug89	6	8	7/7	7/6½	"	S
	7	10	2/½	2/hd	"	E/P
	6	6	4/1½	3/1	"	P
	6	9	3/3	2/1½	"	P
	7	9	7/5½	6/4	"	S

Application

Let's develop a working profile from the worksheet. The summaries from each of the vertical data cells:

Ent: 8.7 average entries
1Call: fourth, approx. 2 to 5 lengths behind the leader
2Call: third, approx. 2 to 4 lengths behind the leader
ESP: Pressers are dominant

Now let's examine each of the categories.

Ent: The average number of entries in these sprints was 8.7, or
9 horses. When related to running positions, the relationships
are clear: the optimal style, or position, is in the top half of the

field at each of the first two calls. With the exception of two consecutive races on August 20, one at 2–5 odds, horses on the lead were severely disadvantaged. Horses in the rear of the field, while not in the ideal position, may be playable depending on separation factors such as class and pace match-ups.

1Call: fourth, 2 to 5 lengths behind. *Beware of averages here.* The average is approximately 2½ lengths and eliminates too many winners. Rather than average the data, establish an acceptable range from which you'll consider betting contenders.

2Call: third, 2 to 4 lengths behind. The second-call position confirms the earlier conclusion: pressers have the advantage.

ESP: Pressers. The ESP data is decisive: favor the pressers and mid-pack sustained types.

This is a limited base and would be strengthened with additional data. Handicappers monitoring their own circuit have more continuous information upon which to base betting decisions. The casual player, or visitor to a new circuit, has scarcely more data than we've developed here. The bottom line: Are conclusions based on such limited data reliable? Let's look at the sprint races on the first day of application, 24Aug89.

1st Arlington

7 FURLONGS. (1.20⅖) CLAIMING. Purse $9,000. Fillies and mares. 3-year-olds and upward. Weight, 3-year-olds, 117 lbs.; older, 122 lbs. Non-winners of a race since July 31 allowed 3 lbs.; of a race since July 15, 5 lbs. Claiming price $16,000; for each $1,000 to $14,000 allowed 2 lbs. (Races where entered to be claimed for $12,000 or less not considered.)

Rock N Roar — **B. f. 4, by Native Uproar—Rockin' Time, by Buckaroo**

Own.—Monfre Charles **117** **Br.—Bohannan John (Ky)** **Tr.—Campbell Michael B** **$16,000**

1989 7 0 1 4 $12,349

1988 8 2 1 2 $34,606

Lifetime 18 2 2 7 $48,865 **Turf 6 0 1 2 $9,572**

23Jly89-6AP 1 1/16 Ⓣ:49^{2} 1:15 1:47^{1}yl 19 119 9^{17} 8^{12} 87¾ 711½ St Leon G^{3} ⒻAw22000 59-27 AlezanneMiss,Evangelical,PureVnill 9

23Jly89—Bumped start.

2Jly89-7AP 1 Ⓣ:48^{3} 1:13^{3} 1:38^{3}fm *2 119 6^{6} 54½ 66½ 68½ Clark K D^{4} ⒻAw19000 73-18 StrightUpLong,Slewsbsqu,Evnglicl 9

16Jun89-8Haw 7½f Ⓣ:23^{4} :46^{4} 1:31^{3}fm 3¼ 116 8^{13} 8^{12} 48½ 34½ Clark K D^{8} ⒻAw23000 78-22 Josette, That's A Doll, Rock NRoar 8

16Jun89—Five wide stretch

4Jun89-8CD 1 1/16 Ⓣ:47^{2} 1:13 1:45^{2}fm 3¼ 112 9^{12} 96½ 53½ 3^{6} Troilo WD^{1} ⒻAw23920 83-11 Obeah, Add, Rock N Roar 10

11May89-6CD 6f :22 :46^{2} 1:10^{4}ft 3 112 53¾ 62½ 3^{3} 3^{6} Troilo WD^{1} ⒻAw23570 83-13 Pozzi, Storm Ryder, Rock N Roar 6

18Mar89-8OP 1 1/16 :47^{4} 1:13^{4} 1:47 ft *7-5 111 87¾ 65½ 4^{4} 2½ Day P^{5} ⒻAw18000 65-24 GorgeousThrt,RockNRor,Prticiptor 9

18Mar89—Five wide.

1Mar89-8OP 1 1/16 :49^{1} 1:15^{1} 1:47^{4}ft 2¼ 116 65½ 64½ 51¾ 31½ Day P^{1} ⒻAw18000 60-32 MssBrbour,GorgousThrt,RockNRor 6

18Nov88-8CD 6½f :23^{1} :47^{3} 1:19^{3}ft 11 111 72¾ 5^{3} 3^{nk} 1^{1} TroiloWD^{12} ⒻAw23270 82-22 RockNRor,MyGiverny,Crter'sCrek 12

18Nov88—Bumped half pole.

29Oct88-6Kee a7f 1:28^{1}ft *2¼e118 10^{7} 74¾ 35½ 35½ Troilo WD^{6} ⒻAw20900 76-20 Sal'sJewel,NturlForest,RockNRor 12

19Oct88-4Kee a7f 1:27^{4}ft *8-5e112 118½ 11^{11} 66½ 36½ Troilo WD^{6} ⒻAw20900 77-18 CreekDancer,Rjb'sTune,RockNRor 12

Aug 18 AP 3f ft :37^{3} B **Jun 30 AP 3f ft :37^{4} B**

FIRST RACE
Arlington
AUGUST 24, 1989

7 FURLONGS. (1.20⅖) CLAIMING. Purse $9,000. Fillies and mares. 3-year-olds and upward. Weight, 3-year-olds, 117 lbs.; older, 122 lbs. Non-winners of a race since July 31 allowed 3 lbs.; of a race since July 15, 5 lbs. Claiming price $16,000; for each $1,000 to $14,000 allowed 2 lbs. (Races where entered to be claimed for $12,000 or less not considered.) 50TH DAY. WEATHER CLEAR. TEMPERATURE 69 DEGREES.

Value of race $9,000; value to winner $5,400; second $1,800; third $990; fourth $540; fifth $270. Mutuel pool $87,564. Perfecta pool $20,804. Quinella pool $25,941.

Last Raced	Horse	Eqt.	A.	Wt	PP	St	¼	½	Str	Fin	Jockey	Cl'g Pr	Odds $1
23Jly89 6AP7	Rock N Roar		4	117	1	7	3hd	41½	22½	11¼	Bruin J E	16000	3.50
6Aug89 10AP4	Sarah's Rose		4	117	6	2	21½	21½	1½	24	Velasquez J	16000	1.20
10Aug89 4AP5	Golden June		5	119	5	5	5½	3hd	3hd	3½	Torres F C	16000	13.10
6Aug89 10AP5	Bobbies Calm		4	117	3	3	61½	51½	41	43	Clark K D	16000	8.20
10Aug89 4AP2	Tiffany Colon		4	117	7	1	12½	11	56	56½	Allen K K	16000	6.60
10Aug89 4AP3	Sharp Type	b	5	117	4	4	7	62	63	69	Razo E Jr	16000	8.70
30Jly89 5AP9	Fox Foot Ginny	b	5	112	2	6	4½	7	7	7	Gomez A5	16000	6.40

OFF AT 1:30. Start good. Won driving. Time, :23, :47⅕, 1:13⅕, 1:26⅕ Track fast.

Official Program Numbers

$2 Mutuel Prices:			
1-ROCK N ROAR	9.00	4.00	2.80
6-SARAH'S ROSE		3.00	2.40
5-GOLDEN JUNE			4.20

$2 PERFECTA (1-6) PAID $26.00. $2 QUINELLA (1-6) PAID $10.20.

Rock N Roar won the first race of the day by pressing the pace setter and asserting herself late. The runaway front runner, Tiffany Colon, stopped badly upon entering the stretch, surrendering the pace to the pressers. Rock N Roar definitely appreciated the drop in class and the return to a main-track sprint. Her two most recent sprints match today's profile, and the basic question was whether the turf races had dulled her speed.

2nd Arlington

7 FURLONGS. (1.20⅖) MAIDEN. CLAIMING. Purse $8,000. 3 and 4-year-olds, Illinois registered, conceived and/or foaled. Weight, 3-year-olds, 117 lbs.; 4-year-olds, 122 lbs. Claiming price $15,000; for each $1,000 to $13,000 allowed 2 lbs.

Almost Mo
Own.—Ladera Farm **117**

Dk. b. or br. g. 3(Mar), by Cojak—Sweet Suzanne, by We Guarantee
Br.—G. A. Buder III, Trustee (Ill) 1989 7 M 1 3 $7,827
Tr.—Belpedio Tori $15,000 1988 0 M 0 0
Lifetime 7 0 1 3 $7,827

9Aug89-2AP	6f	:22⁴	:46³	1:12²ft	8-5	117	76¼	67	45½	34½	Bruin J E 1	S	M15000	74-20	Alln'sSqur,TouchTypng,AlmostMo	12
22Jly89-7AP	6f	:23¹	:47²	1:12³ft	*2¼	115	55½	56½	54½	48¾	St Leon G 8	S	Mdn	68-22	ChiefChuck,SpreBer,StonHrborJim	8
22Jly89—Three wide.																
9Jly89-3AP	7f	:23¹	:46³	1:26⁴ft	3½	115	61½	42½	41½	32½	St Leon G3	S	Mdn	65-23	‡Stvn'sCpt.,WhoYoKddng,AlmstM	10
28Jun89-2AP	6f	:23	:48¹	1:14¹ft	*1	113	52¼	65	48	68	Gryder A T3	S	Mdn	61-35	Post Office, Waydo, Illuminous	12
15Jun89-4Haw	6f	:22²	:46	1:11³ft	9	113	67½	69	55½	2¾	Marquez C H Jr6		Mdn	82-24	Chicago Cop, Almost Mo,Ivajoytoo	7
21Mar89-5GS	6f	:23¹	:48	1:14³m	2½	122	2hd	2½	31	54	Mino O A1		Mdn	65-29	NodblMrtns,JstMssdTwc,SprbInvdr	5
22Feb89-6GS	6f	:22⁴	:46¹	1:11⁴sy	22	122	610	413	410	38	Mino O A8		Mdn	75-24	GllntBrrstr,ThCoolMyrrh,AlmostMo	9

●Aug 21 AP 4f ft :47⁴ H   Aug 6 AP 4f ft :48¹ H   Jly 29 AP 4f ft :48 H   Jly 17 AP 5f ft 1:04 B

SECOND RACE	Arlington	AUGUST 24, 1989	7 FURLONGS. (1.20⅘) MAIDEN. CLAIMING. Purse $8,000. 3 and 4-year-olds, Illinois registered, conceived and/or foaled. Weight, 3-year-olds, 117 lbs.; 4-year-olds, 122 lbs. Claiming price $15,000; for each $1,000 to $13,000 allowed 2 lbs.

Value of race $8,000; value to winner $4,800; second $1,600; third $880; fourth $480; fifth $240. Mutuel pool $91,724. Quinella Pool $38,889. Perfecta Pool $35,771.

Last Raced	Horse	Eqt.A.Wt PP St	¼	½	Str	Fin	Jockey	Cl'g Pr	Odds $1
9Aug89 2AP3	Almost Mo	b 3 117 2 8	5¹	5hd	3½	1¹½	Bruin J E	15000	1.60
9Aug89 2AP8	Stallone	3 117 11 2	8hd	7¹½	2hd	2¹½	Torres F C	15000	69.70
14Aug89 2AP3	Prince Avie	3 114 6 6	6¹½	6¹½	1½	3³	Razo E Jr	13000	8.30
27Nov88 5Cam	What's Your Rush	4 118 1 10	11¹½	10hd	5¹	4¹½	Gomez A	13000	60.90
14Aug89 2AP6	Call Home Rob	b 3 117 7 11	3hd	4²	4hd	5¹½	Sorrows A G Jr	15000	45.30
10Jun89 5Haw6	Bold Ark	4 122 10 3	9¹½	9¹	6²	6½	Focareto S	15000	3.30
10Aug89 5AP10	Judge's Guard	3 117 3 12	12	11⁴	9⁶	7²	Gabriel R E	15000	68.40
14Aug89 2AP5	Double Doers	b 3 117 4 9	4hd	3hd	7hd	8⁴	Gryder A T	15000	10.00
28Jun89 2AP10	Captain Paddington	b 3 113 5 5	1½	1½	8½	9²	Clark K D	13000	61.50
13Aug89 4AP6	Gold Merchant	3 117 8 7	7¹	8hd	11¹	10¹½	Long J S	15000	18.10
24Jly89 2AP8	Notorious Spy	3 113 9 1	2hd	2hd	10hd	11³	Meier R	13000	67.60
	Rockies Hawk	3 117 12 4	10hd	12	12	12	Day P	15000	3.00

OFF AT 1:55. Start good. Won driving. Time, :23⅘, :48¼, 1:15⅘, 1:28½ Track fast.

$2 Mutuel Prices:

2-ALMOST MO	5.20	4.00	3.20
11-STALLONE		33.00	11.00
6-PRINCE AVIE			4.60

$2 QUINELLA (2–11) PAID $147.80. $2 PERFECTA (2–11) PAID $243.00.

Almost Mo won the Second race, a maiden claimer at seven furlongs, employing the identical style of the First-race winner. Her recent record strongly indicated the win and a fit to our profile.

4th Arlington

7 FURLONGS. (1.20⅘) CLAIMING. Purse $6,200. 3-year-olds and upward. Weight, 3-year-olds, 117 lbs.; older, 122 lbs. Non-winners of two races since June 15 allowed 5 lbs.; of a race since then, 5 lbs. Claiming price $7,500; for each $500 to $6,500 allowed 2 lbs. (Races when entered to be claimed for $5,500 or less not considered.)

Trynbestrat

Own.—Long M C Jr — 117

B. c. 4, by Ratification—Strat n Arrow, by Loco Kid
Br.—Long Mack & Brennan Jean (Ark)   1989 5 0 2 0 $2,833
Tr.—Brennan Terry $7,500   1988 1 0 0 0
Lifetime 13 2 5 0 $22,993

13Aug89-2AP	6f :22² :45⁴ 1:11³ft	11 117	4³ 42½ 32½ 42½	Gryder A T⁸	7500	79-19 BrandyCutlass,Reporbate,BoldTry 10
27Jly89-2AP	7f :22¹ :45 1:23²ft	7½ 117	33½ 31½ 2¹ 22½	St Leon G⁶	5000	82-17 Paris Nights,Trynbestrat,Lannuier 11
30Jun89-3AP	6f :23¹ :48 1:13⁴ft	7½ 117	4⁴ 4³ 1hd 22½	St Leon G¹	5000	69-32 Yewillwin, Trynbestrat, Bradie Boy 9
28Jun89-4CD	6½f:22² :46² 1:19²sy	12 116	5⁸ 10⁹ 96½ 99½	St Leon G¹⁰	8000	74-23 Proud Sky, Excelso,ConsciousAim 11
9Jun89-4CD	6½f:22³ :46¹ 1:19²ft	9½ 115	21½ 2hd 41½ 44	St Leon G⁶	6250	79-20 PowerWitnss,SvdbyZro,MilitryMnc 9
5Jun88-7CD	6f :21⁴ :45² 1:10¹ft	18 114	52½ 56 61² 6²¹	Brumfield D⁶	Aw24125	71-17 That'llWork,RySpekin,BrodwyChief 6
27Sep87-10Cby	17⁰:47 1:10³ 1:42¹ft	15 120	55½ 61² 61⁴ 61⁹	Smith M E³	Cby Juv	71-09 SuccssExprss,HousAccount,BgSnoz 8
11Sep87-7Cby	1 :48 1:13¹ 1:40 ft	*4-5 118	1hd 2hd 3½ 2²	Kutz D⁵	Autmn Leaves	80-18 Such Class, Trynbestrat, Le King 5
15Aug87-10Cby	6f :22³ :45⁴ 1:114ft	9-5 117	62½ 42 3¹ 22½	LGrngeDL¹	Eau Claire	85-13 KeyVoyage,Trynbestrat,Mnnington 7
1Aug87-8Cby	6f :23¹ :46² 1:12⁴gd	6-5 118	3½ 2hd 13 14½	Kutz D⁵	Aw9000	82-13 Trynbestrat,SuchClss,HubsAvenger 6

Jly 22 AP 4f gd :49³ B

FOURTH RACE
Arlington
AUGUST 24, 1989

7 FURLONGS. (1.20⅘) CLAIMING. Purse $6,200. 3-year-olds and upward. Weight, 3-year olds, 117 lbs.; older, 122 lbs. Non-winners of two races since June 15 allowed 5 lbs.; of a race since then, 5 lbs. Claiming price $7,500; for each $500 to $6,500 allowed 2 lbs. (Races when entered to be claimed for $5,500 or less not considered.)

Value of race $6,200; value to winner $3,720; second $1,240; third $682; fourth $372; fifth $186. Mutuel pool $131,732. Quinella pool $53,531. Perfecta pool $45,672.

Last Raced	Horse	Eqt.	A.	Wt	PP	St	¼	½	Str	Fin	Jockey	Cl'g Pr	Odds $1
13Aug89 ^{2}AP^{4}	Trynbestrat		4	117	12	3	$5^{\frac{1}{2}}$	$4^{\frac{1}{2}}$	$1^{1\frac{1}{2}}$	$1^{5\frac{1}{2}}$	Smith M E	7500	10.60
9Aug89 ^{5}AP^{8}	Contractor's Tune	b	5	117	1	10	10^{4}	9^{3}	2^{3}	2^{3}	Bruin J E	7500	19.00
21Jly89 ^{6}AP^{9}	Regulative		4	112	5	7	$4^{\frac{1}{2}}$	5^{2}	5^{3}	3^{1}	Gomez A^{5}	7500	21.90
3Aug89 ^{7}AP^{8}	Shady Family		4	117	9	9	12	12	$7^{2\frac{1}{2}}$	$4^{1\frac{1}{4}}$	Marquez C H Jr	7500	27.50
9Aug89 ^{5}AP^{6}	Silver Strike	b	7	113	7	12	11^{2}	$11^{\frac{1}{2}}$	6^{hd}	$5^{3\frac{1}{4}}$	Velasquez J	6500	9.80
13Aug89 ^{2}AP^{3}	Bold Try		6	117	8	4	3^{3}	1^{hd}	3^{hd}	$6^{1\frac{1}{4}}$	Fires E	7500	2.00
9Aug89 ^{5}AP^{7}	Extento	b	5	117	6	11	7^{hd}	6^{hd}	$10^{1\frac{1}{2}}$	$7^{1\frac{1}{4}}$	Diaz J L	7500	11.40
31Jly89 ^{9}AP^{3}	Busy Bask	b	4	117	4	6	6^{hd}	7^{hd}	$9^{\frac{1}{2}}$	8^{1}	Torres F C	7500	2.70
13Aug89 ^{2}AP^{7}	Amillium Walk	b	5	117	10	1	$9^{1\frac{1}{2}}$	$10^{\frac{1}{2}}$	12	$9^{\frac{3}{4}}$	Sorrows A G Jr	7500	9.40
13Aug89 ^{2}AP	Ethics Aside	b	7	114	11	2	2^{hd}	$3^{2\frac{1}{2}}$	11^{2}	10^{nk}	Focareto S	6500	57.20
21Jun89 ^{1}Haw^{5}	Alotizzip	b	4	117	3	5	$1^{\frac{1}{2}}$	$2^{1\frac{1}{2}}$	4^{hd}	$11^{\frac{1}{2}}$	Silva C H	7500	11.20
5Aug89 ^{10}AP^{9}	Done Run Away	b	4	117	2	8	$8^{\frac{1}{2}}$	8^{1}	$8^{\frac{1}{2}}$	12	Johnson P A	7500	31.40

OFF AT 2:48. Start good. Won driving. Time, :22⅘, :46⅘, 1:12⅗, 1:25⅖ Track fast.

$2 Mutuel Prices:				
	12–TRYNBESTRAT	23.20	12.60	7.20
	1–CONTRACTOR'S TUNE		24.60	15.80
	5–REGULATIVE			12.20

$2 QUINELLA (1–12) PAID $284.60. $2 PERFECTA (12–1) PAID $772.40.

The Third was a one-turn mile that we'll address a bit later. The Fourth race was another seven-furlong event, this time for $7500 claimers. The winner, Trynbestrat, was another fit to our profile; but this time the public was looking the other way. They allowed the horse to go off at 10.60–1 while betting Bold Try, who figured to be too close to the early pace, a negative on our profile.

Let's spend a minute with the winner of this race. Betting decisions for this day should be based on the sprint profile:

1Call: fourth, 2 to 5 lengths behind
2Call: fourth, 2 to 4 lengths behind
ESP: Pressers preferred

Now look at the average of Trynbestrat's last three running lines:

1Call: fourth, 3.5 lengths behind
2Call: fourth, 2.3 lengths behind
ESP: Presser

Does this horse's profile look oddly familiar? There's no guarantee that personal bias and judgment won't channel the bet along other lines, *but* consider the enormous value from being so properly channeled in our contender selection. We'll almost certainly cash enough of these to show sizable profits. Take advantage of the profile; it will have a limited life expectancy, and then we'll have to start over again.

5th Arlington

6 FURLONGS. (1.08) MAIDEN. CLAIMING. Purse $8,500. 2-year-olds. Weight, 122 lbs. Claiming price $20,000; for each $1,000 to $18,000 allowed 2 lbs.

Tanksgiving B. c. 2(May), by Tank's Prospect—Se Anda, by Tudor Grey
Br.—Eugene Klein (Ky) 1989 4 M 1 1 $3,480
Own.—Klein E V 122 Tr.—Lukas D Wayne $20,000
Lifetime 4 0 1 1 $3,480
13Aug89-5AP 5½f :22² :46¹ 1:05³ft 2¾e118 5²½ 6⁸ 4⁵½ 3³½ Allen K K2 M25000 84-19 CptinStrbuck,LittlPtrZ.,Tnksgivng 12
29Jun89-1CD 5½f :23 :46⁴ 1:05⁴ft 9½ 110 10¹⁰ 10⁶¼ 10⁹ 5⁶½ 3⁵½ Davis K M3 M30000 86-14 StyingAhed,‡ByouHnri,Tnksgiving 11
29Jun89—Placed second through disqualification
4Jun89-1CD 5½f :23 :47³ 1:06²ft *2¼ 119 6⁴ 5²½ 10⁸¼ 11¹⁶¼ Allen K K4 Mdn 72-15 GnMcCown,MgFortun,RdgcrstRdr 12
18May89-4Hol 5f :21⁴ :44² :56²ft 3¾ 117 8¹¹ 7¹³ 8¹⁴ 9¹⁷¼ McCarron C J2 Mdn 87-07 Magical Mile, Jacodra,SocialJokes 10
18May89—Broke slowly
Aug 3 AP 4f ft :49 B Jly 24 AP 5f ft 1:01 H Jly 15 AP 4f ft :49² B Jun 24 CD 4f ft :50 B

FIFTH RACE Arlington AUGUST 24, 1989 **6 FURLONGS. (1.08) MAIDEN. CLAIMING. Purse $8,500. 2-year-olds. Weight, 122 lbs. Claiming price $20,000; for each $1,000 to $18,000 allowed 2 lbs.**

Value of race $8,500; value to winner $5,100; second $1,700; third $935; fourth $510; fifth $255. Mutuel pool $123,291. Quinella pool, $49,981; Perfecta pool, $48,660.

Last Raced	Horse	Eqt.	A.	Wt	PP	St	¼	½	Str	Fin	Jockey	Cl'g Pr	Odds $1
13Aug89 5AP3	Tanksgiving	b	2	122	4	8	6hd	4hd	4¹	1¾	Day P	20000	.70
	Socially Mort	b	2	122	7	6	5¹½	6³	2½	2½	Sellers S J	20000	14.80
12Jly89 4AP5	Baba Quick	b	2	118	1	4	1hd	1¹	1²½	3⁵	Gryder A T	18000	17.60
	Race the Tape		2	122	10	1	7¹	5hd	5⁶	4²	Clark K D	20000	50.40
3Aug89 7EIP3	Eternal Joy		2	122	9	5	4¹½	2¹	3hd	5³¾	Fires E	20000	4.70
13Aug89 5AP8	Sweet Foyt		2	118	8	2	8½	8²½	7²	6¹¼	Razo E Jr	18000	45.30
2Aug89 4AP7	Payco Kid	b	2	122	11	9	10³	7½	8³	7¾	Torres F C	20000	a-5.90
13Aug89 5AP10	Bim Bam	b	2	122	2	3	2hd	3hd	6½	8²	Sorrows A G Jr	20000	a-5.90
	Da' Ragtime Judge	b	2	122	5	11	11	11	9⁵	9¹¹	Gabriel R E	20000	33.60
3Aug89 4AP10	Incomesfox	b	2	122	3	7	3hd	10³	10-	10	Lindsay R	20000	16.10
12Jly89 4AP11	Timely Win		2	122	6	10	9hd	9¹½	—	—	Allen K K	20000	17.20

Timely Win, Broke down.
a-Coupled: Payco Kid and Bim Bam.

OFF AT 3:16. Start good. Won driving. Time, :23⅕, :47⅘, 1:14⅕ Track fast.

$2 Mutuel Prices:

4-TANKSGIVING	3.40	2.60	2.60
7-SOCIALLY MORT		8.20	6.60
2-BABA QUICK			8.20

$2 QUINELLA (4-7) PAID $22.60; $2 PERFECTA (4-7) PAID $30.20.

The Fifth was a maiden claimer at six furlongs and was taken by Tanksgiving, an odds-on favorite with the right running style. Note the performance of the pace setter Baba Quick. On the biased track, she hit a wall 2½ lengths clear of the field at the eighth pole.

7th Arlington

6 FURLONGS

6 FURLONGS. (1.08) ALLOWANCE. Purse $23,000. Fillies and mares. 3-year-olds and upward which have never won three races other than maiden, claiming or starter. Weight, 3-year-olds, 117 lbs.; older, 122 lbs. Non-winners of two races other than maiden or claiming since May 15 allowed 3 lbs.; of such a race since March 1, 5 lbs.

Water Tester — B. f. 3(Apr), by Water Bank—Try Azimycin, by Clem
Own.—Karp L — 114 — Br.—Donald, Ruby & Gary Wrenn (Ky) — 1989 9 3 2 0 $60,509
Tr.—Kasperski Joseph Jr — 1988 2 1 0 0 $4,800
Lifetime 11 4 2 0 $65,309 — Turf 1 0 0 0

7Jun89-8Haw a7½f Ⓣ:232 :4631:324fm 9½ 119 43 32 57½ 68½ Clark K D2 ⒻAw28750 80-14 ShkRgRuthi,ShowtimDb,FlirtngFlm 9
26May89-9Spt 1 1/16 :49 1:141 1:464ft 12 115 44 34 413 416 RzEJr3 ⒻNat Jky Oak 64-27 Chrlindr,ExquisitMistrss,FlirtngFlm 6
26May89—Bore out turn.
5May89-8Spt 1 :484 1:14 1:422ft 6-5 117 32½ 1½ 1½ 2nk RzEJr5 ⒻMata Hari H 68-27 RugWever,WterTester,FlirtingFlme 6
21Apr89-8Spt 1 :483 1:141 1:404ft *9-5 115 32½ 1hd 12 14 Razo E Jr7 ⒻAw32500 76-21 WterTester,RugWever,ChrfulScrtry 7
2Apr89-6Spt 6f :24 :473 1:131ft 5½ 117 21½ 2½ 1hd 13½ Miller S E7 ⒻAw21000 84-21 Water Tester,Talasassy,DoubleCedi 7
18Mar89-7Spt 6f :24 :474 1:132ft 7½ 115 820 817 817 817¾ Razo E Jr8 ⒻRuffian 65-22 L.B.'sLunch,FlrtngFlm,ChrfulScrtry 8
18Mar89—Bolted
1Mar89-7GP 6f :214 :45 1:114ft 15 121 87½ 713 45 53½ Fires E1 ⒻAw23000 77-22 TrplStrk,Lt'sBFrnds,DonscsPrncss 10
15Feb89-3GP 6f :222 :461 1:121ft *6-5 116 54 42¼ 22 11¾ Chavez J F8 Ⓕ c35000 78-27 WtrTstr,ChrflScrtry,WnnngPrtnrs 10
24Jan89-6GP 6f :223 :462 1:124ft 4 116 42 46 44 21 Gaffalione S6 Ⓕ 25000 74-24 It'saJewel,WaterTester,FlshyHere 12
24Jan89—Checked
10Dec88-9Med 6f :221 :452 1:093ft 6½ 113 21 31 47½ 612¾ Ferrer J C4 ⒻAw20000 81-17 Slewprltiv,SouthrnSoonr,CopprDiv 9
●Aug 21 AP 3f ft :354 H Aug 14 AP 6f ft 1:153 H Aug 5 AP 5f sy 1:021 B Jly 30 AP 6f sy 1:161 Bg

SEVENTH RACE Arlington AUGUST 24, 1989 — **6 FURLONGS. (1.08) ALLOWANCE. Purse $23,000. Fillies and mares. 3-year-olds and upward which have never won three races other than maiden, claiming or starter. Weight, 3-year-olds, 117 lbs.; older, 122 lbs. Non-winners of two races other than maiden or claiming since May 15 allowed 3 lbs.; of such a race since March 1, 5 lbs.**
Value of race $23,000; value to winner $13,800; second $4,600; third $2,530; fourth $1,380; fifth $690. Mutuel pool $127,472. Quin pool $31,140. Per pool $25,055. Tri pool $109,626.

Last Raced	Horse	Eqt.	A.	Wt	PP	St	¼	½	Str	Fin	Jockey	Odds $1
7Jun89 8Haw6	Water Tester		3	114	7	1	51	31	13	1½	Razo E Jr	9.50
30Jly89 8AP7	A Simple Heart		3	114	9	7	73	75	31½	2½	Velasquez J	1.50
31Jly89 4AP4	Five to Six		3	117	6	2	4½	53	21½	34½	Day P	3.90
31Mar89 3SA7	La Sierra		5	117	1	4	33	4hd	51½	42	Silva C H	10.60
31Jly89 1AP1	Cheerful Secretary		3	114	5	5	61	62	63	53	Diaz J L	5.60
31Jly89 4AP6	Princess Fire		4	117	8	6	82	8½	81	6nk	Allen K K	36.40
22Jly89 3AP2	Noetic		3	114	2	3	1½	21½	4hd	7¾	Fires E	8.20
29Jly89 7AP7	Blue Danzig	b	4	119	3	9	9	9	9	81¼	Smith M E	10.60
19Aug89 6AP12	Chapilca		3	113	4	8	2½	1hd	72	9	Clark K D	15.70

OFF AT 4:11. Start good. Won driving. Time, :22⅖, :46⅗, 1:12⅕ Track fast.

$2 Mutuel Prices:			
7-WATER TESTER	21.00	7.00	5.00
9-A SIMPLE HEART		3.20	2.60
6-FIVE TO SIX			3.20

$2 QUIN (7-9) PAID $31.60. $2 PER (7-9) PAID $77.20. $2 TRI (7-9-6) PAID $321.00.

The Sixth was another one-turn mile, but the Seventh, at six furlongs, was taken by Water Tester at 9.50–1. Her running style fits our profile like the proverbial glove. The race was not easy, and there was no guarantee of picking this winner, but the profile steers us in her direction.

The Eighth race was on the turf course, and the final race of the day was another one-turn mile. We'll address both before we complete this chapter. The bottom line of this exercise was that in the five sprint races, *none* deviated from the profile. The data from these races further strengthens our understanding of the track.

Arlington Park Routes

Here's the data from two of the one-turn miles run on 20Aug89:

FIRST RACE
Arlington
AUGUST 20, 1989

1 MILE. (1.32 1/5) CLAIMING. Purse $8,500. 3-year-olds. Weight, 122 lbs. Non-winners of a race at a mile or over since July 31 allowed 3 lbs.; of such a race since July 15, 5 lbs. Claiming price $10,000; for each $500 to $9,000 allowed 2 lbs. (Races for $8,000 or less not considered.) 47TH DAY. WEATHER CLEAR. TEMPERATURE 81 DEGREES.

Value of race $8,500; value to winner $5,100; second $1,700; third $935; fourth $510; fifth $255. Mutuel pool $108,834. Quinella pool $29,243. Perfecta pool $25,309.

Last Raced	Horse	Eqt.	A.	Wt	PP	St	1/4	1/2	3/4	Str	Fin	Jockey	Cl'g Pr	Odds $1
4Aug89 2AP3	Feels Like Far		3	117	2	6	4^{hd}	3^{2}	$3^{2\frac{1}{2}}$	2^{3}	1^{7}	Velasquez J	10000	.80
11Aug89 3AP6	Trogan	b	3	109	6	3	2^{7}	2^{10}	$1^{\frac{1}{2}}$	$1^{\frac{1}{2}}$	2^{nk}	Gomez A5	9000	9.30
11Aug89 5AP6	Mickey's Place		3	117	7	2	$5^{1\frac{1}{2}}$	$5^{\frac{1}{2}}$	4^{8}	4^{8}	$3^{7\frac{1}{2}}$	Sellers S J	10000	18.20
11Aug89 5AP3	Tri For Charlie		3	113	3	5	6^{10}	6^{10}	$5^{3\frac{1}{2}}$	5^{10}	$4^{\frac{3}{4}}$	Smith M E	9000	6.40
2Aug89 3AP3	Peachmeister	b	3	117	4	1	$1^{\frac{1}{2}}$	$1^{\frac{1}{2}}$	2^{6}	3^{hd}	5^{7}	Fires E	10000	2.40
2Aug89 3AP5	Bleu Chanson	b	3	113	1	7	7	7	7	$6^{1\frac{1}{2}}$	6^{6}	Ward W A	9000	33.10
9Aug89 3AP7	Threshold's Image	b	3	117	5	4	3^{1}	4^{1}	6^{2}	7	7	Bartram B E	10000	19.90

OFF AT 1:30. Start good. Won ridden out. Time, :23, :45 4/5, 1:10 4/5, 1:37 3/5 Track fast.

SEVENTH RACE
Arlington
AUGUST 20, 1989

1 MILE. (1.32 1/5) ALLOWANCE. Purse $20,000. Fillies and mares. 3-year-olds and upward, which have never won a race other than maiden, claiming or starter. Weight, 3-year-olds, 115 lbs.; older, 122 lbs. Non-winners of a race other than claiming at a mile or over since May 15 allowed 3 lbs. (Originally scheduled to be run at 1 1/16 miles on the turf). (Originally scheduled to be run at one and one-sixteenth mile on the turf).

Value of race $20,000; value to winner $12,000; second $4,000; third $2,200; fourth $1,200; fifth $600. Mutuel pool $152,834. Qui pool $37,623. Per pool $24,096. Tri pool $129,568.

Last Raced	Horse	Eqt.	A.	Wt	PP	St	1/4	1/2	3/4	Str	Fin	Jockey	Odds $1
10Aug89 8AP3	Brattice Cloth		3	113	2	6	6^{hd}	4^{1}	$1^{\frac{1}{2}}$	$1^{\frac{1}{2}}$	1^{hd}	Bruin J E	1.00
27Jly89 5AP1	Grandma G.		3	115	7	5	5^{2}	$6^{\frac{1}{2}}$	3^{hd}	2^{3}	$2^{3\frac{1}{2}}$	Smith M E	7.00
7Aug89 9AP1	Dibs		3	115	5	8	7^{10}	7^{12}	6^{1}	$3^{3\frac{1}{2}}$	3^{7}	Allen K K	3.50
29Jly89 4Cby1	Miss Kathy S.		4	122	4	2	$2^{\frac{1}{2}}$	$3^{\frac{1}{2}}$	5^{hd}	$4^{2\frac{1}{2}}$	$4^{6\frac{1}{2}}$	Fires E	6.00
4Aug89 4AP2	Miss Harvey		3	113	8	1	$1^{2\frac{1}{2}}$	1^{hd}	2^{1}	5^{3}	5^{1}	Clark K D	8.70
7Aug89 1AP2	Determined to Win	b	3	114	6	4	$4^{\frac{1}{2}}$	5^{hd}	7^{15}	6^{1}	6^{5}	Schaefer G A	17.00
28Jly89 6AP4	Lil Streaker	b	4	114	3	3	3^{2}	$2^{1\frac{1}{2}}$	$4^{\frac{1}{2}}$	7^{12}	7^{15}	Gomez A5	23.70
6Aug89 10RD1	Marine Waltz		6	119	1	7	8	8	8	8	8	Ward W A	42.30

The first race was at one mile, for three-year-olds, with seven horses entered. The winner:

1Call: third, 10½ lengths behind the leader
2Call: third, 6½ lengths behind the leader
ESP: Presser/Sustained

The running style of Feels Like Far appears to be that of a presser. Neatly placed behind a suicidal pace duel, he seemed to press along and wait for the inevitable collapse on the front. He was 10½ lengths behind at the second call, which by itself suggests a Sustained Pace designation. We'll call him both.

Dist	Ent	1Call	2Call	%E	ESP
8	7	3/10+	3/6½	N/A	P/S

The Seventh race was also at eight furlongs, a NW1 for fillies and mares. Eight were entered. The winner:

1Call: fourth, 2 lengths behind the leader
2Call: first by ½ length
ESP: Presser

	Dist	Ent	1Call	2Call	%E	ESP
20Aug89	8	7	3/10+	3/6½	N/A	P/S
"	8	8	4/2	1/½	"	P
"	8	6	5/4½	4/2	"	S/P
"	8	8	5/6½	5/6	"	S
21Aug89	8	8	3/1	2/½	"	P

Route Conclusions

In this example, numerical position and lengths are not as important as several basic conclusions.

First, based on a limited amount of data, we should not consider any horse likely to attempt a "theft" on the lead. The data is clear: Wire-to-wire types are at a severe disadvantage.

Second, *strongly* prefer pressers and sustained runners. As data is added to the worksheet, handicappers can adjust the initial findings. That wasn't necessary during my three-day session.

Third, avoid the deep closers unable to stay in touch with the leaders. These are poor bets most times, at most tracks. The initial data at Arlington Park indicates this track is no exception.

Application

Race 3: A maiden race at one mile. It was won by the 7–5 favorite by pressing the pace and drawing away late.

6th Arlington

1 MILE. (1.32⅕) ALLOWANCE. Purse $24,200 (includes 10% from Illinois Thoroughbred Breeder's Fund). 3-year-olds and upward, Illinois registered, conceived and/or foaled which have never won two races other than maiden, claiming or starter. Weight, 3-year-olds, 115 lbs.; older, 122 lbs. Non-winners of a race other than maiden or claiming at a mile or over since June 1 allowed 3 lbs.

Game Fellow

Ch. c. 3(Apr), by Play Fellow—Shamgame, by Sham
Br.—Schenck J & Vanier HMr–Mrs (Ill)   1989 10 2 1 3 $33,254
Own.—Schenck & Vanier Mmes   115   Tr.—Vanier Harvey L   1988 2 M 0 0
Lifetime 12 2 1 3 $33,254

11Aug89-7AP	1 :45⁴ 1:11¹ 1:38²sy	3½ 115	55½ 34½ 36½ 47¼	Bruin J E ₃	Aw24200	62-33	ChpSnglsss,CblloDlSol,Pocktflfhny 9
4Aug89-7AP	1 1:38 ft ⁴6-5 113	51½ 52 51½ 1ⁿᵒ	Bruin J E ₅	⑤Aw22000	71-23	GameFellow,CashsHeir,MarchStep 10
	4Aug89—Fractional Times Unavailable; Boxed in turn						
23Jly89-7AP	1 :46⁴ 1:12² 1:38 ft	3½e113	64½ 99½ 510 3⁸	Bruin J E ₅	⑤Aw22000	63-25	Wht'sAtStke,Zentherwsu,GmFllow 10
	23Jly89—Bumped start						
9Jly89-2AP	7f :22³ :46 1:25⁴ft	2½ 115	64½ 53½ 1ʰᵈ 15¼	Velasquez J ₇	⑤Mdn	73-23	Game Fellow, Waydo, ArticMystery 9
23Jun89-6CD	6f :21⁴ :46¹ 1:11 ft	6½ 113	63½ 3½ 33 36	Bruin J E ₈	Mdn	82-16	Fsterthnlight,BnnerBerer,GmFllow 9
14Jun89-9CD	6½f :23 :47 1:18²ft	7½ 112	63 5² 54 510½	Allen K K ₉	Mdn	77-17	Polka, Sefa's Music, Baggage Boy 11
	14Jun89—Wide						
19May89-9CD	6f :22¹ :46 1:11³ft	2½ 112	1ʰᵈ 2ʰᵈ 33 58½	Fires E ₅	Mdn	76-17	CddoHill,BreezeEzy,SpctculrSingh 11
8Apr89-3Hia	7f :23² :45⁴ 1:23 ft	4½ 121	84½ 55 22½ 26½	Chavez J F ₄	Mdn	81-11	Compuquin,GmFllow,LttlOrphnAb 11
26Mar89-8Hia	7f :23¹ :46¹ 1:23³ft	9 121	108½ 79½ 69 48½	Lester R N ₃	Mdn	76-14	Roi Danzig, StealingHome,Believe 12
	26Mar89—Bumped st.						
1Mar89-3Hia	7f :23¹ :46¹ 1:24²ft	4½ 121	86½ 87½ 44 36½	Lester R N ₃	Mdn	75-21	KeytotheBot,DevilishGria,GmFllow 9

Aug 17 AP 5f ft 1:02² B   Aug 10 AP 3f ft :38¹ B   Jly 31 AP 5f ft 1:01⁴ H   Jly 21 AP 4f sl :50⁴ B

SIXTH RACE
Arlington
AUGUST 24, 1989

1 MILE. (1.32⅕) ALLOWANCE. Purse $24,200 (includes 10% from Illinois Thoroughbred Breeder's Fund). 3-year-olds and upward, Illinois registered, conceived and/or foaled which have never won two races other than maiden, claiming or starter. Weight, 3-year-olds, 115 lbs.; older, 122 lbs. Non-winners of a race other than maiden or claiming at a mile or over since June 1 allowed 3 lbs.

Value of race $24,200; value to winner $14,520; second $4,840; third $2,662; fourth $1,452; fifth $726. Mutuel pool $132,497.
Quin pl $51,139. Perf pl $56,802.

Last Raced	Horse	Eqt.A.Wt PP St	¼	½	¾	Str	Fin	Jockey	Odds $1
11Aug89 7AP⁴	Game Fellow	b 3 115 4 7	9ʰᵈ	5½	11	1¹	1ʰᵈ	Day P	1.40
11Aug89 7AP²	Caballo Del Sol	b 3 112 5 6	7	7	4ʰᵈ	2⁴	2⁶	Sellers S J	2.50
11Aug89 7AP⁷	Rockaby Gally	b 4 119 3 4	2ʰᵈ	3½	6³	3¹	35½	Silva C H	11.00
13Aug89 6AP⁶	Happy Hotel	4 119 2 3	4¹	2½	31	4½	4½	Razo E Jr	9.80
27Jly89 7AP³	Harham's Imperial	b 6 119 7 1	3½	1ʰᵈ	2ʰᵈ	5½½	5²	Fires E	4.30
11Aug89 7AP³	Pocketfulofhoney	b 4 119 1 5	6²	6½½	5½	6½½	6⅜	Gryder A T	6.50
11Aug89 7AP⁸	Doctor Eugat	5 119 6 2	1½	4ʰᵈ	7	7	7	Meier R	40.60

OFF AT 3:43. Start good. Won driving. Time, :23⅖, :47⅗, 1:13⅘, 1:39⅖ Track fast.

$2 Mutuel Prices:
4-GAME FELLOW 4.80 3.00 2.60
5-CABALLO DEL SOL 3.20 3.00
3-ROCKABY GALLY 4.80
$2 QUIN (4-5) PD $7.40. $2 PERF (4-5) PD $13.60.

Race 6: Game Fellow, the 7–5 favorite, pressed the pace and won late. A strong fit to the profile.

9th Arlington

START / 1 MILE / ARLINGTON / FINISH

1 MILE. (1.32⅕) CLAIMING. Purse $12,500. 3–year–olds and upward. Weight, 3–year–olds, 115 lbs.; older, 122 lbs. Non–winners of a race at a mile or over since July 31 allowed 3 lbs.; of such a race since July 15, 5 lbs. Claiming price $20,000; for each $1,000 to $18,000 allowed 2 lbs. (Races when entered to be claimed for $16,000 or less not considered.)

Navonod's Last — Dk. b. or br. g. 5, by George Navonod—Daring Sword, by Double Edge Sword

Own.—Steinmeitz John — **117** — Br.—Eckler Mr–Mrs John M (Ky) — Tr.—Van Berg Jack C — $20,000

1989 14 4 2 2 $32,776
1988 15 1 3 4 $10,446
Lifetime 38 5 6 8 $47,102

14Aug89-9AP	1	:47	1:122	1:383ft	*2¼	122	42	75½	51¾	21¼	Bartram B E6	20000	67-28	ABuckAThrow,Navonod'sLst,Trver	8
3Aug89-9EIP	1	:464	1:113	1:37 ft	*3-2	117	72½	63¼	53½	53¼	Bass S H5	Aw13800	85-16	Rascal J., Superbest, CinnamonRed	7
23Jly89-9EIP	1	:461	1:111	1:364ft	*2¾	115	33	1hd	14	13¼	Bass S H5	Aw13200	89-13	Nvonod'sLst,SrLghtnng,NrthrnHr	11
13Jly89-9EIP	1	:471	1:131	1:393gd	*2¼	115	611	66	44½	3¾	Bass S H1	Aw13200	74-20	RsclJ.,PuseFortheCus,Nvonod'sLst	6
13Jly89—Checked start															
29Jun89-5CD	1	:463	1:12	1:373ft	3¾	116	48½	43½	2hd	12¼	Bass S H1	13500	81-14	Navonod'sLast,RecklessTop,HeyPt	8
29Jun89—Brushed stretch.															
18Jun89-5CD	1	:463	1:112	1:371ft	7¾	118	57	56¾	31¼	22¼	St Leon G6	10000	81-16	CochFox,Nvonod'sLst,Mtlock'sFrd	8
10Jun89-7CD	1	:462	1:113	1:38 ft	27	116	66¾	75½	94¾	98¼	Bass S H1	13500	71-18	ComlyDncr,WonDuLoup,FourChncs	9
11May89-9CD	1 1/16	:473	1:123	1:452ft	6¼	10810	77	79	59½	510	Johnston M T3	c10000	71-13	RecklessTop,CleverDub,Bob'sDbut	10
19Apr89-6Kee	1 1/16	:484	1:134	1:452m	14	116	1016	1013	911	918½	Bartram B E4	Aw21300	60-26	Baltic Fox, SlickJr.,ShineOnSunny	12
11Apr89-7Kee	1 1/16	:47	1:123	1:454ft	21	112	28	412	56	511½	Garcia J J2	Aw24600	65-21	HeyPli,R.B.McCurry,SubtleMneuver	9

NINTH RACE
Arlington
AUGUST 24, 1989

1 MILE. (1.32⅕) CLAIMING. Purse $12,500. 3–year–olds and upward. Weight, 3–year–olds, 115 lbs.; older, 122 lbs. Non–winners of a race at a mile or over since July 31 allowed 3 lbs.; of such a race since July 15, 5 lbs. Claiming price $20,000; for each $1,000 to $18,000 allowed 2 lbs. (Races when entered to be claimed for $16,000 or less not considered.)

Value of race $12,500; value to winner $7,500; second $2,500; third $1,375; fourth $750; fifth $375. Mutuel pool $126,607. Qui pool $26,291. Per pool $19,968; Tri pool $134,288.

Last Raced	Horse	Eqt.A.Wt	PP	St	¼	½	¾	Str	Fin	Jockey	Cl'g Pr	Odds $1
14Aug89 9AP2	Navonod's Last	b 5 119	6	5	5hd	4½	41	1hd	12½	Bartram B E	20000	7.50
9Aug89 5AP1	Canadian Winter	b 6 117	8	4	63½	31½	21½	21	21½	Diaz J L	20000	1.90
5Aug89 2AP2	High Flanker	b 4 117	3	8	71	6hd	51½	42	3¾	Solomone M	20000	25.30
9Aug89 9AP7	Iwanabeanowner	5 119	1	6	3½	52	71½	63	41½	Day P	20000	3.30
5Aug89 10AP1	Gummo Boy	7 122	4	3	23	2½	1½	3½	51¾	Torres F C	20000	3.90
12Aug89 4AP2	Authentic Hero	5 117	7	2	4hd	72	6½	5hd	63	Bruin J E	20000	5.50
13Aug89 3AP3	Frankie's Pal	b 5 117	2	7	8	8	8	78	7	Lindsay R	20000	14.00
5Aug89 10AP8	Mileage Wise	b 7 117	5	1	14	12	31½	8	—	Clark K D	20000	15.70

Mileage Wise, Eased.

OFF AT 5:05. Start good. Won driving. Time, :23⅘, :47⅕, 1:12⅗, 1:38⅘ Track fast.

$2 Mutuel Prices:			
6–NAVONOD'S LAST	17.00	7.80	5.20
9–CANADIAN WINTER		4.20	3.60
3–HIGH FLANKER			8.60

$2 QUI (6–9) PAID $37.00. $2 PER (6–9) PAID $83.20. $2 TRI (6–9–3) PAID $1,157.60.

Race 9: Navonod's Last, at 7.50–1, sat behind the early leaders and won easily. The two co-second choices were Early Pace types, both perishing late. Navonod's Last was a perfect fit to the profile.

So far, *all* eight races conformed to the profile we constructed from only three days' worth of data. Only one surface or distance remained: the turf course:

	Dist	*Ent*	*1Call*	*2Call*	*%E*	*ESP*
19Aug89	8½	12	10/8	10/6	N/A	S
"	9½	12	9/8½	9/9½	"	S

	Dist	Ent	1Call	2Call	%E	ESP
"	8	11	8/12	8/5½	"	S
20Aug89	8	10	3/2	3/2½	"	P
21Aug89	8	9	4/6	4/2½	"	S

It didn't take genius to unravel the secret of this turf course. With the exception of one pressing performance, the key was to play closers and avoid the Early Pace types. In fact, sprints, routes, and turf races should have been played with an emphasis on Sustained Pace ratings. The one turf race, on August 24:

8th Arlington

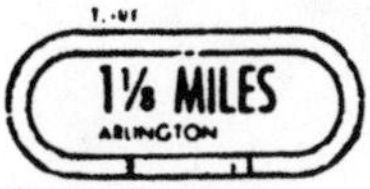

1 ⅛ MILES. (Turf). (1.47¾) ALLOWANCE. Purse $20,000. 3-year-olds and upward which have never won a race other than maiden, claiming or starter. Weight, 3-year-olds, 116 lbs.; older, 122 lbs. Non-winners of a race other than claiming at a mile or over since May 1 allowed 3 lbs.

Grumpy Miller
B. g. 4, by Full Out—Concha Mauina, by Forli
Br.—Miller M W Jr (Ky)
Own.—Hermitage Farm **119** Tr.—Penrod Steven
1989 11 1 2 3 $28,573
1988 11 1 1 5 $29,260
Lifetime 28 2 5 11 $78,513 Turf 1 1 0 0 $6,000

26Jly89-9AP	1 ①:47¹1:13¹1:40 sf	5½ 117	49½ 56	31½ 13	Day P ¹⁰	16000	75-32 GrmpyMllr,BoldLbrtn,Dn'tFlWthM 12
19Jly89-7AP	7f :22⁴ :46³ 1:26¹sl	8½ 117	76 46½	55½ 87¼	Johnson P A ²	25000	63-34 Don'tStiffMe,BstGoods,UndrThSun 9
24Jun89-4CD	6f :21² :45³ 1:13¹ft	*3 117	77¼ 75½	53¼ 44	Bruin J E ²	25000	81-10 NwsComnttor,EsyNEsr,Rchrd'sFrst 8
10Jun89-5CD	1 :46⁴ 1:11⁴ 1:37 ft	*9-5 118	65½ 52	43½ 35½	Bruin J E⁵	25000	78-18 JohnnyCorvtt,B.LinDrv,GrumpyMllr 7
2Jun89-7CD	1¼:47³ 1:13 1:45¹ft	*4-5 112	44½ 22	41½ 44¼	Day P¹	Aw22620	77-18 Trucking Bucks, Win for Jan, Lens 6
2Jun89—Bobbled break.							
19Apr89-6Kee	1¼:48⁴ 1:13⁴ 1:45²m	*3-2 115	41½ 2½	21½ 46½	Perret C⁹	Aw21300	73-26 Baltic Fox, SlickR,ShineOnSunny 12
20Mar89-7Aqu	1½:50 1:14¹ 1:52²ft	3½ 117	2¹ 2ʰᵈ	34½ 3⁹	Cordero A.Jr ²	Aw29000	64-34 Jo'sHunch,BrvndBrght,GrmpyMllr 11
10Mar89-5Aqu	1¼⊡:49 1:14 1:45⁴ft	3 117	3² 3ⁿᵏ	1ʰᵈ 2ʰᵈ	Cordero A.Jr ²	Aw29000	80-24 VlidJourny,GrumpyMllr,SunrisSrvc 8
27Feb89-5Aqu	1¼⊡:48³1:12⁴1:46¹ft	3½ 117	42½ 34	34 34	Fox W I x⁷	Aw25000	74-27 FlowTchnology,VldJrny,GrmpyMllr 8
8Feb89-8Aqu	1¼⊡:49 1:14²1:47³ft	6½ 117	31½ 51½	21 2½	Fox W I Jr ⁴	Aw25000	70-22 O.K.NoProblm,GrmpyMllr,TvolStr 12
Aug 19 AP 4f ft :48² H		Aug 13 AP 4f gd :49² B		Aug 6 AP 4f ft :48 H		Jly 12 AP 4f m :48³ H	

EIGHTH RACE
Arlington
AUGUST 24, 1989

1 ⅛ MILES.(Turf). (1.47¾) ALLOWANCE. Purse $20,000. 3-year-olds and upward which have never won a race other than maiden, claiming or starter. Weight, 3-year-olds, 116 lbs.; older, 122 lbs. Non-winners of a race other than claiming at a mile or over since May 1 allowed 3 lbs.

Value of race $20,000; value to winner $12,000; second $4,000; third $2,200; fourth $1,200; fifth $600. Mutuel pool $150,141.
Quinella pool $51,323. Perfecta pool $55,075.

Last Raced	Horse	Eqt.A.Wt PP St	¼	½	¾	Str	Fin	Jockey	Odds $1
26Jly89 9AP¹	Grumpy Miller	b 4 119 2 3	3½	31½	31½	21½	1½	Fires E	a-2.30
2Aug89 8AP²	Plan To Barter	5 119 5 5	1¹	1½	11½	1½	2ʰᵈ	Gryder A T	2.50
11Aug89 6AP¹¹	Partially Royal	3 115 4 4	61½	61½	4ʰᵈ	46	3½	Velasquez J	6.70
12Aug89¹⁰AP²	Tetcht	b 4 122 3 2	8½	7¹	62½	3½	4¾½	Sellers S J	a-2.30
21Jly89 7AP⁷	Baranof	b 4 119 10 9	7¹	5ʰᵈ	7½	5½	51½	Day P	3.00
11Aug89 6AP⁵	Parrish Express	3 112 6 6	2¹	22	2½	62½	6½	Johnson P A	21.30
12Jly89 7AP²	Not Yet George	b 4 119 9 8	92	10	8ʰᵈ	81½	72	Torres F C	12.10
10Aug89 2AP⁹	Mr. Bonkers	b 5 119 8 1	42	4³	5½	7ʰᵈ	8½	Marquez C H Jr	59.00
26Jly89 7Bel⁴	Lord Summing	3 113 7 10	10	8¹	9¹⁵	9	9	Bruin J E	10.00
11Aug89 6AP¹²	K. O. Kato	b 3 113 1 7	5ʰᵈ	9ʰᵈ	10	—	—	Clark K D	54.50

K. O. Kato, Eased.
a-Coupled: Grumpy Miller and Tetcht.
OFF AT 4:38. Start good. Won driving. Time, :24, :48½, 1:14½, 1:40, 1:52¾ Course good.

$2 Mutuel Prices:				
1-GRUMPY MILLER (a-entry)		6.60	4.00	2.60
4-PLAN TO BARTER			3.80	3.00
3-PARTIALLY ROYAL				3.60

$2 QUINELLA (1-4) PAID $9.60. $2 PERFECTA (1-4) PAID $20.00.

The winner, Grumpy Miller, pressed the pace and asserted himself late to win straight. Every turf race during the three-day session was won from off the pace.

SUMMARY

There were enough potential winners from the Arlington Park profile to virtually guarantee a winning session. In every race during the three-day period, the winner emerged from the final contenders, and that's very often the case. With a reliable track profile, even the most inexperienced handicapper has a chance for winning play. All any handicapper can ask from the contender/selection process is to be pointed in the right direction, and a track profile does exactly that.

CHAPTER IX

Energy Distribution

SOME AGE-OLD PROBLEMS: Why do some horses like certain race-tracks while seemingly detesting others? How to approach the beginning of a race meeting? How to handle the "horses for courses" riddle?

Handicapping "wisdom" generally recommends a wait-and-see attitude in those situations. That's not bad advice. It's certainly better than frivolously risking the bankroll. Is there a better way to solve the problems? There is.

The basic problem can be approached through an understanding of the requirements placed on runners by racing surfaces. In a broader sense, a commonly accepted truth is that turf racing requires a delayed energy output. Sustained pace runners dominate the bulk of turf races, and the inability to finish strongly is a characteristic of turf-course losers. Dirt racing asks for more of an early output. That places a premium on early pace.

The same relationship exists between racetracks. The horse that wires its field at Saratoga will often lose with the same tactics at Belmont Park. Louisiana Downs closers unable to win with a big finish will find the Fairgrounds to their liking.

The problem, in a nutshell, is one of degree. How do we estimate beyond a simple designation as to closers or front-running biases? Measuring *how much* sustained, or *how much* early, will require developing a unit of measurement to be applied universally. It will also require the reader's acceptance that horses are remarkably consistent in their running styles.

In this chapter we'll work toward measuring a horse's total

available energy and then gauging the distribution of that energy in a race. We'll also develop a method for determining what distribution parameters exist at a given racetrack, and how fields match up within those parameters. I will also present some basic conclusions based on an understanding of energy exertion. Now let's develop the measuring device: Total Energy.

TOTAL ENERGY—THE MEASURING STICK

The measurement and application of energy distribution is a concept original to the Sartin Methodology. The realization that a horse distributes unrecoverable energy throughout a race is not a breakthrough idea. It is basic to an understanding of physical exertion. *Measuring* the level of exertion *is* original and represents some of the most creative thinking in modern handicapping. The current Sartin computer programs are emphasizing energy acceleration and deceleration over traditional velocity concepts. They are impressive in their basic insights.

To fully understand the material in this chapter I advise the reader to work through the examples with a handheld calculator. The principles will be vague and virtually impossible to apply without the effort. That's the bad news. The good news? All the math is quite simple and the algorithms easily programmed for a handheld computer.

First, a review of some earlier concepts:

Early Pace: The rate of velocity at the second call. In sprints, it is calculated by dividing the feet in a half-mile (2640) by the second-call time. In routes, the calculation changes only by the number of feet in the pace segment (6 * 660 = 3960).

Last Fraction: The velocity of the final fraction of the race. It is calculated by dividing the number of feet in the fraction by the time of the fraction.

Furlong: One-eighth mile. The basic unit of measurement at the racetrack; 660 feet per furlong.

Beaten Lengths (BL): Ten feet per length. When gained, *add* the distance to the pace segment. When lost, *deduct* from the segment.

Total Energy (TTL): A horse's total available energy based on current condition and basic ability. It is measured by summing Early Pace and the Final Fraction of the horse's representative paceline(s).

Total Energy = Early Pace + Last Fraction
* TTL   = EP + LF*

An earlier discussion advanced the argument for the second call as the pivotal point in a race. Certainly some races are determined earlier or later, but position at the second call decides most races. The problem? Which runners are still capable of winning and which are certain losers? It is entirely dependent upon how much available energy has been utilized prior to reaching the second call. Energy depletion can be measured by the following algorithm:

% Energy Expended = Second Call/Total Energy
* % EARLY   = EP/TTL*

Percentage of energy expended at the second call is determined by dividing second-call velocity by the total energy available. We'll refer to this factor as Percent Early (%E), or early energy. It's simpler than it first appears.

Horse A	22.2	45.4	1:11.4	
(BL)	0	0	0	(beaten lengths)

Early Pace (EP)   = 2640 ft. / 45.8 seconds = 57.64 fps
Last Fraction (LF) = 1320 ft. / 25.8 seconds = 50.76 fps
Total Energy (TTL) = EP + LF 57.64 + 50.76 = 108.4 energy units.
Percent Early (%E) = EP/TTL 57.64 / 108.4 = 53.17%

In the illustration, the runner has used 53.17 percent of his available energy upon reaching the second call. The relationship to other runners, and to the surface, will be discussed in depth after the calculations have been explained.

Horse B	22.2	45.4	1:11.3	
(BL)	3	2	1.5	(beaten lengths)

Early Pace (EP)   = 2640 − 20(2*10) = 2620 ft. / 45.8 seconds = 57.20 fps
Last Fraction (LF)   = 1320 + 5(½ length gained) = 1325 ft. / 25.8 seconds = 51.35 fps

Total Energy (TTL) = EP + LF 57.20 + 51.35 = 108.55 energy units

Percent Early (%E) = EP/TTL 57.20 / 108.55 = 52.69%

In this example, Horse B expended his energy at a smoother rate. The 52.69 percent usually identifies an early pace or presser type. The 53.17 percent from the first illustration will usually be identified with an early pace type. These are general comments and must be considered in the light of a specific race-track.

Now we'll examine a route.

Horse C	47.2	1:12.2	1:45.3	1 1/16 miles
(BL)	7	4	2	(beaten lengths)

Early Pace (EP)   = 3960 − 40(4 * 10) = 3920 ft. / 72.4 seconds = 54.14 fps

Last Fraction (LF)   = 1650(2.5 * 660) + 20(2 lengths gained) = 1670 ft. / 33.2 seconds = 50.30 fps

Total Energy (TTL) = EP + LF 54.14 + 50.30 = 104.44 energy units

Percent Early (%E) = EP/TTL 54.14 / 104.44 = 51.83%

Horse C is typical of the energy expended by a route winner at most racetracks around the country. If his velocity numbers are competitive, he'll be a strong candidate for a win. The last statement deserves more than just a passing comment.

Using the percentage of energy expended at the second call can be a powerful factor in the selection of winners. When considering a field of evenly matched runners, it's often the difference between winning and losing. There is a caution, however. When one or two horses in a race have superior velocity numbers, the energy distribution of the slower horses is meaningless. Horse C will not defeat Secretariat no matter how he distributes his energy.

Now let's look at some actual examples.

Tobin's Wish ✳

GONZALEZ R M		**117**				

B. g. 8, by J O Tobin—Christmas Wishes, by Northern Dancer
Br.—Chase O (Ky)
Tr.—Bonde Jeff
Own.—Lonergan F R–F X & Rita

	1989	4	0	0	2	$2,588
$6,250	1988	7	2	1	2	$25,050

Lifetime   30 8 3 8 $100,498

4May89-9GG   6f :21⁴ :44⁴ 1:10 ft   *2 117   3ⁿᵏ 3ⁿᵏ 31¼ 33½   Campbell B C⁶   6250 85-16 Noon Sun, TouchTime Tobin'sWish 9
4May89--Bumped start
23Apr89-9GG   6f :22¹ :45³ 1:11 gd   *2½ 117   1ʰᵈ 1ʰᵈ 2½ 44½   Campbell B C⁵   6250 80-17 Melchio,Felthorpe Mariner,K.L'sPp 12
19Mar89-7GG   6f :22 .45 1:10¹gd   3½ 112⁵   2¹ 2ʰᵈ 3ⁿᵏ 65¼   Gann S L⁴   10000 83-19 P T.Hustler,SharpWays,GoldTimbre 8
19Mar89--Bumped start

16Feb89-7GG	6f	:21⁴	:44³ 1:10¹ft	2¾	112⁵	2ʰᵈ	2½	21½	32½	Gann S L¹⁰	c8000	85-22 Inswecr,LuckyAdvnc,Tobin'sWish 11
1Jun88-5GG	6f	:21²	:44¹ 1:09 ft	3⅜	117	3¹	3¹	1²	1⁶	Maple S⁸	25000	94-16 Tobin'sWish,Aegen'sBolgr,RcyRichi 8
21May88-9GG	6f	:21²	:44² 1:09⁴ft	3½	117	5⁴	41½	33½	3³	Kaenel J L⁵	32000	87-15 SuperbMoment,LedOn,Tobin'sWish 7
22Apr88-3GG	6f	:21³	:44 1:08³ft	4	117	3²	42½	5³	56½	Castaneda M¹	32000	89-14 DoctorDkot,SuperbMomnt ZrMoro 5
26Mar88-3GG	6f	:21³	:44² 1:09⁴ft	*4-5	117	3½	1ʰᵈ	1½	2²	Castaneda M⁵	32000	88-15 NleesPc,Tobin'sWish,JustTooMuch 5
12Mar88-9GG	6f	:21¹	:43⁴ 1:08³ft	4½	117	3²	3¹	1ʰᵈ	11½	Castaneda M³	25000	96-10 Tobin'sWsh,ShrpPrdcton,ShrSpindd 6
2Mar88-6GG	6f	:21⁴	:44³ 1:10 ft	*2⅜	117	2²	2¹	4³	44½	Diaz A L⁵	25000	84-18 ToothAdn,ShrpPrdcton,AckAck'sJy 8

May 19 GG 4f ft :48⁴ H   Apr 28 GG 4f ft :49¹ H

Tobin's Wish is a tough sprinter who holds his form for extended periods of time. Even in light of what must have been a serious injury in June 1988, he consistently runs his race. Consider his energy distribution pattern:

2Mar88 . . . . . . 53.88%

12Mar88 . . . . . 52.80%

26Mar88 . . . . . 53.74%

22Apr88 . . . . . 53.30%

21May88 . . . . 53.50%

1Jun88 . . . . . . 52.60%

16Feb89 . . . . . 53.77%

19Mar89 . . . . . 53.80%

23Apr89 . . . . . 53.50%

4May89 . . . . . 53.50%

The manner in which this gelding distributes his energy tells us quite a bit about the horse. His normal pattern is to expend between 53.3 and 53.88 percent upon reaching the second call. A number of conclusions can be drawn from his pattern.

1. He is an early pace type runner. His range of Percent Early is high at virtually any track in the country. The style, while perfectly acceptable at Golden Gate Fields, would be an extreme liability at Belmont Park in New York. He is top heavy with early pace.

2. The races of 1Jun88 and 12Mar88 are outside his normal range and should be considered aberrant. Eighty percent of his races fall into the 53.3 to 53.9 percent range and represent his probability of performance. The others represent fields in which he was dominant because of class or velocity considerations. When that's the case, runners often exceed the norm.

3. Horses are generally tied to their intrinsic running style. Age, current condition, and physical infirmities affect velocity

and consistency, but not style. Tobin's Wish, after his extended layoff, returned at one-third his previous claiming value. His energy pattern did not change, although he no longer seemed capable of dominating a field.

    4. If he's to win again, he'll need one of two conditions:

     (a) A racing surface that regularly allows its winners to expend a high level of early energy.

     (b) A field devoid of other early pace runners.

Without the presence of one of these conditions, Tobin's Wish will probably remain winless for an extended period of time.

Magic Door's past performances are a little less consistent, but demonstrate several additional points.

9Oct88	......	51.97%
6Nov88	.....	51.99%
19Nov88	....	50.92%
21Dec88	....	51.69%

    All four races were run at Bay Meadows in the San Francisco Bay area. Unlike its sister track, Golden Gate Fields, Bay Meadows promotes a sustained pace characteristic in its winners. Early pace types can win at the "Bay," but they must possess some late kick. Magic Door apparently did not care for the surface and failed to win a race. He then moved to Golden Gate Fields.

29Jan89	.....	52.51%
26Feb89	.....	53.27%
11Mar89	....	53.51%
1Apr89	.....	52.28%

Magic Door's performances remained consistent. The race on March 11 was run on a muddy surface, and horses usually bog down a bit late. The Percent Early in these races tend to be higher than on dry surfaces. He ran well each time and appears to be a "horse for the course." In all four races his energy expenditure was consistent with his versatility of running style. His two races as an early pace type were over 53 percent; the two races as a presser, 52.40 percent. All four races were surely within acceptable parameters at Golden Gate Fields.

Magic Door's next race was at Turf Paradise in Arizona and followed his usual pattern, a winning effort in 52.99 percent. Next out, he chased an impossible pace (43.2) and then faded from the effort. The 54.28 percent early expenditure does not reflect his style and should not be selected as the paceline for subsequent races. What *should* be considered is his total failure at odds-on.

ESTABLISHING ENERGY PARAMETERS

Percent Early is most effective when used as a supplementary factor in the handicapping process. It will not stand alone. The concept is most effective in selecting and separating contenders. It will seldom isolate *who* to play, but can be deadly accurate in eliminating noncontenders. Day-to-day application is dependent upon the handicapper understanding the nature of his racetrack. In the Magic Door example, Golden Gate Fields definitely required a different energy pattern than did its sister track. That's consistent throughout the country.

The handicapper's advantage lies in an accurate perception of local demands. The task is to establish accurate parameters. Fortunately, that's relatively easy and not time-consuming. Five to ten minutes a day should be adequate.

The Procedure

(1) Using the results charts, calculate daily the early energy expenditure of each of the previous day's winners.

(2) Separate sprints, routes, and turf races and add to a cumulative base. At some racetracks it may be necessary to separate distances within the same distance structure, that is, six, 6½, and seven furlongs.

(3) Calculate the highs and lows for each category and set the boundaries on each side. Do not use aberrant races, and be alert to changes from the norm.

ESTABLISHING PARAMETERS—DEL MAR SPRINTS

Each racetrack has certain definite characteristics that can be anticipated at the beginning of each season. Santa Anita route winners average an early energy output of about 51.85 percent. Sprints average around 52.90 percent. That's consistent from season to season, but *not* week to week. Weather and maintenance activity often initiate significant changes or biases. When that occurs, upsets prevail and most players complain about the lack of form. It will pay to stay in touch with the everyday status of the surface. Two or three days of data is usually enough to establish acceptable boundaries. Races for two-year-olds should be excluded.

Sprints

FIRST RACE
Del Mar
AUGUST 13, 1989

7 FURLONGS. (1.20⅘) CLAIMING. Purse $15,000. 3-year-olds and upward. Weights, 3-year-olds, 116 lbs.; older, 121 lbs. Non-winners of two races since June 15 allowed 3 lbs.; of a race since then, 5 lbs. Claiming price $16,000; for each $1,000 to $13,000 allowed 1 lb. (Races when entered for $12,500 or less not considered). 17th DAY. WEATHER CLEAR. TEMPERATURE 81 DEGREES.

Value of race $15,000; value to winner $8,250; second $3,000; third $2,250; fourth $1,125; fifth $375. Mutuel pool $357,997. Exacta Pool $325,003.

Last Raced	Horse	Eqt.	A.	Wt	PP	St	¼	½	Str	Fin	Jockey	Cl'g Pr	Odds $1
5Aug89 ^{1}Dmr^{1}	Polysemous	b	5	118	9	5	5^{1}	$6^{2\frac{1}{2}}$	4^{2}	$1^{1\frac{1}{2}}$	Davis R G	16000	3.10
5Aug89 ^{1}Dmr^{4}	Exploded Jr.	b	4	113	6	2	3^{1}	2^{1}	$1^{\frac{1}{2}}$	$2^{2\frac{1}{2}}$	Nakatani C S^{5}	16000	4.20
30Jly89 ^{9}Dmr^{4}	Pain		4	116	2	3	1^{1}	1^{1}	$3^{1\frac{1}{2}}$	$3^{\frac{3}{4}}$	Stevens G L	16000	6.00
2Aug89 ^{1}Dmr^{1}	Chief Pal	b	6	117	7	4	$4^{1\frac{1}{2}}$	$3^{\frac{1}{2}}$	2^{hd}	$4^{2\frac{3}{4}}$	Pincay L Jr	16000	5.40
4Aug89 ^{9}Dmr^{9}	Safety Road	b	7	110	3	8	$6^{\frac{1}{2}}$	$5^{\frac{1}{2}}$	5^{2}	5^{nk}	Castanon J L^{5}	13000	23.60
7Aug89 ^{9}LA^{4}	Gallic Writer	b	5	116	1	10	$9^{\frac{1}{2}}$	7^{hd}	6^{1}	6^{3}	Cortez A	16000	50.70
4Aug89 ^{9}Dmr^{10}	Sterling Exchange		8	116	8	7	10	9^{1}	8^{1}	7^{2}	Solis A	16000	23.40
15Mar89 ^{9}SA^{5}	Bucket Head	b	4	111	10	6	$7^{\frac{1}{2}}$	8^{hd}	$9^{1\frac{1}{2}}$	$8^{1\frac{1}{2}}$	Guymon T F^{5}	16000	56.00
30Jly89 ^{9}Dmr^{8}	Tony Aglo		4	116	4	1	$2^{\frac{1}{2}}$	4^{1}	$7^{1\frac{1}{2}}$	$9^{2\frac{3}{4}}$	Valenzuela P A	16000	12.40
5Aug89 ^{1}Dmr^{5}	Fleet Form		6	116	5	9	8^{hd}	10	10	10	Black C A	16000	2.80

OFF AT 2:00. Start good. Won driving. Time, :22⅖, :45⅕, 1:10, 1:22⅘ Track fast.

Official Program Numbers

$2 Mutuel Prices:			
9-POLYSEMOUS	8.20	3.80	3.00
6-EXPLODED JR.		5.40	3.80
2-PAIN			3.80

$2 EXACTA 9-6 PAID $32.60.

Ch. g, by Prijinsky—Violet Charm, by Imbros. Trainer Mollica Michael A. Bred by Mazzulli P P (Cal).

POLYSEMOUS, outrun early and wide down the backstretch, came into the stretch four wide, rallied to get the lead in the final sixteenth and proved best. EXPLODED JR., close up early, vied for the lead on the far turn, battled for comand in the drive and gained the place. PAIN made the early pace, vied for the lead on the far turn and battled for command in the drive before weakening a bit in the final sixteenth. CHIEF PAL, close up early, threatened approaching the stretch while three wide but could not sustain his bid in the drive. SAFETY ROAD, never far back, lacked the needed response in the last quarter. GALLIC WRITER broke slowly. STERLING EXCHANGE, wide down the backstretch, was five wide into the stretch. BUCKET HEAD was four wide into the stretch. TONY AGLO forced the early pace and gave way. FLEET FORM broke slowly and showed little.

Owners— 1, Pessin S or Marilyn; 2, Williams Sheila; 3, Cohen J; 4, Alesia & Cappelli; 5, Sittu S; 6, Sepich E Jr; 7, Cardona & Glaze; 8, Greenman & Wilson; 9, Pejsa A W; 10, Rancho San Miguel.

Trainers— 1, Mollica Michael A; 2, Murphy Marcus J; 3, Young Steven W; 4, Eurton Peter; 5, Tinsley J E Jr; 6, Fenstermaker L R; 7, Stute Melvin F; 8, Greenman Dean; 9, Lerille Arthur J Jr; 10, Vienna Darrell.

Overweight: Chief Pal 1 pound; Safety Road 2.

Fleet Form was claimed by Syndicate Stable; trainer, Ellis Ronald W.

Scratched—Romaxe (9Jly89 ^{1}Hol^{1}).

SECOND RACE
Del Mar
AUGUST 13, 1989

6 FURLONGS. (1.07⅗) CLAIMING. Purse $24,000. 3-year-olds, Weight, 121 lbs. Non-winners of two races since June 15 allowed 3 lbs.; of a race since then, 5 lbs. Claiming price $32,000; for each $2,000 to $28,000 allowed 1 lb. (Races when entered for $25,000 or less not considered).

Value of race $24,000; value to winner $13,200; second $4,800; third $3,600; fourth $1,800; fifth $600. Mutuel pool $560,854.

Last Raced	Horse	Eqt.	A.	Wt	PP	St	¼	½	Str	Fin	Jockey	Cl'g Pr	Odds $1
30Jly89 ^{3}Dmr^{2}	Brilliantized	b	3	117	7	1	3^{3}	$3^{1\frac{1}{2}}$	3^{2}	$1^{1\frac{1}{2}}$	Pincay L Jr	32000	2.90
5Aug89 ^{3}Dmr^{7}	Black Duzy	b	3	116	5	4	5^{hd}	5^{3}	5^{1}	2no	Black C A	32000	6.50
31Jly89 ^{5}Dmr^{2}	Go Dogs Go	b	3	116	1	10	$6^{1\frac{1}{2}}$	$4^{\frac{1}{2}}$	4^{1}	$3^{1\frac{1}{2}}$	Stevens G L	32000	3.30
28Jly89 ^{2}Dmr^{1}	Jungle Jaklin		3	118	9	5	$8^{\frac{1}{2}}$	6^{1}	$6^{1\frac{1}{2}}$	4^{hd}	Solis A	32000	8.10
26Dec88 ^{10}TuP^{11}	Saros Night Wind	b	3	116	10	7	1^{hd}	$2^{1\frac{1}{2}}$	2^{hd}	$5^{1\frac{3}{4}}$	Baze R A	32000	20.90
31Jly89 ^{5}Dmr^{3}	Naturally Weyes	b	3	110	4	2	$2^{\frac{1}{2}}$	1^{hd}	1^{hd}	6^{1}	Nakatani C S^{5}	30000	11.10
22Jly89 ^{2}Hol^{1}	Regally Gold		3	118	6	9	$7^{\frac{1}{2}}$	7^{hd}	7^{2}	$7^{1\frac{1}{4}}$	Davis R G	32000	24.10
5Aug89 ^{3}Dmr^{6}	Burnt Adobe	b	3	116	2	3	4^{1}	$8^{1\frac{1}{2}}$	8^{3}	$8^{1\frac{3}{4}}$	Sibille R	32000	10.70
7Jly89 ^{9}Hol^{7}	Naskra's Waltz		3	116	8	8	10	10	$9^{1\frac{1}{2}}$	9^{3}	Meza R Q	32000	34.30
11Jun89 ^{9}GG^{6}	Mr. Don		3	116	3	6	$9^{1\frac{1}{2}}$	$9^{\frac{1}{2}}$	10	10	Valenzuela P A	32000	4.60

OFF AT 2:40. Start good. Won driving. Time, :21⅘, :44⅘, :57⅗, 1:10⅖ Track fast.

$2 Mutuel Prices:				
	7-BRILLIANTIZED	7.80	4.40	2.80
	5-BLACK DUZY		6.80	4.40
	1-GO DOGS GO			3.00

Ch. g, (Apr), by If This Be So—Brilliant Move, by Effervescing. Trainer La Croix David. Bred by Meadowbrook Farms Inc (Fla).

BRILLIANTIZED, always prominent, took command leaving the furlong marker and drew clear. BLACK DUZY, outrun early, came into the stretch five wide and rallied for the place. GO DOGS GO, outrun early after he broke slowly, came into the stretch four wide, rallied and just missed the place. JUNGLE JAKLIN, devoid of early speed and wide down the backstretch, was going well late. SAROS NIGHT WIND dueled for the lead to the furlong marker and weakened a bit. BURNT ADOBE, in contention early, dropped out of contention before going a half. NASKRA'S WALTZ, wide down the backstretch, was four wide into the stretch. MR. DON showed little.

Owners— 1, Meadowbrook Farms Inc; 2, Flying Lizard Stable; 3, Dye G V Jr; 4, El Rancho de Jaklin; 5, Raub Marella M; 6, Osher B; 7, Liber M; 8, Triple AAA Ranch; 9, Rescigno Josephine; 10, Klinger & Two Rivers Farm.

Trainers— 1, La Croix David; 2, Zucker Howard L; 3, Grissom O Dwain; 4, Fanning Jerry; 5, Raub Bennie; 6, Mulhall Richard W; 7, Garvey Robert W; 8, Owens R Kory; 9, Wright Robert; 10, Mason Lloyd C.

Overweight: Brilliantized 1 pound.

Black Duzy was claimed by Redman L & Iris; trainer, Murphy Marcus J.

13Aug89	*Race*	*Dist*	*2Call*	*Final*	*BL*	*Class*	*Age*	*Sex*	*%Early*
	1	7F	45.1	1:22.4	4	$16,000	3+	M	51.70%

(BL = Beaten lengths at the second call. *Winner's* energy exertion is being measured; there are no final beaten lengths.)

The race was for older $16,000 claiming horses at seven furlongs. The winner was Polysemous, rallying from off the pace. His position at the second call was sixth, 4 lengths off the lead. His energy output was 51.70 percent expended at the second call.

Sprints

13Aug89	*Race*	*Dist*	*2Call*	*Final*	*BL*	*Class*	*Age*	*Sex*	*%Early*
	1	7F	45.1	1:22.4	4	6,000	3+	M	51.70%
	2	6F	44.4	1:10.2	1.5	$32,000	3	M	52.91%

The remaining sprints are from my charts:

3	7F	45.0	1:23.0	3.5	$16,000	3+	M	52.19%
7	6½F	45.0	1:16.1	1.75	NW3 ALW	3+	F&M	52.15%

14Aug89

1	6½F	45.0	1:17.0	0	$16,000	3	M	53.22%
5	6½F	45.3	1:17.0	4.5	NW1 ALW	3+	F&M	51.31%

Let's expand the base by backtracking to 12Aug89:

1	6F	45.2	1:10.0	0	Maiden	3+	M	52.00%
2	6F	44.2	1:10.0	0	$20,000	3	M	53.55%
7	6F	44.3	1:09.1	0	$50,000	3+	M	52.45%

Our mini–data base consists of 9 sprints at distances of six, 6½, and seven furlongs and is already large enough to provide conclusions about Del Mar racing.

The first of our conclusions is that three-year-olds are still too immature to compete with their elders. The three races in that category indicate a lack of finishing ability. Successively, they were 52.91, 53.22, and 53.55 percent. The conclusion will hold over a larger sample. This is not a unique situation, and is even more pronounced in the early part of the racing season. They should be excluded from our data base and moved into one of their own.

Second, according to the winner's average beaten lengths at the second call, there is no bias in running styles. The early energy percentage *does* indicate a bit of a preference for sustained pace, but horses may still go wire to wire.

The parameters . . .

Total Races: 6 (excludes three-year-olds)

(1) 51.70%
(2) 52.19%
(3) 52.15%
(4) 51.31%
(5) 52.00%
(6) 52.45%

6 races averaged: 51.96%

Range of performances: 51.31% to 52.45%

Range of acceptable performances: 51.70% to 52.45% (deletes the 51.31%)

5 races averaged: 52.10%

The range of performance is set to capture the highest probability of winners while eliminating as many entries as possible. Admittedly, this base is very narrow. It does accurately reflect the 1989 Del Mar surface at the midpoint of the meeting. The 51.31 percent at 6½ furlongs (Race 4) was eliminated as an apparent aberration. Del Mar sprinters very seldom win with that number. The larger base confirms the conclusion. The energy range for the meeting was consistently between 51.7 and 52.8 percent, with the ideal expenditure around 52.35 percent.

APPLICATION—SPRINT

The following race was run on 20Aug89:

5th Del Mar

6 ½ FURLONGS. (1.13⅗) 18th Running of THE RANCHO BERNARDO HANDICAP (Grade III). $75,000 added. Fillies and mares. 3-year-olds and upward. By subscription of $75 each, which shall accompany the nomination, and $750 additional to start, with $75,000 added, of which $15,000 to second, $11,250 to third, $5,625 to fourth and $1,875 to fifth. Weights Monday, August 14. Starters to be named through the entry box Friday, August 18, by the closing time of entries. A trophy will be presented to the owner of the winner. Closed Wednesday, August 9 with 15 nominations.

Survive * — **B. m. 5, by Pass the Glass—Elite Khaled, by Prince Khaled**

BAZE R A **116** **Br.—Coffee Dessie F or J (Cal)** **1989 9 2 3 1 $99,100**

Tr.—Mandella Richard **1988 10 1 4 2 $60,450**

Own.—Allred & Hubbard **Lifetime 22 5 7 3 $189,800** **Turf 4 0 1 0 $16,500**

6Aug89-7Dmr 6f :22 $:44^{2}$ $1:08^{4}$ft 3¼ 118 3^{1} 4^{2}¼ 4^{3} 3^{1} DlhoussyE[1] ⒻAw52000 93-14 Skeeter, Kool Arrival, Survive 6

1Jly89-8Hol 6f Ⓣ$:22^{1}$ $:44^{2}1:08^{2}$fm 5½ 117 10^{6}¾ 10^{8}½ 5^{4}½ 4½ DlhssyE[8] ⒻⓈValkyr H 94-11 HastyPasty,Kurbstone,SilentArrivl 12

1Jly89—Wide in stretch

29Apr89-8Hol 7f $:21^{4}$ $:44^{2}$ $1:21^{3}$ft 18 116 6^{7}¼ 7^{7} 4^{4} 2^{1}¾ DlssE[6] ⒻA Gleam H 94-10 Daloma, Survive, BehindTheScenes 7

29Apr89—Grade III; Wide into stretch

19Apr89-8GG 1 $:45^{1}$ $1:09^{3}$ $1:36^{1}$ft 3¾ 117 8^{7} 6^{7}½ 2^{4} 2^{1}½ CpTM[3] ⒻⓈCal GirlsH 82-20 LyricalPirate,Survive,HlloweenBby 8

19Apr89—Forced wide 1/4

26Mar89-8SA a6½f Ⓣ$:22^{1}$ $:45^{1}1:15^{3}$gd 11 116 4^{1}¾ 4^{1}½ 4^{3} 6^{4} Baze RA[9] ⒻLs Cngs H 77-20 ImperilStr,DownAgin,ServN'Volly 10

3Mar89-8SA 6½f $:21^{4}$ $:44^{3}$ $1:16^{2}$gd 7½ 115 6^{6}½ 5^{6}½ 5^{1}¾ 1^{2} Baze R A[3] ⒻAw55000 88-19 Survive, Invited Guest, Saros Brig 6

3Mar89—Wide into stretch

9Feb89-8SA 6f $:21^{4}$:45 $1:10^{3}$sy 3¾ 118 6^{5} 5^{5}½ 2^{3} 1no DlhoussyE[2] ⒻAw41000 85-24 Survive, Humasong, Hasty Pasty 7

26Jan89-8SA 1 $:45^{3}$ $1:10^{1}$ $1:36^{2}$ft 6½ 117 5^{3}¾ 5^{4} 8^{7}¼ 8^{12}½ Baze R A[7] ⒻAw45000 73-16 SetllSmooth,LdyBrunicrdi,SdiB.Fst 8

11Jan89-7SA 6f $:21^{2}$ $:44^{1}$ $1:08^{3}$ft 4 119 8^{6}¼ 8^{5}¾ 3^{3} 2^{3}½ Baze R A[1] ⒻAw40000 91-14 Warning Zone, Survive, HastyPasty 8

30Dec88-5SA a6½f Ⓣ$:21^{4}$:45 $1:16^{1}$gd 3½ 118 6^{7} 6^{6}½ 4^{4} 2^{2}¾ Baze R A[7] ⒻAw40000 75-22 Madruga,Survive,Marian'sCourage 12

30Dec88—Wide into stretch

Aug 14 Dmr 3f ft $:39^{3}$ B **Jly 30 Dmr 5f ft $:58^{4}$ H** **Jly 23 Hol 5f ft $1:02^{1}$ H** **Jly 16 Hol 3f ft $:38^{3}$ B**

Super Avie — Ch. f. 4, by Lord Avie—Super Trip, by Super Concorde
VALENZUELA P A — 117 — Br.—Tricar Sales (Cal) — 1989 1 1 0 0 $19,800
Own.—Friendly Natalie B — Tr.—Fulton Jacque — 1988 9 2 3 2 $153,975
Lifetime 14 5 4 2 $201,325 — Turf 4 1 1 0 $56,625

28Jly89-8Dmr 6f :214 :444 1:094ft 4 116 52½ 1½ 13 11½ DlhoussyE8 ⒻAw36000 89-16 SprAv,StormyBtVld,Shpro'sMstrss 8
10Jly88-8Hol 1⅛:451 1:10 1:483ft 19 121 33½ 2hd 2½ 24 ShmrW6 ⒻHol Oaks 90-10 PtternStep,SuperAvie,ComdyCourt 7
10Jly88—Grade I
25Jun88-8Hol 1 1/16:452 1:10 1:433ft 7½ 118 65½ 45½ 38½ 38¾ PncyLJr8 ⒻPrincess 73-13 ClenLines,FlyingCountess,SuperAvi 8
25Jun88—Grade II; Wide
4Jun88-8Hol 1 1/16Ⓣ:4641:1041:411fm 9¾ 115 42½ 32 42½ 42½ DlssE5 ⒻHnymn H 85-16 Do So, Pattern Step, Jeanne Jones 5
4Jun88—Grade III
14May88-8GG 1 1/16Ⓣ:46 1:1021:433fm*8-5 115 31½ 21½ 13 1nk Olivares F3 ⒻSngsters 84-14 SuperAvie,QuietWk-End,AmyLouis 8
30Apr88-8Hol 7f :22 :45 1:223ft 7¾ 116 84½ 63¼ 34½ 34½ DlhssyE3 ⒻRlbrd 86-14 Sheeshm,AffordblePrice,SuperAvie 9
30Apr88—Grade II
13Apr88-8SA 1⅛Ⓣ:4521:1011:48 fm 5¾ 115 2½ 2hd 3nk 46¼ VelsquzJ7 ⒻⓈPrvdnca 80-16 Pattern Step, Do So, Twice Titled 8
13Apr88—Rank 7/8 turn
23Mar88-8SA a6½f Ⓣ:214 :4421:153fm 5 116 22 32 2½ 22½ VelsquzJ4 ⒻLa Habra 78-18 Sheesham, Super Avie, SadieB.Fast 7
23Mar88—Run in divisions
14Feb88-6SA 6½f :214 :444 1:171ft 4½ 114 54½ 55 34 1nk VelsquezJ9 ⒻAw32000 84-20 SuperAvie,WrningZone,TwiceTitld 10
14Feb88—Bumped start; wide into stretch
1Jan88-8SA 7f :222 :451 1:25 gd 3¾ 118 52½ 52½ 32 2nk VlsJ4 ⒻⓈCal Brs Chp 75-22 Raveneaux,SuperAvie,Pirate'sAngel 7
1Jan88—Bobbled start
Aug 17 Dmr 4f ft :493 H ●Aug 11 Dmr 5f ft :581 H Aug 6 Dmr 3f ft :37 H Jly 25 Dmr 3f ft :361 H

Table Frolic ✻ — B. m. 5, by Never Tabled—Nashua's Frolic, by Nashua
TORO F — 114 — Br.—Sarkowsky H (Cal) — 1989 3 0 0 0 $7,525
Own.—Sarkowsky H — Tr.—Mandella Richard — 1988 14 3 2 2 $111,275
Lifetime 22 5 5 2 $164,700 — Turf 5 0 1 0 $22,500

6Aug89-7Dmr 6f :22 :442 1:084ft 9½ 116 54 55 55½ 42¾ VlenzulPA2 ⒻAw52000 91-14 Skeeter, Kool Arrival, Survive 6
1Jly89-8Hol 6f Ⓣ:221 :4421:082fm 17 117 96½ 97½ 43½ 5½ VlnlPA10 ⒻⓈValkyr H 94-11 HastyPasty,Kurbstone,SilentArrivl 12
28May89-7Hol 6½f :214 :442 1:153ft 7 116 67½ 65½ 63½ 56 VlenzulPA2 ⒻAw45000 91-11 Hasty Pasty, Skeeter, Sadie B.Fast 6
28May89—Pinched at break
17Dec88-7Hol 7f :213 :44 1:22 gd 16 122 77 78½ 76¾ 58¾ Toro F5 ⒻAw35000 85-17 Miss Brio, Bayakoa, Valdemosa 7
30Nov88-8Hol 1 1/16Ⓣ:4721:11 1:412fm 16 117 42 84¾ 910 911½ Pincay LJr8 ⒻAw40000 75-13 WhitMischfII,HollyDonn,RkuPolly 10
5Nov88-9SA 7f :22 :444 1:222ft 13 118 86 96½ 99½ 67¾ GrdrAT10 ⒻⓈEmmiaH 88-13 Valdemosa,NtivePster,OueeeBebe 10
5Sep88-5Dmr 1 :453 1:094 1:34 ft 6¾ 115 32½ 45½ 48 814 Toro F1 ⒻⓈJn Drlng 84-12 Bayakoa,QueenForbes,CaritaTostad 8
20Aug88-7Dmr 6½f :221 :444 1:16 ft 3 117⁵ 32½ 43½ 32 11½ Corral J R5 ⒻAw45000 92-15 TblFrolic,‡QunForbs,MostPrstigous 6
31Jly88-5Dmr 6½f :213 :44 1:143ft 8½ 117 42½ 44½ 54 54¾ ToroF4 ⒻRch Brnd H 95-07 ClbberGirl,QuenForbs,BhindThScns 8
31Jly88—Grade III
1Jly88-8Hol 6f Ⓣ:221 :4421:08 fm 6½ 119 52½ 41½ 1hd 21½ Toro F6 ⒻⓈValkyr H 96-05 SilentArrival,TbleFrolic,VrietyBby 12
1Jly88—Altered path 1/8
Jly 30 Dmr 5f ft :594 H Jly 23 Hol 4f ft :494 H Jly 17 Hol 3f ft :371 H Jun 29 Hol 3f ft :354 H

Kool Arrival — Ro. f. 3(Feb), by Relaunch—Irish Arrival, by The Irish Lord
PINCAY L JR — 114 — Br.—Valenti-Coelho-Fields (Cal) — 1989 6 3 1 1 $248,000
Own.—Coelho-Fields-Valenti — Tr.—Stute Melvin F — 1988 4 2 0 0 $48,613
Lifetime 10 5 1 1 $296,613

6Aug89-7Dmr 6f :22 :442 1:084ft *4-5 117 2hd 1hd 11½ 21 Pincay LJr3 ⒻAw52000 93-14 Skeeter, Kool Arrival, Survive 6
9Jly89-8Hol 1⅛:452 1:094 1:474ft 9 121 1hd 32 47½ 619¾ PncLJr4 ⒻHol Oaks 70-12 Gorgeous, Kelly, Lea Lucinda 6
9Jly89—Grade I
12Mar89-8SA 1 1/16:444 1:091 1:432ft 8-5 117 44 23 22½ 35 PncLJr4 ⒻSt Ata Oks 79-14 ImginryLdy,SomeRomnc,KoolArrivl 7
12Mar89—Grade I; Broke slowly
18Feb89-8SA 1 :461 1:103 1:361ft *2-5e121 11 11½ 11½ 11 PncLJr4 ⒻLs Vrgns 87-19 KoolArrivl,SomRomnc,FntsticLook 7
18Feb89—Grade I; Bumped start
18Jan89-8SA 1 :452 1:094 1:36 ft *3-2 118 11 11½ 13 12¾ PncLJr2 ⒻⓈLa Cntnla 88-17 KoolArrivl,AprlMon,LovAndAffcton 9
4Jan89-8SA 7f :22 :444 1:214ft 2 117 21½ 21½ 14 14½ PincyLJr5 ⒻⓈBrs Chp 91-12 KoolArrvl,ApprovdToFly,Smb'sSng 9
4Dec88-8Hol 1 :451 1:093 1:35 ft 9½e120 11 2hd 2hd 59 BlackCA1 ⒻStarlet 79-13 StocksUp,FntsticLook,OneOfAKlin 8
4Dec88—Grade I; Lugged out
9Nov88-8Hol 6½f :212 :434 1:163ft *1 116 1hd 1hd 2hd 41¾ VlazulPA5 ⒻMoccasin 90-11 Hot Novel, Irishkite, Agotaras 9
29Oct88-9SA 6f :211 :442 1:092ft *4-5 118 1½ 11½ 14 14 VlenzulPA4 ⒻAw27000 91-12 Kool Arrival, Agotaras, Key ToDing 8
29Oct88—Lugged in stretch
7Oct88-6SA 6f :212 :441 1:10 ft *1-2 117 1½ 11 16 14½ ValenzuelPA6 ⒻⓈMdn 88-19 KoolArrival,BessieJne,SpekingPrt 12
Aug 18 Dmr 4f ft :474 H ●Aug 13 Dmr 5f ft :58 H ●Jly 30 Dmr 5f ft :58 H Jly 21 Hol 5f ft :583 H

***Skeeter** — B. f. 4, by Worldwatch—Verbatim's Friend, by Verbatim
STEVENS G L — 117 — Br.—Haras Blackie (Chile) — 1989 6 2 4 0 $87,900
Own.—Van Doren P & Andrena — Tr.—Palma Hector O — 1988 6 4 2 0 $16,996
Lifetime 12 6 6 0 $104,896 — Turf 4 3 1 0 $9,610

6Aug89-7Dmr 6f :22 :442 1:084ft 5¾ 115 42½ 31½ 21½ 11 McCrrnCJ4 ⒻAw52000 94-14 Skeeter, Kool Arrival, Survive 6
28May89-7Hol 6½f :214 :442 1:153ft *7-5 116 32½ 42 42 24½ DlhoussyE4 ⒻAw45000 92-11 Hasty Pasty, Skeeter, Sadie B.Fast 6
28May89—Wide into stretch

4May89-8Hol 6f :221 :444 1:092ft *1 118 2hd 2hd 1hd 21¼ DlhoussyE1 (F)Aw40000 93-15 Hasty Pasty, Skeeter, Sadie B.Fast 6

9Apr89-3SA 6½f :21 :44 1:15 ft *2-3 116 23 22½ 1½ 23 DlhoussyE4 (F)Aw55000 92-14 BehindTheScenes,Skeetr,Humsong 5

25Mar89-3SA 6½f :212 :44 1:151gd *8-5 116 11 1½ 11½ 12¼ DlhoussyE3 (F)Aw42000 94-13 Skeeter,NeverCeeMiss,SteppinErly 6

25Feb89-7SA 6½f :212 :44 1:163ft 12 116 42¾ 45 24 2½ DlhoussyE3 (F)Aw41000 86-14 Humsong,Skeeter,APennyIsAPenny 8

25Feb89—Broke slowly

20Aug88♦7H'podromo(Chile) a1 1:374ft *6-5 117 2no PerezR (F)Cl 1000 Gneas(Gr1) Raika, Skeeter, Galanera 13

6Aug88♦7H'podromo(Chile) a7½f 1:311ft *9-5 117 11½ Perez R (F)ClJrg PbltArtgs Skeeter, Recitation, Forty Dollars 8

26Jun88♦3ClubHipico(Chile a5f :583sf *1-3 123 (T) 17 ManriquezI (F)Alw Skeeter, Por Ti Sandra, Find 9

3Apr88♦7ClubHipico(Chile a6½f 1:16 fm*1-9 117 (T) 22¾ Munoz L (F)Cl Crls Csno Franfina, Skeeter, Espadachina 5

Aug 15 Dmr 5f ft :593 H   Jly 29 Dmr 5f ft 1:014 H   Jly 16 Hol 6f ft 1:143 H   Jly 8 Hol 5f ft 1:002 H

Defend Your Man

B. m. 5, by Raise a Man—In Your Defense, by Good Counsel

NAKATANI C S **110**

Br.—Nrthwst Fms &CulpepperTb's (Ky) 1989 13 6 2 1 $91,150

Tr.—Washington William 1988 5 1 1 0 $14,850

Own.—Johnson-Kuebler-Sokol **Lifetime 22 7 3 2 $110,675**

4Aug89-11LA 6½f :211 :451 1:154ft 4 117 67½ 41¼ 12½ 15½ NtnCS 2 (F)[R]Chapman 96-11 DfndYourMn,ISrHopSo,SngSwtSyl 6

19Jly89-5Hol 6f :221 :453 1:103ft *8-5 119 710 75¾ 66 2no Davis R G 7 (F) 32000 88-18 FriskyDice,DefendYourMn,J.D'sStr 7

14Jun89-9Hol 1 :461 1:113 1:363ft 3¼ 115 64½ 63¾ 63¼ 51¾ Baze R A 4 (F) 45000 78-15 Corvettin, Beseya, Codex's Bride 8

7Jun89-5Hol 6½f :22 :451 1:17 ft *3-2 119 109¾ 85¾ 34 11¼ Davis R G 5 (F) 32000 90-15 DfndYourMn,Mrth'sFstmony,Aflot 10

7Jun89—Wide into stretch

5May89-7Hol 6f :213 :443 1:093ft 5¼ 119 1011 86¼ 24 12¾ Davis R G 2 (F) 40000 93-16 DefendYourMn,MissTwpi,DlwrStrt 10

19Apr89-3SA 1 :452 1:101 1:354ft 3¼ 116 43½ 42 42½ 21½ Davis R G 7 (F) 32000 87-14 GG'sGrl,DfndYorMn,CompltAccord 8

19Apr89—Wide into stretch

9Apr89-1SA 6f :214 :444 1:102ft 6 118 99¼ 99 68½ 43½ Pincay L Jr 9 (F) 40000 82-14 DelwreStret,ShowtimLdy,MissTwpi 9

2Apr89-6GG 6f :214 :444 1:094ft 3¼ 118 77½ 45½ 32½ 11½ HansenRD 2 (F)Aw20000 90-16 DefendYourMn,Mordido,PrningEgl 7

2Apr89—Broke slowly

15Mar89-5SA 7f :222 :45 1:223ft 3¼ 115 84¾ 84¼ 57 34 McCarron CJ 2 (F) 40000 83-14 Taybree, Alfitz, Defend Your Man 10

4Mar89-1SA 6f :213 :451 1:102ft 2¾ 116 64¾ 52¼ 41¼ 12 McCarron CJ 2 (F) 20000 86-12 DefndYourMn,GrySptmbr,MlynLdy 7

4Mar89—Boxed in 3/16

Aug 14 Dmr 5f ft 1:001 H   Jly 29 Dmr 5f ft 1:002 H   Jly 8 Hol 5f ft 1:023 H   Jun 30 Hol 5f ft 1:021 H

Hasty Pasty

B. f. 4, by Flying Paster—Revered, by In Reality

Br.—Cardiff Stud Farm (Cal) 1989 7 3 1 2 $140,625

MCCARRON C J **119** **Tr.—Lukas D Wayne** 1988 13 0 2 2 $52,550

Own.—Spelling A & Candy **Lifetime 26 6 3 5 $294,575** Turf 7 1 2 0 $107,975

12Jly89-8Hol 6f (T):23 :4531:083fm 3 119 22½ 21½ 21½ 21¼ McCrrnCJ2 (F)Aw55000 93-09 WarningZone,HastyPsty,DownAgin 5

1Jly89-8Hol 6f (T):221 :4421:082fm 5½ 120 84½ 43 22 1nk McCrrCJ5 (F)[S]ValkyrH 95-11 HastyPasty,Kurbstone,SilentArrivl 12

28May89-7Hol 6½f :214 :442 1:153ft 2½ 118 43½ 31 2hd 14½ Pincay LJr1 (F)Aw45000 97-11 Hasty Pasty, Skeeter, Sadie B.Fast 6

28May89—Broke out, bumped

4May89-8Hol 6f :221 :444 1:092ft 7½ 117 42½ 31½ 3½ 11¼ Pincay LJr5 (F)Aw40000 94-15 Hasty Pasty, Skeeter, Sadie B.Fast 6

9Feb89-8SA 6f :214 :45 1:103sy 9¾ 115 31½ 33½ 33 33½ VlenzulPA6 (F)Aw41000 81-24 Survive, Humasong, Hasty Pasty 7

26Jan89-8SA 1 :453 1:101 1:362ft 13 117 31 42 33 55¼ Pincay LJr6 (F)Aw45000 81-16 SettlSmooth,LdyBrunicrdi,SdiB.Fst 8

26Jan89—Rank 6 1/2 to 5 1/2

11Jan89-7SA 6f :212 :441 1:083ft 19 117 53 43½ 23 34½ Pincay LJr5 (F)Aw40000 90-14 Warning Zone, Survive, HastyPasty 8

11Jan89—Wide into stretch

30Dec88-5SA a6½f (T):214 :45 1:161gd 17 117 34 44 54½ 47½ Pincay LJr6 (F)Aw40000 70-22 Madruga,Survive,Marian'sCourage 12

15Dec88-8Hol 6½f :213 :443 1:163sy 13 114 31½ 31½ 3nk 57 McCrrnCJ3 (F)Aw27000 85-13 Survive, Young Flyer, Little BarFly 8

10Oct88-7SA 6½f :212 :441 1:152ft 26 114 31 34½ 612 710¼ Gryder AT1 (F)Aw40000 83-16 Bolchina, Comical Cat, SadieB.Fast 8

10Oct88—Lost whip 5/16

Jly 22 Hol 5f ft 1:01 H   Jun 26 Hol 4f ft :481 B   Jun 20 Hol 4f ft :49 H

*Miss Brio

B. m. 5, by Semenenko—Miss Eva, by Con Brio

Br.—Haras Matancilla (Chile) 1989 2 2 0 0 $143,800

DELAHOUSSAYE E **121** **Tr.—Drysdale Neil** 1988 6 2 3 1 $75,950

Own.—Farish W S **Lifetime 15 8 4 2 $249,702** Turf 8 4 1 2 $37,152

28Jan89-8SA 1 1/16 :461 1:101 1:41 ft *7-5 119 23½ 22½ 21½ 1¾ DlhssE6 (F)Sta Mria H 96-14 Miss Brio, Bayakoa, Annoconnor 7

28Jan89—Grade II

16Jan89-8SA 7f :221 :443 1:213ft 2¼ 117 61¾ 63¼ 1hd 12½ DlssE4 (F)St Mnca H 92-15 Miss Brio, Valdemosa, Josette 8

16Jan89—Grade II; Bumped 3/16

17Dec88-7Hol 7f :213 :44 1:22 gd *8-5 116 65½ 66 22½ 12 DlhoussyE6 (F)Aw35000 94-17 Miss Brio, Bayakoa, Valdemosa 7

19Nov88-8Hol 1⅛ :454 1:101 1:48 ft 4¾ 116 2½ 2hd 1hd 23 DlhssyE9 (F)Slvr Blls H 94-11 Nastique, Miss Brio, T. V.OfCrystal 9

19Nov88—Grade II

29Oct88-7Kee 7f :23 :461 1:231ft *4-5 114 51½ 2½ 13 17 Vasquez J11 (F)Aw25500 90-20 MissBrio,FoolforFun,HarlanDncer 12

15Oct88-7Kee 7f :232 :463 1:232ft 2 114 98¾ 74½ 3nk 22 StevensGL1 (F)Aw27800 87-24 Le L'Argent, Miss Brio, Polar Wind 9

3Aug88-7Dmr 1 (T):46 1:1041:344fm 3¾ 116 36 33 23 34½ DlhoussyE4 (F)Aw48000 92-08 Short Sleeves, Galunpe, Miss Brio 7

7Jly88-8Hol 6f :214 :45 1:102ft 8½ 116 512 59 58 2no DlhoussyE3 (F)Aw52000 90-16 BlueJenBby,MissBrio,WindyTriplK. 5

7Jly88—Bumped start; wide 3/8 turn

30Aug87♦7ClubHipico(Chile a1 1/16 1:433fm*3-2e 117 (T) 1¾ BarrerG (F)Pla d Ptrncs(Gr1) Miss Brio, Charnela, White Lady 17

13Jly87♦7ClubHipico(Chile a1 1:424sf — 117 (T) 1 BrrerG (F)CIA L Pena(Gr1) MissBrio,FurthrInformtion,Unvilbl 10

Aug 13 Dmr 5f ft 1:001 H   ●Aug 8 Dmr 7f ft 1:262 H   Jly 25 Hol 7f ft 1:281 H   Jly 20 Hol 6f ft 1:122 H

Behind The Scenes * Dk. b. or br. m. 5, by Hurry Up Blue—Jacinto Rose, by Jacinto
SOLIS A 115 Br.—InternationlThbdBreedersInc (Ky) 1989 6 1 0 3 $77,300
Tr.—Stute Melvin F 1988 12 1 6 2 $147,740
Own.—Alpert D & H Lifetime 36 7 9 7 $315,220 Turf 2 0 0 0

6Aug89-7Dmr 6f :22 :44^{2} 1:08^{4}ft 6½ 118 6^{12} 6^{11} 6^{7½} 5^{3¼} Solis A^{5} ⒻAw52000 91-14 Skeeter, Kool Arrival, Survive 6
6Aug89—Wide into stretch
2Jly89-7Hol 1 :44^{2} 1:09 1:34^{2}ft 5½ 115 6^{12} 6^{7½} 4^{5} 3^{4¾} Solis A^{4} ⒻAw55000 86-13 Rosdor,SettleSmooth,BhindThScns 6
17Jun89-9Hol 1$\frac{1}{16}$:46 1:10^{1} 1:42 ft 12 112 4^{10} 4^{8} 3^{6½} 4^{6} Solis A^{4} ⒻMilady H 84-15 Bayakoa, FlyingJulia,CaritaTostada 5
17Jun89—Grade I
20May89-8Hol 1 :44^{3} 1:08^{1} 1:32^{4}ft 12 114 5^{9½} 5^{7½} 4^{7½} 3^{8} DvsRG^{2} ⒻHwthn H 91-07 Byko,GoodbyeHlo,BehindTheScens 5
20May89—Grade II
29Apr89-8Hol 7f :21^{4} :44^{2} 1:21^{3}ft 6½ 116 7^{8¼} 6^{6} 5^{5} 3^{4½} VIIPA^{1} ⒻA Gleam H 91-10 Daloma, Survive, BehindTheScenes 7
29Apr89—Grade III; Wide into stretch
9Apr89-3SA 6½f :21 :44 1:15 ft 6 111^{5} 5^{8} 3^{5} 2^{½} 1^{3} VlenzulFH^{3} ⒻAw55000 95-14 BehindTheScenes,Skeetr,Humsong 5
30Sep88-12Fpx 1$\frac{1}{16}$:45^{3} 1:11^{1} 1:43 ft 4½ 116 7^{12} 7^{6} 3^{3} 2^{1¼} OrtLE^{2} ⒻLs Mdrns H 95-10 VrityBby,BhndThScns,AFbulousTm 7
18Sep88-11Fpx 1$\frac{1}{16}$:47^{1} 1:12^{1} 1:43^{4}ft *3-2 114 4^{3} 4^{4½} 4^{4} 2^{1½} BlcCA^{8} ⒻⓇE BJhnstn 90-16 CseMoney,BehindThScns,FlyingHill 9
5Sep88-5Dmr 1 :45^{3} 1:09^{4} 1:34 ft *2¾ 115 6^{7½} 6^{6¼} 5^{8} 5^{11¼} Baze RA^{3} ⒻⓇJn Drlng 87-12 Bayakoa,QueenForbes,CaritaTostad8
13Aug88-8Dmr 1$\frac{1}{16}$:46^{3} 1:10^{3} 1:41^{3}ft 10 116 5^{4½} 5^{3} 4^{2} 4^{5¼} BzeRA^{5} ⒻChla Vsta H 86-17 Clabber Girl, Annoconnor, Integra 5
13Aug88—Grade II
Aug 15 Dmr 5f ft 1:01^{2} H Aug 3 Dmr 4f ft :47^{2} H Jly 29 Dmr 5f ft 1:01^{1} H Jly 21 Hol 5f ft 1:00^{1} H

The target energy par (average) from the larger base was 52.35 percent. Horses near that number should be given preference in the selection process. The range was 51.70 to 52.80 percent. Pacelines have been underlined.

Survive: A late-running sprinter who shows no ability in the middle fraction of her races. She's dependent upon early pace *and* presser types to stop in front of her. Both her wins were on off tracks.

Super Avie: A nice filly with a pressing style.

Table Frolic: Another late runner with no turn-time ability. These types are at the mercy of the early runners.

Kool Arrival: A top-class three-year-old with an abundance of early pace.

Skeeter: The layoff appears to have cured her faint heart. She rated kindly in her last, gained on the turn, and then went on to win. A strong contender.

Defend Your Man: She seems badly outclassed. We'll leave her out of this.

Hasty Pasty: She was sharp for several races but is now coming off two turf sprints, a 38-day layoff, and no work in 28 days. She's out.

Miss Brio: Her presence is why this race should be attractive to the bettor. She's a top-class mare, and earlier in the season was at the top of her division. Minor injuries have undoubtedly kept her out of recent racing. This is not her best distance, her condition a question mark, and she cannot be well-meant here. Make it a practice to play against this kind.

Behind The Scenes: A deep closer. Unlike most late-running sprinters, she *can* move on the turn. She doesn't appear to be at her best, however.

The pacelines are all from Del Mar. Energy numbers are more reliable, and current condition more dependable, when pacelines are taken from today's surface.

The Feet-Per-Second Array

	1F	2F	3F	2Call	%Early	Style
Survive	59.54	58.25	54.71	58.89	51.84%	Sustained
Super Avie	59.51	58.36	52.80	58.93	52.74%	Presser
Table Frolic	58.18	58.48	55.02	58.33	51.46%	Sustained
Kool Arrival	59.95	58.97	53.68	59.46	52.55%	Early Pace
Skeeter	58.86	59.37	54.71	59.11	51.93%	Early/Presser
Behind The Scenes	54.54	59.37	57.27	56.95	49.87%	Sustained

The Rankings

In the chapter on running styles (ESP) I stressed the importance of analyzing a race in light of probable positions. The early pace horses have to be identified first. They have the greatest effect on the eventual outcome. Kool Arrival is the only truly dedicated early pace horse in this field. Skeeter's best style is to press the pace and come on late. The early lead most certainly goes to Kool Arrival.

The fps analysis portrays Kool Arrival in the lead at the first call. She then extends the lead over her nearest pursuers with a 58.97 fps turn-time fraction. Only Behind The Scenes and Skeeter make a slight impact on the turn. Kool Arrival will be tough here. Now let's examine the race in light of early energy.

Kool Arrival: At 52.55 percent, she is very close to the target par of 52.35 percent. She's almost a perfect fit for the race. Her pace advantage disappears if her early energy expenditure is above the parameters for the distance. That's not the case here.

Super Avie: Her velocity figures are weaker than the other main contenders. She does, however, have a definite strength: her early energy expenditure. The 52.74 percent pushes the upper limits of our range, but in light of the late expenditure by the other contenders, she'll be forwardly placed at the all-important second call. If she survives class and running style considerations, she may overcome the deficit in pure velocity.

Skeeter: Her last win was aided by a pace battle. The 22.0 first call was followed with a turn-time of 22.2. That strongly suggests Kool Arrival was asked for too much following her lay-off. Skeeter's energy expenditure, while within the parameters, is probably too late to win here. If she's asked for more early pace, it will compromise her best style. The more total energy expended early, the less available for a late run.

Survive: This one epitomizes the one-run sprinter. She will *lose* ground to this field on the turn. She represents a weak play under the best of circumstances. When this kind beats you, just shrug it off and go on. Only on certain tracks, and under certain conditions, should she be bet. Her energy number is acceptable at 51.84 percent; it's her style that's suspect.

Table Frolic: Her 51.46 percent is too late an expenditure to be effective. At Belmont Park she might be tough, but in southern California she'll need too much help from the pace setters. No matter, she was a late scratch.

Behind The Scenes: She's not really in her best form, and the early energy number (49.87%) is more likely to win on a turf course. She may want to route.

The final analysis: The race, by virtue of superior Early Pace numbers, running style, and early energy expenditure, belongs to Kool Arrival. There is no stronger selection type than this filly. Win or lose, she's the right play. An interesting point in the outcome is the finish position of Super Avie. Running style sometimes overcomes velocity numbers. That should not be surprising. The theme of this whole work is pace analysis. Another case of the speed-figure horses being beaten, this time for place.

FIFTH RACE
Del Mar
AUGUST 20, 1989

6 ½ FURLONGS. (1.13⅗) 18th Running of THE RANCHO BERNARDO HANDICAP (Grade III). $75,000 added. Fillies and mares. 3-year-olds and upward. By subscription of $75 each, which shall accompany the nomination, and $750 additional to start, with $75,000 added, of which $15,000 to second, $11,250 to third, $5,625 to fourth and $1,875 to fifth. Weights Monday, August 14. Starters to be named through the entry box Friday, August 18, by the closing time of entries. A trophy will be presented to the owner of the winner. Closed Wednesday, August 9 with 15 nominations.
Value of race $81,375; value to winner $47,625; second $15,000; third $11,250; fourth $5,625; fifth $1,875. Mutuel pool $494,721.
Exacta Pool $537,952.

Last Raced	Horse	Eqt.A.Wt	PP	St	¼	½	Str	Fin	Jockey	Odds $1
6Aug89 ^{7}Dmr^2	Kool Arrival	3 117	3	7	3^{hd}	$1^{\frac{1}{2}}$	1^2	$1^{2\frac{1}{2}}$	Pincay L Jr	3.00
28Jly89 ^{8}Dmr^1	Super Avie	4 117	2	1	$1^{\frac{1}{2}}$	$2^{1\frac{1}{2}}$	$2^{1\frac{1}{2}}$	$2^{1\frac{1}{2}}$	Valenzuela P A	13.80
6Aug89 ^{7}Dmr^3	Survive	5 116	1	4	6^5	$6^{1\frac{1}{2}}$	$4^{1\frac{1}{2}}$	$3^{1\frac{1}{2}}$	Baze R A	9.60
6Aug89 ^{7}Dmr^1	Skeeter	4 117	4	5	$5^{1\frac{1}{2}}$	$4^{\frac{1}{2}}$	3^2	4^{nk}	Stevens G L	6.20
6Aug89 ^{7}Dmr^5	Behind The Scenes	5 115	7	6	7	7	7	5^1	Solis A	'6.60
12Jly89 ^{8}Hol^2	Hasty Pasty	4 119	5	2	$4^{2\frac{1}{2}}$	3^{hd}	$5^{\frac{1}{2}}$	$6^{\frac{1}{2}}$	McCarron C J	4.10
28Jan89 ^{8}SA^1	Miss Brio	5 121	6	3	2^{hd}	$5^{3\frac{1}{2}}$	$6^{\frac{1}{2}}$	7	Delahoussaye E	1.60

OFF AT 4:15. Start good. Won driving. Time, :22¾, :45, 1:09, 1:15½ Track fast.

$2 Mutuel Prices:

4-KOOL ARRIVAL	_____	8.80	4.60	4.80
2-SUPER AVIE	_____		11.80	6.80
1-SURVIVE	_____			5.00

$5 EXACTA 4-2 PAID $290.80.

Ro. f, (Feb), by Relaunch—Irish Arrival, by The Irish Lord. Trainer State Melvin F. Bred by Valenti-Coelho-Fields (Cal).

KOOL ARRIVAL broke slowly, advanced quickly early to reach the front just after going a quarter, shook off SUPER AVIE to open a clear lead in the upper stretch and maintained the advantage through the final furlong SUPER AVIE, away alertly, vied for the early lead, pressed the issue around the far turn while outside KOOL ARRIVAL, then had enough of a response in the drive to gain the place. SURVIVE, patiently handled while being outrun early, rallied after a half but could not gain the necessary ground in the drive. SKEETER, in contention early, moved up to look dangerous at the quarter pole but lacked the needed continued response in the drive. BEHIND THE SCENES, wide down the backstretch, was five wide into the stretch. HASTY PASTY attended the early pace and gave way. MISS BRIO, an early pace factor and four wide into the far turn after being wide down the backstretch, steadily dropped back in the last three furlongs and was four wide into the stretch. TABLE FROLIC (3) AND DEFEND YOUR MAN (6) WERE WITHDRAWN. ALL WAGERS ON THEM IN THE REGULAR AND EXACTA POOLS WERE ORDERED REFUNDED AND ALL OF THEIR PICK SIX AND EARLY TRIPLE SELECTIONS WERE SWITCHED TO THE FAVORITE, MISS BRIO (8).

ESTABLISHING PARAMETERS— HOLLYWOOD PARK ROUTES

Hollywood Park, in southern California, offers two kinds of middle distance races. In addition to the traditional two-turn routes, the 1⅛ mile layout also offers a one-turn mile. The energy requirements are often quite dissimilar. An understanding of the energy expenditure concept provides a significant edge in handicapping. The race we'll look at was 29May89. First, we'll develop the parameters for Percent Early, using ten prior races.

	Dist	2Call	Final	BL	%Early
5–28	8½	1:11.4	1:44.3	1½	51.57%
	8½	1:11.0	1:43.4	0	52.57%
5–27	8½	1:10.2	1:42.2	0	52.17%
5–26	8½	1:11.0	1:42.0	0	51.16%
5–24	8½	1:11.3	1:43.4	1½	51.58%
	8½	1:12.4	1:44.0	1	50.48%
	8½	1:11.1	1:42.3	0	51.41%
5–21	8½	1:11.0	1:43.0	0	51.96%
	8½	1:09.1	1:40.1	0	51.81%
5–20	8½	1:12.1	1:43.3	0	51.07%

This time our mini–data base is large enough to provide insights to Hollywood Park routes. First we'll sort through the data. Two races stand out at the upper and lower extremes. As with most statistical studies, we're well advised to eliminate data at the extremes. That leaves eight usable races. I've eliminated the races at 50.48 and 52.57 percent.

Total Races: 8
(1) 51.97%
(2) 52.17%
(3) 51.16%
(4) 51.58%
(5) 51.41%
(6) 51.96%
(7) 51.81%
(8) 51.07%

8 races averaged: 51.64%

Range of performance: 51.07% to 52.17%

Was there a bias during this period? You bet. No winner came from more than 1½ lengths behind at the second call. Seven of the 10 races were won by the leader at the second call.

APPLICATION—ROUTE

Entries for the 29May89 race:

4th Hollywood

1 1-16 MILES
HOLLYWOOD PARK
FINISH ▲   ▲ START

1 1/16 MILES. (1.40) CLAIMING. Purse $17,000. 4-year-olds and upward. Weight, 121 lbs. Non-winners of two races at a mile or over since April 16 allowed 3 lbs.; such a race since then, 6 lbs. Claiming price $25,000; if for $22,500 allowed 2 lbs. (Races when entered for $20,000 or less not considered).

19May89-5Hol 1 :451 1:092 1:342ft 15 115 64 44¼ 44½ 34¾ Pedroza M A 8 25000 86-08 RoylCmronn,OnoGmmo,Alm'sTbn 12
19May89—Wide final 3/8
29Apr89-1Hol 7f :213 :442 1:223ft 13 117 98 86¾ 73¾ 75¾ Pedroza M A 3 32000 85-10 UnderAndOver,Crftmster,Invoking 10
29Apr89—6 wide into drive
8Apr89-9SA 1 1/16:461 1:102 1:431ft 5½ 116 2hd 2½ 31½ 55 Black C A 2 c25000 80-12 PlesRmit,SpndTwoBucks,K.'sChrgr 8
26Mar89-9SA 1 1/16:453 1:104 1:433ft 8 118 21 1½ 2hd 21¼ Black C A 2 25000 82-16 Whr'sMchis,Alom'sTobin,WritALn 10
19Mar89-9SA 1 1/16:461 1:11 1:44 ft 15 118 3nk 41¾ 87¾ 910¼ Black C A 10 32000 71-16 JgTmDx,BooBoo'sBckro,LmmnJc 12
19Mar89—Broke slowly; bumped start; wide 7/8 turn
26Feb89-9SA 1 1/16:453 1:093 1:433ft 9¾ 1115 811 911 911 56 Valenzuela F H 5 40000 77-14 Ascension, Bizeboy, Instant Cash 12
12Feb89-9SA 1 :464 1:112 1:373gd 3½ 1115 21 2hd 2hd 43¾ Valenzuela F H 5 40000 76-16 Amnotherbrother,InstntCsh,HesBer 8
21Jan89-9SA 1 1/16:463 1:104 1:423ft 4¼ 1115 52¼ 31½ 32 11¾ Valenzuela F H 4 32000 88-12 Aloma's Tobin,AdiosGirl,RichTiger 10
14Jan89-9SA 1 1/16:453 1:101 1:424ft 6¾ 1115 11½ 1½ 2½ 21 Valenzuela F H 3 25000 86-11 MountLagun,Alom'sTobin KmpOut 9
14Jan89—Bumped, checked 3/16
29Dec88-3SA 6f :213 :441 1:084ft 9¼ 116 52¼ 44 67¼ 68¼ Black C A 8 32000 86-12 TddyNtrlly,ChynnTrpc,BmbsBrstng 8
29Dec88—Wide final 3/8
May 11 SA 4f ft :491 H

Telephone Canyon

Dk. b. or br. g. 5, by Assagai Jr—Determining, by Decidedly
DELAHOUSSAYE E 115 Br.—Van Berg J C (Ky) 1989 5 0 0 0 $7,475
Tr.—Passey Blake $25,000 1988 9 1 3 1 $27,855
Own.—Tons of Fun Stable &Fought Lifetime 31 6 7 2 $134,354 Turf 13 3 2 2 $54,269
1Apr89-9SA 1 1/16:463 1:104 1:424ft 11 116 78½ 711 812 813½ Stevens G L 4 32000 73-16 JigTimeDixie,HesBer,PrideOfAndy 10
1Apr89—Bumped start
11Mar89-7SA 1 1/16:463 1:11 1:424ft *3 117 68½ 53½ 54¼ 44½ Pincay L Jr 6 c25000 82-14 SvorFire,ToB.ARuler,TurnAndPress 8
11Mar89—Wide into stretch
26Feb89-9SA 1 1/16:453 1:093 1:433ft 4¼ 117 1112 1112 79¾ 44½ Pincay L Jr 3 40000 78-14 Ascension, Bizeboy, Instant Cash 12
22Jan89-9SA 1 1/16:47 1:11 1:421ft 5½ 116 108¼ 65 64¾ 55¾ Solis A 10 50000 84-14 Sissy'sHeller,Zleucus,FrereJcques 10
22Jan89—Wide 3/8 turn
1Jan89-3SA 1 1/16:462 1:102 1:421ft 12 116 89½ 66½ 56 44¼ Solis A 8 62500 86-10 Ascension,ExoticEgle,Sissy'sHeller 8
31Jly88-8Cby 170Ⓣ:48 1:1131:403fm 5 122 52½ 52¼ 2½ 3¾ Kutz D 3 Aw13000 93-11 Feudal, J. T.'sPet,TelephoreCanyon 8
17Jly88-8Cby 1 1/16Ⓣ:4831:1221:421fm 2 119 56 54½ 32½ 2½ Kutz D 5 Aw13000 90-07 StellarRival,TelephoneCnyon,Feudl 7
3Jly88-9Cby 1 1/16Ⓣ:49 1:1331:424fm 2½ 114 85½ 83¾ 64¼ 52¾ Kutz D 2 Savage H 85-12 I Really Did, StellarRival,SplitRock 9
5Jun88-6Cby 1 1/16Ⓣ:4611:1021:424fm*2-3 119 24½ 22 11 1nk Kutz D4 Lake Isle 88-09 TelephoneCanyon,Feudl,ArthurBlnk 8
30Apr88-9Cby 6½f :223 :451 1:171ft 3½ 122 46 46 31 2hd Martinez F III1 SplW 93-14 Freezem,TelephoneCnyon,OnRtinr 10
May 21 Hol 5f ft 1:002 H May 13 Hol 6f ft 1:123 H May 6 Hol 5f ft 1:01 H

Kentucky Star

Dk. b. or br. g. 5, by Well Decorated—Brokerette, by King's Bishop
VALENZUELA F H 115 Br.—Hillbrook Farm (Ky) 1989 5 0 0 1 $4,100
Tr.—Valenzuela Martin $25,000 1988 5 0 1 1 $9,350
Own.—Flamingo Stable Lifetime 15 1 3 2 $15,846 Turf 7 1 2 0 $2,396
18May89-9Hol 1⅛:463 1:103 1:483ft 38 115 76½ 75¾ 45 35 ValenzuelaFH 12 20000 89-07 Addie's Bro, Mispu, KentuckyStar 12
30Apr89-5Hol 1 :453 1:102 1:353ft 4¾ 116 2hd 2hd 31½ 78½ Valenzuela F H 6 20000 76-13 Ono Gummo, Kamp Out, Kamikaze 7
19Apr89-9SA 1 1/16:452 1:101 1:422ft 4¾ 116 1hd 1hd 31 59 McCarron C J 7 c16000 80-14 Ono Gummo, Kamp Out, Mispu 10
18Mar89-9SA 1 1/16:471 1:113 1:433ft 6¼ 116 53½ 53 43 44¼ Toro F6 20000 79-15 ‡Remar, Sun Club, K.'s Charger 11
19Feb89-9SA 1 1/16:472 1:121 1:444ft 30 116 64½ 64¼ 75¼ 76¾ Toro F7 32000 70-21 Wilmont, Scrapbook, Savor Faire 11
26Mar88-10GG 1⅛Ⓣ:4741:1221:503fm *2½ 119 54 32½ 67 811½ Toro F8 Aw17000 — — PirdAndPintd,Robigus,NorthOfLk 12
18Mar88-7GG 1 1/16:471 1:104 1:433ft *2 119 32 55½ 48 35½ CastanedaM5 Aw17000 75-23 FirstOnTheLin,TioNino,KntuckyStr 8
17Feb88-7SA 1 1/16:462 1:113 1:444ft 7 116 2hd 1hd 2½ 65¾ Toro F1 Aw34000 71-23 Saker,CarolinaNorth,DesertClassic 12
3Feb88-7SA 1 1/16:462 1:104 1:44 ft 17 116 57 55½ 44½ 23½ Toro F5 Aw34000 77-20 Relnd,KentuckyStr,CircleViewDrive 7
3Feb88—Steadied sharply 7 1/2
16Jan88-5SA 1⅛Ⓣ:4641:1141:503fm 6 116 74¼ 54½ 75¼ 65¾ Toro F4 Aw34000 68-26 Silver Dude, Roundlet, Depute 10
May 13 SA 5f ft 1:011 H ●Apr 13 SA 4f ft :462 H Apr 4 SA 4f ft :493 H

Instant Cash

Ch. g. 5, by It's Freezing—Snow Lady, by Raise a Native
PINCAY L JR 115 Br.—Glade Valley Farms Inc (Md) 1989 7 0 1 2 $13,050
Tr.—Kooba Paul $25,000 1988 11 3 1 3 $45,836
Own.—Lebowitz L Lifetime 41 6 7 11 $103,311 Turf 2 0 0 1 $1,760
28Apr89-5Hol 1 1/16:462 1:103 1:431ft 9¾ 117 47½ 45 44½ 31½ Pincay L Jr 8 25000 82-15 LemmonJuic,MountLgun,InstntCsh 8
20Apr89-3SA 1 1/16:462 1:103 1:413ft 5¾ 117 56½ 57 57¼ 610¼ Pincay L Jr 1 32000 83-16 Jazz Island, Rich Tiger, Hanabru 7
9Apr89-9SA 1 1/16:461 1:101 1:43 ft 7 1115 33 34 54¾ 67 Valenzuela F H 6 40000 79-14 Ascension, Black Wing, Adios Girl 8
19Mar89-9SA 1 1/16:461 1:11 1:44 ft 4¾ 116 119 96¼ 74¾ 74½ Baze R A12 c32000 76-16 JgTmDx,BooBoo'sBckro,LmmnJc 12
19Mar89—Steadied 5/16
26Feb89-9SA 1 1/16:453 1:093 1:433ft 17 116 1011 811 69½ 34 Baze R A1 40000 79-14 Ascension, Bizeboy, Instant Cash 12
12Feb89-9SA 1 :464 1:112 1:373gd 8½ 116 85¼ 73½ 53¼ 22 Solis A7 40000 78-16 Amnotherbrother,InstntCsh,HesBer 8
21Jan89-5SA 6½f :213 :434 1:153ft 28 115 88¾ 89½ 810 85¾ Solis A6 50000 86-12 PrcyMc,DonnrPrty,PrsdntsSummt 10
21Jan89—Wide
22Dec88-7Hol 6½f :224 :462 1:183gd 9 116 75 75 43½ 1nk Solis A8 40000 82-27 InstantCash,FrereJacques,ChrltnII 8
22Dec88—Wide 1/4
30Nov88-5Hol 6f :221 :452 1:101ft 54 117 73¼ 74 75½ 75½ Meza R Q5 50000 85-15 BrghtAndRght,KnKnght,LckyMsdd 8
3Nov88-6CD 6f :214 :453 1:11 ft 12 115 45½ 56 63¼ 43¾ Brumfield D3 Aw27070 84-23 Bunbury, DavidL.'sRib,UnitedTimes 6
May 13 Hol 5f ft 1:003 H Apr 17 SA 3f ft :354 H Apr 2 SA 5f ft 1:011 H

Speedy Shannon ✻
Ch. g. 6, by Sadair—Hatchet Miss, by The Axe II
Br.—Meadowbrook Farms Inc (Fla) 1989 2 1 0 0 $6,600
NAKATANI C S 1105 Tr.—La Croix David $25,000 1988 7 1 0 0 $29,450
Own.—Meadowbrook Farms Inc Lifetime 28 7 4 2 $197,892 Turf 3 0 1 0 $10,602
17May89-1Hol 1⅛ :464 1:102 1:493ft 8 1105 11½ 13 12½ 16½ Nakatani C S 10 12500 89-11 SpedyShnnon,Mt.Erin,Convincing 11
27Apr89-5Hol 6f :221 :451 1:094ft 15 117 2hd 21 44 67½ Black C A 3 18000 84-10 Vancealot, Barnhart, Bugarian 8
9Nov88-2Hol 6f :214 :444 1:094ft 33 115 53 76 910 912 Black C A 3 25000 81-11 LoCard,NotableHost,PeacefulImge 9
9Nov88—Wide 3/8
20Oct88-7SA 1 :451 1:094 1:343ft 16 116 66½ 812 820 837¾ Sibille R 7 50000 57-14 L.A.Fire,JustNeverMind,Sissy'sHlr 8
20Oct88—Wide 7/8, 3/8
21Aug88-11Bmf 1 1/16 :452 1:091 1:413ft 9 117 1hd 21½ 68 711¼ Doocy TT 3 Sn Matn H 73-16 NickleBnd,VrietyRod,JustTooMuch 7
4Jly88-5Hol 6½f :213 :44 1:15 ft 25 118 32½ 53¼ 611 614¾ Sibille R 4 Aw52000 88-08 Sebrof,Don'sIrishMelody,HighHook 6
13Feb88-6GG 1 :444 1:082 1:33 ft *2¾ 122 2½ 32 611 613 Doocy T T 3 HcpO 90-10 CarosLove,PerfecTrvel,FstAccount 6
31Jan88-8SA 1 1/16 :46 1:103 1:43 ft 14 112 1hd 2½ 45 515¼ Hawley S 1 Sn Psql H 71-21 SuprDimond,JudgAnglucc,H'sASros 5
31Jan88—Grade II
10Jan88-10BM 1 :47 1:113 1:37 m *3-5 114 11½ 11½ 13 14 Doocy T T 4 Bart H 83-28 SpeedyShnnon,BreWithM,PrfcTrvl 5
26Dec87-10BM 1 1/16 :452 1:09 1:412ft 6¾ 112 2hd 1hd 2hd 11 DoocyTT 6 Hlsdle H 85-14 SpeedyShnnon,SngerChief,Mnzotti 8
Apr 21 Hol 5f ft 1:002 H Apr 9 Hol 5f ft 1:003 H ●Mar 30 Hol 6f ft 1:123 H

Please Remit ✻
Ro. g. 4, by Aggravatin'—Proud Amazon, by Iron Warrior
Br.—Hartstone G D (Cal) 1989 6 1 0 0 $16,625
VALENZUELA P A 115 Tr.—Hess R B Jr $25,000 1988 11 1 0 0 $80,725
Own.—Haurte Mr-Mrs J Lifetime 25 5 1 0 $141,005 Turf 3 0 0 0
20Apr89-3SA 1 1/16 :462 1:103 1:413ft 3 116 43½ 43 46½ 47½ ValenzuelaPA 6 c32000 85-16 Jazz Island, Rich Tiger, Hanabru 7
20Apr89—Wide final 3/8
8Apr89-9SA 1 1/16 :461 1:102 1:431ft 19 116 31½ 31 1hd 12½ Valenzuela P A 8 25000 85-12 PlesRmit,SpndTwoBucks,K.'sChrgr 8
8Apr89—Fanned wide 7/8
31Mar89-9SA 1 1/16 :461 1:111 1:433ft 15 116 88¾ 73¾ 74 65¾ DelahoussyeE 3 c20000 77-17 JazzIsland,ImpossibleStrem,Tbldo 10
31Mar89—Wide into stretch
28Jan89-9SA 1 1/16 :461 1:103 1:423ft 7¾ 115 74¾ 52¾ 99¾1013¼ Pedroza M A 9 c25000 75-14 BooBoo'sBckroo,Rkpsh,K.'sChrgr 12
28Jan89—Wide on turns
15Jan89-9SA 1 :454 1:094 1:35 ft 12 115 96¾ 89¾ 812 714¾ Meza R Q3 40000 78-11 CircleViewDrive,LoclsOnly,Bizeboy 9
15Jan89—Wide into stretch
1Jan89-9SA 1 :454 1:102 1:354ft 5¾ 116 64½ 61¾ 54 44¾ Meza R Q 5 40000 84-10 Reassuring,BigRainbow,RiderMrcus 9
1Jan89—Wide 3/8 turn
1Dec88-7Hol 7f :213 :442 1:222ft 13 117 913 99¾ 99 77 DelahoussayeE 2 50000 85-17 Icy Amber, Zaleucus, GranMusico 10
1Dec88—Wide 3/8
13Nov88-7Hol 1 1/16 :46 1:103 1:422ft 20 113 78½ 78½ 611 714¼ Black C A 3 Aw30000 74-13 Payant, Olympic Native, Galba 9
21Oct88-8SA 1 :45 1:093 1:352ft 22 113 57½ 46½ 35½ 48 Black C A 1 Aw36000 83-18 Shigamba, Captain Valid, Galba 6
21Oct88—Checked 5/16
26Jun88-8GG 1 Ⓣ:463 1:112 1:362fm 8¾ 117 64½ 89¾ 813 817½ KenelJL 4 Au Revoir H 67-18 GrnJudgemnt,CrstingWtr,GoldnFir 8
May 20 Hol 5f ft 1:012 H May 14 Hol 5f ft 1:02 H May 7 Hol 6f ft 1:152 H

Bizeboy
Dk. b. or br. h. 7, by Distant Land—Another Lulu, by Majestic Prince
Br.—Arnold M L (Cal) 1989 6 0 1 3 $17,400
DAVIS R G 115 Tr.—Bernstein David $25,000 1988 20 6 5 2 $99,800
Own.—McAtee R & Melodie Lifetime 63 13 11 11 $231,875 Turf 3 1 1 0 $14,125
7May89-4Hol 1 1/16 :454 1:093 1:421ft *2¾ 115 14 15 13½ 35 Stevens G L 1 25000 84-10 Shoreham, Mount Laguna, Bizeboy 8
1Apr89-9SA 1 1/16 :463 1:104 1:424ft *2¾ 116 11½ 1hd 2½ 67½ Valenzuela P A 6 32000 79-16 JigTimeDixie,HesBer,PrideOfAndy 10
5Mar89-1SA 6½f :211 :44 1:154ft *3¾ 116 1hd 1hd 107¾ 1115½ Pincay L Jr 11 40000 75-07 DonnrPrty,FrrJcqus,InstinctvRson 11
5Mar89—Troubled trip
26Feb89-9SA 1 1/16 :453 1:093 1:433ft 8¾ 116 14 17 16 22¼ Valenzuela P A 7 40000 81-14 Ascension, Bizeboy, Instant Cash 12
29Jan89-9SA 1 1/16 :454 1:094 1:421ft 3½ 116 1½ 1hd 32 36 Valenzuela P A 3 40000 84-16 Armin, Locals Only, Bizeboy 9
15Jan89-9SA 1 :454 1:094 1:35 ft *2¾ 116 12 11½ 11½ 32¾ Pedroza M A 5 40000 91-11 CircleViewDrive,LoclsOnly,Bizeboy 9
15Jan89—Bumped, steadied late
31Dec88-9SA 1 1/16 :454 1:094 1:422ft *8-5 116 13 1½ 2hd 43½ Stevens G L 8 40000 85-10 It'sNotMyJob,FullCharm,FreeWter 9
19Nov88-9Hol 1 1/16 :461 1:102 1:42 ft *2¾ 116 11½ 12½ 17 16½ ValenzuelPA 10 c25000 90-11 Bizeboy, Emperdori, Rakaposhi 12
29Oct88-10SA 1 1/16 :453 1:101 1:422ft *2¼ 118 11½ 11 15 13 Valenzuela P A 7 20000 89-12 Bizeboy, Headline News, Amatar 10
17Sep88-5BM a1⅛ Ⓣ 1:493fm *3 119 11½ 11 11 51¾ Doocy T T 10 40000 85-16 Dncellthedncs,SnsitivCopy,HwiiHy 10
May 19 Hol 5f ft 1:002 H Apr 29 Hol 5f ft 1:02 H

This race will be handicapped with early energy only. It doesn't take a rocket scientist to determine that Bizeboy has the top velocity numbers in the race. I mentioned earlier that running style, as quantified by early energy distribution, will often overpower sheer velocity. It's not only how fast a horse runs, it's also how he distributes his energy. The example should drive home the point.

Unleavened: Only in a match race with the Clydesdales.

Aloma's Tobin: This gelding wants to be near the pace for his best, and that doesn't figure to happen today. His last Percent Early was 51.77.

Telephone Canyon: A deep closer who may be running at the tiring leaders late. Percent Early in his last two were 51.63 and 51.73.

Kentucky Star: A confused sort. He can't seem to make up his mind as to whether he's a closer or an early pace type. His last Percent Early was 51.39.

Instant Cash: He runs forwardly and is showing improvement. The Percent Early in his last was 51.71.

Speedy Shannon: An early pace type. His last race was excellent, but he faces extreme pressure here. The Percent Early in his last was 52.68; and that was *without* pace pressure.

Please Remit: Presser type. His last was a decline in performance, and he drops off a claim. Percent Early in his last was 51.81.

Bizeboy: The guaranteed leader. His final time is excellent, but his recent two Percent Early numbers were 53.68 and 53.19. Both are outside our parameters.

The Rankings

Early Pace: Bizeboy in front for as long as he lasts. Even with the early pace bias, his energy numbers are far too high for this surface at this time. Even in top form, it would be asking a lot for him to win this. Speedy Shannon faces a difficult problem. He can't duel with the other early pace horse, yet his best style is on the lead. His energy number is already too high. A pace battle would only make it higher.

Pressers: Aloma's Tobin, Please Remit, and Instant Cash all possess the right balance of early versus late energy. Aloma's Tobin may not want to be as far back early as he will be in here.

Please Remit doesn't seem all that sharp at the present. Instant Cash appears patient enough to wait.

Sustained: The bias at this track is working against Telephone Canyon and Kentucky Star. They do figure to be running on after most of these have expired.

Pay close attention to Instant Cash in this race. His energy expenditure pattern is nearly perfect. He'll be reasonably close and still have something in the tank late. When the pace setters call it a day, he'll probably be in an ideal position to win the race. The closers are fighting a bias in position and seem to be running for minor awards.

FOURTH RACE
Hollywood
MAY 28, 1989

1 $\frac{1}{16}$ MILES. (1.40) CLAIMING. Purse $17,000. 4-year-olds and upward. Weight, 121 lbs. Non-winners of two races at a mile or over since April 16 allowed 3 lbs.; such a race since then, 6 lbs. Claiming price $25,000; if for $22,500 allowed 2 lbs. (Races when entered for $20,000 or less not considered).

Value of race $17,000; value to winner $9,350; second $3,400; third $2,550; fourth $1,275; fifth $425. Mutuel pool $381,108. Exacta pool $408,558.

Last Raced	Horse	Eqt.A.Wt	PP	St	¼	½	¾	Str	Fin	Jockey	Cl'g Pr	Odds $1
28Apr89 ^{5}Hol^3	Instant Cash	b 5 117	5	5	$5^{1\frac{1}{2}}$	$5^{1\frac{1}{2}}$	4^1	3^2	$1^{\frac{3}{4}}$	Pincay L Jr	25000	2.70
1Apr89 ^{9}SA^8	Telephone Canyon	b 5 116	3	8	$7^{\frac{1}{2}}$	7^{hd}	$7^{\frac{1}{2}}$	6^1	$2^{2\frac{1}{2}}$	Delahoussaye E	25000	7.20
17May89 ^{1}Hol^1	Speedy Shannon	b 6 110	6	4	$2^{\frac{1}{2}}$	2^1	2^3	$2^{\frac{1}{2}}$	$3^{1\frac{1}{2}}$	Nakatani C S^5	25000	6.80
20Apr89 ^{3}SA^4	Please Remit	b 4 116	7	6	6^8	6^6	$5^{\frac{1}{2}}$	5^1	4^1	Valenzuela P A	25000	4.60
7May89 ^{4}Hol^3	Bizeboy	b 7 115	8	1	$1^{1\frac{1}{2}}$	$1^{1\frac{1}{2}}$	$1^{1\frac{1}{2}}$	$1^{2\frac{1}{2}}$	5^1	Davis R G	25000	2.50
20May89 ^{9}Hol^8	Unleavened	b 5 115	1	7	8	8	8	8	$6^{\frac{1}{2}}$	Solis A	25000	12.90
19May89 ^{5}Hol^3	Aloma's Tobin	b 6 115	2	2	4^4	$4^{2\frac{1}{2}}$	$6^{3\frac{1}{2}}$	7^{hd}	$7^{1\frac{1}{2}}$	Black C A	25000	9.70
18May89 ^{9}Hol^3	Kentucky Star	b 5 115	4	3	$3^{\frac{1}{2}}$	3^1	3^1	$4^{\frac{1}{2}}$	8	Valenzuela F H	25000	19.80

OFF AT 3:13. Start good. Won driving. Time, :23, :45$\frac{4}{5}$, 1:10$\frac{4}{5}$, 1:37, 1:43$\frac{3}{5}$ Track fast.

$2 Mutuel Prices:			
5-INSTANT CASH	7.40	4.00	3.40
3-TELEPHONE CANYON		5.60	4.40
6-SPEEDY SHANNON			5.20

$2 EXACTA 5-3 PAID $53.20.

Ch. g, by It's Freezing—Snow Lady, by Raise a Native. Trainer Kooba Paul. Bred by Glade Valley Farms Inc (Md).

INSTANT CASH, outrun early, gained strongly to reach the front a sixteenth out, drew clear between calls soon after passing the sixteenth marker, then withstood TELEPHONE CANYON'S closing charge. TELEPHONE CANYON, far back early after bobbling at the start, came into the stretch five wide and was going fastest of all late but could not get up. SPEEDY SHANNON, close up early and four wide into the clubhouse turn after being steadied slightly off heels nearing the clubhouse turn, prompted the pace through the early going and lacked the needed response in the drive. PLEASE REMIT, outrun early and wide down the backstretch after being four wide into the clubhouse turn, entered the stretch four wide and had only a mild response in the drive. BIZEBOY went to the front at once, moved over to the inner rail before going a quarter, increased his advantage in the upper stretch but gave way in the last furlong. ALOMA'S TOBIN had no apparent mishap. KENTUCKY STAR, close up early, gave way.

The final analysis: As expected, Bizeboy went on a fast pace that spelled destruction for him and his pursuer, Speedy Shannon. Instant Cash waited in fourth. When the leaders expired, he came on to win. His energy output in the race was 52.14 percent, well within the parameters.

ENERGY AND THE "STRETCH-OUT"

Arguably, the most difficult handicapping problem is the sprinter stretching out to a middle distance. It is, at times, seemingly unsolvable. The problem manifests itself in one of two ways:

(1) A runner trying a longer distance for the first time
(2) A runner attempting the distance after tuning up with one or two sprints

The horse attempting a route for the first time is clearly the most difficult of the two scenarios. The handicapper's lot is less than ideal. The betting decision can only be based on two highly inexact factors: breeding and running style. Neither factor is a solid base for risking significant sums of money. Both reduce the bettor to a guessing mode.

An older horse attempting a route forces the player to deal with an equally difficult problem. With one or two sprints as a conditioning base, is the horse ready for the added distance? Again, the answer requires more guesswork than is compatible with a high percentage of winning bets.

Does the bettor pass these situations or attempt another approach? The situations occur so frequently that passing these races is an unsatisfactory solution for the average player. Is there a better way? There must be, or I've just wasted several paragraphs of introduction. We'll approach the problem through an understanding of energy distribution patterns. Consider the following two horses:

| Horse A | 6F | 22.0 | 44.4 | 1:10.1 |
| Horse B | 6F | 22.2 | 45.3 | 1:10.2 |

In a match race between Horses A and B, A appears to be a cinch at six furlongs. If the race were extended to 6½ furlongs, the issue would be less clear. At seven furlongs Horse B's closing ability *may* be decisive; and then again, it may not. In both cases, the demands of the racetrack are the determining factors. The energy numbers for both horses:

| Horse A | 53.13% |
| Horse B | 52.10% |

Assume the following energy parameters for a hypothetical racetrack:

	Target %E	Parameters
6 furlongs	52.85%	52.25–53.35%
6½ furlongs	52.65%	52.10–53.20%
7 furlongs	52.35%	51.90–52.90%

Let's consider our two horses in light of the energy demands of this racetrack.

Six Furlongs

At six furlongs Horse A is clearly the one to beat. It fits the parameters and is relatively close to the target energy par. Horse B is below the parameters and will be expending its energy too late to win at the distance.

6½ Furlongs

An extra half furlong significantly changes the probabilities in this two-horse race. At 6½ furlongs both horses are at the extremes of the energy parameters. Horse A expends his energy too early in the race to be a prime bet; especially if other pace pressure is added to the race. In the two-horse race it still possesses a strong advantage: no other pace pressure. Horse B fits at the bottom of the range of acceptable distribution patterns. To win at this distance, it would need help from other contenders. In light of our hypothetical parameters, B has little chance in the two-horse race.

Seven Furlongs

Stretching this race to seven furlongs changes the scenario in favor of Horse B. It fits the energy pars and is very close to the target/average energy par. Its expenditure pattern is nearly perfect for the expanded distance. Conversely, Horse A expends its energy in an unsuitable manner for the distance. It uses too much energy upon reaching the second call. The last three furlongs of the race should prove too much for it to handle. In the two-horse race, Horse A would be on a clear lead and still be difficult to run down. With other pace pressure, it should not win at seven furlongs.

Let's expand the example:

Horse A   53.13%

Horse B   52.10%

	Target %E	Parameters
6 furlongs	52.85%	52.25–53.35%
6½ furlongs	52.65%	52.10–53.20%
7 furlongs	52.35%	51.90–52.90%
8 furlongs	52.05%	51.45–52.30%
8½ furlongs	51.85%	51.25–52.20%

The scenario changes even more on the stretch-out. Horse A distributes its energy as a pure sprinter and should not be successful in negotiating a route distance. Occasionally, A may find a field entirely devoid of early pace. When that situation occurs, it will probably lead all the way to the wire. More likely, it will face other pace setters and fail to last the distance. Only in soft pace spots should A be considered as a win bet.

Horse B represents a much higher win probability. In sprints it distributes energy in a manner that suggests it wants additional furlongs. Unless a confirmed failure in other route tries, that type of runner is an excellent stretch-out possibility. The distribution of energy is gradual, a necessity in route racing.

Two Major Points Regarding the Stretch-out

1. Sprinters that distribute their energy at the upper limits of acceptable parameters have usually found their best distance. They expend their energy in a manner that will gain position at the four-furlong second call. In a route the runner is imbalanced toward early pace. Too much too soon; not enough late.

2. Sprinters that distribute their energy at the lower limits of the parameters are excellent possibilities on the stretch-out. A more gradual deceleration suggests a willingness to run on. The horse that apportions its energy in an even manner can usually be relied upon to get the longer distances. Beware of

the one-run sprinter; they flatten out badly in routes. As in earlier discussions, the best closer is the one that can sustain its move for more than just a single fraction.

STRETCHING OUT—ROYAL CAMERONIAN

With older horses that may have attempted routes before, or are coming off layoffs, the same reasoning applies. If the race preceding the route is well below the average sprint par, it's a strong indication of current route readiness. Statistical probability indicates the ideal time for the stretch-out is following a two-sprint tune-up. Horses have, supposedly, obtained the necessary conditioning and are ready for longer distances. There is no denying the accuracy of the statistic; it will hold true over time. But it *is* possible to be more accurate in anticipating readiness to run longer.

When returning from a layoff, a horse is usually given one or two races for conditioning purposes. The two races often look like this in terms of energy distribution:

First Race   52.75%
Second Race   51.75%

The first race is indicative of a horse distributing energy as a sprinter. It shows no signs of wanting longer. In the second race the runner ran the final part of the race in a stronger fashion, indicating willingness to run on. That two-race combination is typical of a returning router. There are, however, a great many of these who do not need a second race before a strong route effort. The handicapper emphasizing the apportionment of energy has an enormous advantage in gauging stretch-out possibilities.

The following example is an excellent opportunity to look at two aspects of the same problem.

5th Hollywood

1 MILE. (1.32⅗) CLAIMING. Purse $17,000. 4-year-olds and upward. Weight, 121 lbs. Non-winners of two races at a mile or over since April 2 allowed 3 lbs.; such a race since then, 6 lbs. Claiming price $25,000; if for $22,500, 2 lbs. (Races when entered for $20,000 or less not considered.)

```
Royal Cameronian            B. g. 6, by Temperence Hill—Lucinda Light, by Laser Light
                            Br.—Hill 'N' Dale Farms (Ont-C)              1989  1 0 0 1    $2,400
  GUERRA W A          115   Tr.—Luby Donn                      $25,000   1988 12 1 1 1   $21,425
Own.—Brooke-Kinch-Lovett et al   Lifetime 33 4 7 6 $98,135                Turf  6 0 1 1   $13,070
 6May89-2Hol  6f :213 :443 1:092ft  16 117  67½ 57 43½ 33½  Guerra W A4   25000 90-09 HrdToMiss,KvinsDfns,RoylCmronin 6
 7Aug88-2Dmr 6½f :213 :444 1:16 ft   7¼ 116 1111 97 67½ 48   Olivares F7  c16000 84-13 Gerril,Gypsy'sProphecy,WstBoyII 12
     7Aug88—Wide into stretch
31Jly88-1Dmr  7f :224 :451 1:221ft   5 116  43 21½ 1½ 11¼    Pedroza M A7  10000 91-07 RoylCmronin,IndinSignII,D.D.ThKd 9
12Jun88-2Hol 6½f :22  :45  1:17 ft   5¾ 116  98 96¼ 76¾ 95¼   Gryder A T4   16000 88-09 Lark'sLegacy,AngleArc,StarOrphn 12
 5Jun88-2Hol  7f :223 :453 1:234ft   5¼ 1115 96¾ 53 42½ 21¼  Corral J R10  12500 84-13 Mr.Edlwiss,RoylCmronin,DncnKid 11
     5Jun88—Wide 3/8 turn
12May88-9Hol  1  :451 1:102 1:37 ft  6½ 116  77½ 57 54 54¾   Stevens G L4  20000 73-21 ImprousSprt,Bshop'sRngII,InBold 11
 1May88-7Hol  6f :22  :451 1:102ft  14 116  710 78¾ 78¼ 76¾  Pedroza M A3  40000 83-13 BoldJade,LuckyMasddo,Cliff'sPlce 7
13Apr88-5SA a6½f ⓣ:22 :4441:153fm  68 116  109¼ 96 53 41¾   Sibille R3    70000 79-16 FbulousSond,QpStr,H'sADncngMn 10
 3Apr88-5SA a6½f ⓣ:212 :44 1:144fm  5¾ 116  76½ 67 55½ 66    Toro F5       62500 79-15 Mrvn'sPlcy,GldnGntlt,BmTwnChrl 11
19Mar88-5SA a6½f ⓣ:211 :4321:141fm  25 1115 108¾ 810 67½ 65¼ Valenzuela F H1 75000 83-10 Illuminux,BigChill,H'sADncingMn 12
     19Mar88—Bumped, rider lost stirrup 3/8
  May 14 Hol 5f ft :593 H     Apr 30 Hol 5f ft 1:014 Hg     Apr 24 SA 6f ft 1:15 H     Apr 18 SA 6f ft 1:13 H
```

```
Raider Marcus               Gr. c. 4, by Relaunch—Meet a Queen, by Our Michael
                            Br.—Nahem E (Ky)                             1989  7 1 1 1   $17,850
  NAKATANI C S       1085   Tr.—Rothblum Steve                 $22,500   1988  7 1 1 1   $17,025
Own.—Johns G H              Lifetime 14 2 2 2 $34,875                    Turf  1 0 0 0
22Apr89-5SA a6½f ⓣ:221 :4521:16 fm  7½ 1135 11 2hd 65½ 613   Garcia H J6  Aw32000 66-19 Sinforoso,HombrHombr,GorgHobrt 8
 6Apr89-5SA  6f :211 :433 1:081ft   23 1125 42 56 49 412     Garcia H J1  Aw32000 85-14 SamWho,OurNtiveWish,WickedIde 9
     6Apr89—Lugged in
18Mar89-1SA  6f :212 :443 1:102ft   16 1115 3½ 1½ 11 21½     Garcia H J5    25000 84-15 SuperbMomnt,RidrMrcus,HdlinNws 9
24Feb89-1SA  6f :214 :444 1:102ft  *2½ 115  1½ 2hd 12½ 1no   Stevens G L9  c12500 86-16 RidrMrcus,KngClyd,SwtwtrSprngs 12
 5Feb89-1SA  6f :221 :451 1:113sy   6¼ 1135 43½ 55¾ 611 611  Valenzuela F H6 25000 69-28 GrtForm,MtthwT.Prkr,SprbMomnt 9
29Jan89-5SA  6f :211 :441 1:10 ft   34 1105 43½ 32 55 85     ValenzuelaFH10 40000 83-16 Pialor, EightyBelowZero,QuipStar 12
 1Jan89-9SA  1  :454 1:102 1:354ft  7¾ 1105 32 1hd 21½ 34¾   Valenzuela F H4 35000 84-10 Reassuring,BigRainbow,RiderMrcus 9
     1Jan89—Bumped start
14Dec88-4Hol 6f :213 :451 1:104ft *9-5 1135 54½ 1½ 12 13    ValenzuelFH11 M32000 88-16 RaiderMrcus,GoldenVision,LddyV. 12
     14Dec88—Bobbled start
27Nov88-4Hol 6f :221 :454 1:113gd   3 118  31½ 2½ 21½ 2½     ValenzuelPA11 M32000 83-24 LasForever,RaiderMarcus,CreerDy 12
 3Nov88-2SA  6f :212 :442 1:103ft *9-5 118  55 44½ 45½ 34½    ValenzuelaPA8 M32000 80-18 CervntesSt.,AvergDncr,RidrMrcus 12
     3Nov88—Wide into stretch
  May 15 SA 3f ft :364 H     May 9 SA 5f ft :591 H     May 3 SA 3f ft :353 H     Apr 14 SA 4f ft :463 H
```

Royal Cameronian and Raider Marcus were both bet to about the same odds in a one-mile race on 19May89. Each was attempting the longer distance after a series of sprints. Royal Cameronian further complicated the race because it was only his second start after an eight-month layoff. Most traditional handicappers were waiting for the statistical probability: his *third* race after the layoff. An astute energy player was given an enormous opportunity in this race.

Let's examine Royal Cameronian's comeback race on 6May89. After a long layoff he ran well, with a solid third-place effort. He managed to gain 3½ lengths from the second call to the finish. He then ran evenly through the stretch, indicating he was not being abused. The $64 question: Was the sprint race adequate conditioning for a longer distance?

The energy number for the effort provided an exceptionally accurate picture of the horse's current condition: 51.33 percent. The Hollywood Park average energy for six furlongs was 52.80 percent. In sprinting to a 51.33 percent, Royal Cameronian was clearly telling us three important things about his current condition/ability:

(1) He is *not* a six-furlong horse. His energy figure is far below what could be expected to win a sprint at Hollywood Park.

(2) He probably does not need a second sprint before stretching out to a longer distance; 51.33 percent indicates a willingness to run a longer distance.

(3) If Royal Cameronian has the overall ability to win at the class level, he'll win here. He's a strong fit in the context of energy distribution.

Raider Marcus — Gr. c. 4, by Relaunch—Meet a Queen, by Our Michael

NAKATANI C S — 108^5 — Br.—Nahem E (Ky) — Tr.—Rothblum Steve — $22,500

Own.—Johns G N

Lifetime 14 2 2 2 $34,875

1989 7 1 1 1 $17,850

1988 7 1 1 1 $17,025

Turf 1 0 0 0

22Apr89-5SA	a6½f (T)	:22^1	:45^2	1:16 fm	7¼	113^5	1^1	2^{hd}	65½	61^3	Garcia H J^6	Aw32000	66-19	Sinforoso,HombrHombr,GorgHobrt	8
6Apr89-5SA	6f	:21^1	:43^3	1:08^{1}ft	23	112^5	4^2	5^6	4^9	41^2	Garcia H J^1	Aw32000	85-14	SamWho,OurNtiveWish,WickedIde	9
6Apr89—Lugged in															
18Mar89-1SA	6f	:21^2	:44^3	1:10^{2}ft	16	111^5	3½	1½	1^1	21½	Garcia H J^5	25000	84-15	SuperbMomnt,RidrMrcus,HdlinNws	9
24Feb89-1SA	6f	:21^4	:44^4	1:10^{2}ft	*2½	115	1½	2^{hd}	12½	1no	Stevens G L^9	c12500	86-16	RidrMrcus,KngClyd,SwtwtrSprngs	12
5Feb89-1SA	6f	:22^1	:45^1	1:11^{3}sy	6¼	113^5	43½	55¾	61^1	61^1	Valenzuela F H^6	25000	69-28	GrtForm,MtthwT.Prkr,SprbMomnt	9
29Jan89-5SA	6f	:21^1	:44^1	1:10 ft	34	110^5	43½	3^2	5^5	8^5	ValenzuelaFH^{10}	40000	83-16	Pialor, EightyBelowZero,QuipStar	12
1Jan89-9SA	1	:45^4	1:10^2	1:35^{4}ft	7¾	110^5	3^2	1^{hd}	21½	34¾	Valenzuela F H^4	35000	84-10	Reassuring,BigRainbow,RiderMrcus	9
1Jan89—Bumped start															
14Dec88-4Hol	6f	:21^3	:45^1	1:10^{4}ft	*9-5	113^5	54½	1½	1^2	1^3	ValenzuelFH^{11}	M32000	88-16	RaiderMrcus,GoldenVision,LddyV.	12
14Dec88—Bobbled start															
27Nov88-4Hol	6f	:22^1	:45^4	1:11^{3}gd	3	118	31½	2½	21½	2½	ValenzuelPA^{11}	M32000	83-24	LasForever,RaiderMarcus,CreerDy	12
3Nov88-2SA	6f	:21^2	:44^2	1:10^{3}ft	*9-5	118	5^5	44½	45½	34½	ValenzuelaPA^8	M32000	80-18	CervntesSt.,AvergDncr,RidrMrcus	12
3Nov88—Wide into stretch															

May 15 SA 3f ft :36^4 H   May 9 SA 5f ft :59^1 H   May 3 SA 3f ft :35^3 H   Apr 14 SA 4f ft :46^3 H

Raider Marcus is a frequently encountered type that contributes to the overall difficulty of the problem. He's quick from the gate, and often hangs tough in the late stages of his races. *But* does he really want longer? His pattern of energy distribution provides a crystal-clear answer to the question. His last three races:

22Apr89	53.90%
6Apr89	53.60%
18Mar89	53.92%

None of the three races indicates anything other than an early pace type sprinter. In a reasonably well-contested route, he's a horrible probability. I know of no other approach that will clearly quantify running styles and distance capability. The use of energy solidly distinguishes between the two stretch-out candidates:

Raider Marcus 53.60–53.90%

Royal Cameronian 51.33%

No contest on the stretch-out: Royal Cameronian at $14.60.

FIFTH RACE
Hollywood
MAY 19, 1989

1 MILE. (1.32⅘) CLAIMING. Purse $17,000. 4-year-olds and upward. Weight, 121 lbs. Non-winners of two races at a mile or over since April 2 allowed 3 lbs.; such a race since then, 6 lbs. Claiming price $25,000; if for $22,500, 2 lbs. (Races when entered for $20,000 or less not considered.)

Value of race $17,000; value to winner $9,350; second $3,400; third $2,550; fourth $1,275; fifth $425. Mutuel pool $272,847. Exacta pool $334,941.

Last Raced	Horse	Eqt.	A.Wt	PP	St	¼	½	¾	Str	Fin	Jockey	Cl'g Pr	Odds $1
6May89 ^{2}Hol^{3}	Royal Cameronian		6 115	9	6	4^{1}	2½	2^{4}	1^{2}	$1^{1\frac{3}{4}}$	Guerra W A	25000	6.30
30Apr89 ^{5}Hol^{1}	Ono Gummo		7 115	5	5	3^{hd}	7^{2}	5½	3^{1}	2^{3}	Davis R G	25000	1.60
29Apr89 ^{1}Hol^{7}	Aloma's Tobin	b	6 115	8	3	5^{hd}	6½	$4^{1\frac{1}{2}}$	$4^{1\frac{1}{2}}$	$3^{1\frac{3}{4}}$	Pedroza M A	25000	15.40
2Apr89 ^{3}SA^{5}	Secret Selection		5 115	2	11	12	10½	$6^{1\frac{1}{2}}$	$5^{1\frac{1}{2}}$	4no	McCarron C J	25000	2.80
7May89 ^{4}Hol^{6}	Raw Force		4 115	10	9	11^{2}	11^{2}	8^{2}	6^{1}	$5^{2\frac{1}{2}}$	Black C A	25000	48.60
22Apr89 ^{5}SA^{6}	Raider Marcus		4 108	3	4	1^{hd}	$1^{1\frac{1}{2}}$	1^{hd}	$2^{1\frac{1}{2}}$	6^{1}	Nakatani C S^{5}	22500	8.00
12May89 ^{4}Hol^{1}	Wined Out	b	5 115	12	2	6^{1}	4½	$7^{1\frac{1}{2}}$	$7^{1\frac{1}{2}}$	7^{2}	Solis A	25000	52.50
5May89 ^{4}Hol^{1}	Our Foolish Fancy		4 116	1	10	8^{hd}	3^{hd}	3^{hd}	$8^{3\frac{1}{2}}$	$8^{3\frac{1}{2}}$	Delahoussaye E	25000	29.90
30Apr89 ^{10}TuP^{6}	Marasid		4 115	7	7	7^{hd}	9^{1}	10½	9½	9^{hd}	Valenzuela F H	25000	160.40
30Apr89 ^{5}Hol^{3}	Kamikaze		4 115	6	8	$9^{2\frac{1}{2}}$	8^{hd}	$11^{2\frac{1}{2}}$	10^{4}	10^{5}	Meza R Q	25000	17.00
20Apr89 ^{3}SA^{7}	Armin	b	8 113	11	1	$2^{1\frac{1}{2}}$	$5^{1\frac{1}{2}}$	9½	11^{6}	$11^{7\frac{1}{2}}$	Fernandez A L	22500	23.40
23Apr89 ^{7}SA^{9}	Grand Vizier	b	5 115	4	12	$10^{1\frac{1}{2}}$	12	12	12	12	Cortez A	25000	14.50

OFF AT 3:35. Start good. Won driving. Time, :22⅘, :45⅕, 1:09⅘, 1:21⅗, 1:34⅘ Track fast.

$2 Mutuel Prices:				
	9-ROYAL CAMERONIAN	14.60	5.80	3.80
	5-ONO GUMMO		3.40	2.80
	8-ALOMA'S TOBIN			7.00

$2 EXACTA 9-5 PAID $50.80.

B. g, by Temperence Hill—Lucinda Light, by Laser Light. Trainer Luby Donn. Bred by Hill 'N' Dale Farms (Ont-C).

ROYAL CAMERONIAN, in contention early, opened a clear lead after six furlongs, drew well clear between calls approaching the sixteenth marker and had enough left late to prove best. ONO GUMMO, close up early, dropped back while in traffic approaching the end of the backstretch, was shuffled back while still in traffic going into the far turn, came on in the drive but could not run down ROYAL CAMERONIAN. ALOMA'S TOBIN, never far back, lacked the needed response in the drive. SECRET SELECTION, far back early, steadily improved his position after a quarter but could not gain the necessary ground in the drive. RAW FORCE, quite wide down the backstretch, was four wide into the stretch. RAIDER MARCUS, a pace factor until coming to the furlong marker, gave way. WINED OUT, wide down the backstretch was four wide into the stretch. OUR FOOLISH FANCY, outrun early, made a move on the backstretch while saving ground to get within close range of the lead nearing the far turn but faltered in the drive. MARASID was five wide into the stretch. KAMIKAZE was four wide into the stretch. ARMIN, an early pace factor, faltered badly

ENERGY: SOME FINAL THOUGHTS

The use of energy as an integral part of the handicapping process requires calculating feet-per-second numbers. The principles, however, are not restricted to a feet-per-second methodology. Class, trip, or speed-figure methods will be significantly strengthened by incorporating the ideas in this chapter. The concept of energy distribution contributes to a better understanding of the role of pace in selecting winners. Before leaving this chapter, I should make several additional points concerning the general use of the concepts.

1. Higher-class horses consistently record lower Percent Early numbers than do their lower-class brethren. This is a matter of common sense. The better horses run fast early *and* late. Lower-class runners run nearly as fast early, but much slower in the final fraction. Consider the six-furlong pars for the following class levels at Hollywood Park.

$10,000	45.1	1:10.3
$50,000	44.3	1:09.1

Assume a winning effort from each level, each horse 1½ lengths behind at the second call.

$10,000	52.49%
$50,000	52.02%

The $10,000 claimer, while only 3 lengths inferior at the second call, needed four fifths of a second longer in the final fraction. The result is a considerably higher Percent Early figure for the cheaper horse. That's true at all racetracks. Do not become too restrictive with general energy parameters. Learn to recognize when to concentrate on the higher end of your range and when to accept contenders from the other end of the spectrum.

With young horses the same relationship exists, but in the extreme. Three-year-old fillies, in the early months of the calendar year record the highest energy range on the racetrack. As long as the player is aware of the anomaly, it presents little problem.

2. Within the framework of current form and condition, the paceline selected for your contenders should reflect today's probable pace. Horses that have been badly used in recent races may have energy numbers practically off the scale. Once energy is used, there is no going back. And there is no linear relationship. Two lengths used early in the race may cost many lengths in the end. Once a horse is exhausted, it may wind up distanced in the race. Consider Saros Town's race on 15Jly89:

Saros Town

B. c. 3(Jan), by Saros—Sligo Town, by Baldski

VALENZUELA P A **117**

Br.—Schelb E A (Cal)

Tr.—Gonzalez Juan

Own.—Green Thumb Farm Stable

1989 11 3 3 3 $84,825
1988 0 M 0 0

Lifetime 11 3 3 3 $84,825

3Aug89-3Dmr 6f :22 :443 1:091ft 4 116 1hd 13 15 14 ValenzuelPA² Aw35000 92-14 SrosTown,BurnAnni,TmForAccurcy 6

3Aug89—Drifted out start

```
15Jly89-7Hol   6f :22¹ :45¹ 1:09¹ft  %-5 116   1½  1½  1²  1³   ValenzuelPA³ Aw30000 95-11 Saros Town,NevadaEon,Mehmetski 8
30Jun89-8Hol   6½f:21²  :44¹ 1:16²ft  %-5 116   2²  1½  12½ 3⁴   VlenzuelPA¹ ⊠Aw30000 89-16 WickedIdea,ImperialLad,SrosTown 6
26May89-7Hol   7f :21⁴  :44  1:21³ft  %-5 116   3¹  1hd 11¹ 2²   VlenzuulPA¹ ⊠Aw27800 94-09 Bag Of Magic,SarosTown,OneDrink 8
13May89-6Hol   7f :22¹  :44⁴ 1:21 ft   3½ 119   1¹  11½ 1hd 2⁴   Black C A⁶   Aw27000 95-11 Lode, Saros Town, Splurger    7
29Apr89-3Hol   6½f:22²  :44² 1:15²ft   9-5 119   1½  1hd 1hd 22½  ValenzuelPA³ Aw27800 95-10 Over ThePole,SarosTown,ElGorrion 6
   29Apr89—Bumped break
15Apr89-3SA    6f :21²  :44¹ 1:10 ft   5½ 120   4½  51½ 52½ 53½  ValenzuelPA³ Aw32800 84-15 Bruho, Sabulose, Damaskim       8
   15Apr89—Lost whip late
26Mar89-7SA    1  :46¹ 1:10³ 1:36²ft    9 116   32½ 3nk 3nk 42½  ValenzuelPA⁸ Aw41000 83-16 AdvoctTrnng,Bbytscoldotsd,MorInd 9
   20Mar89—Floated out, wide into stretch
10Mar89-7SA    7f :22¹  :44³ 1:22³ft   *2½ 120  2hd 1hd 21½ 3⁶   VlenzulPA¹ ⊠Aw32800 81-17 Mr. Bolg, Shady Pine, Saros Town 8
25Feb89-6SA    7f :21⁴  :44³ 1:22³ft   2½ 117   21½ 21½ 12½ 13½  ValenzuelPA¹¹ ⊠Mdn 87-14 SarosTown,RoyalAction,ImperiiLd 12
   Sep 2 Dmr 4f ft :47 H          Aug 27 Dmr 5f ft :59³ H        Aug 21 Dmr 5f ft :59⁴ H       Aug 16 Dmr 4f ft :59⁴ H
```

In his two prior races, Saros Town was fully extended to the second call. Consequently, his early energy percentages were higher than what is normally acceptable:

30Jun89	54.43%
26May89	53.51%

On July 15 he was facing a field incapable of reaching the second call in less than 45.0 seconds. Do you think he threw another 44.1 half-mile? Of course not. Only a confirmed quitter would commit suicide in a paceless race. The early energy number for the July 15 win was 51.50 percent, an aberrant situation. That percentage was earned in an unusual pace situation and should also not be considered indicative of his normal energy pattern.

An energy user has to fully understand the impact of today's pace picture on the energy patterns of the contenders. Look for pacelines with a pace comparable to today's situation. The faster a horse runs in the early stages, the higher the Percent Early. On July 15 Saros Town was a virtual cinch; regardless of his recent energy numbers.

3. "Horses for courses" is a real-life situation. Horses do prefer certain racetracks and surfaces. Energy patterns differ from track to track, and present the energy user with opportunities not available to the average bettor.

Saratoga and Belmont are sister tracks in New York, but each requires different characteristics from its winners. Most horses do not fare well over both courses. Sustained pace is usually king at Belmont. Early pace is the dominant style at Saratoga. Front runners who fail on the pace at Belmont are generally strong contenders at Saratoga. The reverse is also true. The application of energy distribution principles can be a loaded gun in the hands of an astute handicapper. Learn to anticipate a horse's performance over a new surface. Every season "horses for courses" is the rationale given for many wake-up performances by horses merely in tune with the energy demands of a racetrack.

4. Also learn to anticipate a successful move from dirt to turf. Runners that consistently run at the lower end of your dirt route parameters are often excellent candidates for the turf course. Turf racing demands a delayed output of available energy. Horses unable to reach contention in dirt routes often come home at generous prices on the turf. Let's invent the following dirt route parameters:

Target %E   51.95%   Range   51.35%–52.40%

Horses recording energy numbers near the target pars have found a home on the surface. Based on our hypothetical parameters, I would consider any horse with an energy output of 51.5 percent or below to be an excellent candidate for a turf-course win. The delayed output of energy indicates a willingness to handle additional furlongs, an important attribute on the turf.

CHAPTER X

The Daily Racing Form Variant

EXPERIENCED HANDICAPPERS are quick to point to the many drawbacks of the *Daily Racing Form* (*DRF*) variants. They are correct in virtually every negative criticism. The *DRF* variant *is* based on too few races each day. Yes, the number fluctuates with weekend cards and better horses. And yes, the *DRF* variant is not based on class pars and must certainly be suspect for that reason also. But the *DRF* variant, while not as dependable as a carefully crafted class/par variant, is generally suitable for our needs.

Our intent is to isolate the pace characteristics of contenders and relate those characteristics to the demands of the racetrack. We're not analyzing final time, which requires an exceedingly accurate variant. The horses we select may not even possess the best final-time ability in the race. Individually, internal fractions are not overly sensitive to a track variant. Nor are compounded ratings greatly affected by minor swings in daily variants. If we can bring day-to-day track speed into fairly close alignment, we'll do very well with our pace ratings.

None of this is to say that an accurate variant will not improve the reliability of the ratings; it will. But it may be asking a lot of the recreational handicapper to commit to the daily task of making track variants. Job and family responsibilities must certainly outweigh the commitment to recreational pursuits. With certain guidelines, and the development of track-to-track pars, the recreational handicapper can make good use of *DRF* variants.

In 1982 Doc Sartin, in his work *Factor Analysis*, developed an approach for the use of *DRF* variants with his fps methodology. By analyzing recent races and their relationship to the *Form* variants, he discovered that .08 fps was equivalent to approximately one point of *DRF* variant. Therefore, a horse running on a day with a variant three points lower than another contender, received a negative adjustment of −.24 (3 ∗ .08) to each of its fractional components. At most tracks, in most instances, those adjustments work remarkably well. At tracks with minimal fluctuations of track speed, they will perform nearly as well as more complex variants.

Interestingly, in his *Total Victory at the Track*, William Scott, coming from an entirely different direction, advanced the idea of using 1 length for every two points of variant. The approximate fps value per length at six furlongs? It's .15 fps or, if applied 2 for 1 as Scott recommends .075 per point of *DRF* variant. Somebody's doing something right.

In 1983 I began to recommend an additional wrinkle to the use of the *Form* variant. Every racetrack has a predictable average *DRF* number, and the daily variant tendency is toward that average. At Santa Anita the averages are 15 in sprints and 18 in routes. Why not use the averages to establish a range of zero adjustments and work up and down from there?

THE APPLICATION

As a concession to the rather loose method used to construct the *Form* variant, we'll use a range of one point above and below the average daily variant. Therefore, the zero adjustment "range" at Santa Anita is 14 to 16 in sprints and 17 to 19 in routes; one point above, and below, the averages. Pacelines selected with a daily variant in that range will be used with no adjustment.

Pacelines from races with higher, or lower, *DRF* variants will be adjusted in the following manner: one length for every two points of variant outside the established parameters. In other words, a variant of 21 in a Santa Anita route must be adjusted downward two variant points (1 length) into the range of 17 to 19. Similarly, a race at 13 must be adjusted upward.

We won't work in half lengths, so we'll round off to the next higher length. With a range of 17 to 19, a paceline with a 22 variant requires 3 points or 1½ lengths of adjustment to move the variant to 19, which is the top of the range. We round upward, thus making the adjustment to the paceline 2 lengths. The final variant for the paceline is "Slow" 2, and we'll adjust the final time of the paceline by that amount. We'll get to the mechanics of that adjustment in a few minutes.

Employing a similar scheme, Scott offers an upgrade that we'll also employ. He reasons, correctly, that when the surface becomes exceptionally conducive to fast races, the times of the horses increase in a disproportionate manner. The 2 for 1 variant adjustment no longer compensates for the speed of the track. To compensate for exceptionally fast tracks, he recommends setting a point below which adjustments should be made on a 1 for 1 basis. I agree.

When the *DRF* variant is more than *four* points below the established range, we'll use 1 length per point of variant for every point greater than four. At Santa Anita (17 to 19), a *Form* route variant of 15 is adjusted at 2 for 1, which is two points or 1 length.

A *Form* variant of 8, however, is adjusted in the following manner:

Range: 17 to 19

Adjustment: 13 to 17 adjusted at 2:1 ratio = 2 lengths

8 to 13 adjusted at 1:1 ratio = 5 lengths

Final: 2 + 5 = 7 lengths, or *Fast 7*

It's not as drastic as it may sound. If the range was based on sound data, it will take an exceptionally fast surface to drive the *DRF* variant more than four points below the bottom of the range. By themselves, exceptionally strong race cards should not drive the variant too far below the range. The reason we chose to use a range rather than an average *DRF* variant was to compensate for strong and weak cards. A weak card may drive the variant well above the range, but continue to use the 2:1 ratio for adjustments. A 1:1 ratio will tend to severely overadjust pacelines. If large adjustments prove to be the rule, the range for zero adjustments should be reexamined.

DRF VARIANTS—SPRINTS

In the following three examples, assume the normal range for the track to be 16–18.

Example 1:   1:10.4 DRF Variant 23
Variant: 23 − 18 = 5 variant points, or 3 lengths *slow*
Adjustment: 1:10.4 is adjusted to 1:10.1, thus compensating
             for the slow racetrack

Example 2:   1:11.2 DRF Variant 15
Variant: One point necessary to bring the variant into the
             16 to 18 range = 1 length.
Adjustment: To adjust the fast racetrack, 1:11.2 is adjusted
             to 1:11.3.

Example 3:   1:09.2 DRF Variant 9
Variant: Seven points below the range requires an adjust-
             ment at a 1:1 ratio. Therefore, the paceline must be
             adjusted by *seven* lengths!
Adjustment: The 1:09.2 on a lightning-fast track is adjusted
             to 1:10.4.

Fractional Times—Sprints

The "splits" or fractional components of races must also be addressed. In sprints we'll apply 50 percent of the final variant to the second call, rounding *downward* to the next whole number. If you expend the effort to calculate a daily variant, you will usually find that a disproportionate amount of that variant is contained in the final fraction. To compensate for that general tendency, and for the rounding upward procedure of the final time variant, we round downward with internal fractions. The fewer the adjustments, the less contaminated the fractions.

Variant adjustments in the first fraction of sprints should be kept to a minimum. While it is often necessary to adjust the first fraction between racetracks as a track-to-track adjustment, daily variants have very little impact on the first quarter-mile of a sprint race. The first quarter, even on "heavy" surfaces, often remains close to the track par whether the overall speed of the track is fast or slow by many lengths. Prove it to yourself by recording the first and third fractions of sprints on a drying-out racetrack and then comparing with normal first and third fractions.

Use 50 percent of the second-call adjustment, but make *no*

adjustment to the first fraction unless a minimum of *3 lengths* are necessary to adjust the second call. Also round these adjustments downward.

Sprint races using a range of 16 to 18 as zero adjustment:

Example 1: 22.1 45.1 1:10.4 DRF Variant 23
Variant: 23 − 18 = 5 variant points, or 3 lengths *slow*
Adjustment: The second-call adjustment is 1½ lengths, rounded to 1 length. There is no first-fraction adjustment. The adjusted line is 22.1 45.0 1:10.1.

Example 2: 22.2 45.3 1:11.2 DRF Variant 15
Variant: The adjustment to the final time is 1 length, making the second-call adjustment ½ length, rounded to 0. There is no first-fraction adjustment. Adjusted paceline: 22.2 45.3 1:11.3.

Example 3: 21.3 44.3 1:09.2 DRF Variant 9
Variant: Five lengths. DRF 16 − DRF 12 = 4 pts at 2:1 = 2 *lengths*
DRF 12 − DRF 9 = 3 pts at 1:1 = 3 *lengths*
Half the final adjustment is 2½ lengths, rounded downward = 2 length second-call adjustment. Also rounding downward, use ½ the second-call adjustment for the first fraction = 1 length.
Adjustment: The 1:09.2 on the fast track is adjusted to: 21.4 45.0 1:10.2.

DRF VARIANTS—ROUTES

Adjust the final time of routes in the identical manner used to adjust sprint races. As with sprints, the 2:1 ratio applies unless the variant is more than four points faster than the established range; then use the same procedure as in sprints.

Fractional Times—Routes

Second Call: Apply 50 percent of the final variant to the second call of the paceline, rounding downward as we did with sprint races.

First Call (1Fr): Use two thirds (67%) of the second-call adjustment. Rounding this adjustment to the next *whole* length.

Some route race examples, also using a range of 16 to 18 as zero adjustment:

Example 1: 46.3 1:11.3 1:44.2 DRF 22
Variant: 22 − 18 = 4 points, or 2 lengths slow
Adjustment: Final Time = 2 lengths
             Second call = 50% of 2 lengths = 1 length
             First call = 66% of 1 length = 2/3 length rounded to
             the next whole number = 1 length at the first call
             Adjusted paceline = 46.2 1:11.2 1:44.0

Readers having difficulty with the direction of the adjustment should remember that faster than par variants require us to *add* time to the paceline; with slower than par variants, *deduct* from the paceline.

Example 2: 45.3 1:10.2 1:42.4 DRF 12
Variant: 18 − 12 = 6 points fast. Four at 2:1 = 2 lengths. Two at
             1:1 = 2 lengths. Total adjustment = fast 4 lengths
Adjustment: Final Time = 4 lengths
             Second call = 50% of 4 lengths = 2 lengths
             First call = 66% of 2 lengths = 1 length
             Adjusted paceline = 45.4 1:10.4 1:43.3

ESTABLISHING PARAMETERS FOR "ZERO ADJUSTMENTS"

In 1989, apparently in response to competing publication, the *Daily Racing Form* began to segregate sprint and route variants. Previously, the *Form* variant was an average of all races (excluding turf) run on a specific day. Sprints and routes were lumped together in a single base, thereby diluting one distance structure with the other. Separating sprints and routes was a step in the right direction, but it has caused a problem of its own.

On any given race day there can be an imbalance of races carded for either sprints or routes, resulting in too narrow a base upon which to base a variant. For example, on 27Oct89, only two routes were carded at Santa Anita, both for two-year-old maiden claimers. In the midst of a series of days with a variant range of 16–19, October 27 shows a 23 DRF variant.

(This has long been the problem with using the *Form* variant from turf races.)

Fortunately for the recreational player, there is a reasonable and relatively painless solution. The following material is a day-to-day record of *DRF* variants for the first 16 racing days of the 1989 Oak Tree season.

Oct.	Sprint	Route
22	11	9
21	17	15
20	16	18
19	14	18
18	13	19
15	13	16
14	15	19
13	18	19
12	16	18
11	11	12
9	13	19
8	(1)8(13)	17
7	14	(2)11(17)
6	15	18
5	16	21
4	15	20

This record of *DRF* variants was accumulated from *Form* results charts, and we'll go through the procedure in a few minutes. First, I should explain the two exceptions to the daily variants: October 7 and 8. Neither day supports the variant from the other distance structure, or the variants from the surrounding days. For example, the 8 assigned to the sprints on October 8 is out of sync with the route variant of 17. Additionally, it is contradictory to the sprint variants from several days before, and after, that date.

When charts are available, take the time to investigate inconsistencies. October 8 featured only two sprint races, one of which was won powerfully by an allowance horse on his way to better things. It seems logical to assume a 13 as a reasonable variant for that day.

Similarly, on October 7 there were only two routes, both featuring powerful winners. The logical variant is probably within the 16 to 18 range, so I arbitrarily assigned a 17.

I set the zero adjustment ranges at:

Sprints	14–16
Routes	17–19

These are not exact averages; they are parameters requiring adjustments to the least number of race days.

Accumulating the Data

There are two readily available sources for the accumulation of a set of usable *DRF* variants: (1) *Daily Racing Form* results charts, and (2) past performances from the same publication. The player with regular access to the *Form* charts has an advantage: the material is neatly summarized.

Using Past Performances

When the sole intent is to set the parameters for zero adjustments, the handicapper can be well served by the past performances of virtually any racing day. In a single racing form, most of *DRF* variants for the entire meeting can be found by searching the p.p.'s of horses competing that day. For example, I've included the records of three horses entered in the second race at Aqueduct on October 28, 1989.

2nd Aqueduct

1 ⅛ MILES. (1.47) CLAIMING. Purse $22,000. 3-year-olds and upward. Weights: 3-year-olds, 119 lbs.; older, 122 lbs. Non-winners of two races at a mile or over since September 15 allowed 3 lbs.; of such a race since then, 5 lbs. Claiming Price $25,000; for each $2,500 to $20,000, 2 lbs. (Races where entered to be claimed for $18,000 or less not considered).

Coupled—Make a Statement and Boutinierre.

Ells Blue Ribbon — **Own.—Tri Pyramid Stable** — **119**

Ch. h. 5, by Mr Redoy—Ribbon Duster, by Dust Commander
Br.—Woodlark Farms Inc (Ky) — 1989 17 6 4 1 $88,495
Tr.—Klesaris Robert P — $25,000 — 1988 9 0 2 0 $6,660
Lifetime 48 12 8 4 $149,863

12Oct89-1Bel	1⅛	:474	1:122	1:50	ft	*9-5	113	75¼	74	36	410	Krone J A 2	30000	67-24	DiamondAnchor,Waterzip,Heritnce	9
23Sep89-3Bel	1 1/16	:472	1:121	1:43	ft	*8-5	115	51¾	52¼	21	13¼	Santos J A 4	22500	87-19	EllsBluRbbon,Boutnrr,Spr'sLstFght	6
9Sep89-1Bel	1 1/16	:454	1:103	1:422	ft	4¼	115	33	22½	2hd	21½	Bailey J D 3	22500	88-15	Onnagata,EllsBlueRibbon,SlickJack	8
28Aug89-5Sar	1⅛	:471	1:113	1:511	ft	*4-5e	117	34	24	47½	614½	Rojas R I 11	25000	64-21	GlmmrGln,CyQudLous,YonklYonkl	12
11Aug89-9Sar	1⅛	:471	1:123	1:51	ft	*2½	114	33½	21	36½	525½	Santos J A 6	30000	54-20	Pauly Boy, Hill Slide, Forecart	8
27Jly89-4Bel	1 1/16	:471	1:124	1:452	ft	*2	115	41½	52	12½	16	Santos J A 1	22500	75-27	EllsBlRbbon,SlckJck GoforCommdr	6
7Jly89-3Bel	1 1/16	:452	1:103	1:441	ft	*1	119	212	28	35½	516¾	Antley C W 6	35000	64-23	Forecrt,WildctTerritory,PinIsingPt	6

Super's Last Fight — Dk. b. or br. g. 5, by Just A Dandy—Super Fighter, by Alley Fighter
Br.—Coppola & Wright (NY)
Own.—Riccio J A 1125 Tr.—Stewart Charles $25,000
Lifetime 56 8 9 11 $121,573

1989	11 2 1 3	$30,871			
1988	21 3 5 4	$54,715			
Turf	1 0 0 0				

12Oct89-1Bel	1⅛ :474 1:122 1:50 ft	12 115	52¾ 64 58½ 614	Cordero A Jr6	32500	63-24	DiamondAnchor,Waterzip,Heritnce	5
2Oct89-1Bel	1 1/16 :462 1:113 1:443sy	2¼ 117	45½ 33 2hd 1nk	Cordero A Jr4	25000	79-26	Supr'sLstFght,SnrsSrvc,TmprncWk	5
2Oct89—Brushed, driving								
23Sep89-3Bel	1 1/16 :472 1:121 1:43 ft	3¼ 117	41½ 62½ 52 33½	Cordero A Jr2	25000	83-19	EllsBluRbbon,Boutnrr,Spr'sLstFght	6
17Aug89-9Sar	1 3/16 :473 1:121 1:58 ft	4 119	66 68 510 59¼	Grabowski JA3	c25000	74-17	SummerTle,SlickJck,MkeSttemnt	10
1Aug89-11FL	1 :463 1:114 1:374ft	3½e 116	55 43 3½ 12½	GrbwskJA2	Ⓢ Aw12100	95-15	Spr'sLstFght,PostTns,Nob'Imprtor	8
22Jly89-4FL	1¼ :503 1:424 2:091ft	3¼ 113	— — — —	GrbowskiJA1	Ⓢ A11000	— —	HickoryCrk,Mr.Trffic,DonAlbrtoJun	6
22Jly89—Lost rider								
15Jly89-5FL	170 :484 1:131 1:431ft	*6-5e 115	63½ 64 44 33½	GrabowskiJA2	Ⓢ 18000	81-15	RdHotLd,UticTrnsit,Supr'sLstFight	7
4Jly89-9FL	1 1/16 :464 1:113 1:454ft	12 114	77¾ 68½ 45 46	GrbsJA2	Ⓢ GnvlybrdrH	81-19	Cousteau, J.R.'sGift,BellbrookRoad	7

Speed Index: Last Race: -13.0 3-Race Avg.: -2.0 7-Race Avg.: -1.2 Overall Avg.: -1.2
Oct 23 Aqu 3f ft :384 B Sep 14 Aqu 3f ft :364 B Sep 11 Aqu 3f ft :364 H Sep 6 Aqu 3f ft :40 B

Glimmer Glen — Ch. h. 5, by Naskra—Twofold, by Timeless Moment
Br.—DearbornLtd&TalbotMKthryn (Ky)
Own.—Sommer Viola 115 Tr.—Martin Frank $22,500
Lifetime 58 12 6 5 $229,320

1989	12 4 0 1	$58,560			
1988	25 6 4 1	$114,640			
Turf	16 1 2 2	$36,200			

14Oct89-1Bel	1⅛ :47 1:114 1:502ft	2½ 117	51¾ 43½ 67 56¼	Santos J A 3	25000	69-26	Mega Silver, FortRiley,BrownBruin	7
6Oct89-1Bel	1 1/16 :464 1:122 1:453ft	4¼ 117	42 31 1½ 12½	Chavez J F 4	17500	74-30	GlimmerGlen,MasterGene,FortRiley	7
23Sep89-3Bel	1 1/16 :472 1:121 1:43 ft	4½ 115	3½ 2hd 31½ 56¾	Vasquez J 3	20000	80-19	EllsBluRbbon,Boutnrr,Spr'sLstFght	6
9Sep89-1Bel	1 1/16 :454 1:103 1:422ft	*8-5 1145	43¼ 32½ 34 45½	Carle J D 6	25000	84-15	Onnagata,EllsBlueRibbon,SlickJack	8
28Aug89-5Sar	1⅛ :471 1:113 1:511ft	11 1125	45 56 22 11½	Carle J D 3	25000	79-21	GlmmrGln,CyQudLous,YonklYonki	12
7Aug89-6Sar	7f :221 :451 1:24 ft	14 113	89 86 811 811¾	Migliore R 2	30000	70-23	ArcticBeat,Samerkano,DesertDevil	10
9Jly89-5Bel	1 1/16 :461 1:112 1:443ft	2¾ 117	35½ 45½ 311 415½	Migliore R 2	35000	63-29	FortRiley,VlidGunner,HsFrquntflyr	6
3Jly89-1Bel	7f :23 :46 1:24 ft	8½ 113	68¾ 67½ 66 65¾	Migliore R 1	45000	76-21	Furicano, SummerTale,ValidGunite	7

Speed Index: Last Race: -5.0 3-Race Avg.: -0.6 6-Race Avg.: -1.8 Overall Avg.: -2.6
Sep 7 Bel tr.t 4f ft :484 B

From the p.p.'s of the three horses we can get a pretty good idea of the route parameters for the 1989 Aqueduct fall meeting.

Ells Blue Ribbon	9Sep89	*DRF* 15
	23Sep89	*DRF* 19
	12Oct89	*DRF* 24
Super's Last Fight	2Oct89	*DRF* 26
Glimmer Glen	6Oct89	*DRF* 30
	14Oct89	*DRF* 26

In actual practice, I suggest using a base of at least 15 days. In the example, however, we'll base our parameters on six races. The variants are, chronologically: 15, 19, 26, 30, 24, and 26. In the absence of additional data, I would assume the 15 to be an aberrant day and base the zero adjustment range on the other five races. The logical range for Aqueduct routes should be *DRF* variants of 24 to 26, and races outside that range should be adjusted to fit those parameters. For the casual player this procedure will allow some degree of order to the subject of varying track speed.

Using Form *Charts*

I'm still aiming at the recreational player, but now, in addition to setting a no-adjustment range, I will impose a minimum of record keeping in exchange for a tighter set of *DRF* variants. From the *Form* charts, keep a daily record of variants and, as I did for the 16-day example earlier in this chapter, apply whatever judgment seems logical to minimize unnecessary fluctuations.

NINTH RACE **6 FURLONGS. (1.08) MAIDEN SPECIAL WEIGHT. Purse $27,000. 2-year-olds. Foaled in New York and Approved by the New York State-Bred Registry. Weight, 118 lbs.**

Aqueduct

OCTOBER 25, 1989

Value of race $27,000; value to winner $16,200; second $5,940; third $3,240; fourth $1,620. Mutuel pool $228,851. Exacta Pool $301,197. Triple Pool $497,790.

Last Raced	Horse	Eqt.	A.	Wt	PP	St	¼	½	Str	Fin	Jockey	Odds $1
	Five Coins		2	115	12	4	8^{3}	$5^{2\frac{1}{2}}$	$2^{2\frac{1}{2}}$	1^{2}	Santiago A	15.10
24Sep89 ^{5}Bel^{2}	Pop Your Top		2	118	2	6	2^{hd}	1^{hd}	$1^{2\frac{1}{2}}$	2^{1}	McCauley W H	1.90
	Indy Carr		2	118	4	14	11^{hd}	11^{3}	6^{hd}	3^{3}	Perret C	9.10
	Sir Lionel		2	118	3	12	$6^{1\frac{1}{2}}$	6^{1}	7^{hd}	4^{nk}	Santos J A	5.20
9Oct89 ^{4}Bel^{4}	King Kenny		2	111	14	8	9^{1}	$9^{1\frac{1}{2}}$	8^{2}	$5^{\frac{1}{2}}$	Aguila G E^{7}	18.70
24Sep89 ^{5}Bel^{3}	Prone		2	118	10	2	4^{1}	4^{3}	3^{2}	6^{5}	Migliore R	3.70
24Sep89 ^{5}Bel^{5}	Cholo		2	118	1	5	3^{1}	$3^{\frac{1}{2}}$	5^{hd}	$7^{\frac{3}{4}}$	Maple E	21.50
	Recipe		2	118	5	7	7^{1}	7^{3}	9^{3}	8^{2}	Bailey J D	6.40
4Oct89 ^{2}Bel	Templeogue	b	2	113	11	1	1^{1}	$2^{2\frac{1}{2}}$	4^{hd}	$9^{1\frac{1}{2}}$	Martinez J R Jr^{5}	31.90
	Dream in Style		2	118	7	10	$12^{1\frac{1}{2}}$	$10^{\frac{1}{2}}$	10^{1}	$10^{\frac{3}{4}}$	Romero R P	30.10
12Oct89 ^{4}Bel^{11}	Ginger's Toys		2	118	9	9	10^{2}	12^{2}	13^{7}	11^{hd}	Carr D	119.10
15Oct89 ^{4}Bel^{7}	Nash	b	2	118	6	3	5^{1}	$8^{1\frac{1}{2}}$	$11^{\frac{1}{2}}$	12^{hd}	Belmonte J F	80.10
28Sep89 ^{7}Bel^{5}	Catrinsez		2	118	13	11	14	14	$12^{2\frac{1}{2}}$	$13^{10\frac{1}{2}}$	Samyn J L	56.40
18Oct89 ^{4}Aqu^{13}	Queen's Testimony	b	2	118	8	13	13^{4}	$13^{\frac{1}{2}}$	14	14	Graell A	211.30

OFF AT 4:24. Start good. Won driving. Time, :22⅗, :46⅕, 1:13⅕ Track fast.

$2 Mutuel Prices:			
12-(L)-FIVE COINS	32.20	15.00	4.00
2-(B)-POP YOUR TOP		3.60	3.20
4-(D)-INDY CARR			6.80

$2 EXACTA 12-2 PAID $178.60. $2 TRIPLE 12-2-4 PAID $2,408.00.

Ch. f. (Apr), by Broadway Forli—Tall Coin, [illegible]

$2 Daily Double 1-12 Paid $125.00 Daily Double Pool $350,470. Attendance 11,306. Total Mutuel Pool $2,860,542. OTB Pool $3,715,791.

(Attendance 11,306. Total Mutuel Pool $6,576,335. Track Attendance 9,186. Track Mutuel Pool $2,521,226. ITW Attendance 2,120. ITW Pool $339,316. OTB Pool $3,715,791.)

Track variant for races 1, 2, 3, 5, 9, it is **21**; for races 4, 7, 8, it is **19**; for race 6 it is **16**.

At the end of each set of daily charts, the *Form* publishes the sprint and route variants for that day. On October 25 at Aqueduct the variants were 21 and 19 for all races but the sixth, a turf route. The 21 variants represented races 1, 2, 3, 5, and 9, and by checking any of those races, we can determine the distance represented by the variant. The ninth race, at six furlongs, tells us the 21 is for sprint races. You'll find the first variant listed is based on the first race of the day, and not on a sprint/route segmentation. Therefore, it's necessary to check the distance of at least one race in the summary.

SUMMARY

The *DRF* variant, within the confines of its own limitations, is quite satisfactory in "ball parking" variable track speed. At tracks with wildly fluctuating variants, it will prove to be less satisfactory than with more consistent racing surfaces.

Fortunately, compounded pace ratings absorb much of the variant, allowing the recreational handicapper to develop reliable figures without the ordeal, or expense, of carefully calculated variants. For the handicapper intent on becoming a "pro," the inconsistencies of the *Form* variant may be intolerable.

In a subsequent chapter I'll outline the procedure for constructing a daily variant. For the examples in the remainder of this book, however, I'll utilize the material from this chapter. To do otherwise is to limit the applications in the book, thereby doing a disservice to methods that can be successfully applied without a professional's commitment.

Before we exit the chapter, let's adjust a few pacelines from the second race at Aqueduct on 28Oct89. We'll set the *DRF* range at 24 to 26.

Ells Blue Ribbon — Ch. h. 5, by Mr Redoy—Ribbon Duster, by Dust Commander
Br.—Woodlark Farms Inc (Ky) — 1989 17 6 4 1 $88,495
Own.—Tri Pyramid Stable — 119 — Tr.—Klesaris Robert P — $25,000 — 1988 9 0 2 0 $6,660
Lifetime 48 12 8 4 $149,863

12Oct89-1Bel	1⅛	:47⁴	1:12²	1:50 ft	*9-5	113	7 5½	7 4	3 6	4 10	Krone J A 2	30000	67-24	DiamondAnchor,Waterzip,Heritnce	9
23Sep89-3Bel	1 1/16	:47²	1:12¹	1:43 ft	*8-5	115	5 1¾	5 2¼	2 1	1 3¼	Santos J A 4	22500	87-19	EllsBluRbbon,Boutnrr,Spr'sLstFght	6
9Sep89-1Bel	1 1/16	:45⁴	1:10³	1:42² ft	4¼	115	3 3	2 2½	2 hd	2 1½	Bailey J D 3	22500	88-15	Onnagata,EllsBlueRibbon,SlickJack	8
28Aug89-5Sar	1⅛	:47¹	1:11³	1:51¹ ft	*4-5e	117	3 4	2 4	4 7½	6 14½	Rojas R I 11	25000	64-21	GlmmrGln,CyQudLous,YonklYonkl	12
11Aug89-9Sar	1⅛	:47¹	1:12³	1:51 ft	*2½	114	3 3½	2 1	3 6½	5 25½	Santos J A 6	30000	54-20	Pauly Boy, Hill Slide, Forecart	8
27Jly89-4Bel	1 1/16	:47¹	1:12⁴	1:45² ft	*2	115	4 1½	5 2	1 2½	1 6	Santos J A 1	22500	75-27	EllsBlRbbon,SlckJck,GoforCommdr	6
7Jly89-3Bel	1 1/16	:45²	1:10³	1:44¹ ft	*1	119	2 12	2 8	3 5½	5 16¾	Antley C W 6	35000	64-23	Forecrt,WildctTerritory,PinlsindPt	6
7Jly89—Lost action															
19Jun89-1Bel	1⅛	:46¹	1:10³	1:49² ft	4¼	113	1 1½	1 1½	2 hd	1 hd	Antley C W 2	30000	80-25	EllsBlRbbon,VldGnnr,GoforCmmdr	8

23Sep89 47.2 1:12.1 1:43.0 *DRF* Variant 19

Adjustment: 24 − 19 = 5 points fast, requiring a one-for-one adjustment of 5 lengths

Second Call: 50% of 5 lengths = 2.5 lengths, rounded down to 2 lengths

First Call: 66% of second-call adjustment = 1.32, rounded to nearest length = 1 length

Paceline: 47.3 1:12.3 1:44.0

9Sep89 45.4 1:10.3 1:42.2 *DRF* Variant 15

Adjustment: 24 − 15 = 9 points fast = 7 lengths

Second Call: 50% of 7 lengths = 3.5, or 3 lengths

First Call: 66% of second-call adjustment = 2 lengths

Paceline: 46.1 1:11.1 1:43.4

Glimmer Glen
Own.—Sommer Viola **115**
Ch. h. 5, by Naskra—Twofold, by Timeless Moment
Br.—DearbornLtd&TalbotMKthryn (Ky) 1989 12 4 0 1 $58,560
Tr.—Martin Frank $22,500 1988 25 6 4 1 $114,640
Lifetime 58 12 6 5 $229,320 Turf 16 1 2 2 $36,200

14Oct89-1Bel	1⅛	:47	1:114	1:502ft	2½	117	51¾	43½	67	56¼	Santos J A 3	25000	69-26	Mega Silver, FortRiley,BrownBruin 7
6Oct89-1Bel	1 1/16	:464	1:122	1:453ft	4¼	117	42	31	1½	12½	Chavez J F 4	17500	74-30	GlimmerGlen,MasterGene,FortRiley 7
23Sep89-3Bel	1 1/16	:472	1:121	1:43 ft	4½	115	3½	2hd	31½	56¾	Vasquez J 3	20000	80-19	EllsBluRbbon,Boutnrr,Spr'sLstFght 6
9Sep89-1Bel	1 1/16	:454	1:103	1:422ft	*8-5	1145	43¼	32½	34	45½	Carle J D 6	25000	84-15	Onnagata,EllsBlueRibbon,SlickJack 8
28Aug89-5Sar	1⅛	:471	1:113	1:511ft	11	1125	45	56	22	11½	Carle J D 3	25000	79-21	GlmmrGln,CyQudLous,YonklYonkl 12
7Aug89-6Sar	7f	:221	:451	1:24 ft	14	113	89	86	811	811¾	Migliore R 2	30000	70-23	ArcticBeat,Samerkand,DesertDevil 10
9Jly89-5Bel	1 1/16	:461	1:112	1:443ft	2¾	117	35½	45½	311	415½	Migliore R 2	35000	63-29	FortRiley,VlidGunner,HsF[illegible]ntfly[illegible] 5
3Jly89-1Bel	7f	:23	:46	1:24 ft	8½	113	68¾	67½	66	65¾	Migliore R 1	45000	76-21	Furicano, SummerTale,VaroGunite 7

Speed Index: Last Race: −5.0 3–Race Avg.: −0.6 6–Race Avg.: −1.8 Overall Avg.: −2.6
Sep 7 Bel tr.t 4f ft :484 B

6Oct89 46.4 1:12.2 1:45.3 *DRF* Variant 30

Adjustment: 30 − 26 = 4 points *slow* = 2 lengths

Second Call: 50% of 2 lengths = 1 length

First Call: 66% of second-call adjustment = ⅔, or 1 length

Paceline: 46.3 1:12.1 1:45.1

Finally, one sprint. For the sake of the example, assume the same 24 to 26 range as typical for the track:

Zio Carlo
Own.—Ferraro T J **113**
B. g. 3(Feb), by Mari's Book—Nurse Lulu, by Jacinto
Br.—Ferraro J W (Fla) 1989 9 2 2 1 $27,900
Tr.—Ferraro James W $15,500 1988 0 M 0 0
Lifetime 9 2 2 1 $27,900

4Sep89-2Bel	6f	:221	:451	1:103ft	*2	119	74¾	54	54	98¼	Migliore R 10	25000	78-18	SoccerTour,EvenFster,PostlStrike 12
27Aug89-1Sar	6f	:221	:46	1:11 ft	4	113	35½	32½	32	33¼	Belmonte J F 1	30000	82-19	IroquoisIndian,T.V.Wizard,ZioCarlo 7
27Aug89—Drifted out														
12Aug89-9Sar	6f	:221	:453	1:111m	*2½	117	1hd	1½	13	12¼	Samyn J L 4	25000	84-13	ZioCarlo,Camadoon,PrinceNapsalot 9
22Jly89-9Bel	6f	:221	:454	1:114ft	3¼	115	21	2hd	2hd	22½	Samyn J L 4	30000	77-23	Bartolono, Zio Carlo, Garabaldlee 11
15Jly89-1Bel	6f	:223	:46	1:111ft	8	119	62¾	41¼	63¼	66¼	Samyn J L 7	50000	77-20	Sayuloveme, JazzCity,BuckMaster 10
7Jly89-4Bel	6f	:223	:463	1:12 ft	*4-5	116	23½	2hd	14½	17¼	Samyn J L 1	M50000	79-23	ZioCarlo,Prospector'sLad,Waccbuc 6
23Jun89-6Bel	7f	:22	:453	1:261sy	6½	114	12	13	2½	55¾	Samyn J L 9	Mdn	65-26	BetWrong,SpceProgrm,SnkeDoctor 9
27May89-6Hia	6f	:221	:46	1:111ft	3	113	52	3nk	2½	24¾	Velez J A Jr 8	Mdn	79-16	CamaRhett,ZioCarlo,PrinceNawed 11
27May89—Swerved in														

●Oct 5 Aqu 3f ft :342 H Sep 30 Aqu 3f ft :373 B

4Sep89 22.1   45.1   1:10.3 *DRF* Variant 18

Adjustment: 24 − 18 = 6 points fast = 4 lengths

Second Call: 50% of 4 lengths = 2 lengths

First Call: 50% of second-call adjustment = 1 length

Paceline: 22.2 45.3 1:11.2

DRF Adjustment Summary

(1) Set the zero adjustment range.

(2) Adjust pacelines into the range, using 2 points of *DRF* variant = 1 length of adjustment.

(3) Pacelines with a *DRF* variant more than 4 lengths faster than the established range must be adjusted at a 2:1 ratio for the first four points, and at 1:1 for the remaining variant points.

Sprints

- Final Time = Adjusted *DRF* variant; round upward
- 2Call   = 50% of final time, adjustment; round downward
- 1Fr   = 50% of 2Call, adjustment (3 length minimum); round downward

Routes

- Final Time = Adjusted *DRF* variant; round upward
- 2Call   = 50% of final time adjustment; round downward
- 1Fr   = 66% of 2Call, adjustment; round to next whole length

CHAPTER XI

The $10,000 Par

SPEED AND PACE HANDICAPPING would be much simpler if, time after time, the same horses competed over the same surface under the same conditions. *It would also be very dull and financially unrewarding.* The ability to adjust runners from different racetracks can be one of the pace handicapper's strongest advantages. Handicappers at Belmont Park must be capable of equalizing races from sister tracks Saratoga and Aqueduct or operate at an extreme disadvantage.

Likewise, a New Jersey handicapper must accurately adjust Monmouth, The Meadowlands, Garden State, and Atlantic City. The pro adds adjustments for New York, Maryland, and Philadelphia shippers into the New Jersey circuit, and so on. Fortunately, the task of acquiring usable adjustments is not as difficult as it first seems.

The works of Andrew Beyer and William Quirin advocate the use of $10,000 claiming races as interchangeable from track to track. In theory, once the $10,000 pars have been determined, handicappers can accurately adjust between racetracks. They're right, within limits. At higher-class racing circuits, the $10,000 claimers from lesser racetracks may not be interchangeable.

Turf Paradise, in Phoenix, runs $10,000 claiming races that seem to be on another planet when compared with Santa Anita. To suggest that a good $10,000 horse from Turf Paradise can ship successfully to southern California is usually wishful thinking. It's not *that* easy. Fortunately, the Turf Paradises are the exceptions. Most $10,000 races *are* interchangeable and provide an excellent base for track-to-track adjustments.

Before proceeding, I ask the reader to accept the following two premises:

1. Between racing circuits of comparable class, a $10,000 horse *is* a $10,000 horse. (New York handicappers should make the same assumption for their lowest claiming level.)

2. Racetracks within two class levels also ship $10,000 horses successfully. Bay Meadows or Longacres $10,000 horses are not greatly disadvantaged on the southern California circuit. The *Daily Racing Form* regularly publishes a track class hierarchy, and it's the responsibility of local handicappers to determine at what level shippers can compete locally. Once determined, a shipper's paceline can be adjusted for track class differences.

In his classic book, *Picking Winners*, Beyer describes the process of par-time construction as exceedingly laborious and worthy of a bottle of scotch whiskey. He may have understated the task; one bottle may not be enough. Constructing the initial pars for a track is not a pleasant undertaking, although once constructed, updating pars is not an ordeal.

Briefly, for the inexperienced handicapper, "pars" are the expected running times for specific class levels. For example, at Hollywood Park $10,000 older male horses usually run 1:10.3 for six furlongs. Not all $10,000 fields are comprised of horses of equal ability, but the *tendency* is toward that final time. Track speed is measured by deviations from the expected pars at varying class levels, and knowledge of the deviation—or "variant"—is the edge gained by many top players.

The processes of creating and updating pars and determining track-to-track adjustments are essentially the same. In the next chapter we'll develop the procedure for constructing a par chart that will reflect the general abilities of horses at all class levels. But for now we're looking for a single class-level par: $10,000.

The Data

Whereas with an entire par chart the intention is to create a daily variant for the racing surface, we'll construct a single par we can use for track-to-track adjustments. Rather than bury ourselves in a stack of race charts, why not use past performances? By opening the *Daily Racing Form* to a few races at the $10,000, the $12,500, and the $16,000 levels, we should have the data necessary to determine our par. Consider this: Where else can you get class levels, running lines, and *Racing Form* variants so neatly summarized? Those races contain horses that have competed regularly at similar class levels, and in their past performances (p.p.'s) should be most of the races run at the current meeting.

Examine the p.p.'s for the Golden Gate claimer Funnyfunnyman:

Funnyfunnyman			B. g. 4, by Shecky Greene—Tapia, by Nijinsky II			
GANN S L		**1105**	Br.—Pease W L (Cal)		1989 10 3 2 2	$19,625;
Own.—Rudolph & Serrone			Tr.—Sharp Lanny Z $18,000		1988 6 1 1 0	$6,950)
			Lifetime 16 4 3 2 $26,575			

25May89-7GG 6f :21³ :44³ 1:10¹ft 11 1125 2³ 3² 2⁴ 43½ Gann S L 4 12500 84-20 MuiLypheorD,French'sLuck,TryBoi 8
13May89-7GG 6f :21³ :44³ 1:09³ft 12 1125 86½ 66½ 67½ 6⁸ Gann S L 8 16000 83-19 IslndDyBrek,VientoDeOro,DvinBoy 9
23Apr89-6GG 6f :21⁴ :45¹ 1:11¹gd 4 117 2½ 1½ 11½ 2½ Doocy T T 4 c12500 82-17 IslndDyBrk,Fnnyfnnymn,DviDoon 11
31Mar89-9GG 6f :21⁴ :44⁴ 1:10⁴ft 5½ 119 21½ 2hd 13 1¹ Doocy T T 6 10000 85-19 Funnyfunnymn,StrkJstc,WckrBskt 12
17Mar89-9GG 6f :21⁴ :44² 1:09⁴ft 6½ 117 2nd 2hd 1½ 32½ Loseth C 2 12500 87-16 Uncultvtd,WckrBskt,Funnyfnnymn 8
26Mar89-9GG 6f :22² :45⁴ 1:11²gd *2½ 117 11½ 1² 1² 1nk Loseth C 2 10000 82-24 Fnnyfnnymn,B.J.'sPockts,PocktRd 9
17Feb89-7GG .6f :21³ :44² 1:10³ft 3½ 117 89½ 4⁸ 33½ 2¹ Loseth C 4 § 8000 85-20 OverDuPlsur,Funnyfunnyrn,BrtCo. 8
  17Feb89—Broke slowly; wide on turn
8Feb89-9GG 6f :21³ :45 1:11²sy *2½ 116 67½ 6⁶ 77½ 64½ Patton D B 2 10000 77-18 Pevikson,JessSteele,He'sMyPlesure 7
  8Feb89—Bumped start
2Feb89-9GG 6f :21³ :44¹ 1:09²m 4½ 117 21½ 21½ 2⁴ 34½ Patton D B 2 16000 87-21 Shmelessly,SportZ,Funnyfunnymn 5
19Jan89-7BM 6f :22² :45² 1:10⁴ft *9-5 117 3¹ 1hd 1⁴ 1³ Warren R J Jr 1 c6250 85-29 Fnnyfnnymn,T.J.Hookm,PracMtthw 8

Neatly displayed are nine races at the approximate $10,000 claiming level. By summarizing the races in the gelding's past performances, and adding from other runners at about the same level, we'll have an accurate look at the 1989 Golden Gate meeting. We will also have a reliable par upon which to base track-to-track adjustments.

Procedure

Together, we'll develop the $10,000 par for six-furlong races at Golden Gate Fields. We'll begin by summarizing Funnyfunnyman's races and then add races from other horses competing at the same class level. First, the format:

Date	1Fr	2Call	Final	Class	Var
25May89	21.6	44.6	1:10.1	12.5	20

(1) To avoid duplication, record the dates of the races used. As other past performances are added, many of the races will be in common.

(2) Use *tenths* of a second for the fractional times. The slight gradations between class levels are more easily represented than with a fifth of a second format. Additionally, many handicappers are using the Quirin pace and speed figures, which require fractional times in tenths of a second.

(3) Record the class levels for each of the races. Once the data base is complete, we'll average for a single class level.

(4) Record the *Daily Racing Form (DRF)* variant. These will also be averaged to a single number.

(5) Do not use races from off tracks. When necessary, other races with aberrant times will be eliminated when we summarize the data.

(6) The performances of the horse represented by the past performances have no importance to the procedure. It is the data from the running lines we want, not an individual horse's ability.

(7) Use older males only. They are the most consistent horses on every racing circuit.

Now, let's construct the $10,000 par for six-furlong races at Golden Gate Fields.

Date	1Fr	2Call	Final	Class	Var
(1) 25May89	21.6	44.6	1:10.1	12.5	20
(2) 13May89	21.6	44.6	1:09.3	16	19
(3) 31Mar89	21.8	44.8	1:10.4	10	19
(4) 17Mar89	21.8	44.4	1:09.4	12.5	16
(5) 17Feb89	21.6	44.4	1:10.3	8	20

The races of April 23, March 2, February 8, and February 2 were eliminated because of the off tracks.

Let's expand the base by adding the past performances of another sprinter from about the same claiming level. Shamelessly's p.p.'s add three more races: 28Apr89, 9Apr89, and 17Mar89.

Shamelessly ✳
GONZALEZ R M
Own.—Murphy P

117

Ch. g. 4, by Fleet Twist—Pin Up Queen, by Pinjara
Br.—Whiting Mr–Mrs P (Cal)   1989 7 2 1 1 $15,125
Tr.—Richman Larry $16,000   1988 11 1 3 0 $10,925
Lifetime   28 4 4 1 $30,238

13May89-6GG 1 :46¹ 1:10⁴ 1:37¹ft   7 117 2¼ 1² 1⁴ 1² Gonzalez R M § 12500 79-19 Shamelessly, Denew, Be ARoadster 9
  13May89—Bumped start

28Apr89-7GG 6f :214 :45 1:111ft 3½ 119 42½ 3½ 11 2½ Loseth C4 10000 82-21 FrncPrinc,Shmlssly,PunctutdMlody 8
28Apr89—Steadied start
9Apr89-1GG 6f :213 :443 1:101ft 11 117 42¼ 41¾ 54½ 612¼ Kaenel J L3 16000 76-16 BoldBrgin,FlyingLiutnnt,P.T.Hustlr 7
17Mar89-6GG 6f :22 :443 1:094ft 2¾ 117 31 3½ 32½ 44¼ Gonzalez R M5 c12500 85-16 Program Search, Swez, Kurri Ten 7
2Mar89-7GG 6f :22 :452 1:111gd *3-2 117 11 2hd 32 33¾ Gonzalez R M3 16000 79-24 Wavering Kite, Swez, Shamelessly 8
11Feb89-7GG 1 1/16 :454 1:104 1:433gd 9 119 2½ 710 824 834 Lambert J1 Aw19000 47-27 DblnO'Bron,MySonnyBoy,Lt'sCrsty 8
11Feb89—Bumped start
2Feb89-9GG 6f :213 :441 1:092m 4½ 117 11½ 11½ 14 14½ Gonzalez R M1 c10000 92-21 Shmelessly,SportZ.,Funnyfunnymn 9
31Dec88-4BM 1 :464 1:122 1:394sy *2½ 117 21 714 — — Kaenel J L3 20000 — — MowshkDncr,ShftySwfty,BngChrry 8
31Dec88—Eased; Wide 3/8 turn
22Dec88-4BM 1 1/16 :461 1:113 1:443sy *3½ 117 14 12 11½ 21½ Gonzalez R M6 16000 67-19 Passino,Shamelessly,FairwayChmp 8
1Dec88-7BM 1 1/16 :47 1:114 1:442ft 11 117 21½ 11½ 22 24 Spencer S J2 12500 66-25 LvBtChmp,Shmlssl,Grgg'sCmmnd 12
1Dec88—Lugged out 7/8
Jun 2 GG 4f ft :482 H May 25 GG 5f ft 1:054 H ●Apr 22 GG 4f ft :464 H

Date	1Fr	2Call	Final	Class	Var
(6) 28Apr89	21.8	45.0	1:11.1	10	21
(7) 9Apr89	21.6	44.6	1:10.1	16	16
(8) 17Mar89	22.0	44.6	1:09.4	12.5	16

That's a total of eight races in the base. Rich's Orphan's p.p.'s add five more races.

Rich's Orphan * Dk. b. or br. g. 6, by Poly Host—Etienne, by Mr Sam S
HUMMEL C R 117 Br.—Rich C W (Cal) 1989 8 1 0 2 $9,025
Own.—Rich C W Tr.—Garrison T W $10,000 1988 10 0 0 1 $2,687
Lifetime 43 4 3 6 $50,077 Turf 1 0 0 0
20May89-7GG 6f :213 :441 1:101ft 11 117 1010 86¾ 810 64 Hummel C R5 10000 84-13 Tellem Ben,OverDuePleasure,Walt 12
6May89-2GG 6f :212 :441 1:101ft 22 117 813 811 59 33 Tohill K S8 12500 85-14 Mr.Medi,MuiLypheorD,Rich'sOrphn 9
8Apr89-6GG 6f :213 :441 1:09 ft 7½ 119 65¾ 87¾ 79¼ 610½ Hummel C R1 10000 83-13 King Skipper, Noon Sun, Walt 11
19Mar89-7GG 6f :22 :45 1:101gd 8½ 119 32 43 53¼ 42¼ Hummel C R1 10000 86-19 P.T.Hustler,SharpWays,GoldTimbre 8
25Feb89-4GG 6f :213 :443 1:101ft 5¼ 117 45 44 44 12½ Hummel C R6 10000 88-16 Rich'sOrphn,KenoKptin,FireSidCht 6
5Feb89-5GG 6f :223 :461 1:114gd 18 117 86¾ 87¼ 65½ 55¾ Hummel C R9 10000 74-24 Doctor Dakota, Punch Bowl,IfyIfy 12
29Jan89-5GG 6f :212 :441 1:094ft 20 117 911 710 76¼ 53¾ Warren R J Jr9 12500 86-14 MriniRed,SupremeStnd,BoldMxicn 9
15Jan89-10BM 6f :223 :452 1:111gd 20 116 76¾ 78¼ 65¾ 33½ Hummel C R8 10000 79-26 DytimeBrgin,MriniRd,Rich'sOrphn 10
31Dec88-9BM 6f :223 :462 1:104sy 17 117 54 64 55½ 57¼ Hummel C R7 10000 77-26 Tiz Stealin, PunchBowl,MarianiRed 9
17Jun88-11Stk 6f :214 :443 1:094ft 5¼ 116 55 66½ 78¼ 64¾ Ochoa J6 10000 94-07 Brecons Charge, Runagate Walt 9
May 5 Stk 4f ft :492 H

(9) 20May89	21.6	44.2	1:10.1	10	13
(10) 6May89	21.4	44.2	1:10.1	12.5	14
(11) 8Apr89	21.6	44.2	1:09.0	10	13
(12) 25Feb89	21.6	44.6	1:10.1	10	16
(13) 29Jan89	21.4	44.2	1:09.4	12.5	14

Thirteen races are a solid base upon which to construct the $10,000 par for the 1989 Golden Gate season. In truth, it can be done with eight or ten. The next step is to summarize the data. Remember, the fractional times are already in tenths of a second.

Date	1Fr	2Call	Final	Class	Var
(1) 25May89	21.6	44.6	1:10.1	12.5	20
(2) 13May89	21.6	44.6	1:09.3	16	19
(3) 31Mar89	21.8	44.8	1:10.4	10	19
(4) 17Mar89	21.8	44.4	1:09.4	12.5	16
(5) 17Feb89	21.6	44.4	1:10.3	8	20
(6) 28Apr89	21.8	45.0	1:11.1	10	21
(7) 9Apr89	21.6	44.6	1:10.1	16	16
(8) 17Mar89	22.0	44.6	1:09.4	12.5	16
(9) 20May89	21.6	44.2	1:10.1	10	13
(10) 6May89	21.4	44.2	1:10.1	12.5	14
(11) 8Apr89	21.6	44.2	1:09.0	10	13
(12) 25Feb89	21.6	44.6	1:10.1	10	16
(13) 29Jan89	21.4	44.2	1:09.4	12.5	14
13 races avg.	21.6	44.5	1:10.1	12	17

The 13-race average reflects the $12,500 claiming par at Golden Gate Fields on a day with a *DRF* variant of 17. The par represents the average performances of older male sprinters and can be used with confidence when adjusting horses to another surface.

The original task, however, was to determine the $10,000 par for this track. A par-time chart is readily constructed from the data we've already accumulated, but track-to-track adjustments should be from a common base: the $10,000 par.

We'll adjust our $12,500 par to the $10,000 by utilizing Quirin's data on par-time charts, a subject we'll explore in the next chapter. His data supports a one-length difference between the $12,500 and $10,000 claiming levels. Therefore, we can confidently adjust the averages by one point at the second call and final time, leaving the first quarter unadjusted. In the next chapter we'll build a par chart for an entire class hierarchy based on the development of $10,000 pars.

Golden Gate's $10,000 sprint par: 21.6   44.6   1:10.2   DRF Var 17

The procedure for route races is identical and resulted in the following $10,000 pars for Golden Gate's three most commonly run route distances:

8F	46.2	1:10.6	1:37.0	18
8½F	46.6	1:10.8	1:43.3	18
9F	46.8	1:11.0	1:50.0	18

TRACK EQUALIZATION

Let's continue the procedure to its logical conclusion.

The edge is considerable to the handicapper able to adjust between tracks on a local circuit. The edge is further enhanced with the ability to accurately assess shippers. Eastern handicappers are well served by maintaining current $10,000 pars for feeder tracks that ship into the local circuits. West Coast handicappers in southern California are rewarded by cashing on high-ability shippers from Bay Meadows and Golden Gate Fields. Northern Californians are rewarded by understanding the relative abilities of Longacres horses shipping in at the conclusion of their race meeting. Consider the possible rewards from the following set of 1989 pars:

$10,000 Sprints					
1989 Golden Gate Fields	6F	21.6	44.6	1:10.2	17
1989 Santa Anita	6F	21.8	45.1	1:10.4	15
1989 Hollywood Park	6F	22.0	45.2	1:10.3	14
$10,000 Routes					
1989 Golden Gate Fields	8.5F	46.6	1:10.8	1:43.3	18
1989 Santa Anita	8.5F	46.8	1:11.5	1:44.3	18
1989 Hollywood Park	8.5F	46.8	1:11.6	1:44.2	16

In the chapter on using the *Daily Racing Form* variant, we developed a procedure for adjusting day-to-day changes in racing surfaces by using the average *DRF* variant attached to each of the pars. For this discussion, we'll just consider the basic differences between tracks.

Let's create the following hypothetical example:

Race date: 21May89

Racetrack: Golden Gate

Distance: six furlongs

Pacelines and surface:

Horse A	22.1	45.2	1:10.4	Golden Gate
Horse B	22.1	45.3	1:11.0	Hollywood Park
Horse C	22.0	45.1	1:11.0	Santa Anita

The basic question: Which is the fastest horse? Let's go through the adjustment procedure and adjust the fractional and final-time components by the differences in the pars.

Horse A: None. The other runners should be adjusted to today's racing surface.

Horse B: Hollywood Park is 2 lengths slower in the first fraction; 3 lengths slower at the second call; and 1 length slower at the final call.
   Paceline: 22.1   45.2   1:11.0
   Adjusted: 21.4   45.0   1:10.4. Faster by 2, 3, and 1 length respectively, thus compensating for the slower surface.

Horse C: Santa Anita is 1 length slower in the first fraction; 2 lengths slower at the second call; and 2 lengths slower at the final call.
   Paceline: 22.0   45.1   1:11.0
   Adjusted: 21.4   44.4   1:10.3

Horse C fights off an early challenge from B, draws off by a length in the middle fraction, and holds on to win by 1 length. This is not an uncommon scenario in California, and the handicapper able to make these adjustments has a decisive edge at the betting windows.

Handicappers should remember that the pars are current estimates and reflect the track at the time of year the data was accumulated. To be reliable over time, the data should be validated periodically. The basic problem with commercially prepared par times is the lag between preparation and application. Too often, handicappers are basing bets on yesterday's reality.

Adjusting between racetracks and racing surfaces (dirt to turf is handled in the identical manner) is a straightforward and common sense procedure. Once the $10,000 pars have been determined, the handicapper has the necessary tools to work through the adjustment puzzle.

Unfortunately, the procedure can take some complicated turns.

At "bullrings" with the additional turns, and at racetracks capable of offering odd distances such as the "one-turn" route, the procedure becomes more complex. Consider the following pars from Hollywood Park:

(1) 8F   45.7   1:10.6   1:36.3
(2) 8½F   46.7   1:11.6   1:44.2

When horses with these two pacelines square off against each other, bettors unfamiliar with the Hollywood Park route structure will lose every play. At first glance, a horse from the one-mile race figures with a 5 length fractional edge en route to a decisive victory. But the line is misleading and the two distances must be equalized.

Adjusting the fractional times is easy: add or deduct 5 lengths in each of the fractional components.

But what about the final-time adjustment? Handicappers employing a feet-per-second methodology using compounded ratings have a definite problem. The final ratings of the two distances will be "apples and oranges," with the mile race rated so much higher as to be unusable.

A *parallel time chart* is of no value in equalization because it extends the approximate rate of velocity from one distance to the other without compensating for the lack of a turn. The one-turn mile has an extended run down a chute into the turn, thus creating artificially fast fractions for a route race. Most charts indicate the eight-furlong equivalent of 1:43.3 to be about 1:37.1. That *would* be true if both pars were for two-turn routes. So, how do we get to the heart of this particular problem?

The key to determining any of these odd distances is "Average Pace" from the Sartin Methodology.

Sprints: Average of the three fractional components
$$AP = 1Fr + 2Fr + 3Fr / 3$$
Routes : Average of Early Pace and Sustained Pace
$$AP = EP + SP / 2$$

Another look at the two pars:

(1) 8F   45.7   1:10.6   1:36.3   AP = 54.76
(2) 8½F   46.7   1:11.6   1:44.2   AP = 54.05

The Average Pace difference is .71, and provides a starting point for our adjustment. Now we need a lengths equivalent for the AP value of .71.

As a "rule of thumb," the value of a length:

sprint = .14 per length

route = .11 per length

In the example, use .11 per length: .71 / .11 = 6.45 lengths. The approximate adjustment necessary to equalize our two pars is *6 lengths*. Let's add 6 lengths to the final time of the mile race and then recalculate the Average Pace figure. We'll also adjust the fractional times by 5 lengths:

$$46.7 \quad 1{:}11.6 \quad 1{:}37.4 \; AP = 54.07$$

Now compare to the 1$\frac{1}{16}$ mile par:

$$46.7 \quad 1{:}11.6 \quad 1{:}44.2 \; AP = 54.05$$

In this example the Average Pace figures are virtually equal, thus requiring no further adjustment to the mile pars. Occasionally, it will be necessary to further adjust the final time by a length or two in order to deliver equal Average Pace figures. Use a trial-and-error procedure, each time adjusting by 1 length and recalculating Average Pace.

With the $10,000 pars firmly in place, we can proceed to the next level: constructing a complete par-time chart.

CHAPTER XII

Par-Time Charts

A THREE-YEAR-OLD FILLY wins a six-furlong sprint in 1:10.4, drawing away down the stretch; the race was a mid-season $32,000 claimer. The handicapper's task: assess the quality of the performance. At Hollywood Park the effort was about par for the level. At Golden Gate Fields it was a couple lengths slower than expected.

In November a three-year-old colt wins a $25,000 claiming race under a hold in 1:09.3. Once again the handicapper's task is to assess the strength of the win. At Santa Anita (Oak Tree) the effort is indicative of a horse about to climb the class ladder.

Handicappers capable of assessing the quality of a performance possess a decisive edge over the crowd. When a future star is unveiled, players with accurate par times are set to follow the horse on its rise to the top of the class hierarchy. When the 1989 champion mare Bayakoa was first switched from turf to dirt, she earned a figure that was off the scale for female stakes performers. Her 10-length allowance win prompted me to suggest to clients that, if kept on the dirt, she was capable of becoming one of the top stakes performers on the West Coast. That was an understatement; she became one of the top mares in recent years.

Likewise, when a claiming horse suddenly begins to improve, class/performance pars indicate where the horse is likely to perform well in its next start. A dependable Horses to Watch list should be based on runners who have exceeded the expected pars for their competitive levels. Gauging a horse's ability to successfully handle a class rise is best determined by matching performance to par. Bettors often shy away from horses climbing in class, and healthy profits are generated from betting those that can successfully climb the class ladder.

The key to an accurate par-time chart is the $10,000 par. Once determined, we can use the Quirin research to expand to other class levels. Based on years of data at each track across the country, Quirin proved a symmetrical relationship exists with par-time charts. The normal gradations, from the lowest-level claimers to the stars on the local circuit, are predictable from track to track. In the following example assume $10,000 claimers as a class par of 100, with the chart escalating at *approximately one point per class level*: $12,500 = 101, $16,000 = 102, etc.

With some exceptions, a top to bottom par chart for sprint and route races is typical of the one on page 272 (fractional times are in *tenths* of seconds).

The route structure typically contains at least one two-step jump in class pars. The first will usually be the step from $16,000 (102) to $20,000 (104). The second jump will usually be the step from NW2 to NW3 allowances. Placement of allowance races varies with the quality of horses running on individual circuits and, for that reason, those levels are not on the hypothetical chart.

At some racetracks the progression may be a bit too orderly. Tracks lower on the track class scale often have idiosyncrasies not common to major racing circuits. Restricted claiming races, starter allowances, and state-bred claiming races (other than Kentucky and California) may not be universal across the country. Occasionally a minor racetrack may have lower-class races with a par superior to a level higher on the chart. These are items of local knowledge best addressed by local handicappers.

If we accept the Quirin data on the symmetrical relationships with a typical par-time chart, we can construct the 1989 chart for Hollywood Park sprints. The $10,000 pars:

$10,000 100 6F 45.2 1:10.3 6½F 45.0 1:17.0 7F 45.0 1:23.1

The quarter-mile times are not displayed because they play no part in constructing the track variant, a subject we'll address after completing the chart.

Missing from the chart are several key pars that are necessary if we're to subsequently use the data in making daily variants. The missing data is on page 273.

Class		Dist	1Fr	2Call	Final
$25,000	104	6F	22.0	45.8	1:11.1
20,000	103	6F	22.1	45.9	1:11.2
16,000	102	6F	22.1	46.0	1:11.3
12,500	101	6F	22.2	46.1	1:11.4
10,000	100	6F	22.2	46.2	1:12.0
8,000	99	6F	22.3	46.3	1:12.1
6,250	98	6F	22.3	46.4	1:12.2

	Dist	1Fr	2Call	Final
105	8½F	46.4	1:12.2	1:44.4
104	8½F	46.4	1:12.3	1:45.0
102	8½F	46.5	1:12.4	1:45.2
101	8½F	47.6	1:12.5	1:45.3
100	8½F	47.6	1:12.6	1:45.4
99	8½F	47.7	1:12.7	1:46.0
98	8½F	47.8	1:12.8	1:46.1

Class		Dist	2Call	Final	Dist	2Call	Final	Dist	2Call	Final
$50,000	107	6F	44.5	1:09.1	6½F	44.3	1:15.3	7F	44.3	1:21.4
40,000	106	6F	44.6	1:09.2	6½F	44.4	1:15.4	7F	44.4	1:22.0
32,000	105	6F	44.7	1:09.3	6½F	44.5	1:16.0	7F	44.5	1:22.1
25,000	104	6F	44.8	1:09.4	6½F	44.6	1:16.1	7F	44.6	1:22.2
20,000	103	6F	44.9	1:10.0	6½F	44.7	1:16.2	7F	44.7	1:22.3
16,000	102	6F	45.0	1:10.1	6½F	44.8	1:16.3	7F	44.8	1:22.4
12,500	101	6F	45.1	1:10.2	6½F	44.9	1:16.4	7F	44.9	1:23.0
10,000	100	6F	45.2	1:10.3	6½F	45.0	1:17.0	7F	45.0	1:23.1

1. Maiden races. These will differ from circuit to circuit, and pars must be determined from local data. The maidens at Santa Anita are equivalent to $20,000 claiming races, while Golden Gate maidens fit the $12,500 claiming par. Fortunately, there are so many maiden races run at every racetrack that pars are readily determined by the methods outlined in the previous chapter.

2. Maiden claiming. The Quirin data suggests that a maiden claiming sprint is 5 lengths slower than the equivalent open claiming level. Routes are 7 lengths slower. Once again, that may vary at individual racetracks and is best determined from local knowledge. In southern California, for example, the actual differences are 7 lengths in sprints and 9 lengths in routes.

3. Nonwinners allowances. NW1, NW2, NW3, NW4, and classified allowances are predictable from level to level, and are consistent with the relationships on the par-time chart. Once the NW1 allowances par is determined, the remainder of the nonclaiming races can be fitted to the chart. NW1's can be written as nonwinners of a race other than maiden or claiming, nonwinners of a specific purse amount, or nonwinners of two races lifetime. They usually fit two levels above the maiden par. If the maiden par is a 103. the NW1 should be 105.

4. Allowances and claiming races restricted to state-breds. With the exceptions of the key breeding states of California, Kentucky, and possibly Florida, these races are the worst on any circuit. Purses are inflated to encourage the program, and runners are often interchangeable with the lowest-level claimers. Pars are determined locally and will vary from state to state.

SPRINT PARS—HOLLYWOOD PARK

Let's complete the sprint pars for Hollywood Park (see chart on page 275).

ROUTE PARS—HOLLYWOOD PARK

The $10,000 pars for Hollywood Park routes are on pages 276 and 277.

		6F			6½F			7F			(7F)*
Stks	111	6F	44.2	1:08.3	6½F	44.0	1:14.4	7F	44.0	1:20.4	112
Cl Alw	109	6F	44.3	1:08.4	6½F	44.1	1:15.1	7F	44.1	1:21.1	110
NW3 Alw	108	6F	44.4	1:09.0	6½F	44.2	1:15.2	7F	44.2	1:21.2	109
NW2 Alw	107	6F	44.5	1:09.1	6½F	44.3	1:15.3	7F	44.3	1:21.3	108
NW1 Alw	105	6F	44.7	1:09.3	6½F	44.5	1:16.0	7F	44.5	1:22.0	106
Maiden	103	6F	44.9	1:10.0	6½F	44.7	1:16.2	7F	44.7	1:22.3	103
50,000	107	6F	44.5	1:09.1	6½F	44.3	1:15.3	7F	44.3	1:21.3	108
40,000	106	6F	44.6	1:09.2	6½F	44.4	1:15.4	7F	44.4	1:21.4	107
32,000	105	6F	44.7	1:09.3	6½F	44.5	1:16.0	7F	44.5	1:22.0	106
25,000	104	6F	44.8	1:09.4	6½F	44.6	1:16.1	7F	44.6	1:22.2	104
20,000	103	6F	44.9	1:10.0	6½F	44.7	1:16.2	7F	44.7	1:22.3	103
16,000	102	6F	45.0	1:10.1	6½F	44.8	1:16.3	7F	44.8	1:22.4	102
12,500	101	6F	45.1	1:10.2	6½F	44.9	1:16.4	7F	44.9	1:23.0	101
10,000	100	6F	45.2	1:10.3	6½F	45.0	1:17.0	7F	45.0	1:23.1	100
Mdn 50K	100	6F	45.2	1:10.3	6½F	45.0	1:17.0	7F	45.0	1:23.1	100
Mdn 32K	98	6F	45.4	1:11.0	6½F	45.2	1:17.2	7F	45.3	1:23.4	97

*7 furlong races usually require an adjustment to the pars at mid-range claiming levels. Hollywood Park pars require the adjustment at $32,000 claiming and at the weakest level: $32,000 maiden claiming.

	8F					8½F	9F	
Stks	113	44.9	1:09.3	1:34.0	45.9	1:10.3	1:41.4	1:48.0	114
Cl Alw	111	45.0	1:09.5	1:34.2	46.0	1:10.5	1:42.1	1:48.2	112
NW3 Alw	110	45.1	1:09.6	1:34.3	46.1	1:10.6	1:42.2	1:48.3	111
NW2 Alw	108	45.2	1:09.8	1:35.0	46.2	1:10.8	1:42.4	1:49.0	109
NW1 Alw	106	45.3	1:10.0	1:35.2	46.3	1:11.0	1:43.1	1:49.2	107
Maiden	104	45.4	1:10.2	1:35.4	46.4	1:11.2	1:43.3	1:50.0	104
50,000	108	45.2	1:09.8	1:35.0	46.2	1:10.8	1:42.4	1:49.0	109
40,000	107	45.2	1:09.9	1:35.1	46.2	1:10.9	1:43.0	1:49.1	108
32,000	106	45.3	1:10.0	1:35.2	46.3	1:11.0	1:43.1	1:49.2	107
25,000	105	45.4	1:10.1	1:35.3	46.4	1:11.1	1:43.2	1:49.3	106
20,000	104	45.4	1:10.2	1:35.4	46.4	1:11.2	1:43.3	1:50.0	104
16,000	102	45.6	1:10.4	1:36.1	46.6	1:11.4	1:44.0	1:50.2	102
12,500	101	45.6	1:10.5	1:36.2	46.6	1:11.5	1:44.1	1:50.3	101
10,000	100	45.7	1:10.6	1:36.3	46.7	1:11.6	1:44.2	1:50.4	100
Mdn 50K	100	45.7	1:10.6	1:36.3	46.7	1:11.6	1:44.2	1:50.4	100
Mdn 32K	98	45.9	1:10.8	1:37.0	46.8	1:11.8	1:44.4	1:51.2	97

8F	45.7	1:10.6	1:36.3
8½F	46.7	1:11.6	1:44.2
9F	46.7	1:11.6	1:50.4

When I was first introduced to the Quirin data on par times, my reaction was that they were too neat, too symmetrical. Remarkably, however, constructing the chart from $10,000 pars came very close to charts constructed from analyzing every race from every season. Accepting Quirin's data greatly reduces the time spent researching charts and past performances for data that will only be marginally more effective.

The pars we've created represent the usual times recorded by older males running over a fast racetrack. Accurate assessment of the performances of females and younger horses requires adjustments to the pars. Fortunately, they are universal and transferable from circuit to circuit.

Fillies and Mares

Sprints: Two lengths slower than the equivalent male class level.

Routes: Four lengths slower in maiden and claiming races. Three lengths slower in nonmaiden, nonclaiming races.

Three-Year-Olds

Before we adjust for the three-year-old's lack of maturity, it's important that we separate claiming and nonclaiming three-year-olds. Nonclaiming three-year-olds require no age adjustment. Older nonclaimers, top class excepted, are usually inferior to the younger allowance and maiden horses. By the age of four years, horses of quality should have long since lost their eligibility for nonwinners allowance races. Unless lightly raced, the older horses in these races are usually culls that may never escape to better things.

Three-year-olds, however, have the potential to develop into top runners, and are often just moving through the conditions of nonwinners races. At major tracks, especially, no adjustment for age is necessary. If your circuit differs, that's local knowledge and provides you with a significant edge. At the stakes level assume the three-year-olds to be *2 lengths* slower than par for the older stakes performers.

Claiming three-year-olds are a different story. Races carded exclusively for these youngsters are considerably weaker than the equivalent class level for older horses. Therefore, adjustments for age are required. We'll use a sliding scale, gradually reducing the adjustments as the calendar year progresses and the horses gain maturity. Once more the Quirin research provides most of the data:

	6F	7F	8F	8½F	9F	
+9					Jan 1	+9
+8					Feb 1	+8
+7				Jan 1	Mar 15	+7
+6				Feb 15	May 1	+6
+5			Jan 1	Apr 15	Jun 1	+5
+4		Jan 1	Apr 15	Jun 1	Jly 1	+4
+3	Jan 1	Mar 15	Jun 1	Aug 1	Sep 1	+3
+2	Apr 15	Jun 15	Aug 15			+2
+1	Jly 1	Aug 15				+1

The adjustments on the chart differ slightly from the Quirin data on a single point. Whereas most published data suggests an end to the use of age adjustments at the end of the calendar year, practical experience suggests otherwise.

There must still be allowances for age, even at the end of the calendar year. End-of-year races restricted to claiming three-year-olds are *at least* 1 length weaker than unrestricted races. The following argument applies:

Beginning January 1 of each season, many of the newly turned four-year-olds will be sharply dropped in class as they seek their proper competitive level. Many will be runners who, prior to December 31, were capable of successfully competing several class levels above the current drop: with three-year-olds! When asked to compete with more seasoned horses, many will need a drop of two or three levels to softer company. It happens every year, at every track. Three-year-old claimers competing at $32,000 in July are often $16,000 claimers the following season.

A few examples:

Example: May 15 at Hollywood Park

Distance: 1¹⁄₁₆ miles

Class: $32,000 claiming

Par: Older male par: 1:11.0 1:43.1 + 5 lengths (adjustment from April 15 to June 1)

3 yr. par: 1:11.0 1:43.1 + 5 lengths = 1:11.5 1:44.1

Example: April 10 at Hollywood Park

Distance: 6 furlongs

Class: $25,000 claiming

Par: Older male par: 44.8 1:09.4 + 3 lengths (adjustment from January 1 to April 15)

3 yr. par: 44.8 1:09.4 + 3 lengths = 45.1 1:10.2

Example: July 1 at Hollywood Park

Distance: One mile

Class: $32,000 claiming for three-year-old fillies

Par: Older male par: 1:10.0 1:35.2 + 4 lengths (female claiming route adjustment) + 3 lengths (three-year-old adjustment from June 1 to August 15) = 7 lengths

3 yr. par: 1:10.0 1:35.2 + 7 lengths = 1:10.7 1:36.4

Example: A good or bad performance? November 5 at Santa Anita for three-year-old fillies

Distance: 1¹⁄₁₆ miles

Class: $25,000 claiming

Time: wire-to-wire in 1:44.0

Par: 1:43.2 (older male par) + 4 lengths female adjustment + 3 lengths age adjustment = 7 lengths

Race par: 1:43.2 + 7 lengths = 1:44.4 par for this age and class level

Evaluation: The filly winning the hypothetical race should appear on your Horses to Watch list. Her performance was 4 lengths better than par for the level, and barring pace disadvantages, she should handle a raise in class.

SUMMARY

The ability to construct and apply a par chart is necessary for complete understanding of the next chapter: "Daily Track Variants." To effectively measure the speed of the track, we must accurately establish pars for races other than those carded for older males. That type of race may only represent part of a day's card and may not provide an adequate sample upon which to base our variants. Therefore, readers having difficulty with the examples should remain with the material until they can readily duplicate the results.

Now on to one of the most illusive of handicapping factors: the care and feeding of a daily track variant.

CHAPTER XIII

Daily Track Variants

AT THE THREE-MINUTE MARK in the betting, the two cofavorites were being held at 3–1 odds. Both were from good barns, and each met most standards for satisfactory form. The two horses:

Horse A   45.0   1:10.3
Horse B   45.1   1:11.0

The betting public, recognizing the apparent superiority of Horse A, begins to "send it in" on the faster horse. On cold dope, the horse looks like the bet of the meeting. Is it time to take the rubber band off the bankroll? Maybe.

The crowd *may* be making a fundamental mistake that is repeated time and again at the racetrack. It is a mistake based on a lack of data. Unless the performances of the two horses are evaluated against the speed of the racing surface over which their clockings were earned, perceived "reality" may be grossly misleading. What is missing in the scenario is a *daily track variant*.

A daily variant is what enables pace and speed handicappers to fully appreciate good performances and downgrade those earned under too-favorable conditions.

Weather and track maintenance activity contribute heavily to fluctuating track speeds. During warm dry spells, most tracks become conducive to artificially fast clockings. Tracks drying out after a winter storm will host artificially slow times, often for days at a time. Maintenance crews cutting the surface or increasing sand content also contribute to slower clockings. Use of the auxiliary rails on turf courses will effect the performances of horses running over that surface.

To effectively evaluate pace and speed performance, clockings must be evaluated against a daily variation from normal track speed.

Let's go back to the A vs B match-up:

| Horse A | 45.0 | 1:10.3 | variant: F2 F2 |
| Horse B | 45.1 | 1:11.0 | variant: S2 S2 |

The pacelines of the two contenders were earned under quite dissimilar conditions. Horse A earned its clocking on a track that was considered "Fast 2" (tenths) at the second call and "Fast 2" (lengths) at the final call. Horse B, however, earned its figures over a track considered "Slow 2—Slow 2."

So, what effect do the variants have on the chances of our two contenders? The adjusted clockings:

Horse A   45.0   1:10.3
    Adjusted: F2 fractional variant = 1 length (two tenths = one fifth)
            F2 final variant = 2 lengths
  Revised times: **45.1   1:11.0**

Horse B   45.1   1:11.0
    Adjusted: S2 fractional variant = 1 length (two tenths = one fifth)
            S2 final variant = 2 lengths
  Revised times: **45.0   1:10.3**

| Horse A | 45.1 | 1:11.0 |
| Horse B | 45.0 | 1:10.3 |

Anybody want to "send it in" on Horse A?

This situation is not atypical. Varying track speed is a fact of racetrack life, and handicappers able to accurately assess the degree of fluctuation have an enormous edge. As the money pours in on Horse A, the value on B grows proportionately. It happens every day, at every track.

In this chapter we'll develop a step-by-step procedure for assessing daily variations in track speed.

Our tools will be the pars we developed in the previous two

chapters. We will continue to use tenths of seconds for fractional times.

Our basic task: to relate actual performance to class pace and speed pars.

The degree that pars and actual performance *differ* will constitute the variant for that day.

The procedure is not difficult. It is, however, a bit like strolling through a mine field. There are traps all along the way that, if not carefully considered, can introduce more than a little error to the figures. I advise the reader not to abandon logic and common sense for the sake of format.

PROCEDURE

We'll be constructing variants for two days from the 1989 Hollywood Park Summer meeting; 3Jly89 and 4Jly89. The procedure:

(1) Determine the appropriate par for each race.
(2) Compare performance in each race to par.
(3) Evaluate apparent inconsistencies.
(4) Assign the daily variants for sprints and routes, usually by averaging the differences between par and actual performance. Emphasis, in order of importance, should be placed on:
  (a) older male claiming races
  (b) older female claiming races

3JLY89 SPRINTS

SECOND RACE
Hollywood
JULY 3, 1989

6 FURLONGS. (1.08) CLAIMING. Purse $11,000. Fillies and mares. 4-year-olds and upward. Weight, 121 lbs. Non-winners of two races since May 14 allowed 3 lbs.; a race since then, 6 lbs. Claiming price $10,000.

Value of race $11,000; value to winner $6,050; second $2,200; third $1,650; fourth $825; fifth $275. Mutuel pool $400,443.

Last Raced	Horse	Eqt.A.Wt	PP	St	¼	½	Str	Fin	Jockey	Cl'g Pr	Odds $1
11Jun89 ^{2}Hol^{2}	Princess Tobin	b 4 118	11	3	3½	3^{1}	2^{1½}	1^{1½}	Castanon A L	10000	2.10
22Jun89 ^{1}Hol^{3}	Nellie Melba	5 115	9	1	1^{hd}	2^{hd}	1½	2^{2½}	Baze R A	10000	3.70
30Nov88 ^{3}Hol^{7}	Princess Deborah	b 4 115	2	4	4^{1½}	4^{1½}	3½	3^{3½}	Sibille R	10000	9.70
14Jun89 ^{11}Stk^{2}	Sabinal Rose	b 4 115	5	11	9^{1½}	7^{hd}	5^{1½}	4^{2}	Fernandez A L	10000	41.60
10Jun89 ^{1}Hol^{7}	Bitatron	b 5 110	6	6	5^{hd}	5^{hd}	6½	5½	Nakatani C S^{5}	10000	6.70
23Jun89 ^{5}Hol^{7}	Kamakhaylyn	b 6 118	3	9	10^{hd}	10^{1½}	7^{1}	6^{hd}	Cedeno A	10000	38.60
8Mar89 ^{1}SA^{12}	Cat Sneaker	4 110	10	2	2^{1½}	1^{hd}	4^{2}	7^{hd}	Garcia H J^{5}	10000	12.70
18May89 ^{1}Hol^{9}	Sparkle Bright	4 110	8	7	7^{1}	6½	8^{1½}	8^{hd}	Meza M D^{5}	10000	46.30
31May89 ^{9}Hol^{4}	Sweetness	b 6 115	7	10	11	11	10^{1½}	9^{2½}	Stevens G L	10000	7.40
18May89 ^{1}Hol^{12}	Northern Edge	4 115	1	8	8^{hd}	8^{1}	9^{hd}	10^{2¾}	Gutierrez St	10000	53.90
17Dec88 ^{8}Mex^{4}	Renatta	b 5 117	4	5	6½	9^{1}	11	11	Pincay L Jr	10000	5.30

OFF AT 2:06. Start good. Won driving. Time, :22⅘, :45⅘, :58⅕, 1:10⅗ Track fast.

THIRD RACE
Hollywood
JULY 3, 1989

6 ½ FURLONGS. (1.15) ALLOWANCE. Purse $31,000. Fillies and mares. 3-year-olds and upward. Non-winners of $3,000 twice other than maiden, claiming or starter. Weights, 3-year-olds, 116 lbs.; older, 122 lbs. Non-winners of such a race since May 1 allowed 2 lbs.; such a race since April 1, 4 lbs.

Value of race $31,000; value to winner $17,050; second $6,200; third $4,650; fourth $2,325; fifth $775. Mutuel pool $294,933, Minus show pool $7,243.25. Exacta pool $367,568.

Last Raced	Horse	Eqt.	A.	Wt	PP	St	¼	½	Str	Fin	Jockey	Odds $1
31May89 ^{7}Hol^1	Bistra		3	116	5	2	3^4	$1^{1\frac{1}{2}}$	1^{hd}	1^4	Baze R A	.40
11Jun89 ^{7}Hol^2	My Treat		3	114	2	3	1^{hd}	2^4	$2^{2\frac{1}{2}}$	$2^{2\frac{1}{2}}$	Black C A	9.10
17Jun89 ^{4}Hol^3	Hickory Crest		4	122	4	5	$4^{1\frac{1}{2}}$	$3^{\frac{1}{2}}$	3^3	$3^{3\frac{1}{2}}$	Pedroza M A	3.50
11Jun89 ^{8}GG^7	Super Misty		3	112	6	1	$5^{3\frac{1}{2}}$	$4^{\frac{1}{2}}$	4^4	4^4	Davis R G	20.10
10Jun89 ^{6}Hol^7	Beware Of The Cat	b	3	116	3	6	6	6	6	$5^{2\frac{1}{2}}$	Stevens G L	10.20
17Jun89 ^{4}Hol^6	J. D's Star	b	4	118	1	4	2^{hd}	5^4	5^1	6	Valenzuela P A	29.50

OFF AT 2:38. Start good. Won ridden out. Time, :21⅘, :43⅘, 1:08⅘, 1:15⅕ Track fast.

FOURTH RACE
Hollywood
JULY 3, 1989

7 FURLONGS. (1.20⅘) CLAIMING. Purse $20,000. 3-year-olds. Weight, 122 lbs. Non-winners of two races since May 14 allowed 3 lbs.; a race since then, 6 lbs. Claiming price $32,000; for each $2,000 to $28,000, allowed 2 lbs. (Races when entered for $25,000 or less not considered.)

Value of race $20,000; value to winner $11,000; second $4,000; third $3,000; fourth $1,500; fifth $500. Mutuel pool $324,822. Exacta pool $375,778.

Last Raced	Horse	Eqt.	A.	Wt	PP	St	¼	½	Str	Fin	Jockey	Cl'g Pr	Odds $1
24Jun89 ^{3}Hol^7	By No Means	b	3	116	7	3	$1^{1\frac{1}{2}}$	1^1	$1^{2\frac{1}{2}}$	$1^{1\frac{1}{2}}$	Solis A	32000	22.90
21Jun89 ^{3}Hol^2	American Force		3	116	8	1	$4^{\frac{1}{2}}$	$3^{\frac{1}{2}}$	$2^{1\frac{1}{2}}$	$2^{2\frac{1}{2}}$	Delahoussaye E	28000	11.30
11Jun89 ^{5}Hol^4	Colorful Hitter		3	116	9	2	$6^{1\frac{1}{2}}$	$5^{1\frac{1}{2}}$	3^2	$3^{3\frac{1}{2}}$	Pedroza M A	32000	3.50
15Jun89 ^{9}Hol^4	Sum Dandy		3	116	4	6	2^{hd}	2^1	5^1	4^1	Baze R A	32000	9.00
24Jun89 ^{3}Hol^6	Restless Galaxy	b	3	115	1	8	8	7^3	$4^{\frac{1}{2}}$	$5^{\frac{1}{2}}$	Davis R G	28000	3.80
2Jun89 ^{1}Hol^1	Agiwin	b	3	119	2	7	7^{hd}	8	$6^{1\frac{1}{2}}$	6^3	Stevens G L	32000	13.70
21Jun89 ^{3}Hol^1	Catfish Purdy	b	3	116	5	4	3^{hd}	4^{hd}	$7^{1\frac{1}{2}}$	$7^{1\frac{1}{2}}$	Black C A	32000	2.50
15Jun89 ^{6}Hol^1	Classy Player	b	3	119	6	5	$5^{1\frac{1}{2}}$	$6^{\frac{1}{2}}$	8	8	Pincay L Jr	32000	6.20
17Jun89 ^{10}GG^8	Waltzing Sass	b	3	116	3	—	—	—	—	—	Sibille R	32000	22.00

Waltzing Sass, Lost rider.

OFF AT 3:10. Start good for all but WALTZING SASS. Won driving. Time, :22, :44⅘, 1:09⅘, 1:22⅘ Track fast.

FIFTH RACE
Hollywood
JULY 3, 1989

6 FURLONGS. (1.08) CLAIMING. Purse $22,000. 4-year-olds and upward. Weight, 122 lbs. Non-winners of two races since May 14 allowed 3 lbs.; a race since then, 5 lbs. Claiming price $40,000; for each $2,500 to $35,000 allowed 1 lb. (Races when entered for $32,000 or less not considered.)

Value of race $22,000; value to winner $12,100; second $4,400; third $3,300; fourth $1,650; fifth $550. Mutuel pool $359,333. Exacta pool $375,197.

Last Raced	Horse	Eqt.	A.	Wt	PP	St	¼	½	Str	Fin	Jockey	Cl'g Pr	Odds $1
24Jun89 ^{5}Hol^3	High Hook		7	117	7	6	6^4	$6^{1\frac{1}{2}}$	4^1	$1^{3\frac{1}{2}}$	Delahoussaye E	40000	2.00
24Jun89 ^{5}Hol^5	Mehmetski		4	117	6	7	7	7	6^4	2^4	Solis A	40000	11.00
22Jun89 ^{7}Hol^2	Rich Tiger	b	4	117	1	3	$4^{\frac{1}{2}}$	4^4	$3^{\frac{1}{2}}$	$3^{\frac{1}{2}}$	Pedroza M A	40000	14.70
31May89 ^{5}Hol^2	Pialor	b	6	117	3	1	$2^{2\frac{1}{2}}$	1^{hd}	1^1	4^2	Olivares F	40000	2.30
17May89 ^{3}Hol^6	Going Easy	b	4	117	5	5	3^{hd}	$3^{\frac{1}{2}}$	5^1	$5^{\frac{1}{2}}$	Baze R A	40000	49.70
11Jun89 ^{3}Hol^5	Eighty Below Zero	b	6	112	2	2	1^{hd}	$2^{1\frac{1}{2}}$	2^{hd}	6^5	Nakatani C S^5	40000	*2.00
25Jun89 ^{3}Hol^6	Circumstantial	b	4	117	4	4	5^4	5^1	7	7	Valenzuela P A	40000	14.10

*—Actual Betting Favorite.

OFF AT 3:45. Start good. Won ridden out. Time, :21⅘, :44⅘, :57⅕, 1:09 Track fast.

SIXTH RACE
Hollywood
JULY 3, 1989

6 FURLONGS. (1.08) MAIDEN. Purse $26,000. Fillies. 2-year-olds. Bred in California. Weight, 117 lbs.

Value of race $26,000; value to winner $14,300; second $5,200; third $3,900; fourth $1,950; fifth $650. Mutuel pool $382,828.

Last Raced	Horse	Eqt.	A.	Wt	PP	St	¼	½	Str	Fin	Jockey	Odds $1
	Roman Point		2	117	6	5	$1^{\frac{1}{2}}$	$2^{1\frac{1}{2}}$	1^1	1^{nk}	Solis A	20.20

16Jun89 ^{6}Hol^{7}	Never A Fee		2 117	8	1	5^{4}	$1\frac{1}{2}$	$2^{1\frac{1}{2}}$	$2\frac{1}{2}$	Cedeno A	12.30
21Jun89 ^{4}Hol^{4}	Saros Treasure	b	2 117	3	3	$4^{1\frac{1}{2}}$	$3\frac{1}{2}$	3^{2}	$3^{2\frac{1}{2}}$	Pedroza M A	1.30
2Jun89 ^{4}Hol^{6}	Florala's Belle		2 117	4	4	3^{hd}	$5^{1\frac{1}{2}}$	$4^{1\frac{1}{2}}$	$4^{4\frac{1}{2}}$	Delahoussaye E	3.50
16Jun89 ^{6}Hol^{3}	Swing Time Gal		2 117	2	7	6^{hd}	$6^{1\frac{1}{2}}$	5^{5}	$5^{5\frac{1}{2}}$	Stevens G L	2.60
9Jun89 ^{6}Hol^{2}	Ararat	b	2 117	1	6	7^{5}	7^{5}	$6^{3\frac{1}{2}}$	6^{3}	Meza R Q	9.90
	Howdy Lynn		2 117	7	2	$2\frac{1}{2}$	4^{1}	7^{1}	7^{1}	Black C A	28.10
	Hartman's Harmony		2 117	5	8	8	8	8	8	Fernandez A L	76.60

OFF AT 4:18. Start good. Won driving. Time, :22⅕, :46, :58⅗, 1:11⅗ Track fast.

SEVENTH RACE
Hollywood
JULY 3, 1989

6 FURLONGS. (1.08) ALLOWANCE. Purse $31,000. 3-year-olds and upward which have not won $3,000 twice other than maiden, claiming or starter. Weights, 3-year-olds, 116 lbs.; older, 122 lbs. Non-winners of such a race since May 1 allowed 2 lbs.; such a race since April 1, 4 lbs.

Value of race $31,000; value to winner $17,050; second $6,200; third $4,650; fourth $2,325; fifth $775. Mutuel pool $355,040. Exacta pool $389,116.

Last Raced	Horse	Eqt.	A.Wt	PP	St	¼	½	Str	Fin	Jockey	Odds $1
7Jun89 ^{7}Hol^{1}	Winchester Drive		4 122	5	3	$2^{1\frac{1}{2}}$	1^{hd}	1^{hd}	$1\frac{1}{2}$	Delahoussaye E	4.20
20Dec88 ^{3}Hol^{2}	Time For Accuracy		5 118	4	6	5^{2}	4^{2}	$3\frac{1}{2}$	2^{hd}	McCarron C J	6.70
14Jun89 ^{7}Hol^{6}	Bag Of Magic	b	4 122	2	4	1^{hd}	2^{1}	$2^{1\frac{1}{2}}$	$3^{1\frac{1}{2}}$	Black C A	8.30
18Dec88 ^{8}Hol^{10}	Queen Mary's Boy		3 112	7	2	4^{hd}	3^{hd}	$4^{1\frac{1}{2}}$	$4\frac{3}{4}$	Solis A	10.70
17Jun89 ^{5}Hol^{1}	Heroic Type		3 116	6	1	6^{3}	5^{3}	$5^{2\frac{1}{2}}$	$5^{2\frac{1}{2}}$	Stevens G L	2.20
10Jun89 ^{7}Hol^{1}	Good Deliverance		4 118	3	7	7	$6^{1\frac{1}{2}}$	6^{8}	6^{17}	Pincay L Jr	1.90
25Jun89 ^{9}Hol^{10}	Short Order		4 113	1	5	$3\frac{1}{2}$	7	7	7	Nakatani C S^{5}	31.80

OFF AT 4:50. Start good. Won driving. Time, :22, :45, :57, 1:09⅗ Track fast.

Three-Year-Old Adjustments

	6F	7F	8F	8½F	9F	
+9					Jan 1	+9
+8					Feb 1	+8
+7				Jan 1	Mar 15	+7
+6				Feb 15	May 1	+6
+5			Jan 1	Apr 15	Jun 1	+5
+4		Jan 1	Apr 15	Jun 1	Jly 1	+4
+3	Jan 1	Mar 15	Jun 1	Aug 1	Sep 1	+3
+2	Apr 15	Jun 15	Aug 15			+2
+1	Jly 1	Aug 15				+1

Adjustments for Females

Sprints: 2 lengths

Routes: 4 lengths in claiming races

3 lengths in nonclaiming races

Hollywood Sprint Pars

Class											
Stks	111	6F	44.2	1:08.3	6½F	44.0	1:14.4	7F	44.0	1:20.4	112
Cl Alw	109	6F	44.3	1:08.4	6½F	44.1	1:15.1	7F	44.1	1:21.1	110
NW3 Alw	108	6F	44.4	1:09.0	6½F	44.2	1:15.2	7F	44.2	1:21.2	109
NW2 Alw	107	6F	44.5	1:09.1	6½F	44.3	1:15.3	7F	44.3	1:21.3	108
NW1 Alw	105	6F	44.7	1:09.3	6½F	44.5	1:16.0	7F	44.5	1:22.0	106
Maiden	103	6F	44.9	1:10.0	6½F	44.7	1:16.2	7F	44.7	1:22.3	103
50,000	107	6F	44.5	1:09.1	6½F	44.3	1:15.3	7F	44.3	1:21.3	108
40,000	106	6F	44.6	1:09.2	6½F	44.4	1:15.4	7F	44.4	1:21.4	107
32,000	105	6F	44.7	1:09.3	6½F	44.5	1:16.0	7F	44.5	1:22.0	106
25,000	104	6F	44.8	1:09.4	6½F	44.6	1:16.1	7F	44.6	1:22.2	104
20,000	103	6F	44.9	1:10.0	6½F	44.7	1:16.2	7F	44.7	1:22.3	103
16,000	102	6F	45.0	1:10.1	6½F	44.8	1:16.3	7F	44.8	1:22.4	102
12,500	101	6F	45.1	1:10.2	6½F	44.9	1:16.4	7F	44.9	1:23.0	101
10,000	100	6F	45.2	1:10.3	6½F	45.0	1:17.0	7F	45.0	1:23.1	100
Mdn 50K	100	6F	45.2	1:10.3	6½F	45.0	1:17.0	7F	45.0	1:23.1	100
Mdn 32K	98	6F	45.4	1:11.0	6½F	45.2	1:17.2	7F	45.3	1:23.4	97

3Jly89 Sprints

Race 2: 6 furlongs for $10,000 older female claimers
Par: Older males 45.2   1:10.3 + 2 length female adjustment
Revised par: 45.4   1:11.0
Performance: 45.8   1:10.3
Fractional differential: S4 (fractions are in tenths)
Final differential: F2

Race 3: 6½ furlongs for NW2 allowance females
Par: Older males 44.3   1:15.3 + 2 lengths female adjustment
Revised par: 44.5   1:16.0
Performance: 43.6   1:15.1
Fractional differential: F9
Final differential: F4

Race 4: 7 furlongs for $32,000 3-yr.-old males
Par: Older males 44.5   1:22.1 + 2 lengths (age adjustment Jun
         15–Aug 15)
Revised par: 44.7   1:22.3
Performance: 44.6   1:22.2
Fractional differential: F1
Final differential: F1

Race 5: 6 furlongs for $40,000 older males
Par: Older males 44.6   1:09.2
Revised par: no adjustment necessary
Performance: 44.6   1:09.0
Fractional differential: 0
Final differential: F2

Race 6: We will avoid using two-year-olds to construct our variants. Younger horses and maiden claimers are to be avoided whenever possible. You will, however, be forced to consider maiden claiming races on days when there is little data with which to work.

Race 7: 6 furlongs for NW2 allowance males

Par: Older males 44.5   1:09.1

Revised par: no adjustment necessary

Performance: 45.0   1:09.3

Fractional differential: S5

Final differential: S2

3Jly89 Sprint Summary

	Par	Actual	Var: Fraction	Final
(2)	45.4 1:11.0	45.8 1:10.3	S4	F2
(3)	44.5 1:16.0	43.6 1:15.1	F9	F4
(4)	44.7 1:22.3	44.6 1:22.2	F1	F1
(5)	44.6 1:09.2	44.6 1:09.0	0	F2
(7)	44.5 1:09.1	45.0 1:09.3	S5	S2

The next step is to evaluate inconsistencies. The initial final time variant is Fast 1.4 (the average of all races), but the bulk of the raw data indicates Fast 2 as a reasonable figure. Let's try and resolve the inconsistency.

Race 3: F9 F4. A powerful win off *exceptional* internal fractions. The winner drew away late, stringing out the field in the process. That's usually the sign of a strong race for the class level.

The opposite is also true. Four or more horses involved in a tight finish usually indicates a weak race for the level.

When the indication is a powerful performance, there are two solid approaches to handling the variant:

1. If the winning margin is 5 *lengths or less*, adjust the winner's margin to 2 lengths; the proven long-term data on the average margin of race winners. Also revise the time of the race accordingly. In the Fourth race, reduce Bistra's winning margin to 2 lengths and adjust the final time by the same amount.

Race 3: 1:15.1 When we reduce the winning margin from 4 to 2 lengths, final time must be adjusted by the same amount: two fifths. Revised: 1:15.3 F2

"Fast 2" for this race supports the data from races 2, 3, and

5, and when averaged with all races, further indicates a Fast 1 variant for the day.

2. An alternate approach is to assume the class of the race to be the next higher level on the class ladder. The Third race should be reevaluated as an NW3:

Par (NW3): 44.2   1:15.2 + 2 lengths female adjustment =

44.4   1:15.4

Actual: 43.6   1:15.1

Differential: *F8 F3*

Depending on the situation, I employ both methods. The first approach is usually preferable, but can become unmanageable when there's a runaway winner. Too often, when a horse draws off to a winning margin *beyond 5 lengths*, the riders of the other horses tend to ease their mounts, falling farther back than necessary. As a result, beaten lengths are superficially inflated and unsatisfactory for our use.

We'll adjust the beaten lengths for Race 3 and settle on Fast 2 for the race.

Race 7: S5 S2. The *opposite* situation. On a day when other races indicate a fast track, a single race points to another conclusion. That's not unusual. Virtually every day features at least one race that does not conform to expected pars. If we average the Seventh race with the others, we could negatively effect what may be an F2 variant. Fast 1.4 rounds to 1 *length* and may introduce an error of 1 length to our figures. We can often do better.

The first five horses in the Seventh race finished within 3 lengths at the wire, usually the sign of a race weaker than par. When you suspect a weak race for any class level, don't hesitate to use the par from the next lower level on the class ladder. In this case, use the NW1 par and reevaluate the race.

NW1 Par: 44.7   1:09.3

Race 7:   45.0   1:09.3

Differential: S3   0

Similarly, when evaluating a restricted stakes race comprised of horses eligible for nonwinners allowances, use the allowance par if the race looks out of line. In short, use a little judgment and common sense, and you won't go far wrong. With experience, you'll make the right call often enough to produce usable variants.

Now to finish the sprint variant using the revised data:

	Par	Actual	Var: Fraction	Final
(2)	45.4 1:11.0	45.8 1:10.3	S4	F2
(3)	44.4 1:15.3	43.6 1:15.1	F8	F2
(4)	44.7 1:22.3	44.6 1:22.2	F1	F1
(5)	44.6 1:09.2	44.6 1:09.0	0	F2
(7)	44.7 1:09.3	45.0 1:09.3	S3	0

In this particular example, there is no change to the average: Total Fast 7 divided by five races=Fast 1.4. Rounded to the nearest whole number, the variant becomes *Fast 1* for the day.

Finally, when working with limited data, consider the claiming races for older horses, especially males, as most important to the procedure. Par charts are based on data from those races because the tendency toward par is greater than with younger or nonclaiming horses. Older claimers have sorted themselves by class and performance and, unlike nonwinners allowance runners, few will go on to stardom. Their running times are highly reliable.

With five races to work from, however, we're probably on solid ground with our Fast 1 designation for 3Jly89.

The fractional variant for the day is the total of fast races F9 less the slow races S7 divided by five races = Fast .4 or 0.

3Jly89 Sprint Variant = 0 F1

RACE SHAPES AND THE HANDICAPPER'S NOTEBOOK

In *Thoroughbred Handicapping—State of the Art*, William Quirin presented an excellent discussion on "race shapes," the normal configurations of pace scenarios in thoroughbred races. The material is insightful and highly beneficial to handicappers employing pace analysis as basic handicapping methodology.

Quirin designated nine individual possibilities for "race shapes":

(1) Slow-Slow (slow at the fractional call–slow at the final call)
(2) Slow-Average
(3) Slow-Fast
(4) Average-Slow
(5) Average-Average
(6) Average-Fast
(7) Fast-Slow
(8) Fast-Average
(9) Fast-Fast

Definitions for Fast and Slow:

	2Call Fast/Slow	*Final Fast/Slow*
Sprints:	2 lengths (4 tenths)	2 lengths
Routes:	3 lengths (6 tenths)	3 lengths

As we record data from each racing day, we will also adjust individual races by the variant and, using Quirin's guidelines, designate the "shape" of each race.

The result of this exercise will be a highly productive Horses to Watch list. Horses exiting a Fast-Fast race, especially claimers, are among the best bets at any racetrack, and often at generous odds. Why not take advantage of the insights gained from constructing daily variants and identify possible key races in advance? The traditional approach is to wait for multiple winners from one of these races and then bet the remaining runners. By then it's too late to take full advantage of those races. You'll be surprised at how many races you'll identify *before* they're generally recognized as key races.

The 3Jly89 Entries in the Handicapper's Notebook

(Races adjusted by the daily variant):

	Par	Adjusted Race	Fraction	Final	Shape
(2)	45.4 1:11.0	45.8 1:10.4	S4	F1	S–A
(3)	44.5 1:16.0	43.6 1:15.2	F9	F3 *1	F–F
(4)	44.7 1:22.3	44.6 1:22.3	F1	0	A–A
(5)	44.6 1:09.2	44.6 1:09.1	0	F1	A–A
(6)	2-yr.-olds	46.0 1:12.0	x	x	x
(7)	44.5 1:09.1	45.0 1:09.4	S5	S3 *2	S–S

3Jly89 Sprint Variant = 0 F1

*1 Bistra's performance exceeded the race par by 4½ lengths at the second call and 3 lengths at the finish; an impressive Fast-Fast performance. She has already exceeded the pace and speed requirements for the next class level and should be included on a Horses to Watch list.

My Treat should also be added to the list. She forced a blistering pace and kept trying throughout, finishing well clear of the third horse. She was still challenging the winner at the stretch call before tiring late. (She won her next start at 7–2 odds!)

*2 Horses coming out of the Seventh race should be avoided in virtually all situations. The shape of the race was Slow-Slow, and any runner from the race should need a sharp drop in class to be competitive in its next start. (All but Good Deliverance ran poorly in subsequent races.)

4JLY89 SPRINTS

Before we calculate route variants, let's complete another day's worth of sprints. The following day, July 4, featured four sprint races.

FIRST RACE
Hollywood
JULY 4, 1989

6 ½ FURLONGS. (1.15) CLAIMING. Purse $11,000. 4-year-olds and upward. Weight, 121 lbs. Non-winners of two races since May 14 allowed 3 lbs.; a race since then, 5 lbs. Claiming price $10,000. 52nd DAY. WEATHER CLEAR. TEMPERATURE 87 DEGREES.

Value of race $11,000; value to winner $6,050; second $2,200; third $1,650; fourth $825; fifth $275. Mutuel pool $389,563.

Last Raced	Horse	Eqt.A.Wt PP St	¼	½	Str	Fin	Jockey	Cl'g Pr	Odds $1
18Jun89 10Pre1	Sandy Mack	b 7 118 12 1	1hd	1½	11	11¾	Desilva A J	10000	8.90
18Jun89 1Hol8	Chary Joy	4 116 11 6	7¼	7²	6¹	2¾	Sorenson D	10000	13.30
16Jun89 1Hol6	Wined Out	b 5 116 5 3	3¹	3hd	2¹½	3¹½	Delahoussaye E	10000	5.10
18Jun89 1Hol3	Smilin' Smiley	b 4 116 1 11	4hd	5hd	4¹½	4hd	Baze R A	10000	8.30
22Jun89 5Hol8	Triteguos	6 111 9 2	5¹	2¹	3½	5¹	Nakatani C S5	10000	7.10
18Jun89 1Hol5	Purr Fect Ideal	4 111 7 9	10hd	11¹¹	8½	6²	Garcia H J5	10000	19.40
18Jun89 1Hol1	Matthew T. Parker	7 113 6 5	6¾	6¹	7¹	7½	Jauregui L H5	10000	6.70

18Jun89 ^{1}Hol^{4}	Blaze Flame	b	7	116	10	7	$11^{\frac{1}{2}}$	$10^{1\frac{1}{2}}$	$9^{\frac{1}{2}}$	8^{nk}	Stevens G L	10000	3.10
8Jan89 ^{1}SA^{8}	Petronack	b	5	116	4	10	8^{hd}	9^{hd}	10^{1}	9^{hd}	Cedeno A	10000	24.60
22Jun89 ^{5}Hol^{7}	Roll A Natural	b	9	116	3	4	$2^{\frac{1}{2}}$	4^{1}	$5^{\frac{1}{2}}$	$10^{1\frac{1}{2}}$	Solis A	10000	11.30
18Jun89 ^{1}Hol^{6}	Jose Sent Me	b	6	116	2	12	$9^{1\frac{1}{2}}$	$8^{\frac{1}{2}}$	$11^{3\frac{1}{2}}$	11^{5}	Valenzuela F H	10000	16.20
28May89 ^{1}GF^{1}	Laurieloy		5	113	8	8	12	12	12	12	Meza M D^{5}	10000	44.70

OFF AT 1:33. Start good. Won driving. Time, :22, :45$\frac{1}{5}$, 1:10$\frac{1}{5}$, 1:16$\frac{3}{5}$ Track fast.

SECOND RACE
Hollywood
JULY 4, 1989

6 FURLONGS. (1.08) CLAIMING. Purse $13,000. Fillies and mares. 4-year-olds and upward. Weight, 122 lbs. Non-winners of two races since May 14 allowed 3 lbs.; a race since then, 6 lbs. Claiming price $16,000; if entered for $14,000, allowed 2 lbs. (Races when entered for $12,500 or less not considered.)

Value of race $13,000; value to winner $7,150; second $2,600; third $1,950; fourth $975; fifth $325. Mutuel pool $481,878.

Last Raced	Horse	Eqt	A	Wt	PP	St	¼	½	Str	Fin	Jockey	Cl'g Pr	Odds $1
23Jun89 ^{5}Hol^{1}	Trust Fund	b	5	116	10	1	3^{2}	$1^{\frac{1}{2}}$	$1^{1\frac{1}{2}}$	1^{1}	Davis R G	16000	7.10
24May89 ^{9}Hol^{11}	Lacrosse	b	4	116	8	7	$7^{\frac{1}{2}}$	6^{2}	$3^{\frac{1}{2}}$	2^{2}	Delahoussaye E	16000	4.40
2Jun89 ^{5}Hol^{2}	Our Ole Lady	b	4	116	9	6	5^{1}	4^{2}	$4^{1\frac{1}{2}}$	3^{nk}	Baze R A	16000	9.80
3Jun89 ^{5}Hol^{5}	Freedom In My Eyes	b	5	117	2	3	$1^{\frac{1}{2}}$	$2^{\frac{1}{2}}$	$2^{1\frac{1}{2}}$	$4^{\frac{1}{2}}$	Pincay L Jr	16000	3.40
23Jun89 ^{5}Hol^{3}	Sovereign Appeal		4	111	3	9	8^{2}	$7^{1\frac{1}{2}}$	$6^{\frac{1}{2}}$	$5^{\frac{1}{2}}$	Nakatani C S^{5}	16000	18.90
11Jun89 ^{2}Hol^{6}	Super Sisters		5	116	4	10	10	9^{1}	$7^{1\frac{1}{2}}$	$6^{1\frac{1}{2}}$	Valenzuela F H	16000	45.60
11Jun89 ^{2}Hol^{1}	Jaklin And Hide		5	114	7	8	$9^{1\frac{1}{2}}$	8^{hd}	8^{2}	$7^{1\frac{1}{2}}$	Jauregui L H^{5}	16000	3.00
11Jun89 ^{2}Hol^{3}	Lager	b	5	116	5	4	2^{hd}	3^{1}	5^{2}	8^{4}	Stevens G L	16000	4.90
22Jun89 ^{1}Hol^{2}	To Be Impressive	b	6	116	1	5	$4^{\frac{1}{2}}$	5^{1}	$9^{1\frac{1}{2}}$	9^{2}	Pedroza M A	16000	28.10
22Jun89 ^{1}Hol^{10}	Miss San Diego		6	109	6	2	$6^{2\frac{1}{2}}$	10	10	10	Meza M D^{5}	14000	27.70

OFF AT 2:06 Start good. Won driving. Time, :22, :45$\frac{1}{5}$, :57$\frac{3}{5}$, 1:10$\frac{3}{5}$ Track fast.

FOURTH RACE
Hollywood
JULY 4, 1989

6 FURLONGS. (1.08) MAIDEN CLAIMING. Purse $16,000. 3-year-olds and upward. Weights, 3-year-olds, 116 lbs.; older, 122 lbs. Claming price $32,000; if for $28,000 allowed 2 lbs.

Value of race $16,000; value to winner $8,800; second $3,200; third $2,400; fourth $1,200; fifth $400. Mutuel pool $407,759. Exacta pool $455,669.

Last Raced	Horse	Eqt	A	Wt	PP	St	¼	½	Str	Fin	Jockey	Cl'g Pr	Odds $1
	Ask The Man		3	116	10	2	2^{1}	$2^{3\frac{1}{2}}$	$1^{2\frac{1}{2}}$	$1^{6\frac{1}{2}}$	Sibille R	32000	5.10
3May89 ^{6}Hol^{7}	Chopem On The Bid	b	3	116	7	9	$11^{1\frac{1}{2}}$	9^{1}	$7^{1\frac{1}{2}}$	$2^{\frac{1}{2}}$	Olivares F	32000	43.50
2Jun89 ^{5}GG^{4}	B. J. Bucks	b	3	116	6	8	$6^{\frac{1}{2}}$	$6^{1\frac{1}{2}}$	5^{hd}	3^{hd}	Davis R G	32000	25.20
8Jun89 ^{2}Hol^{3}	Betsy's Bet	b	3	116	2	1	$1^{\frac{1}{2}}$	1^{hd}	2^{4}	4^{hd}	Stevens G L	32000	2.30
	Dramatic Mac		3	116	1	10	$7^{1\frac{1}{2}}$	$5^{1\frac{1}{2}}$	$3^{1\frac{1}{2}}$	$5^{4\frac{1}{2}}$	Valenzuela P A	32000	23.40
26May89 ^{6}Hol^{11}	Prince Paddy C.	b	3	116	3	12	$10^{\frac{1}{2}}$	7^{1}	8^{3}	6^{hd}	Valenzuela F H	32000	10.30
2Jun89 ^{5}GG^{3}	More Golden	b	3	116	5	3	$4^{2\frac{1}{2}}$	$3^{\frac{1}{2}}$	4^{hd}	7^{hd}	McCarron C J	32000	2.50
	Gray Manner	b	3	114	9	5	3^{hd}	$4^{2\frac{1}{2}}$	6^{1}	8^{4}	Pedroza M A	28000	16.80
	Norman's Mania		3	116	11	4	5^{1}	$8^{1\frac{1}{2}}$	$9^{1\frac{1}{2}}$	$9^{1\frac{1}{2}}$	Solis A	32000	25.10
10Nov88 ^{6}Hol^{5}	Double Tawdry	b	3	116	8	7	$9^{1\frac{1}{2}}$	$10^{1\frac{1}{2}}$	10^{2}	$10^{2\frac{1}{2}}$	Baze R A	32000	8.60
17Mar89 ^{4}SA^{9}	Joropo	b	3	111	4	11	12	$11^{2\frac{1}{2}}$	11^{4}	$11^{5\frac{1}{2}}$	Nakatani C S^{5}	32000	28.80
12Apr89 ^{2}SA^{9}	Fogarty Ynez	b	3	111	12	6	8^{1}	12	12	12	Jauregui L H^{5}	32000	61.30

OFF AT 3:16. Start good. Won ridden out. Time, :22$\frac{1}{5}$, :45$\frac{2}{5}$, :57$\frac{2}{5}$, 1:10$\frac{3}{5}$ Track fast.

SIXTH RACE
Hollywood
JULY 4, 1989

6 FURLONGS. (1.08) MAIDEN. Purse $26,000. 2-year-olds. Bred in California. Weight, 117 lbs.

Value of race $26,000; value to winner $14,300; second $5,200; third $3,900; fourth $1,950; fifth $650. Mutuel pool $455,682.

Last Raced	Horse	Eqt	A	Wt	PP	St	¼	½	Str	Fin	Jockey	Odds $1
23Jun89 ^{4}Hol^{4}	Danno		2	117	8	1	3^{hd}	$2^{1\frac{1}{2}}$	1^{hd}	$1^{\frac{1}{2}}$	McCarron C J	3.40
	Notconned	b	2	112	6	2	1^{hd}	1^{1}	$2^{2\frac{1}{2}}$	$2^{4\frac{1}{2}}$	Nakatani C S^{5}	3.40
	A. Sir Dancer	b	2	117	3	4	$4^{1\frac{1}{2}}$	$4^{\frac{1}{2}}$	$3^{\frac{1}{2}}$	$3^{\frac{3}{4}}$	Pincay L Jr	2.80
8Jun89 ^{4}Hol^{3}	Power Base	b	2	117	7	7	$7^{\frac{1}{2}}$	5^{1}	4^{5}	$4^{4\frac{1}{2}}$	Stevens G L	*2.80
	French Brig		2	117	2	5	$6^{\frac{1}{2}}$	7^{1}	$7^{1\frac{1}{2}}$	$5^{1\frac{1}{2}}$	Davis R G	16.60
23Jun89 ^{4}Hol^{5}	Wayman		2	117	5	3	$2^{1\frac{1}{2}}$	3^{hd}	$5^{1\frac{1}{2}}$	$6^{3\frac{1}{2}}$	Solis A	24.50
	Renegado I	b	2	117	1	6	5^{hd}	$6^{3\frac{1}{2}}$	$6^{\frac{1}{2}}$	7^{hd}	Sibille R	46.60
	Sugar Ray		2	117	4	8	8	8	8	8	Valenzuela P A	9.10

***—Actual Betting Favorite.**

OFF AT 4:24. Start good. Won driving. Time, :22$\frac{2}{5}$, :45$\frac{4}{5}$, :58$\frac{2}{5}$, 1:11 Track fast.

On 4Jly89 there were only two races that we'll consider reliable for our variants: the First, at 6½ furlongs for $10,000 older males; and the Third, at six furlongs for $16,000 older females. To expand the base, we'll also consider the Fourth race, a maiden claimer.

Race 1: 6½ furlongs for $10,000 older males

Par: 45.0   1:17.0

Revised par: no adjustment required

Performance: 45.2   1:16.3

Fractional differential: S2 (fractions are in tenths)

Final differential: F2

Race 2: 6 furlongs for $16,000 older females

Par: Older males 45.0   1:10.1 + 2 length female adjustment

Revised par: 45.2   1:10.3

Performance: 45.2   1:10.3

Fractional differential: 0

Final differential: 0

Race 4: 6 furlongs for $32,000 maiden claimers

Par: 45.4   1:11.0

Revised par: same

Performance: 45.4   1:10.2

Fractional differential: 0

Final differential: F3

Don't attempt to reduce the winning margin in this race to 2 lengths; that approach should be used for races with runners of established class. In maiden claiming races most of the entrants have no class/ability, and winners with any degree of talent often compile large winning margins.

Ask The Man *can* be reevaluated against the next class level (Maiden $50,000) without risking a distortion of the data. He seriously outclassed the culls in this race and belongs at least one level higher on the ladder. We'll reconsider the race and use the result as support for conclusions made from the more reliable races.

Race 6: Avoid 2-yr.-olds

4Jly89—Sprint Summary

Par	Actual	Var: Fraction	Final
(1) 45.0 1:17.0	45.2 1:16.3	S2	F2
(2) 45.2 1:10.3	45.2 1:10.3	0	0
(4) 45.4 1:11.0	45.4 1:10.2	0	F3

The average of the raw fractional and final variants from races 1 and 2 clearly supports the previous day's variant (0=F1). Rather than base our variant on just two races, let's also consider the maiden claiming race: Race 4.

When the runaway victory by Ask The Man in the Fourth race is added to the base, it supports the Fast 2 from Race 1. However, the raw variant does not allow for his easy win. Let's reconsider the race using the Mdn 50K par:

(4) 45.2   1:10.3   45.4   1:10.2   S2   F1

With the additional data, we'll confidently accept Fast 1 as the sprint variant for the day.

The 4Jly89 Entries in the Handicapper's Notebook

(Races are adjusted by the daily variant)

Par	Adjusted Race	Fraction	Final	Shape
(1) 45.0 1:17.0	45.2 1:16.4	S2	F1	A–A
(2) 45.4 1:10.3	45.2 1:10.4	F2	S1	A–A
(4) 45.4 1:11.0	45.4 1:10.3	0	F2	A–F
(6) 2-yr.-olds	45.8 1:11.1	x	x	x

```
4Jly89 Sprint Variant = 0 F1
```

3JLY89—ROUTES

FIRST RACE
Hollywood
JULY 3, 1989

1 1/16 MILES. (1.40) CLAIMING. Purse $13,000. Fillies and mares. 4-year-olds and upward. Weight, 122 lbs. Non-winners of two races at a mile or over since May 14 allowed 3 lbs.; such a race since then, 6 lbs. Claiming price $12,500; if for $10,500 allowed 2 lbs. (Races when entered for $9,000 or less not considered.) 51st DAY. WEATHER CLEAR. TEMPERATURE 85 DEGREES.

Value of race $13,000; value to winner $7,150; second $2,600; third $1,950; fourth $975; fifth $325. Mutuel pool $285,605.

Last Raced	Horse	Eqt.	A.	Wt	PP	St	¼	½	¾	Str	Fin	Jockey	Cl'g Pr	Odds $1
15Jun89 1Hol5	Vigora	b	5	111	7	8	71½	51	4hd	41½	1hd	Davenport C L5	12500	20.80
3Jun89 5Hol4	Sexy Naskra	b	4	116	3	2	2hd	2½	32½	2½	2hd	Black C A	12500	4.70
23Jun89 5Hol5	John's Lady Luck	b	5	116	9	9	81	7½	86	5hd	3¾	Davis R G	12500	3.10
15Jun89 1Hol3	No Se Porque		4	119	1	3	32½	32½	2hd	31	4no	Baze R A	12500	2.20
21Jun89 1Hol7	Exploded's Girl		4	114	4	1	11½	11	11½	1hd	51½	Pedroza M A	10500	17.40
21Jun89 1Hol1	Cozy Road		4	119	5	5	6½	82½	71	62½	6nk	Pincay L Jr	12500	4.60
11Jun89 2Hol10	Maybe Maybenot		5	116	6	6	5hd	61½	6½	7hd	74	Dominguez R E	12500	25.70
1Jun89 2Hol2	Wyoming		4	116	2	4	42½	4hd	5hd	86	86½	Delahoussaye E	12500	7.60
23Jun89 5Hol6	Topside		4	115	8	7	9	9	9	9	9	Valenzuela F H	10500	32.50

OFF AT 1:31. Start good. Won driving. Time, :23⅗, :47⅘, 1:12⅕, 1:38⅘, 1:45⅘ Track fast.

EIGHTH RACE
Hollywood
JULY 3, 1989

1 ⅛ MILES. (1.46⅘) 11th Running of THE SILVER SCREEN HANDICAP (Grade II.) $150,000 added. 3-year-olds. By subscription of $100 each, which shall accompany the nomination, $1,500 additional to start, with $150,000 added, of which $30,000 to second, $22,500 to third, $11,250 to fourth and $3,750 to fifth. Weights, Wednesday, June 28. SHOULD THE WINNER OF EITHER THE KENTUCKY DERBY, THE PREAKNESS OR THE BELMONT BE A STARTER, THE ADDED MONEY WILL BE INCREASED TO $300,000. Starters to be named through the entry box by closing time of entries. Hollywood Park reserves the right not to divide this race. Should this race not be divided and the number of entries exceed the starting gate capacity, highweights on the scale will be preferred and an also eligible list will be drawn. Total earnings in 1989 will be used in determining the order of preference of horses assigned equal weight on the scale. Failure to draw into this race at scratch time cancels all fees. Trophies will be presented to the winning owner, trainer and jockey. Closed Wednesday, June 21, with 17 nominations.

Value of race $163,700; value to winner $102,200; second $30,000; third $22,500; fourth $11,250; fifth $3,750. Mutuel pool $435,871. Exacta pool $415,374.

Last Raced	Horse	Eqt.	A.	Wt	PP	St	¼	½	¾	Str	Fin	Jockey	Odds $1
11Jun89 8Hol1	Raise A Stanza	b	3	115	9	2	2½	21½	3hd	21	1½	Black C A	37.30
11Jun89 8Hol6	Broke The Mold		3	112	8	1	31½	31½	11	11	21¾	Pedroza M A	a-14.60
8Mar89 8SA1	Prized		3	116	2	8	8½	91	7hd	4hd	31	Delahoussaye E	2.30
25May89 8Hol2	Lode		3	115	6	4	5hd	5hd	5hd	62	43	McCarron C J	4.50
11Jun89 8Hol4	Advocate Training		3	115	7	3	11	1hd	2hd	32½	5¾	Baze R A	b-16.90
2Jun89 8Hol2	Annual Date	b	3	115	5	9	93	72	62½	71½	62	Sibille R	b-16.90
27May89 7Spt3	Endow		3	120	11	7	41	41	42½	5½	7¾	Stevens G L	2.60
2Jun89 8Hol3	Runaway Dunaway		3	110	12	10	115	115	92	9hd	8no	Dominguez R E	39.30
20May89 8GG3	Timeless Answer	b	3	113	4	5	61½	6hd	102	102½	9¾	Davis R G	8.00
11Jun89 8Hol2	Exemplary Leader		3	116	3	12	10hd	101½	8½	81½	102¾	Valenzuela P A	a-14.60
2Jun89 9GG1	Strung Up	b	3	112	10	11	12	12	12	119	1110	Solis A	60.10
23Jun89 8Hol2	Malagra		3	113	1	6	7hd	8hd	111½	12	12	Cortez A	6.30

a-Coupled: Broke The Mold and Exemplary Leader; b-Advocate Training and Annual Date.

OFF AT 5:21. Start good for all but EXEMPLARY LEADER. Won driving. Time, :23⅕, :46⅘, 1:10⅘, 1:35⅘, 1:48⅘

NINTH RACE
Hollywood
JULY 3, 1989

1 1/16 MILES.(Turf). (1.38⅘) CLAIMING (Chute start). Purse $42,000. 4-year-olds and upward. Weight, 122 lbs. Non-winners of two races at a mile or over since May 7 allowed 3 lbs.; such a race since then, 5 lbs. Claiming price $150,000; for each $5,000 to $125,000 allowed 1 lb. (Races when entered for $100,000 or less not considered.)

Value of race $42,000; value to winner $23,100; second $8,400; third $6,300; fourth $3,150; fifth $1,050. Mutuel pool $365,064. Exacta pool $466,470.

Last Raced	Horse	Eqt.	A.	Wt	PP	St	¼	½	¾	Str	Fin	Jockey	Cl'g Pr	Odds $1
27May89 9Hol3	Captain Vigors		7	117	6	4	11½	11	11	11½	12	Toro F	150000	3.80
9Jun89 8Hol4	Days Gone By		5	116	2	6	6½	7	5hd	3½	2½	DelahoussyeE	145000	5.70
9Jun89 8Hol2	Individualist	b	6	112	7	5	41½	21	21½	21½	3no	Davis R G	125000	4.50
17Jun89 8Hol1	Rufjan	b	6	117	5	3	51	5hd	7	62½	4no	Pincay L Jr	150000	2.70
27May89 9Hol4	Good Taste		7	117	3	2	2hd	3½	41½	51½	54	Stevens G L	150000	7.50
11Jun89 9Hol5	Bel Air Dancer	b	4	113	1	1	3½	42	3½	4hd	62½	Black C A	125000	20.50
27May89 9Hol5	Five Daddy Five	b	5	117	4	7	7	6hd	61½	7	7	Solis A	150000	3.50

OFF AT 5:53. Start good. Won driving. Time, :24⅘, :48, 1:11⅗, 1:35, 1:41⅗ Course firm.

Hollywood Route Pars

Stks	113	44.9	1:09.3	1:34.0	45.9	1:10.3	1:41.4	1:48.0	114
Cl Alw	111	45.0	1:09.5	1:34.2	46.0	1:10.5	1:42.1	1:48.2	112
NW3 Alw	110	45.1	1:09.6	1:34.3	46.1	1:10.6	1:42.2	1:48.3	111
NW2 Alw	108	45.2	1:09.8	1:35.0	46.2	1:10.8	1:42.4	1:49.0	109
NW1 Alw	106	45.3	1:10.0	1:35.2	46.3	1:11.0	1:43.1	1:49.2	107
Maiden	104	45.4	1:10.2	1:35.4	46.4	1:11.2	1:43.3	1:50.0	104
50,000	108	45.2	1:09.8	1:35.0	46.2	1:10.8	1:42.4	1:49.0	109
40,000	107	45.2	1:09.9	1:35.1	46.2	1:10.9	1:43.0	1:49.1	108
32,000	106	45.3	1:10.0	1:35.2	46.3	1:11.0	1:43.1	1:49.2	107
25,000	105	45.4	1:10.1	1:35.3	46.4	1:11.1	1:43.2	1:49.3	106
20,000	104	45.4	1:10.2	1:35.4	46.4	1:11.2	1:43.3	1:50.0	104
16,000	102	45.6	1:10.4	1:36.1	46.6	1:11.4	1:44.0	1:50.2	102
12,500	101	45.6	1:10.5	1:36.2	46.6	1:11.5	1:44.1	1:50.3	101
10,000	100	45.7	1:10.6	1:36.3	46.7	1:11.6	1:44.2	1:50.4	100
Mdn 50K	100	45.7	1:10.6	1:36.3	46.7	1:11.6	1:44.2	1:50.4	100
Mdn 32K	98	45.9	1:10.8	1:37.0	46.8	1:11.8	1:44.4	1:51.2	97

There were three routes on 3Jly89; the Ninth race, on the turf, will be handled separately.

3Jly89 Routes

Race 1: 8½ furlongs for $12,500 older female claimers

Par: Older males 1:11.5 1:44.1+4 lengths female route adjustment

Revised par: 1:11.9 1:45.0

Performance: 1:12.2 1:45.2

Fractional differential: S3

Final differential: S2

Race 8: 9 furlongs for Grade II 3-yr.-old males

Par: Older males 1:10.3 1:48.0+2 lengths for 3-yr.-old stakes horses

Revised par: 1:10.5 1:48.2

Performance: 1:10.4 1:48.4

Fractional differential: F1

Final differential: S2

3Jly89—Route Summary

Par	Actual	Var: Fraction	Final
(2) 1:11.9 1:45.0	1:12.2 1:45.2	S3	S2
(8) 1:10.5 1:48.2	1:10.4 1:48.4	F1	S2

Two-race average: *Slow 1–Slow 2*

Neither race contained a runaway winner and, since neither conflicts with the other, the variant seems based on solid ground. It does, however, conflict with the Fast 2 we assigned to the sprint races for the day. That's not unusual, and is the reason we separate sprints from routes. Whenever the variant is based on a small sample, it should be validated by races from the previous and/or following day(s). As you'll see shortly, the 4Jly89 races will do us little good. They are all one-turn miles, an odd distance often having no relationship to two-turn routes.

From my notebook, the variants from the previous racing day:

> 2Jly89 Sprints 0 F1—Routes S2 S2

This one's easy. The 2Jly89 data agrees with the sprint and route data from 3Jly89 and 4Jly89. That isn't always the case.

Often you'll have to take your best shot at approximating today's variant by basing a decision on other days with similar sprint and route variants. Had the data from 2Jly89 not supported the two succeeding days, I would have scanned my notebook for other days with sprint variants of *0–Fast 2* and, if not too far out of line with our tentative Slow 1–Slow 2 route variant, would have used the route variant from one of those days.

We'll accept a route variant of *Slow 1–Slow 2* for 3Jly89.

The 3Jly89 Entries in the Handicapper's Notebook

(Dirt sprints and routes)

	Par		Adjusted Race		Fraction	Final		Shape
(1)	1:11.9	1:45.0	1:12.1	1:45.0	S2	0		A–A
(2)	45.4	1:11.0	45.8	1:10.4	S4	0		S–A
(3)	44.5	1:16.0	43.6	1:15.2	F9	F3	*1	F–F
(4)	44.7	1:22.3	44.6	1:22.3	F1	0		A–A
(5)	44.6	1:09.2	44.6	1:09.1	0	F1		A–A
(6)	2-yr.-olds		46.0	1:12.0	x	x		x
(7)	44.5	1:09.1	45.0	1:09.4	S5	S3	*2	S–S
(8)	1:10.5	1:48.2	1:10.3	1:48.2	F2	0		A–A

> 3Jly89 Sprints 0 F1—Routes S2 S2

Horses to Watch:
  3rd: *Bistra* and *My Treat*
  7th: Avoid runners from Slow-Slow configuration

4JLY89—ROUTES

Race 3: 8 furlongs (one-turn mile) for $32,000 older females

Par: Older males 1:10.0   1:35.2 + 4 lengths female route adjustment

THIRD RACE
Hollywood
JULY 4, 1989

1 MILE. (1.32%) CLAIMING. Purse $21,800. Fillies and mares. 4-year-olds and upward. Weight, 122 lbs. Non-winners of two races at a mile or over since May 14 allowed 3 lbs.; such a race since then, 6 lbs. Claiming price $32,000; for each $2,800 to $28,800, allowed 2 lbs. (Races when entered for $25,000 or less not considered.)

Value of race $21,800; value to winner $11,550; second $4,200; third $3,150; fourth $1,575; fifth $525. Mutuel pool $353,253. Exacta pool $480,527.

Last Raced	Horse	Eqt.A.Wt	PP	St	¼	½	¾	Str	Fin	Jockey	Cl'g Pr	Odds $1
25Jun89 2Hol1	Designing Charles	b 4 116	1	8	6$\frac{1}{2}$	4$\frac{1}{2}$	3^1	2$\frac{2}{2}$	12$\frac{1}{2}$	Baze R A	32000	3.60
14Jun89 9Hol8	Sucess Formula	b 6 116	2	4	2$\frac{1}{2}$	1^{hd}	11$\frac{1}{2}$	11$\frac{1}{2}$	2^{11}	Valenzuela P A	32000	4.00
22Jun89 7GG2	Joys Of Spring	b 6 116	3	6	8	8	7^2	31$\frac{1}{2}$	32$\frac{3}{4}$	Stevens G L	32000	6.70
7Jun89 8Hol5	Beautiful Pet	b 4 116	8	2	7$\frac{1}{2}$	6$\frac{1}{2}$	6$\frac{1}{2}$	6^1	4$\frac{1}{2}$	Castanon A L	32000	10.70
4Jun89 4Hol1	Broad Street	7 116	5	5	4$\frac{1}{2}$	5$\frac{1}{2}$	5^1	4$\frac{1}{2}$	52$\frac{3}{4}$	Solis A	32000	2.70
21Jun89 7Hol7	Queens Guard	b 5 116	6	3	3^1	3^1	4$\frac{1}{2}$	7^5	6^{nk}	Sibille R	32000	13.10
16Jun89 5Hol8	War Position	b 4 116	7	1	1^{hd}	2^2	2$\frac{1}{2}$	5$\frac{1}{2}$	7^{11}	Sorenson D	32000	33.60
7Jun89 5Hol4	Oh Marie	6 116	4	7	5^{hd}	7^2	8	8	8	Delahoussaye E	32000	4.30

OFF AT 2:41. Start good. Won driving. Time, :22%, :45, 1:10%, 1:23½, 1:36% Track fast.

FIFTH RACE
Hollywood
JULY 4, 1989

1 MILE. (1.32%) ALLOWANCE. Purse $31,800. Fillies and mares. 3-year-olds and upward. Non-winners of two races. Weights, 3-year-olds, 115 lbs.; older, 122 lbs. Non-winners of a race other than claiming at a mile or over allowed 3 lbs.

Value of race $31,800; value to winner $17,850; second $6,200; third $4,650; fourth $2,325; fifth $775. Mutuel pool $404,495. Exacta pool $465,543.

Last Raced	Horse	Eqt.	A.	Wt	PP	St	¼	½	¾	Str	Fin	Jockey	Odds $1
23Jun89 9Hol	Waviness		3	115	10	3	7hd	71	52½	3½	1¾	Baze R A	15.20
1Jun89 8Hol3	Decora		3	117	11	2	4½	34	31½	2½	21½	Pincay L Jr	3.50
15Jun89 8Hol2	Paper Princess		3	116	3	4	1½	2½	1hd	11½	32	Valenzuela P A	1.80
16Jun89 7Hol2	Duchess Greg		3	112	5	7	3hd	1hd	21½	41½	41½	Davis R G	3.60
30Apr89 9Hol9	Forever Gorgeous		4	119	7	8	8½	82	4hd	53½	53	Valenzuela F H	40.20
14Jun89 3Hol2	Moonlight Ridge		5	117	8	9	101½	101	94	75	61¾	Garcia H J5	19.40
3Jun89 7Hol6	Gabbing Gloria	b	3	116	12	1	61	6½	63½	61½	75	Delahoussaye E	26.40
7Jun89 8Hol7	Durability	b	4	117	6	11	12	12	112	101½	81¼	Jauregui L H5	82.90
4Jun89 3Hol5	Dancinginthepark		4	122	4	10	9hd	91½	81	8½	92½	Solis A	26.20
16Jun89 3Hol5	Road To Happiness		5	122	1	6	52	4hd	101½	114	10¾	McCarron C J	29.60
7Jun89 8Hol3	Jennysport		4	119	2	5	2½	5hd	7½	9½	115½	Stevens G L	6.50
29May89 7GG7	Self Reflection		4	122	9	12	111	11hd	12	12	12	Cortez A	121.90

OFF AT 3:58. Start good. Won driving. Time, :22⅖, :45, 1:09⅖, 1:22⅖, 1:35⅗ Track fast.

SEVENTH RACE
Hollywood
JULY 4, 1989

1 MILE. (1.32⅘) HANDICAP. Purse $55,000. 3-year-olds and upward. Closed with 16 nominations on Friday, June 30 by 5:00 p.m. with no fee. Weights Saturday July 1. Enter Sunday, July 2.

Value of race $55,000; value to winner $30,250; second $11,000; third $8,250; fourth $4,125; fifth $1,375. Mutuel pool $422,698. Exacta pool $472,180.

Last Raced	Horse	Eqt.	A.	Wt	PP	St	¼	½	¾	Str	Fin	Jockey	Odds $1
4Jun89 3GG1	Rahy	b	4	114	6	5	21	1hd	11½	13½	15	Stevens G L	a-2.30
9Jun89 8Hol3	Paramount Jet		4	115	2	9	9hd	96	8½	41	2nk	Baze R A	8.50
29May89 8GG3	Don's Irish Melody	b	6	114	9	1	1½	21½	2hd	21	32¾	Castanon A L	23.20
18Jun89 8Hol3	Mi Preferido		4	119	8	4	51	5hd	62½	6½	4½	McCarron C J	*2.30
17Jun89 6CD2	You're No Bargain		5	116	10	2	41½	4hd	5½	51½	5½	Valenzuela P A	15.70
25Jun89 3Hol3	Dominated Debut		3	108	4	7	7hd	7½	7hd	7hd	6nk	Jauregui L H	42.90
2Jan89 7SA1	Monte Simon		5	116	1	10	10	10	10	9½	72½	Delahoussaye E	a-2.30
10Jun89 8Hol4	Sensational Star	b	5	116	7	3	3½	31	4hd	82	8½	Meza R Q	5.20
10Jun89 8Hol2	Prospectors Gamble	b	4	115	5	6	63	64	32	3½	9nk	Davis R G	4.90
11Feb89 9OP9	Blade Of The Ball		4	113	3	8	87	85	95	10	10	Solis A	32.80

***—Actual Betting Favorite.**
a-Coupled: Rahy and Monte Simon.

OFF AT 4:57. Start good. Won ridden out. Time, :22, :44, 1:08⅖, 1:20⅗, 1:33⅗ Track fast.

EIGHTH RACE
Hollywood
JULY 4, 1989

1 ⅛ MILES.(Turf). (1.45⅗) 50th Running of THE AMERICAN HANDICAP (Chute Start) (Grade I). $300,000 added. 3-year-olds and upward. By subscription of $200 each, which shall accompany the nomination, $2,000 additional to start, with $300,000 added, of which $60,000 to second, $45,000 to third, $22,500 to fourth and $7,500 to fifth. Weights Thursday, June 29. Starters to be named through the entry box by closing time of entries. Hollywood Park reserves the right not to divide this race. Should this race not be divided and the number of entries exceed the starting gate capacity, highweights on the scale will be preferred and also eligible list will be drawn. Total earnings in 1989 will be used in determining the order of preference of horses assigned equal weight on the scale. Failure to draw into this race at scratch time cancels all fees. Trophies will presented to the winning owner, trainer and jockey. Closed Wednesday, June 21, 1989 with 13 nominations.

Value of race $318,600; value to winner $183,600; second $60,000; third $45,000; fourth $22,500; fifth $7,500. Mutuel pool $425,791. Exacta Pool $491,818.

Last Raced	Horse	Eqt.	A.	Wt	PP	St	¼	½	¾	Str	Fin	Jockey	Odds $1
25Jun89 7Hol3	Mister Wonderful II	b	6	115	1	6	51½	63	62	63	1no	Toro F	10.40
18Jun89 8Hol1	Steinlen		6	121	4	1	21½	22	21	1hd	2hd	Stevens G L	.80
29May89 8Hol8	Pranke		5	117	5	5	71½	7½	7½	4½	31½	Pincay L Jr	9.80
18Jun89 8Hol2	Pasakos		4	115	2	7	6½	5½	51½	3½	4nk	McCarron C J	2.90
18Jun89 8Hol5	Skip Out Front		7	116	3	2	32½	31½	32	5hd	51¾	Delahoussaye E	10.30
9Jun89 8Hol1	Splendor Catch		5	116	7	3	11½	11½	1½	21½	62¾	Valenzuela P A	9.10
18Jun89 8Hol7	New Colony	b	6	113	8	8	8	8	8	8	7no	Solis A	76.80
18Jun89 8Hol4	Loyal Double		6	112	6	4	41½	41	4hd	7½	8	Meza R Q	81.40

OFF AT 5:29. Start good. Won driving. Time, :24, :48⅕, 1:11⅖, 1:34⅘, 1:47⅕ Course firm.

NINTH RACE
Hollywood
JULY 4, 1989

1 ⅛ MILES.(Turf). (1.45⅗) ALLOWANCE (Chute start). Purse $31,000. 4-year-olds and upward which have not won $3,000 other than maiden, claiming or starter. Weight, 119 lbs. Non-winners of a race other than claiming at a mile or over allowed 3 lbs. (Winners that have started for a claiming price $25,000 or less in their last three starts and maidens that are non-starters for a claiming price have second preference.)

Value of race $31,000; value to winner $17,050; second $6,200; third $4,650; fourth $2,325; fifth $775. Mutuel pool $344,115. Exacta pool $537,220.

Last Raced	Horse	Eqt.	A.	Wt	PP	St	¼	½	¾	Str	Fin	Jockey	Odds $1
18Jun89 3Hol4	How Very Touching	b	5	119	5	5	53	53	51½	22	1hd	Meza R Q	13.40
18Jun89 3Hol3	Speak High	b	4	116	6	1	1hd	1hd	1½	1hd	2½	McCarron C J	5.30

Date	Track	Horse		wt	pp	st	Calls				Fin	Jockey	Odds
3Jun89	9Hol³	The M. V. P.	b	4 116	2	7	7¹¹	7¹	6ⁿᵈ	4³¹	3¹¹	Olivares F	12.40
18Jun89	9Hol⁶	Sir Willoughby	b	4 119	8	4	3ʰᵈ	4⁴	3ʰᵈ	3ʰᵈ	4²¹	Valenzuela F H	37.70
18Jun89	9Hol⁴	Cranky Kid	b	4 116	9	8	8¹	10¹	10ʰᵈ	6¹¹	5¹	Valenzuela P A	7.30
18Jun89	3Hol⁵	Fools Hat		5 116	11	3	2¹¹	2¹¹	2¹¹	5¹	6²	Cortez A	31.40
18Jun89	9Hol³	The Brazilian	b	4 119	10	6	6²	8¹	9¹¹	7¹	7¹	Pincay L Jr	1.70
15Aug88	6Sar⁵	Find The Cause		5 119	12	12	12	12	12	8¹	8¹¹	Delahoussaye E	6.80
21Jun89	8GG⁵	Spirit Bay	b	5 116	4	9	10¹	11³¹	11³¹	10¹¹	9ⁿᵏ	Baze R A	47.20
18Jun89	3Hol⁶	Duke's Lodge	b	4 119	7	10	11³¹	9¹	8¹	9ⁿᵈ	10³	Davis R G	6.30
18Jun89	3Hol⁸	Just A Gigolo		4 114	1	2	4³¹	3ʰᵈ	4ʰᵈ	11¹	11¹¹	Jauregui L H⁵	88.70
29Mar89	5SA¹¹	Lacquer's Guest		4 119	3	11	9¹¹	6ʰᵈ	7¹	12	12	Stevens G L	18.90

OFF AT 6:03. Start good. Won driving. Time, :23⅖, :47⅖, 1:12½, 1:36½, 1:40⅖ Course firm.

Revised par: 1:10.4 1:36.1

Performance: 1:10.4 1:36.2

Fractional differential: 0

Final differential: S1

Race 5: 8 furlongs (one-turn mile) for NW1 Allowance females

Par: Older males 1:10.0 1:35.2 + 3 lengths female route adjustment

Revised par: 1:10.3 1:36.0

Performance: 1:09.8 1:35.3

Fractional differential: F5

Final differential: F2

Race 7: 8 furlongs (one-turn mile) for older male handicap horses

Par: 1:09.6 1:34.0

Revised par: same

Performance: 1:08.2 1:33.4

Fractional differential: F14

Final differential: F1

4Jly89—Route Summary

	Par		Actual		Var: Fraction	Final
(3)	1:10.4	1:36.1	1:10.4	1:36.2	0	S1
(5)	1:10.3	1:36.0	1:09.8	1:35.3	F5	F2
(7)	1:09.6	1:34.0	1:08.2	1:33.4	(F14)	F1

Three-race average: Fast 6—Fast 1

The sprint variant for this day was Fast 1, and indicates our one-mile variant is based on reality. At Hollywood Park one-turn mile races are more closely related to sprints than two-turn routes. Because of the extended run down the chute and into the turn, the pace of these races is often exceedingly fast. The pace of the Seventh race on 4Jly89 was exceptional.

We won't adjust the winner's beaten lengths in Race 7. The conditions of the race make it difficult to identify the actual class level. An overnight handicap is a rarity at Hollywood Park, and was apparently carded to "dress up" the holiday program. Just take the race at face value and accept the Fast 1 indication.

The *pace* of the Seventh race does present a problem. A Fast 14, if averaged with the other two races, badly distorts the fractional variants of both the other races.

We can approach the problem with several points of logic:

1. The fractional and final variants for both days indicate the track is not exceptionally fast at any call, at any distance. It's logical to assume the *race*, not the *track*, was responsible for the apparently aberrant pace in Race 7.

2. The Third race was a claiming race, usually the most reliable race upon which to base a variant. The pace of the race was run on par, dramatically conflicting with the Seventh race. When possible, lean toward claiming races.

3. If available, examine the past performances of the horses competing in the Seventh race. The makeup of this particular race explains the Fast 14 designation:

Don's Irish Melody, Sensational Star, and Prospectors Gamble are very fast classified allowance sprinters, each capable of throwing a sub 1:09.0 in a sprint race. Their presence in the race assured a blistering pace.

Additionally, Mi Preferido is an exceptionally fast front-running router who was unable to place better than fifth during the early pace of the race.

Exclude Race 7 from your fractional variant calculation.

4Jly89—Route Summary (deleting the fractional time of the Seventh race)

	Par		Actual		Var: Fraction	Final
(3)	1:10.4	1:36.1	1:10.4	1:36.2	0	S1
(5)	1:10.3	1:36.0	1:09.8	1:35.3	F5	F2
(7)	1:09.6	1:34.0	1:08.2	1:33.4	(F14)	F1

Three-race average: Fast 3—Fast 1

The 4Jly89 Entries in the Handicapper's Notebook (Dirt sprints and routes)

	Par		Adjusted Race		Fraction	Final		Shape
(1)	45.0	1:17.0	45.2	1:16.4	S2	F1		A–A
(2)	45.2	1:10.3	45.2	1:10.4	0	S1		A–A
(3)	1:10.4	1:36.1	1:10.7	1:36.3	S3	S2		A–A
(4)	45.4	1:11.0	45.4	1:10.3	0	F2		A–F
(5)	1:10.3	1:36.0	1:10.1	1:35.4	F2	F1		A–A
(6)	2-yr.-olds		45.8	1:11.1	x	x		x
(7)	1:09.6	1:34.0	1:08.5	1:34.0	F11	0	*1	F–A

> 4Jly89 Sprints 0 F1—Routes F3 F1

*1 Rahy's performance in the 7th race is exceptional. In a race loaded with sprinters, he set the Fast 11 pace and then drew off to win with a par figure. A pace setter that can still earn par after a Fast 11 pace should be on our Horses to Watch list. (He won Hollywood Park's Bel Air Handicap in his next start.)

APPLYING THE VARIANTS

Applying the variants is a simple procedure. Adjust the pace-line selected by the fractional (converting back to fifths) and final-time variants for the day of the race.

To adjust the first fraction, use the guidelines we developed for applying the *DRF* variant:

First Fraction:
Sprints: 50% of fractional adjustment, rounded *downward*. Make no adjustment to the first fraction of a sprint race unless the second-call adjustment is at least 3 *lengths*.

Routes: 66% of the fractional adjustment, rounded to the next whole length.

Many recreational handicappers will be content to stop with a final-time variant only. Reliable figures can result by applying that variant in the same manner we used to apply the *DRF* variant:

A review of part of that application:

Sprints
- 2Call = 50% of final time, adjusted; round down
- 1Fr = 50% of 2Call adjusted (3 length minimum); round down

Routes
- 2Call = 50% of final time, adjusted; round down
- 1Fr = 66% of 2Call, adjusted; round to the next whole length

TURF VARIANTS—3Jly89–4Jly89

Most race days feature a single race, perhaps two, over the turf course. The result is an unsatisfactory base upon which to construct variants. The most suitable solution is to project a probable variant from the usual performances of horses competing in those races. But that's an advanced art, requiring daily use of the past performances. It is also time-consuming and loaded with possible pitfalls. We'll discuss that process in the next section.

For now, let's try to construct the 3Jly89 and 4Jly89 variants without adding the burden of projected variants. I advise the reader to cluster several race days into a single turf variant whenever possible. When the data from successive days does not seem greatly dissimilar, use as many days as possible to construct the variant.

NINTH RACE
Hollywood
JULY 3, 1989

1 1/16 MILES.(Turf). (1.39⅘) CLAIMING (Chute start). Purse $42,000. 4-year-olds and upward. Weight, 122 lbs. Non-winners of two races at a mile or over since May 7 allowed 3 lbs.; such a race since then, 5 lbs. Claiming price $150,000; for each $5,000 to $125,000 allowed 1 lb. (Races when entered for $100,000 or less not considered.)

Value of race $42,000; value to winner $23,100; second $8,400; third $6,300; fourth $3,150; fifth $1,050. Mutuel pool $365,064. Exacta pool $466,470.

Last Raced	Horse	Eqt.A.Wt	PP	St	¼	½	¾	Str	Fin	Jockey	Cl'g Pr	Odds $1
27May89 ^{9}Hol^3	Captain Vigors	7 117	6	4	1^{1½}	1^1	1^1	1^{1½}	1^2	Toro F	150000	3.80
9Jun89 ^{8}Hol^4	Days Gone By	5 116	2	6	6^{½}	7	5^{hd}	3^{½}	2^{½}	DelahoussyeE	145000	5.70
9Jun89 ^{8}Hol^2	Individualist	b 6 112	7	5	4^{1½}	2^1	2^{1½}	2^{1½}	3no	Davis R G	125000	4.50
17Jun89 ^{8}Hol^1	Rufjan	b 6 117	5	3	5^1	5^{hd}	7	6^{2½}	4no	Pincay L Jr	150000	2.70
27May89 ^{9}Hol^4	Good Taste	7 117	3	2	2^{hd}	3^{½}	4^{1½}	5^{1½}	5^4	Stevens G L	150000	7.50
11Jun89 ^{9}Hol^5	Bel Air Dancer	b 4 113	1	1	3^{½}	4^2	3^{½}	4^{hd}	6^{2½}	Black C A	125000	20.50
27May89 ^{9}Hol^5	Five Daddy Five	b 5 117	4	7	7	6^{hd}	6^{1½}	7	7	Solis A	150000	3.50

OFF AT 5:53. Start good. Won driving. Time, :24⅘, :48, 1:11⅗, 1:35, 1:41⅘ Course firm.

EIGHTH RACE
Hollywood
JULY 4, 1989

1 ⅛ MILES.(Turf). (1.45⅗) 50th Running of THE AMERICAN HANDICAP (Chute Start) (Grade I). $300,000 added. 3-year-olds and upward. By subscription of $200 each, which shall accompany the nomination, $2,000 additional to start, with $300,000 added, of which $60,000 to second, $45,000 to third, $22,500 to fourth and $7,500 to fifth. Weights Thursday, June 29. Starters to be named through the entry box by closing time of entries. Hollywood Park reserves the right not to divide this race. Should this race not be divided and the number of entries exceed the starting gate

capacity, highweights on the scale will be preferred and also eligible list will be drawn. Total earnings in 1989 will be used in determining the order of preference of horses assigned equal weight on the scale. Failure to draw into this race at scratch time cancels all fees. Trophies will presented to the winning owner, trainer and jockey. Closed Wednesday, June 21, 1989 with 13 nominations.

Value of race $318,600; value to winner $183,600; second $60,000; third $45,000; fourth $22,500; fifth $7,500. Mutuel pool $425,791. Exacta Pool $491,818.

Last Raced	Horse	Eqt.A.Wt	PP	St	¼	½	¾	Str	Fin	Jockey	Odds $1
25Jun89 ^{7}Hol^{3}	Mister Wonderful II	b 6 115	1	6	$5^{1½}$	6^{3}	6^{2}	6^{3}	1no	Toro F	10.40
18Jun89 ^{8}Hol^{1}	Steinlen	6 121	4	1	$2^{1½}$	2^{2}	2^{1}	1^{hd}	2^{hd}	Stevens G L	.80
29May89 ^{8}Hol^{8}	Pranke	5 117	5	5	$7^{1½}$	$7^{½}$	$7^{½}$	$4^{½}$	$3^{1½}$	Pincay L Jr	9.80
18Jun89 ^{8}Hol^{2}	Pasakos	4 115	2	7	$6^{½}$	$5^{½}$	$5^{1½}$	$3^{½}$	4^{nk}	McCarron C J	2.90
18Jun89 ^{8}Hol^{5}	Skip Out Front	7 116	3	2	$3^{2½}$	$3^{1½}$	3^{2}	5^{hd}	$5^{1¾}$	Delahoussaye E	10.30
9Jun89 ^{8}Hol^{1}	Splendor Catch	5 116	7	3	$1^{1½}$	$1^{1½}$	$1^{½}$	$2^{1½}$	$6^{2¾}$	Valenzuela P A	9.10
18Jun89 ^{8}Hol^{7}	New Colony	b 6 113	8	8	8	8	8	8	7no	Solis A	76.80
18Jun89 ^{8}Hol^{4}	Loyal Double	6 112	6	4	$4^{1½}$	4^{1}	4^{hd}	$7^{½}$	8	Meza R Q	81.40

OFF AT 5:29. Start good. Won driving. Time, :24, :48⅕, 1:11⅘, 1:34⅘, 1:47⅕ Course firm.

NINTH RACE
Hollywood
JULY 4, 1989

1 ⅛ MILES.(Turf). (1.45⅗) ALLOWANCE (Chute start). Purse $31,000. 4-year-olds and upward which have not won $3,000 other than maiden, claiming or starter. Weight, 119 lbs. Non-winners of a race other than claiming at a mile or over allowed 3 lbs. (Winners that have started for a claiming price $25,000 or less in their last three starts and maidens that are non-starters for a claiming price have second preference.)

Value of race $31,000; value to winner $17,050; second $6,200; third $4,650; fourth $2,325; fifth $775. Mutuel pool $344,115. Exacta pool $537,228.

Last Raced	Horse	Eqt.A.Wt	PP	St	¼	½	¾	Str	Fin	Jockey	Odds $1
18Jun89 ^{3}Hol^{4}	How Very Touching	b 5 119	5	5	5^{3}	5^{3}	$5^{1½}$	2^{2}	1^{hd}	Meza R Q	13.40
18Jun89 ^{3}Hol^{3}	Speak High	b 4 116	6	1	1^{hd}	1^{hd}	$1^{½}$	1^{hd}	$2^{½}$	McCarron C J	5.30
3Jun89 ^{9}Hol^{3}	The M. V. P.	b 4 116	2	7	$7^{1½}$	$7^{½}$	6^{hd}	$4^{3½}$	$3^{1½}$	Olivares F	12.40
18Jun89 ^{9}Hol^{6}	Sir Willoughby	b 4 119	8	4	3^{hd}	4^{4}	3^{hd}	3^{hd}	$4^{2½}$	Valenzuela F H	37.70
18Jun89 ^{9}Hol^{4}	Cranky Kid	b 4 116	9	8	$8^{½}$	10^{1}	10^{hd}	$6^{1½}$	$5^{½}$	Valenzuela P A	7.30
18Jun89 ^{3}Hol^{5}	Fools Hat	5 116	11	3	$2^{1½}$	$2^{1½}$	$2^{1½}$	$5^{½}$	6^{2}	Cortez A	31.40
18Jun89 ^{9}Hol^{3}	The Brazilian	b 4 119	10	6	6^{2}	8^{1}	$9^{1½}$	7^{1}	$7^{½}$	Pincay L Jr	1.70
15Aug88 ^{6}Sar^{5}	Find The Cause	5 119	12	12	12	12	12	$8^{½}$	$8^{1½}$	Delahoussaye E	6.80
21Jun89 ^{8}GG^{5}	Spirit Bay	b 5 116	4	9	10^{1}	$11^{3½}$	$11^{3½}$	$10^{1½}$	9^{nk}	Baze R A	47.20
18Jun89 ^{3}Hol^{6}	Duke's Lodge	b 4 119	7	10	$11^{3½}$	$9^{½}$	8^{1}	9^{hd}	10^{3}	Davis R G	6.30
18Jun89 ^{3}Hol^{8}	Just A Gigolo	4 114	1	2	$4^{3½}$	3^{hd}	4^{hd}	11^{1}	$11^{1¾}$	Jauregui L H^{5}	88.70
29Mar89 ^{5}SA^{11}	Lacquer's Guest	4 119	3	11	$9^{1½}$	6^{hd}	$7^{½}$	12	12	Stevens G L	18.90

OFF AT 6:03. Start good. Won driving. Time, :23⅘, :47⅘, 1:12⅕, 1:36⅕, 1:48⅘ Course firm.

TURF RACES—3Jly89–4Jly89

This will be an excellent opportunity for readers to test their abilities to work with pars and apply them to the variant process. Before moving ahead to my calculations, spend some time with the three turf races and attempt the variant for the two days.

First the pars. Unlike on their dirt courses, most racetracks do not offer turf races to bottom-of-the-barrel-type runners. Consequently, $10,000 pars must be constructed by matching a higher level par to the par chart and then working *backward* to the $10,000 par. That would be an unnecessary exercise here. Most handicappers maintain turf pars only for class levels competing over the surface. The NW1 turf pars for Hollywood Park:

		2Call	*8½F*	*9F*
NW1 Alw	106	1:11.3	1:41.4	1:48.2

The Exercise:
   Determine the pars for each of the three turf races and then calculate a daily variant for 3Jly89 and 4Jly89. Only one of the pars is easily determined. The other two will test your use of the chart and your understanding of any class hierarchy.

3Jly89 Race 9

Claiming races at this level are found occasionally at major racetracks, but most par charts do not reflect $100,000 claiming races. In truth, these races are hardly claiming races at all. When a horse is claimed, it's front page news in the *Form*.

Readers who reasoned the par to be equivalent to classified allowances have an excellent understanding of basic class hierarchies. That's *exactly* where the race fits on the class ladder.

The numerical par for the level is 111, or *five points* above the NW1 par we've used for the exercise. Let's calculate the exact par:

		2Call	8½F	9F
NW1 Alw	106	1:11.3	1:41.4	1:48.2
Cl Alw	111	1:10.8	1:40.4	

Race 9: 3Jly89 8½ furlongs

Par 111:   1:10.8   1:40.4

Performance: 1:11.4   1:41.2

Fractional differential: S6

Final differential: S3

4Jly89 Race 8

A Grade I race for older males. The pars top out at the stakes level, but to assume all stakes races are the same would be a serious mistake in judgment. The effect on variants is minimal because of the rarity of these races, but the lack of understanding will be costly when evaluating relative class of contenders.

The numerical class par for nine-furlong stakes races is 114, to which we'll add two points for the Grade I designation.

Therefore, par for the Eighth race is 116.

			2Call	8½F	9F
NW1	Alw	106	1:11.3	1:41.4	1:48.2
Gr.I		116	1:10.3		1:46.2

Race 8: 4Jly89 9 furlongs

Par 116:   1:10.3   1:46.2

Performance: 1:11.4   1:47.1

Fractional differential: S11

Final differential: S4

4Jly89 Race 9

A nonwinners of one allowance race. This is the first race in the exercise that is straightforward and easily calculated. The par for the race is 106, the par with which we're working.

Race 9: 4Jly89 9 furlongs

Par 106:   1:11.3   1:48.2

Performance: 1:12.2   1:48.4

Fractional differential: S9

Final differential: S2

3Jly89–4Jly89 Turf Summary

			Var:	
Par		Actual	Fraction	Final
3Jly89				
(9) 1:10.8	1:40.4	1:11.4 1:41.2	S6	S3
4Jly89				
(8) 1:10.3	1:46.2	1:11.4 1:47.1	S11	S4
(9) 1:11.3	1:48.2	1:12.2 1:48.4	S9	S2

Three race average: *Slow 9–Slow 3*

Final Variants for the Two-Day Period

3Jly89	Sprints 0	F1 /	Miles	N/A
	Routes S1	S2 /	Turf	S9 S3

4Jly89	Sprints 0	F1 /	Miles	F3 F1
	Routes N/A	/	Turf	S9 S3

3Jly89 and 4Jly89 presented few problems. There are other days, however, when the variant seems to change as the day progresses. That's characteristic of a racing surface drying out after inclement weather. It can also happen to a track unaffected by adverse weather conditions. Whether the cause is tidal influence, humidity, or the track's water trucks, handicappers must compensate for changing track speed.

The solution is to *cluster* variants from like races. For example:

(1)	6F	S4	S4			
(2)	6½F	S3	S3	Sprints 1–3	S4	S4
(3)	6F	S6	S4			
(5)	6F	S2	S1			
(7)	6½F	S1	0	Sprints 5–9	S1	S1
(9)	6F	F1	S1			

Assume the example to be an Eastern track drying out after a summer rainstorm. The day began with the track 3 or 4 lengths slower than par. As the day progressed, the track showed signs of returning to normal speed. A change is clearly indicated between the third and fifth races. If that change is not addressed, the average of all races will tend to distort both clusters of races. The hour between races 3 and 5 apparently served to dry the track considerably.

Create separate variants for the two clusters: races 1 to 3 and races 5 to 9.

PROJECTED VARIANTS

In recent years much has been written about the use of "projections" to calculate variants. Whereas the use of class pace and speed pars relate performance to general expectations, projected variants attempt to relate performance to the actual abilities of individual fields of horses. The responsibility of handicappers is to evaluate individual runners in a race, keying on the most reliable performers, and then relate their evaluations to actual performances. The task is sizable.

Handicappers willing to assume the burden of projected variants should be aware of the following:

1. The process is extremely time-consuming and requires daily access to past performances.

2. Accurately assessing the current abilities of a field of horses requires a thorough knowledge of form and condition cycles. Today's performance must be related to improving or declining form.

3. Most handicappers will tend to assess runners as though they were pieces on a game board. The tendency will be to assume horses will always live up to expectations and replicate past performance. The result will be neatly ordered variants that will perform poorly in application.

4. To maintain long-term accuracy, it will be necessary to periodically validate variants from previous days. The procedure, while simple, is time-consuming. The handicapper must calculate figures earned by horses in subsequent races and relate those figures to previous races. For example, a horse shows the following pattern:

29Oct89	46.1	1:11.4
15Oct89	46.4	1:12.3
27Sep89	46.3	1:12.2

If the horse reverts to an adjusted 1:12.2 + performance in subsequent races, there should be a cause for concern. The 29Oct89 race may be legitimate; then again, it may not. It would be prudent to assess subsequent performances of other runners from races on 29Oct89, and if necessary, to revise that variant.

A Projected Variant—25Nov89

The actual procedure is not complicated, and a single race should be adequate demonstration:

FIFTH RACE
Hollywood
NOVEMBER 25, 1989

6 FURLONGS. (1.08) CLAIMING. Purse $17,000. Fillies and mares. 3-year-olds and upward. Weights, 3-year-olds, 120 lbs.; older, 122 lbs. Non-winners of two races since October 8 allowed 3 lbs.; a race since then, 6 lbs. Claiming price $32,000; for each $2,000 to $28,000 allowed 2 lbs. (Races when entered for $25,000 or less not considered.)
Value of race $17,000; value to winner $9,350; second $3,400; third $2,550; fourth $1,275; fifth $425. Mutuel pool $305,855. Exacta pool $412,522.

Last Raced	Horse	Eqt.	A.	Wt	PP	St	¼	½	Str	Fin	Jockey	Cl'g Pr	Odds $1
12Nov89 2SA1	J. D's Star	b	4	119	8	1	3hd	21	22	1nk	Solis A	32000	5.30
12Nov89 2SA2	Chip's De Mere	b	4	116	4	3	11½	12½	11½	23	Davis R G	32000	4.30
12Nov89 2SA3	Frisky Dice		4	111	9	2	6hd	3hd	3hd	31	Castanon J L5	32000	5.40
3Nov89 2SA1	Eastern Belief	b	4	114	2	6	52	4½	42	41¼	Nakatani C S5	32000	35.90
15Nov89 7Hol5	Playing Through		5	116	3	9	71½	61½	5½	51½	Stevens G L	32000	5.60
8Nov89 7SA	Lacrosse	b	4	116	7	5	9	71	62	65½	Sibille R	32000	11.10
10Nov89 8SA11	Miss One Mile		5	119	6	7	81½	9	9	7¾	Olguin G L	32000	11.30
22Oct89 9TuP6	Shecky Vous		5	116	1	8	4½	81½	8hd	8hd	Meza R Q	32000	12.80
5Oct89 7SA6	Arcady Miss	b	4	116	5	4	21	51	71½	9	Delahoussaye E	32000	2.70

OFF AT 3:11. Start good. Won driving. Time, :22⅕, :45⅘, :57⅘, 1:10⅕ Track fast.

First, a tentative variant based on par times:

Race 5: 6 furlongs for $32,000 older females

Par: Older males 44.7 1:09.3 + 2 length female adjustment

Revised par: 44.9 1:10.0

Performance: 45.4 1:10.1

Fractional differential: S5

Final differential: S1

Now let's "project" a variant for this race. For purposes of illustration, we'll consider the last two or three races for each of the first six finishers.

5th Hollywood

6 FURLONGS. (1.08) CLAIMING. Purse $17,000. Fillies and mares. 3-year-olds and upward. Weights, 3-year-olds, 120 lbs.; older, 122 lbs. Non-winners of two races since October 8 allowed 3 lbs.; a race since then, 6 lbs. Claiming price $32,000; for each $2,000 to $28,000 allowed 2 lbs. (Races when entered for $25,000 or less not considered.)

Eastern Belief — B. f. 4, by Believe It—Damascene Lady, by Damascus
NAKATANI C S — 1145 — Br.—Phipps O M (Ky) — Tr.—Moreno Henry — $32,000
Own.—Risden A G & L G
1989 5 1 2 0 $18,500
1988 7 M 3 1 $16,346
Lifetime 12 1 5 1 $34,846

3Nov89-2SA	6½f	:221	:452	1:183ft	3½	1155	52½	43½	2½	13	NakatniCS 10	ⒻM32000	81-14	Eastern Belief, Fire Dawn, Zonar	12
20Oct89-6SA	6f	:212	:444	1:111ft	8¼	1135	32½	34	23½	23½	NakatniCS 10	ⒻM45000	78-16	HemetGossip,EstrnBlif,ForbsTims	11
28Aug89-2Dmr	6f	:213	:443	1:11 ft	6¾	121	34	25	24	21½	Stevens GL 3	ⒻM32000	81-14	SouthernSlng,EsternBelief,Siderlli	12
10Jly89-3Hol	6f	:214	:45	1:111ft	12	1175	65	75	67	78¼	DvenportCL 5	ⒻM32000	77-12	BtnInRhhm,MssRcTl,CmpsdOfLht	12
22Jun89-4Hol	6f	:22	:451	1:111ft	5½	1175	62¾	64¼	58¼	49	DvenportCL 9	ⒻM32000	76-12	Bam BamFlash,SwissGold,PageJoi	12

Chip's De Mere
B. f. 4, by Our Blue Chip—Silver de Mere, by Silver Series
DAVIS R G 116
Br.—Millard M (Cal) 1989 12 1 1 2 $23,925
Tr.—Sadler John W $32,000 1988 1 1 0 0 $8,250
Own.—Millard & Rous Mmes
Lifetime 13 2 1 2 $32,175 Turf 1 0 0 0
12Nov89-2SA 6½f :214 :443 1:162ft 9 116 1hd 1hd 1½ 2hd Davis R G4 Ⓕ 25000 92-10 J.D'sStr,Chip'sDeMere,FriskyDice 11
7Oct89-1SA 6f :214 :45 1:11 ft 15 116 31½ 21½ 2hd 32 ValenzuelFH 7 Ⓕ 25000 81-14 Lcrosse,NeverDnceAlon,Chip'sDMr 9
7Oct89—Very wide 3/8
24Sep89-10Fpx 6½f :22 :453 1:171ft 9½ 115 11½ 11½ 11½ 11¼ ValenzuelFH 9 Ⓕ 20000 90-10 Chp'sDMr,RdLghtDsc,JnAndBksRs 9
11Sep89-1Dmr 6f :213 :442 1:093ft 18 116 1hd 1hd 31 55½ McCarron CJ 5 Ⓕ 20000 84-09 NorthrnCch,GoldDcor,RdLghtDsc 10
24Jun89-5GG 4½f Ⓣ:211 :451 :513fm 19 114 6 99¼ 911 98½ Warren R JJr 1 ⒻHcp0 — — Candy Seeker, Dreamt, Debby Kay 9
24Jun89—Steadied 3 1/2

Playing Through
Ch. m. 5, by Messenger of Song—Traditional, by Olden Times
STEVENS G L 116
Br.—Mamakos J L (Cal) 1989 11 3 2 1 $35,325
Tr.—Velasquez Danny $32,000 1988 13 4 2 0 $61,762
Own.—Fritts & Tavaglione
Lifetime 39 8 5 6 $117,322 Turf 1 0 0 0
15Nov89-7Hol 6f :222 :451 1:102ft 8 116 42½ 32½ 33 53½ Baze R A7 Ⓕ 40000 86-10 RunwyBlues,Toulnge,ShowtimeLdy 8
1Nov89-3SA 6f :22 :444 1:093ft 6¾ 1115 2hd 2hd 2hd 41 Nakatani C S8 Ⓕ 40000 89-14 FrostyFreeze,PutTheCase,Toulange 7
15Oct89-1SA 6f :212 :444 1:103ft 2¾ 116 74¼ 42 22 21¾ Baze R A7 Ⓕ 20000 83-13 WndWggns,PlngThrgh,NvrDncAln 11
15Oct89—Checked 3/16
6Oct89-1SA 6f :213 :45 1:103ft 3½ 121 62¾ 11½ 13 15½ Baze R A11 Ⓕ 16000 85-15 PlayingThrough,OkPortl,PlyDncer 12
25Sep89-10Fpx 6f :22 :451 1:112ft *2½ 122 32½ 31 31½ 11¾ Olivares F9 Ⓕ 12500 90-10 PlyngThrogh,MyLovToYo,QnsGrd 10
25Sep89—4-wide into lane

Lacrosse
Ch. f. 4, by Scout Leader—Mark's Mama, by Traffic Mark
SIBILLE R 116
Br.—Beddo H L (NM) 1989 20 2 5 3 $41,757
Tr.—Velasquez Danny $32,000 1988 2 0 0 0
Own.—Mueller-Jucksch-Young
Lifetime 31 5 8 4 $80,210 Turf 1 0 0 0
8Nov89-7SA 1 Ⓣ:4621:0931:341fm 27 117 912 916 924 — Sibille R 7 ⒻAw37000 — — SingSwtSyl,SingngPrt,HthrAndRos 9
8Nov89—Eased
22Oct89-3SA 6f :213 :443 1:093gd 4 116 811 65¾ 64½ 31¾ Sibille R 6 Ⓕ 32000 88-11 J. D's Star,ShowtimeLady,Lacrosse 8
22Oct89—Bumped start
7Oct89-1SA 6f :214 :45 1:11 ft 10 116 911 99½ 63½ 11½ Sibille R 2 Ⓕ 25000 83-14 Lcrosse,NeverDnceAlon,Chip'sDMr 9
7Oct89—Wide into stretch
26Sep89-11Fpx 1$\frac{1}{16}$:48 1:124 1:44 ft 6¼ 116 53½ 56 58 717 Sibille R 8 Ⓕ 25000 74-13 LadyBelief,PlyingTps,FluzieForbes 8
26Aug89-4Dmr 6f :22 :45 1:101ft 3½ 116 87 88¾ 44½ 21¾ DelhoussyE 2 Ⓕ c20000 85-13 Never DanceAlone,Lacrosse,Lager 10

J. D's Star
Dk. b. or br. f. 4, by Star De Naskra—Torpidi, by Torsion
SOLIS A 119
Br.—Monroe Mary (Ky) 1989 15 2 0 1 $31,330
Tr.—Nickerson Victor J $32,000 1988 14 2 7 2 $42,550
Own.—Mr Ed's Stable
Lifetime 32 7 7 3 $87,980 Turf 3 0 1 0 $3,200
12Nov89-2SA 6½f :214 :443 1:162ft 7¾ 118 31½ 32 31 1hd Solis A 3 Ⓕ 25000 92-10 J.D'sStr,Chip'sDeMere,FriskyDice 11
1Nov89-3SA 6f :22 :444 1:093ft 8¼ 114 1hd 43½ 65¾ 6¾ Solis A 5 Ⓕ 35000 84-14 FrostyFreeze,PutTheCase,Toulange 7
22Oct89-3SA 6f :213 :443 1:093gd 12 116 42½ 42 2½ 11¾ Solis A 3 Ⓕ 32000 90-11 J. D's Star,ShowtimeLady,Lacrosse 8
22Oct89—Erratic early
7Oct89-1SA 6f :214 :45 1:11 ft 8 117 2hd 31½ 31½ 53½ Pincay L Jr 5 Ⓕ 25000 79-14 Lcrosse,NeverDnceAlon,Chip'sDMr 9
1Sep89-5Dmr 6½f :221 :451 1:154ft 8¼ 116 41½ 33 34 89¾ Davis R G1 Ⓕ 32000 80-11 Arcady Miss, Go Gaiter,FriskyDice 10
1Sep89—Hopped at start

Frisky Dice
B. f. 4, by Delta Gambler—Kalaska, by Hatchet Man
CASTANON J L 1115
Br.—Marano W F (Cal) 1989 12 2 3 1 $43,375
Tr.—Ellis Ronald W $32,000 1988 3 1 0 0 $8,100
Own.—Black-Black-ClausEtal
Lifetime 15 3 3 1 $51,475
12Nov89-2SA 6½f :214 :443 1:162ft *2¾ 117 52¾ 43½ 43½ 34 Pincay LJr11 Ⓕ c25000 88-10 J.D'sStr,Chip'sDeMere,FriskyDice 11
12Nov89—Wide into stretch
22Oct89-3SA 6f :213 :443 1:093gd 4 1115 65 3nk 42½ 42½ Castanon J L8 Ⓕ 32000 87-11 J. D's Star,ShowtimeLady,Lacrosse 8
22Oct89—Wide final 3/8
25Sep89-11Fpx 6½f :214 :453 1:17 ft 9¾ 120 63½ 53½ 64½ 54 Black C A8 ⒻAw33000 87-10 PreciousVern,OurOlLdy,LightSugr 10
1Sep89-5Dmr 6½f :221 :451 1:153ft 2¾ 118 51½ 53½ 54½ 24½ ♦ McCarron CJ4 Ⓕ 32000 85-11 Arcady Miss, Go Gaiter,FriskyDice 10
♦ 1Sep89—Dead heat; Wide final 3/8
4Aug89-11LA 6½f :211 :451 1:154ft 6¾ 119 51½ 31 68½ 617 BlckCA6 ⒻⓇChapman 79-11 DfndYourMn,ISrHopSo,SngSwtSyl 6

Each of the races in the "Adjusted Races" column *has already been adjusted* by my own pace and speed variants and, if necessary, converted to six-furlong performances. The data in the "Actual" column represents each horse's performance in the Fifth race on 25Nov89.

		Adj. Races		Actual	
Eastern Belief	3Nov89	45.5	1:11.2	46.1	1:11.0
	20Oct89	45.5	1:11.1	"	"
	28Aug89	45.4	1:11.1	"	"
Chip's De Mere	12Nov89	44.8	1:10.1	45.4	1:10.1
	7Oct89	45.1	1:11.0	"	"
Playing Through	15Nov89	45.1	1:10.4	46.4	1:11.1
	1Nov89	44.9	1:10.2	"	"
	15Oct89	45.1	1:10.2	"	"
Lacrosse	22Oct89	45.6	1:10.4	46.7	1:11.3
	7Oct89	46.0	1:11.0	"	"
J.D's Star	12Nov89	45.0	1:10.1	45.9	1:10.1
	1Nov89	45.2	1:11.2	"	"
	22Oct89	45.1	1:10.2	"	"
Frisky Dice	12Nov89	45.2	1:11.0	46.1	1:10.4
	22Oct89	45.1	1:11.0	"	"

Projected Performances

Eastern Belief: This filly is very consistent and the data is clear; 45.5　1:11.1.

Chip's De Mere: She's sharp and shows no evidence of decline. We'll project her to run 44.8　1:10.1.

Playing Through: Two consecutive races in the wrong direction; she's a declining horse. Even her Early Pace numbers are out of line with the performances of the other contenders. It's pointless to use her in our projections.

Lacrosse: She may be another with declining form; 46.0　1:10.4 seems a reasonable projection.

J.D's Star: She's razor sharp and seems to have peaked at about 45.1　1:10.1.

Frisky Dice: Another consistent filly; 45.1　1:11.0

The Variant

Projection vs performance.

	Projection		Actual		Differential	
Eastern Belief	45.5	1:11.1	46.1	1:11.0	S6	F1
Chip's De Mere	44.8	1:10.1	45.4	1:10.1	S6	0
Lacrosse	46.0	1:10.4	46.7	1:11.3	S7	S3
J.D's Star	45.1	1:10.1	45.9	1:10.1	S8	0
Frisky Dice	45.1	1:11.0	46.1	1:10.4	S10	F1

Fractional variant: The average of the five performances is *Slow 7.*

Final-time variant: Drop the probable decliner, Lacrosse, from the calculations. She ran to her normal early fractions, but her final time was another decline in performance. The variant must be based on runners who have "run their race." The tentative final-time variant for the race is: *Fast .5* (½ length).

Leave the final variant at Fast .5 for subsequent averaging with other races on the card. When this race was averaged with other races for the day, the author's final variant was:

> 25Nov89 Sprints   S5 F1

Our original variant for this race, constructed from the par chart, was Slow 5–Slow 1. Although the fractional variants were the same, the projected final variant indicates a different story for the day. Rather than slightly slow for the day, the final times were actually one length fast!

I have intended to impart a sense that this procedure is more of an art than an exercise in mathematics. As an art, it is highly intuitive and requires decisions that a simple application of par times to actual performance does not require. Results can be disastrous if those decisions are not founded on logic and experience. Readers intending to apply the concept should also maintain variants from par-time charts, at least until the projected variants begin to produce acceptable results.

There is a definite "up side" beyond the obvious benefit of more accurate figures. Accurately projected variants *will* provide handicappers with additional faith in their figures, and, when translated to the betting windows, that means a level of betting confidence that may not be possible otherwise.

CHAPTER XIV

Practical Application—25Oct89

IN THIS FINAL CHAPTER, we'll handicap one day at the 1989 Oak Tree at Santa Anita meeting: 25Oct89. There were enough playable races to enable us to apply all the principles developed earlier in the text. The day was representative in terms of betting opportunities and visits to the cashier's window.

Paceline selection will be conservative, usually the most recent race in the past performances. The results should be readily attainable by every reader of this material.

Selection of contenders will also be conservative and well within guidelines established by most traditional handicapping authorities. Individual readers may not always agree with the author's selection of contenders and pacelines, and that's okay. There should be room for individual style in any method of play, and I advise readers not to abandon successful methods for selecting contenders and pacelines.

I advise the reader to work the examples prior to reading my analysis of the races. To facilitate that exercise, I'll include the adjustment criteria, Decision Models and Track Profiles.

Adjustments

Sprints. 6F *(fractions in fifths)*				DRF Adj. Range
Santa Anita	22.0	45.1	1:10.4	14–16
Del Mar	21.4	45.0	1:10.2	13–15
Fairplex	22.0	45.2	1:11.1	10–12

314

Routes. 8½F (fractions in fifths)				DRF Adj. Range
Santa Anita	46.3	1:11.2	1:44.0	17–19
Del Mar	46.1	1:11.1	1:43.2	14–16
Fairplex	46.2	1:11.4	1:44.2	12–14

In each race we handicap, we'll adjust the least number of horses possible. If the bulk of the runners are exiting races at Del Mar, we'll adjust the other horses to that surface, leaving the Del Mar horses unadjusted except for *DRF* Variant adjustments. Likewise, if the bulk of pacelines are from Santa Anita we'll key the other lines to that surface.

Decision Model

	AP	EP	SP	FX
Sprints	2	3	3	3
Routes	2	4	2	n/a

Interpretation:

Sprints: Favor horses with a balance of early pace and average pace. A 3 in Sustained Pace is evidence that faint-hearted early pace types are to be avoided. E and P horses preferred.

Routes: A sustained pace bias. Preferred runners should show an imbalance of Early Pace to Sustained Pace. An Early to Sustained relationship of 3:1 is clearly preferable to a 1:3. We will emphasize S types and P's with strong finishing ability.

Track Profile

Sprints:

1Fr: Top half of field. No deep closers!

2Fr: Top three runners; maximum 2½ lengths behind

Style: P and E respectively

%E:　　Range, 52.10%, to 53.30%

Target: 52.90%

Routes:

1Fr:　　No bias

2Fr:　　Top half of field; maximum 4 lengths behind

Style:　　S and P respectively. E types to be *avoided*. In the 43 non-maiden routes preceding 25Oct89, *one* winner was in the lead at the first call! Only 5 of 43 had gained the lead by the second call! Anybody not yet convinced of the value of an accurate track profile?

%E:　　Range, 51.50% to 52.20%

Target: 51.75%

Finally, before proceeding to the examples, I caution the reader not to be overly concerned about generating numbers that are an exact match to those in this book. The fps numbers and ratings appearing in the text have been generated by a handheld computer. The computer has rounded off its calculations at various stages in the program, and the results may not be an exact match to your numbers. That should be of no concern. The differences will be minimal and relative within a field of runners.

25OCT89—FIRST RACE

The first race of the day was at six furlongs for bottom-of-the-barrel claiming females. As with most of these races, it was possible to quickly narrow the race to its logical contenders. Seven runners possessed no signs of current form/ability, leaving five horses for our consideration. We'll key our adjustments to Santa Anita. Del Mar and Fairplex races will require track-track adjustments.

1st Santa Anita

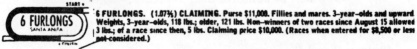

6 FURLONGS. (1.07¾) CLAIMING. Purse $11,000. Fillies and mares. 3-year-olds and upward Weights, 3-year-olds, 118 lbs.; older, 121 lbs. Non-winners of two races since August 15 allowed 3 lbs.; of a race since then, 5 lbs. Claiming price $10,000. (Races when entered for $8,500 or less not considered.)

Lou's Fast
B. f. 4, by Fast—Miss Lady Lou, by Ramadan
Br.—McClary G E (Cal) 1989 5 0 0 0 $750
BAZE R A 116 Tr.—Harte Michael G $10,000 1988 2 1 1 0 $12,000
Own.—Didga Really Stable (Lessee) Lifetime 7 1 1 0 $12,750
25Sep89-10Fpx 6f :22 :451 1:112ft 24 116 11 2hd 11½ 52¾ Sibille R7 Ⓕ 12500 87-10 PlyngThrogh,MyLovToYo,QnsGrd 10
18Aug89-3Dmr 6f :22 :45 1:102ft 59 116 96¾117¾111121219¾ Sibille R11 Ⓕ 25000 66-15 ArcdyMiss,SensOfRomnc,Mordido 12
18Aug89—Hopped at start
22Feb89-5SA 6f :213 :444 1:103ft 17 116 31 64¼1115 1125½ Sibille R6 Ⓕ 25000 59-18 MayFirst,Meanwhile,PreeningEgle 11
10Feb89-5SA 7f :221 :453 1:26 m 75 115 2½ 1hd 2½ 69 Sibille R1 Ⓕ 32000 61-25 Pretty Lake North,Afloat,Barmera 12
12Jan89-5SA 6½f :212 :44 1:161ft 79 116 42½ 43 78 910½ Sibille R7 ⒻAw31000 78-12 CstlCmmssn,ChcltJmbl,BrghtStyl 10
16Nov88-1Hol 7f :22 :452 1:251ft 19 118 32 31½ 11 1½ Sibille R8 ⒻⓈM40000 78-22 Lou'sFast,It'sAttrctive,Helg'sDoll 12
16Nov88—Bumped start
19Aug88-2Dmr 6½f :221 :454 1:184ft 3¾ 116 33 32½ 33½ 21¾ Baze R A6 ⒻⓈM32000 76-15 MjesticLook,Lou'sFst,SweetAdieu 11
Speed Index: Last Race: -3.0 3-Race Avg.: -15.0 7-Race Avg.: -11.1 Overall Avg.: -11.1
●Oct 14 Fpx 4f ft :472 B Sep 10 Fpx 5f ft 1:02 H Sep 3 Fpx 4f ft :483 H

Bravest Star
Dk. b. or br. m. 5, by Captain Courageous—Star Jasmine, by Pia Star
Br.—Pabst Mr-Mrs F L (Wash) 1989 9 1 1 1 $14,455
PEDROZA M A 116 Tr.—Silva Jose $10,000 1988 11 1 0 2 $16,800
Own.—Tricar Stables Inc Lifetime 34 4 4 4 $52,538
29Sep89-7Fpx 6f :22 :46 1:114ft 2¾ 1115 44 43 74¾ 88¾ Castanon J L 5 Ⓕ 10000 79-14 Jaklin'sBarbidoll,Encroach,ShwSy 10
29Sep89—Lugged out
9Sep89-1Dmr 6½f :221 :453 1:172ft *3 1135 1½ 1hd 53 109¼ Castanon J L 8 Ⓕ 12500 72-11 Slade'sLady,Aflot,GreySeptember 11
27Aug89-2Dmr 6f :22 :453 1:11 ft 4½ 1115 1½ 1hd 1hd 1½ Castanon J L 4 Ⓕ 12500 83-15 BrvestStr,MyLdiesTiger,QunsGurd 12
27Aug89—Disqualified from purse money
4Aug89-1Dmr 1 :463 1:12 1:371ft *2 1115 12½ 1½ 22 34½ Castanon J L 1 Ⓕ 16000 75-17 Lady Belief,SnowSpirit,BravestStar 6
4Aug89—Broke out, bumped
28Jly89-5Dmr 6½f :22 :451 1:172ft 5¾ 116 41½ 42½ 42¾ 21¾ Pedroza M A 5 Ⓕ 12500 79-16 Lt'sDrnkDnnr,BrvstStr,FrdmInMEs 7
24Mar89-1SA 7f :222 :454 1:251ft 4 1135 21½ 22 1115 1219¾ Olguin G L 4 Ⓕ c16000 55-20 RobertsReglGirl,Vlhll,NoSePorque 12
12Mar89-2SA 1 1/16 :463 1:114 1:451ft 4½ 1125 12 11½ 11 53 Olguin G L 4 Ⓕ 25000 72-14 Codex'sBride,BrodStret,PlyingTps 12
17Feb89-5SA 1 1/16 :463 1:113 1:444ft 4¾ 1135 12½ 13 16 18 VlenzulFH 10 Ⓕ c16000 77-21 Bravest Star, Topside,OurOleLady 10
25Jan89-9SA 1 1/16 :462 1:113 1:443ft 3e 1105 2½ 32½1113 1117¾ ValenzuelFH 5 Ⓕ 22500 60-17 ExodsFromRom,KssABttor,JlMdm 11
30Dec88-9SA 1 1/16 :463 1:111 1:433ft 10 1115 12½ 13 15 1¾ ValenzuelFH 2 Ⓕ 16000 83-12 BrvstStr,AncintLdy,ColonilTrchry 10
30Dec88—Broke out, bumped
Speed Index: Last Race: -7.0 3-Race Avg.: -8.6 5-Race Avg.: -11.2 Overall Avg.: -10.8
Oct 19 SA 4f ft :493 H

Miss Rock Talk
Dk. b. or br. f. 4, by Acaroid—Hardly, by Rock Talk
Br.—Casse N (Fla) 1989 12 1 3 2 $26,375
NAKATANI C S 1135 Tr.—Moreno Henry $10,000 1988 1 M 0 0
Own.—Stevens S E Lifetime 13 1 3 2 $26,375
5Oct89-1SA 6½f :214 :444 1:171ft 7 118 2½ 21½ 35 810 Pincay L Jr 5 Ⓕ 16000 74-16 Aflot,FceTheKing,SovereignAppel 11
11Sep89-1Dmr 6f :213 :442 1:093ft 12 1135 33 66½ 89½ 911½ Nakatani C S 9 Ⓕ 20000 78-09 NorthrnCch,GoldDcor,RdLghtDsc 10
3Sep89-2Dmr 6f :22 :444 1:102ft *8-5 1165 1½ 15 17 16½ NakatniCS 10 ⒻM32000 86-10 Miss Rock Talk, Dancia,WhiteLine 12
14Aug89-2Dmr 6f :214 :452 1:113ft *2¾ 121 32½ 54½ 45 34½ Pincay L Jr3 ⒻM32000 75-19 ShurFlyng,Dddy'sDoll,MssRockTlk 12
31Jly89-2Dmr 6f :22 :452 1:11 ft 6 122 73¼ 22½ 23 24 Pincay LJr10 ⒻM32000 79-16 Belle Mo, Miss Rock Talk,HiSailor 12
31Jly89—Wide into stretch
23Jly89-2Hol 6f :221 :46 1:12 ft *2¼ 122 3nk 2hd 32 34¼ Pincay L Jr9 ⒻM32000 77-18 BbyDllPjms,SlAwyHny,MssRckTlk 11
10Jly89-3Hol 6f :214 :45 1:111ft 4¾ 122 32 21 22½ 2nk Pincay L Jr3 ⒻM32000 85-12 BtnInRhhm,MssRcTl,CmpsdOfLht 12
7Jun89-2Hol 6f :22 :46 1:123ft 11 122 63¼ 62¾ 54 42¾ Pincay L Jr4 ⒻM32000 75-15 S. S.T.Rose,WhiteLine,Daddy'sDoll 11
7Jun89—Broke thru gate
27Apr89-4Hol 7f :222 :454 1:233ft 13 123 31 32 57 713½ Pincay L Jr1 ⒻM32000 72-10 Foxy Alice,LawnDebut,IceeFreeze 11
27Apr89—Lugged out backstretch
31Mar89-6SA 1 1/16 :464 1:121 1:45 ft 7½ 1135 33½ 812 918 935¼ Garcia H J1 ⒻM45000 41-17 Pirte'sHoorh,BronzeRbl,SnowSpirit 9
31Mar89—Took up 3/8
Speed Index: Last Race: -10.0 3-Race Avg.: -9.0 9-Race Avg.: -8.2 Overall Avg.: -11.6
Oct 22 SA 4f ft :481 H Oct 17 SA 4f ft :492 H Oct 11 SA 4f ft :473 H Sep 30 SA 4f ft :49 H

Princess Deborah
B. f. 4, by L'Natural—Speed Queen, by Tyrant
Br.—Bernheim A P (Cal) 1989 4 0 1 1 $3,850
SIBILLE R 116 Tr.—Bunn Thomas M Jr $10,000 1988 8 2 0 1 $17,262
Own.—Bernheim-Hecht-Karacan Lifetime 16 2 1 3 $24,037
1Sep89-1Dmr 6f :221 :451 1:104ft 12 116 2½ 21½ 21½ 21¾ Sibille R 12 ⒻⓈ 10000 82-11 GloryBond,PrncssDbrh,TB!mprssv 12
9Aug89-9Dmr 6f :22 :45 1:11 ft 7½ 117 2½ 2½ 22 65½ Olivares F 2 Ⓕ 10000 78-14 Knights Bet, Topside, Sweet Adieu 8
20Jly89-5Hol 6f :214 :451 1:114ft 4¼ 116 65 64½ 97½ 108¼ Sibille R 3 Ⓕ 10000 73-23 Renatta, Dr. Leme, Diamond ADay 12
3Jly89-2Hol 6f :221 :454 1:103ft 9¾ 115 42 41¼ 32 33¾ Sibille R 2 Ⓕ 10000 84-10 PrincssTobin,NlliMlb,PrncssDborh 11
30Nov88-3Hol 7f :222 :453 1:24 ft 6¼ 115 2½ 32 712 716¼ Baze R A 3 ⒻⓈ 16000 68-15 PreeningEgle,CoolClrWtr,CozyRod 7
10Nov88-3Hol 6f :221 :46 1:12 ft 5½ 115 52½ 62 41¾ 41¾ Black C A 6 Ⓕ 16000 80-15 MelynLdy,FltMichll,ButifulBgining 9
10Nov88—Bumped start
22Oct88-3SA 6f :212 :441 1:10 ft 28 116 42 911 915 919¾ Solis A 2 Ⓕ 32000 68-12 NstyPster,I'mFlxibl,TouchOfTudor 9
22Oct88—Bore out, wide 3/8 turn, into stretch

90ct88-1SA 6f :213 :45 1:112ft 5½ 1135 34 23 21¼ 4½ Corral J R 2 Ⓒ 20000 88-16 HedToSpd,SpcilFrindship,MissLiz 12
  90ct88—Bumped start
22Sep88-8BM 6f :222 :452 1:103ft 4½ 113 21½ 43½ 912 911 Schacht R 4 ⒻAw16000 75-22 Balclutha, Mordido, Newscene 9
5Sep88-5BM 6f :221 :451 1:102ft 5¼ 116 2nd 2nd 13 13 Schacht R 2 Ⓒ 20000 87-12 PrncssDbrh,SrngWng,OnOrAnnvrsr 8
  Speed Index: Last Race: -7.0   3–Race Avg.: -6.3   10–Race Avg.: -7.5   Overall Avg.: -7.5
  Oct 14 Hol 4f ft :58² H   ●Oct 1 Hol 4f ft :48 H

Oak Portal

Dk. b. or br. m. 6, by Hyannis Port—Oak Harbor, by Polly's Jet
CASTANON J L   Br.—Braun Mr-Mrs C A (Cal)   1989 7 0 1 0 $4,375
Own.—Lebowitz L   **1115**   Tr.—Kooba Paul $10,000   1988 13 1 4 2 $41,475
           Lifetime 54 9 10 5 $139,800   Turf 2 0 1 0 $7,680

6Oct89-1SA 6f :213 :45 1:103ft 9½ 1115 42 43 34½ 25¼ Castanon J L9 Ⓒ 10000 79-15 PlayingThrough,OkPortl,PlyDncer 12
9Sep89-1Dmr 6½f :221 :453 1:172ft 5 117 32 31 43 76¾ Pincay L Jr 4 Ⓒ 12500 74-11 Slade'sLady,Aflot,GreySeptember 11
  9Sep89—Veered in start
27Aug89-2Dmr 6f :22 :453 1:11 ft 8½ 116 31½ 31½ 44 75½ Black C A 2 Ⓒ 12500 77-15 BrvestStr,MyLdiesTiger,QunsGurd 12
12Feb89-2SA 6½f :22 :451 1:173gd 5 116 53 42½ 98½ 811 Pedroza M A 12 Ⓒ 20000 71-16 Alfitz, Buy More,Sovereign·Appeal 12
4Feb89-4SA 6f :222 :463 1:131sy 12 116 3½ 21½ 34 65 Baze R A 2 Ⓒ 25000 67-30 NastyPaster,DistntHour,Holderme 10
14Jan89-1SA 6f :213 :444 1:101ft 5 115 2¹ 2nd 22 41¾ Baze R A 4 Ⓒ 22500 85-11 ManyPasses,Madhuri,NastyPaster 12
6Jan89-7SA 6½f :22 :451 1:18 gd 9½ 1115 53½ 42½ 45½ 55¾ Corral J R 4 Ⓒ 32000 74-20 Afloat,PlayingThrough,Suspiciously 9
  6Jan89—Broke slowly
26Oct88-5SA 6f :214 :442 1:101ft 6½ 1095 43 44½ 45 34½ Valenzuel F H 2 Ⓒ 20000 83-16 MdonnBlu,PlyingThrough,OkPortl 12
  26Oct88—Broke through gate
8Oct88-1SA 6f :213 :45 1:112ft 7 1095 3½ 22½ 2nd 13 Corral J R 1 Ⓒ 22500 81-17 OkPortl,FlyingHighr,ToBImprssiv 12
7Sep88-3Dmr 6f :221 :452 1:103ft 3½ 116 31½ 32½ 35½ 58½ Sibille R 2 Ⓒ 25000 76-17 PlyngThrogh,TBImprssv,MstDrmtc 6
  Speed Index: Last Race: -6.0   3–Race Avg.: -9.6   10–Race Avg.: -6.5   Overall Avg.: -6.5
  Oct 19 SA 4f ft :48 H   Oct 3 SA 4f ft :472 H   Sep 24 SA 4f ft :582 H   Sep 4 Dmr 5f ft 1:00 H

Lou's Fast

ESP: E/P. She's shown willingness to sit just off the early pace and then come on to compete late. She seems versatile enough to fit in most fields at this level.

Paceline: 25Sep89

Adjusted Paceline:

1Fr: 0

2Call: 1 length

Final: 2 lengths

DRF Var: no adjustment required

Revised line: 25Sep89 22.0   45.0   1:11.0

Bravest Star

ESP: F

Paceline: This mare represents the most difficult decision to be made in this race. Her recent two races indicate a decline in form from her 27Aug89 race at Del Mar. The decline may not be as serious as first perceived. The race at Fairplex may have been simply a dislike for the "bullring." Her 9Sep89 effort may have been a combination of a taxing effort in her previous, and the 6½-furlong distance of that race. Too many "mays." A more adventurous paceline selector "may" have selected the 27Aug89 race, but I made her a noncontender.

Miss Rock Talk

ESP: E/P, probably best as E

Paceline: This filly was the betting favorite until the last few minutes, then drifted upward to 7–2 odds. The activity was no doubt based on her powerful win on 3Sep89 at Del Mar. If she repeats that race, she'll win here. The question we have to answer is: *Will* she repeat that race? The answer should be no.

Today's race will be her second consecutive drop in class searching for a field that will allow her to replicate her win. Her last drop produced an improvement to the second call, but her finishing position did not improve. Once this kind begins to drop repeatedly, they often wind up running at lesser racetracks, continuing to drop in class. We'll use the race on 5Oct89 to analyze her effect on today's probable pace.

DRF Var: none required

Princess Deborah

ESP: P

Paceline: If we use this filly as a contender in the race, she'll be our top-rated horse. Her race on 1Sep89 was a strong effort for the level. The decision that must be made by the handicapper is whether or not she'll run back to that race after 55 days without a race. Her pattern is extremely negative.

A layoff over 30 days for these low-level claimers is a definite cause for concern. They win far less than their fair share of races, and should be carefully evaluated. At the beginning of the Oak Tree meeting, a layoff *is* excusable because of the intervening Fairplex meeting. By October 25, however, Oak Tree had carded plenty of opportunities for this filly to cash in on the good form evident in her last race. She is *not* the filly that ran on 1Sep89. Additionally, her workout pattern shows only two four-furlong works since her race. She is not a contender in today's race.

Oak Portal

ESP: P
Paceline: 6Oct89. This mare has more lifetime wins than all the other betting possibilities combined.
DRF Var: none required

Feet-Per-Second Analysis

All three of the remaining contenders are capable of running to the quarter in 22.0 (60.00) seconds, a negative for the E types. In the second fraction, Lou's Fast and Miss Rock Talk continue on with matching rates of velocity, neither able to open a significant lead. Add to this the probable effect of Bravest Star (E) on the early pace, and the race is a setup for a presser or closer. None of the recent races of the E horses we're considering shows the ability to win after a prolonged pace duel.

Energy Distribution

Our range was 52.10% to 53.30%; the pace setters are considerably over the top limit and are unacceptable betting choices. Even Lou's Fast's race of 16Nov88 is 53.56%, also above our parameters. Oak Portal falls just .10 above the acceptable range and is the only acceptable choice.

The Rankings

	AP	EP	SP	FX	%E
Lou's Fast	1	1	3	2	No
Miss Rock Talk	3	2	3	3	No
Oak Portal	2	3	1	1	Yes

Oak Portal fits the preferred running style (E or P) for Oak Tree sprints. Of our contenders, she is the only one fit to the energy demands of the surface, and also exceeds the requirements of our 2–3–3–3 decision model.

Feet-Per-Second Array

	1Fr	2Fr	3Fr	AP	EP	SP	FX	%E
Lou's Fast	60.00	57.34	49.75	55.67	58.64	54.19	54.87	54.10%
Miss Rock Talk	60.32	56.95	48.30	55.16	58.59	53.44	54.31	54.81%
Oak Portal	60.18	55.98	50.58	55.52	58.00	54.29	55.38	53.41%

The remaining question: Are you willing to take 2–1 odds on her?

FIRST RACE
Santa Anita
OCTOBER 25, 1989

6 FURLONGS. (1.07¾) CLAIMING. Purse $11,000. Fillies and mares. 3-year-olds and upward. Weights, 3-year-olds, 118 lbs.; older, 121 lbs. Non-winners of two races since August 15 allowed 3 lbs.; of a race since then, 5 lbs. Claiming price $10,000. (Races when entered for $8,500 or less not considered.) 17th DAY. WEATHER CLOUDY. TEMPERATURE 70 DEGREES.

Value of race $11,000; value to winner $6,050; second $2,200; third $1,650; fourth $825; fifth $275. Mutuel pool $203,212.

Last Raced	Horse	Eq.A.Wt PP St	¼	½	Str	Fin	Jockey	Cl'g Pr	Odds $1
6Oct89 ¹SA²	Oak Portal	6 111 4 6	7²½	3ʰᵈ	2²½	1¹	Castanon J L⁵	10000	2.30
29Sep89 .7Fpx⁸	Bravest Star	b 5 116 10 1	1ʰᵈ	1¹½	1ʰᵈ	2²½	Pedroza M A	10000	8.00
25Sep8910Fpx⁵	Lou's Fast	4 116 9 9	6¹	4ʰᵈ	3ʰᵈ	3²	Baze R A	10000	7.70
5Oct89 ¹SA⁹	Grey September	6 116 7 8	9⁵	8²	5¹½	4½	Patton D B	10000	10.30
5Oct89 ¹SA⁸	Miss Rock Talk	b 4 113 2 5	4¹½	2ʰᵈ	4¹½	5ⁿᵒ	Nakatani C S⁵	10000	3.50
31Aug89 9Dmr¹¹	Northern Edge	4 113 11 2	5ʰᵈ	7¹	6ʰᵈ	6²½	Eldridge P K⁵	10000	20.90
13Apr89 5SA⁹	Becky's Pocketful	b 4 116 6 11	10⁴	10⁶	8½	7³	Dominguez R E	10000	10.80
1Sep89 1Dmr²	Princess Deborah	b 4 116 3 4	3ʰᵈ	6½	7²	8ʰᵈ	Sibille R	10000	8.90
4Oct89 5SA¹¹	Won Ton Ton	3 114 1 7	8ʰᵈ	9³	9³	9²½	Cedeno A	10000	85.10
6Oct89 ¹SA¹²	Walker's Lady	7 116 8 10	11	11	11	10³	Valenzuela F H	10000	25.70
6Oct89 ¹SA¹¹	My Love To You	b 4 116 5 3	2ʰᵈ	5ʰᵈ	10¹½	11	Flores D R	10000	13.80

OFF AT 1:01. Start good. Won driving. Time, :22, :45½, :58¾, 1:11¾ Track fast.

Official Program Numbers\

$2 Mutuel Prices:

4-OAK PORTAL	6.60	4.20	3.00
10-BRAVEST STAR		7.20	5.00
9-LOU'S FAST			4.80

25OCT89—RACES 2 and 4

The second race on the card was for $32,000 maiden claimers and was won by a pace and speed standout from the powerful D. Wayne Lukas stable. The Fourth, another maiden claiming event, this time for two-year-olds, was loaded with first-time starters and runners with poor pacelines.

25OCT89—THIRD RACE

The 1989 Oak Tree meeting featured the introduction of Santa Anita's much ballyhooed turf course. The surface, lightning fast compared to previous years, was conducive to track-record-threatening performances every day from every class level. Without pars or an acceptable profile from past seasons, this author declined to bet races over the surface.

25OCT89—FIFTH RACE

A bettor's delight. A full field of twelve runners with a false favorite. Our friend "Harry" from the earlier chapter made his daily appearance in this race, opening a myriad of betting possibilities. Let's examine "Harry's" offering to the crowd:

5	HARD TO MISS INFLATION HEDGE CRACKSMAN	HARD TO MISS ON EASY STREET QUIP STAR	HARD TO MISS INFLATION HEDGE LARK'S LEGACY	HARD TO MISS CRACKSMAN INFLATION HEDGE	HARD TO MISS INFLATION HEDGE UNREPRESSED	HARD TO MISS INFLATION HEDGE CRACKSMAN	31 7 3

Hard To Miss — Ro. g. 4, by Zein—Florala, by Proper Proof

PINCAY L JR — 118 — Br.—Cameron Margaret (Cal) — Tr.—Fenstermaker L R — $16,000

Own.—Alvarez & Sleepy Stables — Lifetime 42 6 8 8 $160,398

1989	19	4	3	3	$71,327
1988	15	1	2	5	$56,660
Turf	1	0	0	0	$4,219

9Oct89-3SA	6½f	:21³	:44²	1:15²ft	3½	119	11½	11½	21	35¾	Pincay L Jr1	25000	87-13	Romaxe, Wicked Idea, HardToMiss	9
30Sep89-9Fpx	6½f	:22	:45³	1:17¹ft	3	116	2hd	1hd	11½	1¾	Ortega L E 2	25000	90-13	Hard To Miss, Overidge, DonB.Blue	8
23Sep89-10Fpx	6½f	:21²	:45	1:17¹ft	12	116	72¾	65½	63¾	41	Ortega L E8	25000	89-10	HrryAndSpdy,SprbMomnt,RchTgr	10
23Sep89—Lugged in late															
20Aug89-1Dmr	6f	:21⁴	:44³	1:09³ft	7	118	63¼	55	67	68¾	DelahoussayeE6	40000	81-13	Droully'sBoy,PrsdntsSmmt,VgsEgl	7
20Aug89—Wide 3/8 turn															
3Aug89-9Dmr	6½f	:22²	:45	1:15⁴ft	5½	118	3½	32	65¾	88	Davis R G6	40000	81-14	DmscusDrm,UndrAndOvr,KyPrchs	10
3Aug89—Wide into stretch															
2Jly89-8AC	6f	:22	:44¹	1:08³ft	2	124	43	43	53¾	58	EnriquezHF5	A C Xprs	88-14	Rosie's K. T., CesarEduardo,Zarutli	9
11Jun89-8AC	5f	:21³	:43²	:57 ft	9-5	120	2½	31	2hd	1½	EnrzHF8	T J Charro H	92-12	HrdToMiss,CesrEdurdo,ChilliWilli	12
31May89-5Hol	6f	:22	:44⁴	1:09³ft	*2½	117	32½	31½	32	31½	Davis R G6	c40000	92-15	Third Census, Pialor, Hard To Miss	9
31May89—Bumped hard break															
21May89-5Hol	6½f	:21⁴	:44	1:15¹ft	3½	117	41½	42½	2hd	2¾	Davis R G4	c32000	90-05	KevinsDefens,HrdToMiss,HdlinNws	8
6May89-2Hol	6f	:21³	:44³	1:09²ft	2½	117	21½	21½	2½	1½	Davis R G3	c25000	94-09	HrdToMiss,KvinsDfns,RoylCmronin	9

Speed Index: Last Race: 0.0 3–Race Avg.: +0.6 10–Race Avg.: +1.0 Overall Avg.: +1.0

Sep 28 Fpx 5f ft 1:01¹ H

The overwhelming consensus choice and betting favorite in this six-furlong event is Hard To Miss, a hard-trying gelding from the L. R. Fenstermaker barn. His last race, a $25,000 claimer, was an excellent try with fast fractions. He set the pace to the eighth pole and then held on for third in a nine-horse field. His previous two races were a win and close-up fourth at the $25,000 level.

So, where does this runner belong on the class ladder? Anything less than $25,000 represents a bargain claim for interested investors. At $16,000 he should attract claims like bears to honey!

One thing is certain: he *should* attract modern pace handicappers to the race.

With a phony 8–5 shot in the field, there will be more than a few legitimate contenders held at overlaid prices. Don't shy away from the race because of Hard To Miss. The Fifth race was an opportunity to catch the crowd in one of its rare moments of weakness. *Always* attack this type of race aggressively.

Hard To Miss is a noncontender in this $16,000 claimer. We may use his early fractions in our analysis of early pace, but we will *not* bet this negative class dropper.

The Noncontenders

Several runners are racing in soft form. They are:

Quip Star: His recent finishes have been in the rear third of his fields *and*, in the important turn-time fraction, he's been losing ground to the pace of his races. When in form, this guy *gains* in the second fraction.

Biscayne Boy: He's a bit cheaper than these, has been without a race for 31 days, and has only two works in the interim. Additionally, there is enough early pace in here to keep him honest if he should gain the lead.

On Easy Street: Another in poor form. His only in-the-money performance was a win against maiden $32,000 claimers, the worst horses on the grounds.

Lark's Legacy: 1 for 22 over the last two seasons, no race in 39 days, a negative rider switch, a poor workout pattern at a training facility, and a poor barn. Other than those few negatives, this one's a cinch!

Instinctive Reason: His last two races are horrible, his last ten races mostly weak efforts, and his new connections are willing to drop him $9,000 in selling price after only one race.

J.'s Flyer: A terrible horse.

That leaves only five horses for serious consideration:

(1) Inflation Hedge
(2) Fleet Form
(3) Hechizara De Oro
(4) Discovered Gold
(5) King Of Bazaar

None of the pacelines we'll use in this race are from Del Mar, so we'll adjust the Fairplex lines to Santa Anita.

Inflation Hedge	B. g. 5, by Raymond Earl—I'm Booshed, by Tarboosh					
	Br.—Biszantz & Coop (Cal)			1989 10 3 1 1		$25,885
STEVENS G L	**118**	Tr.—Shulman Sanford	$16,000	1988 5 1 0 1		$12,000
Own.—Quezada J		Lifetime 15 4 1 2	$37,885			

40ct89-2SA 6¼f :21³ :44² 1:16¹ft *2½ 118 3¹ 3½ 2¹ 44½ VlenzuelPA² Ⓢ c12500 84-15 Bubb'sBullt,NtrllyMtch,GoStdyLd 11
19Sep89-11Fpx 6¼f :21⁴ :45³ 1:16²ft *2½ 119 4² 3² 32½ 3⁸ Sibille R³ 16000 86-10 CoursngEgl,BlckOrphs,Infl.onHdg 10
19Sep89—Rough start

4Sep89-1Dmr 6f :22 :443 1:084ft *2½ 116 2½ 31½ 44½ 77¾ Solis A9 25000 86-13 Royal Eagle,WellInTheAir,Romaxe 12

4Sep89—Wide into stretch

24Aug89-5Dmr 6½f :22 :443 1:154ft 4¾ 116 1½ 11 11½ 14 ValenzuelPA4 [S] 16000 89-13 InfltionHedg,CityViw,BiddingNtiv 10

24Aug89—Drifted out late

9Aug89-3Dmr 6f :221 :451 1:101ft *2½ 116 42 1hd 12 11¾ Cedeno A2 c10000 87-14 InfltionHdg,D.D.ThKid,BiddingNtiv 8

9Aug89—Broke very slowly

27Jly89-3Dmr 6½f :221 :451 1:161ft 6 117 31 2hd 11½ 21¾ Cedeno A2 [S] 10000 85-16 Contravene,InfltionHedge,VegsKey 8

10Jly89-5Hol 6f :22 :442 1:093ft 29 117 77¼ 76¼ 87½ 63¾ Sibille R4 [S] 16000 89-12 AmzingCourg,InspirdToo,FighAbhil 8

18Jun89-5Hol 6f :214 :45 1:101ft 32 115 74¼ 64½ 77½ 89½ Cedeno A8 20000 80-12 BickerBear,LansMnus,InspiredToo 12

29May89-1Hol 6f :221 :452 1:103ft 9½ 117 1hd 11 11 1hd Cedeno A3 12500 88-13 InfltionHdg,WldPursut,OrchrdSong 6

14May89-1Hol 6f :213 :443 1:101ft 37 116 1hd 1hd 3nk 54¼ Cedeno A9 12500 86-09 InspiredToo,NtivConqust,Silor'sTl 12

Speed Index: Last Race: -1.0 3-Race Avg.: -2.0 10-Race Avg.: -1.3 Overall Avg.: -1.3

Oct 15 SA 6f ft 1:13 H ●Oct 2 SA 3f ft :343 H Sep 16 SA 4f ft :49 H Sep 1 Dmr 3f ft :362 H

ESP: E/P. This one got very good during the summer months before tailing off at the end of Del Mar. He's very versatile, was claimed by a good barn, and his last shows possible form improvement. At the very least he'll have some impact on the early pace scenario.

Paceline: 4Oct89

DRF Var: no adjustment required

***Fleet Form** Ch. g. 6, by Double Form—Fleetsin, by Jim French

CASTANON J L 1095 Br.—Mamakos J (Ire) 1989 4 0 1 1 $6,900

Tr.—Ellis Ronald W $14,000 1988 12 2 1 0 $41,425

Own.—Syndicate Stable Lifetime 36 5 5 5 $107,403 Turf 22 3 3 4 $53,978

15Sep89-9Fpx 6½f :221 :454 1:171ft 2¾ 116 62¼ 41½ 21½ 22 Valenzuela F H1 12500 88-12 SndyMck,FletForm,StrlingExchng 10

15Sep89—Bore out 1st turn

13Aug89-1Dmr 7f :222 :451 1:224ft *2¾ 116 86 107¾ 1011 1016¼ Black C A5 c16000 72-14 Polysemous, Exploded Jr., Pain 10

13Aug89—Broke slowly

5Aug89-1Dmr 6½f :221 :452 1:163ft 11 116 64 63½ 41¾ 52¼ Black C A6 20000 83-15 Polysmous,Droully'sBoy,GrnMsco 11

5Aug89—Steadied 5/16

25Jun89-7GG 4½f (T):212 :44 :513fm 63 113 9 88½ 86½ 31¾ Warren R J Jr4 Hcp0 – – SummerSle,MjesticCper,FletForm 10

17Dec88-9BM 6f :222 :452 1:091ft 7¾ 117 32¾ 32 65 76¾ Diaz A L8 25000 86-16 Cordova Red, Bold Bargair, Renzo 9

20Nov88-5Hol 6½f :214 :443 1:161ft 13 116 73¾ 52½ 33½ 1010½ Black C A10 32000 83-12 Amnothrbrothr,TrpclWhp,FrrJcqs 11

7Nov88-5SA a6½f (T):211 :441 1:152fm 38 116 107¼ 95 118¼ 107¼ Black C A10 70000 75-18 BrightAndRight,Cstnilli,Complicte 12

27Sep88-12Fpx 6½f :212 :45 1:154ft 13 114 66 67½ 67¼ 68¼ PdrozMA5 Gov Cup H 89-11 LttlRdClod,BrodwyPont,Rconntrng 7

3Sep88-3Dmr 6½f :222 :451 1:154ft 4 115 31 1hd 21½ 21¾ McCarron C J6 50000 92-16 KenKnight,FltForm,Amnothrbrothr 6

9Aug88-9LA 6½f :213 :451 1:154ft 4½ 119 56½ 31½ 21 1hd Black C A5 40000 98-13 Fleet Form, Fairly Omen, Bugarian 7

Speed Index: Last Race: 0.0 3-Race Avg.: -5.3 8-Race Avg.: 0.0 Overall Avg.: -0.7

Oct 18 SA 5f ft :593 H Oct 12 SA 5f ft 1:001 H ●Oct 6 SA 3f ft :343 H Sep 11 Dmr 4f ft :474 H

ESP: S. With few exceptions, Fleet Form tends to fall too far behind the early pace to fit our model and profile requirements. He *does* figure to pick up the early pace casualties and noncontenders. He was recently claimed by one of southern California's best young trainers, and figures to continue his improving pattern. In the event the early pace picture falls apart, he may pick up a share of this purse.

Paceline: 15Sep89

Adjusted Paceline:

1Fr: 0
2Call: 1 length
Final: 2 lengths
DRF Var: no adjustment
Revised Line: 15Sep89 22.1 45.3 1:16.4

```
Hechizara De Oro                     Ch. g. 5, by Hechizado—Jolie Gold, by Jolie Jo
  JAUREGUI L H                       Br.—Summit Development (Ky)              1989  7 2 1 1    $19,805
                              1115   Tr.—Webb George H           $16,000      1988 10 2 1 0    $31,915
Own.—Solar Stable                    Lifetime  17 4 2 1  $51,720              Turf  1 0 0 0
10Oct89-7Fpx  6½f :212 :451 1:164ft  3  1145 1hd 1hd 13½ 13½  Castanon J L1   12500 92-09 HechizrDeOro,IndinSignII,AnglArc 10
13Sep89-1Dmr  1   :45 1:094 1:351ft  6¼ 1115 23  2½  1½  54¾  Castanon J L3   12500 85-10 SafetyRoad,NightRomer,SalvteTel 10
31Aug89-1Dmr  6f  :214 :443 1:094ft  4¾ 118  1hd 1hd 2hd 33½  Fernandez AL7  c10000 86-13 HisLegcy,SeeThDrgon,HchizrDOro 12
     31Aug89—Lugged in
12Aug89-8LA   6f  :212 :442 1:101ft  3¾ 116  3nk 1hd 2hd 21½  Fernandez AL10  16000 91-11 Robert'sLd,HchizrDOro,FunHWon 10
5Aug89-10LA   6f  :213 :442 1:092ft  8  114  2hd 2hd 1nk 14   Fernandez A L7  10500 96-12 HchzrDOro,Crcksmn,MrktThFortn 10
2Jly89-1Hol   6f  :214 :444 1:102ft  11 1125 2hd 31½ 43  1011 Jauregui L H1   12500 78-13 FrstToArrv,PublclyPropr,Crcksmn 12
11Jun89-1Hol  6½f :214 :442 1:171ft  16 1125 1hd 2hd 32½ 109½ Jauregui L H1   10000 79-10 Premiere,Contravene,BiscayneBoy 12
9Oct88-4SA    6f  :213 :442 1:094ft  13 1115 44½ 35  33  65   Olguin G L6     20000 84-16 Stn'sBowr,Pppy'sConsl,No'blHost 12
     9Oct88—Bumped start
17Sep88-8Fpx  6½f :203 :451 1:162ft  13 116  42  32½ 56  813½ Fernandez A L1  25000 80-15 Pialor, John's Retreat, Gerril   10
11Sep88-3Dmr  6f  :223 :454 1:111ft  5½ 116  43½ 42  62¾ 72½  Sibille R8      20000 80-17 I'll Be Good,IfyIfy,PeacefulImage 12
     11Sep88—Lugged in
  Speed Index: Last Race: +1.0    3-Race Avg.: +0.6   9-Race Avg.: -2.0     Overall Avg.: -2.3
 Oct 15 Hol 5f ft 1:014 H
```

ESP: E/P. A hard-nosed front runner capable of withstanding prolonged pace duels. With that capability, he should also be able to press the pace from a length or two behind. The question that needs answering is whether he has become strictly a "bullring" specialist. Both his recent wins have been over a ⅝-mile track.

Paceline: 1Oct89
Adjusted Paceline:

1Fr: 0
2Call: 1 length
Final: 2 lengths
DRF Var: One point below the "zero adjustment" range of 10 to 12. We'll adjust the final time by 1 length, with no adjustments to the fractions beyond the required track-track adjustments.
Revised Line: 15Sep89 21.2 45.0 1:16.3

```
Discovered Gold                  B. g. 5, by Stalwart—Near Gold, by Pocket Ruler
                                 Br.—Yoder Mr-Mrs F J (Ky)             1989 13 0 2 1   $13,300
  DAVIS R G               116    Tr.—Marshall Robert W     $16,000     1988 14 0 2 3   $13,330
Own.—Marshall R W                Lifetime  36 1 6 5  $42,100           Turf  6 0 1 0    $3,680
 9Oct89-3SA   6½f:21³ :44² 1:15²ft   44 115  21½ 21½ 34½ 58½  Patton D B2      25000 85-13 Romaxe, Wicked Idea, HardToMiss 9
15Sep89-8BM   6f :22  :44³ 1:09¹ft   5¾ 117  67  66½ 66½ 45   Hansen R D3 Aw16000 88-13 AuditNaughtBe,Tensile,Aron'sDewn 6
    15Sep89—Ducked in start
 9Sep89-6BM   6f :22¹ :44³ 1:08⁴ft   3¾ 115  1hd 2hd 33  69½  Campbell B C1    30000 85-10 DytimBrgin,ZrMoro,Plotting'sHost 6
26Aug89-9BM   6f :22² :45  1:09³ft   13 117  2hd 2hd 21  2nk  Chapman T M5     25000 91-13 MichlD.Mn,DiscovrdGold,CrigRonld 7
12Aug89-9Bmf  6f :22¹ :44² 1:09 ft   9½ 117  2hd 2hd 1hd 31½  Chapman T M6     25000 93-08 SkyBllet,CriJillHjji,DiscoveredGold 6
 1Aug89-10LA  6½f:22¹ :46¹ 1:16³ft   14 119  41¾ 41½ 87¾ 913¾ CastanonAL 2 ⓓMcfdn 78-13 ‡Charlatan,SnowPerch,BearInMind 9
    1Aug89—Placed eighth through disqualification
21Jly89-3Hol  6f :22² :45² 1:11 ft   4¾ 117  2hd 2hd 2hd 2hd  Davis R G2       28000 86-14 GrnMusco,DscovrdGold,FrstToArrv 6
13Jly89-3Hol  5½f:21⁴ :45² 1:04 ft   47 108⁵ 83½ 64¾ 63  45   Jauregui L H5    28000 89-14 SuprbMomnt,DmscusDrm,WrBronz 8
29Apr89-5Hol  7f :21⁴ :44³ 1:22³ft   46 119  3½  3½  76  810½ Pedroza MA6   Aw27000 81-10 HollywoodHys,Freeskte,WickedIde 8
22Apr89-5SA   a6½f ⓣ:22¹ :45²1:16 fm 10 120  31  53½ 54  57½  Solis A4      Aw32000 71-19 Sinforoso,HombrHombr,GcrgHobrt 8
  Speed Index: Last Race: -2.0     3-Race Avg.: -2.0     9-Race Avg.: -1.7     Overall Avg.: -2.6
 Oct 4 SA 4f ft :48² H
```

ESP: E/P. Primarily E, but the 26Aug89 race showed a willingness to continue after apparently beaten on the lead. His style seems closely matched to Hechizara De Oro, although this one has no idea of the location of the winner's circle. He's 1 for 36 lifetime and would press the patience of any thoughtful bettor. However, he does fit the race and may create a problem for any runner needing an easy trip on the lead.

Paceline: 9Oct89

DRF Var: One point below the "zero adjustment" range of 14 to 16. We'll adjust the final time by 1 length, with no adjustments to the fractions.

Revised Line: 9Oct89   21.3   44.2   1:15.3

```
King Of Bazaar                   Ch. g. 5, by Air Forbes Won—Blue Period, by Arts and Letters
                                 Br.—Crutcher Dr R R (Ky)              1989 15 2 1 2   $17,735
  DELAHOUSSAYE E          116    Tr.—Hess R B Jr           $16,000     1988  1 0 0 0
Own.—Five Friends Stable         Lifetime  22 4 1 3  $37,210           Turf  1 0 0 1      $990
12Oct89-5SA   6½f:22¹ :45  1:17¹ft   15 116  85½ 84½ 62¾ 62   DelahoussayeE 7  16000 82-16 Prime Concord, Art'sAngel,Valdad 11
    12Oct89—Crowded last 1/16
28Aug89-1Dmr  6f :22  :44⁴ 1:09 ft   24 116  96¾ 87½ 86½ 56½  Davis R G3       20000 87-14 MuchFineGold,Lrk'sLegcy,Romxe 11
13Aug89-3Dmr  7f :22² :45  1:23 ft  *2½ 118  73¾ 83¾ 54  45¼  Black C A3      c16000 82-14 Kamikaze, Contravene, Shirkee 9
    13Aug89—Lugged in early
 6Aug89-2Dmr  6½f:22  :45  1:16⁴ft   5¾ 118  44  43¾ 33  21½  Olivares F 11    12500 82-14 Mr. Spade,KingOfBazaar,Barnhart 12
    6Aug89—Wide into stretch
16Jly89-4Cby  7½f ⓣ:23 :46⁴1:31 fm   3½ 117  77  84¾ 65  32½  Lozoya D A8     22500 86-09 WnglssFlght,AmcsCror,KngOfBzr 10
29Jun89-7Cby  6½f:22¹ :45  1:16¹ft   3¼ 118  63½ 62  51½ 11½  Lozoya D A7     20000 89-16 KingOfBazr,TexsTrio,WildRedBerry 7
    29Jun89—Lacked room.
18Jun89-8Cby  6½f:22¹ :45  1:16²ft   7¾ 118  65¾ 54¾ 33½ 33   Lozoya D A1   Aw12000 85-13 AlbmSlmmer,Sugr'sBest,KingOfBzr 6
19May89-6Cby  6f :22² :45² 1:10²m    5½ 116  62¾ 31½ 2hd 1nk  Lozoya D A8     12500 94-14 KingOfBzr,Lngoldyon,Dle'sDoublD. 8
    19May89—Five wide
 7May89-11TuP 6½f:21³ :43² 1:14³ft   27 115  106½ 77½ 77¾ 65  EstradJJr8 Sttl Slw H 93-13 ToghOpposton,HndsomIs,PsAKttn 13
26Apr89-11TuP 6½f:23  :45¹ 1:16 ft *9-5 114  2½  42½ 68  43   Salvino D M5  Aw4700 88-19 Lord Felon, Sky Ballet, Mojo Man 7
  Speed Index: Last Race: -2.0     3-Race Avg.: -1.6     9-Race Avg.: +1.6     Overall Avg.: +1.0
 Oct 5 SA 6f ft 1:14³ H     Sep 28 SA 5f ft 1:03⁴ H     Sep 22 SA 5f ft 1:03² H     Aug 25 Dmr 3f ft :39⁴ H
```

ESP: S. He's improving for his new connections, and may have won his last start except for trouble in the last 330 feet.

His style is contrary to the model and profile, so he'll need a lot of help from the early pace runners.

Paceline: 12Oct89. Some handicappers may prefer to use the 6Aug89 race because of the trouble in his last start. That's perfectly acceptable, but after adjustments, the race rates almost identical to the one we're using as his paceline.

DRF Var: no adjustment required

Feet-Per-Second Array

	1Fr	2Fr	3Fr	AP	EP	SP	FX	%E
Inflation Hedge	60.64	58.11	50.62	56.44	59.34	54.98	55.63	53.96%
Fleet Form	58.44	56.83	52.64	55.96	57.62	55.13	55.54	52.25%
Hechizara De Oro	61.68	55.93	52.21	56.51	58.66	55.44	56.94	52.90%
Discovered Gold	60.41	57.89	50.72	56.32	59.12	54.92	55.56	53.82%
King Of Bazaar	57.11	58.20	52.01	55.78	57.66	54.84	54.56	52.57%

Feet-Per-Second Analysis

We should begin the analysis with a brief discussion of the fps characteristics of Fairplex Park. The track features a very short run to the turn in sprint races, requiring an all-out effort to obtain position. As a result, first fraction velocities, especially at 6½ furlongs, can be astoundingly fast. Second fractions are often completed in a more leisurely fashion as runners settle into position for the remainder of the race.

Hechizara De Oro exits that kind of race. In matching today's contenders, the match-up in the first two fractions should be considered in light of the track over which they were run. Hechizara De Oro's first fraction will probably not transfer to Santa Anita, so we won't look for him to open a big early lead.

Of our contenders, Hechizara De Oro and Inflation Hedge should be well placed, with Discovered Gold just off those two. Biscayne Boy and Hard To Miss, both noncontenders, should also ensure a faster than average early pace. Inflation Hedge and Hechizara De Oro have demonstrated they can handle pressure and go on to win. Discovered Gold has shown he hasn't the will to win and, especially without the benefit of an early pace edge, should not be considered as a possible bet.

Fleet Form is clearly the better of the two closers. King Of Bazaar should be eliminated from win consideration.

Energy Distribution

The range was 52.10% to 53.30%. The target energy number was 52.90%. Let's examine each of the contenders.

Inflation Hedge: 53.96%, well over the top limit of our range. For this type to win, it will be necessary to coast on a comfortable lead, saving energy for the latter part of the race. That's not probable in this scenario.

Fleet Form: 52.25%, barely inside the parameters. His energy distribution is acceptable and he remains a definite betting possibility.

Hechizara De Oro: 52.90%. This horse is right on the target energy number, and if he fits the profile and model requirements, is a strong probability for the win.

Discovered Gold: 53.82%. He has the same basic weaknesses as Inflation Hedge.

King Of Bazaar: 52.57%. Well within the parameters, but we've already determined that Fleet Form is the more likely winner of our closers.

Hechizara De Oro, Fleet Form, and King Of Bazaar survive the match-up of energy distribution patterns.

The Rankings

	AP	EP	SP	FX	%E
Hechizara De Oro	1	3	1	1	Yes
Inflation Hedge	2	1	3	2	No
Discovered Gold	3	2	4	3	No
Fleet Form	4	4	2	3	Yes
King Of Bazaar	5	4	5	5	Yes

Decision Model and Track Profile

Only two horses fit the 2–3–3–3 requirements of the decision model: Hechizara De Oro and Inflation Hedge. Both fit the up-close requirements of the track profile, but only Hechizara De Oro passes the Percent Early Energy test. Based on *all* our criteria, he is the horse to beat.

The Betting Decision

One-horse bettors should enthusiastically support Hechizara De Oro. His only cloud is the possibility he may be a "bullring" specialist unable to transfer his form to a one-mile racetrack. If in doubt, demand price. He was sent off at 17.80–1 odds!!

Bettors employing multiple win betting should have also considered Inflation Hedge and Fleet Form. The former had only his energy pattern as a negative, while the latter's style was his only negative.

FIFTH RACE

Santa Anita

OCTOBER 25, 1989

6 FURLONGS. (1.07¾) CLAIMING. Purse $14,000. 3-year-olds and upward. Weights, 3-year-olds, 118 lbs.; older, 121 lbs. Non-winners of two races since August 15 allowed, 3 lbs.; of a race since then, 5 lbs. Claiming price $16,000; if entered for $14,000 allowed 2 lbs. (Races when entered for $12,500 or less not considered.)

Value of race $14,000; value to winner $7,700; second $2,800; third $2,100; fourth $1,050; fifth $350. Mutuel pool $307,142. Exacta pool $358,856.

Last Raced	Horse	Eqt.A.Wt PP St	¼	½	Str	Fin	Jockey	Cl'g Pr	Odds $1
10ct89 7Fpx1	Hechizara De Oro	5 116 7 1	2²	2¹¹	1¹	1¹¹	Black C A†	16000	17.80
15Sep89 9Fpx2	Fleet Form	6 110 6 10	11²	6¹	5¹¹	2ⁿᵏ	Castanon J L⁵	14000	9.50
4Oct89 2SA4	Inflation Hedge	5 118 3 4	4ʰᵈ	5¹	3¹	3¹	Stevens G L	16000	8.00
12Oct89 5SA6	King Of Bazaar	b 5 116 12 8	10ʰᵈ	10¹	7¹	4¹	Delahoussaye E	16000	4.20
9Oct89 3SA5	Discovered Gold	b 5 116 8 9	9ʰᵈ	7¹¹	8¹¹	5¹¹	Davis R G	16000	29.60
9Oct89 3SA3	Hard To Miss	4 118 9 2	3¹	4¹	6ʰᵈ	6¹	Pincay L Jr	16000	1.60
24Sep89 8Fpx4	Biscayne Boy	b 5 111 2 3	1ʰᵈ	1¹	2¹¹	7¹	Nakatani C S⁵	16000	17.40
12Oct89 5SA7	Quip Star	7 116 1 7	5¹¹	3ʰᵈ	4ʰᵈ	8¹	Pedroza M A	16000	14.40
16Sep89 9Fpx4	Lark's Legacy	b 8 111 5 5	7¹¹	9ʰᵈ	9¹¹	9²¹	Davenport C L⁵	16000	12.30
12Oct89 5SA5	On Easy Street	b 4 116 4 12	8ʰᵈ	11¹¹	10¹¹	10¹	Sibille R	16000	13.30
19Sep89 11Fpx5	J.'s Flyer	4 111 11 11	12	12	11¹¹	11²¹	Guymon T F⁵	16000	212.90
9Oct89 5SA9	Instinctive Reason	b 4 116 10 6	6ʰᵈ	8¹	12	12	Solis A	16000	16.80

OFF AT 3:07. Start good for all but ON EASY STREET. Won driving. Time, :21⅖, :44⅘, :57¼, 1:10½ Track fast.

$2 Mutuel Prices:

7-HECHIZARA DE ORO	37.60	17.20	12.40
6-FLEET FORM		11.60	6.20
3-INFLATION HEDGE			5.00

$5 EXACTA 7-6 PAID $881.00.

25OCT89—SIXTH RACE

A sprint for maiden fillies three years and older. Too many first-time starters for a thorough analysis of pace.

25OCT89—SEVENTH RACE

7th Santa Anita

1 MILE. (1.33⅘) CLAIMING. Purse $32,000. 3-year-olds. Weight, 121 lbs. Non-winners of two races at one mile or over since August 15 allowed 3 lbs.; of such a race since then, 5 lbs. Claiming price $50,000; if entered for $45,000 allowed 2 lbs. (Races when entered for $40,000 or less not considered.)

Just Deeds B. g. 3(May), by Beau's Eagle—Shaky Footing, by Shecky Greene
Br.—Dilbeck Ray (Cal) 1989 10 2 0 3 $30,400
NAKATANI C S 1115 Tr.—Mason Lloyd C $50,000 Turf 2 0 0 0
Own.—Dilbeck R Lifetime 10 2 0 3 $30,400
12Oct89-8SA 1 ①:46 1:093 1:34 fm 43 1115 55 67½ 77¾ 89¼ Nakatani CS9 Aw37000 92 — ImmrtlScrpt,LvThDrm,Bbtscldtsd 10
1Sep89-3Dmr 7f :222 :45 1:214ft 4¾ 1115 3½ 2½ 2hd 32¼ Nakatani C S6 62500 91-11 Its Royalty, Comical, Just Deeds 6
24Aug89-3Dmr 1 ①:491 1:124 1:37 fm 22 117 62¼ 43 63¾ 63½ Pincay L Jr5 Aw38000 82-09 Friendly Ed, Strung Up, One Drink 8
24Aug89—Wide throughout
11Aug89-8Dmr 7f :214 :441 1:213ft 42 115 65½ 76¼ 65 65½ Black C A7 ⓈRl Gd Dl 88-15 Mr. Bolg, Timeless Answer, Bruho 7
11Aug89—5 wide into lane
9Jly89-9Pln 6f :224 :452 1:103ft *1 117 41½ 53½ 57 56½ Chapman T M3 HcpO 82-18 BearInMind,Doncreer,PlusOrMinus 6
24Jun89-7GG 6f :214 :45 1:101ft 6½ 117 42½ 41½ 31 1¾ ChapmanTM6 Aw20000 88-16 Just Deeds, Comical, Bin Of Ice 7
24Jun89—Bumped start
10Jun89-8GG 6f :212 :44 1:093ft 8¼ 117 43 31½ 31½ 32 ChapmanTM6 Aw20000 89-11 Desert Rival, Vote, Just Deeds 8
27May89-7GG 6f :214 :443 1:092ft 9¾ 117 95 63¾ 54¾ 34½ Kaenel J L5 Aw20000 87-15 Mr. Don, Rip Curl, Just Deeds 10
6May89-6GG 1 :461 1:094 1:351ft 33 109 21½ 22 26 48¼ Gryder A T2 HcpO 81-14 AvengingForce,BseCmp,Beu'sAllinc 7
23Apr89-4GG 6f :221 :453 1:113gd 29 118 11 2hd 1hd 1½ ChapmnTM4 ⓈM20000 81-17 JustDeeds,KingoftheByou,GryWhl 12
23Apr89—Broke in a tangle
Speed Index: Last Race: -5.0 1-Race Avg.: -5.0 1-Race Avg.: -5.0 Overall Avg.: -0.5
Oct 18 SA 3f ft :353 H Oct 6 SA 7f ft 1:301 H Sep 30 SA 6f ft 1:143 H Sep 20 SA 3f gd :37 H

Its Royalty B. c. 3(Mar), by Native Royalty—Cuidado Jan, by Introductive
Br.—AIBAIncThbd&OwnsRE&Sns (Ky) 1989 4 1 1 0 $25,250
SIBILLE R 116 Tr.—Mulhall Richard W $50,000 1988 7 M 0 2 $10,975
Own.—Arnold & Fulmer Lifetime 11 1 1 2 $36,225
1Sep89-3Dmr 7f :222 :45 1:214ft 15 116 59 57 33 12½ DelahoussayeE 5 62500 93-11 Its Royalty, Comical, Just Deeds 6
20Feb89-5SA 1 1/16 :474 1:121 1:433ft 39 115 1110 106¾ 75½ 68 Sibille R 9 Aw35000 75-19 ExemplryLeder,Copet,BrirticChief 11
3Feb89-3SA 1 1/16 :461 1:112 1:444ft 4¼ 116 811 76½ 43 2nk DelahoussayeE 6 40000 77-17 ScoutOffFortune,ItsRoylty,DimeTim8
3Feb89—Bumped start
11Jan89-2SA 1 :462 1:114 1:381ft *7-5 117 43 31½ 1½ 13 † DelahoussyeE 1 M32000 77-14 ItsRoyalty,Naskra'sWltz,Dr.Hughes 9
11Jan89—Disqualified from purse money; Broke out, bumped
14Dec88-3Hol 1 1/16 :472 1:122 1:454ft 5½ 118 75¼ 64½ 34 3¾ DelahoussyeE 4 M32000 70-16 LuckIsSweet,Dramtized,ItsRoylty 12
14Dec88—Wide 3/8
3Nov88-4SA 1 1/16 :464 1:123 1:451ft *2 117 43 32½ 37 310 Stevens G L 4 M40000 65-18 LeliaLove,TropicWarrior,ItsRoylty 12
3Nov88—Veered out, bumped start, again at 7 1/2
16Oct88-6SA 1 1/16 :462 1:113 1:454ft 9½ 117 79 56¾ 49 410¼ Baze R A 6 Mdn 62-16 SnowsInPris,Pster'sImge,P.cerRex 12
16Oct88—Broke in a tangle
5Oct88-2SA 1 :471 1:122 1:381ft 16 117 813 59 56½ 47½ Ortega L E 5 Mdn 69-21 MrThnGrn,LghtThWrld,ExmplryLdr 8
5Oct88—Steadied start
12Sep88-6Dmr 6f :223 :46 1:104ft 7¾ 118 89¼ 76½ 57 47 Ortega L E 7 M62500 77-19 Gum, Charlie O., Pope's Warning 9
12Sep88—Veered in start
29Aug88-6Dmr 6f :22 :453 1:112ft 35 118 74½ 64½ 74¾ 52¾ Ortega L E 11 M50000 78-18 LoddJn,Bbytscoldtsd,StrctCnfdnc 12
29Aug88—Bumped start
Speed Index: Last Race: -6.0 3-Race Avg.: -7.0 7-Race Avg.: -12.0 Overall Avg.: -8.8
Oct 20 SA 6f ft 1:15 H Oct 15 SA 6f ft 1:132 H Oct 10 SA 5f ft 1:004 H Sep 29 SA 6f ft 1:16 H

Rolling Donut
DAVIS R G
Own.—Naify Valerie
B. c. 3(Feb), by Flying Paster—Etzel, by Silent Screen
Br.—Rancho Jonata (Cal)
116 Tr.—Headley Bruce $50,000
Lifetime 10 1 2 1 $32,550
1989 7 1 0 0 $19,250
1988 3 M 2 1 $13,300

11Oct89-7SA 1 :461 1:103 1:354ft 6½ 120 52½ 41½ 53 77 McCarronCJ 5Aw34000 81-12 PrinceColony,KingTufn,ClevrRturn 9
19Aug89-5Dmr 6½f :221 :442 1:153ft 4½ 116 66¾ 69 46 45½ McCarronCJ 9Aw32000 84-14 Wily, Doncareer, Explosive Dream 9
16Apr89-7SA 1 1/16 :462 1:11 1:43 ft 8½ 118 31½ 32 45 56 Meza R Q 2 Aw36000 80-16 NotorousPlsur,ImprlLd,PrncColony 6
1Apr89-7SA 1 :454 1:101 1:363ft 7 119 95¾ 87½ 68½ 69¾ Black C A7 Aw36000 75-16 Malagr,NotoriousPlesure,AnnulDte 9
8Mar89-8SA 1⅛ :46 1:103 1:484ft 35 115 89 95¾ 76½ 68 Black C A6 Ⓢ Brdbry 77-15 Prized,CarolLover,ExemplaryLeder 10
8Mar89—Checked, altered path 1/4
19Feb89-6SA 1 1/16 :464 1:114 1:453ft 4 117 811 65½ 21½ 1½ Black C A7 Mdn 73-21 RollngDont,StylshBlvr,NrthrnDrm 11
8Jan89-8SA 7f :221 :443 1:204ft 53 114 118½118½ 69½ 614½ Black CA11 Ⓢ Brs Chp 81-13 PstAgs,VryPrsonbly,FlyngCntnntl 11
29Dec88-6SA 7f :223 :452 1:231ft *1 118 31½ 21½ 2hd 2½ Black C A3 Mdn 83-12 ShdyPine,RollingDonut,PtTheTnor 9
29Dec88—Lugged in early
10Dec88-2Hol 1 :453 1:112 1:371ft *2½ 118 42½ 31 1hd 2½ Black C A8 Mdn 76-15 Goldonrube, Rolling Donut,Copeta 12
10Dec88—Wide final 3/8
26Nov88-3Hol 7f :214 :45 1:23 ft 4½ 118 95½ 63½ 35 34½ Black C A10 ⓈMdn 85-12 DontsToDollrs,FstDlSol,RollngDnt 10
Speed Index: Last Race: -7.0 3-Race Avg.: -6.6 6-Race Avg.: -7.1 Overall Avg.: -5.9
Oct 22 SA 3f ft :35 H Oct 7 SA 4f ft :483 H Oct 1 SA 7f ft 1:261 H Sep 25 SA 7f ft 1:28 H

Shady Pine
PINCAY L JR
Own.—Winner C N & Anne
Ch. c. 3(Apr), by Flying Paster—Bold Take, by Bold Forbes
Br.—Jones A U (Cal)
116 Tr.—Aguilera Humberto $50,000
Lifetime 15 1 4 1 $46,425
1989 11 0 4 1 $31,575
1988 4 1 0 0 $14,850
Turf 2 0 0 0

13Sep89-2Dmr 1 :443 1:091 1:344ft 4½ 116 911 910 916 922¼ McCarron C J 5 50000 70-10 LteExpress,John'sReveng,KingTufn 9
13Sep89—6-wide into lane
1Sep89-3Dmr 7f :222 :45 1:214ft 6 116 44 45½ 59 510¾ Solis A 2 62500 82-11 Its Royalty, Comical, Just Deeds 6
1Sep89—Lugged out
7Aug89-3Dmr 1 :454 1:104 1:371ft 3¾ 116 58½ 54½ 53½ 2no Solis A 3 62500 80-20 ByNoMens,ShdyPin,ScoutOfFortun 5
7Aug89—Lugged out
31Jly89-7Dmr 6½f :214 :442 1:153ft 19 116 99¾ 86½ 56½ 38½ Solis A 3 ⓈAw30000 81-16 T. V. Screen, Comical, Shady Pine 9
31Jly89—Wide into stretch
14Jly89-5Hol 1 :443 1:09 1:352ft 9 116 611 68½ 49½ 27 Solis A 6 62500 79-16 CourgeousPirte,ShdyPine,FettlKttl 7
27Apr89-7Hol 1 Ⓣ:4641:11 1:36 fm 16 117 1116111110151118½ Solis A 7 Aw28000 65-16 Skisit,Presidential,Plymeonmortim 12
29Mar89-8SA a6½f Ⓣ:213 :44 1:144fm 50 114 1117111611181121½ ShoemkerW 2 Baldwin 63-18 TenciousTom,MountinGhost,Gum 11
29Mar89—Steadied start
10Mar89-7SA 7f :221 :443 1:223ft 8 120 66½ 56½ 55½ 25 Solis A 3 ⓈAw32000 82-17 Mr. Bolg, Shady Pine, Saros Town 8
10Mar89—Erratic backstretch; wide in stretch
20Feb89-5SA 1 1/16 :474 1:121 1:433ft 8½ 116 83¾ 61¾ 86¾ 810¾ Solis A 6 Aw35000 72-19 ExemplryLeder,Copet,BrirticChief 11
20Feb89—Wide final 3/8
27Jan89-6SA 6½f :213 :44 1:17 ft 70 120 87¼ 76¼ 54½ 21¾ Solis A 4 ⓈAw32000 83-21 MyLuckyLynnie,ShadyPine,Mr.Bolg 8
27Jan89—Lugged out; wide into stretch
Speed Index: Last Race: -20.0 3-Race Avg.: -8.3 4-Race Avg.: -8.5 Overall Avg.: -7.9
Oct 22 Hol 3f ft :374 H Oct 15 Hol 5f ft 1:014 H ●Oct 5 Hol 6f ft 1:133 H Sep 26 Hol 5f ft 1:022 H

Scout Of Fortune
DELAHOUSSAYE E
Own.—Hinds T F
B. c. 3(Apr), by Run of Luck—Tepee Time Gal, by Any Time Now
Br.—Hinds T F (Cal)
116 Tr.—Robbins Jay M $50,000
Lifetime 16 5 0 5 $86,200
1989 13 5 0 4 $83,575
1988 3 M 0 1 $2,625
Turf 2 0 0 0

6Oct89-9SA 1 :461 1:104 1:37 ft 5¾ 115 22 22 21½ 1½ DelahoussayeE2 40000 82-18 ScotOfFrtn,SrsNghtWnd,HnstOnyx 9
13Sep89-2Dmr 1 :443 1:091 1:344ft *3 117 55½ 77 69 59½ Pincay L Jr4 50000 83-10 LteExpress,John'sReveng,KingTufn 9
13Sep89—Lugged out 3/8
23Aug89-5Dmr 1 1/16 Ⓣ:4641:1131:431fm 11 114 79½101210111012¾ Stevens G L2 75000 71-16 CourgousPrt,Lyscnt,RunwyDunwy 10
7Aug89-3Dmr 1 :454 1:104 1:371ft *6-5 115 47 44 43½ 3hd Stevens G L1 60000 80-20 ByNoMens,ShdyPin,ScoutOfFortun 5
7Aug89—Wide into stretch
16Jly89-7Hol 1 1/16 Ⓣ:4731:1121:413fm 23 113 52½ 74¾ 75½ 66¾ BlckCA7 Ⓢ Bstle Dy H 79-16 ArtWork,LiveTheDrem,TnciousTom 7
30Jun89-7Hol 1 1/16 :463 1:104 1:44 ft 10 116 36 35½ 1½ 14½ Stevens G L5 50000 80-16 ScoutOfFortun,GoBobrib,HourFndr 7
15Jun89-5Hol 1 :444 1:093 1:353ft 7¾ 116 84½ 88½ 610 611¾ DelahoussayeE7 62500 73-19 DominatedDebut,Lyscent,WellAwre 9
10May89-9Hol 1 1/16 :472 1:123 1:433ft *2½ 117 2½ 2½ 1hd 32 Pincay L Jr4 50000 80-12 BrllntEquton,FttlKttl,ScotOfFortn 6
25Mar89-3GG 1 :462 1:111 1:37 gd 2¾ 116 21 31½ 55½ 45½ Chapman T M1 HcpO 74-21 AvngingForc,AmdoTucci,‡PririCptn 5
25Mar89—Placed third through disqualification
4Mar89-6GG 1 :454 1:103 1:362ft 2¾ 117 21 21 2hd 11 ChapmanTM5 Aw19000 83-15 ScoutOfFortun,HnoHno,MrvlosMn 9
Speed Index: Last Race: 0.0 3-Race Avg.: -2.3 8-Race Avg.: -4.2 Overall Avg.: -5.2
Oct 20 SA 5f ft 1:001 H Oct 1 SA 5f ft 1:00 H Sep 24 SA 5f ft 1:012 H Sep 2 Dmr 4f ft :482 H

Playmeonemoretime
CASTANON J L
Own.—Jhayare Stables
B. g. 3(Mar), by L'Enjoleur—Protest, by Rash Prince
Br.—Crescent Farm (Ky)
111[5] Tr.—Bellase Wallace $50,000
Lifetime 16 1 1 2 $49,125
1989 7 0 0 1 $6,450
1988 9 1 1 1 $42,675
Turf 4 0 0 1 $4,200

14Oct89-5SA a6½f Ⓣ:211 :4231:131fm 27 1095 42½ 41¾ 44 77 Nakatani CS7 Aw34000 86-07 Movnglkwnnr,KngAlobr,JstoBrwn 11
7Jun89-7Hol 6f :221 :452 1:094ft 4 117 63 41½ 43½ 46½ Pincay L Jr7 Aw30000 86-15 WinchesterDrive,SnowPerch,Dringl 7
7Jun89—Wide final 3/8

18May89-8Hol 1 1/16 ⓣ:47 1:1111:423fm 9¾ 117 72¾ 62¾107¾1010¾ Davis R G6 Aw28000 70-19 Presidential, Mr. O. P., Tokatee 10
18May89—Wide
27Apr89-7Hol 1 ⓣ:4641:11 1:36 fm 4¼ 117 32 32 21½ 3hd DelhoussyeE2 Aw28000 84-16 Skisit,Presidentil,Plymeonnortim 12
15Mar89-8SA a6½f ⓣ:213 :4421:151fm 13 115 44 75¼ 53¾ 66¾ Davis R G8 Aw37000 76-17 Irish,Movinglikeawinner,VlintPete 10
15Mar89—Jumped track marks after start; steadied 4 1/2
5Mar89-7SA 1 :451 1:093 1:353ft 6¼ 116 1hd 2½ 44 811 McCarronCJ3 Aw35000 79-07 RunwyDunwy,NotoriousPlesur,Copt 8
18Feb89-3SA 6½f :214 :45 1:17 ft *2¼ 119 1hd 3nk 41¾ 66¾ McCarronCJ 6Aw32000 78-19 Gntlmn'sStyl,HroicTyp,ClssicKnght 9
29Dec88-8SA 6f :204 :434 1:094ft 8 115 35 33 21 43½ McCrrnCJ 2 Sn Miguel 85-12 RisAStnz,DoublQuick,Movnglkwnnr 8
3Dec88-3Hol 6½f :22 :443 1:163ft 8¾ 120 43 42½ 44 53½ DelhoussyeE4 Aw24000 88-12 Houston,SundySilence,ThrTimsOldr 7
3Dec88—Wide final 3/8
25Nov88-5Hol 1 :45 1:102 1:362sy 14 114 54 55¼ 79¾ 719¼ GrydrAT4 Hst Th Flg 62-23 MuscMrc,DoublQck,CrownCollcton 9
25Nov88—Grade II; Run in divisions
Speed Index: Last Race: –14.0 2–Race Avg.: –14.5 2–Race Avg.: –14.5 Overall Avg.: –5.9
Oct 9 SA 5f ft 1:004 H Oct 3 Hol 6f ft 1:144 H Sep 28 Hol 5f gd 1:02 H Sep 13 SLR tr.t 5f ft 1:011 H

Radar Alert
SORENSON D **116**
Own.—Vail S H
Ch. g. 3(Mar), by Radar Ahead—Gold Martyr, by Gold Admiral II
Br.—Vail S H (Cal) 1989 4 1 0 0 $13,775
Tr.—Needham Lloyd $50,000 1988 0 M 0 0
Lifetime 4 1 0 0 $13,775
13Sep89-2Dmr 1 :443 1:091 1:344ft 17 116 78 45 33½ 41½ Olivares F3 50000 91-10 LteExpress,John'sReveng,KingTufn 9
13Sep89—Bumped at 1/16
3Sep89-3Dmr 6f :214 :443 1:084ft 30 1135 74½ 73¾ 54¼ 45½ Castanon J L1 32000 88-10 Mr. Baldski, Racer Rex, Go DogsGo 8
18Aug89-2Dmr 6f :221 :451 1:103ft 33 116 41½ 54½ 54¼ 1no Sibille R3 ⓢM32000 85-15 RadarAlert,PappyYokum,OhDtFox 11
27May89-4Hol 6f :221 :452 1:094ft 76 115 2hd1116111910243 Solis A6 M50000 67-10 True Potential, Interpol, Le Roc 12
Speed Index: Last Race: +1.0 1–Race Avg.: +1.0 1–Race Avg.: +1.0 Overall Avg.: –6.0
Oct 21 GD tr.t 6f ft 1:124 H Oct 16 GD tr.t 6f ft 1:12 H ●Oct 10 GD tr.t 5f ft 1:023 H Oct 5 GD tr.t 3f ft :37 H

Ask The Man
STEVENS G L **116**
Own.—Doe-Segal-Vallone et al
Ch. g. 3(May), by Glamor Kid—Bubblin Belle, by Wild Lark
Br.—Procter J & W L (Tex) 1989 5 2 1 0 $33,785
Tr.—Canani Julio C $50,000 Turf 1 0 0 0 $1,025
Lifetime 5 2 1 0 $33,785
30Sep89-10Fpx 6½f :213 :45 1:17 ft 3¾ 111 31½ 31½ 2hd 24½ Castanon JL1 Aw33000 86-13 Charlatan,AskTheMn,CleverReturn 7
8Sep89-3Dmr 1 ⓣ:4741:1211:37 fm 4¾ 116 2hd 1hd 1½ 55¼ Sibille R1 80000 81-14 Strogien, Beau's Alliance, Lyscent 6
8Sep89—Rank 7/8 turn
30Aug89-5Dmr 1 :444 1:093 1:36 ft 3¾ 116 2hd 12 13 12 Sibille R1 c40000 86-13 AskThMn,BtOutOfHll,Bonni'sMrk 10
7Aug89-5Dmr 6f :211 :441 1:091ft 3¾ 115 45 52¾ 42½ 45 Sibille R7 Aw32000 87-15 M Single M,Doncareer,LoadedJuan 8
4Jly89-4Hol 6f :221 :452 1:102ft 5 116 2½ 2hd 12½ 16½ Sibille R10 M32000 89-12 AskThMn,ChopmOnThBd,P.J.Bcks 12
Speed Index: Last Race: –1.0 1–Race Avg.: –1.0 1–Race Avg.: –1.0 Overall Avg.: –0.8
●Oct 20 SA 4f ft :464 H Oct 14 SA 5f ft 1:014 H Oct 8 SA 3f ft :364 B Sep 28 SA 3f ft :353 H

Well Aware
SOLIS A **116**
Own.—Murphy-Sssell-SigbndMmes
Ch. c. 3(Mar), by Inverness Drive—Andover Cottage, by Affiliate
Br.—Polk A F Jr (Ky) 1989 14 2 2 2 $36,493
Tr.—Murphy Marcus J $50,000 1988 10 1 2 0 $13,489
Lifetime 24 3 4 2 $49,982 Turf 3 0 0 0
13Sep89-2Dmr 1 :443 1:091 1:344ft 7 116 31½ 33½ 57½ 610½ DelahoussyeE 9 c50000 81-10 LteExpress,John'sReveng,KingTufn 9
13Sep89—Fanned wide 3/8
1Sep89-3Dmr 7f :222 :45 1:214ft 14 115 2½ 3½ 44 48½ Sibille R 3 60000 85-11 Its Royalty, Comical, Just Deeds 6
23Aug89-5Dmr 1 1/16 ⓣ:4641:1131:431fm 47 116 21 2½ 33 77 Sibille R 7 80000 77-16 CourgousPrt,Lyscnt,RunwyDunwy 10
7Aug89-3Dmr 1 :454 1:104 1:371ft 6½ 116 11½ 11 2½ 4½ Sibille R 2 62500 79-20 ByNoMens,ShdyPin,ScoutOfFortun 5
7Aug89—Bumped late
15Jun89-5Hol 1 :444 1:093 1:353ft 32 116 3½ 21½ 34 36½ Sibille R 8 62500 79-19 DominatedDebut,Lyscent,WellAwre 9
4Jun89-7Hol 1 ⓣ:4511:0941:351fm 123 116 2½ 3nk 44 109¼ Sibille R 5 95000 78-10 FrindlyEd,ArtWork,DoublProsprty 12
6May89-3Hol 6f :22 :45 1:094ft 34 116 52¼ 53½ 43½ 65¾ Pedroza M A2 62500 86-09 Gntlmn'sStyl,NmbrOnTto,FrstLylty 9
19Apr89-8SA 1⅛ ⓣ:4641:12 1:49 fm 104 116 42 42½ 911 918½ Sibille R1 ⓢLa Puente 63-19 BrokeTheMold,Irish,ExemplryLedr 9
19Apr89—Rough start
25Mar89-10TuP 1 1/16 :47 1:111 1:443ft 4¾ 122 1hd 1hd 2hd 2¾ Krasner S11 Tu P Dby 74-18 Stalaxis, Well Aware, Stage King 12
11Mar89-10TuP 1 :463 1:11 1:373ft 6 122 3nk 3½ 32 1¾ Krasner S7 Dby Trl 81-18 WellAware,SilkyDiamond,RoyalPln 8
Speed Index: Last Race: –9.0 3–Race Avg.: –4.0 5–Race Avg.: –4.2 Overall Avg.: –6.7
●Oct 19 Hol 5f ft :594 H Oct 14 Hol 6f ft 1:144 H Oct 9 Hol 7f ft 1:274 H Oct 4 Hol 4f ft :481 H

The Seventh race was for three-year-olds at one mile. Based on our understanding of the track profile, we will *not* consider betting E type runners.

The Noncontenders

It's Royalty: After a decisive sprint win at a higher level, trainer Mulhall opted to give the runner 55 days off—an exceedingly negative sign with a powerful claiming winner. Additionally, when Mulhall returns the horse to the races, he drops him in class and switches from a top rider to a journeyman. Too many negative signs.

Shady Pine: The presence of Pincay in the saddle will attract a lot of attention to this horse, but its last two starts are too bad to be excused.

Playmeonemoretime: A bad horse exiting weak races. With the exception of a single turf effort on 27Apr89, he has no race that would impact a field of runners at this class level.

Well Aware: Forty-two days off after the claim, three races in a row that would not threaten this field, and a running style that guarantees defeat on this surface. He may improve off the claim, but his style is still against him here.

That leaves the following horses as possible contenders:

(1) Just Deeds
(2) Rolling Donut
(3) Scout Of Fortune
(4) Radar Alert
(5) Ask The Man

We'll continue to adjust the runners to Santa Anita's pars.

Just Deeds — B. g. 3(May), by Beau's Eagle—Shaky Footing, by Shecky Greene

NAKATANI C S — 1115 — Br.—Dilbeck Ray (Cal) — Tr.—Mason Lloyd C — $50,000 — 1989 10 2 0 3 $30,400 — Turf 2 0 0 0

Own.—Dilbeck R — Lifetime 10 2 0 3 $30,400

12Oct89-8SA	1	Ⓣ:46 1:093 1:34 fm	43	1115	55	67½	77¾	89¼	Nakatani CS9	Aw37000	92 —	ImmrtlScrpt,LvThDrm,Bbtscldtsd	10
1Sep89-3Dmr	7f	:222 :45 1:214ft	4¾	1115	3½	2½	2hd	32¼	Nakatani C S6	62500	91-11	Its Royalty, Comical, Just Deeds	6
24Aug89-3Dmr	1	Ⓣ:491 1:124 1:37 fm	22	117	62¼	43	63¾	63½	Pincay L Jr5	Aw38000	82-09	Friendly Ed, Strung Up, One Drink	8
24Aug89—Wide throughout													
11Aug89-8Dmr	7f	:214 :441 1:213ft	42	115	65½	76¼	65	65½	Black C A7	ⓈRl Gd Dl	88-15	Mr. Bolg, Timeless Answer, Bruho	7
11Aug89—5 wide into lane													
9Jly89-9Pln	6f	:224 :452 1:103ft	*1	117	41½	53¼	57	56¼	Chapman T M3	HcpO	82-18	BearInMind,Doncreer,PlusOrMinus	6
24Jun89-7GG	6f	:214 :45 1:101ft	6¼	117	42½	41½	31	1¾	ChapmanTM6	Aw20000	88-16	Just Deeds, Comical, Bin Of Ice	7
24Jun89—Bumped start													
10Jun89-8GG	6f	:212 :44 1:093ft	8¼	117	43	31½	31½	32	ChapmanTM6	Aw20000	89-11	Desert Rival, Vote, Just Deeds	8
27May89-7GG	6f	:214 :443 1:092ft	9¼	117	95	63¾	54¾	34½	Kaenel J L5	Aw20000	87-15	Mr. Don, Rip Curl, Just Deeds	10
6May89-6GG	1	:461 1:094 1:351ft	33	109	21½	22	26	48¼	Gryder A T2	HcpO	81-14	AvengingForce,BseCmp,Beu'sAllinc	7
23Apr89-4GG	6f	:221 :453 1:113gd	29	118	11	2hd	1hd	1½	ChapmnTM4	ⓈM20000	81-17	JustDeeds,KingoftheByou,GryWhl	12
23Apr89—Broke in a tangle													

Speed Index: Last Race: –5.0 1–Race Avg.: –5.0 1–Race Avg.: –5.0 Overall Avg.: –0.5

Oct 18 SA 3f ft :363 H Oct 6 SA 7f ft 1:301 H Sep 30 SA 6f ft 1:143 H Sep 20 SA 3f gd :37 H

ESP: On the basis of limited data, I would suggest a P designation.

Paceline: 1Sep89

Adjusted Paceline:

1Fr:	minus 1 length
2Call:	minus 1 length
Final:	minus 2 lengths
DRF Var:	Two points below the "zero adjustment" range of 13 to 15. We'll adjust the final time by 1 length, with no additional adjustments to the fractions.

Revised Line: 1Sep89 22.3 45.1 1:22.2

Now that we've adjusted the paceline to the Santa Anita surface, it will be necessary to utilize the sprint to route adjustment for *that* track. We'll use the pars to calculate the adjustment as we did in the chapter on the Sartin Methodology.

Santa Anita	22.0	45.1	1:10.4	14–16
Santa Anita	46.3	1:11.2	1:44.0	17–19

	1Fr	*2Fr*	*3Fr*	*AP*	*EP*	*SP*	*FX*	*%E*
Sprint Par				56.12	58.40	54.98		
Route Par				54.25	55.46	53.03		

Differential: −1.87 −2.94 −1.95

We'll apply each of the three adjustments to Just Deeds's pace ratings when we create the fps array.

Rolling Donut B. c. 3(Feb), by Flying Paster—Etzel, by Silent Screen
DAVIS R G 116 Br.—Rancho Jonata (Cal) 1989 7 1 0 0 $19,250
Tr.—Headley Bruce $50,000 1988 3 M 2 1 $13,300
Own.—Naify Valerie Lifetime 10 1 2 1 $32,550
11Oct89-7SA 1 :461 1:103 1:354ft 6½ 120 52¼ 41½ 53 77 McCarronCJ 5 Aw34000 81-12 PrinceColony,KingTufn,ClevrRturn 9
19Aug89-5Dmr 6½f :221 :442 1:153ft 4¼ 116 66¾ 69 46 45½ McCarronCJ 9 Aw32000 84-14 Wily, Doncareer, Explosive Dream 9
16Apr89-7SA 1 1/16 :462 1:11 1:43 ft 8¼ 118 31½ 32 45 58 Meza R Q 2 Aw36000 80-16 NotorousPlsur,ImprlLd,PrncColony 6
1Apr89-7SA 1 :454 1:101 1:363ft 7 119 95¾ 87¼ 68½ 69¾ Black C A7 Aw36000 75-16 Malagr,NotoriousPlesure,AnnulDte 9
8Mar89-8SA 1⅛ :46 1:103 1:484ft 35 115 89 95¾ 76¼ 68 Black C A6 Ⓡ Brdbry 77-15 Prized,CaroLover,ExemplaryLeder 10
8Mar89—Checked, altered path 1/4
19Feb89-6SA 1 1/16 :464 1:114 1:453ft 4 117 811 65¼ 21½ 1½ Black C A7 Mdn 73-21 RollngDont,StylshBlvr,NrthrnDrm 11
8Jan89-8SA 7f :221 :443 1:204ft 53 114 1110¾1110½ 69½ 614½ Black CA11 Ⓢ Brs Chp 81-13 PstAgs,VryPrsonbly,FlyngCntnntl 11
29Dec88-6SA 7f :223 :452 1:231ft *1 118 31½ 21½ 2hd 2½ Black C A3 Mdn 83-12 ShdyPine,RollingDonut,PtTheTnor 9
29Dec88—Lugged in early
10Dec88-2Hol 1 :453 1:112 1:371ft *2½ 118 42½ 31 1hd 2½ Black C A8 Mdn 76-15 Goldonrube, Rolling Donut,Copeta 12
10Dec88—Wide final 3/8
20Nov88-3Hol 7f :214 :45 1:23 ft 4¼ 118 95½ 63½ 35 34¼ Black C A10 Ⓢ Mdn 85-12 DontsToDollrs,FstDlSol,RollngDnt 10
Speed Index: Last Race: −7.0 3–Race Avg.: −6.6 6–Race Avg.: −7.1 Overall Avg.: −5.9
Oct 22 SA 3f ft :35 H Oct 7 SA 4f ft :483 H Oct 1 SA 7f ft 1:261 H Sep 25 SA 7f ft 1:28 H

ESP: P
Paceline: 11Oct89

DRF Var: Five points below the "zero adjustment" range of 17 to
19. We'll adjust the final time by 3 lengths, the second call by 1
length, and the first fraction by 1 length.

Revised Line: 11Oct89   46.2   1:10.4   1:36.2

Scout Of Fortune
B. c. 3(Apr), by Run of Luck—Tepee Time Gal, by Any Time Now
Br.—Hinds T F (Cal)
DELAHOUSSAYE E   **116**   Tr.—Robbins Jay M $50,000
Own.—Hinds T F
Lifetime 16 5 0 5 $86,200

Date															
1989	13	5	0	4									$83,575		
1988	3	M	0	1									$2,625		
Turf	2	0	0	0											

6Oct89-9SA 1 :46¹ 1:10⁴ 1:37 ft 5½ 115 2² 2² 2¹½ 1½ DelahoussayeE² 40000 82-18 ScoutOfFrtn,SrsNghtWnd,HnstOnyx 9
13Sep89-2Dmr 1 :44³ 1:09¹ 1:34⁴ft *3 117 55½ 77 6³ 59½ Pincay L Jr⁴ 50000 83-10 LteExpress,John'sReveng,KingTufn 9
   13Sep89—Lugged out 3/8
23Aug89-5Dmr 1½①:46⁴1:11³1:43¹fm 11 114 79½18¹²10¹¹¹10¹²½ Stevens G L² 75000 71-16 CowrgousPrt,Lyscnt,RunwyDunwy 10
7Aug89-3Dmr 1 :45⁴ 1:10⁴ 1:37¹ft *8-5 115 4⁷ 4⁴ 43½ 3hd Stevens G L¹ 60000 88-20 ByNoMens,ShdyPin,ScoutOffortun 5
   7Aug89—Wide into stretch
16Jly89-7Hol 1½①:47³1:11²1:41³fm 23 113 5²½ 74½ 75½ 66½ BlckCA⁷ BBstle Dy H 79-16 ArtWork,LiveTheDrem,TnciousTom 7
30Jun89-7Hol 1 :46³ 1:10⁴ 1:44 ft 10 116 3⁶ 35½ 1½ 14½ Stevens G L⁵ 50000 88-16 ScoutOffortun,GoBobrib,HourFndr 7
15Jun89-5Hol 1 :44¹ 1:09³ 1:35³ft 7½ 116 84½ 88½ 6¹⁰ 6¹¹½ DelahoussayeE⁷ 62500 73-19 DominatedDebut,Lyscent,WellAwre 9
10May89-9Hol 1½:47² 1:12³ 1:43³ft *2½ 117 2½ 2½ 1hd 32 Pincay L Jr⁴ 50000 88-12 BrllntEquton,FttlKttl,ScotOffortn 6
25Mar89-3GG 1 :46² 1:11¹ 1:37 gd 2½ 116 2¹ 3¹½ 55½ 45½ Chapman T M¹ HcpO 74-21 AvngingForc,AmdoTucci,¾PririCptn 5
   25Mar89—Placed third through disqualification
4Mar89-6GG 1 :45⁴ 1:10³ 1:36²ft 2½ 117 2¹ 2¹ 2hd 1¹ ChapmanTM⁵ Aw19000 83-15 ScoutOffortun,HnoHno,MrvlosMa 9
Speed Index: Last Race: 0.0   **3-Race Avg.: -2.3**   **8-Race Avg.: -4.2**   **Overall Avg.: -5.2**
Oct 20 SA 5f ft 1:00¹ H   Oct 1 SA 5f ft 1:00 H   Sep 24 SA 5f ft 1:01½ H   Sep 2 Dmr 4f ft :48² H

ESP: P, although he also seems comfortable in the role of S
Paceline: 6Oct89
   DRF Var: no adjustment required

Radar Alert
Ch. g. 3(Mar), by Radar Ahead—Gold Martyr, by Gold Admiral II
Br.—Vail S H (Cal)
SORENSON D   **116**   Tr.—Needham Lloyd $50,000
Own.—Vail S H
Lifetime 4 1 0 0 $13,775

Date															
1989	4	1	0	0									$13,775		
1988	0	M	0	0											

13Sep89-2Dmr 1 :44³ 1:09¹ 1:34⁴ft 17 116 7⁸ 45 33½ 41½ Olivares F³ 50000 91-10 LteExpress,John'sReveng,KingTufn 9
   13Sep89—Bumped at 1/16
3Sep89-3Dmr 6f :21⁴ :44³ 1:09⁴ft 30 113⁵ 74½ 73½ 54½ 45½ Castanon J L¹ 32000 88-10 Mr. Baldski, Racer Rex, Go DogsGo 8
18Aug89-2Dmr 6f :22¹ :45¹ 1:10³ft 33 116 41½ 54½ 54½ 1no Sibille R³ SM32000 85-15 RadarAlert,PappyYokum,OhDtFox 11
27Aug89-4Hol 6f :22¹ :45² 1:09⁴ft 76 115 2hd11¹⁶11¹⁹10²⁴½ Solis A⁶ M50000 67-10 True Potential, Interpol, Le Roc 12
Speed Index: Last Race: +1.0   **1-Race Avg.: +1.0**   **1-Race Avg.: +1.0**   **Overall Avg.: -6.0**
Oct 21 GD 6f ft 1:14 H   Oct 16 GD 6f ft 1:12 H   •Oct 10 GD 6f ft 1:02³ H   Oct 5 GD 6f ft :37 H

ESP: S. Forty-two days off after a strong performance, and a
switch to a journeyman rider seldom used on the circuit, should
be cause for concern.
   Paceline: 13Sep89
   Adjusted Paceline:

1Fr:	minus 2 lengths
2Call:	minus 1 length
Final:	minus 3 lengths
DRF Var:	Four points below the "zero adjustment" range of 14 to 16. We'll adjust the final time by 2 lengths, the second and first calls by 1 length each.

Revised Line: 13Sep89   45.3   1:09.3   1:35.4

Ask The Man
STEVENS G L
Own.—Doe-Segal-Vallone et al

116

Ch. g. 3(May), by Glamor Kid—Bubblin Belle, by Wild Lark
Br.—Procter J & W L (Tex)
Tr.—Canani Julie C $50,000

1989 5 2 1 0 $33,785
Turf 1 0 0 0 $1,025

Lifetime   5 2 1 0 $33,785

30Sep89-10Fpx	6½f :21³ :45 1:17 ft	3½ 111	3½½ 3½½ 2ʰᵈ 24½	Castanon JL¹	Aw33000	86-13 Charlatan,AskTheMn,CleverReturn 7
8Sep89-3Dmr	1 ⊕:47⁴1:12¹1:37 fm	4½ 116	2ʰᵈ 1ʰᵈ 1½ 55½	Sibille R¹	80000	81-14 Strogien, Beau's Alliance, Lyscent 6
8Sep89—Rank 7/8 turn						
30Aug89-5Dmr	1 :44¹ 1:09³ 1:36 ft	3½ 116	2ʰᵈ 12 13 12	Sibille R¹	c40000	86-13 AskThMn,BtOutOfHll,Bonri'sMrk 10
7Aug89-5Dmr	6f :21¹ :44¹ 1:09¹ft	3½ 115	45 52½ 42½ 45	Sibille R⁷	Aw32000	87-15 M Single M,Doncareer,LoadedJuan 8
4Jly89-4Hol	6f :22¹ :45² 1:10²ft	5 116	2½ 2ʰᵈ 12½ 16½	Sibille R¹⁰	M32000	89-12 AskThMn,ChopmOnThBd,B.J.Bcks 12

Speed Index: Last Race: -1.0   1-Race Avg.: -1.0   1-Race Avg.: -1.0   Overall Avg.: -0.8
●Oct 20 SA 4f ft :46⁴ H   Oct 14 SA 5f ft 1:01⁴ H   Oct 8 SA 3f ft :36⁴ B   Sep 20 SA 3f ft :36³ H

ESP: E
Paceline: 30Aug89
Adjusted Paceline:

1Fr: minus 2 lengths

2Call: minus 1 length

Final: minus 3 lengths

DRF Var: One point below the "zero adjustment" range of 14 to 16. We'll adjust the final time by 1 length with no additional adjustments to the fractions.

Revised Line: 30Aug89   45.1   1:09.4   1:36.4

Feet-Per-Second Array

	1Fr	2Fr	3Fr	AP	EP	SP	FX	%E
Just Deeds	N/A	N/A	N/A	54.57	55.35	53.57	n/a	52.49%*
Rolling Donut	56.41	54.50	49.31	54.14	55.75	52.53	n/a	53.06%
Scout Of Fortune	56.70	53.65	51.14	54.52	55.64	53.39	n/a	52.10%
Radar Alert	56.14	56.25	51.81	55.08	56.17	53.99	n/a	52.02%
Ask The Man	58.38	53.69	48.88	54.77	56.73	52.81	n/a	53.71%

*Just Deeds's pace ratings adjusted by sprint-route adjustments.

Feet-Per-Second Analysis

The final fractions (3Fr) of Ask The Man and Rolling Donut are unacceptable at a track favoring off-pace horses. Ask The Man, at 3–2 odds, was an excellent horse to bet against.

Energy Distribution

Range: 51.50% to 52.20%. Target par 51.75%.

Just Deeds: 52.49% in a seven-furlong sprint. His %E is on the low side of the sprint parameters (52.10% to 53.30%), which usually indicates the horse may be capable of a strong route performance.

Rolling Donut: 53.06% is far out of our range.

Scout Of Fortune: 52.10% is an acceptable energy pattern.

Radar Alert: 52.02% is also an acceptable pattern of energy distribution.

Ask The Man: 53.71% is an unacceptable pattern.

Three betting possibilities remain: Just Deeds, Scout Of Fortune, and Radar Alert.

The Rankings

	AP	EP	SP	%E
Radar Alert	1	2	1	Yes
Ask The Man	2	1	4	No
Just Deeds	3	5	2	Yes
Scout Of Fortune	3	4	3	Yes
Rolling Donut	5	3	5	No

The model is 2–4–2, and only Radar Alert is an exact fit. Bettors able to excuse the layoff after his powerful try at Del Mar will play him enthusiastically. The negative rider switch and the layoff should be cause for concern and this author elected to pass on the horse. (He won his next start at 9–2 odds.)

Let's reexamine the rankings with Radar Alert removed as a betting possibility:

	AP	EP	SP	%E
Ask The Man	1	1	3	No
Just Deeds	2	4	1	Yes
Scout Of Fortune	2	3	2	Yes
Rolling Donut	4	2	4	No

Now, Just Deeds and Scout Of Fortune *both* fit the decision model. The model is based on races previously handicapped in this manner, and in no way did we alter the contenders just to fit preconceived notions.

The remaining decision was to choose between Just Deeds, with ratings that suggest a stretch-out win, and the proven winner over the course: Scout Of Fortune. By removing Ask The Man as a betting possibility, generous profits could be made by betting both the remaining contenders.

SEVENTH RACE Santa Anita OCTOBER 25, 1989 — 1 MILE. (1.33⅘) CLAIMING. Purse $32,000. 3-year-olds. Weight, 121 lbs. Non-winners of two races at one mile or over since August 15 allowed 3 lbs.; of such a race since then, 5 lbs. Claiming price $50,000; if entered for $45,000 allowed 2 lbs. (Races when entered for $40,000 or less not considered.)

Value of race $32,000; value to winner $17,600; second $6,400; third $4,800; fourth $2,400; fifth $800. Mutuel pool $249,198. Exacta pool $302,302.

Last Raced	Horse	Eqt.	A.Wt	PP	St	¼	½	¾	Str	Fin	Jockey	Cl'g Pr	Odds $1
6Oct89 9SA1	Scout Of Fortune		3 116	5	2	33	31	42½	3hd	12¼	Delahoussaye E	50000	3.50
12Oct89 8SA8	Just Deeds		3 111	1	3	42½	41½	3½	43½	21½	Nakatani C S5	50000	12.40
13Sep89 2Dmr6	Well Aware	b	3 116	9	4	11	12½	23½	21½	3¾	Solis A	50000	25.10
14Oct89 5SA7	Playmeonemoretime		3 111	6	1	21½	24	11	11½	41	Castanon J L5	50000	18.70
13Sep89 2Dmr4	Radar Alert		3 116	7	6	8hd	8hd	71½	61½	51¼	Sorenson D	50000	10.00
30Sep89 10Fpx2	Ask The Man		3 116	8	9	75	75	5hd	51	61¾	Stevens G L	50000	1.50
11Oct89 7SA7	Rolling Donut		3 116	3	7	61	6½	61½	71½	7no	Davis R G	50000	7.30
13Sep89 2Dmr9	Shady Pine	b	3 117	4	8	9	9	8	8	8	Pincay L Jr	50000	18.00
1Sep89 3Dmr1	Its Royalty	b	3 116	2	5	5hd	5½	—	—	—	Sibille R	50000	6.20

Its Royalty, Lame.

OFF AT 4:11. Start good for all but ASK THE MAN. Won driving. Time, :22⅘, :45⅘, 1:10⅕, 1:23⅗, 1:36⅗ Track fast.

$2 Mutuel Prices:			
5-SCOUT OF FORTUNE	9.00	4.80	3.80
1-JUST DEEDS		10.40	8.80
9-WELL AWARE			11.00

$5 EXACTA 5-1 PAID $273.50.

25OCT89—EIGHTH RACE

8th Santa Anita

7 FURLONGS. (1.20) 4th Running of THE CASCAPEDIA HANDICAP. $75,000 added. Fillies and mares. 3-year-olds and upward. By subscription of $75 each, $750 additional to start, with $75,000 added, of which $15,000 to second, $11,250 to third, $5,625 to fourth and $1,875 to fifth. Weights, Friday October 20. Starters to be named through the entry box by the closing time of entries. A trophy will be presented to the owner of the winner. Closed Wednesday, October 18, 1989 with 12 nominations.

Behind The Scenes *
Dk. b. or br. m. 5, by Hurry Up Blue—Jacinto Rose, by Jacinto
SOLIS A 115
Br.—InternationlThbdBreedersInc (Ky) 1989 9 1 1 3 $93,175
Tr.—Stute Melvin F 1988 12 1 6 2 $147,740
Own.—Alpert D & H
Lifetime 29 7 10 7 $331,095 Turf 2 0 0 0

29Sep89-12Fpx 1 1/16 :451 1:111 1:443ft 2¾ 116 98¾ 87 66¼ 610 Solis A1 ⒻLs Mdrns H 78-15 Corvettin, Sticky Wile, Survive 9
13Sep89-7Dmr 7f :223 :451 1:212ft 3 117 53 33 32½ 21¾ Solis A4 ⒻⓇLne Drlng 93-08 Survive,BehindTheScenes,Holderm 6
20Aug89-5Dmr 6½f :222 :45 1:151ft 17 115 79¾ 77½ 78 55¾ SolisA7 ⒻRch Brdo H 86-13 Kool Arrival, Super Avie, Survive 7
20Aug89—Grade III; Wide
6Aug89-7Dmr 6f :22 :442 1:084ft 6½ 118 612 611 67½ 53¼ Solis A5 ⒻAw52000 91-14 Skeeter, Kool Arrival, Survive 6
6Aug89—Wide into stretch
2Jly89-7Hol 1 :442 1:09 1:342ft 5½ 115 612 67½ 45 34¾ Solis A4 ⒻAw55000 86-13 Rosdor,SettleSmooth,BhindThScns 6
17Jun89-9Hol 1 1/16 :46 1:101 1:42 ft 12 112 410 48 36½ 46 Solis A4 ⒻMilady H 84-15 Bayakoa, FlyingJulia,CaritaTostada 5
17Jun89—Grade I
20May89-8Hol 1 :443 1:081 1:324ft 12 114 59½ 57½ 47½ 38 DvsRG2 ⒻHwthn H 91-07 Byko,GoodbyeHlo,BehindTheScens 5
20May89—Grade II
29Apr89-8Hol 7f :214 :442 1:213ft 6½ 116 78¼ 66 55 34½ VllPA1 ⒻA Gleam H 91-10 Daloma, Survive, BehindTheScenes 7
29Apr89—Grade III; Wide into stretch
9Apr89-3SA 6½f :21 :44 1:15 ft 6 1115 58 35 2½ 13 VlenzulFH3 ⒻAw55000 95-14 BehindTheScenes,Skeetr,Humsong 5
30Sep88-12Fpx 1 1/16 :453 1:111 1:43 ft 4½ 116 712 76 33 21¼ OrtLE2 ⒻLs Mdrns H 95-10 VrityBby,BhndThScns,AFbulousTm 7

Speed Index: Last Race: +1.0 3-Race Avg.: +1.6 5-Race Avg.: +3.0 Overall Avg.: +0.9

Oct 21 SA 5f ft 1:011 H Oct 14 SA 4f ft :472 H Oct 8 SA 5f ft 1:001 H Sep 22 SA 4f ft :49 H

Linda Card * Dk. b. or br. f. 3(Mar), by Noble Monk—Pick Up Your Cards, by Piaster
TORO F 114 Br.—Hi Card Ranch (Cal) 1989 10 5 1 1 $117,718
Tr.—Dutton Jerry 1988 3 1 1 0 $7,200
Own.—Hi Card Ranch Lifetime 13 6 2 1 $124,918

8Sep89-8Dmr 1 1/16 :454 1:10 1:412ft 5¾ 118 11½ 11½ 46 49½ Baze R A5 ⒻⓇTry Pns 83-11 AffrmdClssc,ApprovdTFly,StckyWl 5
4Aug89-8Dmr 7f :224 :451 1:222ft *8-5 116 11½ 11½ 11½ 12½ Baze R A5 ⒻⓈFlt Trt 90-17 LindaCard,PperPrincess,ThnksTissr 6
2Jly89-11Pln 170:461 1:103 1:404ft *4-5 119 15 16 12½ 1no LbrtJ4 ⒻⓈPln Sen H 90-12 LindaCard,MoonlitDesert,BigSquw 8
9Jun89-8GG 6f :212 :434 1:09 ft *2-3 119 1½ 12 15 18 Lambert J2 ⒻHcp0 94-20 LindaCard,ReasonToRage,Hon'sLss 5
10May89-8GG 6f :211 :44 1:094ft 2 118 1½ 1hd 1hd 31 Lambert J1 ⒻHcp0 89-15 Manon Letsgo,Conclaire,LindaCard 5
10May89—Bobbled start
23Apr89-8GG 6f :212 :441 1:10 gd 8½ 117 2½ 1hd 2½ 2nk LmbertJ8 ⒻⓈMiss Cal 89-17 Yugo Marie, Linda Card, Flom 12
23Apr89—Ducked out start
24Mar89-8GG 1 :46 1:11 1:383gd *2½ 118 11 2hd 21½ 46½ LbrtJ3 ⒻⓇPcfca Iv H 65-27 LunarBeuty,CrystlBounty,BoldCost 6
24Mar89—Lugged out early drive
18Feb89-8GG 1 :462 1:111 1:38 ft 3¾ 115 1hd 2hd 3½ 43 LmbrtJ3 ⒻSrty Br Cp 72-19 LovAndAffcton,IcTrffls,FlmMcGon 6
18Feb89—Stumbled start; lugged out 1st turn, backstretch
29Jan89-8GG 1 :46 1:104 1:374ft *2½ 118 16 16 15 16 Lambert J5 ⒻHcp0 76-14 LindaCrd,CrystlBounty,FbulousJoy 6
29Jan89—Lugged out
2Jan89-7BM 6f :223 :463 1:122m 13 113 14 12 13 16 LambertJ1 ⒻⓇInv Stk 77-33 LindaCard,CrystlBounty,SolrSoring 8
Speed Index: Last Race: +7.0 3–Race Avg.: +8.3 5–Race Avg.: +8.2 Overall Avg.: +1.0
●Oct 20 SA 6f ft 1:123 H ●Oct 14 SA 6f ft 1:131 H Oct 6 SA Ⓣ 5f fm 1:003 H (d) ●Sep 29 BM 5f ft 1:01 H

A Penny Is A Penny B. f. 4, by Temperence Hill—Raise a Penny, by Raise a Native
SIBILLE R 115 Br.—Milam & Smith (Ky) 1989 5 2 0 2 $53,550
Tr.—Vogel George 1988 7 2 1 3 $41,540
Own.—Hughes & Yeder Lifetime 12 4 1 5 $95,090 Turf 1 0 0 1 $6,150

9Sep89-7Dmr 6½f :22 :443 1:153ft 3½ 117 3½ 1½ 1hd 1½ Sibille R2 ⒻAw40000 90-11 APnnyIsAPnny,NvrCMss,Rcr'sFolly 7
15Jly89-11Sol 6f :221 :441 1:093ft *2 112 2½ 41¾ 74¼ 77¼ EspdlMA1 ⒻVclBrCpH 85-16 Flyinmyway,MissMaiTi,AmoreCielo 7
25Feb89-7SA 6½f :212 :44 1:163ft 2½ 118 74¾ 76¾ 55¾ 33 Sibille R1 ⒻAw41000 84-14 Humsong,Skeeter,APennyIsAPenny 8
25Feb89—Wide final 3/8
27Jan89-7SA a6½f Ⓣ:213 :4441:153fm 3½ 118 32½ 2hd 11 31¼ Sibille R7 ⒻAw41000 80-19 Green'sGlry,Mdrug,APnnyIsAPnny 8
27Jan89—Wide into stretch
7Jan89-5SA 6f :214 :444 1:093ft 3¾ 118 64 2½ 21 12½ Sibille R10 ⒻAw35000 90-14 APnnyIsAPnny,Humsong,SlwJnFll 10
18Nov88-8BM 1 :464 1:113 1:381gd 2½ 114 66 65 42 1½ LamanceC2 ⒻAw17000 77-29 APnnyIsAPnny,MrVstArtst,ButflPt 7
12Oct88-7SA 1 1/16 :462 1:104 1:434ft 13 115 32 34 55¼ 53½ Sibille R7 ⒻAw34000 78-19 LdyBrunicrdi,Nikishk,ComdyCourt 11
19Sep88-11Fpx 6f :214 :444 1:10 ft 4¾ 115 44½ 611 37 3½ SorensonD5 ⒻAw32000 96-10 DlwrStrt,Suspcosly,APnnyIsAPnny 8
4Jun88-7Hol 6½f :214 :444 1:163ft 26 120 74¼ 52 33½ 35¼ PedrozMA8 ⒻAw33000 90-16 FrtntBrbr,ChrryD'r,APnnyIsAPnny 9
4Jun88—Wide into drive; jumped mirror reflection at finish
8May88-6Hol 6f :22 :454 1:111ft 3½ 115 51½ 42 22 12 Sibille R3 ⒻMdn 86-13 APnnyIsAPnny,LovWthHny,IcyTs 10
Speed Index: Last Race: +1.0 3–Race Avg.: 0.0 7–Race Avg.: +2.1 Overall Avg.: +1.7
Oct 21 SA 4f ft :464 B Oct 15 SA 4f ft :472 H Oct 9 SA 3f ft :362 B Oct 3 SA 5f ft 1:012 H

Hasty Pasty B. f. 4, by Flying Paster—Revered, by In Reality
PINCAY L JR 118 Br.—Cardiff Stud Farm (Cal) 1989 9 3 1 2 $140,625
Tr.—Lukas D Wayne 1988 13 0 2 2 $52,550
Own.—Spelling A & Candy Lifetime 28 6 3 5 $294,575 Turf 8 1 2 0 $107,975

11Oct89-8SA a6½f Ⓣ:212 :43 1:124fm 23 118 105¾ 87¼ 87 73¾ DvsRG7 ⒻAtmn Dys H 91-05 WrnngZon,DownAgn,StormyBtVld 11
11Oct89—Wide into stretch
20Aug89-5Dmr 6½f :222 :45 1:151ft 4 119 4¾ 32 57 66¾ McCrrCJ5 ⒻRchBrdff 85-13 Kool Arrival, Super Avie, Survive 7
20Aug89—Grade III
12Jly89-8Hol 6f Ⓣ:23 :4531:083fm 3 119 22½ 21½ 21½ 21½ McCrrnCJ2 ⒻAw55000 93-09 WarningZone,HastyPsty,DownAgin 5
1Jly89-8Hol 6f Ⓣ:221 :4421:082fm 5½ 120 84½ 43 22 1nk McCrrCJ5 ⒻⒼValkyrH 95-11 HastyPasty,Kurbstone,SilentArrivl 12
28May89-7Hol 6½f :214 :442 1:153ft 2½ 118 43½ 31 2hd 14½ Pincay LJr1 ⒻAw45000 97-11 Hasty Pasty, Skeeter, Sadie B.Fast 6
28May89—Broke out, bumped
4May89-8Hol 6f :221 :444 1:092ft 7½ 117 42½ 31½ 3½ 11½ Pincay LJr5 ⒻAw40000 94-15 Hasty Pasty, Skeeter, Sadie B.Fast 6
9Feb89-8SA 6f :214 :45 1:103sy 9½ 115 31½ 33½ 33 33½ VlenzulPA6 ⒻAw41000 81-24 Survive, Humasong, Hasty Pasty 7
26Jan89-8SA 1 :453 1:101 1:362ft 13 117 31 42 33 55¾ Pincay LJr6 ⒻAw45000 81-16 SettlSmooth,LdyBrunicrdi,SdiB.Fst 8
26Jan89—Rank 6 1/2 to 5 1/2
11Jan89-7SA 6f :212 :441 1:083ft 19 117 53 43½ 23 34½ Pincay LJr5 ⒻAw40000 90-14 Warning Zone, Survive, HastyPasty 8
11Jan89—Wide into stretch
30Dec88-5SA a6½f Ⓣ:214 :45 1:161gd 17 117 34 44 54½ 47½ Pincay LJr6 ⒻAw40000 70-22 Madruga,Survive,Marian'sCourage 12
Speed Index: Last Race: -2.0 3–Race Avg.: +5.0 5–Race Avg.: +4.8 Overall Avg.: +1.7
Oct 19 SA 5f ft 1:004 B Oct 6 SA 4f ft :483 H

```
Survive *                              B. m. 5, by Pass the Glass—Elite Khaled, by Prince Khaled
  BAZE R A                     118     Br.—Coffee Dessie F or J (Cal)          1989 12 3 3 3   $156,100
Own.—Allred & Hubbard                  Tr.—Mandella Richard                    1988 10 1 4 2    $60,450
                                       Lifetime 25 6 7 5 $246,800              Turf  4 0 1 0    $16,500
29Sep89-12Fpx 1 1/16:451 1:111 1:443ft *8-5 118 77 43 31½ 31½ BzeRA4 ⒻLs Mdrns H 87-15 Corvettin, Sticky Wile, Survive 9
13Sep89-7Dmr 7f :223 :451 1:212ft *1-2e117 21 11½ 11½ 11½ BzeRA2 ⒻⓇJne Dring 95-08 Survive,BehindTheScenes,Holderm 6
20Aug89-5Dmr 6½f:222 :45 1:151ft 9½ 116 64¾ 66 45½ 33¾ BzRA1 ⒻRch Brdo H 88-13 Kool Arrival, Super Avie, Survive 7
  20Aug89—Grade III
6Aug89-7Dmr 6f :22 :442 1:084ft 3½ 118 31 42½ 43 31 DlhoussyE1 ⒻAw52000 93-14 Skeeter, Kool Arrival, Survive 6
1Jly89-8Hol 6f Ⓣ:221 :4421:082fm 5½ 117 106¾108½ 54½ 4½ DlhssyE8 ⒻⓈValkyr H 94-11 HastyPasty,Kurbstone,SilentArrivl 12
  1Jly89—Wide in stretch
29Apr89-8Hol 7f :214 :442 1:213ft 18 116 67½ 77 44 21¾ DlssE6 ⒻA Gleam H 94-10 Daloma, Survive, BehindTheScenes 7
  29Apr89—Grade III; Wide into stretch
19Apr89-8GG 1 :451 1:093 1:361ft 3¾ 117 87 67½ 24 21½ CpTM3 ⒻⓈCal GirlsH 82-20 LyricalPirate,Survive,HlloweenBby 8
  19Apr89—Forced wide 1/4
26Mar89-8SA a6½f Ⓣ:221 :4511:153gd 11 116 41¾ 41½ 43 64 Baze RA9 ⒻLs Cngs H 77-20 ImperilStr,DownAgin,Serv'N'Volly 10
3Mar89-8SA 6½f:214 :443 1:162gd 7½ 115 65½ 56½ 51¾ 12 Baze R A3 ⒻAw55000 88-19 Survive, Invited Guest, Saros Brig 6
  3Mar89—Wide into stretch
9Feb89-8SA 6f :214 :45 1:103sy 3¾ 118 65 55½ 23 1no DlhoussyE2 ⒻAw41000 85-24 Survive, Humasong, Hasty Pasty 7
  Speed Index: Last Race: +3.0   3-Race Avg.: +3.6   6-Race Avg.: +5.1   Overall Avg.: +3.7
 Oct 20 SA 5f ft 1:011 H    Oct 14 SA 4f ft :481 H    ●Sep 24 SA tr.t 4f ft :484 H    Sep 8 Dmr 5f ft 1:004 H
```

```
Akinemod                               B. f. 3(Apr), by Time to Explode—Lady Paese, by Sir Gaylord
  STEVENS G L                  115     Br.—Klugman J (Cal)                     1989 4 3 0 0    $51,300
Own.—El Rancho De Jaklin               Tr.—Fanning Jerry                       1988 0 M 0 0
                                       Lifetime 4 3 0 0 $51,300
10Oct89-5SA 6f :213 :44 1:084ft *4-5 117 11½ 12 13 13 VlenzulPA6 ⒻAw34000 94-11 Akinemod, Jo's Joy, Put The Case 8
31Aug89-8Dmr 6f :213 :44 1:09 ft 9-5 116 11 11½ 13 12¾ VlenzulPA3 ⒻAw32000 93-13 Akinemod, PaperPrincess,Jig'sJove 8
  31Aug89—Lugged out 1/2
13May89-4Hol 6½f:213 :442 1:161ft 2½ 116 11½ 13½ 15 18½ ValenzuelPA2 ⒻⓈMdn 94-11 Akinemod,DesrtProwlr,PriclssCndy 8
30Apr89-4Hol 6f :22 :451 1:103ft 2 115 54½ 52½ 43 47 Stevens G L6 ⒻMdn 81-13 PperPrincess,MissMlibu,DpEnough 9
  30Apr89—Steadied 1/4
  Speed Index: Last Race: +5.0   3-Race Avg.: +5.3   4-Race Avg.: +2.5   Overall Avg.: +2.5
 Oct 19 SA 5f ft :592 H    Oct 7 SA 4f ft :483 B    ●Oct 1 SA 6f ft 1:11 H    Sep 25 SA 6f ft 1:141 H
```

```
Miss Tawpie                            Dk. b. or br. m. 5, by Miswaki—Tawpie, by In Reality
  FLORES D R                   117     Br.—Saiden A (Ky)                       1989 16 5 3 4   $144,300
Own.—Saiden A                          Tr.—Barrera Lazaro S                    1988  7 2 2 1    $44,650
                                       Lifetime 25 7 5 6 $192,275              Turf  4 2 1 0    $43,275
25Sep89-12Fpx 6½f:212 :444 1:154ft *1-2 122 31½ 21 11 14 FlrsDR1 ⒻBngls NBds 97-10 Miss Tawpie, Valid Allure, Skeeter 4
18Sep89-12Fpx 6½f:214 :45 1:152ft 16 122 2½ 2½ 11½ 16 FlorsDR6 ⒻⓇPio Pico 99-08 Miss Tawpie, Table Frolic, Skeeter 7
25Aug89-8BM 6f :221 :443 1:082ft 7½ 114 65 67½ 57 47½ FrzierRL3 ⒻSpctclr H 89-11 WarningZone,SprrowLke,TbleFrolic 6
27Jly89-8Dmr 1 Ⓣ:4721:12 1:37 fm 12 115 11½ 21 43 54½ Cortez A6 ⒻAw55000 81-18 Dvie'sLmb,MriJesse,RintreeRenegd 7
6Jly89-9Hol 1 Ⓣ:47 1:1111:353fm 4½ 115 2½ 2hd 21 1hd Cortez A7 ⒻAw35000 86-10 Miss Tawpie, Ardglen, Sticky Wile 8
21Jun89-5Hol 6f Ⓣ:221 :4431:09 fm 6 118 31 34½ 43½ 12 Cortez A2 ⒻAw31000 92-12 Miss Tawpie, Jo'sJoy,DucklingPark 7
11Jun89-7Hol 6f :22 :451 1:104ft 2½ 120 53 53 53¼ 31 Cortez A6 ⒻAw31000 86-10 Many Passes, MyTreat,MissTawpie 6
26May89-9Hol 1 1/16 Ⓣ:46 1:1021:41 fm 5¾ 116 11½ 1½ 11 22 Cortez A8 Ⓕ 62500 87-10 MissRoylMont,MissTwp,Ironcomb 10
14May89-3Hol 1 :45 1:093 1:342ft 3¼ 114 2hd 11½ 13 16 Cortez A3 Ⓕ 47500 91-09 MissTawpie,Soonermoon,SssySlew 7
5May89-7Hol 6f :213 :443 1:093ft *2¼ 116 86½ 98¼ 97½ 22¾ Cedeno A3 Ⓕ 40000 90-16 DefendYourMn,MissTwpi,DlwrStrt 10
  5May89—Wide into stretch
  Speed Index: Last Race: +7.0   3-Race Avg.: +4.6   5-Race Avg.: +3.2   Overall Avg.: +1.2
 Oct 20 SA 5f ft :593 H    Oct 13 SA 5f ft 1:003 H    Oct 6 SA 4f ft :462 H    ●Sep 14 SA 4f ft :471 H
```

```
Corvettin                              Dk. b. or br. f. 4, by Don B—Imparity, by Figonero
  NAKATANI C S                 116     Br.—Hudon E A Jr (Cal)                  1989 11 5 0 2   $142,875
Own.—Hudon E A                         Tr.—Luby Donn                           1988  4 1 1 0    $12,750
                                       Lifetime 15 6 1 2 $155,625              Turf  2 0 0 0
29Sep89-12Fpx 1 1/16:451 1:111 1:443ft 6¾ 117 66 54 41¾ 1nk NtnCS 7 ⒻLs Mdrns H 88-15 Corvettin, Sticky Wile, Survive 9
17Sep89-11Fpx 1 1/16:461 1:104 1:43 ft 6¼ 114 32 31 1hd 11¾ OlrsF 2 ⒻⓇE B Jhnstn 96-10 Corvettin, Sticky Wile, Beseya 8
25Aug89-3Dmr 1 :45 1:093 1:341ft 11 117 21½ 21 31½ 34¼ Olivares F 2 ⒻAw42000 91-10 Voila, Sugarplum Gal, Corvettin 5
11Aug89-11LA 1 1/16:453 1:103 1:411ft 5½ 117 64½ 65 47 49¾ OlivresF 5 ⒻLs Palmas 89-01 KpOnTop,TropiclStphni,HllownBby 7
14Jun89-9Hol 1 :461 1:113 1:363ft 8¼ 117 53 41¾ 42 11 Pincay L Jr 5 Ⓕ 50000 80-15 Corvettin, Beseya, Codex's Bride 8
  14Jun89—Wide final 3/8
28May89-9Hol 1 1/16 Ⓣ:4611:1021:411fm 22 116 48 79½ 711 712½ DlhoussyE 3 ⒻAw32000 75-09 Marian'sCourage,Petali,YoungFlyer 8
3May89-8Hol 6½f:214 :443 1:17 ft 21 117 69½ 67½ 34 1no DlhoussyE 4 ⒻAw28000 90-15 Corvettin, Lori's Light,ManyPasses 6
2Apr89-5SA a6½f Ⓣ:212 :4421:162fm 47 118 119½119¾109¼ 88¾ Baze R A 7 ⒻAw37000 68-24 Barmera,RunwyBlues,BobOleLight 12
20Feb89-6GG 6f :221 :452 1:104ft 13 118 1½ 1hd 1½ 1hd GonzlzRM 3 ⒻAw18000 85-21 Corvttin,MrVistArtist,I'mLittlNippr 7
4Feb89-3GG 1 :46 1:12 1:381m 9½ 118 3½ 45 — — LamanceC2 ⒻAw19000 — — JanealJones,LollipopLies,ShanMdel 5
  4Feb89—Eased
  Speed Index: Last Race: +5.0   2-Race Avg.: +5.5   2-Race Avg.: +5.5   Overall Avg.: -2.0
 Oct 17 SA 6f ft 1:14 H    Oct 9 SA 5f ft 1:022 B    Sep 7 Dmr 5f ft 1:001 H
```

Seattle Meteor
DELAHOUSSAYE E 114
Own.—Buckland Farm

B. f. 3(Apr), by Seattle Slew—Northern Meteor, by Northern Dancer					
Br.—Buckland Fm D B A EvansTM (Ky)		1989	9 0 2 0		$71,495
Tr.—Speckert Christopher		1988	7 3 1 1		$307,558
Lifetime 16 3 3 1 $379,053			Turf	3 0 1 0	$12,170

60ct89-7SA   6$\frac{1}{2}$f :22^1 :45^1 1:16^{2}ft *8-5 117   810 76$\frac{1}{2}$ 64$\frac{1}{4}$ 56$\frac{1}{2}$ Pincay LJr^7 ⑤Aw38000 81-15 ReluctntGust,BrightAsst,Rcr'sFolly 8
   60ct89—Stumbled at start
9Sep89-7Dmr   6$\frac{1}{2}$f :22 :44^3 1:15^{3}ft *2$\frac{1}{2}$ 117   712 69 55 41$\frac{1}{4}$ Pincay LJr ⑤Aw40000 89-11 APnnyIsAPnny,NvrCMss,Rcr'sFolly 7
   9Sep89—Off very slowly
13Aug89-5Dmr   1 ①:47^{2}1:12 1:36^{3}fm 25 118   915 911 97$\frac{3}{4}$ 87$\frac{3}{4}$ B[?]CA^6 ⑤Sn Clmnt H 80-15 Drby'sDughter,StickyWile,3IDrling 9
   13Aug89—Broke against bit
9Jly89-8Hol   1$\frac{1}{16}$:45^2 1:09^4 1:47^{4}ft *25 121   33$\frac{1}{4}$ 43 37 5$\frac{11}{4}$ BlckCA^5 ⑤Hol Oaks 83-12 Gorgeous, Kelly, Lea Lucirda 6
   9Jly89—Grade I
10Jun89-6Hol   7f :21^4 :44^2 1:21^{2}ft 25 122   66$\frac{1}{2}$ 56$\frac{1}{4}$ 56$\frac{1}{4}$ 45$\frac{1}{4}$ BlackCA^5 ⑤Railbird 92-13 ImaginaryLady,Kiwi,StormyButVlid 7
   10Jun89—Grade III; Wide backstretch
13May89-8Hol   1 ①:45^{3}1:09^{4}1:34 fm 3$\frac{1}{4}$ 119   75$\frac{1}{4}$ 84$\frac{3}{4}$ 811 716$\frac{3}{4}$ GuerraWA^7 ⑤Senorita 77-10 RluctntGust,FormidblLdy,GnrlChrg 9
   13May89—Wide into drive
1Apr89-11Lrl   1$\frac{1}{16}$:46^4 1:11^1 1:43 ft   6$\frac{1}{4}$ 114   56$\frac{1}{4}$ 55$\frac{1}{4}$ 54$\frac{3}{4}$ 54$\frac{1}{4}$ Rocco J^2 ⑤Pim Oks 90-19 Open Mind, Dreamy Mimi, Seraglio 7
5Mar89-10GP   1$\frac{1}{16}$:48^2 1:12^3 1:43^{4}ft   5$\frac{1}{4}$ 121   2$\frac{1}{4}$ 2$\frac{1}{4}$ 3$\frac{1}{4}$ 2^3 RrRP^6 ⑤Bonne Ms 79-20 Open Mind, SeattleMeteor Surging 6
   5Mar89—Grade II
15Feb89-9GP   1$\frac{1}{16}$ ①:46^{2}1:10^{4}1:42^{4}fm *2 121   44$\frac{1}{4}$ 33 1$\frac{1}{4}$ 2^{nk} SntosJA^7 ⑤Hrcmsbrd 86-17 DarbyShuffle,SeattleMeteor,Imago 8
5Nov88-5CD   1$\frac{1}{16}$:47 1:12^3 1:46^{3}m   4 119   8$\frac{1}{2}$ 76$\frac{1}{4}$ 63$\frac{1}{2}$ 53$\frac{3}{4}$ RrRP^4 ⑤Br Cp Juv F 71-20 OpenMind,DarbyShuffle,LeLucind 12
   5Nov88—Grade I

Speed Index: Last Race: -4.0   3-Race Avg.: +0.3   3-Race Avg.: +0.3   Overall Avg.: -2.0
Oct 18 SA 4f ft :49^1 H   Oct 2 SA 5f ft 1:01^4 H   Sep 26 SA 5f ft 1:01 H   Sep 20 SA 4f gd :49^1 H

The Eighth race was The Cascapedia Handicap named after one of the truly great mares of recent years. At seven furlongs, the race attracted an odd collection of classified allowance and restricted-stakes types. This type of end-of-season race is an ideal spot for high potential three-year-olds to continue their development and, at the same time, get tested for class.

It would be just enough of a test for Akinemod to prove her quality.

The Noncontenders

Behind The Scenes: Her last race was dull at every call, at a track she's enjoyed in the past. Additionally, she comes from too far back to win over this course at this time.

Hasty Pasty: Her recent have been dull and her work tab spotty.

Corvettin: Shortening up after a series of routes, the last of which she showed no early speed.

Seattle Meteor: She has some back class but is extremely trouble prone. In her last she showed little down the stretch, and her style is against her in this race.

The following horses are contenders:

(1) Linda Card

(2) A Penny Is A Penny

(3) Survive

(4) Akinemod

(5) Miss Tawpie

Runners will be adjusted to the Santa Anita surface.

Linda Card ✱

Dk. b. or br. f. 3(Mar), by Noble Monk—Pick Up Your Cards, by Piaster
Br.—Hi Card Ranch (Cal)
Tr.—Dutton Jerry

TORO F   **114**

1989 10 5 1 1 $117,718
1988 3 1 1 0 $7,200

Own.—Hi Card Ranch

Lifetime 13 6 2 1 $124,918

8Sep89–8Dmr	1⅟₁₆ :454 1:10 1:412ft	5½ 118	11½ 11½ 46 49½	Baze R A⁵	ⓒⒼTry Pns	83-11 AffrmdClssc,ApprovdTFly,StckyWl 5
4Aug89–8Dmr	7f :224 :451 1:222ft	*8-5 116	11½ 11½ 11½ (12½)	Baze R A⁵	ⓒⒼFt Trt	90-17 LindaCard,PperPrincess,ThnksTissr 6
2Jly89–11Pla	17⁰ :461 1:103 1:404ft	*4-5 119	15 16 12½ 1ʰᵈ	LbrtJ⁴	ⓒⒼPln Sen H	90-12 LindaCard,MoonlitDesert,BigSquw 8
9Jun89–8GG	6f :212 :434 1:09 ft	*2-3 119	1½ 12 15 18	Lambert J²	ⓐHcpO	94-20 LindaCard,ReasonToRage,Hon'sLss 5
18May89–8GG	6f :211 :44 1:094ft	2 118	1½ 1ʰᵈ 1ʰᵈ 31	Lambert J¹	ⓐHcpO	89-15 Manon Letsgo,Conclaire,LindaCard 5
18May89–Bobbled start						
23Apr89–8GG	6f :212 :441 1:10 gd	8½ 117	2½ 1ʰᵈ 2½ 2ⁿᵏ	LmbertJ⁹	ⓒⒼMiss Cal	89-17 Yugo Marie, Linda Card, Flom 12
23Apr89–Ducked out start						
24Mar89–8GG	1 :46 1:11 1:383gd	*2½ 118	11 2ʰᵈ 21½ 46½	LbrtJ³	ⓒⒼPcfca Iv H	65-27 LunarBeuty,CrystlBounty,BoldCost 6
24Mar89–Lugged out early drive						
18Feb89–8GG	1 :462 1:111 1:38 ft	3½ 115	1ʰᵈ 2ʰᵈ 3½ 43	LmbrtJ³	ⓐSrty Br Cp	72-19 LovAndAffcton,IcTrffls,FlmMcGon 6
18Feb89–Stumbled start; lugged out 1st turn, backstretch						
23Jan89–8GG	1 :46 1:104 1:374ft	*2½ 118	16 16 15 16	Lambert J⁵	ⓐHcpO	76-14 LindaCrd,CrystlBounty,FbulousJoy 6
23Jan89–Lugged out						
2Jan89–7BM	6f :223 :463 1:122m	13 113	14 12 13 16	LambertJ¹	ⓒⒼlnv Stk	77-33 LindaCard,CrystlBounty,SolrSoring 8

Speed Index: Last Race: +7.0   3–Race Avg.: +8.3   5–Race Avg.: +8.2   Overall Avg.: +1.0
●Oct 20 SA 6f ft 1:123 H   ●Oct 14 SA 6f ft 1:131 H   Oct 6 SA ① 5f fm 1:00³ H (d)   ●Sep 29 BM 5f ft 1:01 H

ESP: E

Paceline: 4Aug89

Adjusted Paceline:

1Fr:	minus 1 length
2Call:	minus 1 length
Final:	minus 2 lengths
DRF Var:	Two points above the "zero adjustment" range of 13 to 15. We'll adjust the final time by 1 length with no additional adjustments to the fractions. This is the first time we've adjusted one of our contenders in this direction.

Revised Line: 4Aug89   23.0   45.2   1:22.3

Her first fraction in the paceline race is deceptively slow. Seven-furlong races are often run with slow first fractions before accelerating on the turn. When we analyze the race, we'll give additional consideration to her usual first-fraction speed.

A Penny Is A Penny — B. f. 4, by Temperence Hill—Raise a Penny, by Raise a Native

SIBILLE R 115 — Br.—Milam & Smith (Ky) — 1989 5 2 0 2 $53,550

Own.—Hughes & Yedor — Tr.—Vegel George — 1988 7 2 1 3 $41,540

Lifetime 12 4 1 5 $95,090 — Turf 1 0 0 1 $6,150

9Sep89-7Dmr 6½f :22 :443 1:153ft 3½ 117 3½ 1½ 1hd 1½ Sibille R2 ⒻAw40000 90-11 APnnyIsAPnny,NvrCMss,Rcr'sFolly 7
15Jly89-11Sol 6f :221 :441 1:093ft *2 112 2½ 41¾ 74¼ 77½ EspdlMA1 ⒻVclBrCpH 85-16 Flyinmyway,MissMaiTi,AmoreCielo 7
25Feb89-7SA 6½f :212 :44 1:163ft 2½ 118 74¾ 76¾ 55¾ 33 Sibille R1 ⒻAw41000 84-14 Humsong,Skeeter,APennyIsAPenny 8
25Feb89—Wide final 3/8
27Jan89-7SA a6½f Ⓣ:213 :4441:153fm 3¾ 118 32½ 2hd 11 31¼ Sibille R7 ⒻAw41000 80-19 Green'sGlry,Mdrug,APnnyIsAPnny 8
27Jan89—Wide into stretch
7Jan89-5SA 6f :214 :444 1:093ft 3¾ 118 64 2½ 21 12½ Sibille R10 ⒻAw35000 90-14 APnnyIsAPnny,Humsong,SlwJnFll 10
18Nov88-8BM 1 :464 1:113 1:381gd 2½ 114 66 65 42 1½ LamanceC2 ⒻAw17000 77-29 APnnyIsAPnny,MrVstArtst,ButflPt 7
12Oct88-7SA 1 1/16 :462 1:104 1:434ft 13 115 32 34 55¼ 53¼ Sibille R7 ⒻAw34000 78-19 LdyBrunicrdi,Nikishk,ComdyCourt 11
19Sep88-11Fpx 6f :214 :444 1:10 ft 4¾ 115 44½ 611 37 3½ SorensonD5 ⒻAw32000 96-10 DlwrStrt,Suspcosly,APnnyIsAPnny 8
4Jun88-7Hol 6½f :214 :444 1:163ft 26 120 74¼ 52 33½ 35¼ PedrozMA8 ⒻAw33000 90-16 FrtntBrbr,ChrryD'r,APnnyIsAPnny 9
4Jun88—Wide into drive; jumped mirror reflection at finish
8May88-6Hol 6f :22 :454 1:111ft 3½ 115 51½ 42 22 12 Sibille R3 ⒻMdn 86-13 APnnyIsAPnny,LovWthHny,IcyTs 10

Speed Index: Last Race: +1.0 3-Race Avg.: 0.0 7-Race Avg.: +2.1 Overall Avg.: +1.7

Oct 21 SA 4f ft :464 B Oct 15 SA 4f ft :472 H Oct 9 SA 3f ft :362 B Oct 3 SA 5f ft 1:012 H

ESP: P/S. She can press the pace or come from mid-pack.
Paceline: 9Sep89
Adjusted Paceline:

1Fr:	minus 1 length
2Call:	minus 1 length
Final:	minus 2 lengths
DRF Var:	Two points below the "zero adjustment" range of 13 to 15. We'll adjust the final time by 1 length, with no additional adjustments to the fractions.

Revised Line: 9Sep89 22.1 44.4 1:16.1

Survive ✻ — B. m. 5, by Pass the Glass—Elite Khaled, by Prince Khaled

BAZE R A 118 — Br.—Coffee Dessie F or J (Cal) — 1989 12 3 3 3 $156,100

Own.—Allred & Hubbard — Tr.—Mandella Richard — 1988 10 1 4 2 $60,450

Lifetime 25 6 7 5 $246,809 — Turf 4 0 1 0 $16,500

29Sep89-12Fpx 1 1/16 :451 1:111 1:443ft *8-5 118 77 43 31½ 31½ BzeRA4 ⒻLs Mdrns H 87-15 Corvettin, Sticky Wile, Survive 9
13Sep89-7Dmr 7f :223 :451 1:212ft *1-2e117 21 11½ 11½ 11¾ BzeRA2 ⒻⒼJne Dring 95-08 Survive,BehindTheScenes,Holderm 6
20Aug89-5Dmr 6½f :222 :45 1:151ft 9½ 116 64¾ 66 45½ 33¾ BzRA1 ⒻRch Brdo H 88-13 Kool Arrival, Super Avie, Survive 7
20Aug89—Grade III
6Aug89-7Dmr 6f :22 :442 1:084ft 3½ 118 31 42½ 43 31 DlhoussyE1 ⒻAw52000 93-14 Skeeter, Kool Arrival, Survive 6
1Jly89-8Hol 6f Ⓣ:221 :4421:082fm 5½ 117 106¾108½ 54¼ 4¼ DlhssyE8 ⒻⒼValkyr H 94-11 HastyPasty,Kurbstone,SilentArrivl 12
1Jly89—Wide in stretch
29Apr89-8Hol 7f :214 :442 1:213ft 18 116 67½ 77 44 21¾ DlssE6 ⒻA Gleam H 94-10 Daloma, Survive, BehindTheScenes 7
29Apr89—Grade III; Wide into stretch
19Apr89-8GG 1 :451 1:093 1:361ft 3¾ 117 87 67½ 24 21¼ CpTM3 ⒻⒼCal GirlsH 82-20 LyricalPirate,Survive,HlloweenBby 8
19Apr89—Forced wide 1/4
26Mar89-8SA a6½f Ⓣ:221 :4511:153gd 11 116 41¾ 41½ 43 64 Baze RA9 ⒻLs Cngs H 77-20 ImperilStr,DownAgin,Serv'N'Volly 10
3Mar89-8SA 6½f :214 :443 1:162gd 7½ 115 68½ 58½ 51¾ 12 Baze R A3 ⒻAw55000 88-19 Survive, Invited Guest, Saros Brig 6
3Mar89—Wide into stretch
9Feb89-8SA 6f :214 :45 1:103sy 3¾ 118 65 55½ 23 1no DlhoussyE2 ⒻAw41000 85-24 Survive, Humasong, Hasty Pasty 7

Speed Index: Last Race: +3.0 3-Race Avg.: +3.6 6-Race Avg.: +5.1 Overall Avg.: +3.7

Oct 28 SA 5f ft 1:011 H Oct 14 SA 4f ft :481 H ●Sep 24 SA tr.t 4f ft :484 H Sep 8 Dmr 5f ft 1:004 H

ESP: S/P
Paceline: 13Sep89
Adjusted Paceline:

1Fr: minus 1 length

2Call: minus 1 length

Final: minus 2 lengths

DRF Var: Five points below the "zero adjustment" range of 13 to 15. We'll adjust the final time by 3 lengths, the second call by 1 length, and no adjustment to the first fraction.

Revised Line: 13Sep89 22.4 45.3 1:22.2

Akinemod
B. f. 3(Apr), by Time to Explode—Lady Paese, by Sir Gaylord
STEVENS G L 115 Br.—Klugman J (Cal) 1989 4 3 0 0 $51,300
Tr.—Fanning Jerry 1988 0 M 0 0
Own.—El Rancho De Jaklin Lifetime 4 3 0 0 $51,300
11Oct89-5SA 6f :213 :44 1:084ft *4-5 117 11½ 12 13 (13) VlenzulPA6 ⓕAw34000 94-11 Akinemod, Jo's Joy, Put The Case 8
31Aug89-8Dmr 6f :213 :44 1:09 ft 9-5 116 11 11½ 13 12¾ VlenzulPA3 ⓕAw32000 93-13 Akinemod, PaperPrincess,Jig'sJove 8
31Aug89—Lugged out 1/2
13May89-4Hol 6½f :213 :442 1:161ft 2½ 116 11½ 13½ 15 18½ ValenzuelPA2 ⓕⓈMdn 94-11 Akinemod,DesrtProwlr,PriclssCndy 8
30Apr89-4Hol 6f :22 :451 1:103ft 2 115 54¾ 52½ 43 47 Stevens G L6 ⓕMdn 81-13 PperPrincess,MissMlibu,DpEnough 9
30Apr89—Steadied 1/4
Speed Index: Last Race: +5.0 3-Race Avg.: +5.3 4-Race Avg.: +2.5 Overall Avg.: +2.5
Oct 19 SA 5f ft :592 H Oct 7 SA 4f ft :483 B ●Oct 1 SA 6f ft 1:11 H Sep 25 SA 6f ft 1:141 H

ESP: E
Paceline: 11Oct89

DRF Var: Three points below the "zero adjustment" range of 14 to 16. We'll adjust the final time by 2 lengths and the second call by 1 length. No adjustment to the first fraction.

Revised Line: 11Oct89 21.3 44.1 1:09.1

Miss Tawpie
Dk. b. or br. m. 5, by Miswaki—Tawpie, by In Reality
FLORES D R 117 Br.—Saiden A (Ky) 1989 16 5 3 4 $144,300
Tr.—Barrera Lazaro S 1988 7 2 2 1 $44,650
Own.—Saiden A Lifetime 25 7 5 6 $192,275 Turf 4 2 1 0 $43,275
25Sep89-12Fpx 6½f :212 :444 1:154ft *1-2 122 31½ 21 11 (14) FlrsDR1 ⓕBngls NBds 97-10 Miss Tawpie, Valid Allure, Skeeter 4
18Sep89-12Fpx 6½f :214 :45 1:152ft 16 122 2½ 2½ 11½ (16) FlorsDR6 ⓕⓇPio Pico 99-08 Miss Tawpie, Table Frolic, Skeeter 7
25Aug89-8BM 6f :221 :443 1:082ft 7½ 114 65 67½ 57 47½ FrzierRL3 ⓕSpctclr H 89-11 WarningZone,SprrowLke,TbleFrolic 6
27Jly89-8Dmr 1 Ⓣ:4721:12 1:37 fm 12 115 11½ 21 43 54½ Cortez A6 ⓕAw55000 81-18 Dvie'sLmb,MriJesse,RintreeRenegd 7
6Jly89-9Hol 1 Ⓣ:47 1:1111:353fm 4½ 115 2½ 2hd 21 1hd Cortez A7 ⓕAw35000 86-10 Miss Tawpie, Ardglen, Sticky Wile 8
21Jun89-5Hol 6f Ⓣ:221 :4431:09 fm 6 118 31 34½ 43½ 12 Cortez A2 ⓕAw31000 92-12 Miss Tawpie, Jo'sJoy,DucklingPark 7
11Jun89-7Hol 6f :22 :451 1:104ft 2¼ 120 53 53 53¼ 31 Cortez A6 ⓕAw31000 86-10 Many Passes, MyTreat,MissTawpie 6
26May89-9Hol 1 1/16 Ⓣ:46 1:1021:41 fm 5¾ 116 11½ 1½ 11 22 Cortez A8 ⓕ 62500 87-10 MissRoylMont,MissTwp,Ironcomb 10
14May89-3Hol 1 :45 1:093 1:342ft 3¼ 114 2hd 11½ 13 16 Cortez A3 ⓕ 47500 91-09 MissTawpie,Soonermoon,SssySlew 7
5May89-7Hol 6f :213 :443 1:093ft *2½ 116 86½ 98¼ 97½ 22¾ Cedeno A3 ⓕ 40000 90-16 DefendYourMn,MissTwpi,DlwrStrt 10
5May89—Wide into stretch
Speed Index: Last Race: +7.0 3-Race Avg.: +4.6 5-Race Avg.: +3.2 Overall Avg.: +1.2
Oct 20 SA 5f ft :593 H Oct 13 SA 5f ft 1:003 H Oct 6 SA 4f ft :462 H ●Sep 14 SA 4f ft :471 H

ESP: P/S
Paceline: 25Sep89
Adjusted Paceline:

1Fr: 0
2Call: 1 length
Final: 2 lengths
DRF Var: no adjustment required
Revised line: 25Sep89   21.2   44.3   1:15.2

Feet-Per-Second Array

	1Fr	2Fr	3Fr	AP	EP	SP	FX	%E
Linda Card	57.39	58.92	53.22	56.50	58.14	55.68	55.30	52.21%
A Penny Is A Penny	59.23	58.62	52.54	56.80	58.92	55.73	55.89	52.86%
Survive	57.45	58.33	53.80	56.53	57.89	55.84	55.63	51.83%
Akinemod	61.11	58.40	52.80	57.41	59.72	56.26	56.95	53.07%
Miss Tawpie	60.98	57.11	53.89	57.27	58.96	56.43	57.43	52.24%

Feet-Per-Second Analysis

Two obvious inconsistencies exist in this race.

1. Linda Card's fractional array is somewhat distorted as a result of her seven-furlong win at Del Mar. We should spend a few minutes with her pattern. Anyone not convinced of the impact of early pace in a race should memorize Linda Card's fractional array. In her Del Mar race she was allowed to set a leisurely pace of 57.39 fps to the quarter, thus crushing the hopes of any horse hoping to catch her in the stretch.

Her acceleration on the turn of that race, a 58.92 fps turn-time fraction, was a direct result of a soft first quarter. A front-running type able to control both the first two fractions is the modern pace handicapper's dream. Unless the horse is a confirmed quitter, it will win again and again.

Linda Card's final fraction of 53.22 fps reflects a fresh horse in the stretch.

Do not expect that performance in this race.

2. Miss Tawpie's first fraction is distorted as a result of the characteristics of the Fairplex "bullring." Pace handicappers should not upgrade her chances because of the first fraction, nor should she be downgraded because of an apparently weak second fraction. Both are misleading. Her performance in this race should be predicated on her final figure and energy distribution pattern.

Early Pace Analysis

Akinemod, with Linda Card and A Penny Is A Penny in closest pursuit. Akinemod's incredible turn-time fraction following a first fraction of 61.11 fps virtually guarantees the defeat of her closest pursuers. The readers of this book should never miss a pace situation this favorable. If she handles the seven furlongs, Akinemod is virtually a "cinch" in this race. We'll estimate her ability to get the seven furlongs by analyzing her energy distribution pattern.

Energy Distribution

Linda Card: 52.21%. Her Percent Early is misleading because of the manner in which it was earned. Even if capable of leading in here, she won't slow down the pace as she did at Del Mar. Her energy pattern is okay for this race, but she's not quick enough to handle Akinemod.

A Penny Is A Penny: 52.86%. Her energy number is at the target number for this track.

Survive: 51.83%. Her Percent Early is characteristic of a closer, which is exactly her role in here. She'll be running late, but her energy number is below our acceptable range of 52.10% to 53.30%.

Akinemod: 53.07%. She fits solidly in our Percent Early range. If the race contained another E type with matching fractions, the 53.07% might indicate inability to survive the seven furlongs, but this race does not fit that scenario.

Miss Tawpie: 52.25%. Acceptable on the low end of the range, and indicates she'll also be running late.

The Rankings

	AP	EP	SP	FX	%E
Akinemod	1	1	2	2	Yes
Miss Tawpie	2	2	1	1	Yes
A Penny Is A Penny	3	2	4	3	Yes
Linda Card	4	4	5	5	Yes
Survive	5	5	3	4	No

Akinemod looks to be the best bet of the Oak Tree meeting. She is a developing three-year-old in a field of runners who have already found their best level. If she's as good as she looks, she'll move on to better things.

Based on her high early energy pattern (53.07%), her future appears to be sprinting. Perhaps, with additional maturity, she'll learn to ration her speed more evenly and successfully negotiate additional furlongs.

The Final Decision

The *Form* selectors considered the race wide open, apparently skeptical of Akinemod's ability to get the seven furlongs. This author arrived at the track practically salivating over the opportunity to play this standout.

During the Santa Anita and Oak Tree meetings, I have the pleasure of sharing a box with Lee Rousso and James Quinn. Both are outstanding professional handicappers.

Rousso brings a number of skills to the task of selecting winners. The two most spectacular are an uncanny ability to estimate early pace standouts, and the ability to evaluate track biases. The former clearly cost an odds point or two on Akinemod. For the benefit of his telephone service and seminar clients, and much to my disappointment, Lee declared Akinemod to be the most certain winner of the day. Thanks, Lee.

James Quinn combines pace and speed figures with a well-documented expertise on class requirements, especially with developing three-year-olds. Quinn calmly stated that Akinemod would not lose. Period. At least he was low-key with his opinion!

It was apparent early in the day that Akinemod was not going to be overlaid in the race. She did, however, go off at 8–5, winning as she pleased. The strong second choice, Miss Tawpie, finished second and completed a generous $83.00 exacta.

EIGHTH RACE
Santa Anita
OCTOBER 25, 1989

7 FURLONGS. (1.20) 4th Running of THE CASCAPEDIA HANDICAP. $75,000 added. Fillies and mares. 3-year-olds and upward. By subscription of $75 each, $750 additional to start, with $75,000 added, of which $15,000 to second, $11,250 to third, $5,625 to fourth and $1,875 to fifth. Weights, Friday October 20. Starters to be named through the entry box by the closing time of entries. A trophy will be presented to the owner of the winner. Closed Wednesday, October 18, 1989 with 12 nominations.

Value of race $82,650; value to winner $48,900; second $15,000; third $11,250; fourth $5,625; fifth $1,875. Mutuel pool $313,047. Exacta Pool $302,606.

Last Raced	Horse	Eqt.	A.	Wt	PP	St	¼	½	Str	Fin	Jockey	Odds $1
11Oct89 ^{5}SA^{1}	Akinemod		3	115	6	1	$1\frac{1}{2}$	$1^{1\frac{1}{2}}$	1^{3}	$1^{2\frac{3}{4}}$	Stevens G L	1.70
25Sep89 ^{12}Fpx^{1}	Miss Tawpie		5	117	7	2	5^{1}	$5^{2\frac{1}{2}}$	2^{1}	$2\frac{1}{2}$	Flores D R	6.10
11Oct89 ^{8}SA^{7}	Hasty Pasty		4	118	4	4	4^{1}	4^{1}	4^{1}	$3^{1\frac{1}{2}}$	Pincay L Jr	9.40
29Sep89 ^{12}Fpx^{3}	Survive		5	118	5	5	$6^{3\frac{1}{2}}$	$6^{1\frac{1}{2}}$	6^{hd}	$4\frac{3}{4}$	Baze R A	2.80
29Sep89 ^{12}Fpx^{1}	Corvettin	b	4	116	8	3	8^{7}	8^{6}	$7^{1\frac{1}{2}}$	5^{hd}	Nakatani C S	13.70
29Sep89 ^{12}Fpx^{6}	Behind The Scenes		5	115	1	9	9	9	9	$6\frac{3}{4}$	Solis A	†8.90
8Sep89 ^{8}Dmr^{4}	Linda Card	b	3	115	2	8	$2^{2\frac{1}{2}}$	$2^{1\frac{1}{2}}$	3^{hd}	$7^{1\frac{1}{4}}$	Toro F	16.80
9Sep89 ^{7}Dmr^{1}	A Penny Is A Penny		4	115	3	7	3^{hd}	$3\frac{1}{2}$	$5^{1\frac{1}{2}}$	$8\frac{1}{2}$	Sibille R	26.60
6Oct89 ^{7}SA^{5}	Seattle Meteor		3	116	9	6	7^{hd}	$7\frac{1}{2}$	8^{1}	9	Delahoussaye E	8.30

OFF AT 4:43. Start good. Won ridden out. Time, :22⅕, :44⅘, 1:09⅗, 1:22⅖ Track fast.

$2 Mutuel Prices:

6–AKINEMOD	5.40	3.80	3.20
7–MISS TAWPIE		6.60	5.00
4–HASTY PASTY			7.00

$5 EXACTA 6–7 PAID $83.00.

25OCT89—NINTH RACE

The ninth race on the card was at one mile for $12,500 claimers. The ranking categories and energy figures went to Reason To Study as he attempted to repeat a win at the $10,000 level. The second-rated horse was Greek Turf, also attempting to repeat a win for $10,000. Neither horse was able to overcome Eratone, a four-year-old gelding dropping from nonwinners-one allowances.

Eratone
DAVIS R G **116**
Own.—Baccala & Ross

Ch. g. 4, by Exclusive Era—Last Bell, by Nicaray
Br.—Two Ton Tony Farm (Cal) **1989 6 1 0 1 $14,170**
Tr.—Sadler John W **$12,500** **1988 1 M 0 0**
Lifetime 7 1 0 1 $14,170

15Oct89-4SA	6½f	:21^{3}	:44^{1}	1:16^{2}ft	20	118	$8^{8\frac{3}{4}}$	$8^{7\frac{1}{4}}$	$8^{9\frac{1}{4}}$	$8^{12\frac{1}{2}}$	Black C A $\underline{1}$	Aw31000	75-13	BlueEyedDnny,Portl,TimForShmns	9
15Oct89—Broke in a tangle															
17Sep89-10Fpx	6½f	:22	:45^{1}	1:16 ft	8¾	117	$9^{4\frac{3}{4}}$	$8^{7\frac{1}{2}}$	$8^{7\frac{1}{2}}$	8^{11}	Pedroza MA $\underline{9}$	Aw32000	85-06	LoadedJun,OneDrink,WorkTillDwn	10
17Sep89—Wide 1/2															
10Sep89-5Dmr	6f	:21^{3}	:44^{2}	1:09 ft	22	113^{5}	8^{15}	$8^{9\frac{1}{4}}$	$8^{6\frac{1}{2}}$	$5^{4\frac{1}{2}}$	CastnonJL $\underline{6}$	[S]Aw33000	88-09	AddedFeathers,IntoTheMct,Comicl	8
10Sep89—Steadied start															
18Aug89-4Dmr	6f	:22	:45^{3}	1:10^{3}ft	10	119	$8^{6\frac{1}{4}}$	$7^{3\frac{1}{4}}$	$5^{2\frac{1}{2}}$	1^{2}	Davis R G $\underline{9}$	[S]M28000	85-15	Eratone, Interpol, Mild Reproach	12
18Aug89—Wide final 3/8															
3Aug89-2Dmr	6f	:22^{2}	:45^{3}	1:11 ft	7	122	5^{4}	$5^{2\frac{1}{4}}$	$4^{2\frac{1}{2}}$	$4^{5\frac{1}{2}}$	ValenzuelaPA $\underline{3}$	M32000	77-14	Clvinist,MildRproch,BigMoLttlMo	12
3Aug89—Jostled start															
22Jly89-1Hol	6f	:22^{2}	:45^{3}	1:11 ft	4	122	$7^{3\frac{3}{4}}$	5^{5}	5^{6}	$3^{6\frac{3}{4}}$	Davis R G $\underline{9}$	M32000	79-16	DnweProspctor,MildRproch,Erton	12
22Jly89—Wide final 3/8															
3Sep88-5BM	6f	:22^{3}	:45^{3}	1:09^{4}ft	29	118	$9^{6\frac{1}{2}}$	9^{14}	—	—	Diaz A L $\underline{7}$	Mdn	— —	LibraWlk,Steven'sLed,Checkerino	10
3Sep88—Eased															

Speed Index: Last Race: (—) 3–Race Avg.: (—) 12–Race Avg.: (—) Overall Avg.: –6.3

Oct 6 SA 6f ft 1:14^{4} H ●Sep 27 Fpx 5f ft 1:01^{4} H

NINTH RACE
Santa Anita
OCTOBER 25, 1989

1 MILE. (1.33⅘) CLAIMING. Purse \$13,000. 3-year-olds and upward. Bred in California. Weights, 3-year-olds, 117 lbs.; older, 121 lbs. Non-winners of two races at one mile or over since August 15 allowed 3 lbs.; of such a race since then, 5 lbs. Claiming price \$12,500; if entered for \$10,500 allowed 2 lbs. (Races when entered for \$10,000 or less not considered.)
Value of race \$13,000; value to winner \$7,150; second \$2,600; third \$1,950; fourth \$975; fifth \$325. Mutuel pool \$226,862. Exacta pool \$363,012.

Last Raced	Horse	Eqt.A.Wt	PP	St	¼	½	¾	Str	Fin	Jockey	Cl'g Pr	Odds $1
15Oct89 ^{4}SA^{8}	Eratone	b 4 116	3	5	$5^{3\frac{1}{2}}$	$5^{3\frac{1}{2}}$	$4^{1\frac{1}{2}}$	3^{1}	1^{1}	Davis R G	12500	4.10
13Oct89 ^{9}SA^{1}	Greek Turf	b 4 116	1	1	1^{1}	$2^{1\frac{1}{2}}$	1^{hd}	2^{hd}	2^{1}	Baze R A	12500	3.90
21Sep89 ^{9}Fpx^{1}	Pirate's Adventure	3 113	4	2	2^{1}	1^{hd}	2^{hd}	1^{hd}	3^{1}	Black C A	12500	7.20
31Aug89 ^{7}Dmr^{9}	Knight Regent	b 4 116	6	4	$3^{\frac{1}{2}}$	3^{1}	3^{hd}	$4^{2\frac{1}{2}}$	$4^{2\frac{3}{4}}$	Stevens G L	12500	2.50
5Oct89 ^{9}SA^{1}	Reason To Study	b 6 116	7	6	$7^{\frac{1}{2}}$	7^{1}	6^{hd}	6^{3}	$5^{2\frac{1}{2}}$	Solis A	12500	4.30
13Oct89 ^{9}SA^{2}	Diego Dandy	b 5 116	2	3	$4^{1\frac{1}{2}}$	$4^{1\frac{1}{2}}$	5^{4}	$5^{1\frac{1}{2}}$	6^{3}	Sibille R	12500	13.30
12Oct89 ^{5}SA^{8}	Aliso Boy	4 116	5	8	8	8	8	7^{1}	7^{2}	Sorenson D	12500	20.80
13Oct89 ^{1}SA^{4}	Builder's Boy	3 110	8	7	$6^{2\frac{1}{2}}$	$6^{1\frac{1}{2}}$	7^{1}	8	8	Castanon J L^{5}	12500	11.80

OFF AT 5:13 Start good. Won ridden out. Time, :22⅗, :46⅕, 1:11⅖, 1:24⅕, 1:37⅕ Track fast.

\$2 Mutuel Prices:			
3-ERATONE	10.20	6.80	5.00
1-GREEK TURF		5.00	3.40
4-PIRATE'S ADVENTURE			4.20

\$5 EXACTA 3-1 PAID \$148.00.

SUMMARY

The results of this day are not atypical. I chose to use 25Oct89 because it offered the opportunity to demonstrate most of the tools presented in the text *and* because a winning day reinforces the learning experience. As with any method, there will be losing days—many of them. Handicappers unable to come to grips with that fact are destined to travel a rocky road. Top players have learned to look beyond a single day, winning or losing, and base their estimation of success or failure on a larger sample. You should too.

In the progression from neophyte to journeyman, the handicapper eventually sheds the "How did you do today?" test of success or failure. When the outcome of a single day no longer has a severe impact on your emotional state, it's a sign you've matured as a player.

The principles in this book will serve you well in your progression. They've been proven time and again at all tracks across the country. They are *not* provincial in their application.

A *Track Profile* was the key to winning at Arlington Park in Illinois, *and* at Santa Anita in California.

Negative class drops should be aggressively attacked at Longacres *and* at Gulfstream Park; the logic is the same regardless of geography.

Early Pace horses with first fraction *and* also *turn-time* advantages are superior plays; most times, at most tracks.

The use of *pars* to equalize tracks and surfaces is universal and provides the opportunity to gain a significant edge over the crowd. Current pars for a circuit featuring lots of shippers can lead to enormous profits.

A *Decision Model* is an outstanding vehicle for relating personal handicapping skills to the realities of the track. *Everywhere.*

The ability to effectively relate the *Energy Distribution* demands of a racetrack to the horses competing in a race is a powerful concept at *all* types of tracks, east *and* west.

Finally, the handicapper willing to expend the effort to calculate feet-per-second figures will be well served by the pace ratings from the *Sartin Methodology.*

Handicappers on both coasts, and everywhere in between, should be able to successfully apply the principles and concepts in *Modern Pace Handicapping.*